WILLS, TRUSTS, AND FUTURE INTERESTS

WILLS, TRUSTS, AND FUTURE INTERESTS

By

LAWRENCE H. AVERILL, JR.
Charles C. Baum Distinguished Professor of Law
University of Arkansas at Little Rock

BLACK LETTER SERIES®

WEST GROUP

ST. PAUL, MINN.
2000

610 Opperman Drive
P.O. Box 64526
St. Paul, MN 55164–0526
1–800–328–9352

Printed in the United States of America

ISBN 0–314–21106–3

TEXT IS PRINTED ON 10% POST CONSUMER RECYCLED PAPER

To all of the law students who, over the past thirty-five years, have taken my decedents' estates and trusts classes and who have inspired my continuing enthusiasm for the course.

*

PREFACE

Projects often do not turn out the way they were originally intended. This Black Letter is a perfect example of this phenomenon. Intended as a multi-author project, it has ended as a single author publication. Commitments to new projects drained this work of its co-author, Professor Lawrence W. Waggoner, Lewis M. Simes Professor of Law of the University of Michigan Law School. With Professor Waggoner's assumption of duties as the Reporter for the RESTATEMENT (THIRD) OF PROPERTY (WILLS AND OTHER DONATIVE TRANSFERS), the time necessary to properly manage and complete this project had to take a precedence over the Black Letter project. By the time the completed draft of the Black Letter was finished, he found himself unable to fully participate to the extent that he felt co-authorship warranted.

His participation merits express recognition, however. The future interests material of the Black Letter is organizational and substantively based on Professor Waggoner's ESTATES IN LAND AND FUTURE INTERESTS IN A NUTSHELL (West Group, Publishing Co., 2d ed. 1993). Portions quoted from this NUTSHELL are reprinted by permission of the author. In addition, Professor Waggoner merits my sincere appreciation for reviewing portions of the Black Letter text and making valuable suggested changes to it.

Several students assisted me in various ways over the time this work was in progress. Those deserving mention include Kimberly G. Allison, Michael J. Lamoureux, Christopher A. Stratton. I thank them for their willingness to eagerly complete tasks that I did not want to do myself.

For whatever it is worth, the finished product is the by-product of my more than thirty years of accumulated wisdom garnered from teaching in the area of decedents' estates, trusts and estate planning. I hope it proves useful to the students who use it.

LAWRENCE H. AVERILL, JR.

Little Rock, Arkansas
December 1, 1999

*

PUBLISHER'S PREFACE

This "Black Letter" is designed to help a law student recognize and understand the basic principles and issues of law covered in a law school course. It can be used both as a study aid when preparing for classes and as a review of the subject matter when studying for an examination.

Each "Black Letter" is written by experienced law school teachers who are recognized national authorities in the subject covered.

The law is succinctly stated by the authors of this "Black Letter." In addition, the exceptions to the rules are stated in the text. The rules and exceptions have purposely been condensed to facilitate quick and easy recollection.

If the subject covered by this text is a code or code-related course, the code section or rule is set forth and discussed wherever applicable.

FORMAT

The format of this "Black Letter" is specially designed for review. (1) **Text.** First, it is recommended that the entire text be studied and, if deemed necessary, supplemented by class texts and notes. (2) **Capsule Summary.** The Capsule Summary is an abbreviated review of the subject matter which can be used both before and after studying the main body of the text. The headings in the Capsule Summary follow the main text of the "Black Letter." (3) **Table of Contents.** The Table of Contents is in outline form to help you organize the details of the subject and the Summary of Contents gives you a final overview of the materials. (4) **Practice Exam Questions.** The Practice Examination Questions in Appendix B gives you the opportunity of testing yourself with the type of questions asked on an exam and comparing your answers with model answers.

In addition, a number of other features are included to help you understand the subject matter and prepare for examinations:

Perspective: In this feature, the authors discuss their approach to the topic, the approach used in preparing the materials, and any tips on studying for and writing examinations.

Analysis: This feature, at the beginning of each section, is designed to give a quick summary of a particular section to help you recall the subject matter and to help you determine which areas need the most extensive review.

Index of Key Terms: This feature is designed to illustrate, through fact situations, the law just stated. This, we believe, should help you analytically approach a question on the examination.

Illustrations: This feature is designed to refamiliarize you with the meaning of a particular legal term. We believe that the recognition of words of art used in an examination helps you to better analyze the question. In addition, when writing an examination you should know the precise definition of a word of art you intend to use.

Text Correlation Chart: This feature permits the student to correlate the material in this "Black Letter" to the material included in the primary texts for this area of law. This tracking feature assist the student in organizing the materials for the particular course being taken.

We believe that the materials in this "Black Letter" will facilitate your study of a law school course and assure success in writing examinations not only for the course but for the bar examination. We wish you success.

THE PUBLISHER

SUMMARY OF CONTENTS

*

TABLE OF CONTENTS

PART TWO. INTESTATE SUCCESSION AND RELATED DOCTRINES

PART THREE. TESTAMENT TRANSFERS

PART SIX. TRUSTS

PART EIGHT. FUTURE INTERESTS AND PERPETUITIES

PART NINE. THE FIDUCIARY OBLIGATION

APPENDICES

*

CAPSULE SUMMARY

PART ONE: GRATUITOUS TRANSFERS IN PERSPECTIVE

I. SCOPE AND HISTORY OF GRATUITOUS TRANSFERS

The law of gratuitous transfers of assets or property concerns: succession of property at death, including intestacy, testacy and will substitutes; trust creation, purpose and administration; future interests and perpetuities; and, administration of decedents' estates. Planning for retirement and incapacity is also involved.

II. ADMINISTRATION OF ESTATES AND TRUSTS

A. The Judicial Involvement in Property Transmission

When persons die owning assets at death, some form of an administrative process is necessary to resolve the rights of decedent's creditors and successors. The word probate not only refers to the formal process of proving and deciding a will's validity but also to all matters appropriately before the probate courts.

The primary reasons for having an administration of a decedent's estate are to establish title to property, facilitate the collection of assets and claims, and resolve tax and creditor claims, if any. The process of administration is divisible into five parts: opening; inventory and appraisement; creditor settlement; property management and sale; and, distribution and closing.

A person may employ other techniques, called will substitutes, for disposing of property. These techniques pass an interest at the owner's death directly to the designated beneficiary. The transfers can be completed without a will or intestacy law and without probate administration. Will substitutes include survivorship interests, trust interests, contractual arrangements, life insurance proceeds, retirement programs, and nondescendable future interests.

B. Court versus Noncourt Transactions

Whereas decedent's probate estate requires that assets pass through a court procedure regardless of the desires of the interested persons, decedent's will substitutes are handled privately without court involvement unless litigation between the interested parties arises over the interest. Although probate may be less efficient and slow at times, nonprobate procedure may lack procedural protection for adversely affected interested persons and may offer less predictability when litigation develops.

C. Jurisdictional Issues

Probate courts must have jurisdiction over the persons or property involved in the proceeding, and the subject matter. The jurisdictional facts for the probate court usually involve domicile of decedent, location of property, and other relevant contacts with the locale. Under the federal Constitution, proper jurisdiction over the persons and property depends on minimum contacts with the state, adequate notice, and an opportunity to be heard. Under some circumstances, the traditional notice by publication in probate matters must be supplemented with additional notice techniques. Subject matter jurisdiction varies by state but is commonly broadly defined.

III. JUDICIAL PROCEDURE AND EVIDENCE

A. Parties and Pleadings

The parties and pleadings for probate matters are usually specified by state probate code. Parties and pleadings in will substitute litigation must conform to the civil procedural rules set for the court of proper jurisdiction.

B. Burdens of Proof and Presumptions

As with all litigation, the burdens of proof and presumptions are very important to the outcome of the case.

C. Introduction to Interpretation

Interpretation refers to the process of searching for the donor's actual intention by looking to the text of the document and extrinsic evidence. Construction refers to the process of attributing intention from constructional preferences and rules of construction. Interpretation and construction are part of a single process. Actual intention, when sufficiently established, always overcomes attributed intention.

D. Substantive Evidence Rules: Restrictions on Admissibility

The evidence rules for litigation concerning lifetime gratuitous transfer are controlled by the normal evidence and procedurals rules for civil litigation. The evidence rules for litigation concerning wills follows a unique and more restrictive approach regarding admissibility. The inherent fact that the testator is dead and the so called sanctity of the statute of wills has been used to justify the distinction.

With few exceptions, provisions mistakenly omitted from a will are not provable. On the other hand, courts have provided some kind of remedy when words are mistakenly included in a will.

A mistake in the inducement is remedied only if (1) testator was laboring under a mistake as to the facts; (2) knowing the truth, testator would have made a different disposition; and (3) these facts should appear in the will itself.

If testator mistakenly executes the wrong document, courts have split on whether to deny probate because testamentary intent is entirely lacking or to permit reformation of the will to conform to testator's intent.

A group of authorities now take the position that any ambiguity should be resolved by construing the text of any donative document, will or trust, in accordance with the donor's intention to the extent that the donor's intention is established by a preponderance of the evidence. Thus a donor's intention should control the meaning of a donative document to the extent that it is sufficiently established by the evidence.

IV. PROFESSIONAL RESPONSIBILITY

A. General Application of Ethical Standards

The practice of the law of gratuitous transfers covers the entire scope of the rules of professional ethics. Generally, the estate planning attorney must exercise for the client the professional duties of competence, diligence, communication, confidentiality, and loyalty. Pervasive ethical issues arising for estate practitioners include competence, beneficiary liability, undue influence, conflicts of interest and client identification.

B. Competence

An estate planning attorney must exercise for the client the legal knowledge, skill, thoroughness and preparation reasonably necessary for the representation. Generally, malpractice liability springs from the attorney-client relationship and includes fraud, breach of fiduciary duty, and negligence. Courts have held that an attorney is liable to persons outside the attorney-client relationship who are injured by negligent representation.

C. Confidentiality

The attorney must maintain a client's confidences. Confidentiality applies not merely to matters communicated in confidence by the client but also to all information relating to the representation, whatever its source. An attorney may disclose such information only if authorized or required by the Rules of Professional Conduct or other law. Confidentiality begins at first interview, lasts beyond employment, and even beyond death.

D. Loyalty

Generally, an attorney can not represent a client if the representation of that client will be directly adverse to another client or if the representation of that client may be materially limited by the attorney's responsibilities to another client or to a third person, or by the attorney's own interests. Clients may consent to the representation despite the conflict if they consent after full disclosure of any conflict or potential conflict. Full disclosure requires revelation of all of the facts and implications of the representation to all affected clients.

Conflicts may be of the nature that require that the attorney decline the representation. If an actual and nonconsentable conflict of interest arises after the representation has begun, the attorney should withdraw from further representation of all clients in the transaction.

E. Estate Planning

Neither an attorney nor the attorney's associates in the same firm should draft a will for a legal stranger in which the attorney takes a devise. When drafting a will for a relative, the attorney should not receive a disproportionate share in relation to the familial relationship.

Although joint representation of clients in estate planning matters is common and beneficial, the attorney should be sensitive to potential conflicts of loyalty and confidentiality that may develop during the joint representation.

Attorneys who represent fiduciaries of trusts and estates also may see conflicts develop between the fiduciary and the beneficiaries. Issues such as confidentiality and privilege may arise in litigation between the parties. The question is whether the attorney represents the fiduciary who engaged the attorney, the beneficiaries of the fiduciary entity, or the entity itself. Three views on the matter have been advocated: (1) the fiduciary is the sole client; (2) the attorney represents the estate and must protect the interests of both the beneficiaries and the fiduciary; and (3) the representation issue must be worked out and documented at the outset of the representation.

PART TWO: INTESTATE SUCCESSION AND RELATED DOCTRINES

I. ESTATE PLAN BY OPERATION OF LAW

A. General Patterns of Intestate Succession

When a person owning property dies without creating effective inter vivos or testamentary instruments for the disposition of all of that property, the person dies intestate. Intestate inheritance is a statutory estate plan by operation of law. It applies to both partial and total intestacy. Generally, the statutes direct distribution of the intestate's estate to certain relations in a pattern thought to represent a pattern that an average person would have designed had that person's desires been properly manifested.

The persons protected or benefitted by the statute generally include:

- Those persons related to the intestate by blood, called relationship by *consanguinity*. This includes an intestate's descendants, ancestors and collateral relations.
- Those persons related to the intestate by marriage, called relationship by *affinity*. The primary, and under most laws, the only person to inherit by affinity is the surviving spouse. In a few jurisdictions, others related by affinity (the spouse's consanguine relations) may inherit in order to avoid escheat.
- A person not related by consanguinity or affinity, may be able to inherit if that person is adopted according to the adoption statutes.

The intestate's surviving spouse, descendants and parents are the standard preferred beneficiaries. In varying degrees, other ancestors and collateral relations are also protected if the preferred relations cannot take. Most intestacy statutes protect consanguine relations up to grandparents and their descendants. Some go further and allow inheritance to the determinable nearest of kin. All states recognize that the property escheats to the state if no one qualifies to take under the intestacy provisions.

Generally, intestacy statutes distribute the net intestate estate among classes of decedent's relatives according to a set of prioritized contingencies. These contingencies anticipate foreseeable circumstances and are applied until all property is allocated. Within the contingencies, classes of relatives are used to identify the distributees. Typical classes of relatives entitled to take as distributees including the decedent's "surviving spouse," "descendants," "parents," "brothers and sisters," "grandparents" and "uncles and aunts." The term "descendant" includes all of a person's lineal descendants at all generations.

With a few exceptions, the statutes apply equally to both real and personal property. There are no preferences depending on the taker's gender. Decedent's debts and the family protections (homestead, allowances and exemptions) are paid prior to intestacy distribution.

B. Shares of the Takers

Share of Surviving Spouse: If a decedent is survived by a spouse, the spouse takes a significant share in all states ranging from one-third of the estate to all the estate. The statutory trend is to raise the spouse's share.

Under the UPC, the surviving spouse takes all the intestate estate (1) if the decedent is also survived by children who are all children of the decedent and the spouse; or, (2) if the decedent is not survived by descendants and parents notwithstanding other surviving blood relations of the decedent. In all other circumstances the spouse takes a large threshold amount ranging from $100,000 to $200,000 before having to share the remainder of the estate with decedent's descendants or parents. The threshold amounts guarantee the surviving spouse will take all the estate except in large estates.

Share of Issue: In all states, after allocating the share of any surviving spouses, the remaining part of an intestate estate passes to the intestate's surviving descendants, if any survive. If no spouse survives, descendants take all of the estate. Representation is recognized for decedent's descendants.

Share of Ascendants and Collaterals: Except for parents who share with a surviving spouse under some statutes, ascendants and collateral relations take only if no spouse and no descendants survive. Ascendants are ancestors including parents, grandparents, etc. Collateral blood relatives are related to the decedent by consanguinity through common ancestry, *e.g.,* siblings, aunts/uncles, great aunts/great uncles and their descendants.

Usually parents take before siblings; grandparents before uncles and aunts. Usually surviving descendants of collaterals may take by representation if the statutorily designated collateral did not survive, *e.g.,* nephew takes in place of sibling.

C. Representation

Representation permits persons who are of more remote degree of kinship to an intestate to take some share from the estate even though there are relatives of closer degree of kinship to the intestate.

The two general principles of representation are: (1) descendants of more remote degree from the decedent cannot inherit if their ancestor, who is related in a closer degree to the decedent, can take.; and (2) descendants of more remote degree from the decedent can inherit if their ancestor, who is related in a closer degree, cannot take even though there are other descendants of closer degree.

Various representation systems define the root generation in different ways. The four primary methods of applying representation are as follows:

Per stirpes: the initial division of the estate is made at the generation nearest to the decedent, regardless of whether there are any members of that generation who are alive. The number of primary shares is the number of living persons in that nearest generation, plus the number of deceased persons in that generation who have descendants who survive. The latter are permitted to represent their ancestor. The same approach is taken in dividing the estate of each deceased member's share among these descendants.

Per capita with per capita representation: the initial division of the estate is made at the first generation with a living member. Representation is recognized for living descendants of that generation. The number of primary shares is the number of living persons in the first generation with a surviving member, plus the number of deceased persons in that generation who have descendants who survive. The same approach is taken in dividing the estate of each deceased member's share among these descendants.

Per capita at each generation: the estate is divided into primary shares at the first generation with one or more living members. Representation is recognized for living descendants of this generation. The number of primary shares is the number of living persons in the first generation with a living member plus the number of deceased members with living descendants. After the living members are allocated their shares, the remaining estate as a whole is combined and divided in the same way among the living descendants of the deceased descendants of the previous generation, and so on.

Per capita with per stirpes representation: the initial division of the estate is made at the first generation with a living member. If all persons in that first generation survive the decedent, each in that generation take per capita. If one or more in that generation did not survive the decedent but left descendants who did, a pure per stirpes approach is then taken, using the first generation as the root generation.

When the specific allocations of the intestacy statutes are not applicable to an intestate, some statutes distribute the estate *per capita*. Under this system the closest relation is determined by degree of relationship and all persons of equal degree share equally. No representation is allowed for the descendants of persons in the applicable generation.

D. Ancestors and Collaterals

Counting degrees of relationship of one to a decedent is the process of determining next of kin in intestacy. The predominant method for counting degrees is the civil law system. Under this system the degree of kinship is the total of (1) the number of the steps counting one for each generation, from the decedent up to the nearest common ancestor of the decedent and the claimant, and (2) the number of steps from the common ancestor down to the claimant. Claimants having the lowest degree count are entitled to the property. All of equal degree share per capita.

E. Escheat

All states recognize escheat when a decedent has no identifiable relatives. Under escheat the property becomes the property of the state. Some statutory systems, like the UPC, require escheat if certain specified relations are not able to take. Some only provide for escheat if relations of the decedent cannot be found.

II. TAKER QUALIFICATIONS

A. Questions of Status

Because all intestate succession statutes describe their beneficiaries in terms of relational classifications such as "descendant," "heirs," and "surviving spouse," it is necessary to determine what qualifies a person for such status. If one meets the status requirements, a secondary question is whether inheritance is by, from and through the relevant relations. For example, if one has the status of a child, does that person inherit from and through the parent or will the parent inherit from and through the child. Relationships raising questions of status include adopted, nonmarital, posthumous, and half-blooded relations.

B. Survivorship and Simultaneous Death

At common law, to take, an heir must survive the decedent "for an instant of time." Mere survival by any measurable time is enough. When a question arises whether a person survived for inheritance purposes, the answer depends on matters of evidence and standards of proof.

The original Uniform Simultaneous Death Act created a rebuttable presumption of survival of each property owner when "there is no sufficient evidence" of the order of death. Unfortunately, the presumption only applies when there is not sufficient evidence to rebut the presumption. For intestacy, UPC Section 2–104 (and the comparable section in the new Uniform Simultaneous Death Act) requires that every taker must survive the decedent's death or the transfer activating event by 120 hours. If one does not survive by 120 hours, one does not take by intestacy unless one is the last heir.

C. Consanguinity

Collateral blood relations can be whole blooded or half blooded. Half blood relations have one common ancestor but not both relevant ancestors as whole blooded relations. The UPC and most other jurisdictions make no distinctions between the inheritance share of whole or half-blooded relations.

A posthumous heir, *i.e.*, one conceived before the intestate's death but born after that death, could take at common law. Most states permit posthumous children to take. UPC Section 2–108 permits posthumous persons to take if they survive by 120 hours from the time of birth. Consequently, the posthumous child must survive the decedent by 120 hours and live 120 hours after the child's birth.

D. Affinity

Affinity means relationship by marriage. With only limited exception, the only person related by affinity who can take in intestacy is the surviving spouse. Other persons related by affinity, including step children and other in-laws, do not take in intestacy.

E. Adoption

The three types of adoption circumstances affecting succession include formal adoption, virtual adoption, and equitable adoption. A formal adoption is one approved through a statutory adoption process and in many states is the only type given recognition. All states today have formal adoption procedures recognizing the status of adoption. The effect of adoption on inheritance rights varies among the states. Most grant adopted persons full status as a child of the adopted parents.

The UPC recognizes that there are two primary types of adoption circumstances: the "new family adoption," and the "stepparent adoption."

The "new family adoption," concerns the adoption of a child by an entirely new family, usually a husband and wife. Here, the UPC severs the relationship of the adopted child from that child's natural parents: it grafts a new relationship between the adopted child and the adopting parents for inheritance purposes. The adopted person inherits from and through that person's adopting parents and vice-versa.

The "stepparent adoption" concerns the adoption of a stepchild by a stepparent while one of the natural parents continues as a normal custodial parent of the child. The other natural parent continues in a noncustodial relationship. Here the adopted stepchild is permitted to inherit from and through the adopting stepparent. In addition, the child is permitted to inherit from and through both natural parents. The adopting stepparent inherits from and through the adopted stepchild. The custodial natural parent may also inherit from and through the child if that natural parent openly treated the child as that person's child and did not refuse to support the child during the child's years when support is legally mandated. The noncustodial parent and that parent's relatives cannot inherit from or through the adopted child.

Virtual adoption concerns a situation where there is a promise between the natural parent and the nonparent that if the natural parent will give custody to the nonparent, the nonparent will adopt the child. If the natural parent, the child and the nonparent perform the agreement, the agreement is enforceable by the child as a contract on a third party beneficiary theory, or as a means of establishing an inheritance right. Equitable adoption concerns a situation where a parent-child relationship appears to exist for a period of time although formal adoption never occurred. Upon proof by clear and convincing evidence that the child is the equivalent of an adopted child, some courts have granted inheritance rights to the equitably adopted person.

F. Definition of Spouse

The spousal relationship is a very important status for inheritance and related purposes. Most spousal relationships are created by a formal marriage. Marriages recognized by the law of the place of the marriage are generally recognized in other jurisdictions. Even common law marriages, which are relationships formed by an agreement to marry and followed by cohabitation, if valid where entered, are usually valid in states that do not recognize them if created locally. The putative spouse can also generally inherit as a spouse even though the actual marriage was either void or voidable.

G. Cohabitors

Cohabitors, those who live together in some form of an established, lasting, but nonmarital relationship, have had mixed judicial success when seeking a division of property due to the dissolution of the living arrangement. Successful actions have been based on implied contract, *quantum meruit* or constructive trust. A few states recognize cohabitation without marriage for inheritance purposes. Without authorizing legislation, courts have not granted same-sex couples intestate rights between each other. A statutory alternative method of recognizing probate and other rights between nonmarried persons is to create a new status. Hawaii enacted a statute that creates a new status caller "reciprocal beneficiary relationship." It extends "certain rights and benefits which are presently available only to married couples to couples composed of two individuals who are legally prohibited from marrying under state law." Beyond this specific protection, survivors of same-sex relationships are left to claims based upon contractual theories used by heterosexual cohabitors.

H. Nonmarital Children

Nonmarital children are consanguine children born to an unmarried mother. Although denied inheritance at common law, under statutes in all states they are permitted to inherit subject to proof of paternity. Under UPC Section 2–114(a) the marital status of the parents is not determinative. The child inherits by, from and through the parents if paternity is proved by a preponderance of evidence during the parents' lifetimes or by clear and convincing evidence after death. A nonmarital parent and kindred do not inherit from and through the nonmarital child unless the natural parent openly treated the child as a child and did not refuse to support the child during minority.

Some states have statutes specifically granting full relational status to children conceived by artificial insemination when the mother is married to the father whether or not the father's sperm was used for the conception. Beyond this, the law is unknown and unsure.

III. BARS TO INHERITANCE

A. Effect of Prior Transactions on Inheritance Rights

Advancements: The common law advancement is an irrevocable inter vivos gift of money or property, real or personal, to a child by a parent that enables the child to anticipate the child's inheritance from the parent to the extent of the gift. Some states have extended the doctrine to other heirs in addition to the intestate's children. For example, the UPC uses "heir" and defines that term to include children, descendants, collaterals, spouses. Whereas under some statutes one has to be heir or next of kin at time of advancement, under the UPC the donee must be an heir to the time of death.

The key that makes a gift an advancement is the donor's intent. There must be an intent to advance at the time of the gift. No changes of intent by the donor may occur that are more onerous on donee. The problem when a gift is claimed to be an advancement has been proof of intent. A donor seldom indicates that intent clearly. Courts have had to rely on oral evidence and often it was conflicting. Generally, courts admit a wide range of evidence including donor's records and declarations.

Presumptions are used when admissible evidence of intent is lacking, *e.g.,* some courts presume that a gift is an advancement if it was substantial but presume the gift was not an advancement if it was of nominal value or for support of the donee. The value of the advancement is determined as of the time of the donee's possession or enjoyment or as of the donor's death, whichever occurs first.

UPC Section 2–109(a) provides that a gift is a formal advancement only if either (1) the donor "declared in a contemporaneous writing;" or, (2) the heir "acknowledged in writing;" or (3) the gift indicates that it must be taken into account in computing the division or distribution of decedent's intestate estate. No words of art such as "advancement" must be used by the donor. Whereas at common law a gift was treated as an advancement only if the donor died totally intestate, the UPC provision applies to partial intestacy, too, so long as evidentiary requirements of intent are met.

An heir who received an advancement must participate in a "hotchpot" estate in order to also take his or her intestate share from the intestate's estate. The two principles of this hotchpot are: (1) participation in the hotchpot is optional on the part of advancees, but (2) if they want to take from the estate, they must participate: they have an *equitable election*. If the heir participates, the value of the advancement is added to the value of the distributable estate for calculation purposes only and from the appropriate calculations the heir's distribution directly from the intestate's estate equals the excess of the heir's intestate share over the value of the advancement received. If the value of the heir's advancement exceeds the heir's intestate share from the hotchpot calculations, the heir would neither participate in the hotchpot nor receive an intestate share from the estate. The heir, of course, may keep the advancement.

Transfers of assets from one to an heir may be characterized as a loan. An enforceable loan is an asset of the estate and must be repaid. A debtor-heir may set-off the value of any inheritance against the loan and may raise defenses available to any creditor.

<u>Releases of Expectancies:</u> A release of an expectancy is an agreement between the expectant heir and expectant intestate from whom the heir expects to inherit. The agreement releases the expectant heir's inheritance when the intestate dies. The agreement must be for fair consideration. If the consideration is found to be unfair, the agreement may be treated as an advancement. Releases have been found to bind the expectant heir's descendants if the expectant heir predeceases the intestate. Some courts require a release to be in writing.

<u>Assignments of Expectancies:</u> An assignment of an expectancy is an assignment between a third party and an expectant heir of a person. Fair and equitable consideration is required: a gratuitous assignment is void. Because assignments do not bind the expectant heir's descendants if the expectant heir predeceases the intestate, the value for an assigned interest is low, which then raises an issue of fair and equitable consideration. Assignments of expectancies are not desirable financial arrangements and are strictly construed by courts.

B. Misconduct

Although disqualification for misconduct is a principle of equity that bars a wrongdoer from profiting from the wrongdoing, most personal misconduct is not a basis for disinheritance in the absence of a statute. The primary exception concerns when a person is murdered by an heir.

Generally, the law does not allow a murderer to take a benefit from the victim. Most states have some legislation concerning some of the issues. Sometimes statutes are limited to rights in intestacy, testacy and life insurance benefits. Despite limited statutory coverage, courts have applied the equitable doctrine of constructive trust to prevent a murderer from benefitting. Unfortunately without a comprehensive statute many issues remain unanswered and must be resolved through costly litigation.

UPC Section 2–803 deals solely but comprehensively with disqualification for homicide. The nature of the crime that initiates the forfeiture is a felonious and intentional killing of another person. A criminal conviction equals conclusive evidence of wrongdoing but an acquittal is not binding and a civil action may be separately instituted.

> The provision applies to the intestate share, elective share, pretermitted spouse or heir share, or family protection. It also applies to all benefits bestowed in wills, trusts, contractual agreements, multiple-party accounts, and TOD security registrations. Depending on the issue, the murderer is treated as if he or she disclaimed or predeceased the victim.
>
> Protection is provided for bona fide purchasers and other unknowing third persons who deal with the murderer because there may be a long delay in instituting proceedings accusing a person of murdering another and even after institution of the case, the result may be in doubt for a long period of time.

C. Termination of Marital Status

Whether a person is a surviving spouse is very important in determining inheritance rights and responsibilities. A person is not a surviving spouse of the decedent if the person and the decedent have been divorced or their marriage annulled unless they remarry and are married on the date of the decedent's death. Although a decree of separation does not terminate the husband-wife status, a complete property settlement entered into after or in anticipation of separation or divorce operates as a disclaimer of the spouse's elective share, family protections, rights under intestate succession and provisions in wills executed before the property settlement unless a contrary intent appears on the agreement.

Sometimes the validity of the divorce is raised. In response, UPC Section 2–802(b)(1)–(3) recognizes a kind of estoppel concept. It provides that a marriage ends when the surviving person has either consented to, participated in, sought or completed some volitional act other than the formal divorce causing the marital relationship to be terminated.

D. Disclaimer

Disclaimer, or renunciation, concerns the disavowal of a property interest, imputed to be held by a person. A disclaimer is usually made in order for the person to avoid taxes, creditors, spendthrift provisions, and sometimes spousal protections. At common law a person could not disclaim an interest passing by intestacy, but could disclaim an interest passing by will. Disclaimer statutes now define the consequences and procedures for an effective disclaimer.

Disclaimer statutes deal specifically with the time within which a disclaimer must be made, the formality for executing one, the procedure necessary to follow, the disclaimer's effect, and what constitutes waiver of the disclaimer privilege.

UPC Section 2–801 permits, under defined procedures, all persons to whom property devolves by whatever means to disclaim their interest in the property. The disclaimer may be made by any competent person, a conservator for a disabled person, a guardian for a minor or incapacitated person, an agent under a durable power of attorney, or a decedent's personal representative. A valid disclaimer may be made only by a written instrument that describes the property disclaimed, declares the fact and extent of the disclaimer and is signed by the disclaimant or that person's proper representative.

A person is barred from renouncing, however, if the person made commercial use of the property or interest, waived the right to disclaim in writing; accepted the property or interest or benefits from it; or had the property sold under a judicial sale before the disclaimer became effective.

Absent expression of contrary intent, the testamentary and intestacy interests pass as if the disclaimant had predeceased the decedent or donee. For interests devolving by nontestamentary instruments and contracts, the interest devolves as if the disclaimant had predeceased the effective date of the instrument or contract.

E. Alienship

Most states and UPC Section 2–111 eliminate alienage as a status issue for intestate succession.

F. Negative Wills

At common law if a person executed a will that disinherited the person's heir but for whatever reason that did not pass all of decedent's property, the heir would still be able to take the intestate property. UPC Section 2–101(b) provides that if a decedent has excluded or limited the right of an heir to succeed to that person's intestate property, the exclusion or limit is binding even if the decedent dies intestate. The disinherited heir's share in intestacy passes as if that heir had disclaimed the interest. This means that the disinherited heir's descendants may take by representation but only the share the heir would have received.

PART THREE: TESTAMENT TRANSFERS

I. EXECUTION OF WILLS

A. Will Formality Overview

A *will* or *testament* is a lawful procedure by a competent testator acting voluntarily that conforms to a specified form and that disposes of property to a competent donee, or makes other directions, or both. A *codicil* is a properly executed will that amends a primary will but which might have to stand on its own if the "primary" will is not effective.

Minors and adults lacking testamentary capacity cannot execute valid wills. A person's power to execute a will is a nondelegatable power although the power to revoke can be granted if set forth in the will proper (conditional will).

A will is effective only after the death of the testator (testator must have intent to dispose of property at time of death and not before), and remains ambulatory and revocable during the testator's lifetime.

Compliance Standards: Courts have held that the execution formalities for wills are no greater than the applicable statute requires. Concomitantly, courts do not object to greater formalization than the statute requires. Finally, any type of will recognized by an applicable statute validates the will. On the other hand, most courts follow the concept of strict construction, *i.e.*, an instrument must satisfy all the formalities set out in the statute. Under this standard, each act or condition required by a wills statute may be important.

As a ground for contesting a will, execution formalities of the statute have been heavily litigated. Courts in these cases are faced with a policy conflict between respect for legislative intent as expressed in the wills statute versus the denial of testator's clearly expressed intent for failure to conform to an execution formality. Consequently, even when strict construction is the interpretive rule, courts tend to adopt a sort of reasonable compliance corollary rule in order to relax some incidental formalities in the statutes, *e.g.*, the "conscious presence" test to satisfy the requirement that the witnesses must sign in the testator's presence.

A few courts have adopted a substantial compliance standard. It permits probate of an otherwise defectively executed will if the proponents prove that the document adequately expresses the decedent's testamentary intent, and the execution procedure actually completed sufficiently approximates the execution requirements and purposes of the relevant statute of wills. This standard will not provide relief when a major execution requirement is lacking such as less than sufficient witnesses or no signature of the testator.

UPC Section 2–503 contains a dispensing power provision that permits a court to dispense with one or more statutory formalities even if they have not been followed, so long as the document's proponents establish by clear and convincing evidence that the testator intended the document to constitute the decedent's will or other will-related instruction.

Notwithstanding some modernization of wills statutes, current wills statutes generally retain the same basic formalities of the English Statute of Frauds (1677), and the Wills Act of 1837. These include a writing, testator's signature and witnesses who sign the instrument. Details concerning attestation have been refined. In addition, states have added other types of instruments that qualify as wills and which require different formalities.

The common types of wills recognized in the United States include:

- Ordinary Executed Will: the standard will that generally requires a writing, signature of the testator, and witnessing by several witnesses.
- Holographic Will: a will handwritten and signed by the testator with no requirement of witnesses.
- Nuncupative Will: an oral will announced under specified conditions.
- Self-proved Will: A will executed in a manner similar to the ordinary executed will and which also includes a notarization requirement.
- Foreign Will: recognition that a written will executed under the laws of another state or jurisdictions that has relevant contacts with the will or testator, is valid in the local state whether or not the formalities of the local statutes of wills are satisfied.
- International Will: a will executed under special execution procedures that makes it valid in all jurisdictions which join an international convention or which enact the appropriate act.

B. The Formal Requirements of Attested Wills

A testator must have testamentary capacity. Consequently, the testator must be an adult (usually 18 years old) and be of sound mind at time of execution.

The testator must have testamentary intent (*animus testandi*) which means the testator must intend that the instrument presently operate as his or her last will when the testator signed the instrument or when the last act of execution was performed. Testamentary intent is found from the face of the instrument or admissible relevant evidence.

The standard requirement for an attested will is that it be in writing which means that any inscription which results in a readable and fairly permanent record is satisfactory.

The testator must sign the will. Any visible mark is valid as long as testator intends it to be the signature and completes all testator intended to complete. Proxy signatures are usually permitted so long as the proxy signs in the testator's presence and at testator's "direction."

A few states require the testator to sign at the end of the will. Under this requirement, a will may be invalid if a court determines a significant part of the will follows the signature. Under the UPC and some other will statutes, the will need only be signed—top, bottom or margin.

Signature authentication requirements vary by state. Common requirements include:

- Testator must sign in the presence of the witnesses;
- Testator must acknowledge either the signature (this may require that the witnesses see it, too) or that testator has signed the will;
- Testator must sign or acknowledge in the presence of all of the witnesses at the same time;
- Testator must publish the will, *i.e.*, testator declares to the witnesses that the instrument is the testator's will;
- Under UPC Section 2–502(a)(3) testator must either sign in the witnesses' presence, acknowledge the signature, or acknowledge the will.

Witnessing: Attested wills require that they be witnessed. Witnesses must be "credible" or "competent" at the time of execution. Except for wills in Pennsylvania, witnesses are required to sign the will.

Generally, witnesses must sign in the testator's presence. Some courts require that witnesses sign in the testator's "line of sight." A "conscious presence" test has been recognized by other courts. Conscious presence constitutes a closeness in space (physically close to testator), time (contemporaneously with other execution processes), and action (in the nature of a single action). UPC Section 2–502(a)(3) merely requires that witnesses sign within a "reasonable time after" attestation or acknowledgment. Wills statutes that follow the Wills Act of 1837 require that the witnesses sign in the joint presence of the testator and the other witnesses.

Interested Witness Rule: At common law a will was invalid if a necessary witness was interested, *i.e.*, took a *direct pecuniary benefit* by the terms of the will. The rule applied only if the witness was interested at the time of execution: an interest developing after execution did not fall under the rule. Most states have "purging statutes," which validate the will but take away the witness' interest. Under these provisions, the will is valid but the interested necessary witness may only take the lesser of the will devise or other inheritable interest, *e.g.*, intestate interest or devise in another prior valid but revoked will. UPC Section 2–505(b) abolishes the interested witness restriction and restricts the undue influence concern to a direct contest for undue influence.

An attestation clause, usually found at the end of a will, recites that the proper execution processes were followed and that the witnesses certify that the instrument has been executed before them. Their use has several benefits:

- It may by prima facie evidence of the facts which it contains;

- It can help the unsure witness remember the witnessing better;
- It offers a valuable and forceful form of impeachment if a witness offers testimony against the will.

With similar benefits, the UPC and many other states recognize the "self-proved will." Its execution requirements are similar to the procedure for an ordinary witnessed will but includes a notarized affidavit executed by the testator and the witnesses.

C. Unattested Wills

There are two basic forms of unattested wills: *holographic* and *nuncupative* wills.

A holographic will is an unattested will written entirely in the handwriting of and signed by the testator. Witnesses are not needed. Typically, the will must be "entirely" handwritten. UPC Section 2–502(b) merely requires that "material portions of the document are in the testator's handwriting."

When nonholographic material appears on the face of the will, two basic theories of interpretations have developed concerning this requirement: (1) Under the intent theory the issue is determined on whether the testator intended that the nonholographic matter be a part of his will, and if not, the will is valid; (2) Under the surplusage theory the issue is whether there is enough remaining in the testator's hand to give the will effect and if so, then the nonholographic parts will be held to be surplusage.

Oral or nuncupative wills are given limited recognition in twenty states. The statutes are typically limited to military personnel or others facing imminent death and to disposing of personal property or to a set value of property.

D. Special Wills

Foreign Wills: Most states, as well as the UPC, recognize that wills, which are executed according to the requirements of certain factually connected jurisdictions, are valid locally. Some of these statutes limit the choice of law reference to wills that are in written format, and at least one requires that the will be signed by the testator. These statutes have been interpreted to apply only to execution requirements and not to other substantive issues concerning the will's effectiveness.

International Wills: The International Wills Act establishes a special procedure for executing a will to ensure the will is valid in all jurisdictions that join an international convention or that enact the Act. If the Act's requirements are followed, the will may be probated immediately.

II. REVOCATION OF WILLS

A. Revocation Requirements

Generally, will revocation must follow the revocation statute requirements. There are three principal elements for a testator's directed revocation of a will: (1) an authorized act or instrument; (2) an intent to revoke (*animus revocandi*); and (3) legal capacity of the testator. As with questions of will execution and validation, revocation requirements may raise policy issues: the conflict between defeating testator's intent and conforming to statutory mandates.

Revocation by Physical Act: Wills may be revoked by physical act such as burning, tearing, canceling, obliterating, or destroying the will. Courts require that some act, however minimal in nature, must be done to the will that basically fits the definition of the physical method used by the testator. For example, the mere burning of the edges of will satisfies the statute: canceling, however, may require actual marks that touch the writing of the will. The testator must complete the act intended and must have intended to revoke through the completed act. Once revocation is complete, reexecution or other proper revival must be accomplished to reestablish the will's validity.

Because physical revocation is inherently ambiguous, courts have freely admitted extrinsic evidence.

Partial revocation by physical act is permitted by most revocation statutes including the UPC. Some states prohibit revocation in part by physical act either in the statutes or by court decision.

Partial revocation by physical act, if permitted, can generate numerous interpretation and litigation problems. Forbidding partial physical revocation, however, may effectively prevent carrying out a testator's clearly indicated intent and thus potentially be harmful to intent enforcing concepts. Where partial revocation by physical act is permitted, courts distinguish between revocation and modification. Whereas revocation requires satisfaction of the revocation statute: modification requires satisfaction of the execution statute.

Revocation by Subsequent Instrument: Wills may be expressly revoked in whole or in part by a properly executed subsequent will. No words of art are necessary to revoke.

When the subsequent will does not specifically revoke but is inconsistent, in whole or in part, with a prior will, a question arises whether the inconsistencies revoke the provisions, or whether the prior provisions are merely superseded. If both wills are probated after the testator's death, the subsequent will prevails. The question is important, however, if the subsequent will is revoked before the testator's death. Of course, the result depends on testator's intent, but often this is not adequately expressed. If the inconsistent later will merely superseded the prior will, revocation of the later will or its provisions reinstates the prior will or its provisions. If the later will revoked the prior will or its provisions, the prior will is effective only if reexecuted or if the doctrine of revival is applicable.

UPC Subsections 2–507(b)-(d) establish reverse presumptions rebuttable by clear and convincing evidence. If the subsequent will "makes a complete disposition" of the estate, the inconsistencies are revocations and replace the prior will terms. If the subsequent will "does not make a complete disposition" of the estate, the inconsistencies are merely supersession and supplement to the prior will terms. The continuing life of the prior will depends on whether inconsistencies are effective.

Revocation by Changed Circumstances: At common law, a man's will was revoked if he subsequently married and had issue; a woman's will was revoked if she subsequently married. Most states have abolished these rules and have adopted a rule that the testator's testamentary provisions for the ex-spouse are revoked if there has been a divorce and a property settlement.

Subject to a court order or contract between the decedent and the former spouse, divorce under UPC Section 2–804 revokes all provisions in a will and all gratuitous inter vivos transfers that benefit the former spouse and spouse's relatives. It also severs joint survivorship interests between the decedent and the former spouse and converts them into tenancies in common. Nonrevoked provisions are given effect as if the former spouse and relatives of the former spouse disclaimed the revoked provisions, or with regard to appointments, predeceased the decedent. Remarriage to the spouse revives provisions for spouse, etc.

B. Reestablishing Revoked or Apparently Revoked Wills

Revival of Revoked Wills: The issue of whether the revoked will is revived by the revocation of the revoking instrument arises in at least three situations: (1) Will #2 wholly revokes Will #1 and Will #2 is revoked by physical act; (2) Will #2 partially revokes Will #1 and Will #2 is revoked by physical act; or, (3) Will #2 wholly revokes will #1 and Will #2 is revoked by Will #3.

The three basic theories for revival are:

- Revival by operation of law: The prior will is automatically revived regardless of the testator's intent.
- Revival depends upon the testator's intent: Although revocation takes effect immediately upon execution of the revoking instrument, the earlier will is revived if the testator intended to revive it.
- Revival only by republication: The prior will is revived only if it is republished or reexecuted.

UPC Section 2–509 adopts three separate rules:

(1) If a will, which wholly revokes a previous will, is then physically revoked, revival of the earlier will occurs only when those who seek revival present evidence that the testator intended the previous will to be revived.

(2) If a will, which partially revokes a previous will, is then physically revoked, revival of the earlier will is presumed unless those who contend that no revival occurred introduce evidence showing the testator did not intend revival of the prior instrument.

(3) If a will, which wholly revokes a previous will, is then revoked by a subsequent will, the revoked portions of the prior will are revived only if testator's intent to revive them appears from the terms of the latest will.

Dependent Relative Revocation [DRR]: Under DRR, the revocation of a will, which was brought about by mistake, is ignored and the revoked will is admitted to probate. This result is grounded on the basis that the intent to revoke was conditional. The inference of conditional intent is a fiction and will not contradict unambiguous revocation.

DRR is a judicial remedial doctrine that functions on the bases of "second best": the result does not conform to testator's actual intent but attempts to find a preferred result. For example, if a testator cancels or destroys a will while laboring under a material mistake of law or fact regarding the will, it may be presumed that the testator preferred the old will to intestacy. Thus, the old will will be admitted to probate in absence of evidence overcoming the presumption. The doctrine applies to partial and/or total or complete revocation.

III. DEFINING THE SCOPE OF THE WILL

A. Policy of the Statute of Wills

The policy of the Statute of Wills demands that the will consist only of appropriate materials included in the execution process. Consequently, if a devise in a will does not adequately describe the beneficiary and the property on its face, the devise is invalid unless an exception applies.

B. Integration of Wills

The doctrine of integration provides that when a will consists of multiple pages, only pages that were intended by the testator to be part of the will and that were present at the time of execution are part of the will.

C. Republication by Codicil

The republication by codicil doctrine provides that when a will is republished by codicil, it to speaks as of the date of the republishing as though originally executed at that time. The doctrine has relevance anytime the date of the will is an important reference point to a rule of construction or doctrine.

D. Incorporation by Reference

The incorporation by reference doctrine permits a document, not properly executed as a will, to be made part of the will for certain purposes only. Any sort of document may be incorporated. The requirements for incorporation by reference are:

(1) A will executed as required by statute.

(2) A distinct reference to a written document in the will itself. Lenient courts say the reference must be so definite and precise as to permit the document to be identified by parol evidence. Strict courts say the reference must be such as to identify the document beyond any doubt.

(3) The document must in fact be in existence at the time the will is executed.

(4) The will must show or state that the document is in existence at the time the will is executed. This requirement has not been strictly enforced.

(5) The will must show an intention to incorporate the document as part of the will. The entire document need not be incorporated: it may be incorporated in whole or part.

(6) When the document is offered, it must be shown to be the document referred to in the will, corresponding to the description in the will.

If a holographic will incorporates a non-holographic writing into the will, some courts treat the incorporated document as a physical part of the will and thereby destroy the holographic nature of the will; other courts say that integration and incorporation by reference are distinct concepts with their own safeguards and that a proponent of a will need only satisfy one or the other doctrine, not both.

UPC Section 2–510 substantially codifies the doctrine of incorporation by reference as described above. The one exception is that requirement (3) is not a prerequisite.

E. Reference to Facts of Independent Significance

The doctrine of independent significance permits certain evidence outside the will to be admitted to interpret the will if the evidentiary fact, be it an act or event, has significance other than to pass property at death. The doctrine applies regardless of whether the testator or third persons can affect the act or event subsequent to the will's execution. The degree of significance a devise is said to have, however, may depend on matters such as convenience versus whimsy and the degree of certainty from misuse. For example, compare a devise "to my spouse," versus a devise "of contents of shoe boxes to persons named on the box." A "spouse" clearly has significance other than to pass property at death, but the "shoe boxes" appear to have no significance other than to pass the contents at death. UPC Section 2–512 codifies a broad statement of the common law rule.

IV. WILL CONTESTS AND WILL SUBSTITUTE SUITS

A. Proving the Will

At probate the sole question is the judicial proof of the will. The two common types of probate are: *Ex parte* probate or probate in common form where no notice is given at the initiation of the proceedings; and, probate *in solemn form* where notice to all interested parties is required at initiation. By election of interested persons depending on their needs, the UPC includes both types.

B. Limitations on the Rights of Probate and Contest

A person who contests the probate of a will must be "interested" or "aggrieved." An *interested person* is one who would be directly benefitted financially if the will is denied probate. For example, an heir can contest a will that disinherits him or her, and a devisee of a prior will can contest a subsequent will that revokes the devise.

An *anticontest clause* is a clause in a will which provides that if a devisee under a will unsuccessfully contests the will, the devisee forfeits that devise. A variation provides that a devise is forfeited if the devisee files a claim against the estate. The devisee is given an election: either take under the will as provided or contest and defeat will. If the contest is successful the no-contest provision fails with the will. Courts take the position that the clauses are either valid whether or not there is probable cause for the contest, or valid only if there was no probable cause for the contest. UPC Section 2–517 adopts the probable cause rule.

C. Grounds of Contest

The general grounds for contesting a will include:

- improper execution
- forgery
- failure of capacity
- nontestamentary intent
- revocation
- undue influence
- fraud and
- legality

Contests Concerning Execution and Revocation of Wills: A will can be contested on the ground that it was not executed according to the proper formalities of the applicable statute of wills. Similarly, a will can be contested if it was revoked by the testator according to the terms of the revocation statute. Of course, a forged will can be contested.

Testamentary Intent: A will can be contested if it was not executed with testamentary intent. Testamentary intent must exist when the testator signed the instrument, or when the last act of execution was performed. For most wills this is not an issue because they state that they are wills on their face.

Testamentary Capacity: A will can be contested for lack of testamentary capacity if the testator is not of the age of majority or is not of sound mind at the time of execution. Requiring a sound mind is explained on the basis that it is better to distribute property according to intestate laws than according to the desires of a person who is so deficient or unbalanced mentally that he or she does not appreciate the significance of the disposition.

Testator is of sound mind for testamentary purposes only when:

Testator has the ability to know (can understand and carry in testator's mind in a general way):

(1) The nature and extent of testator's property;

(2) The persons who are the natural objects of his or her bounty;

(3) The disposition which testator is making of testator's property;

Testator must also be capable of:

(4) Appreciating these elements in relation to each other; and,

(5) Forming an orderly desire as to the disposition of testator's property.

A person who fails the above test of ability suffers from a *mental deficiency* and can not execute a valid will. Although the test is subjective and pragmatic, the real problems, when capacity is an issue, are ones of fact, proof, and in some states, of the province of the jury. The ultimate question is not fairness, compassion or brilliance, but the rational character of the testator's mind.

A will may also be contested if the testator is suffering from an *insane delusion*. An insane delusion is a false belief that is the product of a diseased mind unto which one adheres against evidence and reason *and which affects the disposition*.

Undue Influence and Duress: A will can be contested for *undue influence* and *duress*. Undue influence is influence that destroys testator's free agency at the time when the instrument is made, and that substitutes the will of another for that of the testator. Undue influence is a subjective evaluation whether *this testator* was overcome, not whether an average testator would be overcome. Undue influence is not actions or words of kindness, persuasion, pleas, friendship, advice or courting favors, even if the intent is to obtain testamentary benefits. On the other hand, physical coercion is not necessary. Undue influence is usually proved by inference with circumstantial evidence. The four elements of undue influence are:

(1) A testator subject to such influence because of some frailty;

(2) An opportunity to exercise the influence through access, communication, and contacts;

(3) A disposition to exercise the influence or willingness to do something wrong or unfair; and,

(4) A will appearing to be the effect of the influence because it contains an "unnatural" distribution pattern or unusual inclusion or exclusion.

When there is a confidential relationship between testator and the alleged influencer, most courts do not presume undue influence but require that some suspicious circumstances also be shown to raise the presumption. A presumption may arise if the alleged undue influencer and confidant drafts testator's will. By contrast, there is a presumption of undue influence for gifts made to one in a confidential relation with the donor.

Duress concerns the imposition of improper pressure on the testator which overcomes testator's will and takes away testator's free agency. The pressure may be manifested by physical coercion or some other improper threat.

Fraud: A will can be contested for a *fraud* committed against the testator when it can be shown that false representations were designed to and did deceive the testator into making a will different in its terms from that which he or she would have made had testator not been misled. The ground is similar to a tort action for deceit. There must be intent to deceive the testator: an innocent misrepresentation of the fact does not constitute fraud. The "risk of non persuasion" in a fraud contest is on the contestants.

Fraud must relate either to *fraud in the execution* of a will or to *fraud in its inducement*. *Fraud in the execution* concerns a fraud perpetrated in the execution or misrepresentations as to the character or contents of the instrument. The fraud must be made directly upon the testator: Fraud on the witnesses is not enough. Misrepresentation of contents not induced by the beneficiary is not ground for judicial relief, unless under the circumstances redress would be given for mistake alone. *Fraud in the inducement* concerns knowingly false statements made directly to the testator before the execution concerning material facts outside the will.

Mistake: Testator may have been mistaken as to the nature of the instrument executed, called a "mistake in the execution." Or, a testator may have been mistaken as to facts outside the instrument itself, called a "mistake in the inducement." Mistake in the execution would be a ground for contest whereas mistake in the inducement ordinarily would not be.

D. Inter Vivos Transfers

Generally, inter vivos transfers including trusts can be reformed or rescinded for fraud, duress, undue influence and sometimes unilateral mistake. If evidence is clear, unilateral mistake is ordinarily a sufficient ground for rescission or reformation although some courts have been more restrictive depending upon the situation.

V. CONSTRUCTIONAL PROBLEMS OF DISPOSITIONS

A. General Comment

The application or nonapplication of the following rules of construction can be controlled by the testator by express provision in the will.

B. Classification of Testamentary Gifts

Types of Devises: Many distributive doctrines depend on the types of devises involved. The four types of testamentary gifts are as follows:

- Specific bequests and devises are gifts of some particular thing or parcel of land.
- General bequests are ones which are payable out of the general estate, *e.g.*, "$1,000 to A."
- Demonstrative devises are devises, typically of an amount of money, payable primarily from a particular source, fund or container and if that source fails or is inadequate, then from the general assets of the estate.
- Residuary gifts are gifts of whatever remains of the estate after the payment of all obligations and after all other bequests and devises have been satisfied.

Courts have not consistently applied these definitions.

C. Class Gifts

A class gift is one in which the donor intends that the number of donees is subject to fluctuating by way of decrease or increase or both between the time of the gift and the time it vests. Common class gift terms include "children," "brothers," "sisters," "cousins," and "descendants."

As long as the class remains open, it is not possible to determine definitively the exact share of any class member in the subject matter of the disposition. It is necessary to determine (1) when the class closes and reaches its maximum membership; and, (2) when the class reaches its minimum membership. An increase in membership is most frequently caused be birth of members of the class. A decrease in the membership of a class is most frequently caused by the failure of a class member to survive to some specified time or event.

D. Lapse and Antilapse

Survivorship: A devisee must survive the decedent in order to take under the will. When the question of one's survival materially affects the distribution of an intestate's estate, the timing of death becomes a disrupting and litigable issue.

At common law, to take, a devisee must survive the decedent by any measurable time. Whether one survives becomes a matter of evidence and the standard of proof.

Testators can control the terms of survival in the will by specifying a period of time, *e.g.*, thirty days, after the death of the testator that the devisee must live to take. UPC Section 2–702 adopts a default survivorship rule for all types of gratuitous transfers including wills, trusts, etc. requiring all takers to survive by 120 hours of decedent's death or the transfer activating event.

Lapse and Void Devises: A devise lapses when a devisee dies between the execution of a will and the death of the testator. A devise is said to be void when the devisee died before the execution of the will. Lapsed or void devises either: (1) pass to a specifically named alternative devisee (a gift-over); (2) if no gift-over devise, to the residuary devisee; or (3) if no gift-over or residuary devise, by intestacy.

Antilapse Statutes: Antilapse statutes, which exist in all states, are not antilapse but actually substitutional and do not create a future interest. These statutes substitute the devisee's issue for the devisee, with the issue taking in their own right. The statutes usually limit the antilapse protection to selected family categories such as children or descendants. In addition, the statutes do not apply if the testator adequately indicates lapse should occur. Some statutes only protect against lapse and not void devises. Others cover both. Some cover class gifts; others do not.

Antilapse under the UPC: UPC Section 2–603 applies to any devisee (1) who is a grandparent or lineal descendant of a grandparent of the testator or the donor of a power of appointment and (2) who is a stepchild of the testator or the donor of a power of appointment. All covered relatives must survive testator, but not their ancestor who is devisee, by 120 hours. It applies if the devisee dies before the will, after the will or, if a devisee is treated as predeceased or disclaimed. It applies both to void and lapsed class gifts, but not to class gifts that are inherently representational, *e.g.*, "heirs," "issue."

UPC Section 2–604(a) provides that if lapse still occurs, the devised property becomes part of the residue. If the residue is to more than one person, but one dies and the devise fails, the lapsed devise is divided between the other residuary beneficiaries in proportion to their interests in the residue.

Survivorship Rules for Will Substitutes: Although survivorship problems can arise in inter vivos gratuitous transfers, the law in nonUPC states is usually undeveloped. The UPC contains several important provisions dealing with these problems for will substitutes. The UPC establishes a set of rules of construction that are applicable unless a contrary intent is provable or expressly stated on the instrument. UPC § 2–701.

E. Ademption

Ademption by Extinction: When the subject of a specific devise—the property given—is not in the estate at the time of testator's death, the gift fails under the doctrine of ademption by extinction. With a few exceptions, courts hold that ademption does not depend on testator's intent.

Ademption is avoided only if avoidance is expressed on the face of the will. Sometimes courts, however, have avoided ademption by construction of the devise or by tracing the devise to other assets. Courts also hold that changes in form, if not substantial, do not cause an ademption. For example, courts have held that a specific devise of stock is adeemed when the stock devised was converted to bonds and when stocks or bonds were converted to notes. On the other hand, specific devises of stock that split or that were only reclassified have been held not to be adeemed.

UPC Section 2–606 provides that the specific devisee has a right to specifically devised property or any part of it that exists in testator's estate at death. Concomitantly, the specific devisee has a right to assets that represent, in part or in whole, the remaining interest which the testator retains at death in the specifically devised property. If the specifically devised property is not in the estate at testator's death, the devisee is entitled to a general pecuniary devise equal to the value of the specifically devised property less the value of any actual portion of the devise remaining in the estate at testator's death and of the interests representing the devise under the provision but only to the extent clear and convincing evidence shows ademption is inconsistent with testator's intent.

In addition, transactions made for an incapacitated testator by or with a lifetime conservator or agent under a durable power of attorney are not adeemed and the specific devisee is entitled to the dollar amount of the devise equal to the net sale price, condemnation award or the value of the insurance proceeds.

Ademption by Satisfaction: Under the common law, the doctrine provides that a general or residuary devise is adeemed in whole or in part when a testator makes an inter vivos gift to the devisee after the execution of the will. As with advancements, the purpose is to prevent a devisee from receiving a double share. Testator's subjective intent in making the gift is key but frequently difficult to judicially establish. Courts use presumptions to settle the issue when evidence of intent is lacking.

UPC Section 2–609 codifies the ademption by satisfaction doctrine and formalizes its proof requirements. A gift is satisfaction of a devise only if either:

(1) the will provided for the deduction, or

(2) the testator "declared in a contemporaneous writing," that the gift is in satisfaction of the devise, or

(3) the devisee "acknowledged in writing" that the gift is in satisfaction of the devise, or

(4) the required writing indicates that the gift must be deducted from the value of the devise.

Although no words of art such as "satisfaction" need be used, the gist of the declaration must indicate the testator intended the gift to constitute what the law calls satisfaction.

When the devisee of a formal satisfaction fails to survive the donor, the formal satisfaction affects the devisee's descendants' share if the descendants take as substitute devisees under the UPC's antilapse provisions, unless the testator's contemporaneous writing expressly provides that the gift is not to affect the descendants' devise.

F. Accessions

Accession concerns changes in the property that occurred both before and after the death of the testator. Before death, accessions include rules that a specific devisee takes property at its distribution market value, takes land with improvements, and takes stock splits of specifically devised stock. Post-death accession issues concern the productivity of assets devised and how that productivity must be distributed. Thus, on distribution, devisees of specific devises receive all post death accessions, income, etc., attributable to the asset.

UPC Section 2–605 concerns accession issues raised by devises of securities. If certain conditions are met, it allows the devisee of securities to take a wide range of corporate accessions including, for example, shares acquired (1) because of stock dividends, (2) from merger restructuring, and (3) from reinvestment. It makes no difference whether the devise is characterized as specific or general. Cash distributions prior to death, however, are not part of the devise. UPC Section 3–904 follows the general rule and provides that cash devises earn interest beginning one year after decedent's death.

G. Abatement

Abatement problems arise anytime an estates lacks, for whatever reason, sufficient funds to satisfy all devises in a will. In the absence of a specific order indicated in the testator's will, the order of abatement for personal (and in most states, real) property is as follows: (1) intestate property; (2) residuary legacies; (3) general legacies; and (4) specific and demonstrative legacies. For example, all intestate property would abate before any type of testamentary devise. Within each class of testamentary devise, the assets abate ratably.

UPC 3–902(a) provides similarly. The UPC personal representative, however, is given authority to alter the normal order if necessary to carry out the testator's intent. Finally, the UPC contains other special abatement provisions for abatement caused by the election of a surviving spouse and from payment of estate taxes.

All jurisdictions have provisions that determine the proper order for paying debts, claims, and expenses when estates are insolvent. UPC Section 3–805, for example, provides that if the applicable assets of the estate are insufficient to pay all claims in full, the personal representative shall make payment in the following order:

(1) costs and expenses of administration;

(2) reasonable funeral expenses;

(3) debts and taxes with preference under federal law;

(4) reasonable and necessary medical and hospital expenses of the last illness of the decedent, including compensation of persons attending him;

(5) debts and taxes with preference under other laws of this state; and,

(6) all other claims.

No preference is given in the payment of any claim over any other claim of the same class, and a claim due and payable is not entitled to a preference over claims not due.

H. Miscellaneous Matters

Exoneration: The common law recognized a rebuttable presumption that loans or liens held on property devised by will should be discharged because the personal estate benefitted from the loan. UPC Section 2–607 reverses the presumption and provides that specific devises pass "subject to any mortgage interest existing at the date of death, without right of exoneration, regardless of a general directive in the will to pay debts."

Right of Retainer: Right of retainer refers to the right of a personal representative of a decedent's estate to reduce a devise by an amount equal to the debt owed to the estate by that devisee. A majority of courts have permitted the retainer even if the debt is barred by the Statute of Limitations or if the devisee has declared bankruptcy. UPC Section 3–903 recognizes the right of setoff against debts owed the estate but allows the debtor all defenses.

PART FOUR: LIFETIME TRANSFERS

I. WILL SUBSTITUTES

A. Testamentariness and Will Substitutes

Will Substitute Definition: A will substitute is a property transfer device, such as an inter vivos trust, that passes title at death without being subject to the formalities of the Statute of Wills, or to the probate administration processes. Ideally, the transfer avoids both requirements.

Testamentariness: A basic problem concerns what powers reserved by the grantor in the will substitute will cause the transfer to be declared testamentary and thus subject to the requirements of the Statute of Wills. The most common test courts use to determine whether a will substitute is testamentary is the *present transfer test* which attempts to determine whether the donor made a present transfer of an interest. Thus, that if an instrument is intended to become presently binding and nothing is left for the grantor to do to complete the transaction, then it need not be regarded as of a testamentary character. The two most significant factors that courts take into consideration are (1) the extent of the powers, and (2) the nature of the instrument, if any, which directs the disposition of the property to be made on the donor's death. Imparting importance to the form of the instrument is consistent with the purpose of the Statute of Wills to prevent fraudulent claims.

B. Joint Ownership

Joint Tenancy With Right of Survivorship: Joint tenancy with right of survivorship is a widely recognized nontestamentary form of ownership with its own particular requirements. When a joint tenant dies that tenant's title passes to the surviving joint tenant outside the probate process and without court administration.

Tenancy in Common: Tenancy in common is a form of co-ownership in a piece of property. On the death of a cotenant, the cotenant's interest passes through the cotenant's probate estate.

C. Contractual Survivorship

Pay on Death Provisions (POD): Clauses in various contractual arrangements usually have been held to be nontestamentary. For example, a partnership agreement may provide that on the death of a partner, that partner's partnership interest passes automatically to the surviving partner(s) or to one or more other designated persons. In contrast, POD provisions used in purely gratuitous arrangements have been characterized as testamentary. UPC Section 6–101 alters this distinction and confers nontestamentary status on the most common types of provisions sometimes found in inter vivos commercial transactions, *e.g.,* provisions to pay obligations to a designated person on the death of the obligee or to waive a debt on the event of the death of the obligee. This section establishes the validity of many common provisions found in insurance policies, pension plans, annuity contracts, trust agreements and other family arrangements.

Multiple Party Accounts: Accounts held in the name of multiple parties are common financial arrangements that take several forms:.

- Joint accounts, *e.g.,* an account payable to "A or B";
- Trust accounts, *e.g.*, an account held as "A in trust for B"; and,
- Accounts payable on death or POD accounts, *e.g.*, an account held as "A payable on death to B."

Joint Accounts: Although the ordinary joint bank deposit arrangement is not a true joint tenancy, the surviving party to the account has been permitted to take on the bases of contract or trust principles.

Trust Accounts: The trust account or "Totten Trust" refers to an account that is held in the name of one or more parties as trustee for one or more beneficiaries. Despite the unlimited control over the account by the depositor, and that the sole purpose of the arrangement is to pay the remainder of the account to the "beneficiary," these accounts have been readily upheld under the characterization of being a revocable trust. In effect, these are pay-on death accounts.

Pay-on Death Accounts: A Pay-on Death or POD account refers to an account that is payable on request to one person, usually the depositor, during his or her lifetime and on that person's death, to one or more POD payees to whom the account is payable. Courts have a split as to their validity.

Multiple Party Accounts under the UPC: UPC Article 6 specifically recognizes the validity of survivorship for multiple-party, POD, and trust accounts. Significantly, the right of survivorship cannot be changed by the will of a depositor or of any other person.

Life Insurance, Annuities, and Related Arrangements: Life insurance of all kinds is consistently held to be nontestamentary. The beneficiary obtains his or her interest upon the theory of a contract or a trust for his or her benefit. With only a few exceptions, life insurance and related beneficiary designations are not alterable by will and must be changed according to the terms of the contract.

D. Conditional Deeds

Conditional deeds are inter vivos transfers of property wherein the grantor retains interest in the property. Typical reservations include the grantee survive the grantor, the conveyance takes effect only upon the grantor's death, and the instrument is revocable by the grantor, or a combination of these conditions. When all three reservations appear in the same instrument, the deed has usually been held testamentary. There is a decided split of authority as to the effect of each provision taken singly.

E. Nondocumented Gratuitous Transfers

Formal Requirements of Gifts: An owner (donor) of personal property may make a gift of that property to another person (the donee) by delivering it to the donee, or to a third person for the donee, with the manifested intention that the donee be the owner of the personal property. The donee's acceptance of the gift is required to complete the gift. Delivery is the formality that explains the act of the donor. Delivery may be actual or constructive or symbolic.

Gifts Causa Mortis: A gift causa mortis is a gratuitous transfer of personal property by the donor to another person in apprehension of imminent death. It is presumed the gift is a revocable gift within a reasonable time after the donor is no longer in apprehension of imminent death.

F. Gifts to Minors

Because minors lack legal capacity to manage property, property ownership by minors requires a system of property management usually called guardianship. Guardianships require court involvement including appointment, periodic review, limitations on management, and necessary authorization.

Under the Uniform Transfer to Minors Act a gift may be made to a custodian in the name of the minor according to the terms of the Act. The Act fully defines the custodian's duties and powers and the rights of the minor. Under the Act, when the minor attains the age of 21 or dies, the conservatorship ends and the property is transferred to the beneficiary or to his or her estate, if dead.

II. PLANNING FOR RETIREMENT AND INCAPACITY

A. General Concepts and Techniques

Anticipating the Incapacity: Because adults, either because of physical or mental decline, may need assistance at some point in life in either personal or financial decision making or both, planning ahead for these potential incapacities is an important responsibility for the estate planner. The revocable inter vivos trust [*see infra,* Part 6.IV], the durable power of attorney [*see infra*, 4.II.B], and the advanced healthcare directives [*infra* Part 4.II.C.], are devices commonly used to deal with this problem.

B. Durable Powers of Attorney

Authorizing Statutes: Durable powers, which are recognized in all states, are significant alternatives for conservatorships. They permit persons to anticipate the problem of diminished or full incapacity without the need for court involvement. They have become essential estate planning tools.

The UPC Model: UPC adopts the civil law rule for all written powers of attorney which means all actions by the attorney in fact in good faith and according to the written power of attorney are valid even though such actions take place after the principal's death, disability or incompetence so long as the attorney in fact did not have actual knowledge of the happening of such an event. Such valid actions bind the principal and the principal's heirs, devisees and personal representative. Parties dealing with the attorney in fact are protected in the absence of fraud. An affidavit executed by the attorney in fact that recites no knowledge of revocation or termination caused by death, disability or incompetence is conclusive proof of nonrevocation or nontermination of the power.

True Durable Power: The UPC also permits the true durable power to specifically provide that the disability of the principal does not affect the power of the appointed attorney in fact to act. The qualifying language permits the power to either provided that disability or incapacity of the principal does not affect the power or that the power of attorney becomes effective upon the disability or incapacity of the principal.

Exercises of the Power: All actions taken according to the durable power during a period of disability or incompetence of the principal have the same binding and beneficial effect as if the principal was not disabled. Durable powers remain effective until a time explicitly expressed in the instrument, or until terminated by the death of the principal, whichever first occurs.

Other Responsibilities: An appointed conservator has the same power over the attorney in fact as the principal would have had if incapacity or disappearance had not occurred, including the power to revoke, suspend or terminate any part or all of the power. The principal may include in the durable power a nomination of the attorney in fact to serve as conservator if protective proceedings are commenced.

C. Health Care Decisions

The Health Care Dilemma: A conflict can arise between one's normal desire to extend life and the desire to die because of personal and financial reasons.

Constitutional Protection of Liberty to Body Integrity: With only limited exceptions, a conscious person has complete domain over the person and no one can administer care that is not wanted. On the other hand, decisions concerning health care will be made by others notwithstanding the presence or absence of health care instructions.

The Need for an Advanced Health Care Directive: The Advanced Health Care Directive permits the person to have some input into health care decisions once the ability to make one's own decision is gone. Because the state is allowed to establish a procedure and to set a burden of proof for determining the desires of the person, the existence or nonexistence of a health care directive is significant.

Advanced Health Care Directives: The two basic types of health care directives are the living will and the health care durable power of attorney or health care proxy.

Living Will: A living will is a document that expresses an individual's desires regarding health care, including the withholding or withdrawal of life-sustaining treatment, under certain prescribed circumstances when the individual is no longer personally able to make those decisions.

Health Care Durable Power of Attorney or Health Care Proxy: The health care durable power of attorney or health care proxy is used instead of or in conjunction with a living will. It appoints a person as agent who is empowered to make health care decisions, including the withholding or withdrawal of life-sustaining treatment, for the principal under certain prescribed circumstances when the individual is no longer personally able to make those decisions.

Scope and Exercise of Living Will: Any competent adult may complete a written declaration directing the withholding or withdrawal of life sustaining procedures under certain circumstances. The declarant may choose not to prolong his or her life if the individual:

- has "an incurable and irreversible condition" that will result in declarant's death within a relatively short time; or
- becomes unconscious and, to a reasonable degree of medical certainty, will not regain consciousness, or
- faces likely risks and burdens of treatment that would outweigh the expected benefits.

Health Care Instructions: The declarant may choose what procedures may be required, withheld or withdrawn, including the use or nonuse of:

- life support systems;
- artificial nutrition and hydration systems or procedures; and
- treatment for alleviation of pain or discomfort.

Notice of the Living Will: To be effective, declarants must inform other relevant family members and health care providers of the existence of their living wills.

Formalities for Execution and Revocation of Living Wills: Living wills must be in writing and signed by the declarant and witnessed. They may be revoked by a writing, signed by the declarant.

Health Care Durable Power of Attorney or Health Care Proxy: A health care durable power appoints an agent or surrogate who has authority to make decisions concerning medical treatment and health care when the attending physician determines decisions can no longer be made by the individual. Although a sense of the principal's particular desires concerning medical care should be indicated, the agent is to do what is in the individual's best interests, taking into account the principal's personal values when no instructions are provided.

D. Physician Assisted Suicide

The Assisted Suicide Issue: The basic legal issue is whether state laws making assisted suicide a felony violate the terminally ill patient's constitutional rights. The argument is that where the patient is in the final stage of terminal illness, the state has no interests prohibiting a physician from prescribing medication to be self administered for the purpose of hastening death particularly where those who are on life support systems are permitted to hasten their deaths by withdrawing life maintaining support systems.

The Supreme Court held that respondents' asserted "right" to assistance in committing suicide is not a fundamental liberty interest protected by the Due Process Clause. An assisted suicide statutory ban rationally relates to legitimate government interests. Such interests include, *e.g.,* prohibiting intentional killing and preserving human life; protecting the medical profession's integrity and ethics and maintaining physicians' roles as their patients' healers; protecting the poor, the vulnerable elderly, from indifference, prejudice, and psychological and financial pressure to end their lives. In *Vacco v. Quill*, the Court held that neither the assisted suicide ban nor the law permitting patients to refuse medical treatment treats anyone differently from anyone else or draws any distinctions between persons. Everyone, regardless of physical condition, is entitled, if competent, to refuse unwanted lifesaving medical treatment; no one is permitted to assist a suicide. The distinction between letting a patient die and making that patient die is important, logical, rational, and well established: It comports with fundamental legal principles of causation.

Assisted Suicide Legislation: Oregon legalized physician assisted suicide for competent, terminally ill adults. Other states have rejected such proposals. The Federal Assisted Suicide Funding Restriction Act prohibits the use of federal funds in support of physician assisted suicide. The law is under development.

E. Public Programs for Incapacity and Retirement

The Programs: Social Security, Medicare, Supplemental Security Income and Medicaid are the primary sources of governmental benefits for retired and disabled persons. SSI and Medicaid are financial need based programs.

Social Security: Social Security is a retirement program that workers, employers and the self-employed pay for with their Social Security taxes. Qualification depends on work history and the amount of benefit is based on earnings. Social Security also protects workers who become severely disabled and eligible family members . Disabled means a severe physical or mental condition that prevents them from working and that is expected to last for at least 12 months or to result in death. Benefits continue only for as long as the worker is disabled and cannot work.

Medicare: Medicare is a health insurance program for aged persons to complement the retirement, survivors and disability insurance benefits. Medicare consists of three parts: Hospital Insurance (HI), known as "Part A," Supplementary Medical insurance (SMI), known as "Part B, and the Medicare+Choice program, 'Part C.' "

Part A is financed primarily through a mandatory payroll deduction ("FICA tax"). Almost all employees and self-employed workers in the U.S. work in employment covered by the Part A program and pay taxes to support the cost of benefits for aged and disabled beneficiaries.

Part B is financed through: (1) set premium payments usually deducted from the monthly Social Security benefit checks of those who are enrolled in Part B program, and (2) through contributions from general revenue of the U.S. Treasury. Beneficiary premiums are currently set at a level that covers 25 percent of the average expenditures for aged beneficiaries.

The Part C program is financed from the Part A and Part B trust funds in proportion to the relative weights of benefits of those Parts to the total benefits paid by the Medicare program.

Medicare Coverage: Part A is provided automatically to persons age 65 and over who are entitled to Social Security or Railroad Retirement Board benefits. Individuals who have received such benefits based on their disability, for a period of at least 24 months, are also entitled to these benefits.

Part B primarily covers the cost for physician services and covers certain other non-physician services, such as ambulance services, clinical laboratory tests, diagnostic tests, flu vaccinations, prescription drugs which cannot be self-administered, certain other health services not supplied by Part A.

Part C or Medicare+Choice plans will be risk-based plans offered by Qualified Health Maintenance Organizations, Provider–Sponsored Organizations, Preferred Provider Organizations, and other certified public or private coordinated care plans and entities.

Non-covered Services: Medicare does not include long term nursing care or custodial care, and certain other health care needs, *e.g.*, dentures and dental care, eyeglasses, hearing aids, most prescription drugs, etc. Some of these noncovered services may be offered in Part C plans.

Supplemental Security Income (SSI): SSI disability benefits are paid to people who have a disability and who do not own much or have a lot of income. To qualify for

SSI the applicant must have limited countable monthly income of countable assets, *e.g.,* $2,000. Assets held in irrevocable trusts are not countable but actual income payments from the trust to the beneficiary will be counted under the SSI income limit test. Distribution of in-kind income that does not result in the beneficiary's direct receipt of a basic needs, *e.g.,* food, clothing or shelter, is not counted.

Medicaid: Medicaid is a Federal–State matching entitlement program that pays for medical assistance for certain vulnerable and needy individuals and families with low incomes and resources. Medicaid is the largest source of funding for medical and health-related services for America's poorest people.

Medicaid Coverage: Under broad national guidelines each State: (1) establishes its own eligibility standards; (2) determines the type, amount, duration, and scope of services; (3) sets the rate of payment for services; and (4) administers its own program. Medicaid policies for eligibility, services, and payment are complex, and vary considerably even between similar sized or adjacent States. Medicaid eligibility or services, or both, within a State can also change during the year.

Generally, to qualify for medicaid an applicant must (1) be eligible according to the categorically needy test; (2) have income below the state's income test; and (3) have assets valued below the state's asset test.

F. Long Term Care Planning

The Long Term Care Planning Setting: Financing the costs of long term care is of crucial importance to elderly individuals. Other than long term care insurance, the alternative to personally financing nursing home care is the federal Medicaid program.

Estate Depletion: In order to obtain public assistance through medicaid to finance long term care, individuals must reduce the value of any personal estate below poverty limits.

Estate Planning Goal: An estate planning goal for these clients is both to preserve the client's access to public benefits, and assets and control.

Qualifying for Medicaid: For Medicaid eligibility purposes, asset protection planning involves the transfer of assets, creation of certain trusts, conversion of excess resources to exempt assets, and outright gifts. Medicaid rules provide that for eligibility purposes, all assets that could be liquidated to provide for the individual's basic needs, such as food, shelter and clothing, must be considered, unless exempt. Exempt assets for eligibility purposes under both SSI and Medicaid include, *e.g.,* the family home, household goods and personal effects with a total equity of $2,000. Many states also deny Medicaid if the applicant receives too much income, *e.g.,* in 1997 the annual limit was $1,453.

Smart Spend–Down: A "smart spend-down" concerns a effort to purchase or make exempt expenditures including, *e.g.,* medical equipment, adapted or new vehicle, prepay health insurance.

Transfer Restrictions: Inter vivos transfers of the applicant's (or spouse's) assets to trusts by the applicant or others for the applicant are counted for Medicaid eligibility purposes if payment could be made to or for the applicant under any circumstance (including the exercise of trustee's discretion).

Ineligibility Period: Any gift of assets by the applicant to individuals within 36 months of Medicaid application (or within 60 months for transfers to trusts), triggers a period of Medicaid ineligibility, even if the applicant retains no interest in the donated property.

Qualifying Trusts: There are two types of trusts creatable with the applicant's own assets that do not count for Medicaid eligibility purposes.

> Under Age 65 Disability Trust: Trusts created by parents, grandparents, legal guardians or courts for the benefit of a disabled individual under the age of 65 are exempt if the trust provides that, at the beneficiary's death, the state will receive amounts remaining in the trust up to Medicaid benefits provided by such state. Additional amounts added to the trust do not affect eligibility unless transferred after the beneficiary reaches age 65.

> Pooled Account Trust: Pooled Account Trusts are pooled asset trusts that are managed by non-profit associations and hold the assets of disabled individuals in separate accounts. Any amount remaining in the account at the beneficiary's death must be paid to the state up to the benefits provided by Medicaid.

Estate Recovery Program: States must establish estate recovery programs to recover the cost of Medicaid benefits from the probate estate of any deceased recipient who was in-patient in a nursing facility, or who received nursing home care or other long term care services, if the recipient was 55 years or older when the recipient received such benefits. The states can also recover nonprobate property in which the individual had any legal title or interest at the time of death (to the extent of such interest), including assets conveyed through joint tenancy, tenancy in common, survivorship, life estate, living trust or other arrangements. No recovery is permitted until the applicants surviving spouse dies or if there is a surviving child who is under age 21, blind or disabled.

Federal Crime for Asset Transfers: It is a federal crime to give away assets or set up trusts for purposes of qualifying for Medicaid. Conviction may result in a fine of not more than $10,000 or imprisonment for not more than one year, or both.

Third Party Special Needs Trusts (SNT): Inter vivos or testamentary trusts may be created and funded by third parties for the benefit of disabled individuals without affecting the beneficiary's eligibility for Medicaid, if the purposes of the trusts are to improve upon the beneficiaries' quality of life by providing for those otherwise unprovided supplemental needs, such as more sophisticated medical, rehabilitative, recreational or educational aid. No distributions for basic support provided under governmental assistance programs may be made. Although not counted as an asset for Medicaid, actual income distributions from the trust are counted under the income test.

G. Organ Donation

Summary of the Law: When a person dies it is presumed that that person's organs may not be taken without the person's prior consent or the consent of the relevant survivors. State law controls the requirements for making an effective organ and tissue donation. Generally, an intention to make a gift may be indicated by signing a donor card. Some states require the cards to be witnessed. Specific requests by the donor concerning purposes and organs to be donated may be indicated.

Organ Donation Benefit: Organ and tissue donation are very beneficial because a single person can donate up to eight organs (the heart, liver, pancreas, kidneys, lungs and small intestine), as well as tissue (skin, bone, bone marrow, corneas and heart valves). The single donor will on average benefit three or more recipients.

Need for Organs: Due to increased organ transplant capabilities, long waiting lists exist for some organs.

Estate Planning for Organ Donations: Organ donation considerations should be a part of all estate planning representations.

PART FIVE: POWERS OF APPOINTMENT

I. INTRODUCTION TO POWERS

A. Definition of Power of Appointment

Definition: A power of appointment is the authority, held by a nonowner, to designate recipients of beneficial interests in or powers of appointment over the appointive property. The appointive property is the property or property interest subject to a power of appointment. The property interest subject to appointment need not be an absolute-ownership interest. Powers of appointment put flexibility into the donor's original disposition to allow it to be molded to meet changing conditions.

Parties to a Power of Appointment:

- Donor: The donor (creator) is the person who created the power of appointment.
- Donee: The donee (powerholder) is the person upon whom the power of appointment was conferred.
- Objects: The objects are the persons expressly designated in the instrument creating the power for whom the power can be exercised.
- Appointee: The appointee is the person the donee appoints. The appointment makes the appointee the owner of the appointed property interest.

- Takers in Default: The taker in default is the person who takes the appointive property to the extent the power is not effectively exercised. The taker in default has a property interest that is subject to the power of appointment.

The Doctrine of "Relation Back": The doctrine of "relation back" says the donee's appointment is deemed to relate back to and become part of the donor's original instrument. Because the exercise of a power is the completion of the terms of a transfer that started with the creator of the power, it passes the appointed interest directly from the donor to the appointee.

Personal Nature of Powers of Appointment: Powers of appointment are personal to the donee. Except when trustees hold powers, the donee is not a fiduciary and is under no duty to exercise a power of appointment. An unexercised power dies with the donee's death and does not pass to the donee's successors in interest.

B. Creation of a Power of Appointment

Intent to Create a Power of Appointment: A power of appointment is created when the transferor manifests an intent to create a transfer device the law calls a power of appointment. Powers may be presently exercisable, or exercisable by will, or both.

Formalities for Creating Powers of Appointment: The requisite formalities for creating a power of appointment are the formalities required by law for the type of transfer made by the donor *e.g.,* a power of appointment created in a will must be executed as a will.

Determining the Donee's Intent: When an instrument does not specifically indicate whether a power of appointment is exercised, relevant admissible evidence will be considered to determine the donee's intent.

Exercise Formalities: To exercise a power effectively, a donee must indicate an intent to exercise it and comply with the requirements of exercise imposed by the donor and by rules of law.

C. Different Kinds of Powers of Appointment

General versus Special (Nongeneral) Powers: A general power permits the donee to appoint the property to the donee, personally, to the donee's creditors, to the donee's estate, or to creditors of the donee's estate. A special power, or nongeneral power is any power that is not a general power. A donee of a nongeneral power may appoint only to a particular group of persons.

Donee's authority is presumptively unlimited. The donee's authority regarding appointees and the time and manner of appointment is limited only to the extent the donor effectively manifests an intent to impose limits. All powers must be in existence before they are exercisable.

Exercise Instructions: Powers are categorized as to when they may be exercised.

A power of appointment is presently exercisable if the donee may immediately exercise it at the time in question by deed or by will. A power of appointment is not presently exercisable if it may only (1) be exercised by a will, called a testamentary power, or (2) at the time in question cannot be exercised until some event or passage of time occurs.

A "non-exclusive" power is a special power in which the donee is required to appoint some part to each of the members of the class. An "exclusive" power is a special power in which the donee may appoint to some members of the class and exclude others. The donor's intent determines whether a power of appointment is exclusive or non-exclusive. General powers are characterized as exclusive powers because objects of the power are unlimited. Most courts apply a constructional preference for the "exclusive" power if there is ambiguity in what the donor intended.

If the donee of a non-exclusive power appoints in a manner inconsistent with the principles of the non-exclusive power, the appointment is invalid in toto, and the property passes to the takers in default, or if there are no takers in default designated, the appointed property passes in equal parts to the class of permissible appointees.

Collateral Powers and Powers in Gross: The donee has a purely collateral power if the donee holds no interest in the property except the power. The donee has a power in gross if the donee holds both an interest in the property and a power that if exercised would dispose of the interest that the donee does not hold.

II. EXERCISE OF A POWER OF APPOINTMENT

A. Exercise of a Power of Appointment

Exercise Requirements Imposed by the Donor: A donor may impose various restrictions on the donee's exercise of the power, *e.g.,* donee must make a specific reference to the power in order to exercise it. Failure to comply with any formal requirement imposed by the donor may prevent exercise even though the donee clearly manifested an intent to exercise.

Blanket Appointments: A donee, who by deed or will and who manifests an intention to exercise all powers the donee holds, will be held to have manifested an intent to exercise both general and non-general powers that are exercisable by the deed or the will unless formal limits imposed by the donor are not satisfied. A mere manifestation to dispose of all of the donee's property, however, does not exercise any power held by the donee.

Appointive Assets Identified in Dispositive Instrument of Donee: A donee's disposition, by deed or will, of the property that is covered by a power is inferred to manifests an intent to exercise the power.

Other Circumstances Indicating Donee's Intended Exercise of Power: All surrounding circumstances existing at the time of the execution concerning the formulation of the donee's deed or will are relevant to determine whether donee intended to exercise the power. Sympathies for the appointee will be a factor.

Testamentary Exercise of After-acquired Power: A donee's manifestation to exercise powers includes powers acquired after the execution of the donee's will unless the exercise of the after-acquired powers is specifically excluded. If the donee dies before the donor creates the power, however, it never comes into existence and thus the donee's will does not exercise it.

Exercise of Power of Appointment under the UPC:

- When the document creating a power of appointment does not explicitly require specific reference, a will that contains a general residuary clause exercises the power only (1) if the document creating the power fails to contain an effective gift in default of exercise, or (2) if the testator-donee's will manifests an intention to include the property that is subject to the power as part of the residuary or general disposition clause and the power is a general and nongeneral testamentary power.

- When the document creating a power of appointment explicitly requires that the power may only be exercised by a specific reference to the power in the exercising document, it is presumed the donor wanted to prevent an inadvertent exercise of the power. The donor's intent as to the requirements for exercise, and the donee's intent as to the exercise, are left to extrinsic evidence.

B. Excessive Appointment–Fraud on Power of Appointment

Appointment to Non-object of Non-general Power: An appointment of a beneficial interest by the donee to a non-object is ineffective. Attempts to benefit non-objects through the appointment are described as a "fraud on the power" or "fraudulent appointment."

The definition of the limited class is significant because the broader the class of objects, the less likely an appointment will be ineffective. A distinction is recognized between a positively defined limited class and a very wide range of objects.

The inclusion of adopted children, nonmarital, stepchildren, and persons related by affinity depends on rules of construction operative in the controlling jurisdiction when proper drafting has not defined their inclusion or exclusion.

General Power Exclusion: The excessive appointment doctrine is inapplicable to general powers because the donee is free to appoint by deed to the donee personally or by will to the donee's estate. Thus, there are no non-objects.

C. Interests Creatable by Exercise of Power of Appointment

Permissible Appointment under General Power: The donee of a general power of appointment may appoint a fee or any lesser or qualified legal estate. The donee is permitted to create any power in another directly that could be created indirectly in another by appointing to the donee or the donee's estate and then creating the power in connection with a disposition of owned property.

Permissible Appointment under Non-general Power: Unless the donor indicates otherwise, the donor of a non-general power may make any appointment benefitting objects of the power that the donee could make of owned property in favor of those objects including: (1) creating a general power in an object of the non-general power, or (2) creating a non-general power in any person to appoint to an object of the original non-general power.

> Donor can make the appointment personal to the donee and then the donee is not allowed to exercise the power by creating a power.

D. Contract to Appoint Power of Appointment

Presently Exercisable Power: The donee who holds a presently exercisable power of appointment may contract to make an appointment in the future if neither the contract nor the promised appointment confers a benefit upon one not an object of the power. Such a contract is not valid if the contract or the promised appointment confers a benefit on a non-object.

Power Not Presently Exercisable: The donee of a power of appointment that is not presently exercisable cannot contract to make an appointment in the future that is enforceable by the promisee.

E. Time of Exercise of Power of Appointment

Attempted Appointment Before Creation of Power: A power of appointment cannot be effectively exercised before the power is created or before a condition precedent to the power's exercise has been satisfied. This rule does not prevent the exercise of a testamentary power by a will executed prior to the creation of the a power so long as the will becomes effective after the power's creation.

F. Appointment to Deceased Persons

Death of Objects Prior to Effective Exercise: The appointment by donee to a person who is dead is ineffective except as provided by an applicable antilapse statute. The appointment to the dead person's estate is effective if the dead person's estate is a proper object of the power. The donee's appointment to an alternative taker if the originally named appointee dies before some specified time is valid only if the alternative appointee is an object of the power and is not dead at the time of appointment.

Antilapse Statutes and Powers of Appointments: Many antilapse statutes are silent about their application to powers of appointments and their exercise.

UPC Antilapse Provision: The UPC specifically applies its substitute gift protection to the exercise of powers of appointment. Exercised testamentary powers are protected by the substitute gift presumption if the appointee comes within the protected class of a grandparent or a lineal descendant of a grandparent or a stepchild of the donor of a power of appointment exercised by the testator's will or of the testator who is donee of the power. The rule applies to general and special powers so long as the appointee is in the protected class. The exercise may be to an individual or a class and the substitute taker need not be a member of the class of permissible appointees so long as the appointee is a permissible appointee and meets the relational threshold requirement.

III. NONEXERCISE OF POWERS OF APPOINTMENT

A. Release and Disclaimer of Powers of Appointment

Release of Powers of Appointment: A donee of a general or a non-general power of appointment created by the donee can be released, in whole or in part, by the donee of the power unless the donor effectively manifest an intent that it not be releasable. If a power is properly released, the property passes at the time and to the persons who would have taken if the power were never exercised.

Disclaimer of Power by Donee: The donee of a power of appointment can disclaim all or some part of the power if the procedures of the relevant disclaimer statute are followed.

Lapse of Power: If the donor of a power of appointment requires that the power be exercised within a specified time or it will cease to exist, failure of the donee to exercise the power within the specified period of time causes the power to lapse. A lapse is the equivalent of a release.

Methods of Release: A releasable power may be released, for example, by following any method authorized by the donor of the power, or by delivering the release to a person who could be adversely affected by an exercise of the power, or communicating an intent to release the power in any other appropriate manner.

B. Disclaimer by Object or Appointee

Disclaimer by Object of Power: Objects of the power may disclaim within a reasonable time after the creation of the power.

Disclaimer by an Appointee: Appointees can disclaim the interest appointed in the appointee's favor. The appointee can disclaim the interest within a reasonable time after the exercise of the power. The fact that a person accepted the status of being an object of the power does not prevent a disclaimer of the status of an appointee.

IV. DONEE'S CREDITORS AND SPOUSAL ELECTIONS

A. General Application

Third Person Rights Against the Donee: Whether creditors and spouses of donees of powers of appointment can reach appointive assets to satisfy their claims depend on whether (1) the power of appointment held by the donee is a general or special power, and (2) it has been exercised.

B. Creditors of the Donee

Non-general Power: Because a donee of a non-general power is not considered to be the owner of the appointive assets, creditors of that donee cannot subject the appointive assets to the payment of the claims or to the expenses of administration of the donee's estate even if the donee exercises the power.

Fraudulent Conveyance: Fraudulent transfers of assets by an owner of property into a trust are reachable by the owner's creditors even though the owner only reserved a non-general power.

General Power Not Created by Donee:

Unexercised General Power of Appointment: Generally in the absence of a controlling statute, appointive assets covered by an unexercised general power of appointment that was created by some person other than the donee cannot be subjected to payment of claims of the donee's creditors. Until the donee exercises the power, courts say the donee has not accepted sufficient control over the appointive assets to give the donee the equivalent of ownership. Several state statutes permit creditors to subject the property over which the donee holds a general power of appointment whether or not the power has been exercised.

Exercised General Powers: An exercised power is one that has been effectively exercised in favor of appointees other than takers in default.

- Exercised general testamentary powers are subject to the payment of claims against the donee's estate.
- Exercised general inter vivos powers are subject to the payment of the claims of creditors of the donee to the same extent as any fraudulent conveyance of donee's personally owned assets would be.

The donee's exercise of a general power, whether testamentary or inter vivos, is considered to be identical to full ownership of property. These rules apply regardless of whether the donor or the donee manifested a contrary intent.

General Power Created by Donee: Creditors of the donee or claimants against the donee's estate may get at appointive assets that were subject to a general power of appointment held and created by the donee whether it is presently or not presently exercisable. Persons cannot put their property beyond the reach of creditors merely by transferring the assets to a trust and retaining a general power of appointment.

Consequences of Donee's Bankruptcy: Section 541(b)(1) of the Bankruptcy Code excludes from the bankruptcy estate all non-general powers and all general powers to appoint by will. The bankruptcy estate includes the donee's general powers that are presently exercisable because they are inherently exercisable for the benefit of the bankrupt. A spendthrift clause does not change this rule.

C. Spousal Rights in Appointive Assets

Spouses Rights Absent a Statute: The donee's spouse is not entitled to treat the appointive assets as owned by the donee or as part of the donee's estate for elective share purposes if those assets are subject to a power not created by the donee.

Statutory Spousal Rights of Surviving Spouse: Some spousal protection statutes specifically provided that property over which the deceased spouse had a general power of appointment is included in the deceased spouse's estate for a spouse's elective share if the deceased spouse was both the donor and donee of the power. Common law right of dower does not attach to appointive assets.

PART SIX: TRUSTS

I. TRUSTS: DEFINITIONS AND CHARACTERISTICS

A. Trust Characteristics

An express trust is a fiduciary relationship with respect to property, arising as a result of a manifestation of an intention to create that relationship and subjecting the person who holds title to the property to duties to deal with it for the benefit of charity or for one or more persons, at least one of whom is not the sole trustee.

Fragmentation of Trust Interests: Trusts always separate "legal ownership" from "equitable ownership." Trusts usually have their equitable trust interests divided between present and future beneficiaries, *e.g.*, in trust for A for life, remainder to B.

Trust Distinctions: Occasionally, the nature of a transaction is unclear and a question arises whether it creates an express trust or some other device. Characterization of the arrangement may be determinative of rights and duties between the parties to the transaction or of liabilities or priorities regarding third parties. Sometimes it is beneficial for a party to the transaction to contend a trust exists, sometimes another legal device. Courts have not consistently characterized ambiguous transactions.

Nontrust Security Arrangements: Generally, security interests such as mortgages, pledges and legal or equitable liens are not "trusts" even when trust concepts are used and some rules applicable to trust relationships are applied. Under special circumstances, arrangements of this nature have been held to be trusts when the property had to be segregated and not commingled with the "trustee's" own assets.

Estate–Planning Uses of Trusts

Testamentary trusts are used to provide property management for beneficiaries, allow for successive estates, protect future interests, permit flexibility regarding unanticipated situations, and save taxes.

Inter vivos trusts are used to avoid probate and agency pitfalls and to save taxes.

B. The Trustee

The Trustee's Title: The trustee holds legal title to the property and administers the trust property. A trustee is a fiduciary.

Trustee Designation: The trustee or successor trustees are usually named in the trust. Otherwise, a court may appoint the trustee. Individuals, corporate fiduciaries, and governments may be trustees. Infants, incompetents, aliens, nonresidents/foreign corporations, and unincorporated associations may have special capacity problems in qualifying as trustees. Trusteeships are terminated only by court order or as set out in the instrument or by law.

"A trust will not fail for want of a trustee." Once a trust is established, the failure or absence of a trustee will not affect the continuation of the trust since a successor will ordinarily be appointed to carry out the settlor's intention. The limited exceptions to this rule include when the trusteeship (its duties) is considered personal to the person appointed and when a trustee is not appointed and there is a question whether there has been a transfer.

Successor Trustee: The trust or a court may name a successor trustee. The court will consider the desires of beneficiaries, settlor's intent, and furtherance of sound administration

C. The Trust Property

Specific Res: A trust must have a specific identifiable res: it must be transferable and be ascertainable. The issue is whether the property of the trust is described with such definiteness and certainty that the trustee and the court can be sure that the intended trust is carried out.

Property Interests: Trusts may be created with the transfer of fee simples, terms of years, life estates, contingent remainders (some states prohibit this), vested remainders, other future interests, and contractual rights. Tort claims and contingent remainders can be held in a trust but not transferred to a trust.

> Trusts of certain shares of stock or of certain capital, including all future profits realized from trading that stock or capital, are effective at the date of creation. In addition, a trust is created if the settlor transfers into the trust an enforceable contract including future earnings from the contract. What is not permitted is merely a gratuitous promise to pay income in the future. Here, no trust exists until income is received and transferred into the trust.
>
> The res requirement serves evidentiary and cautionary purposes. It improves the reliability of proof and probative safeguards for the settlor, trustee and beneficiary against unworthy disputes over rights, responsibilities and title. It also serves a cautionary function for the settlor by emphasizing the importance of the act and by exhibiting a clear expression of finality of intent. It also limits and puts in focus the trustee's substantial fiduciary duties.

D. The Beneficiaries

Cestui Que Trust: The cestui que trust, or beneficiary, is the one for whom the trust property is held. The beneficiary has in personam and in rem rights: personal rights against the trustee, and equitable ownership of the trust res.

Definite Beneficiary: There must be a definite beneficiary identifiable at the time of creation or within the Rule Against Perpetuities who can receive the beneficial interest from and judicially enforce the trust against the trustee. Charitable trusts have a different beneficiary rule.

The definite beneficiary rule is justified because only those who stand in the position of a beneficiary under a private trust have the right to come into court and challenge the way it is administered. Thus, it is argued that without a definite beneficiary there would be no one able to enforce the administration of the trust. Only beneficiaries may enforce a trust but any beneficiary can do so. The proper question might be: "Is there at least one clear beneficiary?"

Relational Terminology Used in Trusts: Relational terminology used to describe the beneficiary must permit beneficiary identification on the basis of facts of independent significance for trusts created in wills. Definiteness, however, depends on provable intent of the settlor.

Special Group Language: Group categories including, *e.g.,* "relatives," "family," "neighbors," "friends," have caused litigation. How they are defined may determine whether the description is definite enough.

Unborn Beneficiaries: Although there is old contrary authority, the modern rule is that a trust can be validly created even if all beneficiaries are unborn, unascertained, or both. For example, if S transfers assets "to T, in trust, for T and his children for the life of T, remainder to T's children" and at time of transfer T was childless, a valid trust is established. If T dies childless, S or S's estate will take the defeasibly vested reversion.

E. Trust Purposes

Trust Purpose and Public Policy: Trusts can be created for any purpose that is not deemed contrary to public policy. Improper purposes include, *e.g.,* the trust that supports the commission of a criminal or tortious act by the trustee, or an activity that is against "public policy."

> Public policy prohibitions include trust purposes that, *e.g.,* restrict marriages, encourage divorce or neglect of parental responsibilities, or require a change of religious beliefs.
>
> "Public policy" cannot be defined because it changes almost as rapidly as society in general changes. It has been stated that the exercise of public policy by a court goes to the maximum of the exercise of its inherent powers.
>
> When conditions are found to be illegal, courts have refused to enforce the condition, removed the condition, or held that the trust fails and thus the condition fails too.

Before a trust purpose is invalid, the acquisition or retention of the beneficial interest must be dependent upon devisee's future conduct which the disposition is intended to influence. Thus any condition that must be met at the moment of creation of the trust does not invalidate the trust if there is no attempt to affect future conduct after death.

If the settlor anticipates that the originally suggested trust may be held to be invalid and provides for an alternate gift, courts will follow the settlor's intent. Settlor's manifested intention, as to the disposition to be made of the property if the condition should be held illegal, will be followed.

A particular condition may be valid or invalid depending on the subjective purpose of the settlor in inserting it in the trust terms even though the effect of the condition would be the same regardless of settlor's motivation.

F. Comparisons with Other Transactions

Constructive Trusts: Constructive trusts are judicial remedies. Courts may impose a constructive trust for fraud, mistake, breach of implied or express promise, justified reliance, unjust enrichment, wrongful acquisition. The constructive trust decree ordinarily requires the defendant to deliver possession of and convey title to the property and to pay the plaintiff profits received or rental value during the period of wrongful holding and otherwise to adjust the equities of the parties after taking an accounting.

Constructive trusts must involved property, and have someone who could be called a settlor, a trustee and a cestui que trust. The court implies a trust intent to prevent an "unjust enrichment."

Resulting Trusts: Resulting trusts arise from the nature of the circumstance. The character of the transaction raises an inference that the transferor did not intend for the transferee or "trustee" to receive the beneficial interest. Consequently, the "trustee" is held to hold the property or appropriate portions thereof subject to a duty to reconvey to the settlor, settlor's estate or successors in interest. Trust intent is presumed or inferred from the nature of the transaction. The risk of non persuasion is upon the alleged beneficiary.

The two most typical types of resulting trusts include: (1) the express trust that fails or makes an incomplete disposition of the trust property; and (2) the purchase money resulting trust where A buys land but has title put in B's name. In the latter situation, courts presume a gift when there is a gratuitous transfer to one who is the natural object of such a transfer, *e.g.*, wife or other close relation, but presume a trust when it is a transfer to a legal stranger rather than a close relation.

II. TRUST FORMALITIES: CREATION AND TERMINATION

A. Intent to Create a Trust

Trust Intent: The settlor must properly manifest an intention to create a trust relationship at the time of transfer or creation.

Informality of Intent: Although particular words or phrases need not be used, there must be an outward expression of the settlor's intention. A settlor's secret intent is not sufficient to create a trust. A trust is created if in substance the settlor intends to create the relationship that lawyers know as a trust.

Precatory Words: Mere precatory words do not satisfy the trust intent requirement. Transferor must manifest an intention to impose enforceable duties on the transferee. Admissible extrinsic evidence can prove trust intent was present. Surrounding circumstances can indicate trust intent.

Active and Passive Trusts: If a trustee merely holds title as custodian for the beneficiary, or holds title as custodian and makes nondiscretionary distribution of the trust property to the beneficiary, the trust is passive and the Statute of Uses, if applicable, executes it. Trusts may be passive when created or may become passive later.

If the trustee has affirmative duties, such as collecting rents and profits, exercising responsibility for trust investments, and generally managing the trust property, the trust is active and the Statute of Uses does not execute it.

B. Formalities for Trusts

Formalities in General: A trust may be created if the least possible formalities applicable to the situation are satisfied. An imperfect gift, however, will not be converted into a trust because the transfer lacks trust intent.

Settlor's Capacity: The settlor must have testamentary capacity to create a trust by will. An inter vivos trust requires that Settlor have the same capacity as one needs to make a gift. If the trust is created by contract, then contractual capacity suffices.

Possible Remedies: Trust formality problems present a court with three possible approaches and remedies: (1) permit trust be proved and enforce it; (2) enforce the formality and let the "trustee" take personally; or, (3) prevent unjust enrichment of the transferee and reinstate the status quo.

Inter Vivos Trusts: Inter vivos trust are either created by transfer, declaration of trust, or contract.

Distinct Circumstances: Litigation results may vary depending on whether one of the following distinct factual situations is involved:

A → T → C

A → T
↖ ← ↙

A → A → C

Formalities in Creation

No Writing Requirement: Oral trusts may be proved by clear and convincing evidence if neither the Statute of Frauds nor the Parol Evidence Rule is applicable.

Parol Evidence Rule: Although extrinsic evidence is not admissible to contradict or vary the terms of an instrument which states the complete expression of the settlor's intention, courts take the view that even an absolute conveyance does not unequivocally manifest an intention that the grantee should take the property for his or her own benefit, because it does not purport to show whether the grantee is to take it for personal benefit or for the benefit of someone else. The trust is supplemental with regard to a matter on which the instrument is silent. The standard of proof has been held to require clear and convincing evidence.

Statute of Frauds: Generally, the Statute of Frauds requires all trusts of real property to be in a writing that is signed by the settlor, manifests trust intent, and identifies the trust property, the beneficiaries, and the purposes of the trust. Trust agreements not complying with the Statute are unenforceable but are not void. Exceptions to the writing requirement and other remedies may apply.

Restitution: The Statute of Frauds does not prevent a suit for restitution by the transferor based on the principle of preventing unjust enrichment. The "trustee" who orally promised to hold the property in trust would be unjustly enriched if permitted to keep the property for personal benefit.

Specific Enforcement: The direct or specific enforcement of the oral promise for the intended beneficiaries and of the trust purposes is prevented by the Statute of Frauds unless a recognized exception applies.

Part Performance: Part performance that provides sufficient corroboration of the parol evidence of the trust may permit the oral trust to be directly proved and enforced. Part performance includes, for example, the situation where the beneficiary took possession of the property and changed position in reliance on the trust's existence.

Fraud or Duress: A transferee who procured the property by fraud or duress will be compelled to hold the property on constructive trust for the transferor or for the intended beneficiaries and purposes. Fraud requires proof that the transferee made a conscious misrepresentation and did not intend to perform the trust at the time of the agreement. A mere breach of contract will not suffice.

Undue Influence: If the transferee at the time of the transfer and oral trust exercised undue influence over the transferor, the transferee will be held to hold the property on constructive trust for the intended beneficiaries and purposes.

Confidential Relationship: If the transferee at the time of the creation of the oral trust stood in a confidential or fiduciary relationship with respect to the transferor, the transferee will be held to hold the property on constructive trust for the intended beneficiaries and purposes. "Confidential relationship" concerns any relationship in which one person gains the confidence of another and purports to act or advise with the latter's interest in mind. Even a close family relationship or friendship may be one under certain circumstances.

Contemplation of Death: An oral trust made by the transferee to a transferor who is in fear of fairly imminent death will be enforced by a constructive trust for the beneficiary.

Two Separate Agreements: If an oral trust of land was declared and the trustee agreed to sell the land and to hold the proceeds in trust, the transferee's oral promise to hold the land in trust is unenforceable because of the failure to comply with the Statute of Frauds; but the transferee's oral promise in regard to the proceeds is not within the Statute of Frauds and is enforceable. The transferee's promises are severable.

Limitations on Taking Advantage of the Statute of Frauds Defense: Only the trustee and trustee's successors in interest can take advantage of any failure to comply with the Statute of Frauds. Successors include a purchaser or other transferee, the personal representative of transferee-decedent's estate, the transferee's heirs, devisees, and bankruptcy trustee. Other persons, including trustee's creditors, attached or otherwise, cannot raise the Statute of Frauds if the trustee agrees to perform the trust.

Trusts Created by Will:

General Formality Requirements for Testamentary Trusts: Testamentary trusts generally must satisfy all the requirements of an express inter vivos trust and be included in a valid will.

Secret and Semi–Secret Trusts

Semi–Secret Trust: A partially-secret or semi-secret trust is a bequest or devise which clearly provides that the devisee is not to get the beneficial interest but does not adequately indicate the true beneficiary under the appropriate Statute of Wills. Some courts have declared these trust ineffective because of the Statute of Wills and have mandated a resulting trust for the decedent's estate. Other courts have held the trust property should be held upon a constructive trust for the agreed purposes and persons.

Secret Trust: A "secret trust" is a devise of property to a person absolutely, without reference to any intended trust, but the devisee prior to the testator's death agreed with the testator to hold the property upon a certain trust. The "secret trust" doctrine holds that when a testator devises property in reliance upon an agreement or understanding with a devisee either before, or after the will was executed, that the latter holds it in trust, the devisee holds the property upon a constructive trust for the person for whom the devisee agreed to hold it.

Analysis of the Rules: Both secret and semi-secret trusts should be enforceable for the beneficiaries using the constructive trust device. Only if relief runs in favor of the intended beneficiaries can the unjust enrichment principle be consistently applied. In both situations, the trust should be carried out if the trustee is willing and in cases where the trustee balks, constructive trust relief should be in favor of the intended beneficiary.

Estate Planning Aspects: Despite general recognition of secret trusts, their litigation risks are too great to use them as a planning device.

Pour-over Trusts: A pour-over devise is a provision in a will that directs the distribution of property into a trust.

Validation Problems: Prior to authorizing legislation, pour-over devises were contested on the basis that they did not comply with the Statute of Wills because the will did not identify the beneficiaries.

Pour-Over Statutes: Pour-over statutes exist in one form or other in all or nearly all states. The UPC and Uniform Act's version validates a devise when the trust is amendable or revocable or even if the trust is actually amended after the execution of the will or the testator's death. The devise is valid notwithstanding the existence, size or character of the corpus of the trust during the testator's lifetime.

Inter-Vivos or Testamentary Trust: The Uniform Act gives the testator the option whether to treat the trust as a testamentary trust under the testator's will or to allow it to be governed by the terms of the trust and by its terms and provisions including amendments made to the trust before or after the testator's death. Unless the testator's will indicates otherwise, the property devised will be administered under the terms and conditions of the trust and not as a new testamentary trust.

Revocation: If both the trust and the will are revoked, the pour-over trust is revoked too. If the trust is revoked but the will is not, the UPC and Uniform Act declare the trust revoked.

C. Trust Revocation and Termination

General Rule of Revocability: Settlor cannot revoke an inter vivos trust unless a power of revocation is expressly reserved or may be implied from language contained in the instrument or unless grounds for reformation or rescission exist. Several states provide a trust is revocable unless it is expressly made irrevocable.

Termination by the Terms of the Trust: Trusts terminate when the terms of the trust provide it is to terminate at the end of a certain period of time or upon the happening of a certain event.

Trust Purpose Impossibility or Illegality: A Trust will be terminated if the trust's purposes become impossible or illegal to accomplish.

Merger: Except for circumstances when a material purpose of the trust would be defeated (such as when the trust is a discretionary trust), a trust terminates if the legal title and the entire beneficial interest merges in one person who is not under an incapacity.

Settlor Termination: A settlor, who is the sole beneficiary of a trust and is not under an incapacity, can terminated the trust even though the purposes of the trust have not been accomplished and even though the settlor has not retained a power to revoke.

Beneficiary Termination: The beneficiaries can compel the termination of the trust if all beneficiaries consent and none is under an incapacity unless the continuance of the trust is necessary to carry out a material purpose of the trust.

Trustee Termination: A trustee can terminate a trust when this power is expressly or impliedly conferred upon trustee by the terms of the trust, *e.g.*, when the purpose is no longer present.

III. REVOCABLE TRUSTS

A. Definition and Application of Revocable Trusts

Definition: A revocable trust is an inter vivos trust in which the settlor either expressly, impliedly or by law, holds and reserves the right to revoke.

Basic Formalities: Revocable trusts require the same formalities as other inter vivos trusts. *See supra*, Part 6.II.B.2.

Applications: Revocable trusts are important estate planning devices. They serve as will substitutes and as dispositive instruments at the settlor's death.

Revocable trusts avoid the costs and delays of the probate process, provide property management for the settlor, offer greater privacy for the estate plan, avoid continual probate court supervision, and save or postpone taxes.

B. Settlor Control over Revocable Trusts

Method of Revocation: Settlor can revoke the trust only by following the manner or circumstances specified in the trust, or in any manner that sufficiently manifests the intention of the settlor to revoke the trust if not specified.

Concept of Testamentariness: When a settlor of an inter vivos trust reserves powers over the trust and its res until death, issues have been litigated over what powers reserved in the trust instrument cause the transfer to be testamentary and thus have to be executed according the Statute of Wills.

Powers Reserved by Settlor: Recent decisions hold inter vivos trusts valid even where settlors have retained complete control, and where other beneficiaries usually, if drafting is competent, have only future interests that are not only defeasible (by revocation or amendment) but also contingent upon surviving the settlor and maybe other events as well.

Validity Theories: A common explanation concerns the question whether the deed presently passes an interest on its execution. If the trust is intended to become presently binding and nothing is left for the settlor to do to complete the transaction, the trust is not testamentary.

Scholars argue that the real issue is the Statute of Wills and whether the settlor satisfied the underlying purposes of the wills execution formalities.

Validity Limitations: A few cases indicate that not every trust type transfer will be upheld if the court questions the seriousness of a particular settlor's trust intention.

Statutory Validation: Several states have statutes expressly providing that revocable trusts are not testamentary dispositions. The common pour-over legislation also impliedly recognizes the validity of revocable trusts.

IV. TRUST INTERESTS AND RELATIONSHIPS

A. Enforceability of Beneficial Interests

General Principles:

Beneficiary Rights: The beneficiary has both in personam and in rem rights: personal rights against the trustee, and equitable ownership of the trust res.

Impartiality Between Beneficiaries: The trustee must act impartially in dealing with the beneficiaries. This obligation requires careful consideration when making payments among beneficiaries and in allocating principal and income.

Improper Payments: The trustee is liable for overpayment or wrongful payment even though trustee acted in good faith. Misinterpretations and mistakes of law or fact are generally no defense. The trustee should apply to the proper court for instructions when in reasonable doubt.

Discretionary Distributions: Nature of the Fiduciary Relationship

Range of Discretion: Some trusts give the trustee discretion to make distributions among the beneficiaries. Discretion can concern selection of the recipients among a group of beneficiaries, and what the benefit can include be it income, principal or both. The trustee has what is called an "invasion power" when the trustee has discretion to invade the principal for the life beneficiary or income or principal for the remainder beneficiary

Reasons for Discretion: Discretion may be granted to save income taxes, death taxes, and to provide distributive flexibility to deal with changed circumstances that the settlor could not foresee.

Meaning of Uncontrolled Powers: Nonfiduciary powers of appointment are exercisable arbitrarily and without explanation so long as persons outside the class of objects are not benefitted directly or indirectly. When a trustee is given discretion, however, the preliminary question is not whether there is review but the degree of the review. A fiduciary power in a trust is never beyond the power of the court to review.

Simple Versus Absolute Discretion: If the trustee is given simple discretion over distributions, judicial intervention is not warranted merely because the court would have differently exercised the discretion. If the settlor manifests an intention that the discretion of the trustee shall be uncontrolled, the words are said to dispense with the standard of reasonableness. The difference between simple and extended discretion is out of degree, not kind.

B. Transfer of a Beneficiary's Interest

Transfers In General

Voluntary Assignment: A beneficiary can transfer his or her trust interest. The transferee acquires only the interest which the beneficiary owned.

Rights of Creditors of a Beneficiary: A trust beneficiary's judgment creditors can reached the beneficiary's trust interest through a creditors' bill. The creditor cannot reach the trust property itself except where the debtor is the sole beneficiary of a trust and can presently demand conveyance of the trust property.

Restraints on Alienation: A spendthrift spends improvidently or wastefully. Trusts are often used to protect the "spendthrift" from his or her own lack of discretion or ability. Restrictions on alienation are essential to provide this protection.

A spendthrift trust is one in which, either because of a direction of the settlor or because of statute, the beneficiary is unable to transfer his or her right to future payments of income or capital (a voluntary transfer), and the beneficiary's creditors are unable to subject the beneficiary's interest to the payment of their claims (an involuntary transfer). The beneficiary need not be and usually is not a spendthrift.

Scope of the Spendthrift Protection: Spendthrift provisions do not restrain alienability or creditor's rights with respect to property after it is received by the beneficiary from the trustee, but merely restrain rights to future payments under the trust.

Policy Considerations: Policy concerns weigh the economic and sociological effect upon both the community and the beneficiaries by permitting spendthrift restraints, and whether these effects are desirable. Typically, voluntary creditors are not harmed by spendthrift trusts and the beneficiary's interests are seldom alienable for a fair price.

Statutory Spendthrift Recognition: New York statutes automatically prohibit voluntary assignments of express trusts and protect creditors only "in excess of the sum necessary for the education and support of the beneficiary." California statutes permit spendthrift provisions but protect creditors "in excess of the amount that is or will be necessary for the education and support of the beneficiary." New York's interpretation of "need" has permitted protection for extravagance whereas California's interpretation only protects reasonable amounts.

Discretionary and Related Trusts

Discretionary Trusts: When the trustee has discretion whether to pay to or apply income or principal for a beneficiary, the beneficiary's creditor cannot compel the trustee to pay any part of the income or principal.

Limitation on Discretionary Payments: Absent the application of a valid spendthrift provision, the trustee should not pay over or apply any part of the trust property to the beneficiary with knowledge of the transfer of the interest or of a proceeding by beneficiary's creditor to reach that interest. The trustee who makes such payments is personally liable to the transferee or creditor for the amount paid to or applied for the beneficiary.

Support and Education Trusts: By its nature, a trust interest which provides that the trustee must pay or apply only so much of the income and principal or either as is necessary for the education or support of the beneficiary, cannot be transferred by the beneficiary nor reached by his or her creditors. A creditor cannot compel the trustee to pay anything to the creditor and the trustee may pay to or apply for the beneficiary so much of the property as is necessary for his or her education or support even if the trustee knows of the conveyance or of the creditor's claim. The restriction even protects the beneficiary who becomes bankrupt.

Special Limitations

Public Policy Limitation: The beneficiary's interest in spendthrift or support (but not a discretionary trust) trusts may be reached by claimants if considerations of public policy so require. Thus, the beneficiary's interest can be reached by certain claimants in satisfaction of their enforceable claims such as, for example, alimony, child support, necessities, and claims of the United States or State.

Theory of Limitation: Courts recognize that the interests of particular claimants should be protected over the interests of the beneficiary. Where the beneficiary benefitted by the claimant's actions, the beneficiary is unjustly enriched if the claim is not allowed.

Claimant Procedure: The proper court has discretion as to how much trust income may be applied for the claimant's benefit and how much the beneficiary may receive.

V. TRUST MODIFICATION AND TERMINATION

A. Trust Modification and Termination by the Settlor

Revocation and Modification of Trust by Settlor: Generally, a trust is not revocable or modifiable by the settlor, unless these powers were expressly or impliedly reserved. Settlor can revoke the trust only by following the manner or circumstances specified in the trust, or in any manner that sufficiently manifests the intention of the settlor to revoke the trust if not specified.

Reformation and Rescission by the Settlor: Any trust can be reformed or rescinded upon the same grounds as a transfer free of trust, *i.e.*, fraud, duress, undue influence or sometimes unilateral mistake. Courts determine whether it would be inequitable not to permit the settlor to set it aside. The settlor's burden of proof is by clear and convincing evidence.

B. Trust Modification and Termination by the Trustee

Trustee Termination: A trustee may terminate a trust when a power to do so is expressly or impliedly conferred upon him or her by the terms of the trust or when discretionary power of invasion of principal would cause termination because all of the property is distributed. Powers of invasion are reviewable on exercise.

Trustee Wrongful Termination: When a trustee wrongfully terminates a trust, consenting sui juris beneficiaries are precluded from recovering from the trustee for breach of trust, but nonconsenting and unknown beneficiaries are not.

Trustee Modification: A trustee can modify a trust to the extent permitted by the terms of the trust and if not provided by the terms of the trust, the trustee may seek modification by the appropriate court. In emergencies, the trustee may modify without court approval if the trustee reasonably believes that there is a pressing need and there is no opportunity to apply to the court for permission to deviate.

C. Trust Modification and Termination by the Beneficiaries

Beneficiary Consent: If all of the beneficiaries of a trust consent and all are sui juris, they can compel the trust's termination (or modification) unless the continuance of the trust is necessary to carry out an unfulfilled material purpose of the trust.

Under the *Claflin* doctrine, however, where a trust's continuance is necessary to carry out a material purpose of the trust, the beneficiaries cannot compel the termination of the trust even if they all consent and are sui juris.

Settlor and Beneficiaries Consent: The settlor and all the beneficiaries may consent to modification or termination even if a material purpose has not been fulfilled. Similarly, if the settlor is or becomes the sole beneficiary of a trust and is not under an incapacity, the settlor can terminate the trust even though material purposes of the trust have not been accomplished.

Determination of a Material Purpose:

General Principles: Whether a material purpose exists is a question of interpretation of the trust instrument in light of all the circumstances. It is presumed that there is no material purpose unless trust language or evidence of the circumstances indicate otherwise.

Successive Beneficiaries: If all of the beneficiaries are sui juris and consent to the termination of the trust, they can compel its termination even when there are successive beneficiaries, *i.e,* in trust for A for life, remainder to B.

Material Purpose Trusts: Typical material purposes include provisions that (1) postpone enjoyment of the trust interest, (2) protect against improvidence, such as a spendthrift clause, (3) provide for the beneficiary's support, or (3) confers discretion upon the trustee as to the method of distribution.

Beneficiary Nonconsent: If one or more of the trust beneficiaries do not consent to its termination or are not sui juris, the trust beneficiaries cannot terminate a trust

Representing Minors, Unborns and Unascertained Beneficiaries: Some courts and statutes permit representatives, *e.g.,* guardians ad litem, to provide the consent for minor or other incapacitated persons.

Virtual representation: When beneficiaries have common interests, the doctrine of virtual representation may permit certain persons of a large group to represent all in that group.

D. Trust Modification and Termination by the Court

Equitable Deviation from Trust Administrative Provisions

Changing Circumstances: Ordinarily, the trustee, if properly empowered, can adjust the operation of the trust to many changed circumstances. When changes are drastic or the trust instrument is inflexible, the trustee may seek court approval for modifications to administrative provisions that will accommodate the circumstances.

Judicial Modification Criteria: In order to obtain Court modification, proponents of change must show (1) there are circumstances that have occurred either unknown to not anticipated by the settlor, (2) failure to approve a modification would defeat or substantially impair the accomplishment of the purposes of the trust, and (3) the request is to modify an administrative provision of the trust and not its distributive provisions.

Deviation from Distributive Provisions

General Rule Against Deviation: The court cannot properly authorize modification of distributive provisions when another nonconsenting trust beneficiary is deprived of all or apart of that interest, even though the other beneficiary's interest is contingent.

Anticipating Vested Interests: Modification of dispositive provisions is permitted when the time or manner of enjoyment is modified without changing the beneficiary, *e.g.,* when the trust provides "income to A until age 30, and then principal is to be paid to A," the principal might then be advanced to A prior to age 30 in case of need.

Invasion for Support and Education: Several states have statutes that allow the court to invade principal for the life beneficiary for the beneficiary's support and education if that purpose is otherwise insufficiently provided. The settlor can expressly prohibit invasion.

VI. CHARITABLE TRUSTS

A. History of Charitable Trusts

Charitable Trusts at Common Law: Most states recognize charitable trusts as part of their Common Law: some states have specific statutes that define charities.

B. General Nature of Charitable Trusts

Definition of Charitable Trust: A charitable trust is a trust in which the property is devoted to purposes the law deems appropriately beneficial to the community. Thus, a charitable trust is a trust established for a charitable purpose.

Special Benefits of a Charitable Trust: Charitable trusts enjoy several special benefits not enjoyed by private trusts:

- May last longer than the period of the Rule Against Perpetuities;
- May accumulate income beyond the period of the Rule Against Perpetuities;
- Purposes may be changed under the cy pres doctrine;
- If recognized, has charitable immunity; and
- Receives special tax exemption and benefits.

Mixed Private and Charitable Trusts: Mixed private and charitable trusts are valid if the private and charitable portions or estates are separately valid as their type of trust and the private portions are limited to the Rule Against Perpetuities.

C. Charitable Purpose

Definition of Charitable Trust: "Charitable purpose" has no exact definition and no fixed standard. It changes from time to time and community to community.

Appreciable Social Benefit: Generally, a charitable trust is a trust the performance of which will, in the opinion of the court, accomplish an appreciable amount of social benefit to the public or some reasonably large class thereof. Neither motive nor "morality" is relevant. The key is to evaluate the purpose to which the property is applied.

Additional Distinctions: Although the meaning of charitable is not a popularity contest or limited to universal beliefs, a line must be drawn between purposes believed to be irrational and those merely believed to be unwise. The test is what the rational persons may believe. Concepts of contemporaneous "public policy" also affect decisions.

Political Objectives: When the trust's charitable purpose has a political objective, a line must be drawn between objectives which are merely political and objectives which are of general social significance.

All or Nothing Rule: When words such as "charitable," have been included with terms such as "benevolent," "philanthropic," or "fraternal," courts have held that all the terms of purpose used must qualify as charitable purposes. If not, a court might hold that the whole trust fails as a charitable trust. Other courts uphold the trusts if the evidence indicates the settlor intended the ambiguous phraseology to have the legal equivalence of "charitable."

D. Illegal and Public Policy Limitations

Illegal Purpose: A trust cannot be created for an illegal purpose, *e.g.,* using trust property in violation of criminal law, or to induce crime.

Against Public Policy: A trust purpose may not be charitable if it seeks a result contrary to public policy. "Public policy" lacks a firm definition and depends upon the conceptions of public policy tested in time and location.

E. Indefinite Beneficiary

The Indefinite Beneficiary Rule: A charitable trust may not be created for a specifically identified beneficiary. That only one or a few persons actually benefit from a charitable trust does not necessarily make the trust noncharitable. A charitable trust may fail because the class of persons who can benefit is so narrow that the community has no interest in the performance of the trust. Even so, if the purpose of the trust is to relieve poverty, promote education, advance religion or protect health, the class need not be as broad as it must be where the benefits to be conferred have no relation to any of these purposes.

Actual Versus Potential Beneficiaries: A trust may be valid even if all beneficiaries are known if they are a large enough group. Conversely, a trust may fail even if the beneficiaries are unknown if they are too small a group. On the other hand, a large group of beneficiaries may cause a trust to fail if the actual benefit to the public is insignificant. When the actual benefit from the trust is de minimis or insubstantial, courts have made the distinction sometimes between being generous or benevolent but not charitable.

F. Interrelated Factors

The determination of charitability may depend upon an interrelationship between the various charitable trust criteria and indefiniteness of beneficiary. The greater the perceived social benefit, the less concern the reviewer will show concerning the legality of the purpose or the size of the class of beneficiaries.

G. Discriminatory Trusts

Discriminatory Charitable Trusts: Settlors of charitable trusts may express conditions and limitations on the use of trust funds without special legal consequences. Occasionally, the settlor's condition or limitation concerns matters that affect conflicting public policies. The most predominant of these concern charitable trusts that discriminate on the basis of race, gender, or religion.

Legal Issues for Discriminatory Trusts: The primary legal issue has been whether the trust involves "state action" for Fourteenth Amendment purposes. If a state entity is directly involved with the administration of the trust, the state action requirement is met and the trust may not discriminate.

If there is no state action, discriminatory clauses have been upheld. Neither the special benefits nor the judicial enforcement of charitable trusts constitute state action for constitutional protection.

H. Cy Pres

Definition of the Cy Pres Doctrine: Cy pres permits a court to alter the current charitable purpose if the trust purpose of a charitable trust is or becomes impossible or impracticable, or illegal to carry out, or fully accomplished, and the settlor manifested a more general intention. The change should be tailored to satisfy the general charitable intention of the settlor. The doctrine permits the court to direct the application of the trust property to a different charitable purpose from the original one.

Cy Pres Procedure: Cy Pres requires the court to determine:

- That the originally specified purpose has become impossible, illegal, impracticable or fully satisfied;
- That the settlor had a general charitable intent; and,
- What modifications would be made under the cy pres power.

Cy Pres Initiation: Cy pres suits are begun by the trustees and make the Attorney General of the state a party, as the representative of the people of the state.

Old Trust Inclination: If a general charitable purpose is not found, a trust might be terminated rather than cy presed. Old trusts generally receive a generous interpretation concerning a general charitable purpose because termination will require the difficult task of identifying the settlor's successors.

I. Honorary Trusts

Definition of Honorary Trust: A honorary trust is a trust for a specific purpose where no beneficiary is actually named and the designated purpose cannot be considered charitable. Despite the absence of a definite beneficiary, honorary trusts have sometimes been held valid.

UPC Honorary Trust: The UPC both legitimatizes and limits the duration of honorary trusts. Section 2–907(a) allows a settlor to transfer property in trust for any lawful non-charitable purpose, either as specified in the instrument or as selected by the trustee. This provision applies to any transfer in trust that does not qualify as either private or a charitable trust. The honorary trust, however, may last for no more than twenty-one years.

"Bona fido" Law: The UPC permits assets to be transferred in trust for the care of designated domestic or pet animals. Section 2–907(b) validates trusts for pets, but limits their duration to the lives of the covered animals living when the trust is created. On termination, the trust must be transferred according to its creating instrument or the relevant clauses of the transferor's will or by intestacy. If excessive funds are transferred into the trust, the court may adjust the funds and order the excess distributed as it would be if the trust ended.

J. Charitable Corporations

Charitable Corporations: Charitable corporations are non-profit corporations which were organized for charitable purposes

Charitable Corporation's Purpose: Property may be devoted to charitable purposes by transferring it to a charitable corporation. The property or its income may be used for one or more of the purposes for which the corporation is organized

Trust Characteristics: Ordinarily, charitable trust principles and rules apply to charitable corporations. The property must be used for the designated charitable purposes. Cy pres is applicable to gifts to charitable corporations. The managing board of a charitable corporation are not technically "trustees" because they do not hold title to the property of the corporation.

K. Supervision of Charitable Trusts

The Beneficial Interest of a Charitable Trust: The state or the community is the actual beneficiary and thus the trust is enforced by a public officer, usually the Attorney General. The designated beneficiaries do not hold the beneficial interest and cannot agree to terminate a charitable trust even though they may all agree.

PART SEVEN: REGULATION OF DISPOSITION

I. POLICY LIMITATIONS ON FREEDOM OF DISPOSITION

A. Interrelated Public Policies

Three interrelated public policies affect the regulation of gratuitous transfers:

- intestacy, which reflects a policy that combines normality of intention and the supposed better intention;
- the family protections, which combines the policies of *parens patriae*, assumed intent, and forced heirship;
- forced or elective heirship, which combines the policies of *parens patriae* and forced intention.

B. Allowances, Homesteads, and Exemptions

The three basic types of family protections are allowances, homesteads and exemptions. They protect certain persons from testamentary omission, creditors, and financial problems caused by delay in administration. They are limited to selected beneficiaries and in amount. The UPC includes a version of each type, with a combined total protective amount of $43,000.

C. Surviving Spouse Protection from Disinheritance

Although the vast majority of married persons pass substantial portions of their estates to their surviving spouses, there is a need to provide a safety net so that unfairly disinherited surviving spouses can protect their merited interests in their deceased spouse's estate.

Types of Protective Devices

Dower: Common law dower and curtesy were the historical spousal protection devices. Typically, dower, the prevailing concept, was limited to a life interest in one-third of the real estate held seized by the deceased spouse during marriage. States that retain the concept have expanded it to include personal property and have often enlarged the fractional interest in the estate from a life estate to one in fee.

Forced Shares: A common alternative or substitute system is the forced share device. Forced share usually provides that if a decedent spouse does not pass to the surviving spouse a minimum arbitrary percentage, *e.g.*, one-half, of the decedent's probate estate, the surviving spouse may elect to take the forced share, in fee.

Community and Quasi Community Property: Nine states have community property systems which basically provide that property gained during a marriage is owned equally by each spouse. Community property is a property division system among married persons based on a partnership theory of marriage and not merely a post-death safety-net. It operates as a protection from inter vivos disposition as well as testamentary disinheritance.

Fixed Share Augmented Estate: The original 1969 UPC contained a spousal protection scheme that provided a fixed ⅓ share of an augmented estate. The augmented estate concept expands the scope of property that is subject to the calculation for the elective share and that is subject to satisfying the share.

Accrual Share Augmented Estate: The 1990 UPC adopts an accrual-type elective share under which the elective share percentage ascends from a low of three percent of the augmented estate after the first year of marriage to a high of fifty percent of the augmented estate after fifteen years of marriage. The UPC also includes a $50,000 supplemental or minimum safety-net monetary amount for a surviving spouse below which the elective share cannot equal regardless of the length of the marriage.

The accrual approach theorizes that marriages are similar to economic partnerships and that the partnership interest of both spouses should increase in the other spouse's assets as the marriage endures. This reciprocal maturing interest attaches to all of the assets of both spouses, not merely the assets acquired during the marriage. This approach roughly accords with the ways that married persons treat their assets: few spouses distinguish their separate from their marital property when making gifts or devises to others.

Definition of the Protectable Estate:

Dower and forced share are primarily concerned with the decedent's probate estate. This limitation permits not only easy avoidance of the protection by use of lifetime transfers but also may over-compensate the surviving spouse. With limited success, courts have allowed a surviving spouse to recover a protective share against property transferred during decedent spouse's lifetime if the transfer was made with intent to defraud or which was illusory. Notwithstanding these concepts, many courts, in the absence of statutory regulation, have permitted a married person to make absolute and unconditional lifetime gifts of his or her personal property even though the effect is to deprive the spouse of dower or forced share.

The UPC's augmented estate incorporates a device which prevents easy avoidance of the elective share protection and which prevents the surviving spouse from receiving more than the circumstances merit. The augmented estate includes four distinct segments:

Segment 1 of the Augmented Estate: Segment 1 includes what normally is thought of as the decedent's gross probate estate less enforceable claims, funeral and administration expenses, and the family protections.

Segment 2 of the Augmented Estate: Segment 2 includes all properties over which decedent immediately prior to death retained certain interests, powers or relationships, including, for example, trusts over which decedent retained power to revoke until death.

Segment 3 of the Augmented Estate: Segment 3 includes all of decedent's nonprobate property which the surviving spouse gratuitously received or derived from the decedent by reason of the latter's death, including, *e.g.*, property received by survivorship.

Segment 4 of the Augmented Estate: Segment 4 includes (1) all of the surviving spouse's individual property and (2) the surviving spouse's Segment 2 property (the spouse's nonprobate transfers to others) as if that spouse predeceased decedent, to the extent these properties are not included in Segments 1 and 3.

The sum of the value of these four segments equals the augmented estate and the surviving spouse's elective share equals the elective share percentage times the augmented estate.

Election Procedure by the Surviving Spouse: Generally, either the surviving spouse elects to take the applicable spousal protection, or the spouse takes under the decedent's estate plan. Some states presume that if no election is made, the spouse elects the estate plan; others presume the spouse takes the spousal protection. Whatever the election is, it must be made within the time frame of three to nine months.

Effect of Spouse's Election: When a spouse elects the spousal protection rather than the estate plan, the intended beneficiaries must suffer abatement of their devise or gift. A pro rata sharing among levels of contributors is a common method for the abatement.

Funding the Elective Share under the UPC: The UPC explains how the elective share is to be funded. First, amounts received or attributable to the surviving spouse are deducted. If these amounts do not satisfy the elective share, then the deficiency is funded with the nonspousal portions of Segment 1 and Segment 2 transfers less the value of certain irrevocable transfers made by decedent within the two year period prior to death. If the elective share amount still remains unsatisfied, the irrevocable transfers must contribute. Only the original recipients and their gratuitous donees are liable for contribution and a recipient may either pay the value of the amount of contribution due or give up the proportional part of the nonprobate reclaimable asset received.

Permissible Avoidance of the Spousal Protection: In recognition of the underlying philosophy of freedom of disposition and clarity of title and ownership, the UPC excludes several categories of nonmarital interests and completed lifetime transfers made by either spouse. These include, for example, transfers for which either spouse received adequate and full consideration in money or money's worth; and, transfers made with the written consent or joinder of the surviving spouse.

Marital Agreements: Antenuptial and postnuptial agreements and waivers of a right of election between spouses also waive the elective share if the agreements are (a) in writing, (b) voluntary, and (c) not unconscionable. In addition, a waiver of "all rights" or equivalent language, waives all rights to elective share and the family protections in the other spouse's estate and renounces all interests passing from the other spouse by intestacy or by a will executed before the agreement.

D. Unintentional Disinheritance

Pretermitted Issue of Decedent: Forced heirship protection is recognized only in Louisiana. In all other states persons may disinherit their relatives including their children. Mere omission from the will is sufficient except for pretermitted heir statutes. Pretermitted heir statutes are designed to avoid *unintentional* failure of a testator's natural and probable intention of including all descendants. They establish rules of construction against unintentional disinheritance. Wills and the surrounding circumstances are interpreted liberally in favor of the omitted person.

Pretermitted heir statutes differ as to time of application and scope of coverage. For example, the statutes differ as to the time of birth of the pretermitted heir vis à vis the date of the will. Some statutes apply to those covered persons who are born after the will was executed and some to persons born both before or after the will was executed.

Some statutes cover only testator's children, while a few expand coverage to grandchildren. Inclusion or exclusion of adopted persons within the protected class is another variant. A few statutes limit evidence of testator's intent to the face of the will while others admit extrinsic evidence to resolve ambiguity.

When a pretermitted person protected by the statute exists, most states permit the person to take the equivalent of an intestacy forced share against the estate.

Omitted Children under the UPC: The UPC Section 2–302(b) includes a very precise omitted child protection that is designed to reduce litigation and judicial misinterpretation.

Level 1 Requirements:

- The protection is limited to pretermitted children and does not protect disinheritance of other descendants and relatives.
- The child must be born or adopted after the execution of the will that disinherits the child.
- Intent to disinherit must not appear on the "face of the will."
- The disinherited or omitted child must not have been provided for by transfers outside the will intended to be in lieu of testamentary provision.

Level 2 Requirements:

- If the testator had no children living when the will was executed, the omitted child takes an intestate share from the estate unless the natural or adopted child's parent is "devised all or substantially all" of the estate, survives the testator, and is entitled to take under the will.
- If the testator had one or more children living when the will was executed, the pretermitted child takes a representative pro rata share or interest from the total value of the interests devised to the pre-existing children, if any. The interest of the pre-existing children's devises abate pro rata according to their respective interests.

Omitted or Pretermitted Spouse: Most states rely upon their spousal protection provisions if a spouse is omitted by a premarital will. Under UPC Section 2–301, however, if decedent's only will is a premarital will the surviving spouse takes from the estate no less than an intestate share subject to significant limitations. Although omission is not required no share is allowed if:

- The will or evidence indicates that the will was executed in contemplation of the marriage, or
- The will expressly shows an intent to exclude the spouse from a subsequent marriage, or

- The surviving spouse received transfers outside will intended to be in lieu of a testamentary gift.

In addition, the automatic intestate share is limited to the portion of the estate not passing to devisees who are decedent's children or descendants of those children born before the marriage and who are not children of the surviving spouse. All others devisees are subject to pro rata abatement caused by the exercise of this provision.

E. Other Public Policy Regulations and Prohibitions

Improper Beneficiary: A few states restrict gifts to charitable organizations if they exceed a monetary maximum or percentage maximum of the decedent's estate and are made within a particular time prior to death, *e.g.*, thirty days.

Public Policy Limitations: Courts have restricted certain testamentary gifts that are found to be against public policy. Sometimes conditions in wills requiring the beneficiary to meet certain conditions have been struck. Generally, courts will enforce personal conduct conditions on devisees if the condition must be satisfied at death and there is no *in terrorem* effect.

II. VOLUNTARY REGULATION OF DISPOSITION

A. Will Contracts

There are three basic types of will contracts:

- to will or devise;
- to die intestate; and
- not to revoke.

Persons contending they are a beneficiary of a will contract face one or more substantiation barriers:

- A Statute of Frauds which requires contracts to will real property to be in writing; or,
- A specific statute that requires all will contracts to be in writing; or,
- A requirement that the contract be proved by clear and convincing evidence; or,
- Because specific performance is usually the remedy sought, the will contract must be supported by fair and reasonable consideration.

Formality for Will Contracts: If a contract is not in writing as required, part performance and estoppel concepts have been applied. For example, some courts find that either part performance or estoppel applies when a promisor dies passing the property to the other promisor in conformity with the oral contract and the surviving promisor accepts the benefits of the agreement.

Joint and Mutual Wills: A joint will may infer a contract whereas mutual wills do not.

Remedies for Breach of Will Contracts: Although will contracts are generally enforced as a claim against the estate and usually are suits for specific performance, courts have at times confused or mixed the law of wills and contract. For example, in the enforcement of a contract not to revoke, courts have probated the revoked will, which is a form of specific performance as applied in a probate environment.

Scope of Will Contracts: If a contract not to revoke is provable, interpretive issues arise as to the survivors' rights with the property covered by the agreement as well as the rights of persons dealing with the survivor.

Will Contracts under the UPC: UPC Section 2–514 sets specific alternative formalities that must be satisfied before either contracts to will or devise, not to revoke a will or devise, or to die intestate are provable. The agreement must be expressed either by material provisions of the contract in the will, or by express reference in the will plus corroborating extrinsic evidence, or by a separate contract in writing signed by decedent. No presumption of contract arises from the execution of mutual or joint wills.

B. Settlement Agreements

Agreements to settle disputes between persons concerning the distribution of a decedent's estate are valid and not against public policy. A settlement agreement, however, binds only those made a party to it, and may be invalid if it interferes with the rights of others. Two types of agreements are most common: (1) not to contest a will and (2) not to probate a will. Both are usually recognized although a few courts hold that the probate court owes a duty to the testator to see that testator's will, if valid, is admitted to probate.

Enforcement of the settlement agreement may take several forms:

- When there is a breach by the heir, the devisees may (1) seek an injunction against a contest by heirs, or (2) plead the settlement agreement in bar of the contest, or, (3) seek a subsequent damage action against the heirs for breach of contract.
- When there is a breach by the will beneficiaries, a suit for specific performance has been permitted.

C. Doctrine of Equitable Election

The equitable election doctrine provides that a person cannot accept benefits accruing to him or her by a will and at the same time refuse to recognize the validity of the will in other respects. The application of the doctrine is dependent on the intent of the testator. Intent may be inferred from circumstance. The application of an election is similar to that of one who has received an advancement. The advancee has an election to participate in the hotchpot calculation and share in the estate, or not participate, thus keep only the advancement and not share in the estate.

PART EIGHT: FUTURE INTERESTS AND PERPETUITIES

CLASSIFICATION OF ESTATES AND FUTURE INTERESTS

A. Introduction to Estates in Land and Future Interests

Fragmentation of Ownership: Property law recognizes both whole and divided ownership.

Whole Ownership: Whole ownership is outright ownership of property and refers to ownership in fee simple absolute for land and absolute ownership for personalty.

Divided or Fragmented Ownership: Divided or Fragmented Ownership allows two or more persons to have simultaneous interests in the property as a whole. It involves an abstract allocation of the incidents of ownership among the owners.

Ownership fragmentation concerns either concurrent interests, separate legal and equitable interests, or sequentially ownership between present and future interests.

Basic Terminology: A present or possessory estate entitles the owner to possession of the property. A future interest in property is a nonpossessory interest that might or will become possessory at some future time.

B. The Importance and Process of Classification

Classification Process: Classification is a process of fixing the proper label or labels to a property interest.

Hierarchy of Estates: The hierarchy of estates is a system of technical and almost indistinguishable distinctions. The classification of interests determined legal consequences. Thus, form controlled over substance.

Quantum of Estates: The descending order of the quantum of possessory estates is: (1) the fee simple estates (2) the fee tail, (3) the life estate, (4) the term of years, (5) the estate from period to period, (6) the estate at will, and (7) the estate at sufferance.

Freehold and Nonfreehold Estates: Freehold estates include: (1) the fee simple estates, (2) the fee tail, and (3) the life estate. Nonfreehold estates include: (1) the term of years, (2) the estate from period to period, (3) the estate at will, and (4) the estate at sufferance.

Particular Estate: The particular estate denotes any estate that is less than a fee simple.

The Importance of Present and Future Interests: Future interest analysis today primarily concerns trusts and the division of equitable title between income beneficiaries and corpus beneficiaries.

C. The Process of Classification

Possessory Estates and Future Interests Classified: The classification of estates uses the concept of defeasance.

Defeasance: Defeasance means that the holder of the estate will lose that estate upon the happening of a specified event. Possessory estates that are subject to defeasance are subject to either a condition subsequent or a limitation.

"Condition Subsequent": A "condition subsequent" terminates a possessory by cutting it off upon the happening of the specified event. "Condition subsequent" language includes, *e.g.,* "on condition that" or "provided that," followed by such words as "but if" or "and if."

"Limitation": A "limitation" terminates possessory estates naturally or by their own terms. Limitation language includes, *e.g.,* "until," or "so long as," followed by such words as "at," "upon," or "then." A "special" limitation subjects an estate to possible termination in addition to that normally characteristic of the estate and is not certain to happen.

Possessory Estates: The four fee simple estates can be divided into two general categories.

Fee Simple Absolute: The estate in fee simple absolute is unlimited in duration and is not subject to any special limitations, conditions subsequent, or executory limitations. A fee simple absolute is never followed by a future interest.

Defeasible Fee Simple: The three defeasible fee simple estates include the fee simple determinable, the fee simple subject to a condition subsequent, and the fee simple subject to an executory limitation. The defeasible fee simple estate terminates upon the happening of an event specified in the grant.

Fee Simple Determinable: The fee simple determinable is a fee estate subject to a special limitation that automatically terminates or expires if the specified event happens, *i.e.,* possibility of reverter (if reversionary) or an executory interest (if nonreversionary). The terminating event is an event that is not certain to happen.

Fee Simple Subject to a Condition Subsequent: The fee simple subject to a condition subsequent is a fee estate that is subject to divestment in favor of a reversionary future interest called a right of entry or power of termination. The happening of the specified event empowers the grantor or grantor's successor in interest to divest the estate by exercising the right of entry.

Fee Simple Subject to an Executory Limitation: The fee simple subject to an executory limitation is a fee estate that is subject to divestment in favor of a nonreversionary future interest called an executory interest. The happening of the specified event divests the estate.

Fee Tail: The fee tail estate terminates if and when the line of the tenant in tail's issue fails. In almost all states, the fee tail estate is abolished or altered.

Life Estates: Life estates expire naturally on the death of the measuring life. Unless the life estate is a life estate measured by the life of another (pur autre vie), the measuring life is the life tenant.

The phrase "equitable life estate" is sometimes used to describe the interest of a trust beneficiary who has the right to the income from a trust for his or her lifetime.

Term of Years: Terms of years expire naturally on the expiration of the term. They are defeasible estates that are subject to a limitation.

The phrase "equitable term" is sometimes used to describe the interest of a trust beneficiary who has the right to the income from a trust for a term.

Prematurely Defeasible Life Estates and Terms of Years: Life estates and terms of years can be made prematurely defeasible, so that they might end before the expiration of the life or term, by adding a special limitation to the grant or a condition subsequent, *e.g.*, "to A for life or until A remarries."

Reversionary and Nonreversionary Future Interests: Future interests are classified by type, described in terms of vesting, and identified by the type of possessory estate they might or will later become.

Identifying Type: The five types of future interests are: (1) remainders, (2) executory interests, (3) reversions, (4) possibilities of reverter, and (5) rights of entry. Executory interests are further divided into springing and shifting executory interests.

Labeling Vesting Categories: The four vesting categories are: (1) indefeasibly vested, (2) vested subject to complete defeasance, (3) vested subject to open, and (4) contingent.

Future Possessory Estate: When the future interest becomes possessory, the range of interests is the same as it is for interests that start out as possessory estates.

Steps to Identification: (1) Determine whether the future interest is reversionary or nonreversionary, (2) identify the future interest by type, and (3) classify it in terms of vesting and in terms of the type of possessory estate it might or will become.

Reversionary or Nonreversionary Distinctions: A reversionary future interest is either a reversions, a possibility of reverter, or a right of entry. A nonreversionary future interest is either a remainder or an executory interest. It is reversionary, if transferor retained a future interest. It is nonreversionary if a future interest is created in a transferee than the transferor.

The reversionary or nonreversionary classification is fixed at the time of creation. Post-creation transfers do not change reversionary interests into a nonreversionary interest or vice versa.

The Nonreversionary Future Interests–Remainders and Executory Interests:

Conventional Definitions: A nonreversionary future interest is either a remainder or an executory interest. It cannot be a reversion, a possibility of reverter, or a right of entry.

Differentiating Remainders from Executory Interests:

Remainders become possessory, if at all, upon the natural termination of the preceding vested estate. The preceding vested estate must have been created when the future interest was created, be a possessory estate, and be a "particular" estate.

Executory interests become possessory, if at all, by cutting short or divesting the preceding vested estate or interest. The preceding vested estate or interest need not have been created when the future interest was created, can be a possessory estate or a future interest, and can be a fee simple estate or a particular estate.

The possessory estate succeeded by a single nonreversionary future interest is a remainder if the possessory estate is a fee tail, a life estate, or a term of years, or an executory interest when the possessory estate is a fee simple subject to defeasance.

Because a remainder cannot follow a fee simple estate, a fee simple must always be followed by an executory interest, even when the fee simple is subject to a special limitation.

All the future interests are executory interests when a defeasible fee simple is followed by more than one nonreversionary future interest, only one of which can become possessory.

Post–Creation Changes in Classification: Executory interests can become remainders, contingent remainders can become vested remainders, and remainders can become executory interests. Thus an executory interest can vest before becoming possessory by changing into a remainder. Although an executory interest cannot vest until it vests in possession, an executory interest can vest before becoming possessory by changing into a remainder.

II. CONSEQUENCES OF CLASSIFICATION

A. Introduction to Consequences of Classification

Current Classification Consequences: The two types of consequences that continue to turn on future interest classification are that contingent future interests (1) may be inalienability and (2) are subject to the Rule Against Perpetuities. If contingent future interests are inalienable, inalienability flows directly and automatically from contingency whereas contingent future interests, which are subject to the Rule Against Perpetuities, do not necessarily violate it.

B. Alienability of Future Interests

Two Divisions of Alienation of Future Interests: Alienation of future interests is divided into transferability at death and by inter vivos transfer.

Transferability at Death By Intestacy or Will:

Descendability: All future interests are "descendible" which means they are capable of passing by intestacy.

Devisability: Reversions, remainders, and executory interests are devisable by will. Possibilities of reverter and rights of entry are devisable in most jurisdictions.

Descendability and Devisability of Contingent or Defeasible Interests: Future interests that are contingent or vested subject to defeasance are descendible and devisable only if the condition precedent or subsequent has not been extinguished by the beneficiary's death.

Voluntary Alienability During Life: Reversions and vested remainders, including those subject to divestment, are alienable inter vivos. Contingent remainders and executory interests are inalienable.

Transferability of Contingent Remainders and Executory Interests: The three ways of transferring contingent remainders and executory interests are:

Contract to Convey: If for adequate consideration and all conditions precedent are satisfied, a contract to convey the interest is specifically enforceable.

Estoppel By Deed: A deed that contained a covenant of warranty estopped the grantor if and when the conditions precedent are later satisfied.

Release: The release of an inalienable future interest to the holder of the interest that would be defeated by the satisfaction of the conditions precedent attached to the released interest is enforceable. Any valid instrument capable of transferring an interest in land is sufficient to release a future interest.

Current Transferability: The vast majority of states hold that all contingent future interests are alienable. About seven states still follow the common law rule of inalienability. A small number of states hold remainders and executory interests that are contingent as to person (interests created in unborn or unascertained persons) are still inalienable, but those that are contingent as to event are alienable.

Understanding Alienability: A future interest that is contingent as to person is not truly alienable because there is no one who can transfer the interest. Thus alienability of future interests that are contingent as to persons are alienable only in regard to unascertained persons, not in regard to unborn persons.

Inter vivos Alienability of Possibilities of Reverter and Rights of Entry: Jurisdictions are divided on the alienability of possibilities of reverter and rights of entry are inalienable inter vivos.

Creditors' Rights in Future Interests: If a future interest is voluntarily alienable, it is also subject to the claims of creditors before and after death of interest holder. Although this rule applies to both vested and contingent interests, a few states hold that contingent remainders and executory interests are not subject to the claims of creditors. When the sale price of a future interest that is subject to conditions is substantially lower than its potential value to the debtor if the interest vests or becomes possessory, the interest cannot be reached by the debtor's creditors. Courts may, however, impose a lien on the future interest until the contingencies are satisfied, if ever. Under section 541 of the Bankruptcy Reform Act of 1978, creditors of a bankrupt should be able to seek claims from all types of future interests, including those that are immune from the claims of creditors under state law.

C. Summary Comparison of Three Future Interest Rules

A following table compares the three feudally-based rules that affect future interests:

Destructibility Rule	Rule in Shelley's Case	Inter Vivos Worthier Title
A legal contingent remainder in land is destroyed if it has not vested by the time of the termination of the preceding freehold estate	A remainder in land that is purportedly created in the life tenant's heirs or the heirs of the life tenant's body, and that is of the same quality as that of the life estate, is held by the life tenant	When a transferor, by an inter vivos conveyance, purports to create a future interest in the transferor's own heirs, the transferor is presumed to intend to retain a reversionary interest
Rule of law	Rule of law	Rule of construction by majority view
Merger causes destructibility and if it takes place, precedes the application of the Rule	Merger usually takes place and applies after the operation of the Rule, not before	Merger is not relevant
Inter vivos and testamentary transfers	Inter vivos and testamentary transfers	Inter vivos transfers only
Only to land	Only to land	Land and personalty
Applicable only to remainders	Applicable only to remainders	Applicable to remainders and executory interests
Applicable only to legal contingent remainders	Applicable to legal and equitable remainders, but the remainder and the preceding estate must be of the same quality	Applicable to legal and equitable future interests; can be of different quality from prior estate
Identity of the remainder person irrelevant so long as remainder is contingent (preceding estate must be a freehold)	Remainder must purportedly be created in the heirs or heirs of the body of the ancestor who is given the preceding freehold estate	Remainder must purportedly be created in the heirs of the transferor if land, the next of kin of the transferor if personalty
Abolished in well over half the states. Statutory abolition is commonly not retroactive; crucial date is when the prior freehold terminated.	Abolished in over three-fourths or more of the states. Statutory abolition is commonly not retroactive; crucial date is effective date of deed or death of testator.	Specifically abolished in only a few states. Statutory abolition is commonly not retroactive. Crucial date is effective date of deed.

D. The Destructibility of Contingent Remainders

Statement of the Destructibility Rule: [*See* Chart, in 8.II.C., *supra*.]

E. The Rule in Shelley's Case

Statement of the Rule in Shelley's Case: [*See* Chart, in 8.II.C., *supra*.]

F. The Doctrine of Worthier Title

Statement of the Worthier Title Doctrine: [*See* Chart, in 8.II.C., *supra*.]

Effect of a Worthier Title Doctrine Application: Under the Worthier Title Doctrine, the grantor owns the reversionary interest during grantor's lifetime; consequently, the grantor's heirs-apparent have no interest, only an expectancy. Thus the grantor retains an alienable interest, grantor's creditors can subject the reversionary interest to the payment of their claims, and grantor's testate or intestate successor take the interest on grantor's death.

Trust Termination: The Worthier Title Doctrine can sometimes permit the grantor of an inter vivos trust who is the life beneficiary but who did not reserve a power to revoke the trust, to terminate the trust because the grantor is sole beneficiary owning both the income interest for life and the reversion that follows it.

G. Express and Implied Conditions of Survival

Survivorship and Future Interests: Courts have had numerous problems determining whether remainder beneficiaries must survive to the time of distribution or merely to the time of the creation of the future interest. Absent clearly expressed intent by the interest creator concerning survivorship, the general common law rule holds that survivorship to date of distribution is not presumed: that is if the remainder beneficiary died between date of creation and date of distribution, the interest passes to the beneficiary's estate for distribution according to the beneficiary's will or by intestacy if no will. The nonsurvivorship presumption applied only to remainders to named individuals or to single-generation classes. The Common Law subjects the future interest to a multiple-generation class to an implied requirement of survival to the distribution date.

> UPC Provisions: The UPC reverses the presumption and provides that there is an implied requirement of survivorship, to the date of distribution for future interests held in trust. In addition, the survivorship requirement is extended to 120 hours after the time of distribution. The new presumption is only applicable to future interests in trust and therefore does not apply to nonequitable interests such as "to A for life, remainder to B."

Antilapse and Future Interests: The common law remedy to lapse of passing the remainder interest through the nonsurviving beneficiary's estate did not depend upon the existence of descendants surviving the beneficiary. The UPC includes an "antilapse" presumption in favor of descendants of the nonsurviving remainder beneficiaries.

UPC Provisions: The UPC provides that if a remainder beneficiary fails to survive the date of distribution, a substitute gift arises for the beneficiary's descendants, if any survive. This is an "antilapse" rule for future interests in trusts. It protects descendants of all remainder beneficiaries in trusts regardless of their relationship to the transferor. It does not apply to multiple-generation class gifts, *e.g.*, "descendants," "issue," that inherently possess a nonlapsing affect because representation is allowed for descendants of predeceased ancestors in the class.

The antilapse protection is merely a rule of construction subject to transferor control. But a mere survivorship requirement in the instrument will not rebut the presumption.

III. CLASS GIFTS

A. Definition of a Class Gift

What is a Class Gift?: A class gift is a gift of property to a group of persons identified by a group label, *e.g.*, "children," "nephews." Not all gifts to a group of persons are class gifts, however.

Subject to Fluctuation: The distinguishing feature of a class gift is the ability of the designated group to fluctuate in number either by an increase in the number of takers (caused by births or adoptions), and/or through a decrease in the number of takers (caused by deaths).

A gift to a group identified only by a group label, *e.g.*, "my children," is likely a class gift. A gift to a group that also identifies the takers by name, number, or both, *e.g.*, "to my children, A, B, and C," is likely not a class gift. A gift to a static group is a not a class gift but is a separate gift of a fractional share of the property to each member of the original group. Although these rules are merely presumptions, the presumptions are seldom rebutted.

Fluctuation in Number Limited: The ability to fluctuate in number need not continue forever and once the time of possession has arrived, fluctuation comes to an end. The ability of a given class gift to increase might expire before its ability to decrease expires, and vice versa. Indeed, some class gifts might never be able to increase, only decrease, and vice versa.

Decrease in Class Membership: A class may decrease in membership if the gift is subject to a requirement of survivorship but it will not decrease after the time to which survival is required. The deceased class member's lost share is added to the shares of those other members of the class who become entitled to participate. Class gifts create an implicit gift over to the other members of the class.

Immediate Testamentary Class Gifts: An immediate testamentary gift in fee simple absolute to a class is subject to decrease between the time of the execution of the will and of the testator's death but not thereafter.

Future Interest Class Gifts: A class gift that is a future interest rather than an immediate fee simple absolute cannot decrease beyond the testator's death unless survival of the life tenant is expressly imposed or a statute requires.

Increase in Class Membership: Class gift members may increase in number. For example, persons born as members of a class prior to the date the class closes are included in the class for distribution purposes. Each time a new entrant joins a class, the shares of the existing class members are reduced.

B. Class Closing

Subject to Open: A class can increase as long as new entrants can join the class. The class "closes" to further increase, at the earlier of (1) the physiological or natural closing of the class; or (2) the artificial or premature closing of the class brought about by application of the so-called rule of convenience.

Physiological Closing: The physiological closing of a class occurs when the possibility of births (or, if adopted members are within the class description, adoptions) becomes extinct.

Artificial or Premature Closing of a Class: The "rule of convenience" may close a class artificially or prematurely. Although the rule of convenience is only a rule of construction and yields to a contrary intent, contrary intent can seldom be shown. Once a class is closed by the rule of convenience, new entrants cannot join the class even though they otherwise fit the class label.

The Rule of Convenience: The rule of convenience closes a class when the property must be distributed. The Rule prevents the current distributees from receiving a defeasible possessory estate, part of which might have to be returned if new members of the class were admitted. The rule only applies to class gifts that did not close physiologically by the time of distribution.

Immediate Class Gifts: An immediate class gift closes at the date the gift becomes effective, if at least one member of the class is in existence. Thus a class gift taking effect in possession at the termination of a life estate closes at the death of the life tenant.

An immediate class gift by will does not close at the testator's death if at the testator's death there are no class members "in being." In this situation the class remains open until it closes physiologically.

Postponed Class Gifts: The postponed class gifts closes when a distribution of the property must be made. When a postponed class gift is preceded by a life estate, the general rule is that the class closes on the life tenant's death.

Sequential Distribution Class Gifts: Sequential distribution class gifts (*e.g.,* those that condition distribution on class members reaching a particular age) close as soon as one class member becomes entitled to receive a share.

IV. THE RULE AGAINST PERPETUITIES

A. Basic Requirements of the Rule Against Perpetuities

Statement of the Common Law Rule: A common formulation of the Rule provides: "No interest is good unless it must vest, if at all, not later than twenty-one years after some life in being at the creation of the interest."

Intended to curtail the deadhand control of wealth and to facilitate the marketability of property, its application engendered continual criticisms.

The Rule does not directly restrict the duration of an interest but restricts the time during which an interest can remain contingent. The Rule requires an initial certainty of vesting of all of the interests at their creation. All interests created in a governing instrument had to be tested against the Rule. If an interest is not certain of vesting within the Rule, the concept of infectious invalidity might cause the entire transfer to fail.

The Present Status of the Rule Against Perpetuities: Substantially more than half the states have reformed the common law Rule Against Perpetuities (Rule) in one way or another and, almost fifty percent of the states have enacted the Uniform Statutory Rule Against Perpetuities (1986) (USRAP).

Classifications and the Rule Against Perpetuities: The classifying of future interests in a disposition sorts out which interests, if any, are subject to the Rule.

Triggering Concern of Rule Against Perpetuities: The sole concern of the common law Rule is whether a future interest in property is certain to vest or fail to vest (terminate) within the time allowed (the perpetuity period).

Interests Subject to the Rule: The Rule potentially applies if a transaction creates a future interest in property. The subject matter may be land or personalty and the interest may be legal or equitable. Legal relationships such as long-term contracts are generally exempt. The Rule applies only to contingent remainders and executory interests. It does not apply to reversions, vested remainders, possibilities of reverter, or rights of entry.

A contingent remainder or an executory interest is valid only if there are no post creation events that would permit the interest to remain nonvested beyond the Rule.

Class Gifts and the All-or-Nothing Rule: Class gifts are subject to the Rule and a class gift is either completely valid or completely invalid. The "all or nothing" rule does not allow some class members to have valid interests if other class members have invalid interests.

The "Perpetuity Period": The common law perpetuity period is "life in being plus twenty-one years." It may be extended by the period of gestation of an actual pregnancy.

The "perpetuity period" is not a set length of time. Validity at common law does not depend on when the interest actually vests or terminates. Validity under the Rule turns on a projection regarding the various times in the future when the interest might vest or terminate.

The Twenty-one Year Part of the Period: The twenty-one year part of the perpetuity period can stand on its own. Thus a testamentary transfer "to my grandchildren who are living twenty-one years after my death" would be valid. But it probably cannot come first, followed by a life that is in being twenty-one years after the creation of the interest. The measuring life must be in being at the creation of the interest.

The Meaning of "Must Vest If At All": The phrase "if at all" means that the contingencies must be guaranteed to be finally resolved within the perpetuity period. Thus the Rule prohibits interests that might remain contingent beyond the perpetuity period. Conversely, the Rule validates interests that must vest or terminate within the perpetuity period.

The Life-in-Being Part of the Period: The life in being or measuring life must be a human being who was "in being" at the creation of the interest. This means that the measuring life must have been alive or in gestation when the interest was created. Lives in being must be identifiable and discoverable.

Persons Qualified as the "Measuring" Life: Invalid interests fail because there is no measuring life to make them valid. The goal of the search is to find one person for whom there is no invalidating chain of possible post-creation events. The process for determining whether a validating life exists is to postulate the death of each individual connected in some way to the transaction. If one individual can be found for whom there are no invalidating chain of possible events, that individual can serve as the validating life.

When dispositions of property create more than one interest that is subject to the Rule, the validity of each interest must be tested separately and a validating life must be found for each interest.

Only Insiders Need be Considered: Only insiders or persons who are connected in some way to the transaction need to be considered because only they will have a chance of supplying the causal connection demanded by the requirement of initial certainty.

Insiders include the transferor, if living, the beneficiaries of the disposition, including but not restricted to the taker or takers of the challenged interest, the objects and donee of a power of appointment, persons related to the foregoing by blood or adoption, especially in the ascending and descending lines, and anyone else who has any connection to the transaction.

The validating life need not be a devisee or mentioned in the instrument so long as the person is inherently involved in the lives in being determination.

Survivor of Group: The validating life can be a later-to-be-determined member of a group of individuals. The validating life is the life of the member of the group who turns out to live the longest.

Beneficiary of the Interest as the Validating Life: The beneficiary of an interest can sometimes be the validating life. This is applicable particularly when the beneficiary must reach an age exceeding twenty-one or survive to a particular point in time that exceeds twenty-one years.

Executory Interests Following Defeasible Fees: An executory interest following a defeasible fee is subject to the Rule and will be invalid unless there is a validating life.

Time of Creation: The time of creation of the property interest in question is crucial because the creation point fixes the time when the validating life must be "in being," and limits the facts and circumstances that can be taken into account in determining validity. An interest is valid only if, at the point of its creation, with the facts and circumstances then existing taken into account, the interest is certain to vest or terminate within a life in being plus twenty-one years.

Testamentary Transfers: Because property interests created by will are created when the testator dies, the validating life for testamentary transfers must be a person who was alive (or in gestation) when the testator died, and the facts and circumstances that are relevant to the validity of an interest created by will are those existing at the testator's death.

Inter Vivos Transfers: Property interests created by inter vivos transfer are created when the transfer becomes effective for purposes of property law generally, *e.g.,* the date of delivery of the deed or the funding of the trust. The validating life for inter vivos transfers must be a person who was alive (or in gestation) when the transfer became effective. The facts and circumstances that are relevant to the validity of an interest created by inter vivos transfer are those existing at that time. There are exceptions in certain cases when an interest is subject to a power.

Facts and Circumstances: The facts and circumstances existing at creation can be just as important in determining the validity of an interest as the contingencies attached to that interest.

Postponement Principle: For purposes of interests created in revocable inter vivos transfers, the creation time is postponed to the time when the power to revoke expires, *e.g.,* death of the settlor, date power released. The time of creation is also postponed if the interest is destructible, pursuant to the uncontrolled volition, and for the exclusive personal benefit of the person having such a power of destruction, *e.g.,* person holds an unqualified and currently exercisable power to make himself or herself the beneficial owner of the interest in question.

Constructional Preference for Validity: Most courts find that where an instrument is subject to two or more plausible constructions, one of which causes a Rule violation and the other of which does not, the construction that does not result in a Rule violation should be adopted.

The Consequences of Invalidity: Unless the doctrine of infectious invalidity applies, only the interest held invalid under the Rule is stricken from the disposition. All other valid interests created by the disposition take effect as if the invalid interest had never been created.

When the invalid interest is a remainder interest following a life estate or a term of years or is an executory interest following a fee simple determinable, its invalidity will probably cause a gap in the disposition. For inter vivos transfers, the gap will be filled by a reversion or a possibility of reverter. For testamentary transfers, the gap will be filled by the residuary clause or, by intestate succession if no residuary clause or it is invalid.

When the invalid interest is an executory interest (other than one following a fee simple determinable), the effect will cause the condition subsequent to be stricken, too.

Separability: When an interest is expressly subject to alternative contingencies, the principle of separability provides that the invalidity of one of the interests does not invalidate the other. It is applicable only when the transferor has expressly stated the contingencies in the alternative and is not recognized where alternative contingencies are merely implicit.

Infectious Invalidity: The doctrine of infectious invalidity provides that the invalidity of an interest may be held to invalidate one or more otherwise valid interests. Its application depends on case by case analysis whether the general dispositive scheme of the transferor will be better served by eliminating only the invalid interest or by eliminating other interests as well.

Technical Violations: The required certainty of vesting or terminating within the Rule may invalidate some interests even though they do not violate the policy of the Rule, *e.g.,* the fertile octogenarian, the administrative contingency, and the afterborn spouse.

Fertile Octogenarians: The term "fertile Octogenarians" refers to persons who are infertile, young or old, male or female. Generally, courts and authorities hold that all persons are conclusively presumed to be capable of having children throughout their entire lifetimes, regardless of their age or physical condition.

The Administrative Contingency: An "administrative contingency" concerns the performance by a fiduciary of some administrative function, the completion of which probably will not but might take more than twenty-one years, *e.g.,* "distribution upon the settlement of an estate."

The Afterborn Spouse: The "afterborn spouse" refers to the fact that an unnamed spouse, *e.g.,* "widow," of a beneficiary is excluded from serving as the validating life because the person assuming the status might turn out to be someone who was conceived and born after the creation of the interest. Probability is not considered. If no other validating life can be located, the questioned interest is invalid. Some courts avoid this problem by construing the reference to "widow," etc., as only referring to the person fitting that status when the will was executed or the date of the interest's created.

Perpetuity Saving Clauses: A typical perpetuity saving clause provides:

The trust hereby created shall terminate in any event not later than 21 years after the death of the last survivor of my descendants who are in being at the time this instrument becomes effective, and unless sooner terminated by the terms hereof, the trustee shall, at the termination of such period, make distribution to the persons then entitled to the income of this trust, and in the same shares and proportions as they are so entitled.

Perpetuity saving clauses eliminate the fear that a trust or other property arrangement will violate the Rule. Perpetuity saving clauses do not typically govern the term of the trust; they operate as a back-stop just in case the actual term of the trust exceeds the time allotted by the saving clause.

The clause is composed of the lives in being, the perpetuity-period, and gift over components. Each component is designed to assure the gift made in the clause qualifies under the Rule. The number of individuals specified as the measuring lives must not be so large that it would cause it to be impracticable to determine the death of the survivor.

B. Perpetuity Reform

The Need to Reform the Rule: Although there was nearly universal agreement that the Rule should be reformed, early reform efforts were not generally enacted. Now, with the enactment by nearly half the states of the Uniform Statutory Rule Against Perpetuities Act (USRAP), the perpetuity environment has been dramatically altered.

Checkerboard Reform of the Rule: In addition to the USRAP, reform efforts include: (1) total repeal of the Rule, (2) creation of an immediate judicial reformation power for interests that will not vest within the Rule, (3) creation of wait and see or deferred judicial reformation power for interests that do not vest within the Rule, and (4) substitution of a specific period of time or period in gross within which all conditional interests must vest.

Abolition of the Rule: A growing number of states have abolished application of the Rule.

The Wait-and-See Reform of the Rule: Wait-and-see reform proposed that the basis of validity under the Rule be shifted from possible to actual post-creation events. The wait-and-see element is applied only to interests that are potentially invalid under the common-law Rule. These potentially invalid interests are valid if they actually vest within the permissible vesting period. They are invalid only if they remain in existence but are still nonvested at the expiration of that period.

Criticism of Wait-and-See: The wait-and-see method has been criticized because it puts the validity of property interests in abeyance because no one can determine whether an interest is valid or not. Actually, it merely subjects the nonvested future interest to an additional contingency and only the status of the affected future interest is deferred.

The Permissible Vesting Period: The most significant controversy over wait-and-see concerns how to determine the period of time during which contingencies can be validly satisfied. The wait-and-see approach requires that a permissible vesting period be determined.

Pre–USRAP Wait-and-See: Several states enacted wait-and-see type legislation. These efforts only partially resolve Rule problems and raised issues of their own.

In 1983, the Restatement (Second) of Property adopted the wait-and-see method of perpetuity reform that uses a predetermined list of lives for determining the wait-and-see measuring lives. If a property interest is still in existence but nonvested at the expiration of the permissible vesting period, the transferred property must be disposed of in the manner which most closely effectuates the transferor's manifested plan of distribution and which is within the limits of the Rule.

Immediate Reformation Method of Perpetuity Reform: Some courts are statutorily authorized or directed to cure any violation of the Rule by reforming the disposition to make it valid. Reformation is permitted at any time. Under this power, courts have merely reformed age contingencies or periods in gross that exceed twenty-one by changing the prescribed age to twenty-one. Courts have not inserted a saving clause into the governing instrument which would have been a more faithful reformation to the transferor's intention.

Specific–Statutory–Repair Method: Two states, have enacted precise provisions directed specifically to deal with the fertile-octogenarian problem, the administrative contingency problem, the afterborn spouse problem, and age contingencies exceeding twenty-one.

The fertile-octogenarian problem is resolved by providing that (1) persons above 65 and below 13 are deemed incapable of having a child; (2) evidence is admissible regarding the incapacity of having a child by a living person who is under 65; and (3) the possibility of having a child or more remote descendant by adoption shall be disregarded.

The administrative-contingency problem is resolved by presuming that all the typical administrative contingencies, *e.g.,* the probate of a will, must happen, if at all, within the perpetuity period.

The afterborn-spouse problem is resolved by presuming that an interest in an unnamed spouse, *e.g.,* the "widow," of another person refers to a person who was living at the date that the Rule commences to run.

Age contingencies exceeding twenty-one are resolved by providing that when an interest is invalid because it depends upon any person attaining or failing to attain an age exceeding twenty-one years, the age shall be reduced to twenty-one regarding every person to whom the age contingency applies.

C. The Uniform Statutory Rule Against Perpetuities (USRAP)

Development and Status of USRAP: USRAP was promulgated in 1986, and made a part of the UPC. [References to the USRAP are to the UPC citations.] By mid–1999, it has been enacted in twenty four states.

Basic Operation: Under section 2–901 of the USRAP, a non-vested interest is valid if it is certain to vest or terminate either no later than twenty-one years after the death of a living individual or within ninety years after its creation. The first arm codifies the common law Rule. The second arm is a form of a wait and see approach tied to a specific length of time. It applies specifically to non-vested property interests, general powers of appointment that are not presently exercisable because of a condition precedent, and nongeneral powers of appointment such as testamentary powers of appointment.

Lives in Being under USRAP: The USRAP disregards the possibility that an individual may have a child born after the individual's death and thus, eliminates the common law lives in being extension granted to children en ventre sa mere. This extension is eliminated because under the new rule it is unnecessary for purposes of validating interests under the perpetuity rule.

Date of Creation of Interest: Section 2–902(a) of the USRAP provides that the time of creation for most non-vested property interests or powers of appointment is determined under general principles of property law. Thus, non-vested interests created in a will are created on the date of the testator's death. Those created in an inter vivos transfer, are created as of the effective date of the transfer. In addition, two special circumstances are resolved. If a person may personally exercise a power to become the unqualified beneficial owner of the property subject to the interest, the non-vested interest or power of appointment is created for purposes of the perpetuity period when that unqualified power terminates. These rules apply also to property added to the interest after the original duration date.

Reformation Under USRAP: Section 2–903 of the USRAP includes a judicial reformation procedure exercisable by the courts when transfers violate its perpetuity period. The court's power to reform does not arise until the transfer is invalid under the perpetuity period which means the non-vested interest has not vested within either of the durational periods of the perpetuity period.

Deferred Reformation: A deferred reformation power reduces "temperature testing" law suits over a perpetuity question, permits the transferor's plan to fully work out, rejects the prospective analysis of vesting determinations, and adopts the retrospective analysis approach. The court should know more about how the donor would reform the instrument had the donor known the instrument created an invalid transfer.

Exceptions to Deferred Reformation: Two exceptions to the post-validity reformation requirement are recognized. Under section 2–903(2), if a class gift may vest in the future but the time for actual possession or enjoyment of a share of the estate in a class member has arrived, those of the class entitled to immediate possession or enjoyment may seek reformation of the instrument so that their possession or enjoyment may occur immediately.

A reformation action is also permitted although the perpetuity period has not expired if it is clear it will expire before the property vests. This exception would cover the unlikely case where a donor created a transfer that would not vest until a period of time has passed clearly beyond the Rule.

Reformation Remedy: In a reformation action, the court must reform the document. It cannot hold that the transfer is invalid. Under section 2–903, the court must reform the transfer in a "manner that most closely approximates the transferor's manifested plan of distribution." There is no doctrine of infectious invalidity. Courts should make as little alteration to the disposition as possible, *e.g.*, the maximum number of persons who could take at the time of reformation should be permitted, and age requirements above twenty-one should be reduced only to the point where it will satisfy the rules.

D. Class Gifts under the Rule Against Perpetuities

General Rule: "All or Nothing": Class gifts are subject to the Rule and are either completely valid or completely invalid. If the interest of any potential class member might vest beyond the Rule, the entire class gift is invalid.

All-or-Nothing Rule under the USRAP: Although the USRAP does not abrogate the all-or-nothing rule, the class gift is valid if the interests of all class members vest within ninety years. If some class members' interests do not vest within ninety years, the disposition can be reformed to validate the interests of all class members who are conceived (or adopted) before the ninety-year mark.

Two Exemptions from the All-or-Nothing Rule: The two types of class gifts that are exempt from the all-or-nothing rule are the specific-sum class gifts and the gifts to subclasses. They are exempt because the underlying rationale of the all-or-nothing rule does not apply to them.

Specific–Sum Class Gifts: A specific-sum class gift is one that gives a specific sum of money to each class member, *e.g.*, "$10,000 to each child of A." Class members whose interest will vest within the Rule take, those whose interest will not vest, fail. The USRAP saves the interests of any persons in the class who are born (or adopted) within the ninety-year period following the creation date.

Gifts to Sub–Classes: The all-or-nothing rule does not apply to gifts to subclasses which requires that the takers must be described as a group of subclasses, and the share going to each subclass must be certain to be finalized within a life in being plus twenty-one years. The USRAP also validates gifts to subclasses but also applies the ninety-year period to all of the interests and reforms the document if invalidity is still applicable.

E. Powers of Appointment Under The Rule Against Perpetuities

General Application of the Rule: If a power of appointment violates the Rule, the power is invalid, and the disposition takes effect as if the power had never been created. If the power itself is valid, some or all of the interests created by its exercise may violate the Rule and be invalid.

The USRAP validates exercises of powers that are either valid under the Rule or under the ninety-year wait-and-see period.

Presently Exercisable General Powers: A presently exercisable general power is treated as the equivalent of a vested property interest in the donee and is, therefore, not subject to either the common-law Rule or the USRAP.

Validity of the Exercise: For perpetuity rule purposes, the donee of a general power presently exercisable is considered to have created the appointed interests. Thus, for purposes of the Rule, the creation date for the appointed interests is when the exercise becomes effective.

General Powers Not Presently Exercisable Because of a Condition Precedent: A general power not presently exercisable because of a condition precedent is invalid unless the condition precedent must be resolved one way or the other within the Rule.

Validity of Nongeneral Powers and General Testamentary Powers:

Common Law Rule: A nongeneral power and a general testamentary power are valid only if they are exercisable within the Rule.

Theory of Relation Back: The theory of relation back provides that any property interest created by the donee's exercise of a nongeneral power or of a general testamentary power is created by the donor when the donor created the power. Because no such property interest can vest until the power is exercised, the requirement of certainty of vesting means the power cannot be exercised beyond the Rule.

USRAP Approach: USRAP provides that even if a nongeneral or a general testamentary power is invalid under the Rule, the power is valid if it is actually exercised within ninety years after it was created.

Fiduciary Powers: Discretionary powers, *e.g.*, a trustee's power to invade the corpus of the trust for the benefit of the income beneficiary, held by fiduciaries are nongeneral powers of appointment, for perpetuity purposes. They are invalid if they might be exercised beyond the Rule. Under the USRAP, these powers can be exercised for ninety years. Purely administrative fiduciary powers are not subject to either the common law Rule or the USRAP.

Validity of the Exercise of Nongeneral and General Testamentary Powers: The relation back theory is applicable to determining the validity of interests created by the exercise of nongeneral powers and general testamentary powers. Any property interest created by the donee's exercise of the powers is treated as created by the donor when the donor created the power.

The Second–Look Doctrine: The "second look" doctrine holds that although the exercise of nongeneral powers or of general testamentary powers are treated as created when the power was created, the facts existing when the power was exercised can be taken into account. No useful purpose would be served by holding appointed interests to be invalid because of what might have happened after the power was created but which at the time of exercise can no longer happen.

F. Charitable Gifts And Commercial Transactions Under The Rule Against Perpetuities

Charitable Gifts: If contingent charitable future interests are preceded by interests created in one or more charity, the future interest is exempt from the Rule and the USRAP. In addition charitable future interests that are vested are not subject to the Rule.

Future interests created in charities that follow noncharitable interests are subject to the Rule and the USRAP. Under the common law, a condition precedent that might not be satisfied within the Rule invalidates the charitable interest. The USRAP gives the charitable interest ninety years in which to vest.

Commercial Transactions: Generally, the Rule is not an appropriate policy instrument to control commercial arrangements. When commercial transactions contractually create property interests, however, the Rule is applicable. The perpetuity argument is usually raised by one of the parties who does not want to perform his or her part of the contract.

Options in Gross: An option in gross is a contract right to purchase property held by an optionee who has no possessory interest in the property. Specifically enforceable options to purchase are equitable property interests which are invalid if they are exercisable beyond the Rule.

Rights of First Refusal (Preemptive Rights): Rights of first refusal obligate the owner to offer the property first to the preemptioner if the owner decides to sell. Rights of first refusal have been held invalid if they are exercisable beyond the Rule.

Options Appurtenant to Leasehold Interests: Options to renew a lease and to purchase leased property are exempt when held by the lessee. Thus, even though exercisable beyond the Rule, options appurtenant are valid.

Leases to Commence in the Future: A lease to commence at a fixed time in the future is valid but a lease scheduled to commence in the future is invalid if it is subject to a contingency that might occur beyond the Rule.

USRAP and Commercial Transactions: The USRAP specifically excludes all common law or statutory exceptions. Generally, the USRAP maintains that a perpetuity rule which concerns gratuitous transfers is not appropriate to apply to transactions with consideration. Certain transactions, however, that are in the nature of donative transfers despite their nongratuitous characterization are covered by the USRAP. Purely administrative or management powers, powers to appoint a fiduciary, and discretionary trustee powers to distribute principal to an indefeasibly vested beneficiary are excepted.

PART NINE: THE FIDUCIARY OBLIGATION

I. CONCEPT OF THE FIDUCIARY

A. The Fiduciary

The Fiduciary Relationship: A fiduciary is a person having a duty, created by his or her undertaking, to act primarily for another's benefit in matters connected with that undertaking. The fiduciary stands in great confidence and trust and owes a high degree of good faith to the beneficiary. The term, fiduciary, includes the trustee, guardian, and executor or personal representative.

B. The Personal Representative

The Representative Concept: An official administration of a decedent's estate requires appointment of a personal representative or multiple personal representatives. The office of personal representative carries significant responsibilities and status in the administration of a decedent's estate. Responsibilities include collection of assets, settling of claims, and final distribution of the estate.

Legal Status: The personal representative is recognized as the estate's legal entity, an officer of the court, a fiduciary and title holder of the decedent's personal property.

Specific Titles: A personal representative named in the will is called an "executor." One appointed in an intestate estate is called an "administrator." An administrator cum testamento annexo (c.t.a.) is a personal representative appointed when an executor fails to qualify or is not named in the will. An administrator de bonis non (d.b.n.) is the personal representative who succeeds an administrator. An administrator c.t.a. d.b.n. is the successor to the executor or an administrator c.t.a.

Particular titles primarily concern questions of the personal representative's qualification and authority. State laws, for example, sometimes make distinctions between whether the personal representative is an executor or an administrator.

UPC Terminology: This term, "personal representative," is used exclusively to refer to all persons who perform substantially the same function including executors, administrators, successor personal representatives and even special administrators.

Priority and Disqualification for Appointment: State statutes typically phrase qualification in the form of a priority list and disqualification with respect to a candidate's particular prohibited status. UPC section 3–203 illustrates:

Priority Order for Appointment of a Domiciliary Personal Representative	
Priority Rank	**Description of Candidates**
1	Persons named in will (including named successors and nominated selectees under a power in the will).
2	Surviving spouse who is a devisee (or the surviving spouse's selectee).
3	Other devisees (or the devisees' selectee).
4	Surviving spouse (or the surviving spouse's selectee).
5	Other heirs (or the heirs' selectee).
6	Any creditor forty-five days after death.

Disqualification: Non–UPC states are very specific as to when a person is disqualified or incompetent to serve either as an administrator or as an executor or both. Persons typically disqualified or barred from appointment, include minors, persons convicted of infamous crimes, or persons adjudged incompetent because of drunkenness, improvidence, mental incapacity or integrity. UPC section 3–203(f) disqualifies persons under the age of twenty-one and those found unsuitable by a Court in a formal proceeding.

Domiciliary Foreign Personal Representative: The personal representative appointed in the decedent's domicile has priority over all other persons for appointment in a nondomiciliary jurisdiction unless the decedent's will nominates different persons for different jurisdictions. Domiciliary foreign personal representative may also nominate another person who immediately assumes first priority for appointment.

Special Administrator: A special administrator may be appointed if there is a delay in granting letters testamentary or there are grounds for removal of the named personal representative.

C. The Trustee

Trustee Qualification: Any competent natural person or legal entity capable of taking title to property may be a trustee. Individuals, corporate fiduciaries, and governments are eligible. Some states bar infants, incompetents, aliens, nonresidents/foreign corporations, or unincorporated associations from serving as a trustee.

To have and retain capacity the trustee must be capable of taking title to property, of continuing to hold the title to the property, and of administering the trust. Incompetence, disqualification, renunciation or resignation, does not affect the validity of the trust, because the court will appoint a replacement trustee.

Grounds for Removal: Trustees may be removed for lack of capacity, serious breach of trust, refusal to account, commission of a crime, long continued absence, favoritism to one or more beneficiaries; and other related reason. Mere friction between the trustee and the beneficiary is not a sufficient ground for removing the trustee unless it interferes with the proper administration of the trust.

Disclaiming versus Resigning: A trustee may disclaim the position and assume no responsibility. Once a trustee accepts, the trustee cannot resign except (a) with the permission of a proper court; or (b) in accordance with the terms of the trust; or (c) with the consent of all the beneficiaries, if they have capacity to give such consent.

D. The Guardian

Concept and Necessity of Guardianship: Guardianship involves protection for the person who is under some type of disability which causes that person to be unable to manage his or her own personal or business affairs or both. Persons who suffer from disabilities include minors, mental incompetents, or other incompetents. A minor's disability is presumed by law depending upon age. Other disabilities require voluntary action by the disabled person or legal proceedings to determine the incompetency status.

Guardianships serve two distinct functions, *i.e,* guardianship of property and guardianship of the person. Guardianship of the property manages (receives and expends) the ward's property or estate for the purposes of the guardianship. Guardian of the person concerns custody or physical control over the ward. The same person may be permitted to serve in both capacities.

Guardian of Minors: A guardian for a minor is not necessary unless the minor is unmarried and all parental rights of custody have been terminated or suspended. The natural or adoptive parent is automatically the guardian of the person of his or her minor natural and adopted children. A parent would have to be removed by the proper court before any other person could be appointed guardian of that parent's minor children. The UPC and some other states permit the parent of an unmarried minor to appoint a guardian for the minor by will or by any other writing which is signed by the parent and attested by at least two witnesses.

When a guardian of a minor must be appointed, the court must appoint the person whose appointment would be in the best interest of the minor. Minors fourteen or older, may nominate who they want as guardian but the nomination need not be accepted.

Guardian of Incapacitated Persons: Incapacitated persons concern adults who for any reason lack sufficient understanding or capacity to make or communicate responsible decisions, *e.g.,* persons suffering from mental illness, mental deficiency, physical illness or disability, chronic use of drugs and chronic intoxication.

Under the UPC, the spouse or parent of an incapacitated person may appoint a guardian for the person by will or by any other writing which is signed by the spouse or parent and attested by at least two witnesses. Spouse's appointment prevails over parent's appointment. Appointment in the will of the last parent to die prevails over the first to die.

Conservator of the Estate: The guardian of the property or conservator deals with the management of the protected person's estate.

Usually, the conservator must be an individual or a corporation possessing trustee powers. It is common for statutes to list specific priorities for the Court's consideration in making an appointment. Between persons of equal priority, the Court has discretion to select the one best qualified if more than one is willing to serve. In addition, for good cause shown, the Court has discretion to ignore these priorities and to appoint anyone, including a person with less or without any priority.

II. DUTIES OF FIDUCIARIES

A. The General and Common Duties of a Fiduciary

The General and Common Duties of a Fiduciary: An abbreviated list of duties for a fiduciary include the duties of:

- loyalty,
- not to delegate,
- to take control of assets and to render accounts,
- to segregate property,
- to use reasonable care and skill,
- to treat all of the beneficiaries impartially when carrying out the many duties of administration, and
- to account.

Trustee's Primary Duty: The primary duty of a trustee is to administer the property of the trust for the beneficiaries.

Personal Representative's Primary Duty: The primary duty of a personal representative is to administer the property in the estate first for the benefit of the creditors of the estate and second for the distributees. A personal representative is primarily involved in a liquidation process. Thus, notice to creditors and completing an inventory of decedent's assets are of primary importance. Ordinarily a personal representative does not have a duty to keep the property productive.

Drafting Considerations: the governing instrument may affect most of the duties of fiduciaries. Global exceptions and waivers to duties should not be granted in the instrument. Exceptions and waivers should be tailored to the needs of the estate or trust.

B. Standard of Care, Skill and Prudence

Definition of Standard of Care: Under the Restatement (Second) of Trusts, a trustee must exercise the care and skill that a person of ordinary prudence would exercise in dealing with his or her own property. Generally, courts also use this definition as a standard of care for other fiduciary relationships.

Meaning of the Word "Prudence": Prudence means "caution." This means how a prudent trustee would act in administering the property of others or how he would act in conserving the property.

UPC Standard: Under the UPC a personal representative, conservator, and trustee must act as a prudent person dealing with the property of another.

Non-Varying Standard: Unless the settlor or testator reduces the amount of skill and prudence, the standard will not be lowered. That a particular fiduciary does not possess the necessary skill or prudence is not a defense. Exculpatory clauses have been strictly construed.

Higher Standard Enforced: The fiduciary, who possesses or represents that it possesses greater than ordinary skill and more than ordinary facilities, must exercise the greater skill and use the better facilities.

C. Duty of Loyalty

Principle of Loyalty: The duty of loyalty requires the fiduciary to administer the estate or trust solely in the interest of the beneficiaries. The fiduciary is not permitted to place personal interests in a position where it would be for the fiduciary's own benefit to violate the duty to the beneficiaries. The duty of loyalty is broadly applied. It prohibits the trustee not only from purchasing trust property individually but also from using trust property for personal financial or other purposes.

Self-Dealing Strict Liability: The duty of loyalty is strictly construed against the fiduciary. Courts use the "no-further-inquiry" rule which means if a fiduciary engages in self-dealing, the conduct is per se illegal. The fiduciary will be surcharged for any profit and any loss, or required to return the assets if still available, regardless of the substantive fairness of the deal and regardless of the fiduciary's good faith. The only defense to self-dealing is consent of the beneficiaries after full disclosure. Fairness, reasonableness and good faith may be defenses if the fiduciary puts itself in a position of conflict of interest that does not include self-dealing.

Rationale Behind This Strict Rule: The strict rule against self-dealing is a prophylactic rule which demands that fiduciaries not allow themselves to assume a position of conflict. It strives to avoid potential conflicts and requires undivided loyalty. All temptation is removed from one acting as a fiduciary to serve the fiduciary's own interest when in conflict with the obligations of the trust or estate.

It also protects the beneficiaries from having to prove bad faith, wrongdoing or unfairness by the trustee under circumstances where the issues are presented a long time after the event and the fiduciary has had the opportunity to cover its tracks. No countervailing reasons exist to allow a conflict and the strict rule exhibits clarity and administrative efficiency.

Arguments Against the Strict Rule: Others contend the strict rule gives beneficiaries a windfall when loss is caused by a decline in general market valuations. It makes even the innocent non-earmarking trustee an insurer against all losses to the beneficiaries and thus may discourage otherwise responsible individuals and institutions from accepting a fiduciary office. A rule of reasonableness is said to sufficiently protects beneficiaries against risks of loss.

Court Approval: When it is advantageous for a fiduciary to self-deal with the estate or trust, the trust should seek approval from the appropriate court. Courts, after reviewing all of the relevant facts, can approve the transaction. Sometimes they have approved them post facto when an emergency arose.

Drafting Solution: When self-dealing may be necessary or desirable for all concerned, provisions in the governing instrument can expressly permit it.

D. Duty Not to Delegate

Statement of the No Delegations Rule: Under the modern law as expressed by the Restatement (Second) of Trusts, a trustee is under a duty not to delegate the doing of acts which the trustee can reasonably be required personally to perform. A trustee has a duty personally to perform the responsibilities of the trusteeship except as a prudent person might delegate those responsibilities to others. The trustee has fiduciary discretion to delegate fiduciary authority and in such manner as a prudent investor would delegate under the circumstances.

Requirement of Supervision: Even if delegation is permitted, the trustee must exercise general supervision over any agent's conduct.

Total Delegation of Trust Duties: Unless the trust instrument permits, a trustee may not properly commit the entire administration of the trust to an agent, co-trustee, or other person.

E. Duty to Identify and Segregate Trust Property

Extent of Duty to Identify and Segregate: Trustees have the duty (1) to keep the trust property separate from trustee's own property; (2) to keep the trust property separate from property held upon other trusts; and (3) to identify and earmark the trust property as property of the trust.

Prohibition on Commingling Other Property: A trustee must not commingle trust funds with trustee's own funds. The terms of the trust, however, may permit commingling of trust property and the trustee's own property

When authorized, a bank trustee can properly deposit into a single common trust account the funds of several trusts, provided that it keeps an accurate record of the contributions of the separate trusts.

Earmarking Trust Assets: A trustee must earmark trust property as trust property which means that titled or documented asset should be held and recorded in the name of the trustee as trustee.

Consequences of Failure to Identify and Segregate: A trustee is will not be liable for a technical breach of trust that involves a trustee taking title to the trust property in trustee's individual name in good faith if no loss results or if the loss is caused by events and circumstances not related to the failure to segregate. The trustee is liable for the full amount of the loss and interest thereon, if trustee took title in trustee's own name in bad faith with intent to misappropriate the property.

F. Duty to Take Control of Assets and to Make Accounts

Personal Representative Requirement to Collect and Appraise the Estate: The decedent's personal representative must identify and take into his or her possession the decedent's estate as can be found. The personal representative must prepare within a specific period of time an inventory of the estate and must file it with the court or send it to interested persons or both.

Inventory: The inventory of the estate must list the decedent's assets with reasonable detail indicating the fair market value and the amount of any encumbrance existing as to each asset.

Appraisal Process: In some states appraisers must be hired or appointed by the court to value the property of the estate. The UPC permits the personal representative to personally value the assets at fair market value or may employ other qualified and disinterested appraisers as is required under the circumstances.

Subsequently Discovered Property: The personal representative must prepare a supplementary inventory and appraisement if subsequent property is discovered or the value or description of property on the original inventory is erroneous or misleading.

G. Duty to Account

Personal Representative's Accounts: When states require a formal administration procedure for a decedent's estate, the personal representative must file periodic accountings of transactions that occurred during the period.

Final Closing and Accounting: When an estate closes, a full accounting of the actions and transactions occurring during the administration is usually required. Notice to interested persons is required. If interested persons object, a hearing will be held to resolve disputes. After all disputes are settled or no one objects, the court then approves the accounting, closes the estate, and discharges the personal representative.

UPC Accountings: The UPC does not contain a standard accounting requirement unless interested persons file a petition for an accounting. A request for a final accounting is part of this formal closing process. After notice to all devisees and the personal representative and a hearing, the court may approve the accounting and order the discharge of the personal representative.

Trustee's Accounts: A trustee is under a duty to keep and render accounts and to furnish the beneficiary information at reasonable times. These accounts must show in detail the nature and amount of the trust property and the administration thereof.

Failure to Keep Accounts: A trustee is liable for any loss or expense resulting from trustee's failure to keep proper accounts. The trustee has the burden of proof to show that the trustee is entitled to the claimed credits.

Court Supervised Trusts: In some states when a trustee is appointed by a court, the trustee may be required to submit the accounts at designated intervals to the proper court for its approval.

Proceeding for Accounting: Persons financially interested in the trust administration, including both income and remainder beneficiaries, may bring suit to review or to force an accounting.

Trust Provisions Waiving Accounts: The trust instrument may relieve the trustee from the necessity of keeping formal accounts. Notwithstanding, the beneficiary may, by suit, require the trustee to account and to show that the trustee faithfully and dutifully performed the trust. The trustee will be liable for whatever remedies may be appropriate due to any breach of trust.

Trustee's Record Keeping: Trustees must keep records that are so complete and accurate that the trustee can prove faithfulness to the trust. If the trustee does not keep records, all evidentiary presumptions and doubts are resolved against the trustee.

Unless the instrument manifests an intention that the property should be held free of trust, courts do not allow exculpatory provisions to create a virtual license to the trustee to convert the fund to trustee's own use and thereby terminate the trust.

Consequences for Failure to Account: If the trustee fails to account as required, the trustee may be:

- removed,
- deprived of trustee's compensation
- liable for costs of suit requiring him to account.

Res Judicata for Prior Accountings: Court approved accountings are final only to matters determined by and before the court. The trustee's duty is to make the fullest measure of disclosure.

Informal Accounting Reports: When the trustee presents to beneficiaries a written statement that is merely a brief condensed outline of the work of the trustee during the stated period, the beneficiaries are bound only if the trustee made a proper disclosure in the accounting of the conduct in question in the administration of the trust.

III. POWERS OF FIDUCIARIES

A. Powers Concept

Interrelationships of Fiduciary Concepts: A fiduciary's powers, duties and liabilities are different ways of saying the same thing. The scope of a trustee's powers depend upon the scope of the trustee's duties: liability springs only from breach of duties.

Powers of the Personal Representative: Under less progressive systems for the administration of decedent's estates, the personal representative is required to seek an order by the appropriate court either when initiating an action or when obtaining approval for it, or at both times. In addition, the personal representative lacks any degree of broad powers necessary to administer the estate. Failure to seek court authority may burden the personal representative with severe potential liability. This red tape costs the successors time and money.

Estate Planning Relief: Will provisions limiting court involvement, broadening the personal representative's powers, and exculpating the personal representative from certain liabilities typically constitute a substantial and significant portion of a well drafted will in these states.

UPC Approach: The UPC and other states have greatly expanded the personal representative's powers. Consequently, except as restricted by the terms of the will or requested by interested persons and ordered by a court, the personal representative is to administer the estate as rapidly as possible without court supervision or intervention. To achieve this end, the personal representative is granted the same power over the title to decedent's property that an absolute owner would have and more specifically all personal representatives are authorized to perform twenty-seven specified actions.

Exercise Standard: All of these powers must be exercised "reasonably for the benefit of interested persons."

Powers of Trustee: A trustee may exercise all powers conferred by the specific terms of the trust and any other power necessary or appropriate to carry out the purposes of the trust which are not expressly or impliedly forbidden. The nature and extent of a trustee's duties and powers are primarily determined by the terms of the trust including any form of judicially provable intent. It can be assumed that the settlor intends to confer upon the trustee the powers necessary to carry out the purposes of the trust.

Implied Powers: The trustee who has neither express power nor statutory authority, may be held by a court to have implied powers inferred from the language of the trust instrument, the purpose of the trust, and the character of the trust's assets.

Forbidden Power: A trustee must not exercise any power if the terms of the trust forbid a trustee from exercising a power. If a forbidden power must be exercised to save the trust, a court might order the trustee to exercise it.

Uniform Trustees Powers Act (UTPA): The UTPA applies to "trusts" that contemplate general trust administration whether they are inter vivos or testamentary, or characterized as charitable, or private trust.

Prudent Trustee Concept: Section 1(3) of the Act adopts the prudent person concept as a pervasive regulator of trustee action. Thus, the trustee must determine whether it has the necessary power to act: if the trustee makes this determination in good faith and within the bounds of reasonable judgment, a court should be precluded from substituting its judgment for that of the trustee. On the other hand, the act's conferral of a power does not mean the trustee should exercise it. Only if the power conferred ought to be exercised, is the trustee permitted to exercise it.

Listed Powers: UTPA's long list of powers that the trustee may exercise covers every primary power a trustee would need to use to properly administer the trust. These powers include, for example, power to sell, lease and mortgage trust assets and even the power to borrow in general.

UTPA Powers That Were Prohibited at Common Law: The specific powers provided to a trustee significantly alter some of the common law rules concerning expressed or implied powers including matters of loyalty and other conflicts of interest, delegation powers, segregation of trust property, investment power.

Trustee Unanimity: Although at common law multiple trustees had to act with unanimity unless otherwise provided in the instrument, the UTPA makes unanimity unnecessary. If a third person requires unanimity, however, UTPA permits the trustees to achieve it without making the dissenting trustee a part of the action.

Settlor's Limitation on Powers: The UTPA allows a settlor to limit a trustee's powers except that the settlor probably cannot restrict the rule which requires third persons dealing with the trustee to have actual notice of a breach of trust in order to be liable.

B. The Investment Function

Investment Standard: A fiduciary must invest and manage the funds of the trust as a prudent investor would, in light of the purposes, terms, distribution requirements, and other circumstances of the trust. The trustee must possess and exercise ordinary intelligence in the investment function. The fiduciaries, who possesses more skill than an individual of ordinary intelligence, must use that higher level of skill.

Bases of Judging Fiduciary Investments: The two bases for judging a fiduciary's investments are:

- Whether the investment is of a type in which the fiduciary may properly invest under the law of the applicable jurisdiction.
- Whether the particular investment chosen from the permissible type is proper.

Under the first, compliance with the general fiduciary standards of care, skill and prudence is not a defense. Under the second, the fiduciary may defend investment actions by showing compliance with the skill, care, and caution exercised by the fiduciary.

The Investment Function of an Executor or Administrator: Normally the personal representative does not have an investment function. It may be granted or implied from the will.

Interrelationship Between Powers and the Investment Function: Sometimes a question arises whether a certain action by the personal representative is an exercise of a permissible power or an act of investment. The UPC permits the personal representative to invest funds, which are not needed to meet currently payable debts and expenses or distributions, in investments that are reasonable for use by trustees generally.

The Investment Function of a Trustee: Normally, a trustee must use reasonable care and skill to make the trust property productive in a manner that is consistent with the fiduciary duties of caution and impartiality. If property is unproductive, it needs to be made productive or sold unless the trust instrument requires or the circumstances indicate otherwise.

Limited Investment Policy: A few states have statutes, called legal-list statutes, that restrict all or part of a trust's investments to particular types of investments unless the settlor grants broader investment authority in the trust.

Prudent Person Rule: The prudent person rule provides:

> A trustee to invest trust funds must conduct him or herself faithfully and exercise sound discretion, and must observe how men of prudence, discretion and intelligence manage their own affairs, not in regard to speculation, but in regard to the permanent disposition of their funds, considering the probable income, as well as the probable safety of the capital to be invested.

Under the test, speculative investments are prohibited. In addition, the trustee's investments must be evenly balanced between the claims of the life tenant and those of the remaindermen.

Second Restatement of Trust Rule: Section 227 of the Restatement (Second) of Trusts "prudent-man rule" declares that it is the trustee's duty "to make such investments and only such investments as a prudent man would make of his own property having in view the preservation of the estate and the amount and regularity of the income to be derived." Most states have codified this rule or a close proximity to it.

When a trust document grants the trust authority to select investments "in the trustee's discretion," the trustee is limited by the "prudent trustee" rule regardless of the rule in the state

Investment in Stock of Companies: The prudent investor rule allows investments in a corporate security when the corporation has acquired by reason of the amount of its property, and the prudent management of its affairs, such a reputation that cautious and intelligent persons commonly invest their money in such security as permanent investments.

Diversification: Most but not all states require that a trust fund be diversified. Diversification has several meanings.

Restrictive Application: Some states link diversification to protecting the security of trust funds. Under this definition, the trust investment portfolio need not be diversified but invested in the most conservative investments such as federal government securities. Protection from risk of loss through default is the only consideration.

Expansive Definition: Diversification requires the trustee to invest in a wide range of investments in order to take advantage of the many attributes of the investment market place including purchasing power, beneficiary impartiality, and diversifiable risk.

Non-Legal Investments: If investments become improper as to type, the trustee must get rid of them. Non-legal investments included within the original trust must be sold within a reasonable period unless the trust specifically permits retention.

The Prudent Investor Rule: The Restatement (Third) Trust, Prudent Investor Rule (PIR) was promulgated to eliminate archaic investment rules and to provide flexibility to trustees in their investment decisions.

Purpose and Goals of the Prudent Investor Concept: The new investment rules accept modern investment experience and research, without either endorsing or excluding any particular theories of economics or investment. They are intended to be general and flexible enough to adapt to changes in the financial world. They protect the trustee and provide guidance for court review of trustee actions. They encourage the expert trustees to pursue challenging, rewarding, non-traditional strategies, and provide guidance and safe harbors for the less sophisticated trustees. The importance and usefulness of modern portfolio theory is recognized.

First Principle of Modern Portfolio Theory: The value (price) of an asset is a function of two factors: the rate of total return (*i.e.*, ordinary income and capital appreciation) that the asset is anticipated to generate, and the risk that the actual return will fall short of the anticipated return.

The risk of shortfall of total return leads to a focus upon assets as integral parts of a whole portfolio rather than to a focus upon each asset in isolation. Thus, assets are not labeled as inherently prudent or imprudent.

Whether a trustee has discharged its duties depends upon the manner in which the trustee has made investment decisions, not portfolio performance.

Shortfall of Total Return: The risk of shortfall of return is divided into two categories: market risk and nonmarket risk.

- Market risk is the risk that the return in the market in which the asset is situated will fall short of the anticipated return, *e.g*, change in the monetary policy of the Board of Governors of the Federal Reserve System, or a general economic downturn. Modern portfolio theory espouses that the market compensates the investor for market risk. Generally, a higher rate of return corresponds to a higher market risk of a shortfall.

The trustee should attempt to assemble a portfolio that maximizes return at any level of risk. Conversely, the trustee should attempt to assemble a portfolio that minimizes risk at any level of return.

- Nonmarket Risk is the risk that something may occur particularly with respect to the particular asset that may increase or decrease its return, *e.g,* the chief executive officer of a particular firm dies, or an earthquake or flood renders a plant inoperable. Modern portfolio theory espouses that the extent this risk may cause a shortfall of return, it is a nonmarket risk. The duty to diversify for the purpose of eliminating nonmarket risk is a centerpiece of the Rule.

  Evaluating Risks: A trustee usually has a duty to incur what risk is necessary to obtain a return that preserves real values. Thus, inflation is a risk and must be considered.

  Risk Tolerance: Risk tolerance is the tolerance that a trust has to the volatility of return. This tolerance depends on an estimate of distribution obligations of the trust including both its regular distribution requirements and any irregular distributions that may in fact become necessary or appropriate. The trust's obligations depend on the terms of the trust, as affected by the needs of one or more of the beneficiaries.

  Duty to Diversify: The Rule imposes a duty upon the trustee to eliminate the risk that is unique to each asset by imposing a duty to diversify. The duty to diversify also reduces the importance of nonmarket risk. Diversification elevates the importance of market risk and leads to the conclusion that the chief duties of the trustee are to determine and implement the mix of market risk and reward that is appropriate for the trust.

Second Principle of Modern Portfolio Theory: Modern portfolio theory contends that an investor is not able to outperform the market at whatever mix of risk and reward the investor is seeking. Attempts to do so are futile, counterproductive and wasteful. Thus, a trustee's investment strategy is prohibited from incurring costs that are not reasonable in amount. The theory sanctions passive investment strategies and challenges active investment strategies that produce inferior returns. Investments such as index funds that tend to mimic a market as a whole are encouraged.

C. Allocating Receipts and Expenditures Between Principal and Income

The Allocation Problem: All fiduciaries must allocate expenses or income among beneficiaries. In making allocations, trustees must use reasonable care and skill and act with impartiality between conflicting beneficiaries. Generally, receipt and expenses must be characterized as either income or principal or a combination of both.

Sources of Allocation Rules: There are three basic sources for allocation rules:

- Instructions included in the relevant transfer instrument.
- If none, the fiduciary follows relevant state statutes.
- If neither, the trustee must allocate in a reasonable and equitable manner, taking into account the interests of both income and principal beneficiaries.

Uniform Principal and Income Acts: Several Uniform Acts deal with four general problems affecting the rights of beneficiaries:

- The allocation of income earned during the administration of an estate.
- The allocation of income interests between income and principal for any trust at its beginning.
- The allocation of income interests at the end of a trust.
- The allocation of income between principal and income for interests received during administration of the trust.

Conflicting Interests Between Beneficiaries: When a settlor of a trust provides for both income and remainder beneficiaries, the income beneficiaries have the right to trust income: the remainder beneficiaries have the right to the principal when the trust terminates. The allocation of income and expenses against these beneficiaries' interests places them in conflict. Income beneficiaries want high rates of return, remainder beneficiaries want asset appreciation. An investment that is good for one type of beneficiary may not benefit the other. Similarly, each type of beneficiary wants expenses to be charged against the other beneficiaries' interest and not his or her own.

Special Allocation Rules under the Revised Act:

Examples of income include:

- Rent and other related payments;
- Interest and similar appreciation;
- Cash dividends;
- Net business and farming profits;
- Net receipts from mineral or natural resource interests less that value allocated to principal for depletion purposes;
- A 4% per year return taken from proceeds of the sale of underproductive property.

Examples of principal include:

- Proceeds from the sale of corpus;
- Repayments of loans and other return of corpus;
- Eminent domain proceeds;
- Insurance proceeds on principal assets;
- Stock dividends, stock splits, and capital gains, depreciation distributions, and other similar corporate capital distributions;
- A portion of production payments from natural resources for depletion purposes;
- A portion of gross receipts, (no more that 50%) of net receipts from a royalty, working net profit or any other mineral or natural resources interest;
- Receipts from other depletable assets to the extent such receipts exceed 5% per year of the asset's inventory value;
- Receipts from the disposition of underproductive property less the income portion;
- Any allowance for depreciation.

Examples of expenses against income include:

- Ordinary administration, management, or preservation of trust property expenses;
- A reasonable allowance for depreciation upon property other than a beneficiary's residence;
- One-half of the court costs, attorney's fees, and other fees on periodic judicial accountings unless the court otherwise directs;
- One-half of the trustee's regular compensation, whether based on a percentage of principal or income;
- All reasonable expenses incurred for current management of principal and application of income; and,
- Any income tax.

Extraordinary Expense Against Income: Unusually high charges against income may be charged in a reasonable manner over a reasonable period of time so that income distributions can be regularly maintained.

Examples of charges against principal include:

- One-half of a trustee's regular compensation;

- Expenses reasonably incurred concerning principal;
- Costs of investing and reinvesting principal;
- Payments to reduce the balance of an indebtedness;
- Expenses for the preparation of property for rental or sale;
- Litigation expenses maintaining and defending the trust, and concerning trust property;
- Charges not charged against income;
- Extraordinary repairs or expenses for capital improvement;
- Capital gain and similar taxes;
- Estate or inheritance taxes, including interest and penalties thereon; and,
- Business operating losses.

Income Earned During the Administration of an Estate: Specific devisees receive the income from the property specifically devised to them, reduced by expenses clearly allocated to that property. The remaining net income is payable to all other beneficiaries except those who receive proportional pecuniary legacies. All debts, funeral expenses, estate taxes, attorney's fees, fiduciary commissions, and court costs are charged against the principal of the estate unless the will provides otherwise.

IV. LIABILITY OF FIDUCIARIES AND OTHERS

A. General Fiduciary Liability

Nature of Liability: Fiduciaries are not insurers of loss but are liable to:

- Beneficiaries for breaches of trust for violations of duty, and
- Third persons for problems caused by contracts and torts occurring during the administration of the estate or trust.

Proper Party: An action may be brought against all types fiduciaries by a beneficiary, a creditor of the estate or trust, and a successor or co-fiduciary.

Status of Claim: Judgments against fiduciaries are not preferred claims unless a claimant is granted a lien on certain property of the fiduciary or where the claimant can trace particular trust property into the hands of the fiduciary.

Measure of Damages to Beneficiary: The fiduciary for breach of trust is liable for:

- Any loss or depreciation in value of the property of the estate or trust resulting from the breach;
- Any profit made by the fiduciary through the breach; and
- Any profit which would have accrued to the property of the estate or trust if there had been no breach.

Offsetting a Loss by a Gain: A fiduciary can not directly offset a loss with a gain but can offset gain from sale of asset on which surcharge is made for losses.

Joint and Several Liability: Multiple fiduciaries are liable jointly and severally to the beneficiaries. Fiduciaries who pay the claim have a right to indemnification from the other fiduciaries based on the degree of culpability of the respective fiduciary.

Fiduciary Defenses: Breaches of the trust are generally not defendable on good faith and reasonable exercise of care and skill. Answers to fiduciary reasonable doubt should be sought by a petition for instructions from the appropriate court. Actions taken pursuant to the court instructions are protected if the trustee obtained the instruction in good faith and upon full disclosure.

Beneficiaries Consent to the Breach: If beneficiaries consent to the fiduciary's action they are estopped from action unless the fiduciary concealed material facts or acted in a manner not consistent with the fiduciary's relationship to the beneficiaries. Generally, nonconsenting beneficiaries are not bound unless a consenting beneficiary virtually represent the former.

Exculpatory Provisions: Clauses that attempt to relieve fiduciaries of liability are limited in effectiveness. Although they may exculpate the fiduciary from liability for nonvolitional behavior, they do not relieve them of liability for:

- Bad faith, intentionally, or reckless breaches of trust;
- Profits gained by the trustee from a breach of trust.

UPC Rule of Liability: UPC section 3–712 makes a personal representative liable as that of a trustee to interested persons for any damage or loss from a breach of a fiduciary duty in the improper exercise of a power.

B. A Fiduciary's Liability to Third Parties

Common Law Rule of Personal Fiduciary Liability: Although the fiduciary is personally liable upon contracts, tax assessments and torts relating to the property and its management, it will be reimbursed from the estate for its expenses if the fiduciary's administration was proper. Actions in tort or contract are brought and judgment entered in the fiduciary's individual capacity. Courts rationalized these rules on the basis that the nature of the original liability and then the liability of the estate might cause a clash of interests between the trustee in its individual capacity and in its representative capacity. Holding the fiduciary personally liable is sometimes influenced by the availability of insurance for the fiduciary.

Avoiding Personal Liability: Personal contract liability could be avoided by specific terms of the contract if the contract was one proper to the fiduciary's administration.

Judgment Enforcement: The judgment creditor can reach the assets of the estate in equity through subrogation but the creditor's rights are dependent upon the fiduciary's right of indemnification.

UPC Rule of Liability: UPC section 3–808 makes the estate a "quasi-corporation" for purposes of a personal representative's personal liability to third persons on contracts, from ownership or control of the estate's property and from torts arising out of the administration of the estate. Thus, the personal representative is liable not individually but only as an agent would be liable.

Specific UPC Rules: A personal representative is personally liable:

- Under authorized contracts only when expressly provided in the contract or when the representative capacity of the personal representative is not revealed in the contract; and,

- For torts or for obligations arising from property ownership or control only when the personal representative is personally at fault.

Fiduciary Liability Issue: Third persons may sue the estate for such claims in the name of the personal representative in a representative capacity regardless of the personal representative's personal liability. The personal representative's personal liability to the estate may be litigated during the third person's initial action against the estate or in any other appropriate proceeding such as a proceeding for an accounting.

C. Third Party Liability to Trust or Beneficiary

Parties to the Action: The fiduciary brings an action against a third person who owes or has injured the estate unless a beneficiary has a possessory right which has been interfered with, or a trustee neglects or declines to act. Then, the beneficiary may bring the action personally.

Liability for Trustee's Breach of Trust

Nature of the Liability: If a third person joined with a fiduciary in committing a breach of trust, that person is liable to the beneficiaries. When the question concerns the purchase by a third person of trust property from a trustee who commits a breach of trust in making the transfer, the third person may have to return the property or its value or the proceeds of resale if that person did not pay value or had notice of the breach. The "value" need not be the fair market value but it must be greater than would put a person on notice of a breach or that a reasonable inquiry should be made.

Notice of Breach of Trust: Liability depends on whether the third party had notice of the breach of trust. Some courts have held that a third person has notice if the third person had knowledge of facts that would cause a reasonable person to make an inquiry into the trustee's actions and it was likely that the breach of trust would have been discovered upon reasonable inquiry. Consequently, third persons have become very cautious and conservative in dealing with fiduciaries such as personal representatives.

Remedial Uniform Acts: By enacting various uniform laws many states have reduced the potential liability of third persons for the breach of trust by a fiduciary in particular commercial transactions. Under these acts, a third person who purchases a trust asset for value from a trustee, takes good title unless he or she had actual knowledge or reason to believe that the transfer is in breach of trust. The third person is not bound to inquire whether the trustee has power to act or is properly exercising the power.

UPC Rule of Third Person Liability: UPC section 3–714 provides that if a person deals with or assists a personal representative in good faith and for value, that person is protected as if the personal representative properly exercised a power. Third persons, when knowingly dealing with a personal representative, are also not required to

- Inquire into the existence or the propriety of exercise of a power, or
- See to the proper application of funds or property delivered to the personal representative.

Only actual knowledge of any will or court restriction on the personal representative's powers, will cause the third person to be liable for breach of the restriction.

PART TEN: TAXATION

I. TAXATION OVERVIEW

A. The Place for Taxation

Accumulation of Wealth and the Imposition of Taxes: The current federal gift and estate tax system is a thorough and comprehensive system to tax the accumulation of wealth. It comprehensively applies to will substitutes as well as testamentary disposition. Today in the federal tax system, there are few "loopholes" for tax avoidance that have not been intentionally engrafted into the law.

Tax Triumvirate: The relevant parts of the federal taxation systems are the income tax, the gift tax and the estate tax.

Although the three types are substantially complementary, they overlap to some extent. A transaction, for example, might be subject to a gift tax and at donor's death be part of donor's gross estate for estate tax purposes. Estate planning decisions require analysis whether a particular transaction has gift tax, estate tax and income tax consequences.

Federal Transfer Tax System Overview: Both probate and nonprobate transfers are subject to either (1) the federal gift tax, (2) the federal estate tax, and (3) the federal generation skipping transfer tax. The tax is usually imposed on the donor or the donor's estate. Lifetime or deathtime gifts of money or other property are not taxable to donees as income.

II. GIFT AND ESTATE TAXES

A. Unified Transfer Tax System

History of Unified Tax: Although prior to 1976 the federal estate and gift taxes operated independently rather than cumulatively, in 1976 Congress adopted an unified tax system that accumulates all taxable gifts over the person's lifetime and adds them to the value of the taxable estate at death. In our progressive tax system, unification of the calculation of the estate and of the tax rate permits maximum tax collection and reduces the advantages of splitting large estates between lifetime and deathtime transfers.

Lifetime Giving Advantages: Certain lifetime gifts retain tax advantages. Outright inter vivos gifts of $10,000 or less per donee per year are excluded from all transfer taxation. Whereas the estate tax is calculated on the value of the estate including that portion of the estate that will be used for payment of the estate taxes, gift taxes paid on inter vivos gifts are not included in the valuation of the taxable estate if the gift is made prior to three years before the donor's death. Although the tax savings may be significant for large estates, the savings must be compared to the loss of the investment return on the amount of any gift taxes paid. Finally, lifetime gifts lock in the date of gift value for the asset given. If assets are appreciating in value, locking in their value can save taxes when the total tax burden is calcutated after donor's death.

Unified Tax Rate Schedule: The current gift and estate tax rate schedule is:

CHART 10–II–1

PROGRESSIVE RATE OF FEDERAL GIFT AND ESTATE TAXES		
TAXABLE BASE OR ESTATE	PERCENT OF TAX ON EACH DOLLAR ABOVE BASE	TAX ON TAX BASE
$1	18%	$0
$10,000	20%	$1,800
$20,000	22%	$3,800
$40,000	24%	$8,200
$60,000	26%	$13,000
$80,000	28%	$18,200
$100,000	30%	$23,800
$150,000	32%	$38,800
$250,000	34%	$70,800
$500,000	37%	$155,800
$750,000	39%	$248,300
$1,000,000	41%	$345,800
$1,250,000	43%	$448,300
$1,500,000	45%	$555,800
$2,000,000	49%	$780,800
$2,500,000	53%	$1,025,800
$3,000,000	55%	$1,290,800
$10,000,000	60%	$5,140,800
$21,040,000	55%	$11,764,800

Marginal Tax Rate: Although there are tax brackets that run from 18 and 37 percent, the actual marginal rate that a taxpayer will pay is 37 percent due to the unified credit which eliminates tax liability below its equivalent exemption value. In 2000 that equivalent exemption equals $675,000. In 2006, the marginal rate goes up to 41% as the exemption amount becomes $1 million. .

1997 Tax Act: Between 1998–2005, the unified credit and its equivalent exemption increases as follows:

Chart 10–II–2

Unified Tax Exemption and Credit

Year	Exemption	Unified Tax Credit
Prior to 1998	$600,000	$192,800
1998	$625,000	$202,050
1999	$650,000	$211,300
2000 and 2001	$675,000	$220,550
2002 and 2003	$700,000	$229,800
2004	$850,000	$287,300
2005	$950,000	$326,300
Thereafter	$1,000,000	$345,800

B. The Federal Gift Tax

Accumulative Effect of Taxable Gifts: Although taxable gifts must be reported and the tax must be paid on an annual basis, all taxable gifts, both present and past, are totaled for purposes of calculating current taxable gift. The gift tax rate applicable to that amount is used to figure the tentative tax and the current tax on taxable gifts for preceding years. The latter tax is subtracted from the former tax to set the balance. The balance is reduced by any unused unified credit. The result equal the tax due.

Definition of a Gift: All transfers for less than adequate and full consideration in money or money's worth are considered gifts to the extent the value of the property exceeded the value of the consideration. Adequate and full consideration in money or money's worth requires a sale, exchange, or other transfer of property made in the ordinary course of business (a transaction which is bona fide), at arm's length, and free from donative intent.

Annual Exclusion: Qualified gifts valued up to a cumulative value of $10,000 or less made by a donor during a calendar year to each separate donee are excluded from the donor's taxable gifts. Certain transfers for educational expenses or medical expenses are also not subject to gift taxation regardless of their amount.

Gift splitting: The donor and the donor's spouse may elect to treat gifts as having been made one-half by the donor and one-half by the donor's spouse thus permitted them to transfer $20,000 per year to a donee tax free. The total gift may be from the property of one or both spouses.

Qualified Gifts: To qualify for the annual exclusion, gifts must be of a present interest in property. A gift of a future interest such as a gift of a remainder interest does not qualify for the annual exclusion. Gifts of a present income interest, however, qualify to the extent of the income interest's present value.

2503(c) Exception: IRC § 2503(c) allows the annual exclusion if a donor makes a gift in trust giving a trustee the discretion to distribute or accumulate the income from the property as long as the property and any accumulated income is distributed when the minor attains 21. The trust must also provide that if the minor dies before attaining 21, the property and any accumulated income must be paid to the minor's estate or as the minor directs under a general power of appointment.

Valuations: Gift tax valuations must be accurate and may require an appraisal for assets that are not publicly traded.

Donee's Basis: The donee's tax basis for gifts of capital assets equals the donor's basis subject to adjustment for transfer expenses and gift taxes incurred and subject to the limitation that basis cannot exceed fair market value as adjusted at the date of the gift.

Allowable Deductions: The value of gifts for gift tax purposes are reduced by any allowable deductions, such as the marital or the charitable deduction.

Spousal Joint Interests: A transfer of individually owned or purchased property by one spouse into the names of both spouses as joint tenants with right of survivorship qualifies for the gift tax marital deduction.

Taxable Gift: The taxable gift equals the total value of the gift less the annual exclusion and the applicable deductions. The tax is calculated and any unused unified credit is deducted. The result is the tax due.

Nontaxable Lifetime Transfers: When a donor reserves a power to revoke a transfer, the gift is incomplete and is not subject to gift taxation. In addition, a transfer may continue to be treated as an incomplete gift and the donor as owner, if the donor retained the right to choose who will enjoy the property.

Powers of Appointment: Releases of or exercises by a donee of a general power of appointment constitutes a gift. A power to consume or to invade trust property limited by an ascertainable standard relating to the "health, education, support, or maintenance of the donee," and one that can be exercised only in conjunction with the donor of the power or an adverse party are excluded.

The 5 and 5 Power: A release or exercise of a general power of appointment over an amount which does not exceed the greater of $5,000 or 5 percent of the aggregate value of the property subject to the power at the time of the lapse is not a taxable gift.

C. The Estate Tax

Lifetime and Deathtime Application: The estate tax taxes both the net probate estate and will substitutes which otherwise could be used as tax avoidance devices. The estate tax provisions specifically deal with common will substitutes such as life insurance, joint tenancies and joint accounts, pension death benefits, revocable trusts, and even irrevocable trusts with a retained life estate.

The Gross Estate Definition: The decedent's gross estate includes the value of the decedent's probate estate, specified will substitutes, property over which the decedent held a general power of appointment, and certain transfers (QTIPS) for which a marital deduction was previously allowed.

Probate Estate: The decedent's gross estate includes the value of all of decedent's transmissible property that passes at death by will or by intestacy. Transmissible property includes property owned in fee, as tenants in common, or in a transmissible remainder interest but not income interests that expire on the death of the income beneficiary.

Lifetime Gifts Within Three Years of Death: The value of outright gifts of property that the donor owns in full are not part of the gross estate even if made minutes before death. There are two major exceptions.

Selected Transfers: When the value of the gift for gift tax purposes varies greatly over the value of the gift for estate tax purposes, such a gift made within the three years period is part of the gross estate. The rule applies to transfers made within three years of death of life insurance, and any interest in which the donor retained a life interest, takes effect at death, or is revocable.

Gift Tax Gross–Up Provision: The amount of any gift tax paid by the decedent on gifts made by the decedent (or the decedent's spouse) during the three-year period ending on the date of the decedent's death are includable in the decedent's gross estate. This means there is a tax on the gift tax. The rule applies regardless of donor's motive or expectations of death.

Retained Property Interests: When a donor does not part with complete ownership of the property, the donor is treated as owning the property at death for estate tax purposes.

Retention of an Income Interest: If a donor gratuitously transfers a remainder interest, while retaining the right to the income for life, the value of the transferred property at the donor's death is included in the gross estate. The value of the remainder interest transferred is subject to the gift tax.

Retention of a Reversionary Interest: The value of any reversion held by the donor at death is part of the gross estate. When donor's retained reversionary interest terminates at the donor's death, the value of the reversion may also be part of the gross estate if (1) the donor made a transfer of an interest in which possession or enjoyment of the property can, through ownership of the interest, be obtained only by surviving the donor; (2) the donor retained a reversionary interest in the property; and (3) the value of the reversionary interest immediately before the donor's death exceeds 5 percent of the value of the property.

Revocable and Other Retained Powers: If a donor transfers property (usually in trust) and reserves a power to revoke it, the value of the property is included in the donor's gross estate.

When the donor makes a transfer but retains the power to decide who can enjoy the property or its income, some value of the property is included in the donor's gross estate even though the donor relinquished the right to enjoy personally the property or the income it produces.

Powers of Appointment: The value of property over which the decedent held as a donee a general power of appointment is included in decedent's gross.

Donees, who at death hold nongeneral powers of appointment over property, will not have that property included in their gross estates.

Jointly Held Property: There are special estate tax consequences for jointly held property that is subject to a right of survivorship, *i.e.,* property held in joint tenancy with right of survivorship, property held in tenancy by the entirety by spouses, joint bank accounts, and jointly held U.S. Savings Bonds.

Joint Tenancy Created by Gift: Decedent's estate includes a fractional share of the property equal to the decedent's fractional cotenancy interest in the decedent's gross estate, if the decedent's jointly held interest was created as a gift or devise from a person who did not also become a joint tenant.

Spousal Joint Tenancy: One half of the value of property held jointly by spouses is included in the estate of the first spouse to die regardless of how much the decedent spouse contributed to its purchase. A marital deduction is allowed for the value of property included in the gross estate that passes to the surviving spouse in a qualified manner.

The percentage-of-consideration rule: For all jointly held property owned by unmarried tenants who acquire the property by purchase the value of the portion of the jointly held property included in the decedent's gross estate is determined by multiplying the property's value by the percentage of consideration the decedent is deemed to have provided. The decedent is presumed to have provided all the consideration for the jointly held property. The decedent's estate has the burden of proving the amount of consideration, if any, that the surviving cotenant or cotenants provided.

Life Insurance: Proceeds from life insurance on the decedent's life are included in the gross estate if at the decedent's death the decedent retained an "incident of ownership." Incidents of ownership mean "the right of the insured or his estate to the economic benefits of the policy." To avoid inclusion of life insurance proceeds, decedent must (1) relinquish all rights over the policy during life, and (2) assure that the proceeds are not paid to the estate or available to pay creditors of the estate. In addition, this action must have occurred more than three years prior to decedent's death.

Annuities: Four types of annuity contracts have varying estate tax consequences:

- Nonrefund-single-life annuities that are fully exhausted at the decedent's death are not part of the decedent's probate or gross estate.
- If the annuity contract pays a refund of a portion of the cost upon the decedent's premature death, to the decedent's estate or to a designated beneficiary, it is included in the gross estate.
- If the annuity contract is a joint-and-survivor annuity that obligates the company to make payments to the annuitants and upon the death of either, to make payments to the survivor for life, the value of thesurvivor's right to future payments is included in thedecedent's gross estate.
- If the annuity contract is a self-and-survivor annuity by which the insurance company obligates itself to make payments to the decedent and to the designated beneficiary only after the decedent's death, the value of the survivor's right to future payments is included in the decedent's gross estate. If the designated beneficiary dies first, however, the annuity is not included in the decedent's gross estate because the annuity is exhausted at decedent's death.

These rules apply to benefits under employee retirement and pension plans and individual retirement accounts.

III. DEDUCTIONS FROM THE GROSS ESTATE

A. General Scope

The Various Deductions: The IRC specifically recognizes the marital deduction, the charitable deduction, the deduction for funeral and administration expenses, bona fide claims against the decedent's estate, and the deduction for certain losses during administration. Federal estate taxes are not deductible.

B. Expenses, Debts, and Losses

Expenses of Administration: Decedent's allowable funeral expenses and, subject to certain limitations, the expenses of administering property that was included in the decedent's gross estate may be deducted. When administration expenses are also allowable income tax deductions, the executor must elect whether to deduct the expenses as either estate tax or income tax deductions. Decedent's outstanding bona fide debts also may be deducted.

Decedent's bona fide mortgage obligations incurred for adequate and full consideration in money or money's worth, are either deductible or constitute a reduction in the value of the property subject to the mortgage, depending upon whether the decedent was personally liable for the payment of the underlying debt.

Casualty and Theft Losses: Casualty and theft losses incurred during the administration of the estate are deductible so long as the loss is not reflected in the valuation of the property where the alternate valuation date was elected.

C. Marital Deduction

The Unlimited Marital Deduction: Federal estate and gift tax law treat married couples as a taxable unit and thus interspousal transfers are ignored. An estate or gift tax is assessed only when one or the other of the spouses transfers property to someone outside the marital unit.

Qualified Devise or Gift: To qualify for the marital deduction:

- The decedent must be a citizen or resident of the United States.
- The decedent must be survived by a spouse.
- The property must "pass" from the decedent to the surviving spouse.
- The value of the property interest must be included in the decedent's gross estate.
- The property interest must be a qualified type.

Nondeductible Terminable Interest: The marital deduction is not allowed for terminal interests passing to the surviving spouse. A terminable interest is an interest that will either fail or terminate on: (i) the mere lapse of time; (ii) on the occurrence of an event or contingency; or (iii) on the failure of an event or contingency to occur. Life estates, terms of years, and annuities are terminable interests.

Recognized exceptions require that the interests passing to the surviving spouse will result in gift or estate taxation when that spouse transfers them during life or at death. The life estate general power of appointment and the QTIP are the most common. Trusts are usually used for exercising these exceptions.

Life Estate General Power of Appointment: The qualified interest rule is satisfied if the donee spouse receives an income interest for life and the power to appoint the property alone to any person and in all events. Any unconsumed income and the trust corpus will be subject to the surviving spouse's estate tax. The donee spouse's gift of the life interest or appointment of remainder interest will be a gift taxable to the surviving spouse.

The spouse must have an absolute right to be paid the current income at least annually. The trust corpus must produce a current income stream or, the spouse must have the right to compel the trustee to convert any nonincome producing property into property that will produce a fair current return.

Although the power must be unrestricted, a general power only exercisable by will is sufficient. The trustee can also be given additional fiduciary powers to distribute the trust principal to the spouse so long as the trustee does not have a power to appoint any part of the property to any person other than the surviving spouse.

The donor spouse may grant to the surviving spouse a lifetime power to appoint to a class of beneficiaries, such as the donor's lineal descendants. The exercise of this nongeneral power during life will result in a gift tax, because its exercise operates as a release of the general testamentary power.

Qualified Terminal Interest Property (QTIP): A donor can obtain a marital deduction by transferring a life estate in property to the spouse if the donor (for gift tax purposes) or the donor's executor (for estate tax purposes) elect to have the life estate treated as a qualified terminable interest, and no person, not even the spouse, can have a power to appoint any part of the property to any person other than the surviving spouse during the spouse's life. Any disposition of any portion of the life estate is treated as a transfer of the entire remainder interest and thereby assures that the remainder interest is subject to gift taxation. The value of the property at the spouse's death is included in the spouse's gross estate.

The life estate requirements permit the trustee to have a power to distribute principal to the spouse during the spouse's life. The spouse cannot have, however, a lifetime power to appoint to anyone other than the spouse.

Estate Trust: The less popular "estate trust" permits income to be accumulated and taxed for income purposes to the trust but upon the death of the spouse, the trust property must then be paid to the estate of the surviving spouse. It has the great disadvantage in that it puts the trust assets through the formalities and delays of the administration of the surviving spouse's estate and subjects the property to the surviving spouse's creditors.

D. Charitable Deduction

Gift and Estate Tax Unlimited Charitable Deduction: The value of all outright gifts by a person to a qualifying charitable organization is deductible for estate and gift tax purposes. A calculatable deduction from gift and estate taxes is available if the donor establishes a trust giving a charity either an income interest (a charitable lead trust) or a remainder interest (a charitable remainder trust). To qualify, the charities must actually receive interests reasonably related to the amount claimed as a deduction.

Combined Charitable and Marital Deduction: A marital deduction is allowable for certain charitable remainder trusts as long as the trust has no noncharitable beneficiaries other than the surviving spouse. The entire value of this type of trust is deductible by the decedent spouse's estate by combining the charitable and marital deductions and because the surviving spouse receives only an income interest, no portion of the trust property is included in the surviving spouse's estate at death.

IV. FEDERAL GENERATION-SKIPPING TRANSFER TAX

A. Generation–Skipping Transfer Tax

Description and Application: The federal generation-skipping transfer tax (GSTT) is designed to tax wealth at least once in each generation. A tax is paid whenever property skips a generation or passes through a generation in a form that would allow it to escape gift or estate taxation in the skipped generation.

GSTT Special Terminology: The key interlocking definitions include:

Skip Person: A skip person is a natural person assigned to a generation two or more generations below the transferor's generation. A non-skip person is a person who is not a skip person.

Transferor: The transferor of a testamentary bequest is the decedent: the transferor of an inter vivos gift is the donor.

Interest: A person has an interest in property held in trust if he or she has a present right to receive income or principal from a trust or, if he or she is a permissible recipient of income or principal from a trust.

Generation Assignments: Individuals are assigned to generations based either on their degree of relationship to the transferor or on the difference in age between the transferor and the individual.

Spouses: Transferor's spouse is always assigned to the transferor's generation and a spouse of any lineal descendants is assigned to the generation of that descendant, no matter what the spouse's age.

Other Persons: All other people are assigned to generations based on age differences. Transferor's generation ends at an age 12½ years younger than the transferor. The next generation begins at an age 12½ years younger than the transferor and extends for 25 years. Each succeeding generation is a succeeding 25 year period.

GST Exemption: Every transferor has a flat lifetime exemption from the GSTT called the GST exemption. The exemption is indexed for inflation and for 1999, the exemption is $1,010,000. Allocation of the GST exemption may be made among the applicable lifetime or testamentary transfers of property as the transferor chooses.

Applicable Tax Rate: The applicable rate is the maximum Federal estate tax rate at the time of the transfer (now 55%) multiplied by the inclusion ratio.

Inclusion Ratio: The inclusion ratio equals the number one (1) minus a fraction, the numerator of which is the amount of the GST exemption allocated to this transfer and the denominator of which is the value of the transferred property. If no GST exemption is allocated to a transfer, the inclusion ratio will be 1. When the allocated GST exemption equals or exceeds the value of generation-skipping transfer, the applicable rate equals zero and thus, the rate of tax is zero.

Taxable Events: The three types of generation-skipping transfers include direct skips, taxable terminations, and taxable distributions.

Direct Skips: A direct skip is a transfer to a skip person of an interest in property that is also subject to the estate or gift tax.

Taxable Termination: A taxable termination occurs when an interest in trust property terminates as a result of death, lapse of time or otherwise, unless immediately after such termination, a nonskip person has an interest in the property or unless at no time after the termination may a distribution (including a distribution upon termination) be made from the trust to a skip person.

Taxable Distributions: A taxable distribution is any distribution from a trust to a skip person other than a taxable termination or a direct skip.

Nontaxable Events: Some gifts to skip persons are exempt from the GSTT.

Gift Tax Exclusions: Gifts that qualify for the annual exclusion or the tuition-or-medical-expense exclusion are not subject to the generation-skipping transfer tax.

Predeceased Parent Exception: Transfers to a grandchild or a grandniece are not generation-skipping transfers if the donee's parent was dead at the time of the transfer. The exception applies to transfers to collateral relations if the transferor has no living descendants at the time of the transfer.

Tax Exclusive and Tax Inclusive Applications:

Tax Exclusive Direct Skips: The GSTT on a direct skip is computed on a tax exclusive basis and thus the tax is on the transferor or on the trustee. Transferor's tax payment is treated as a taxable gift for gift tax purposes.

Tax Inclusive Taxable Distributions and Taxable Terminations: Taxable distributions and taxable terminations are tax inclusive and thus the tax is imposed on the recipient or the trust. If the trustee makes a taxable distribution and pays the tax out of the trust, the amount of the tax paid is itself a part of the taxable distribution for GSTT purposes.

PERSPECTIVE

ABOUT THE SUBJECT MATTER

This BLACK LETTER explains the law related to the gratuitous transfer of property. Gratuitous transfer law covers a wide and diverse range of legal matters including:

- Succession of property at death, including intestacy, testacy and will substitutes;
- Retirement and incapacity concerns, including social security and medicare;
- Trust creation, purpose and administration;
- Future interests and perpetuities;
- Fiduciary Administration; and,
- Taxation of Gratuitous Transfers.

Several observations about this course may be useful. First, in its totality, the subject covers widely diverse areas of law that are inseparably intertwined in practice. Wills and succession tend to be filled with a large number of picayune rules and concepts. Trust law is more expansive with many generalities. Future interests requires thorough understanding of basic principles and their careful application. Transfer taxation is a study of a tightly crafted statutory system designed to impose taxes across a wide range of transfer techniques. In addition to these differences, the sources of the laws varies:

the laws of wills, succession, fiduciary administration, and transfer taxation are based primarily on statute: the laws of trusts and future interests are primarily court or common law based.

ABOUT THIS BOOK

The goal of this book is to provide the student with a basic understanding of the law of the above subjects. The style of writing is designed to explain the materials. Quotes are kept to a minimum. The intent is to have the text be easy to read and easy to comprehend. Charts, problems and illustrations are placed throughout the book for the purpose of improving comprehension.

Much of the law of the subject, particularly the areas of intestate succession, wills, and the administration of estates, is based on state statutes. Although professors across the country vary as to the source of the statutes they emphasize in their classes, this BLACK LETTER emphasizes the UPC where applicable. Statutes of other jurisdictions are cited or discussed where appropriate and beneficial to understanding. The UPC offers an excellent teaching tool because it is comprehensive in content and coverage and provides a model for change.

ORGANIZATION OF BLACK LETTER

The Black Letter is divided into ten relevant parts that relate to the commonly segregated parts of gratuitous transfer law. These parts are:

Part One: Gratuitous Transfers in Perspective

Part Two: Intestate Succession and Related Doctrines

Part Three: Testament Transfers

Part Four: Lifetime Transfers

Part Five: Powers of Appointment

Part Six: Trusts

Part Seven: Regulation of Disposition

Part Eight: Future Interests and Perpetuities

Part Nine: The Fiduciary Obligation

Part Ten: Taxation

COURSE COVERAGE AND ORGANIZATION

The particular courses that cover the area of gratuitous transfer law vary greatly among the many law schools. Courses may be scheduled as a single three or four credit hour survey course, or as a combination of two, three or four credit hour classes. At least one course will cover the basic areas of wills, intestacy, and trusts. Some courses will cover fiduciary administration or future interests or both. The taxation of gratuitous transfers (or an introduction to it) is also included in many courses. **Because this Black Letter covers all of these relevant areas, it can be a valuable study aid for use for all of the related course formats.** The materials in this Black Letter can be easily accommodated to any class organization.

COURSE MATERIALS

This Black Letter is also tailored to be a valuable study aid for use with all of the major casebooks in the area of gratuitous transfers (wills, trusts, future interests, fiduciary administration, taxation of gratuitous transfers). Although all course texts vary to one degree or another, the table of contents of this Black Letter should provide an easy guide to correlating the subject matter. In addition, Appendix C correlates the subparts of this Black Letter with the pages of the major casebooks.

PREPARING FOR EXAMINATIONS

Generally, proper study for an examination in a course requires that the student follow the structure laid down by the professor in the course. Study and preparation techniques vary greatly among students. A student should use and refine techniques that the student finds successful.

One technique that many suggest is to physically integrate class notes, class materials and this BLACK LETTER into a single outline. Study for the exam from this self-prepared outline by condensing it into smaller versions leaving out all material the student believes has been learned. The more times the outline is condensed, the more the student has learned and understood. Generally, the greater the knowledge and understanding, the better the performance on the test.

ADDITIONAL READING MATERIAL

A text of this size cannot deal with all aspects or nuances of the law of gratuitous transfers. If additional study is desired, the reference materials and literature is substantial. The Restatements of Trusts and Property been very influential. Both are maturing into their third versions. These Restatements are cited frequently throughout this Black Letter and are valuable resources.

Many other reference resources are also available. A selected bibliography of a few of the other reference texts that should be available through law school bookstores include:

Intestacy, Wills and Administration:

Atkinson, Wills (West Group, 2d ed. 1953). ISBN: 0–314–28333–1

Uniform Probate Code

Averill, Uniform Probate Code in a Nutshell (West Group, 4th ed. 1996). ISBN: 0–314–07083–4

Trusts:

BOGERT, TRUSTS (West Group, 6th ed. 1987). ISBN: 0–314–35139–6

Future Interests:

SIMES, FUTURE INTERESTS (West Group, 2d ed. 1966).

WAGGONER, ESTATES IN LAND AND FUTURE INTERESTS IN A NUTSHELL (West Group, 2d ed. 1993). ISBN: 0–314–02770–X

Transfer Taxation:

MCNULTY, FEDERAL ESTATE AND GIFT TAXATION IN A NUTSHELL (West Group, 5th ed. 1994). ISBN 0–314–04247–4

PEAT & WILLBANKS, FEDERAL ESTATE AND GIFT TAXATION: AN ANALYSIS AND CRITIQUE (West Group, 2d ed. 1995). ISBN 0–314–06777–9

General Coverage:

MCGOVERN, KURTZ & REIN, WILLS, TRUSTS AND ESTATES INCLUDING TAXATION AND FUTURE INTERESTS (West Group, 1988). ISBN: 0–314–36114–6

MENNELL, WILLS AND TRUSTS IN A NUTSHELL (West Group, 2d ed. 1994). ISBN: 0–314–04025–0

PART ONE

INTRODUCTION TO GRATUITOUS TRANSFERS

*

I

SCOPE AND HISTORY OF GRATUITOUS TRANSFERS

Analysis

A. SCOPE OF SUBJECT

1. SUBJECT MATTER CONTENT

Generally the subject matter of this BLACK LETTER concerns the law of gratuitous transfers of assets or property. More specifically the course covers:

- Succession of property at death, including intestacy, and testacy;
- Lifetime transfers including retirement and incapacity planning;
- Trust creation, purpose and administration;
- Future interests and perpetuities; and,
- Fiduciary Administration.
- Taxation of gratuitous transfers.

2. STATUTORY PREFERENCES

Much of the law of the subject, particularly the areas of intestate succession, wills, and the administration of estates, is statutory. Teachers vary as to the source of the statutes they emphasize. Some emphasize the statutes of the jurisdiction in which the course is taught; the Uniform Probate Code (hereafter referred to as UPC) may be used for comparison or as a paradigm. Others emphasize the UPC; the situs law may be used for comparison, cross-referenced or in combination with the UPC. This BLACK LETTER will follow the latter approach, emphasizing the UPC where applicable but integrating statutes of other jurisdictions where appropriate and beneficial to understanding.

B. BRIEF HISTORY

1. EARLY HISTORY

The law of succession and estates is as ancient as civilization. Research indicates that the earliest law was family-oriented rather than individual centered. As societies became more complex, individual ownership and disposition law developed. Clearly by the time of the establishment of the United States, succession law gave significant recognition to individual ownership and freedom of disposition. The ancestor of our law is England, with Roman law and civil law of the European continent as shirt-tail relations. None of these relationships are pure. All descended concepts have been modified or reformulated. From a distance, broad similar characteristics are identifiable; but on closer inspection significant differences are patent.

2. CURRENT DESIGN

Today, English history of wealth transmission is more significant for its underlying principles than for its rules. The recognition in the United States that the individual has power to determine his or her successors is one of the paramount legacies from English law. The creation of the trust device for holding property also persevered and flourished in our jurisprudence. Certainly, the intricacy and precision of future interest rules continued in our law. The idea of an administration of an estate was accepted by the States and cultured far beyond its original design and purpose.

3. MODERN REFORM

In the United States, significant reform of succession law occurred when each state entered the union in the 18th and 19th centuries. England did not reform until the twentieth century and its reform was more dramatic and relevant to modern society than was the earlier reform in the States.

Major comprehensive reform did not really come to the states until the late 1960's when the UPC was promulgated. The Original UPC was promulgated in 1969 by the National Conference of Commissioners on Uniform State Laws (Uniform Law Commission). Minor amendments were made to the 1969 version over the next two decades. The Uniform Law Commission undertook a major overhaul of Article VI of the Code in 1989 and of Article II in 1990. Article VI covers nonprobate transfers on death, and Article II covers intestacy, wills, and other donative transfers. A few minor amendments to the 1989–1990 version have been made in the years following 1990. The 1989–1990 period marks the division between the Original and the Revised UPC. **Unless otherwise noted, references to the UPC in this BLACKLETTER are to the Revised UPC, *i.e.*, to the UPC as it currently exists.**

Even though the UPC has not swept the country, it has constituted a significant source of reform through all of the states. The influence and the use of the UPC is growing in a variety of ways. *See* Anderson, *Influence of the Uniform Probate Code*, 8 U. Puget Sound L. Rev. 599 (1985). Enactment as a UPC in full with some amendments has occurred in more than a third of the states. Piece-meal enactment of segments or sections of the UPC for inclusion into another probate code or law has occurred in nearly all of the other states. It is also referred to as a model of modern policy by courts which are interpreting their own non-UPC provisions. *See, e.g., First Church of Christ, Scientist v. Watson*, 239 So.2d 194 (Ala. 1970). Finally, it is referred to as secondary or persuasive authority for determining proper rules of construction for the common law. *See, e.g., Russell v. Estate of Russell*, 534 P.2d 261 (Kan. 1975); *In re Will of Ranney,* 589 A.2d 1339 (N.J. 1991); *Thompson v. Potts*, 423 N.E.2d 90 (Ohio 1981); *Smith v. Smith*, 519 S.W.2d 152 (Tex.Civ.App. 1974).

Another source of reform is the Restatement (Third) of Property (Wills and Other Donative Transfers). Although this new Restatement is not yet complete, the first volume, which covers intestacy, execution and revocation of wills, and post-execution events affecting wills, was published in 1999. The new Restatement is a major source of law reform and will be referred to throughout this BLACK LETTER.

4. TRUST LAW DEVELOPMENT

Trust law has not received as much legislative attention as has the law of decedents' estates. For most states, trust law developed in the common law tradition, incrementally through court decisions with a smattering of legislative involvement particularly in the area of investments and administrative powers. Possibly because of the absence of statutory restraints, trust law has kept a degree of currentness and has adjusted to the times. One area in which the common law of trusts did not keep up with the times is the area of permissible trust investments. This inadequacy is now addressed in a new prudent investor rule, which is contained in a special volume of the Restatement (Third) of Trusts and in the Uniform Prudent Investor Act. Because trusts are often affected by taxation issues, drafters and courts have striven to accommodate the changing world of tax law. Few states have comprehensive trust codes. The Uniform Law Commission is currently developing a comprehensive Uniform Trust Act, and the American Law Institute is continuing to work on the Restatement (Third) of Trusts.

II

ADMINISTRATION OF ESTATES AND TRUSTS

Analysis

A. THE JUDICIAL INVOLVEMENT IN PROPERTY TRANSMISSION

1. CONSEQUENCES OF DEATH

When a person accumulates property and does not completely dispose of it during the person's lifetime, the person's death leaves an "estate" for which the continuing ownership must be resolved between creditors and successors. Efforts taken to resolve ownership require some kind of administration process. This process may be a private matter among the interested parties, a public matter under the auspices of the court or quasi courts, or a combination of the two.

2. ADMINISTRATION PROCESSES

Court involvement depends on each state's system for administering decedents' estates. It may or may not require significant court involvement. To the extent that there is court involvement, the process is largely public in nature. The court required processes constitute a judicial bureaucracy.

3. PROBATE

Over time the word "*probate*" has had a variety of meanings. Technically, "probate" refers to the process of proving and deciding the validity of a will before a court having competent jurisdiction. More generally, it refers to all matters appropriately before the probate courts. BLACK'S LAW DICTIONARY.

4. INHERITABLE INTERESTS

The types of interests requiring an administration process include all inheritable interests owned by decedent at death that do not pass to others by will substitute. They include interests that pass according to decedent's will or according to intestacy statute. Thus, for example, all property owned by decedent in fee is included.

5. WILL SUBSTITUTES

Certain types of interests do **not** require administration. These interests are referred to as "will substitutes" because they pass an interest at the death of the owner directly to the designated beneficiary. In addition, they require no valid will or intestacy law to identify the beneficiaries.

Will substitute interests include property in which decedent held a lifetime interest but which pass according to the rules applicable to the particular will substitute, *i.e.,* survivorship interests, trusts interests, contractual arrangements, life insurance proceeds, retirement programs, and nondescendable future interests such as a remainder interest following a life estate.

The "administration" of will substitute interests is usually privately resolved by the interested persons. An official administration supervised by the courts is unnecessary. Court involvement is limited to resolving litigation initiated by the parties.

6. FUNCTION AND NECESSITY OF ADMINISTRATION

The primary reasons for having an administration of a decedent's estate are to:

- Establish title to property of the decedent in the successors;
- Facilitate the collection of assets and claims against others;
- Provide a method to determine and pay taxes in order to clear up tax lien problems; and,
- Permit the closing of creditors' claims against the decedent's estate—providing for their determination and payment or for them to be barred under a non-claim statute.

7. PARTS OF PROBATE

The estate administration process can be better understood if one knows what matters have to be resolved. A person's financial relationship with the person's own property might be characterized as a partnership between the person and the estate. The death of the person causes a dissolution of the partnership. A liquidation of the assets of the estate is necessary. The administration process is generally divided into six parts: opening, inventory and appraisement, creditor settlement, property management and sale, distribution, and closing.

The following lists the usual necessary steps for liquidation:

- Take care of funeral and burial arrangements;
- Gather information on the status and extent of the decedent's estate;
- Make an inventory and appraisement of the assets in the estate;
- Notify and identify creditors and obligations owed to other persons;
- Provide basic support for surviving family members during the liquidation process;
- Determine tax obligations and complete and file necessary tax returns;
- If necessary, manage the estate's assets during liquidation;

- Liquidate sufficient portions of the estate to pay obligations, debts, and taxes;
- Pay obligations, debts and taxes;
- Determine shares of eventual successors;
- Distribute remaining assets and funds to successors in appropriate shares;
- Complete final accounting of transactions during the administration process;
- Discharge the personal representative; and,
- Terminate the liquidation process.

B. COURT VERSUS NONCOURT TRANSACTIONS

1. COURT INVOLVEMENT WITH PROPERTY TRANSFERS

Generally, decedent's estates are administered to some degree through a court procedure that lasts from death until final distribution of the assets, regardless of the desires of the interested persons. Will substitutes are handled privately without court involvement unless litigation between the interested parties arises over an interest. This difference has given rise to the estate planner's cry "avoid probate."

2. COURT VERSUS NONCOURT DISTINCTIONS

Whereas probate may be less efficient and slow at times, nonprobate procedure may lack procedural protection for interested person who are adversely and wrongfully harmed and may offer less predictability when litigation develops. Probate law gives interested persons a specific forum in which to litigate matters and the substantive rules are more settled and determinable. Consequently, the cost difference between probate systems and will substitute techniques may be one of degree and not kind and may economically disappear when all factors are considered.

The decision to employ one technique or another or to use a combination of techniques must be determined individually, based on the desires of the client and the demands of the desired estate plan.

C. JURISDICTIONAL ISSUES

1. THE PROPER COURT

Depending on the jurisdiction, the court concerned with probate matters may be called the "probate court," "orphans' court," "surrogate's court," "court of ordinary" or by the name of the court in the jurisdiction that has general or some other subject matter jurisdiction. THOMAS E. ATKINSON, WILLS § 4 (West Group 2d ed. 1953) [hereinafter ATKINSON, WILLS].

2. JURISDICTIONAL FACTS

The territorial reach of a court's jurisdiction is usually based on one of the following factors:

- The relevant person *e.g.*, decedent, was domiciled in the state;
- The relevant property of a non-domiciliary is located in the state;
- The relevant property is under the control of a fiduciary who is subject to the laws of the state; or,
- The person, the contractual device, or the fiduciary relationship is within the state.

The latter two jurisdictional facts refer respectively to minors or incapacitated persons residing within the state, to the existence of multiple party accounts and security registrations located in the state, and to trusts subject to administration in the state.

3. SUBJECT MATTER JURISDICTION

There are differences between the laws of the various states concerning the subject matter jurisdiction of the court or courts assigned to deal with succession to property issues. Generally, these courts are given subject matter jurisdiction over all matters related to succession including the probate of wills, administration of the decedents' estates, interpretation of wills, determination of heirs and successors, the estates of protected or disabled persons, the protection of disabled persons and the administration of trusts. *E.g.*, UPC § 1–302(a). In addition, the court is usually empowered to take all "necessary and proper" action for the purpose of administering justice in any matters properly before it. *E.g.*, UPC § 1–302(b).

4. IN PERSONAM AND IN REM JURISDICTION

As in any other judicial proceeding, probate courts must have jurisdiction over the persons or property involved in the proceeding. The federal Constitution defines the outermost limits of a state's power over persons and things outside its borders, and thus determines the scope of a particular court's personal jurisdiction.

Grounds for asserting personal jurisdiction include the presence of the person or thing involved in the litigation within the forum's territorial boundaries or the consent of the party. In addition, personal jurisdiction may be based upon certain relationships that exist between the place where the underlying transaction took place, the parties, and the state where suit is brought. The Court has shifted the focus of *in personam* jurisdiction from a state's physical power over the defendant to the defendant's minimum contacts with the state. *See International Shoe Company v. State of Washington,* 326 U.S. 310 (1945). In *Hanson v. Denckla,* 357 U.S. 235 (1958), in determining the jurisdiction of a state court over a trust with multi-state contacts, the Supreme Court limited *in personam* jurisdiction to contacts that take the form of a purposeful affiliation between the defendant and the forum.

Finally, the due process requirement prohibits a court from exercising its adjudicatory authority unless the persons whose rights will be affected have been given adequate notice and an opportunity to be heard. *See Mullane v. Central Hanover Bank & Trust Co.,* 339 U.S. 306 (1950).

For many actions taken during the administration of an estate, notice by publication was the principal method required. In *Tulsa Professional Collection Services v. Pope*, 485 U.S. 478 (1988), the Supreme Court considered the constitutionality of this type of notice and gave some answers to the problem. It held that a nonclaim statute, which barred creditors' claims not filed within two months after notice by publication only, is unconstitutional as applied to known or reasonably ascertainable creditors. Many jurisdictions have amended their notice statutes for creditors to include a period "in gross" after which all claims are barred regardless of notice and to provide for notice to known creditors in order to shorten the period within which creditors must apply. Whether *Pope* applies to other estate administration notice requirements has not been answered. It might be suggested that wherever rights are cut off, the *Pope* rule applies.

D. REVIEW QUESTIONS

1. What is the process of proving and deciding the validity of a will before a court having competent jurisdiction called?
2. A will substitute passes an interest at the death of the owner directly to the designated beneficiary. True or False?
3. What are the parts of probate?
4. Compare and contrast probate and nonprobate procedure.
5. What are the grounds for asserting personal jurisdiction?

III

JUDICIAL PROCEDURE AND EVIDENCE

Analysis

A. PARTIES AND PLEADINGS

1. PROPER PARTIES

The proper parties for court matters concerning gratuitous transfers depend upon the nature of the proceeding and the court before which it occurs. Obviously in probate and estate administration, the fiduciary, *e.g.,* executor, personal representative, is an essential party for all proceedings for or against the estate. Generally, interested persons, those who have a financial stake in the proceeding, are proper persons to institute proceedings before the proper court. When *in rem* and *quasi in rem* proceedings are involved, guardians ad litem will be necessary to cut off or set rights of unknown or other incompetent interested persons.

Will substitute litigation involves the parties as required by normal civil procedure rules. Actions take a variety of forms. They may involve suits to establish constructive trusts or other ownership interests, or rectify breaches of fiduciary responsibilities. Sometimes the fiduciary for the estate is the initiator or merely a party to the suit.

2. PLEADINGS

For probate matters, the pleadings are usually specified in the statutes governing estate administration matters. They range from information type filings to full litigation petitions.

Pleadings in will substitute litigation must conform to the civil procedural rules established by the court of proper jurisdiction.

B. BURDENS OF PROOF AND PRESUMPTIONS

1. BURDEN OF PROOF

The burden of proof of a matter refers to the litigating party's duty to produce evidence sufficient to justify a verdict or result in regard to matters at issue. It has two elements: the risk of non-persuasion and the burden of going forward with the evidence.

The risk of non-persuasion refers to the obligation of a party to so move the trier of fact that the particular issue may be regarded as established, normally by a preponderance of the evidence. This burden does not shift from one party to the other. It is important in the instructions to the jury.

The burden of going forward with the evidence concerns the quantum of the evidence necessary to have an issue submitted to the jury. It may shift from one party to the other. It is important when one moves for a directed verdict. It is not explained to the jury.

The original burden of going forward is upon the party who has the risk of non-persuasion, though the latter may satisfy it by the introduction of evidence that either establishes a prima facie case or that gives rise to a rebuttable presumption.

2. PRESUMPTIONS

Presumptions are rules of law that accord probative value to specific facts in evidence or draw particular inferences as to the existence of facts that are not actually known but which arise from other facts that are known or proven. They are created by statute or court decision based on reason and human experience. Some presumptions are rebuttable while others are irrebuttable.

A rebuttable presumption is a presumption that may be rebutted by evidence. It shifts the burden of proof. It contains elements of both a presumption of fact and a presumption of law; sometimes referred to as a mixed presumption.

An irrebuttable presumption exists when an ultimate fact is presumed to be true upon proof of a particular fact or set of facts, and no evidence, no matter how persuasive, can rebut it.

C. INTRODUCTION TO INTERPRETATION

1. INTERPRETATION AND CONSTRUCTION

Interpretation refers to the process of searching for the donor's actual intention by looking to the text of the document and extrinsic evidence. It has sometimes been distinguished from construction, which is said to refer to the process of attributing intention from constructional preferences and rules of construction. With this distinction, the process of interpretation is sometimes thought to occur first, followed by construction only when interpretation fails. Actually, interpretation and construction are neither completely distinct processes, nor are they applied sequentially. *See* Restatement (Third) Property, Donative Transfer § 11.3 cmt. c (Tent. Draft. No. 1, 1995).

2. SINGLE PROCESS

Interpretation and construction actually work as a single process. *See* Restatement (Third) of Property, Donative Transfer § 11.3 cmt. a (Tent. Draft. No. 1, 1995). Distinguishing between actual and attributed intention may be useful in determining which governs when the two processes conflict. When actual intention is sufficiently established, it always overrides attributed intention. Determining whether the intent is "sufficiently established" is the principal problem. Consequently, constructional preferences and rules of construction govern in default of sufficient and persuasive evidence of contrary actual intention.

D. SUBSTANTIVE EVIDENCE RULES: RESTRICTIONS ON ADMISSIBILITY

1. EXTRINSIC EVIDENCE GENERALLY

In most regards, litigation concerning the gratuitous transfer of property and the rights, obligations, and duties between the parties are governed by normal evidence and procedural rules applicable to other forms of civil litigation. Consequently, the appropriate jurisdiction's rules or codes of civil procedure and rules of evidence govern during the litigation processes.

Rules of Evidence in Probate Courts: With regard to litigation concerning the proof and interpretation of wills, courts have usually employed some different rules, particularly in regard to the admissibility of evidence. The inherent distinguishing factor identified by courts is that the testator is dead and can no longer provide either evidence of intent or take further action concerning a matter that the testator has confirmed in writing. Thus the writing is given special significance in wills litigation: it is often "protected" from the vagaries of extrinsic evidence and other proofs.

Rules of Evidence for Inter Vivos Transfers: The same attitude concerning evidence admissibility has not prevailed in regard to inter vivos instruments even if these instruments require interpretation or establishment after the creator's death.

The distinction between these approaches may be best explained as a vestige of common law "dead-man's acts" and the sanctity of the Statute of Wills.

2. THE ULTIMATE OBJECT OF THE PROCESS

The two proclaimed objectives of the evidence process are that the donor's intention controls the meaning of donative documents; and, donor's intent is given effect to the maximum extent allowed by law. Although meeting these objectives would seemingly demand a liberal admissibility approach, other factors have moved courts to restrict admissibility of extrinsic evidence. In the process of the litigation two interrelated issues arise: (1) Is evidence admissible? and (2) What remedy will the court approve? When the remedy sought is considered drastic, *e.g.*, add an inadvertently omitted clause to will, courts may exercise their concern about the remedy by excluding the evidence that may sympathetically and persuasively demand it. If the court does not want to delve into reformation, the court might take the easy way out and decline to accept the persuasive evidence.

3. MISTAKE: OMISSION, INCLUSION AND MISDESCRIPTION

a. Mistaken Omission

Generally, courts will not provide a remedy if a provision is mistakenly omitted from a will. The rationale is the Statute of Wills requires the terms of the will to be in writing. Limited avoidance of this rule may be possible if construction of the words in the will cure the problem. Generally, this avenue is restricted to future interest constructions. Courts have taken the same no-remedy approach even with respect to mistakes as to the legal effect of a will provision.

b. Misdescription

When a will mistakenly misdescribes a person or a thing, evidence is admissible to explain the intention of the testator if there is an ambiguity. Although courts have customarily distinguished between latent and patent ambiguities, no legal consequences attach to the distinction. The terms are used for descriptive purposes only. *See* Restatement (Third) of Property: Donative Transfers § 11.1 cmt. a (Tentative Draft No. 1, 995)

A latent ambiguity is one that is not apparent merely from reading the text of the donative document but becomes apparent from extrinsic evidence. A patent ambiguity is one that is apparent on the face of the document. There is no clear line between the concepts of latent and patent ambiguities. It is a question of characterization. Court distinctions between patent and latent ambiguities often relate to the court's willingness to speculate as to what testator meant to do. The characterization may depend on the trustworthiness of the extrinsic evidence. For example, "greed" evidence is less acceptable than "clarification" evidence.

Illustration 1: T's will states: "I devise $5,000 to my cousin John." Evidence extrinsic reveals that T had no cousin named John when T executed the will but did then have a nephew named John and a cousin named James. A court that makes the latent-patent distinction would characterize this as a latent ambiguity and admit extrinsic evidence to resolve the ambiguity. Other courts would admit relevant extrinsic evidence without characterizing the ambiguity.

Illustration 2: T's will states in article III "I devise Meadowacre to John," and in Article VI states: "I devise Meadowacre to James." These clauses raise a patent ambiguity. A few courts might say testator's intent must be resolved solely by reading the document as an entirety or by rules of construction. Other courts might admit extrinsic evidence to resolve the ambiguity.

c. Mistaken Inclusion

If words are mistakenly included in a will, courts have recognized three options:

i. Deny probate to the words (American courts have rejected entire provisions; English courts have rejected individual words if mistakenly included);

ii. Reject the entire will (May be appropriate when circumstances show that the testator did not know of any of the contents); or,

iii. Probate as written (presumption that the will contained the provisions intended by the testator).

4. MISTAKE IN THE INDUCEMENT

A mistake in the inducement is an error as to facts outside the instrument itself. It includes the misconception as to the nature, condition or extent of one's property or as to the conduct or status of the beneficiaries or heirs.

a. Admissibility of Extrinsic Evidence for Mistakes in the Inducement

The classic and restrictive test for admissibility of extrinsic evidence was set out in *Gifford v. Dyer*, 2 R.I. 99 (1852). This case held that extrinsic evidence is admissible only if the following specific conditions are met:

i. The testator must have been laboring under a mistake as to the facts;

ii. If the truth had been known, testator would have made a different disposition; and

iii. These facts should appear in the will itself.

An exception to this exception is that evidence will not be admitted even if the test may be met if the mistake is solely dependent on testator's knowledge.

b. Mistakes in the Inducement under the UPC

The UPC has a specific statutory mistake in the inducement exception: "if at the time of execution of the will the testator *fails to provide* in his [or her] will for a living child *solely because* he [or she] *believes the child to be dead,* the child is entitled to share in the estate as if the child were an omitted after-born or after-adopted child." UPC § 2–302.

5. MISTAKE IN THE EXECUTION

If the testator mistakenly executes the wrong document, courts have differed on whether to permit a remedy. Some have corrected the mistake by reforming the wills: others have denied probate because testamentary intent is entirely lacking. *Compare In re Pavlinko's Estate*, 148 A.2d 528 (Pa. 1959), *with In re Snide*, 418 N.E.2d 656 (N.Y. 1981).

Mistakes of this nature are capable of satisfactory proof because the error generally appears upon the face of the document signed, *e.g.*, mutual wills misexecuted. This issue is litigated at the time of probate or contest of the will.

6. ADMISSIBILITY AND THE TYPE OF PROCEEDING

Some courts seem to be more receptive to admitting evidence at probate. This may be explainable because evidence has to be admitted to prove the validity of the will.

It is a sort of "foot in the door" theory. Once some relevant evidence is admitted, other relevant evidence ought to be admitted even to correct a mistake. Other courts, however, state this is not a valid distinction.

7. RECENT DEVELOPMENTS CONCERNING EVIDENCE ADMISSIBILITY

Recently, commentators and some courts have disputed the evidence admissibility distinctions discussed above. As the Comment to Section 11.2 of the Tentative Draft of the THIRD RESTATEMENT OF PROPERTY, DONATIVE TRANSFERS, states: "The line between deleting and changing, transposing, or supplying words is artificial and difficult to defend." Thus, the RESTATEMENT takes the position that any ambiguity should be resolved by construing the text of any donative document, will or trust, in accordance with the donor's intention to the extent that that intention is established by a preponderance of the evidence. The donor's intention controls the meaning of a donative document to the extent that it is sufficiently established. RESTATEMENT (THIRD) PROPERTY, DONATIVE TRANSFER § 11.3 cmt. a (Tent. Draft. No. 1, 1995). In addition, if the intention of an individual donor conflicts with a rule of construction or a constructional preference, the intent of the donor controls if sufficiently established. *Id.* On the other hand, if a contrary intention cannot be established, a rule of construction or constructional preference controls in interpreting the meaning of an ambiguous portion of the document.

8. OPPOSING POSITIONS ON ADMISSIBILITY

Strict construction courts place emphasis upon the written word, its usual and indeed its technical meaning. They stress rules of construction and precedent. Opinions typically declare that they cannot disturb the plain meaning of words and that the meaning must be obtained from the four corners of the instrument. But as Wigmore opined: "The 'plain meaning ...' is simply the meaning of the people who did *not* write the document...." 9 J. WIGMORE, LAW OF EVIDENCE § 2462, at 191.

Liberal construction courts emphasize the element of the testator's intention. They are more inclined to consider extrinsic evidence to determine the intent. They criticize the importance of rules or precedents—"no will has a sibling, especially an identical twin."

These are not two well defined approaches. Frustratingly, a court may take one approach in one case, and the other in another controversy.

9. MAGNITUDE OF THE EXTRINSIC EVIDENCE PROBLEM

It must be remembered that the person who knows most about these matters is dead. Greedy heirs or other persons are not an unknown phenomenon. From these factors, courts are fearful of the burden of having to rewrite every "abnormal" will.

There are also the concerns about the burden of the costs of litigation. Often this burden falls on the estate, or on property over which litigation occurs, or on the successors to claim and protect their largess. A strong policy of the Statute of Wills is to limit litigation when its formalities have been duly met.

E. REVIEW QUESTIONS

1. In probate and estate administration, who is an essential party for all proceedings for or against the estate?

2. What type of guardian is appointed in quasi in rem and in rem proceedings to cut off or set rights of unknown or other incompetent interested persons?

3. What is the litigating party's duty called that requires evidence sufficient to justify a verdict or result in regard to matters at issue?

4. The burden of proof has two elements which are the risk of non-persuasion and the burden of going forward with the evidence. True or False?

5. What process searches for the donor's actual intention by looking to the text of the document and extrinsic evidence.

*

IV

PROFESSIONAL RESPONSIBILITY

Analysis

A. GENERAL APPLICATION OF ETHICAL STANDARDS

1. ETHICAL CONCERNS

The area of law covered by the subject matter of this text concerns the entire scope of the rules of professional ethics. From client acquisition to case termination, from office practice through the whole course of litigation practice, ethics issues may concern the estate attorney practitioner. Attorneys are facing an increasing number of claims against them based upon conflicts and violations of ethics or rules of professional conduct.

Every state and jurisdiction in the United States has an explicit set of rules governing professional ethics for attorneys. Generally, in the representation of clients, the attorney must exercise the professional duties of competence, diligence, communication, confidentiality, and loyalty.

2. PERVASIVE ETHICAL ISSUES

Several pervasive ethical issues arise for estate practitioners.

- The standard of competence for attorneys who are not specialists and for those who are specialists.
- Negligent representations and the liability of the attorney to beneficiaries of the client. This is often a problem of whether privity of contract is necessary and whether the relevant statute of limitations has run.
- The ethical and substantive issues of undue influence where the attorney receives a gift from a client by the terms of an instrument that the attorney drafted.
- The issue raised by joint representation of clients in estate planning matters where possible conflicts of interest may arise.
- The question of who the attorney represents in trust and estate administration when conflicts arise between the fiduciary and the beneficiaries.

3. CLIENT–ATTORNEY RELATIONSHIP

Ethical standards generally arise out of the attorney-client relationship which is contractual in nature. As with contracts generally, an express agreement is not necessary for formation: an agreement may be implied from the circumstances. MODEL RULES OF PROFESSIONAL CONDUCT, Scope. (Hereinafter MODEL RULES). Indeed, the reasonable perceptions of the "client" may be given the most weight by a court. *See, e.g., DeVaux v. American Home Assurance Co.*, 444 N.E.2d 355 (Mass. 1983).

4. MALPRACTICE

The general term "malpractice" when applied to the legal profession includes fraud, breach of fiduciary duty, and negligence. Note, *Attorney Malpractice,* 63 Colum. L. Rev. 1292 (1963).

Most negligent malpractice litigation against attorneys springs directly from the attorney-client relationship. In addition, a significant number of state courts have held that an attorney is liable to persons outside the attorney-client relationship who are injured by negligent representation. For example, in *Ogle v. Fuiten,* 466 N.E.2d 224 (Ill. 1984), the Illinois Supreme Court held the complaint filed by beneficiaries of a will alleged to have been negligently drafted by the defendant attorney sufficiently stated traditional elements (1) of a negligence theory in tort by virtue that the attorney prepared wills in a manner so that the intended contingent beneficiaries received no benefit at all, and (2) of third-party beneficiary breach of contract theory with allegations that the purpose of the employment of the attorney was to draft wills not only for benefit of testators, but for the benefit of intended contingent beneficiaries.

B. COMPETENCE

An attorney must provide competent representation to the attorney's clients. "Competent representation requires the legal knowledge, skill, thoroughness and preparation reasonably necessary for the representation." Model Rules 1.1. Generally, it is presumed that the competence can be achieved by reasonable preparation. The standard of competence is that of the general practitioner unless the attorney is held out to be a specialist. One court indicated that a generalist who undertakes legal work that should be referred to a specialist will be held to the same standard of care as the specialist. *Horne v. Peckham*, 158 Cal. Rptr. 714 (Cal. App.1979).

C. CONFIDENTIALITY

There are two distinct but related confidentiality concepts involved: the ethics issue of confidentiality and the evidence issue of attorney-client privilege. The attorney-client privilege is a rule of evidence that determines whether an attorney may be called as a witness against a client or compelled to produce evidence. Unif. R. Evid. 502, 503. The rule of ethics concerned with confidentiality is a much broader and more limited concept. It requires an attorney to keep all information related to representation confidential. The attorney may be required to reveal this information if properly requested in litigation or by judicial process.

D. LOYALTY

1. BASIC RULES

An attorney owes a duty of loyalty to the client and this means that in representing the client the attorney must avoid conflicts of interest. The ethics standards prohibit an attorney from representing a client if the representation of that client will be directly adverse to the representation of another client. Model Rule 1.7(a). In addition, an attorney may not represent a client if the representation of that client may be materially limited by the attorney's responsibilities to another client or to a third person, or by the attorney's own interests. Model Rule 1.7(b).

Conflicts Avoidance and Resolution: The attorney, or the firm, should maintain a compilation or list containing certain basic information such as the names of all existing clients and the matters being handled for each client.

2. DECLINING REPRESENTATION

Conflicts may be of the nature that require that the attorney decline the representation. If an actual conflict of interest arises after acceptance of the representation such that the attorney is unable to exercise independent professional judgment because of divided loyalties, the attorney should withdraw from further representation of either client in the transaction.

3. CONSENT OF THE CLIENTS

The prohibitions against simultaneous representation of multiple clients may be avoided if each client consents after full disclosure of the conflict or potential conflict. For consent to be effective, however, the attorney must fully disclose all of the facts and implications of the representation to all affected clients. The attorney has the burden of affirmatively disclosing all relevant facts. The attorney must explain "the nature of the conflict of interest in such detail so that they can understand the reasons why it may be desirable for each to have independent counsel, with undivided loyalty to the interests of each of them." Consent must be express and based upon actual knowledge: it will not be implied nor can it rest on constructive knowledge. Preferably, the client's consent should be in writing.

E. ESTATE PLANNING

1. ATTORNEYS AND UNDUE INFLUENCE

There are several general rules. Do not draft a will for a legal stranger in which you take a devise. *See* Model Rule 1.8(c). A person in the same firm cannot prepare the instrument either because of the imputation rule under Rule 1.10 of the Model Rules. If you are not a legal stranger, do not draft a will for a client in which you receive a disproportionate share in relation to the legal relationship. The risks are too great to take. In the *State v. Beaudry*, 191 N.W.2d 842 (Wis. 1971), *cert. denied* 407 U.S. 912 (1972), the court held that an attorney could not draw a will for a client, whether a relative or not, in which he or she or a member of his family was a beneficiary if the amount bequeathed was more than what he or she would receive by intestacy. In *Magee v. State Bar*, 374 P.2d 807 (Cal. 1962), the attorney not only lost the devise but almost lost his license to practice law.

2. JOINT REPRESENTATION AND LOYALTY ISSUES

The representation for estate planning purposes of certain clients who have generally common interests may promote better representation, economy, coordination, harmony, fact gathering and needs of clients. These benefits, however, must be weighed against the potential conflicts of loyalty and confidentiality that may develop during joint representation. An "engagement agreement" that explains the possible conflicts is advisable.

<u>Common Joint Representations</u>: It is common for an attorney to be approached by one spouse about doing an estate plan for both spouses. Both spouses are clients of the attorney and both need to be treated as such. Conflicts can arise when an attorney prepares an estate plan for spouses including, for example, when one or both spouses have children by another marriage.

Another joint representation that can raise conflicts is when parent and child are represented by the same attorney. Two situations are common where conflicts between parents and children can arise: (1) parents may overreach when engaging in estate planning involving their minor children; (2) children may overreach when engaging in estate planning involving aged or infirm parents.

3. IDENTIFYING THE CLIENT

An attorney who represents a fiduciary (trustee, personal representative, or guardian) or, who assists in the administration of an estate, may face the significant ethical issue "to whom does the attorney's duties and loyalties run, and with what ancillary or derivative obligations?" *See* Report of the Special Study Committee on Professional Responsibility, *Counseling the Fiduciary*, 28 Real Prop., Prob. & Trust J. 825 (1994). Although real conflicts seldom arise because all the parties have common interests or the identity of the real client is clear, conflicts may arise that raise the question whether the attorney represents the fiduciary who engaged the attorney, the beneficiaries of the fiduciary entity, or the entity itself. A particular ethical issue when the conflict occurs concerns questions of confidentiality and work product privilege. For example, if the fiduciary's wrongful conduct is revealed to or discovered by the attorney in the course of the representation, what is the attorney's duty to reveal or not reveal this information? Can the knowledge be sought through the discovery process if litigation arises between the beneficiaries and the fiduciary?

Illustration: T is the executor of the estate of his deceased wife, W, and the trustee of three separate testamentary trusts created under W's will for the primary benefit of the T's three daughters. One of the daughters, M, filed suit against T for breach of fiduciary duties relating to her trust. M claims that T mismanaged the trust, engaged in self-dealing, diverted business opportunities from the trust, and commingled and converted trust property. T's other two daughters have not joined in the lawsuit. M attempted to depose T's attorney, L, who has represented T in his capacity as executor and trustee since W's death. L also represented T in many other matters unrelated to the trusts and estate during that period. Before M filed suit, L was compensated from trust and estate funds for T's fiduciary representation. L refused to answer questions about the management and business dealings of the trust, claiming the attorney-client and attorney-work-product privileges. M subsequently moved to compel responses, and T moved for a protective order. Does the attorney have to answer?

Conventional wisdom and case law seem to view the fiduciary as the sole client and thus communications between the attorney and the fiduciary are confidential and privileged. *See, e.g., Huie v. Honorable Nikki DeShazo, Judge*, 922 S.W.2d 920 (Tex. 1996); American Bar Association Standing Committee on Ethics and Professional Responsibility Formal Op. 94–380. A growing number of authorities support the notion that derivative duties are owed to the beneficiaries. *See generally*, Restatement of the Law Governing Attorneys § 73(4) cmt. h (T.D. No. 7, 1994). Of this position, some champion an entity approach whereby the attorney represents the estate and must protect the interests of the beneficiaries as well as the fiduciary. *See, e.g.*, Jeffrey N. Pennell, *Ethics, Professionalism, and Malpractice Issues in Estate Planning and Administration*, C126 ALI–ABA 67 (1995). Others say that you must distinguish between representation in a "representative" capacity and "individual" representation. This distinction should be worked out and documented at the outset of the representation. The attorney must make the beneficiaries aware that the scope of the attorney's duties does not include watching out for their individual interests, and that they need to secure independent counsel for this purpose. Failure to so inform them that they are responsible for protecting their interests may amount to malpractice. *See, e.g., Linck v. Barokas & Martin*, 667 P.2d 171 (Alaska 1983); Model Rule 1.7 cmt. 12.

F. REVIEW QUESTIONS

1. What are the general professional duties an attorney must exercise in his or her representation of a client?
2. The attorney-client relationship is contractual in nature. True or False?
3. An attorney may never draft a will for a parent in which he or she takes a devise. True or False?
4. What does competent representation by an attorney require?
5. What is the rule of evidence that determines whether an attorney may be called as a witness against his or her client or compelled to produce evidence?
6. The ethics standards prohibit an attorney from representing a client if the representation of that client will be directly adverse to the representation of another client. True or False?

PART TWO

INTESTATE SUCCESSION AND RELATED DOCTRINES

*

I

ESTATE PLAN BY OPERATION OF LAW

Analysis

A. GENERAL PATTERNS OF INTESTATE SUCCESSION

1. ESSENCE OF INTESTACY

When someone dies without a valid will, the decedent's property passes by intestate succession according to a statutory scheme. *See, e.g.,* UPC § 2–101(a).

Intestate succession is recognized by all fifty states and territories at least for the benefit of certain relatives. An intestate succession statute is an estate plan by operation of law. It applies to both partial and total intestacy. The theoretical purpose of intestate succession statutes is to distribute a decedent's wealth in a pattern that represents a close approximation of that which an average person would have designed had that person's desires been properly manifested.

To accomplish this task on a general basis, legislatures have developed objective rather than subjective programs. Relevant factors that help design the intestacy scheme include the legislators' personal experiences, their ideas of fairness, convenience, vicarious intent, and their personal expectations. On a broader policy basis, legislatures consider protecting the family financially, securing title, encouraging family relationships and property accumulation. Attitudes change as these ideas and policies change.

2. CLASSES OF PROTECTED PERSONS

The persons protected or benefitted by the statute generally include:

- Persons related to the intestate by blood, called relationship by consanguinity. This includes an intestate's descendants, ancestors and collateral relations.
- Persons related to the intestate by marriage, called relationship by affinity. The primary, and under most laws, the only person to inherit by affinity is the surviving spouse. In a few jurisdictions, others related by affinity (the spouse's consanguine relations) may inherit in order to avoid escheat.
- Persons, although not related by consanguinity or affinity, inherit because they were adopted according to the adoption statutes.

3. SELECTION AND DISTRIBUTION TECHNIQUES

The vast majority of intestacy statutes distribute the net intestate estate among decedent's relatives according to a set of prioritized contingencies. These contingencies anticipate foreseeable circumstances and are applied until all property is allocated. The surviving spouse, descendants and parents of the intestate are the standard preferred beneficiaries. In varying degrees, other ancestors and collateral relations are also protected after the preferred relations. Except for the surviving spouse, inheritance is usually limited to consanguine or adoptive relations. Occasionally, the surviving spouse's consanguine relations may take if the decedent's consanguine relations cannot. *See* Ark. Code Ann. § 28–9–215 (1987).

The relational range of consanguinity necessary in order to take in intestacy varies among the states. Most intestacy statutes protect consanguine relations through grandparents and their descendants. Some make no express relational cutoff point and if the specified relations in the statute cannot take, pass the intestate's estate to the determinable nearest of kin. All states recognize that the property escheats to the state if no one qualifies who can take under the intestacy provisions.

4. PRIORITIZED CONTINGENCIES

The prioritized contingencies divide the relatives into classes, which are in turn scaled on a specific priority list. Except as will be explained under the concept of "representation," relatives included in a relational class that is closer to the decedent take to the exclusion of those in a relational class that is more distant from the decedent.

The specific classes of relatives whose members are entitled to take as distributees under the UPC include the decedent's "surviving spouse," "descendants," "parents," "descendants of decedent's parents," "grandparents" and "descendants of grandparents." *See, e.g.,* UPC §§ 2–102, 2–103.

Descendants: A key term in many of the classes of relatives described as taking a share is the word "descendant." UPC § 2–103. This word is defined to include all of a person's lineal descendants at all generations. UPC § 1–201(9). Consequently, when the UPC, for example, refers to a decedent's descendants, it means the decedent's children, grandchildren, great grandchildren, etc. When it refers to the descendants of the decedent's parents, it means the decedent's siblings (i.e., brothers and sisters), nephews and nieces, grandnephews and grandnieces, etc. *See* Chart 2–1–1. A reference to the descendants of grandparents means the decedent's uncles and aunts, first cousins, first cousins once removed in the descendancy, etc.

Sometimes the word "issue" is used. The terms "issue" and "descendants" have been held to be synonymous. *In re Radt's Will*, 167 N.Y.S.2d 817, 818 (Sur. Ct. 1957). Although the term "issue" has a biological connotation, many state intestacy statutes provide that an adopted child is the "issue" of the adopted parents. The drafters of the UPC used the term "descendant" because it recognizes inheritance rights beyond biological relations, *i.e.,* adoption. UPC § 2–102 cmt.

Chart 2–1–1 diagrams an abbreviated decedent's family tree.

CHART 2–1–1								
ABBREVIATED RELATIONSHIP DIAGRAM								
Great Great Grandparents (4)								
Great Great Aunt/Uncle (5)		Great Grandparents (3)						
First Cousin Twice Removed (6)		Great Aunt/Uncle (4)		Grandparents (2)				
Second Cousin Once Removed (7)		First Cousin Once Removed (5)		Aunt/Uncle (3)		Parents (1)		
***Third Cousin* (8)**		***Second Cousin* (6)**		***First Cousin* (4)**		Sibling (2)		DECEDENT
Third Cousin Once Removed (9)		Second Cousin Once Removed (7)		First Cousin Once Removed (5)		Nephew/ Niece (3)		Child (1)
Third Cousin Twice Removed (10)		Second Cousin Twice Removed (8)		First Cousin Twice Removed (6)		Grand Nephew/ Niece (4)		Grandchild (2)
Third Cousin Three Times Removed (11)		Second Cousin Three Times Removed (9)		First Cousin Three Times Removed (7)		Great Grand Nephew/ Niece (5)		Great Grandchild (3)
(1) Full cousins are in bold-italics. Cousins above full cousins are "in the ascendancy"; Cousins below full cousins are "in the descendancy."								
(2) Numbers in parentheses constitute the degree of relationship to Decedent using the Civil Law method of counting degrees.								
(3) The relatives that are included in the shaded portion of this Chart are those covered by the *UPC Umbrella*. Relatives and descendants of relatives included in this *Umbrella* are covered by the intestacy and other distribution provisions in the UPC.								
Excerpted from AVERILL, UNIFORM PROBATE CODE IN A NUTSHELL 33 (4th ed. 1995).								

5. OTHER ATTRIBUTES OF INTESTACY

Most intestacy statutes apply to both real and personal property, although a few still apply different distribution patterns to each kind of property. A few states have special provisions concerning ancestral property. There are no preferences depending on the gender of the distributee. Debts of decedent and the family protections (homestead, allowances and exemptions) are paid prior to intestacy distribution.

B. SHARES OF THE TAKERS

1. SHARE OF SURVIVING SPOUSE

The share of the surviving spouse raises several policy questions. The primary issues concern: (1) the share the spouse takes when there are surviving descendants of the intestate, and (2) the share the spouse takes when there are no surviving descendants of the intestate but other consanguine relatives of the decedent, such as parents and siblings, survive. The legislative trend is to increase the share of the spouse in these two situations. Many recently enacted intestacy statutes allocate the entire estate to the surviving spouse if all descendants surviving are descendants of the decedent-surviving spouse relationship or if no descendants of the decedent survive, even if parents and siblings survive.

On the other hand, the increased number of multi-family families, where one or more of the spouses have descendants from a prior relationship, raises policy issues concerning the protection of these descendants from the potential disinheritance when the surviving spouse dies. Unless there is adoption, the surviving spouse is usually not a blood relation to these descendants. They are only step-descendants to that spouse and the friction that sometimes develops between stepparents and stepchildren is well known.

UPC Response: The UPC offers one type of response to these conflicting policy concerns. Under the UPC, depending upon the existence of specified relations to the decedent, a surviving spouse is accorded substantial shares if the decedent dies intestate.

(1) The maximum share that a surviving spouse will take equals the total net intestate estate and the minimum share equals the first $100,000[1] of the net estate plus 1/2 anything exceeding that amount in the estate.

(2) The surviving spouse takes all the intestate estate in two situations. First, the surviving spouse takes all the estate if the decedent is also survived by children who are all children of the decedent and the spouse. This provision reflects the recommendations made from several studies that indicated testators usually follow this approach in their wills. The theory is that since intestacy portions should closely track the distribution patterns of the typical testator, the findings were incorporated into the UPC.

1. In the Official Text of the UPC all monetary amounts for the spouse in the intestacy provision are put in brackets to indicate that individual legislatures can select their own monetary thresholds. In this BLACK LETTER the brackets are removed.

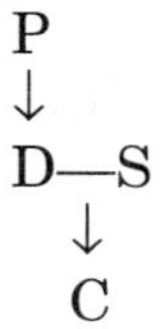

Illustration 1: A decedent's surviving spouse takes the entire intestate estate if all of the decedent's surviving descendants are also descendants of the surviving spouse and there is no other descendant of the surviving spouse who survives the decedent.

Second, the surviving spouse takes all the estate if the decedent is not survived by descendants and parents notwithstanding that other blood relations of the decedent also survive. In this situation, it also makes no difference if the surviving spouse has descendants who are not descendants of the decedent.

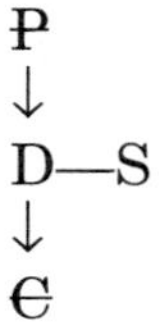

Illustration 2: A decedent's surviving spouse takes the entire intestate estate if no descendant or parent of the decedent survives the decedent.

(3) Between the above two situations lie three special familial circumstances.

(a) If parents survive but no descendants survive, a surviving spouse takes the first $200,000 of the net estate plus 3/4 anything exceeding that amount in the estate.

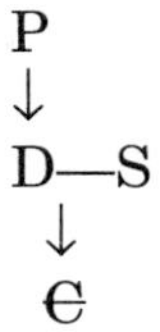

Illustration 3: A decedent's surviving spouse takes the first $200,000, plus three-fourths of any balance of the intestate estate, if no descendant of the decedent survives the decedent, but a parent of the decedent survives the decedent.

(b) Addressing the phenomenon of growing numbers of multi-relationship children, the UPC reduces the share of a surviving spouse in order to provide for descendants who are not the surviving spouse's descendants. Notwithstanding the reduction, the surviving spouse's share is substantial.

If the decedent is survived by one or more descendants who are also descendants of the surviving spouse and by one or more descendants of the surviving spouse who are not descendants of the decedent, the surviving spouse takes the first $150,000 of the net estate plus 1/2 of anything exceeding that amount remaining in the estate.

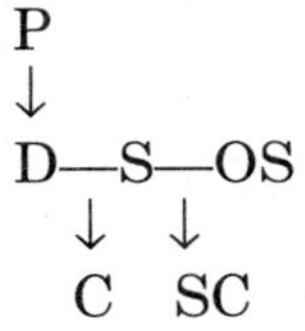

Illustration 4: A decedent's surviving spouse takes the first $150,000, plus one-half of any balance of the intestate estate, if all of the decedent's surviving descendants are also descendants of the surviving spouse and the surviving spouse has one or more surviving descendants who are not descendants of the decedent.

If decedent is survived by one or more descendants who are not descendants of the surviving spouse, the surviving spouse takes the first $100,000 of the net estate plus 1/2 of anything exceeding that amount in the estate. In this situation, it makes no difference if the decedent is survived by descendants who are also descendants of the surviving spouse.

```
      P
      ↓
OS—D—S
 ↓
 C
```

Illustration 5: A decedent's surviving spouse takes the first $100,000, plus one-half of any balance of the intestate estate, if one or more of the decedent's surviving descendants are not descendants of the surviving spouse.

(4) The large monetary prioritized amounts insure that a surviving spouses will take the entire estate in most cases. Limited protection is accorded to decedent's descendants of relationships other than the one existing at death and to decedent's parents only in relatively large estates.

2. SHARE OF ISSUE

In all states, after allocating the share of any surviving spouses, the remaining part of an intestate estate passes to the intestate's surviving descendants, if any survive. If no spouse survives, descendants take all of the estate. For a discussion of how the shares are to be divided *see infra* Part 2.I.C.

3. SHARE OF ASCENDANTS AND COLLATERALS

If neither spouse nor descendants survive the decedent, statutes allocate shares to ascendants and collateral relations by different methods. Ascendants are ancestors including parents, grandparents, etc. Collateral blood relatives are neither ascendants nor descendants but are those who are related to the decedent by consanguinity through common ancestry. Typical members of these relatives include siblings, aunts/uncles, great aunts/great uncles and their descendants. Surviving ancestors sometimes take in preference to collaterals, *e.g.,* parents take the estate before any share passes to siblings. Some statutes permit surviving collaterals to share with the nearest common surviving ancestor of decedent, *e.g.*, parents and siblings equally share the estate. Usually surviving descendants of collaterals may take by representation if the statutorily designated collateral did not survive, *e.g.,* in the previous example, if a sibling did not survive the decedent but a descendant of the sibling did, the descendant may take the share of the estate the sibling would have taken.

C. REPRESENTATION

1. DEFINITION OF REPRESENTATION

A common problem with allocating intestacy shares is that sometimes a person, who the intestacy statute designates should take, does not survive the decedent but descendants of that person do survive. Because a person must survive the decedent to take in intestacy it is necessary to determine whether a surviving descendant of that person may take by representation the share of the deceased ancestor. *See* Part 2.II.B.

Representation permits persons who are of more remote degree of kinship to an intestate to take some share from the estate even though there are relatives of closer degree of kinship to the intestate. The most common problem has been the determination of the generation that is to be considered the root generation for purposes of setting the stock shares of the more remote relatives who are able to represent their ancestors. The various systems that define representation differ in one or more ways in making this generation determination.

2. GENERATIONS AND STOCKS

An understanding of the various systems may be aided if one visualizes a family and divides it on vertical and horizontal graphic formats. The vertical classification refers to a descendant's family tree or stocks of lineal ancestors and descendants. The horizontal classification refers to a descendant's degree of relationship to the decedent. Each degree of relationship is a separate generation.

Chart 2–1–2

Generations and Stocks

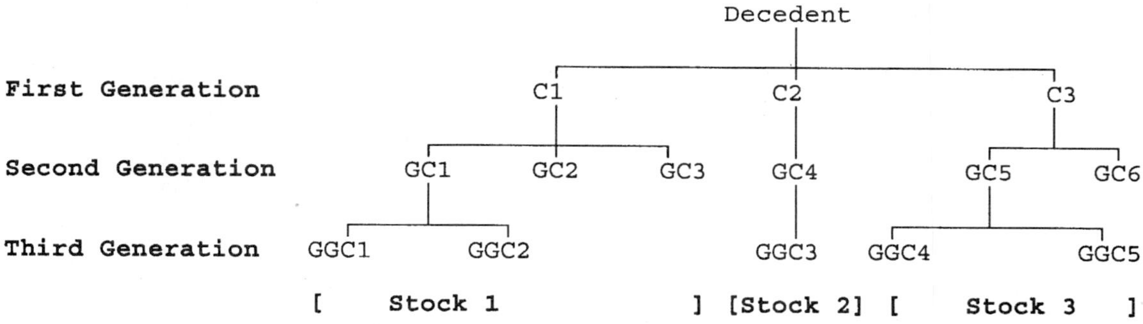

Because Chart 2–1–2 deals with a decedent's own descendants, the starting point for examining the vertical-horizontal subclassifications is with the decedent's three children. As the chart indicates vertically, each child constitutes a separate stock within which that child's own descendants are listed and graphed on a generation by generation basis. Child C1, grandchildren GC1, GC2, GC3, and their more remote descendants constitute one stock. (Stock 1). The same description is applicable to C2 and C3 and their respective descendants. (Stocks 2 and 3). As the chart indicates horizontally, all of the decedent's descendants are classified also by degree or generation. Under this subclassification decedent's children constitute a separate generation, the grandchildren another and each generation of more remote descendants other generations. Therefore, C1, C2 and C3 are all in the same horizontal class, *i.e.*, the First Generation. All the grandchildren would also constitute a horizontal class of their own, *i.e.*, the Second Generation. The same type of vertical and horizontal analysis is also relevant to decedent's collateral relatives. By using these two classification systems, it is possible under the various representation systems to determine the descendants who are to take and their individual shares.

3. GENERAL PRINCIPLES OF REPRESENTATION

Two general principles apply when using the above subclassifications.

- First, with respect to descendants in the same stock, descendants of more remote degree from the decedent cannot inherit if their ancestor, who is related in a closer degree to the decedent, can take. In other words, using Chart 2–1–1, GC1 will not be able to take anything by intestacy if C1 can take. The same rule would apply to the other grandchildren if their respective ancestor is able to take.

- Second, descendants of more remote degree from the decedent can inherit if their ancestor, who is related in a closer degree, cannot take even though there are other descendants of closer degree. In other words, using Chart 2–1–1, GC1 will be able to take by intestacy if C1 cannot take. GC1 can take even if C2 and C3 can take because GC1 is allowed to represent GC1's ancestor. This is called the bootstrapping effect of the doctrine of "representation."

4. TYPES OF REPRESENTATION SYSTEMS

Several types of representation systems have been used and currently are being used:

a. Per Stirpes

The initial division of the estate is made at the generation nearest to the decedent, regardless of whether there are any members of that generation who are alive. The number of primary shares is the number of surviving persons in that nearest generation, plus the number of deceased persons in that generation who have descendants who survived. The latter are permitted to represent their ancestor. The same approach is taken in dividing the estate of each deceased member's share among the deceased member's descendants.

b. Per Capita with Per Capita Representation

The initial division of the estate is made at the first generation in which one or more members survived. Representation is recognized for surviving descendants of that generation. The number of primary shares is the number of surviving persons in the first generation with a surviving member, plus the number of deceased persons in that generation who have descendants who survive. The same approach is taken in dividing the estate of each deceased member's share among the deceased member's descendants. This was the system adopted in the original UPC § 2–106, and is used in a large number of jurisdictions either by statute or court interpretation.

c. Per Capita at Each Generation

The estate is divided into primary shares at the first generation in which one or more members survived. Representation is recognized for the descendants of this generation who survived. The number of primary shares is the number of surviving persons in that first generation with surviving members plus the number of deceased persons in that generation who left surviving descendants. After the surviving members of the primary generation are allocated their shares, the remaining estate as a whole is combined and divided in the same way among the surviving descendants of the deceased descendants of the previous generation, and so on. This system was adopted in the 1990 UPC and has been enacted in several non UPC states.

d. Per Capita with Per Stirpes Representation

The initial division of the estate is made at the first generation in which a member survived. If all persons in that first generation survived the decedent, each in that generation take per capita. If one or more in that generation did not survive the decedent but left descendants who did, a pure per stirpes approach is then taken, using the first generation as the root generation. *E.g., Maud v. Catherwood,* 155 P.2d 111 (Cal. App. 1945). This system has been adopted for intestate distribution in a small number of states under the judicial construction of an intestacy statutes providing that: "if all the descendants are in the same decree of kindred to the decedent they share equally, otherwise they take by right of representation" West's Ann. Cal. Prob. Code § 222. The phraseology has also been interpreted in a manner similar to "per capita with per capita representation." *E.g., Balch v. Stone*, 20 N.E. 322 (Mass. 1889).

Illustration 6:

Situation 1:

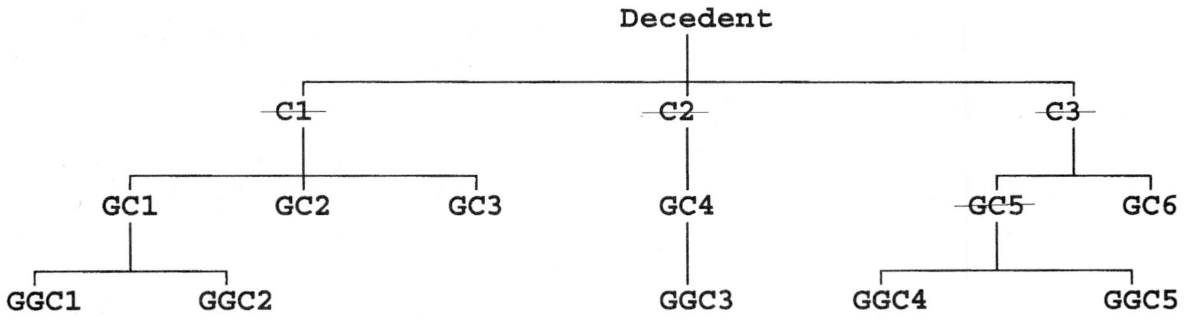

Decedent is predeceased by the following: C1, C2, C3, and GC5. Net estate is valued at $108,000. Of the surviving descendants, who, in what fractions and amounts, will take under:

a. Per stirpes?

b. Per capita with per capita representation?

c. Per capita at each generation?

Answer Situation 1:

<table>
<tr><th>Situation 1</th><th>Per stirpes</th><th>Per capita with per capita representation</th><th>Per capita at each generation</th></tr>
<tr><td>GC1</td><td rowspan="3">⅓ of ⅓ =1/9 = $12,000</td><td rowspan="5">1/6 = $18,000</td><td rowspan="5">1/6 = $18,000</td></tr>
<tr><td>GC2</td></tr>
<tr><td>GC3</td></tr>
<tr><td>GC4</td><td>⅓ = $36,000</td></tr>
<tr><td>GC6</td><td>½ of ⅓ = 1/6 = $18,000</td></tr>
<tr><td>GGC4</td><td rowspan="2">½ of ½ of ⅓ = 1/12 = $9,000</td><td rowspan="2">½ of 1/6 = $9,000</td><td rowspan="2">½ of 1/6 = $9,000</td></tr>
<tr><td>GGC5</td></tr>
<tr><td colspan="4">Note that in this situation "per capita with per capita representation" is the same as "per capita at each generation."</td></tr>
</table>

Situation 2:

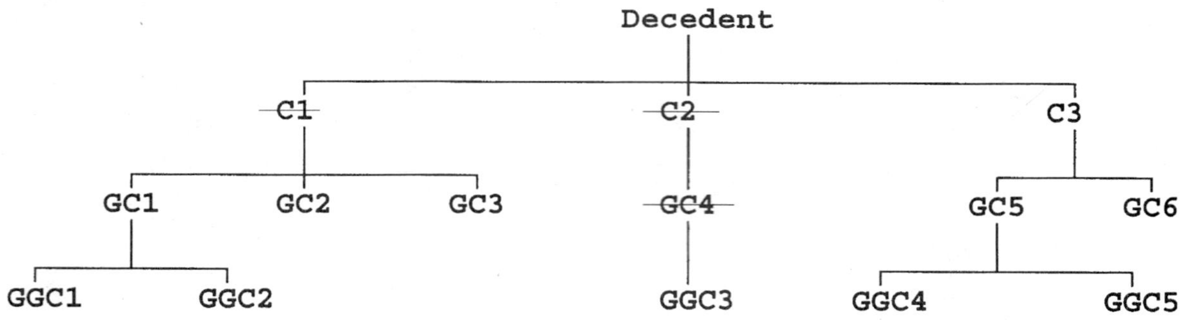

Decedent is predeceased by the following: C1, C2 and GC4. Net estate is valued at $108,000. Of the surviving descendants, who, in what fractions and amounts, will take under:

a. Per stirpes?

b. Per capita with per capita representation?

c. Per capita at each generation?

Answer Situation 2:

<table>
<tr><th>Situation 2</th><th>Per stirpes</th><th>Per capita with per capita representation</th><th>Per capita at each generation</th></tr>
<tr><td>C3</td><td>⅓ = $36,000</td><td>⅓ = $36,000</td><td>⅓ = $36,000</td></tr>
<tr><td>GC1</td><td rowspan="3">⅓ of ⅓ =1/9 = $12,000</td><td rowspan="3">⅓ of ⅓ =1/9 = $12,000</td><td rowspan="4">¼ of ⅔ = 2/12 or 1/6 = $18,000</td></tr>
<tr><td>GC2</td></tr>
<tr><td>GC3</td></tr>
<tr><td>GGC3</td><td>⅓ = $36,000</td><td>⅓ = $36,000</td></tr>
<tr><td colspan="4">Note: in this example, per stirpes derives the same distribution pattern as per capita with per capita representation.</td></tr>
</table>

5. NONREPRESENTATION

In some circumstances, intestacy statutes do not permit representation and use a *per capita (without representation)* system. This system divides an intestate's estate by the number of persons who survive by the method described by the statute. An equal share is given to each of a number of persons, all of whom are in equal degree to the decedent without reference to their stocks or the right of representation. No representation is allowed for the descendants of persons in the applicable generation. This system is employed normally only after specificity of the intestacy statute is exhausted and applies to distant collateral relations when it is necessary to count degrees of relationship.

D. ANCESTORS AND COLLATERALS

1. PARENTELIC SYSTEM

The UPC and most intestacy statutes use the "parentelic system" for determining heirs other than the surviving spouse. Under this kind of system, one must determine the nearest ancestors who either survive intestate or who leave issue surviving intestate. Once those relatives are identified, the property is distributed to the closest surviving ancestors or if none survive, to their surviving issue, by representation. *See* RESTATEMENT (THIRD) OF PROPERTY (WILLS AND OTHER DONATIVE TRANSFERS) § 2.4 (1999).

2. COUNTING DEGREES

The process of determining next of kin in intestacy requires counting degrees of relationship of one to a decedent. This process is referred to as determining the propinquinity of relations. It does not come into play until it is discovered that the property is not disposed of under the specific terms of the intestacy statute.

3. PRIMARY METHODS OF COUNTING DEGREES

a. Civil Law System

The degree of kinship is the total of (1) the number of the steps counting one for each generation, from the decedent up to the nearest common ancestor of the decedent and the claimant, and (2) the number of steps from the common ancestor down to the claimant. *See* Chart 2–1–3. Claimants having the lowest degree count are entitled to the property. All of equal degree share per capita.

Chart 2–1–3

Civil Law Degree Counting

Relation	Degree of Kinship
Sibling	2
Nephew/Niece	3
Aunt/Uncle	3
First Cousin	4
Great Uncle	4
Second Cousin	6

b. Modified Civil Law System

A few states modify the civil law system by counting in the same way but providing that only those of lowest degree who are related to the closest ancestor take per capita. *See, e.g.,* Neb. Rev. Stat. Ann. §§ 30–2303, 2305, 2306 (1995).

E. ESCHEAT

1. ESCHEAT DEFINITION

In all states when a decedent has no relatives, the property escheats to the state. The possibility of escheat depends on the extent to which the intestacy statute allows distant heirs to take. Some contend that the state should not allow distant relatives, called "laughing heirs," to take because decedent is unlikely to have known of these relatives and it is unrealistic to contend that the decedent would want them to benefit. Others add that state purposes for escheat properties is preferable to benefitting distant relatives. On the other hand, some contend that any relative should inherit if that person is the closest relation and can prove that relationship. Thus, the state never should benefit so long as someone can show the kinship or necessary relationship.

2. ESCHEAT UNDER THE UPC

The UPC cuts off inheritance if there is no surviving spouse and no surviving grandparent or descendant of a grandparent. This feature is designed to simplify proof of relationship and to cut off so-called "laughing heirs" who, as very distant relatives, are far beyond the normal confines of the modern family unit and the probable donative intent of the decedent. The relational limitation on inheritance has been held valid against an equal protection contention by an intestate's second cousin and closest heir. *See Estate of Jurek v. State,* 428N.W.2d 774 (Mich. Ct. App. 1988).

3. NEXT OF KIN STATUTES

Many states, after exhausting the persons specified in their intestacy statutes, pass the estate "to the person of the closest degree of kinship with the decedent." *See, e.g.*, MONT. CODE ANN. § 72–2–113(1)(e) (1995). These states use one of the degree counting techniques for determining the closest relative.

Even under the UPC's system, escheat is not very likely considering the large class of people who can qualify and the length of time in which they have to qualify. Under all the systems, finding the relatives is the most difficult problem: not whether or not there are some. In addition, under every system a person is able to benefit even the most distant relatives if that person so provides in a valid will or will substitute.

Illustration 7: Assume decedent is survived only by those collaterals mentioned. Using CHART 2–1–1 for reference, which of the living collateral claimants under the following three Problems would receive decedent's intestate property using:

(1) the civil law system

(2) the modified civil law system

(3) the parentelic system

(4) the Uniform Probate Code

Problem 1:

Grandniece, First Cousin, Great Uncle.

Problem 2:

First Cousin twice removed (in the descendancy), First Cousin once removed (in the ascendancy), Second Cousin.

Problem 3:

Second Cousin, Third Cousin.

Problem 1 Answer	Grandniece	First Cousin	Great Uncle
Civil law system	Per capita [4]	Per capita [4]	Per capita [4]
Modified civil law system	All [4]	[4]	[4]

Parentelic system	All		
Uniform Probate Code	All		

Problem 2 Answer	**First Cousin twice removed [in the descendancy]**	**First Cousin once removed [in the ascendancy]**	**Second Cousin**
Civil law system	[6]	All [5]	[6]
Modified civil law system	[6]	All [5]	[6]
Parentelic system	All		
Uniform Probate Code	All		

Problem 3 Answer	**Second Cousin**	**Third Cousin**
Civil law system	All [6]	[8]
Modified civil law system	All [6]	[8]
Parentelic system	All	
Uniform Probate Code	Escheats to State	

F. REVIEW QUESTIONS

1. An intestate succession statute is an estate plan by operation of law. True or False?
2. Most intestacy statutes protect consanguine relations through great-grandparents and their descendants. True or False?
3. "Descendant" includes all of a person's lineal descendants at all generations. True or False?
4. In all states, after allocating the share of any surviving spouses, the remaining part of an intestate estate passes to the intestate's surviving descendants, if any survive. True or False?
5. What is the term for ancestors including parents and grandparents?
6. A person must survive the decedent to take in intestacy. True or False?
7. What is the process of determining next of kin in intestacy?
8. In all states, what occurs when the decedent dies intestate with no relatives?

II

TAKER QUALIFICATIONS

Analysis

A. QUESTIONS OF STATUS

1. RELATIONAL CLASSIFICATION

All intestacy statutes describe their beneficiaries in terms of relational classifications such as "parent," "grandparent," "descendant," "heirs," and "surviving spouse." Determining who falls into these categories is a question of status. Because of the importance of this problem for intestate succession and other related purposes, state statutes may also include specific provisions concerning the status of relations such as step-descendants, step-ancestors, half-bloods, posthumous heirs, adopted persons, persons born out of wedlock and spouses.

2. BY, FROM AND THROUGH

A common thread among these distinct categories is the reference to the inheritance "by, from and through" a person.

CHART 2–2–1

BY, FROM AND THROUGH

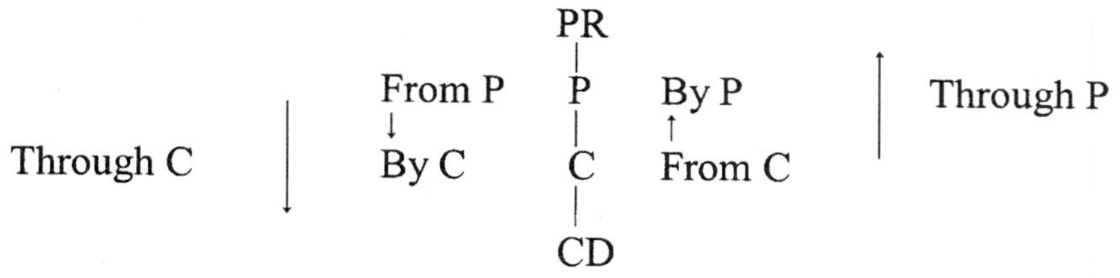

Legend: C = Child; CD = Child's Descendant; P = Parent; PR = Parent's Relatives.

Reproduced from AVERILL, UNIFORM PROBATE CODE IN A NUTSHELL 54 (4th ed. 1995).

Using the Chart 2–2–1, if by, from and through inheritance is applicable, there is inheritance by C from P and through P from P's other descendants and P's ancestors and collateral relations: conversely, there is inheritance by P from C and through C from C's descendants. In addition, CD inherits from P through C and P's ancestors and collateral inherit from C through P.

B. SURVIVORSHIP AND SIMULTANEOUS DEATH

1. SURVIVORSHIP AT COMMON LAW

At common law, an heir, to take, must survive the decedent "for an instant of time." Mere survival by any measurable time is enough. When a question arises whether a person survived for inheritance purposes, the answer depends on matter of evidence and standards of proof.

2. SIMULTANEOUS OR NEAR SIMULTANEOUS DEATH

A problem with the survivorship rule arose when reciprocal heirs, *e.g.*, husband would take from wife if husband survived wife and vice versa, died under simultaneous or near simultaneous circumstances. A Uniform Act was promulgated to address this problem. Under the original Uniform Simultaneous Death Act, a rebuttable presumption of survival of each property owner arises when "there is no sufficient evidence" of the order of death. It only applies when there is not sufficient evidence to rebut the presumption. The evidence of the order of death has in several case tested the presumption and have been held to rebut it.

See infra, Part 3.V.G. for the discussion of the survivorship rules regarding transfers of property under instruments such as wills and other will substitutes.

3. SURVIVORSHIP UNDER THE UPC

For intestacy, UPC Section 2–104 (and the comparable section in the revised Uniform Simultaneous Death Act) takes a different approach. It requires that every taker must survive the decedent's death or the transfer activating event by 120 hours. For intestacy, the 120 hour requirement is irrebuttable—if one does not survive by 120 hours, one does not take by intestacy unless one is the last heir. In addition, the UPC requires that survival by 120 hours be established by clear and convincing evidence.

C. CONSANGUINITY

1. WHOLE BLOODS AND HALF BLOODS

Consanguinity means relationship by blood. Whole blood relatives are blood relations who have the same common ancestors. Half bloods are blood relations who have one common ancestor but not both relevant ancestors. Half-blooded relatives are always collateral relations. Most jurisdictions including the UPC make no distinctions between the inheritance share of whole or half-blooded relations. A few require different allocations such as one-half the share of a whole blooded relation.

2. POSTHUMOUS

A posthumous heir is a blood relation who was conceived before the intestate's death but born after that death. A posthumous heir could take at common law. Statutes in some states limit inheritance to posthumous children or other descendants of the intestate and specifically exclude collateral relatives. *See* ARK. CODE ANN. § 28–9–210 (1987)

UPC Rule: The UPC Section 2–108 provides that an individual in gestation "at a particular time" who survives by 120 hours from the time of birth is treated as surviving the particular time. The survivorship period refers to the time of the birth and not the time of the death of the intestate. The section applies to descendants and collaterals of both males and females. The purpose of this rule is to prevent property from passing from the intestate to the estate of a child who has died shortly after birth. Consequently, a child in gestation 120 hours after the intestate's death must survive the time of birth by 120 hours to be treated as an heir.

D. AFFINITY

Affinity means relationship by marriage. The most common example of relationship by affinity is the husband and wife relationship. The husband is related to his wife by affinity and vice versa. With a few statutory exceptions, the only inheritance in intestacy by persons related by affinity is by a surviving spouse. Thus with only a few exceptions, other persons related by affinity, including step children and other in-laws, do not take in intestacy.

E. ADOPTION

1. TYPES OF ADOPTIONS

Three types of adoption that affect succession are formal adoption, virtual adoption, and equitable adoption.

2. FORMAL ADOPTION

Formal adoption arises when the adoption has been approved through a statutory adoption process. The rule often recognized is that "as adoption is only permitted by virtue of legislative grant, no rights of inheritance exist unless the legislative requirements have been complied with." Atkinson, Wills § 23, at p. 91. Although adoption was not recognized at common law, all states today have formal adoption procedures recognizing the status of adoption. The effect of adoption on inheritance rights depends on the law of the individual states.

The inheritance rights of an adopted child have been a common subject of inheritance legislation. The legislation throughout the fifty-plus jurisdictions in this country varies significantly in scope and content. A few only protect inheritance rights between the persons to the adoption and do not extend it to other relations. Most recognized inheritance beyond those who were a part of the adoption proceedings and grant inheritance through the adopting parent and the adopted child.

3. ADOPTION UNDER THE UPC

The UPC includes a provision for adopted persons that attempts to deal with the primary issues faced from an inheritance standpoint. *See* UPC § 2–114(b).

a. General Rule

Section 2–114(b) of the UPC establishes the general rule that for purposes of inheritance by, from, or through the child, an adopted child is the child of the adopting parents and not of the child's natural (genetic) parents. This general rule applies to what may be described as a "new family adoption."

> New Family Adoption: A "new family adoption" arises when a natural parent or both natural parents voluntarily put the child up for adoption and an entirely new family, usually a husband and wife, adopt this child. In this situation, the UPC severs the relationship of the adopted child from that child's natural parents: it grafts a new relationship between the adopted child and the adopting parents for inheritance purposes. [See Chart 2–2–2]. The adopted person inherits by, from and through that person's adopting parents and vice-versa. UPC § 2–114(b). Inheritance rights between the adopted child and the natural parents and vice-versa are severed. UPC § 2–114(b). A total severance of the inheritance relationship is accomplished.

Using Chart 2–2–2 for reference, if any of AC's adopted family died intestate and AC was entitled to a share, AC, or AC's descendants if AC did not survive, inherit from AC's adopting parents, AP, and from the adopting parents' relations through AP if AP did not survive. The reverse is also applicable. If AC or AC's descendants died, AP would inherit from AC and from AC's descendants through AC if AC did not survive. In addition AP's other relations would inherit from AC through AP if AP did not survive. In the new family adoption situation, however, inheritance rights between AC and AC's natural parents, NP, are severed. AC will not inherit from or through NP and NP will not inherit from or through AC.

CHART 2–2–2

NEW FAMILY ADOPTION

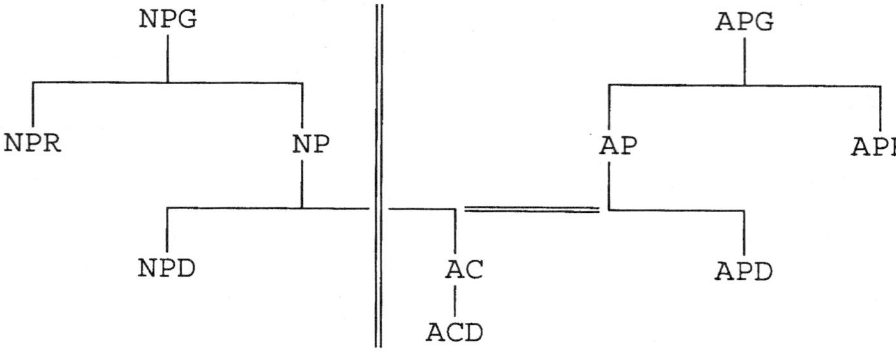

Legend: AC = Adopted Child; AP = Adopting Parents; NP = Natural Parents; _D = Descendants; _G = Ancestors; _R = Collateral Relations; ‖ = Adoption wall; == Adoption bridge

b. Stepparent Exception

UPC Section 2–114(b) creates an exception for stepparent adoptions. Subsection (b)(i) provides that a stepparent adoption does not sever the relationship between the adopted stepchild and the child's natural parent who has custody of the child and who married the child's stepparent. Subsection (b)(ii) provides that a stepparent adoption does not sever the adopted stepchild's right to inherit from and through the other natural parent. Subsection (b)(ii) does not expressly provide that the other natural parent (and that parent's family) continues to inherit from and through the adopted stepchild. The absence of such an express provision means the general rule—the rule that severs the relationship between an adopted and the child's natural parents—continues to apply.

Chart 2–2–3

Stepparent Adoption

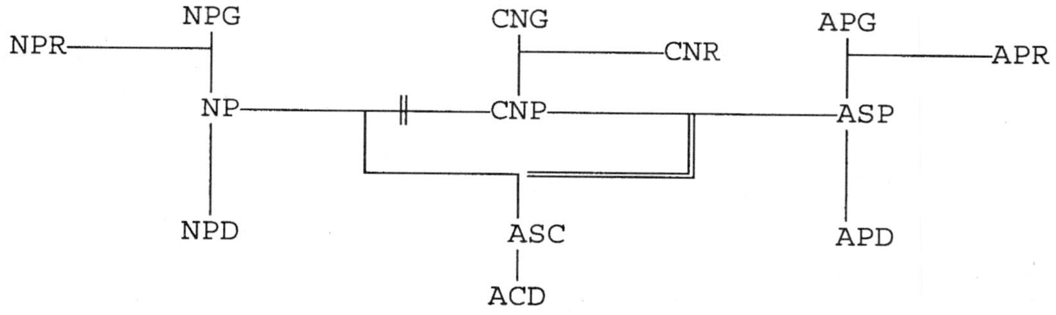

Legend: ASC = Adopted Stepchild; ASP = Adopting Stepparent; CNP = Custodial Natural Parent; NP = Noncustodial Natural Parent; _D = Descendant; _G = Ancestors; N_ = Natural Relationship; _P = Parent; _R = Collateral Relations; ‖ = Adoption wall; == Adoption bridge

Using Chart 2–2–3 for reference, the adopted stepchild, ASC inherits from three parents: the two natural parents, CNP and NP, and the adopting stepparent, ASP. ASC is capable of inheriting from relatives of any of the three parents through the parent if any or all of these parents failed to survive. The adopting stepparent, ASP, and the natural custodial parent, CNP will inherit from and through ASC. Neither natural parent NP and nor NP's relations will inherit from ASC.

4. VIRTUAL ADOPTIONS AND EQUITABLE ADOPTION

Virtual adoptions have been recognized for inheritance purposes where there is a promise between natural parent and nonparent that if the natural parent will give custody to the nonparent, the nonparent will adopt the child. If the natural parents, the child and the nonparents perform the agreement, the agreement is enforceable by the child as a contract on a third party beneficiary theory, or as a means of establishing an inheritance right. Atkinson, Wills § 23, at p. 91.

Equitable adoption is also a circumstance driven relationship. A typical situation includes attributes of a parent child relationship has existed, *e.g.*, support, custody, care and concern for needs, control, filial obedience of child, mutual love and affection; the relationship existed from a young age; and there were representations to others that child was a natural or adopted child. Courts require proof by clear and convincing evidence that the child is the equivalent of an adopted child. The issue is sometimes characterized as one of contract law but wills evidentiary rules also sometimes are used. If proof is satisfied, the child may be able to take an intestate share.

Comment: Virtual and equitable adoptions are sympathetic situations where some but not all courts exercise their equitable powers and provide a remedy for the child. Even if recognized, these relationships raise issues of, by, from, and through the "adoptive" and "adopted" persons. In addition, they expose the estate to the costs of litigation that the statutory adoption formality was intended to prevent. Although the UPC does not specifically recognize the concepts of equitable and virtual adoption and other similar remedial inheritance devices, the courts in UPC jurisdictions are free to apply these doctrines. *See, e.g.*, Atkinson, Wills § 23, at pp. 91–92.

F. DEFINITION OF SPOUSE

1. FORMAL MARRIAGE

To inherit as a spouse, a person must be characterized as a spouse under the appropriate law. Most spousal relationships are created by a formal marriage. The form and requirements for formal marriages are set by the law of the jurisdiction in which the marriage was contracted or celebrated. If a marriage is valid by that law, generally it will be valid in the forum state for inheritance purposes unless it violates the strong public policy of the state which had the most significant relationship to the spouses and the marriage at the time of the marriage. Restatement (Second) Conflict of Laws § 283 (1971).

2. OTHER MARITAL TYPE RELATIONSHIPS

Other methods of marriage formation are also recognized including the common law spouse and the judicially or societal spouse called the putative spouse.

Common Law Spouse: A common law marriage is one not solemnized as a formal marriage but created by an agreement to marry, or an understanding of marriage, followed by cohabitation. Although these marriages are invalid in a majority of states, a common law marriage valid where entered is valid in other states except in the unusual situation where invalidity is required by the strong policy of another state which had the most significant relationship to the spouses and the marriage at the time of the marriage. If valid, a spouse of a common law marriage is considered a spouse for inheritance purposes.

Putative Spouse: A putative spouse is a person whose marriage was solemnized in proper form and celebrated in good faith by one or both parties, but whose marriage, by reason of some legal infirmity, is either void or voidable. Christopher L. Blakesley, *The Putative Marriage Doctrine*, 60 TUL. L. REV. 1 (1985). Generally, states protect those persons who went through a marriage ceremony in the good faith belief notwithstanding the marriage's nullity. The rationale is that the good faith party is entitled to an equitable apportionment of the personal and real property accumulated by the couple's joint efforts: a putative spouse ought to recover a fair share of the fruits of the skill, industry and toil which that spouse contributed to the relationship.

G. COHABITORS

1. COHABITORS

Cohabitors are two persons who live together in some form of established lasting relationship which exhibits the characteristics of a marriage. These may include same sex or opposite sex couples whose relationships do not qualify as official marriages.

Most of the litigation concerning property rights between cohabitors concerns division of property upon dissolution of the living arrangement. Court decisions range from recognition of rights on theories such as implied contract, *quantum meruit* or constructive trust to rejection of rights on grounds of public policy (illegal or immoral) or that the matter is a legislative prerogative. *Compare Marvin v. Marvin*, 557 P.2d 106 (Cal.1976) (express or implied contract provable) *with Rehak v. Mathis*, 238 S.E.2d 81 (Ga. 1977) (contract unenforceable if founded on illegal or immoral foundation).

There are few states that recognize cohabitation without marriage for inheritance purposes. Claims by cohabitors against decedents' estates are usually based on express or implied contract or *quantum meruit* bases. *See infra* Part 7.II.A.

2. SAME-SEX COUPLES

Same-sex couples are currently denied inheritance rights between each other. Survivors of such relationships are left to claims based upon contractual theories used by heterosexual cohabitors. *See, e.g., Whorton v. Dillingham*, 248 Cal. Rptr. 405 (Ct. App. 1988).

Same sex marriages are not presently recognized under the laws of any state of the Union. Although the Supreme Court of Hawaii [*Baehr v. Lewin*, 852 P.2d 44 (Haw. 1993)] held that under the equal protection provisions in the Hawaiian Constitution, the refusal to allow same-sex marriage is unconstitutional because the State failed to justify the distinction by showing a compelling state interest,[1] most decisions have upheld the state's power to limit marital status to heterosexual couples. *See, e.g., Dean v. District of Columbia,* 653 A.2d 307 (D.C. App.1995); Baker v. Nelson, 191 N.W.2d 185 (Minn.1971), *appeal dismissed*, 409 U.S. 810, (1972). In 1997, a lower court in New York held that marriage is limited to opposite sex couples and that the gender classification serves a valid public purpose. The court reiterated that neither the due process, nor the equal protection clause of the 14th Amendment, nor a right of privacy is offended by New York's gender classification of persons authorized to marry. *Storrs v. Holcomb*, 645 N.Y.S.2d 286 (Sup. Ct. 1996), *aff'd on different grounds,* 666 N.Y.S.2d 835 (App. Div. 1997). *See also Matter of Cooper,* 592 N.Y.S.2d 797 (App. Div. 1993) (Survivor of same-sex relationship, alleged to be a "spousal relationship," is not entitled to right of election against decedent's will under New York spousal protection statute).

3. RECIPROCAL BENEFICIARY LEGISLATION

An alternative method of recognizing probate and other rights between nonmarried persons is to create a new status. In 1997 Hawaii enacted a statute that creates a new status called "reciprocal beneficiary relationship." HAW. REV. STAT. ANN. §§ 572C–1 to–7 (Supp. 1998). This Act extends "certain rights and benefits which are presently available only to married couples to couples composed of two individuals who are legally prohibited from marrying under state law." HAW. REV. STAT. ANN. § 572C–1. Under the Act, reciprocal beneficiaries have the same rights and obligations that are conferred through marriage. *Id.*, § 572C–6. These rights and obligation include rights of inheritance and spousal protections, to health benefits, to hold property as tenants by the entirety, and to make health-care decisions on behalf of the other. To achieve this status, both parties must be at least eighteen years old, not be married or a party to another reciprocal beneficiary relationship, be unable to marry, consent free of force, duress, or fraud, and sign the declaration of the reciprocal beneficiary relationship. The declaration may be registered with the state director of health. Registration is necessary to qualify for some of the rights such as the spousal protection and the ability to hold property as tenants by the entireties. *See* 1997 Hawaii Laws Act 383. Other states are considering similar legislative approaches.

In 1999, the Supreme Court of Vermont held that under its equal protection provision same sex couples may not be denied "secular benefits and protections offered married couples." *Baker v. State of Vermont*, 1999 WL 1211709 (Vt. 1999). The Court retained jurisdiction to permit the Vermont legislature to consider and enact constitutionally consistent legislation.

H. NONMARITAL CHILDREN

1. NONMARITAL CHILDREN

Nonmarital children are consanguine children who were born to an unmarried mother. At early common law "bastards" could not inherit. Later, inheritance by,

1. The Hawaii litigation was made moot by the adoption of a constitutional amendment that provides: "The legislature shall have the power to reserve marriage to opposite-sex couples." HAW. CONST. Art. I, § 23.

from and through the mother was permitted. Today, the primary issue concernspaternity and its requirements. The Supreme Court has held that a state may not discriminate against nonmarital children by requiring marriage but may require paternity and a high level of proof. *See Trimble v. Gordon,* 430 U.S. 762 (1977); *Lalli v. Lalli,* 439 U.S. 259 (1978).

2. NONMARITAL PERSONS UNDER THE UPC

UPC Section 2–114(a) provides that a child may inherit by, from and through the parents whether or not the parents were married to each other. Paternity may be proved by a preponderance of evidence during the parent's lifetime or by clear and convincing evidence after death. UPC § 2–114(c), however, provides that a nonmarital parent and kindred do not inherit from and through the nonmarital child unless the natural parent openly treated the child as a child and did not refuse to support the child during minority.

3. PATERNITY

Maternity has not been an issue because the woman who bears the child is presumed to be the mother. Paternity, however, may be an issue and may be established by several methods. Presumptions of paternity of the husband exist if the child is conceived and born during a marriage or if the husband marries the mother while the latter is pregnant. Otherwise, paternity may be shown by relevant conduct concerning the representations and relationships the child had with the parent after birth or by DNA evidence.

4. ASSISTED CONCEPTION

The rights of children conceived by methods other than sexual intercourse are less firmly established. Some state have statutes specifically granting full relational status to children conceived by artificial insemination when the mother is married to the father notwithstanding whether the father's sperm was used for the conception. Beyond this the law is unknown and unsure. In 1993 the Uniform Laws Commission promulgated the UNIFORM STATUS OF CHILDREN OF ASSISTED CONCEPTION ACT (1993). This Act primarily concerns the security and well being of those children born and living as a result of assisted conception. The Act establishes the relational status for any child conceived and born after the "fertilizing [of] an egg of a woman with sperm of a man by means other than sexual intercourse or (ii) implanting [of] an embryo, but ... does not include the pregnancy of a wife resulting from fertilizing her egg with sperm of her husband." Basically the child, conceived under assisted conception, is accorded virtually the same rights in property and inheritance as though conceived by natural means.

I. REVIEW QUESTIONS

1. To take at common law, an heir must survive the decedent by 120 hours unless one is the last heir. True or False?

2. Affinity means relationship by blood. True or False?

3. What do we call blood relatives who have one common ancestor but not both relevant ancestors?

4. This type of heir is a blood relation who was conceived before the intestate's death but born after that death.

5. What is a relationship by affinity? Give examples.

6. Name the three types of adoption that affect succession.

7. What do we call a person whose marriage was solemnized in proper form and celebrated in good faith by one or both parties, but whose marriage, by reason of some legal infirmity, is either void or voidable?

8. Nonmarital children are consanguine children who were born to an unmarried mother. True or False?

III

BARS TO INHERITANCE

Analysis

A. EFFECT OF PRIOR TRANSACTIONS ON INHERITANCE RIGHTS

1. THE DOCTRINE OF ADVANCEMENT

The doctrine of advancement recognizes that lifetime gifts may have post death consequences and must be considered in order to foster equality among equals. Unfortunately, there is far less uniformity on this issue than desired.

a. History of Advancement

The Statute of Distribution of 1670 provided that any settlement of land, or advancement of personalty to a child by an intestate, should be taken into account in the distribution of the personalty in order to make the shares of all children "equal as near as can be estimated." On account of primogeniture, the statute provided that settlements of land on the heir at law did not reduce his share in the personalty. ATKINSON, WILLS § 129 (Personalty). There were no advancements under the Statute of Distribution if the gift was to a collateral.

At common law, an heir's intestate share would be affected if the heir received an advancement from the intestate during the latter's lifetime. By common law definition, an advancement meant an irrevocable inter vivos gift of money or property, real or personal, to a child by a parent that enables the child to anticipate the child's inheritance from the parent to the extent of the gift. ATKINSON, WILLS § 129.

b. Scope of the Advancement Concept

The relatives who are within the advancement doctrine depend on the terms of the relevant statute. ATKINSON, WILLS § 129, at p. 722. Many states have extended the doctrine to other heirs in addition to the intestate's children. For example, the UPC uses "heir" and that term is defined to include children, descendants, collaterals, and spouses. Under some statutes, one has to be an heir or next of kin at time of advancement. The UPC requires the donee to be an heir at the time of death.

c. Proof of Intent

There must be an intent to make an advancement at the time of the gift. The donor cannot subsequently change an outright gift into an advancement, but can change an advancement into an outright gift. Under the common law rule, the problem was proving intent. Because the intent of the donor at the time of the gift is the determinative factor, not all such gifts are so characterized. Seldom, however, does one find that a donor has clearly indicated that intent. The transferring document, if there even is one, will seldom specifically indicate one way or the other.

When admissible evidence of intent was lacking, courts developed various presumptions. For example, a court might presume all gifts are advancements unless rebutted by admissible evidence; others might presume all gifts are not advancements unless rebutted by admissible evidence. Some courts presume that a gift was an advancement if it was substantial but presume the gift was not an advancement if it was of nominal value or for support of the donee.

The burden of proof for intent ranges from a preponderance of the evidence to a clear and convincing evidence standard. Generally, the courts admit a wide range of evidence, including donor's records and declarations. Value of the gift for advancement calculation purposes is set at the date of gift or the date of death, usually depending on when the donee obtains enjoyment of the property. Under the UPC, valuation of a formal advancement is determined at the time of the donee's possession or enjoyment or at the donor's death, whichever occurs first. UPC § 2–109(c).

d. Advancement Formality

Under the UPC and other similar type statutes, a gift is an advancement only if any one of several formalities is satisfied. A gift is a formal advancement if either the donor "declared in a contemporaneous writing" or the heir "acknowledged in writing" that the gift is an advancement. UPC § 2–109(a). The required writing may, rather than declaring the gift is an advancement, merely indicate that the gift must be taken into account in computing the division or distribution of decedent's intestate estate. No words of art such as "advancement" need be used by the donor. The gist of the declaration must indicate that the donor intended that the gift constitutes under legal principles what lawyers call advancements. There is also no specific requirement that the written declaration of intent to make a formal advancement be communicated to the donee at the time of the gift. It could be a contemporaneous written note or indication that the gift is a formal advancement which is included with the donor's personal records. Of course, the writing must be available or provable after the donor's death when distribution decisions are made.

e. Intestate Condition of the Decedent's Estate

At Common Law a gift would be treated as an advancement only if the donor died totally intestate. Partial testacy destroyed advancement consequences because the testator was presumed to have considered advancements in the calculations of the bequest. The UPC provision applies to partial intestacy, too, so long as evidentiary requirements of intent are met. *See* UPC § 2–609.

f. The Hotchpot

An heir who received an advancement and who also wants to take an intestate share from the intestate's estate must participate in a "hotchpot" estate. A hotchpot is a fictional estate created merely for calculation purposes: it does not ever actually exist but is used to determine the proper distribution amount from estates that do exist. There are two principles of these calculations: (1)

participation in the hotchpot is optional on the part of advancees, but (2) if they want to take from the estate, they must participate: they have an equitable election. If the heir participates, the value of the advancement is added to the value of the distributable estate for calculation purposes only. From the appropriate calculations the heir's distribution directly from the intestate's estate equals the excess of the heir's intestate share over the value of the advancement received. If the value of the heir's advancement exceeds the heir's intestate share from the hotchpot calculations, the heir neither participates in the hotchpot nor receives an intestate share from the estate. The heir, of course, keeps the advancement.

Illustration 1: I gave $6,000 to G, a grandchild. I properly indicated that the gift was an advancement on G's inheritance. At the time of the gift, C1, G's parent and I's child, was still alive. I died intestate with a distributable estate valued at $24,000. I was survived by two children, C2 and C3, and by G but not by C1. How should I's estate be distributed?

Answer to Illustration: Under a rule that a gift is an advancement only if the donee was an heir at the time of the gift, the estate would be divided equally between, C2, C3, and G. G would take a full share ($8,000) by representation because at the time of the gift G was not an heir and would not have inherited if I had died at that moment. Under the UPC, however, if the intent to make an advancement was properly indicated in a contemporaneous writing, G would have to account for the $6,000 advancement previously received. Here the hotchpot estate would now be worth $30,000, C2, C3, and G would each be entitled to a third or $10,000. G's advancement of $6,000 would be deducted and thus G would take $4,000 from the estate, and C2 and C3 would get $10,000 each. If G's advancement in this illustration had been $12,000 or more, however, G would not have participated in the hotchpot because G would not take anything from the estate. G, of course, gets to keep the $12,000.

2. CHARACTERIZATIONS OF PREDEATH TRANSFERS TO AN HEIR

Transfers of assets from one to an heir may be characterized in three different ways: unconditional gift, an advancement, or a loan. The characterization is significant to the post death consequences of the transfer. If the transfer is an unconditional gift, the heir takes the appropriate intestate share without deduction or obligation to return the gift. If an advancement, the heir will have to participate in the hotchpot to take any share from the estate. The advancement will reduce or even eliminate any share from the intestate's estate. No return of the gift is necessary. Although some statutes require a writing, there are no statutes of limitations on advancements.

A loan is an asset of the estate and must be repaid. An heir may be able to set off the loan against the intestate share but if the loan is greater than the share, the heir will have to pay back to the estate the difference. Loans, however, are subject to statutes of limitation, and the heir is usually allowed to raise any defenses available to any creditor.

3. RELEASES AND ASSIGNMENTS OF EXPECTANCIES

a. Releases of Expectancies

A release of an expectancy is an agreement between an expectant heir and the expectant intestate, the person from whom the heir expects to inherit. The agreement releases the expectant heir's inheritance. On the death of the intestate, the heir will not take the normal intestate share. The agreement must be for fair consideration which is said to require enough consideration to support specific performance. Consideration must bear some reasonable relationship to the estimated value of the expectancy relinquished. RESTATEMENT OF PROPERTY § 316 (1940). If the consideration is found to be unfair, the agreement may be treated as an advancement. Releases have been found to bind the expectant heir's descendants if the expectant heir predeceases the intestate. Some courts require a release to be in writing when their law requires advancements to be in writing. ATKINSON, WILLS § 130, p. 726, fn. 5.

b. Assignments of Expectancies

An assignment of an expectancy is an assignment between an expectant heir of a person and a third party. Fair and equitable consideration is required: a gratuitous assignment is void. Consent of the expectant intestate is not necessary. Assignments do not bind the expectant heir's descendants if the expectant heir predeceases the intestate. Thus, the assignee takes the significant risk that the heir will not outlive the intestate. This means the value for the assigned interest is going to be low, which will raise an issue of whether the assignment is supported by fair and equitable consideration. Assignments of expectancies are not desirable financial arrangements and are strictly construed by courts.

B. MISCONDUCT

1. DISQUALIFICATION FOR MISCONDUCT

The disqualification for misconduct concept is a principle of equity that bars a wrongdoer from profiting from the wrongdoing. Generally, personal misconduct is not a basis for disinheritance. For example, only a few states restrict inheritance of a person who deserts his or her family from taking from the spouse or from the children. The typical scenario, however, concerns the rights of an heir or beneficiary to take from a person whom he or she murdered. Most states have either statutes or court decisions dealing with this issue.

Disqualification Statutory Provisions: When a state has a statute that attempts to disqualify a wrongdoer from taking benefits due to the wrongdoing, a significant number of common issues are relevant.

- What constitutes the type of wrongdoing that activates the disqualification, *e.g.*, murder, desertion, adultery?
- What interests and relationships are covered, *e.g.*, intestacy, contractual, fiduciary appointments?
- What is the disposition of property or effect on relationship, *e.g.*, treat wrongdoer as predeceased, revoke appointment?
- Is conviction of the wrongdoing necessary?
- What is the admissibility of conviction in civil preceedings?
- What is the effect of acquittal in civil proceedings?
- If a civil suit is brought, what is the standard of proof?
- How are persons dealing with a murderer affected, *e.g.*, are *bona fide* purchasers protected?
- What is the effect of minority status of the murderer, *e.g.*, does juvenile status for criminal prosecution purposes preclude disqualification?

Most non UPC states leave many of these issues unresolved. The UPC in Section 2–803 attempts to answer many of them.

2. HOMICIDE

a. Typical Scenarios

The two most typical situations where an heir murders a person from whom the murderer will inherit are (1) child murders parent, and (2) spouse murders spouse.

CHART 2–3–1

HOMICIDE SCENARIOS

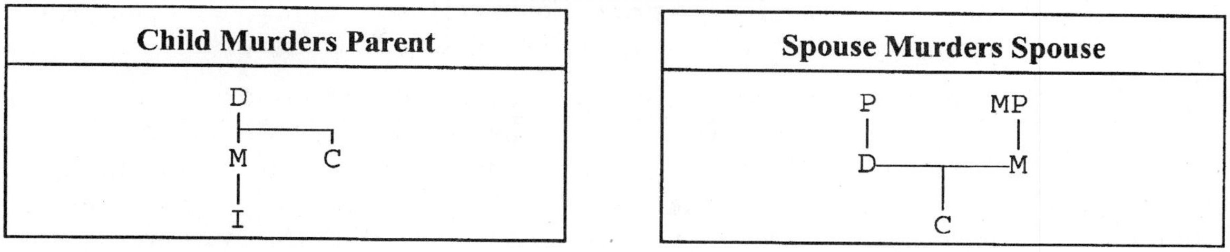

The problem of whether a murderer may derive benefit from (or assume a responsibility due to) the wrongful act applies to a wide range of issues. For example, can the murderer take from the deceased by intestacy, under deceased's will, as beneficiary of insurance contracts on deceased's life, as survivor of survivorship interests with the deceased, or as beneficiary of other contractual interests? In addition, issues arise whether the murderer can serve as executor under deceased's will or trustee of a trust established by deceased. Most states have some legislation concerning some of these matters. Sometimes it is limited, however, to rights in intestacy, testacy and life insurance benefits.

Although a state may have a statute that is not comprehensive in dealing with the consequences of homicide for succession purposes, courts have occasionally found it appropriate to apply judicially imposed preclusion rules. Some courts have used the equitable doctrine of constructive trust. In *Neiman v. Hurff*, 93 A.2d 345 (N.J. 1952), the court held that the murderer has only a life estate in survivorship property and on the murderer's death the property passes according to victim's will. Similarly, the court in *In re Estate of Mahoney's*, 220 A.2d 475 (Vt. 1966) found a constructive trust over the survivorship interest in favor of the victim's heirs. Courts have even applied equity concepts despite statutory provision to the contrary. In *Estate of Karas*, 485 A.2d 1083 (N.J. App. Div. 1984), the court held that although the relevant statute divided survivorship interest equally between victim and murderer, a constructive trust would be imposed on the murderer's half for the benefit of victim's beneficiaries as if the victim had survived.

b. UPC Disqualification Provision

Section 2–803 of the UPC deals solely with disqualification for homicide. It covers all kinds of property interests and relationships including inter vivos transfers, powers of appointment, fiduciary appointments, survivorship interests, life insurance, and, revocable benefits under instruments. All of these benefits are treated as having been revoked as far as they benefit the murderer.

(1) Felonious and intentional killing: Under the UPC, the wrongdoing that activates the provisions is the felonious and intentional killing of another person. Whereas a criminal conviction equals conclusive evidence of wrongdoing, acquittal is not binding because a civil action concerning the nature and perpetrator of the crime may take place under a preponderance standard of proof. Some statutes require conviction before the statutory restriction on succession takes effect.

(2) Disposition of property or effect on relationship: The murderer forfeits all statutory benefits conferred on the murderer by the UPC in regard to a decedent's estate. UPC § 2–803(b). This includes any intestate share, elective share, pretermitted spouse or heir share, or family protection. The provision also revokes all benefits conferred on the murderer by the terms of any and all revocable governing instruments executed by the decedent. UPC § 2–803(c)(1). It applies to all benefits bestowed in wills, trusts, contractual agreements, multiple-party accounts, and TOD security registrations. The murderer is treated as if he or she disclaimed or predeceased the victim depending on the issue.

(3) Persons who deal with murderer. Protection for bona fide purchasers and other unknowing third persons who deal with the murderer recognizes that there may be a long delay in instituting proceedings accusing a person of murdering another and even after institution of the case, the result may be in doubt for a long period of time. In addition to the notice requirement to bind purchasers of property sold by a surviving joint tenant with right of survivorship, the UPC includes provisions protecting other payors, bona fide purchasers and other third persons who deal with the murderer prior to notice of the claim against the murderer. UPC § 2–803(d), (h), and (i).

C. TERMINATION OF MARITAL STATUS

1. IMPORTANCE OF MARITAL STATUS

A person's marital status is very important in determining inheritance rights and responsibilities. These rights and responsibilities include, for example, distribution in intestacy, elective share rights, revocation of wills, family protection rights, priority for appointment as personal representative, and appointment of a guardian for an incapacitated person. *See* UPC § 2–802(b). Generally, the requirements for marriage depend on the law of domestic relations. *See* Part 2.II.F.

2. NONSPOUSAL STATUS

A person is not a surviving spouse of the decedent if the person and the decedent have been divorced or their marriage annulled. *See* UPC § 2–802(a). This rule does not apply, of course, if they remarry and are married on the date of the decedent's death. It also does not apply to a decree of separation that does not terminate the husband-wife status.

Notwithstanding the absence of a final divorce or annulment, unless a contrary intent appears on the agreement, a complete property settlement entered into after or in anticipation of separation or divorce operates as a disclaimer of the spouse's elective share, family protections, rights under intestate succession and provisions in wills executed before the property settlement. *See* UPC § 2–213.

3. DEFINITION OF DIVORCE

Sometimes the status of the divorce is in question. Under UPC Section 2–802(b)(1)-(3), in addition to a spouse who has obtained a valid divorce or an annulment, the term "surviving spouse" also does not include:

- A person who obtained or consented to a final decree of divorce or of annulment even though the decree is not valid in the UPC state, unless that person has subsequently remarried the decedent, or subsequently lived together as husband and wife. UPC § 2–802(b)(1).

- A person who participated in a marriage ceremony with a third person following a valid or invalid decree of divorce or annulment. UPC § 2–802(b)(2).
- A person who participated as a party to a valid proceeding which terminated all marital property rights. UPC § 2–802(b)(3).

These three situations are based on the concept of estoppel. In each one, the surviving person has either consented, participated in, sought or completed some volitional act other than the "divorce" that causes the marital relationship to be terminated. Because the rights of a surviving spouse under the UPC are substantial, it is very important that only those who legally and equitably should be considered a surviving spouse are able to take these benefits.

D. DISCLAIMER

1. DISCLAIMER DEFINITION

A disclaimer (also called a renunciation) is a refusal to accept a donative transfer. It is an important estate planning device. A disclaimer is usually made to avoid some burden the disclaimant did not want to assume or cause. These burdens include, for example, the avoidance of taxes, creditors, spendthrift provisions, and sometimes spousal protections.

2. COMMON LAW DISCLAIMERS

At common law a person could not disclaim an interest passing by intestacy, but could disclaim an interest passing by will. Today, disclaimer statutes in most states define the consequences and procedures for an effective disclaimer. Despite general recognition for tax avoidance purposes, disclaimers still receive less than universal acceptance. For example, in *Molloy v. Bane*, 631 N.Y.S.2d 910 (App. Div. 1995) a disclaimer of an intestate share of a daughter's estate, which was potentially valuable because of the possibility of a wrongful death suit, justified termination of the disclaimant's Medicaid benefits for failure to pursue available resources as required by New York regulations.

3. DISCLAIMER STATUTES

Disclaimer statutes typically cover common ground. They deal specifically with the time within which a disclaimer must be made, the formality for executing one, the procedure necessary to follow, the effect of the disclaimer, and what constitutes waiver of the disclaimer privilege.

4. DISCLAIMERS UNDER THE UPC

Section 2–801 of the UPC is a comprehensive disclaimer provision. The UPC permits, under defined procedures, all persons to whom property devolves by whatever means to disclaim their interest in the property. UPC § 2–801(a). The right to disclaim exists regardless whether the transfer instrument permits disclaimers and even if the transfer instrument restricts transfers or prohibits disclaimer or both. The disclaimer may be made either personally by any competent person, or by persons who represent the disclaimant. A representative of a person includes not only a conservator for a disabled person but also a guardian for a minor or incapacitated person, an agent under a durable power of attorney and a decedent's personal representatives. A disclaimer may be made for an incapacitated or protected person by that person's representative if made according to applicable procedures for protected persons.

Disclaimer Formality: A valid disclaimer may be made only by a written instrument that describes the property or interest disclaimed, declares the fact and extent of the disclaimer and is signed by the person disclaiming or that person's proper representative. UPC § 2–801(c).

Notice of Disclaimer: If the interest concerns devolution at death, the necessary writing must be filed in the court where the deceased owner's or deceased donee of the power's estate is being administered or where it could have been administered if none has been commenced. UPC § 2–801(b)(2). A copy of the disclaimer must also be delivered or mailed by registered or certified mail to any personal representative or other fiduciary of the decedent or donee. If the interest concerns devolution under a nontestamentary instrument or contract, the necessary writing must be delivered in person or by certified mail to the person holding legal title or possessing the interest disclaimed. Disclaimers of real property interests may also be recorded in the office where deeds are recorded in the county where the real estate is situated. UPC § 2–801(b)(4).

Timing for Disclaimer: The timing of the disclaimer is also crucial. If the interest concerns devolution at death, the UPC requires that the disclaiming instrument must be filed not later than nine months after the death of the decedent or the donee of the power when a present interest is disclaimed or not later than nine months after the event determining the taker of the property or interest is finally ascertained and that interest is indefeasibly vested when a future interest is disclaimed. UPC § 2–801(b)(1)–(2).

Waiver of Disclaimer Capability: Even if the time periods have not run, certain specified actions by the person attempting to disclaim will bar the right to disclaim. UPC § 2–801(e). Specifically, a person is barred from disclaiming if the person: (1) used the property or interest in any commercial manner such as selling or pledging it; (2) waived the right to disclaim in writing; (3) accepted the property or interest or benefits from it; or (4) had the property sold under a judicial sale before the disclaimer becomes effective. Significantly, written waivers of the right to disclaim bind the persons waiving and all persons claiming through or under them. UPC § 2–801(d)(3).

Effect of Disclaiming: Unless the decedent or the donee has properly indicated otherwise, the disclaimed interest, which devolves by will, by exercise of a power in a will, or by intestacy, passes as if the disclaimant had predeceased the decedent or donee. UPC § 2–801(d)(1). A similar rule applies to interests devolving by nontestamentary instruments and contracts except the interest devolves as if the disclaimant had predeceased the effective date of the instrument or contract. UPC § 2–801(d)(2). An exception to this approach applies where the persons who take the disclaimant's interest would share in that interest by representation or other rule if the disclaimant had failed to survive the decedent. In order to prevent manipulation of the size of shares passing to representatives, the disclaimant's actual interest passes by representation to the representative takers.

Illustration 2: If D died intestate survived by G1 and G2, grandchildren of A and B who are D's two predeceased children, and by C, a surviving child who has two surviving grandchildren, G3 and G4, C's disclaimer of C's ⅓ intestate share could not be increased effectively to a total of ⅓ of the estate to G3 and G4 by way of the per capita at each generation rule that would treat all grandchildren equally had no children survived. In this situation, C's ⅓ share would pass equally to G3 and G4. This rule also protects C's ⅓ share for G3 and G4 if A and B had had a total of more than four children.

5. FEDERAL DISCLAIMER STATUTE

Because of the checker-board coverage of disclaimers by states, Congress enacted a federal disclaimer law that must be followed for tax avoidance purposes. I.R.C. § 2518. If disclaimers are being used for estate and gift savings purposes, disclaimants must scrupulously obey the requirements of I.R.C. Section 2518 as well as state law. Significant differences exist concerning the timing of disclaimers particularly in the disclaiming of future interests. *See* S. Alan Medlin, *An Examination of Disclaimers Under UPC Section 2–801,* 55 Alb. L. Rev. 1233 (1992)

In outline terms Section 2518 provides that a disclaimer is effective for estate and gift tax purposes if (1) disclaimant disclaims in a writing, (2) the writing is received by the transferor within nine months after the later of creation day, or the day disclaimant reaches 21, (3) the disclaimant has not accepted any interest or benefit therefrom and (5) the interest passes without directions to decedent's spouse, or to nondisclaimant.

E. ALIENSHIP

During the 1940s and '50s many states enacted reciprocity statutes. These statutes provided that alien persons may inherit in the state only if citizens of the state can inherit from a citizen of the alien's nation. They were called "Iron–Curtain" acts since their consequences were to deny inheritance to citizens of communist countries that would not permit local citizens to inherit. The validity of these status is in doubt today.

The Supreme Court struck down such a statute as unconstitutional because it constituted a state interfering with international affairs that is a federal power. *See Zschernig v. Miller*, 389 U.S. 429 (1968). Most states and UPC Section 2–111 eliminate alienship as a status issue for intestate succession

F. NEGATIVE WILLS

1. DISINHERITANCE BY FIAT

The common law generally stated that one could not disinherit an heir by fiat. ATKINSON, WILLS § 36, at p. 145. Consequently, if a person executed a will that disinherited the person's heir but for whatever reason that will did not pass all of decedent's property, the heir would still be able to take the intestate property.

Illustration 3: T's will states "I give all my property to X. I intentionally disinherit my son C and do not want my son to take anything from this estate" C would be disinherited if X is capable of taking at T's death. But if X died prior to T and did not leave someone who could take in his or her place according to the law of lapse or antilapse, C would take all the estate passing by intestacy

2. NEGATIVE WILL PROVISIONS

The UPC includes a provision recognizing what might be considered the negative will as far as intestacy is concerned. It provides that if a decedent has excluded or limited the right of an heir to succeed to that person's intestate property, the exclusion or limit is binding even if the decedent dies intestate. For example, using the above example, C would not take even if X's devise lapsed. The share of the disinherited heir passes as if the heir disclaimed the interest. UPC § 2–101(b). Mere omission from the will would not be considered the expressed disinheritance required under this section. On the other hand, a will that states that an heir is disinherited or that an heir shall only receive a certain amount from the estate and no more, would constitute the type of disinheritance for which this section would operate. As mentioned, the disinherited heir's share in intestacy passes as if that heir had disclaimed the interest. This means that the disinherited heir's descendants may take by representation but only the share the heir would have received. UPC § 2–101, Comment.

G. REVIEW QUESTIONS

1. What is an irrevocable inter vivos gift of money or property, real or personal, to a child by a parent that enables the child to anticipate the child's inheritance from the parent to the extent of the gifts called?

2. At common law, a gift would be treated as an advancement if the donor died totally or partially intestate. True or False?

3. An assignment of an expectancy is an assignment between an expectant heir of a person and a third party. True or False?

4. Personal misconduct is a basis for disinheritance. True or False?

5. A person is not a surviving spouse of the decedent if the person and the decedent have been divorced or their marriage annulled. What is this status called?

6. What does the negative will provision in the UPC provide?

PART THREE

TESTAMENT TRANSFERS

*

I

EXECUTION OF WILLS

Analysis

- 5. *Testator's Acknowledgment*
- 6. *Witnessing*
    - a. *General Witnessing Requirements*
    - b. *Line of Sight Test*
    - c. *"Conscious Presence" Test*
    - d. *Witness Competency*
    - e. *Interested Witness Rule*
    - f. *Purging Statutes*
- 7. *Attestation Clauses and Procedures for Execution*
- 8. *Self–Proved Wills:*
- 9. *Recommended Method of Executing a Will*

C. *Unattested Wills*
- 1. *Holographic Wills*
- 2. *Nuncupative Wills*

D. *Special Wills*
- 1. *Foreign and International Wills*
    - a. *Foreign Wills*
    - b. *International Wills*
- 2. *Statutory Wills*

E. *Review Questions*

A. WILL FORMALITY OVERVIEW

1. WILL DEFINITION AND CHARACTERISTICS

A *will* or *testament* disposes of property owned at death (or acquired by the decedent's estate after death). To be valid, the maker must be competent, must be acting voluntarily, and must make the will in accordance with procedures set forth by statute.

A *codicil* is a will with a special purpose. Normally the special purpose is to amend a primary will. Even if there is a primary will, the codicil must be properly executed according to a valid will execution procedure. Because it must be executed as a will, it may be able to stand on its own if the "primary" will is not effective.

The power to make wills is limited. Because of capacity requirements, persons (minors) who have not attained the set statutory age required for will execution and persons who lack testamentary capacity cannot execute valid wills. The power to execute a will is a nondelegatable power. A will remains ambulatory and revocable during the testator's lifetime.

Many have written about the merits, demerits and proper utility for formalities. *See, e.g.*, Ashbel G. Gulliver & Catherine J. Tilson, *Classification of Gratuitous Transfers*, 51 YALE L.J. 1 (1941). Identified purposes for formalities include protective, evidentiary, ritual, channeling, and administrative functions. Thus formalities can provide (1) protection for the testator, (2) reliable proof and evidence, (3) an environment that accentuates finality of intent and execution, (4) assurance that the document will receive the anticipated legal recognition, and (5) administrative judicial efficiency. Considering the solemnness, importance, and finality of a will, it has been common for states to set out elaborate formalities necessary to be followed in order to satisfy and to produce a recognizable and valid will. The dilemma created by legal formalities is that failure to satisfy a crucial formality may cause the instrument to fail and thus cause an intent denying rather than intent enforcing result.

2. COMPLIANCE STANDARDS

a. General Requirements

Courts have held that wills need no more formalities than the applicable statute requires. *See, e.g., Lemayne v. Stanley*, 3 Lev. 1 (1691); *but cf. Estate of McKellar*, 380 So. 2d 1273 (Miss. 1980). In addition, courts do not invalidate a will because it was executed with greater formalities than the statute requires. Finally, any type of will recognized by an applicable statute validates the will.

Each act or condition required by a wills statute may be important, however. One must dissect the statutory requirements of the applicable wills statute.

Each "action" word may have importance. There are sufficient differences between the many wills statutes applicable in this country that reliance on generalizations concerning proper will execution requirements must be exercised with caution.

Because the validity or invalidity of an instrument such as a will is so important to the distribution of an estate, the determination of validity has been a highly litigated issue. Opponents of wills are likely to offer any reason to deny probate. Consequently, the formalities of the execution statute have been a fertile breeding ground for these arguments. Courts that face this litigation are put in a policy bind. On the one hand, the court is conscious and respectful of legislative intent as expressed in the appropriate wills statute. If the legislature has set out a particular formality to follow, it is not for the court to ignore. On the other hand, the invalidation of a will because of a failure on the part of the testator to conform to a technical formality may appear extremely picayune and callous when the result is contrary to the clearly expressed and finalized intent of the testator.

b. Strict Compliance

Generally, courts have followed the concept of strict compliance, *i.e.*, an instrument must satisfy all the formalities set out in the statute. *See* 2 William J. Bowe & Douglas H. Parker, Page on the Law of Wills § 19.4. "Whether the courts profess to follow the harsher rule, or whether they profess to follow the milder rule, they generally agree on the result which they reach. The testator must perform each of the acts which is required by the statute in order to execute a valid will; and the courts rarely require more." Id. at 68.

c. Reasonable Compliance

Even when strict compliance is the court's philosophy, some courts have been willing to ignore or generously interpret some incidental formalities in the statutes. *See, e.g., In re Demaris' Estate*, 110 P.2d 571 (Or. 1941), where the court adopted the "conscious presence" test to satisfy the requirement that the witnesses must sign in the testator's presence. In another example, a statute might require the testator to "request" the witnesses to witness the will. The word "request" may be liberally interpreted to mean the circumstances must indicate that the testator wanted the witnesses to witness the will. The testator need not have actually verbally requested the witnesses to do so. *See, e.g., Hollingsworth v. Hollingsworth*, 401 S.W.2d 555 (Ark. 1966). This might be referred to as a reasonable compliance standard for these incidental formalities.

A statutory formality that is described by a term that has more than one plausible meaning–such as the word "presence" or the word "request"–is more likely to receive a reasonable construction than a formality that has only one plausible meaning–such as a requirement that a will be witnessed by "two" witnesses.

d. Substantial Compliance

The substantial compliance standard is a judicially developed approach to the will execution problems. It permits probate of an otherwise defectively executed will if the proponents prove that the document adequately expresses the decedent's testamentary intent, and the execution procedure actually completed sufficiently approximates the execution requirements and purposes of the relevant statute of wills. Rather than an afterthought, the doctrine is a positive approach to execution issues. *Cf. In re Ranney*, 589 A.2d 1339 (N.J. 1991) (allowing relief, although the court applied a literal interpretation to its wills act requirements under a separate court-developed substantial compliance doctrine that permits formal probate of a document despite execution deficiencies if clear and convincing evidence shows substantial compliance with the statutory requirements).

e. Dispensing Powers

The UPC contains a dispensing power provision. Its provision permits a court to dispense with one or more statutory formalities even if they have not been followed, so long as the proponents of the document or writing establish by clear and convincing evidence that the testator intended the document to constitute the decedent's will or other will-related instructions. UPC § 2–503. The provision is unspecific as to which formalities may be dispensed with. With the exception that there must be a document or a writing added upon a document, all other formalities are subject to the dispensing remedy.

f. Harmless Error Rule

The RESTATEMENT (THIRD) OF PROPERTY expressly adopts a harmless error rule for will execution formalities. Adopting the philosophy that will formalities are meant to facilitate intent-serving purpose, not to be ends in themselves, the Restatement provides that "A harmless error in executing a will may be excused if the proponent establishes by clear and convincing evidence that the decedent adopted the document as his or her will." RESTATEMENT (THIRD) OF PROPERTY: WILLS AND OTHER DONATIVE TRANSFERS § 3.3 (1999). The harmless error rules is based on the principle that mistake in execution should not defeat intention nor work unjust enrichment. The question is whether an execution defect was harmless in relation to the purpose of the statutory formalities, not in relation to an isolated individual statutory formality. In evaluating the purposes of all of the execution formalities, the Restatement recognizes "a hierarchy" among the formalities. While a writing is essential and excusing testator's signature is difficult but not insuperable, excusing attestation defects may be an easy matter. *See* RESTATEMENT (THIRD) OF PROPERTY: WILLS AND OTHER DONATIVE TRANSFERS § 3.3 cmt. b (1999).

3. EVOLUTION OF WILLS ACTS

For the three hundred year-period following the Norman Conquest, only personal property was disposable by will. Testamentary disposition of real property was later permitted under the first English Statute of Wills, enacted in 1540. This statute made land devisable "by last will and testament in writing," but required no signature or other formalities.

a. Statute of Frauds

The Statute of Frauds, enacted in 1677, imposed stringent formalities upon the testamentary disposition of land. It required that wills of realty be in writing, signed by testator and attested and subscribed by three or more witnesses.

Statute of Frauds, 1677, 29 Car.2, c.3, Sec.5.

[A]ll devises and bequests of any lands or tenements shall be in writing and signed by the party so devising the same or by some other person in his presence and by his express directions and shall be attested and subscribed in the presence of the said devisor by three or four credible witnesses or else they shall be utterly void and of none effect.

b. Wills Act of 1837

The Wills Act of 1837 brought uniform formality to the testamentary disposition of both realty and personalty. This Act required that a will be in writing, that the testator sign it at the end and that it be witnessed by two or more witnesses who must sign in the presence of the testator.

Wills Act, 1837, 7 Wm. 4 & 1 Vict. c.26, Sec. 9.

[N]o will shall be valid unless it shall be in writing and executed in manner hereinafter mentioned; (that is to say,) it shall be signed at the foot or end thereof by the testator, or by some other person in his presence and by his direction and such signature shall be made or acknowledged by the testator in the presence of two or more witnesses present at the same time, and such witnesses shall attest and subscribe the will in the presence of the testator, but no form of attestation shall be necessary.

c. Comparison of Wills Acts

Under the Statute of Frauds, there was no requirement that the testator sign the will in any specific place; there was a requirement of three witnesses, although each could attest separately. In contrast, the Wills Act required a signature "at the foot or end" of the will and attestation by two witnesses, both of whom had to be present when the will was signed or acknowledged by the testator.

4. CURRENT WILLS ACTS

From these statutes, the modern law of wills execution developed. Some states followed the Statute of Frauds approach, whereas others followed the Statute of Wills.

Notwithstanding some modernization of wills statutes, our current wills statutes generally retain the same basic formalities: the will must be in writing, the testator must sign it, and the will must be signed by a specified number of attesting witnesses. Details concerning attestation vary from state to state. In addition, many states recognize certain types of unattested wills.

The following briefly describe the several types of wills common in most American jurisdictions.

- Attested Will: This is the standard will and it generally requires a writing, signature of the testator, and several attesting witnesses.
- Holographic Will: Holographic wills are wills that are handwritten and signed by the testator. They do not require attesting witnesses.
- Nuncupative Will: Nuncupative wills are oral wills announced under specified conditions as set out by the statute.
- Self-proved Will: A self-proved will is one that is executed as an attested will but which includes a notarized affidavit.
- Foreign Will: Most, if not all, states recognize that a written will executed under the laws of other states or jurisdictions that have relevant contacts with the will or testator are valid in the local state whether or not the formalities of the local will's statutes are satisfied. *See infra.* Part 3.I.D.3.
- International Will: The international will is a will executed under special execution procedures that make the will valid in all jurisdictions that join an international convention or that enact the appropriate act. The latter procedure is incorporated in Uniform International Wills Act (Hereinafter referred to as the International Wills Act). UPC §§ 10–1001 through–1010. *See infra.* Part 3.I.D.3.

5. UPC WILLS

The UPC adopts a comprehensive scheme for will execution. First, four different types of wills are recognized and their actual individual formalities have been pared down to minimum levels. Most executed instruments will satisfy one or more of the types of formalities. Second, the UPC provides an escape device in that the court is accorded a dispensing authority for formalities not followed so long as the standard of proof is met. This covers the occasional case where clear unfairness occurs if the will is not recognized. Third, the UPC provides a model form to follow. This is the self-proved will and it has its own attributes and advantages if proper practice follows its formalities to the letter.

The UPC recognizes four separate and alternative will execution techniques. Successful satisfaction of any one of these techniques produces a probatable will in the UPC state. The four types of wills include the ordinary witnessed will [UPC § 2–502(a)], the holographic or handwritten will [UPC § 2–502(b)], the foreign will [UPC § 2–506], and the international will [UPC Art. II, Pt. 10, UNIFORM INTERNATIONAL WILLS ACT]. The UPC also includes a special procedure for executing a fifth kind of will called the self-proved will, which although not essential for basic validity is useful to follow for purposes of easing proof of execution requirements in contested will cases. UPC § 2–504. Significantly, the UPC does not include recognized procedures for nuncupative or other types of special wills.

B. THE FORMAL REQUIREMENTS OF ATTESTED WILLS

1. TESTAMENTARY CAPACITY

A testator must be an adult to execute a valid will. Adulthood status is a chronologically determined age and usually is set at 18 years. Testator must also be of sound mind at time of execution. *See infra.* Part 3.IV.C.4. All types of wills require proper testamentary capacity.

2. TESTAMENTARY INTENT

The testator must have testamentary intent (animus testandi) to have a valid will. Thus, the testator must intend that the instrument presently operate as his or her last will. Testamentary intent must exist when the testator signed the instrument or when the last act of execution was performed. Because most wills state that they are wills, ordinarily testamentary intent is presumed. There need not be any words of art, however. Any instrument may be a will if there is testamentary intent. When testamentary intent is a question, courts look first to the face of the instrument. If that does not provide the answer, the court's sources of intent will depend on the admissibility of relevant evidence. *See* Part 3.IV.C.3.

3. REQUIREMENT OF A WRITING

The standard requirement for an attested will is that it be in writing. The "writing" requirement is satisfied by inscription on a medium that allows the markings to be detected. A tape recording has been denied probate in a reported case. *Estate of Reed*, 672 P.2d 829 (Wyo. 1983) (Not a valid holographic will). On the other hand under Federal Rules of Evidence recordings are treated as writings. Fed. R. Evid. 1001

4. TESTATOR'S SIGNATURE

Most testators sign their normal signature, but any visible mark can constitute a testator's signature as long as the testator (1) intends it to be a signature and (2) completes all the writing the testator intended to complete.

a. Proxy Signatures

Proxy signatures are usually permitted as well. Under the UPC, the other person, who is the proxy, must be in the testator's "conscious" presence and must sign at testator's "direction."

A distinction must be made when the testator fixes a mark (an "X") upon the will and then someone writes testator's name along side at a later time. Here, the "X" is regarded as the personal signature of the testator rather than the testator's name that was added for purposes of identification.

b. Sign at the End Requirement

A requirement under the Wills Act type of statute and still under the statutes of a few states is that the will must be signed at the end. Most courts say the logical end. Clauses that are merely formal in nature do not invalidate a will although they may appear after the testator's signature, *e.g.*, date, compensation of the executor, or the attestation clause. Another approach to the requirement is to validate the will when it is not signed at the end if the only clauses that follow the signature are nondispositive provisions. *Clark v. National Bank of Commerce*, 802 S.W.2d 452 (Ark 1991).

Matter of Winters, 98 N.Y.S.2d 312 (N.Y. App. Div. 1950), emphasizes the serious problem that can occur with the "signing at end" requirement. In that case the court held the entire will invalid because the clause that appointed the executor appeared after the signature. The New York statute was later amended to invalidate only clauses following the signature unless the will is incomprehensible without the post-signature clauses.

The effect of provisions that appear after the signature may depend on timing. If added before signing, and intended to be part of the will (integrated and not surplusage), the will may be void as not signed at the end. If clause was added after signing, however, only the clause is void.

c. Sign Anywhere Requirement

Under the UPC and many other will statutes, there is no required place for testator's signature. The will need only be signed—top, bottom or margin. There must be evidence that the testator intended it to be his or her signature and had testamentary intent. Thus, when the signature appears in an unusual place of the instrument, there may be an evidence problem in proving a will was intended.

A problem may arise where the testator signed the will in the exordium, *i.e.*, "I, S. Testator, hereby make my last will." The problems are of testamentary intent and finality. In *Estate of McKellar,* 380 So.2d 1273 (Miss. 1980), the Mississippi Supreme Court affirmed the holding that testator's purported will was not properly executed where testator's signature only appeared in the exordium on page one of a five page document, none of three witnesses to instrument stated that they saw or read or heard of the entire document before signing, and none of witnesses either saw testator affix her signature on document or heard her acknowledge that she had previously or at any time signed or affixed her signature to the document. In effect the Court added many requirements that the statute did not require.

5. TESTATOR'S ACKNOWLEDGMENT

Statutory requirements vary regarding authentication of the signing by the testator. Some require the testator to sign in the presence of the witnesses. Some permit the testator to acknowledge either the signature (this may require that the witnesses see it, too) or that testator has signed the will. Others require signing or acknowledgment in the presence of all of the witnesses at the same time. A few require publication which requires the testator to declare to the witnesses that the instrument is the testator's will.

Acknowledgment under the UPC Section 2–502(a)(3) may be satisfied if the testator either signs in the witnesses presence, or acknowledges the signature, or acknowledges the will.

6. WITNESSING

a. General Witnessing Requirements

Attested wills require that they be witnessed.

Except for wills in Pennsylvania [*see Estate of Dawson*, 120 A. 828 (Pa. 1923)], the witnesses are required to sign the will. The same problems concerning the location for the signatures is applicable to the witnesses signatures as to the testator's signature. *See infra.* Part 3.I.B.2.

b. Line of Sight Test

Generally, the witnesses must sign in the presence of the testator. Litigation has developed over the meaning of presence. The predominant interpretation follows the line of sight test, *i.e.,* at the time of execution the testator, if the testator had looked, must have been able to see the witness sign the will whether or not the testator actual sees the witness sign. *In re Beggan's Will,* 59 A. 874 (N.J. Prerog. Ct. 1905). Although this test is generous when the testator and the witnesses are in the same room, it does not validate wills where the testator was in another room that is in close proximity to the room in which the witnesses signed.

c. "Conscious Presence" Test

The "conscious presence" test has been recognized by some courts to deal with the latter problem. In applying this doctrine, the Court in *Cunningham v. Cunningham,* 83 N.W. 58 (Minn. 1900), stated:

The signing was within the sound of the testator's voice; he knew what was being done; the act occupied not more than two minutes; the witnesses returned at once to the testator; their signatures were pointed out to him; he took the instrument into his own hands, looked it over, and pronounced it satisfactory. The whole affair, from the time he signed the will himself down to and including his expression of approval, was a single and entire transaction; and no narrow construction of this statute, even if it has met the approval of the courts, should be allowed to stand in the way of right and justice, or be permitted to defeat a testator's disposition of his own property.

Although the UPC does not require the witnesses to sign in testator's presence, a witness must sign within a "reasonable time after" attestation or acknowledgment. UPC § 2–502(a)(3). Generally, the courts have refused to allow witnesses to sign after the death of the testator. *Estate of Royal v. Royal*, 826 P.2d 1236 (Colo. 1992).

Wills statutes that follow the Wills Act of 1837 require that the witnesses not only sign in the testator's presence but also in the presence of each other.

d. Witness Competency

States generally require witnesses to be "credible" or "competent." Occasionally, issues of the competency of a witness to the will arises, *e.g.*, mental deficiency, drug abuse, age. There has been a debate whether this issue is one of evidence or a substantive issue of wills execution. Most states have held it to be the latter with a tinge of evidence rules and concepts being applied. Some states require will witnesses to be of a certain age, *e.g.*, 18. *See* ARK. CODE ANN. § 28–25–102 (1987).

e. Interested Witness Rule

At common law a will was invalid if a necessary witness was interested, which meant the witness takes a *direct pecuniary benefit* by the terms of the will. At common law even the decedent's spouse was not a competent witness—unity of legal identity. This rule is probably not followed today but the statutory law would apply. Evidence rules have abolished all the old prohibitions, but most states have special competence requirements for witnesses of wills.

Whether a witness is an "interested" witness or not is determined at the time of execution. Subsequent changes do not affect the will. Becoming a beneficiary after execution will not raise the interested question. On the other hand, disclaiming of the benefit after death does not remove the interest. *Estate of Parsons*, 163 Cal. Rptr. 70 (Ct. App. 1980).

f. Purging Statutes

In what are called "purging statutes," most states modified the common law rule by validating the will but by removing the witness' interest. If a necessary witness takes a *direct pecuniary benefit* by the terms of the will, the witness may take the lesser of the devise or other inheritable interest, *e.g.*, intestate interest or devise in another prior valid but revoked will. Many cases discuss what constitutes an interest under this rule. For example, there is a split of authority whether a beneficiary's spouse is an interested witness.

If the will gave a necessary witness a devise of $1,000, but the witness would have inherited $500 had the testator died intestate, the will is valid but the witness may take no more than the $500 intestate share. On the other hand, if the will gave a necessary witness a devise of $500, but the witness would have inherited $1,000 had the testator died intestate, the will is valid but the witness may still only take the $500 devise under the will.

The major problems with both the common law and the purging statute rules are that they defeat intent without otherwise inspecting the real circumstances and they constitute an undesirable backdoor attack of undue influence which avoids ordinary burden of proof problem faced by will contestants. In addition, neither rule is effective because each is easily avoided by anyone bent on undue influence. The most prevalent effects of purging rules are to deny testator's intent, harm innocent devisee/witnesses, and increase litigation

UPC Section 2–505(b) abolishes the interested witness restriction and puts the issue in a more appropriate situation where contest is in order. It also adopts the evidence rule for witnesses.

7. ATTESTATION CLAUSES AND PROCEDURES FOR EXECUTION

An attestation clause is a clause, usually at the end of a will, which recites that the proper execution processes were followed and that the witnesses certify that the instrument has been executed in their presence. There are several benefits of using an attestation clause in a will. First, because the clause usually recites all of the required formalities, it may aid in the establishment of the will at probate or contest. Second, some state rules provide that the clause is prima facie evidence of the facts which it contains. Third, it can help the unsure witness remember the witnessing better. Finally, it also offers a valuable and forceful form of impeachment if a witness offers testimony against the will.

8. SELF-PROVED WILLS

The UPC and many other states provide for a special will called the "self-proved will." UPC § 2–504. The execution requirement is similar to the procedure for an ordinary witnessed will but includes a notarized affidavit executed by the testator and the witnesses.

UPC Self-proved Will Provision: Under the UPC self-proved will provision, two alternative affidavits are included. Both types of affidavits describe the formalities and facts that were followed and observed in execution and require the will to be notarized. The first type of affidavit form permits the self-proved will affidavit to be a part of the will itself and actually constitutes the execution thereof. UPC § 2–504(a). In using this form, the testator and the witnesses execute the affidavit and the will simultaneously. UPC § 2–504, Comment. The second affidavit form is to be executed separately from and subsequently to the execution of the ordinary witnessed will. UPC § 2–504(b). When using this form, the testator and the witnesses execute the will separately and then subsequently in a separate or continuous proceeding complete and sign the affidavit.

Under the UPC the effect of executing a self-proved will is not substantial. A self-proved will is subject to the same treatment as any other validly executed will. Its principal distinguishing features are to permit the will to be admitted to probate in a formal testacy proceeding without the necessity of testimony of one of the subscribing witnesses. UPC § 3–406(a). In addition, it provides that the signature requirements are conclusively presumed; other execution requirements are rebuttably presumed. UPC § 3–406(a). It still is subject to contest for grounds such as revocation, undue influence, lack of testamentary capacity, fraud and even forgery. UPC § 3–406, Comment. Notwithstanding its limited significance, use of one or the other of these forms should become standard practice for attorneys who draft and supervise the execution of wills.

In addition to the affidavit, the execution process for a self-proved requires that three additional execution formalities be followed which are not required for the ordinary witnessed will:

- The testator must declare to the witnesses that the will is testator's last will;
- The witnesses must sign as witness to testator's will; and
- The witnesses must sign in the testator's presence and hearing.

Additional formalities increase the risks that they will not be followed. This may cause a will to be found to be invalid. For example, it has been held that where the testator signs the will only in the place reserved for the affidavit, the will neither meets the requirements of the self-proved will or those required for an ordinary witnessed will. *Orrell v. Cochran*, 695 S.W.2d 552 (Tex. 1985). Other courts have overlooked such errors and have probated the wills. *See Will of Ranney,* 589 A.2d 1339 (N.J. 1991). In *Ranney*, the Supreme Court of New Jersey held that although the testator signed only in the place reserved for the affidavit, the will could be admitted to probate if execution substantially complied with the statutory requirements. It also held that this signature did not literally satisfy the statutory requirement that at least two persons must witness either the signing or testator's acknowledgment of signature or of will itself.

Section 2–204(c) of the UPC corrects this problem by providing "A signature affixed to a self-proving affidavit attached to a will is considered a signature affixed to the will, if necessary to prove the will's due execution."

9. RECOMMENDED METHOD OF EXECUTING A WILL

Because superfluous formalities are not objectionable, it is common to execute a will with extra formalities. Extra formalities may assist in getting a will probated in other states that have different formalities than the state where the will is executed. When supervising the execution of a will, the attorney should consider observing the following procedures:

- Before any execution process occurs the attorney should be sure that the testator has examined the will in its entirety and understands its terms;

- The pages of the will should be firmly fastened together;
- Only one will should be executed and several copies should be made after execution;
- The proper sequence in execution should be followed: the testator should sign, then the witnesses should sign immediately in order;
- Two adult persons who are younger and who know the testator but are not devisees of the will should be used as witnesses;
- The execution process should be made a serious ceremony in order that the witnesses will remember the event. (For example, ask the testator to read aloud the testimonium before signing: then ask the first witness to read aloud the attestation clause or affidavit, whichever is used);
- If the will is "self-proved," make sure the proper execution procedures are followed and the necessary affidavit properly executed (It helps to be able to have a notary available at the time of execution so that the affidavit can be executed immediately);
- Put the executed will in a safe place: in the testator's safety-deposit box.

C. UNATTESTED WILLS

1. HOLOGRAPHIC WILLS

A holographic will is an unattested will written and signed in the handwriting of the testator. Its recognition is solely by statute. Half of the states permit, half do not. [But note the conflict of laws statutes, *see* UPC § 2–506]. Some statutes require that the will be "entirely" handwritten. UPC Section 2–502(b) only requires that "material portions of the document be in the testator's handwriting."

When nonholgraphic material appears on the face of the will, two basic theories of interpretations have developed concerning this requirement. One theory is called the intent theory. It is based upon whether the testator intended that the matter be a part of his will, and if not, the will is valid. The second theory, called the surplusage theory, is based upon whether there is enough remaining in the testator's hand to give the will effect and if there is, then the nonholographic parts will be held to be surplusage. These interpretations concern a court attitude toward extrinsic evidence and the part it plays in will determination.

All holographic will statutes require that the will be signed by testator: Some say at the end of the will. Holographic wills must, of course be made with testamentary intent. Sometimes this has been a problem when the testator's signature does not appear at the end but, for example, is only found in the exordium or in the opening line of will. Courts have said this document may lack finality and testamentary intent. Some courts have even said that extrinsic evidence is not admissible to prove the intent. *In re Estate of Johnson*, 630 P.2d 1039 (Ariz. Ct. App. 1981). Section 2–502(c) of the UPC resolves this problem by providing "Intent that the document constitute the testator's will can be established by extrinsic evidence, including, for holographic wills, portions of the document that are not in the testator's handwriting."

It is clear that witnesses are not needed. Although some statutes require the will to be dated, this requirement has been found to be for juxtapose purposes only and the date need not be valid. On the other hand, a holographic will cannot be wholly typed and there is no provision for a proxy signature.

2. NUNCUPATIVE WILLS

The majority of states and the UPC do not recognized oral wills. Twenty states give limited recognition to nuncupative or oral wills. American College of Trust and Estate Counsel, *ACTEC STUDY 1, Will Requirements of Various States* (Dec. 1996). The statutes typically limit oral wills to disposing of personal property or to a set value of property. Almost all the statutes limit oral wills to testators who are soldiers or sailors or who are in their last sickness or in imminent peril of death. Usually, the testator must actually die from the sickness or the peril. There are witnessing requirements and frequently the oral will must be put in writing within a specified period of time after announcement and must be probated within a set period, such as six months, after testator's death.

D. SPECIAL WILLS

1. FOREIGN AND INTERNATIONAL WILLS

In our modern mobile society, the question of the validity of wills executed according to the wills execution laws of other states or countries is an important consideration. If a will is executed according to the law of a different jurisdiction than the one in which it must be proved, a serious question of validity may arise. The principal problem is how to protect a person's reasonable expectations concerning an instrument that the person wants and believes to be a valid will. Execution requirements can vary significantly between states and nations. Other nations, in particular, set widely varying will execution requirements that differ from those that generally prevail in the United States. Two solutions to this problem have been brought forward:

a. Foreign Wills

The first type is a special choice of law rule with regard to the probate of foreign wills properly executed according to the wills' execution laws of other states or countries. Most states have a statute that specifically recognizes a will executed according to the requirements of other jurisdiction. The statutes may limit the choice of law reference to wills that are in written format and at least one requires that the will be signed by the testator. These statutes have been interpreted to apply to execution requirements, not other substantive issues concerning the will's effectiveness.

The UPC's broad choice of law rule is typical. It provides that in addition to recognizing the validity of any foreign instrument that happens to be executed according to any of the UPC's techniques, a **written** will is also valid if executed in compliance with the law of any of the following jurisdictions: (1) the place of execution; (2) the testator's domicile at the time of execution; (3) the testator's place of abode at the time of execution; (4) the place of the testator's nationality at the time of execution; (5) the testator's domicile at the time of death; (6) the testator's place of abode at the time of death; or (7) the testator's nationality at the time of death. UPC § 2–506. If a written instrument is a valid will under the laws of any of these jurisdictions, then the will is valid and may be probated in a UPC state.

b. International Wills

The second type of statutory provision concerns the Uniform International Wills Act. UPC §§ 10–1001 through–1010. This Act establishes a special execution procedure for executing a will so that the will will be valid in all jurisdictions that join an international convention or that enact the Act.

The application of the International Wills Act is not dependent upon the place of execution, the location of assets or the nationality, domicile or residence of the testator. UPC § 2–1002(a). Its procedures are independent of that status. If the proper execution procedure is followed, the will is presumed to be valid under the Act. On the other hand, the fact that a will is not validly executed under the Act does not affect its formal validity under other will statutes and acts. UPC § 2–1002(b). Nor would execution under the Act preclude the probate of such will under other wills acts or provisions including the choice of law provision.

Basic requirements of an international will are (1) the will must be in writing, (2) the testator must declare that the document is testator's will and that testator knows its contents in the presence of three people, (3) the testator (or a proxy) must sign the will or acknowledge testator's signature, and (4) the witnesses and the authorized person must attest the will by signing it in the presence of the testator.

Similar to an attestation clause, or self-proved will affidavit, the Act sets out a form of a certificate that must be signed by the authorized person and that recites the requirements under the Act for valid execution of an international will. UPC § 2–1005. Three copies of this certificate must be executed. Probate of the will with a certificate attached should be immediate since the certificate is conclusive of the formal validity of the instrument as a will. UPC § 2–1006.

Of course, such a will can be contested under formal testacy proceedings on the grounds of lack of capacity, fraud, undue influence, revocation, substantive ineffectiveness, and even forgery and genuineness. UPC §§ 2–1005, cmt.; 2–1007; 2–1006; 2–1006 cmt.

2. STATUTORY WILLS

Several states recognize special wills where the terms of the will are set out in a statute. One type provides one or more will forms (some with trusts) that permit the testator to fill in relevant information in blanks provided. *See e.g.,* CAL, PROB. CODE §§ 6200–48. Another type is the incorporation by reference approach where the testator incorporates statutory dispositive provision into the will. *See* UNIFORM STATUTORY WILL ACT (1984). Both require normal ordinary witnessed will execution processes. The Uniform Statutory Will Act is generally regarded as a failure, and the Uniform Law Conference no longer promotes it as a uniform act.

E. REVIEW QUESTIONS

1. What is a will called that amends a prior will?
2. A will is effective on the date of execution? True or False?
3. What statute requires that wills of realty be in writing, signed by the testator and attested and subscribed by three or more witnesses?
4. What type of will is handwritten, signed by the testator and does not require a witness?
5. The testator must have testamentary intent to have a valid will. True or False?
6. How does the "line-of-sight" test differ from the "conscious presence" test?
7. What are nuncupative wills?

*

II

REVOCATION OF WILL

Analysis

A. REVOCATION REQUIREMENTS

1. GENERAL PRINCIPLES OF WILL REVOCATION

a. Revocation Statute

The principal source of permissible methods of revocation is the revocation statute. Wills are created according to statutory formalities. Conversely, they may be revoked only by following statutory formalities.

b. Three Principal Elements of Revocation

There are three principal requirements for revoking a will: (1) an authorized act or instrument; (2) an intent to revoke (*animus revocandi*); and (3) legal capacity of the testator. Similar to court construction problems with will execution and validation, revocation requirements may raise policy issues: the conflict between defeating testator's intent versus conforming to statutory mandates.

2. REVOCATION BY PHYSICAL ACT:

a. General Physical Revocation Requirements

A will may be revoked by physical act. For example, the UPC uses the common laundry list approach of itemizing the various methods for accomplishing physical revocation. *See, e.g.,* UPC § 2–507(a)(2). According to this list a testator may physically revoke a will by either burning, tearing, canceling, obliterating, or destroying the will. One needs to examine carefully any applicable revocation statute on this matter. For example, some statutes omit "canceling" and "obliterating."

Proxy Revocation: Generally, statutes permit a testator to physically revoke a will by proxy so long as the revocatory act is done in testator's presence and by testator's direction. The UPC allows proxy revocation but only requires that the proxy perform the act in the testator's "conscious presence" and by the testator's direction.

Evidence Issues: Physical revocation is inherently ambiguous. Consequently, courts have freely admitted extrinsic evidence. Courts have varied, however, on admissibility of testator's declarations.

b. Nature of the Physical Act

Generally, courts have required that some act must be done to the will that is listed in the revocation statute. Normally, the physical act need not be of a substantial degree if the intent to revoke is present. In addition, the testator must have completed the act intended and must have intended to revoke through the completed act. Once the act and intent is completed, testator cannot merely change his or her mind. Reexecution or other proper revival must be accomplished to reestablish the will's validity.

Sometimes issues have arisen concerning the sufficiency of particular acts taken by testators to physically revoke a will. For example, merely burning the edges of will has satisfied the burning requirement. Tearing has been similarly interpreted to require mere small tears on will itself. On the other hand, the requirement for canceling has been strictly applied. Some courts have required that the testator's marks touch the writing of the will.

Illustration 1: T's writes a notation in the margin of the will that states: "This will is revoked." When the will was offered for probate, contestants argue the will was revoked. The court held that this attempted revocation was not an effective revocation because the markings did not touch the text of the will. To cancel a will, the words of cancellation must "touch the words of the will." *See Kronauge v. Stoecklein,* 293 N.E.2d 320 (Ohio Ct. App. 1972). Because the will was defectively revoked, the will retained continued validity and was probated despite the clearly expressed intent of the testator.

c. UPC on the Nature of the Physical Act

UPC Section 2–507 gives meaning to the revocatory acts and reduces the necessary actions. It states: "A burning, tearing, or canceling is a 'revocatory act on the will,' whether or not the burn, tear, or cancellation touched any of the words on the will." A writing, such as "This will is revoked" in the margin, would satisfy this standard. *See also* RESTATEMENT (THIRD) PROPERTY (WILLS AND OTHER DONATIVE TRANSFERS) § 4.1, cmt. g (1999).

d. Partial Revocation

Partial revocation by physical act is permitted by most but not all revocation statutes. UPC Section 2–507(a) states that "A will or any part" may be revoked by physical act. Some states expressly prohibit revocation in part by physical act. *See* IND. CODE § 29–1–5–6. Other statutes do not expressly permit it and have been interpreted to forbid it. N.Y. EST. POWERS & TRUSTS § 3–4.1.

Partial revocation by physical act, if permitted, opens up a significant number of interpretation and litigation problems. On the other hand, to forbid partial physical revocation may effectively prevent carrying out a testator's clearly indicated intent and thus, potentially be harmful to intent enforcing concepts.

Where partial revocation by physical act is permitted, courts recognize a distinction between revocation and modification. Revocation requires satisfaction of the revocation statute: modification require satisfaction of the execution statute. This issue arises when testator lines through selected bequests in a will but does not revoke the whole will. Generally, courts allow the residue to benefit from the markings but not permit revision of the devise.

Illustration 2: T has five children and a surviving spouse. T's will provides: [Assume lapse is applicable if devisee does not survive] *"I give my stock to my children, Tom, Dick, and Mary."* T, with a pen, crossed-out the name "Dick" years after the will was executed. The apparent intent of this act was to increase the specific devise to Tom and Mary and to exclude the gift to Dick. Rather than a third of the stock, Tom and Mary would each take half of the stock. Most courts would consider this alteration a proper revocation.

Similarly if T crosses out all three names, the alteration seeks to convert a specific devise into a class gift thus adding beneficiaries, *i.e.*, the two children not provided for originally. This alteration changes the fundamental nature of the gift and might be considered a modification and therefore require reexecution to be valid. Under this interpretation it would appear that either the entire gift is revoked or the original devise is valid under Dependent Relative Revocation. *See infra* Part 3.II.B.2.

The Restatement (Third) of Property rejects the position that there is a difference between revocation of a complete devise and either rearranging of shares within a single devise or rewriting the terms of the will by deleting selected words. *See* RESTATEMENT (THIRD) PROPERTY (WILLS AND OTHER DONATIVE TRANSFERS) § 4.1, cmt. i (1999). The Restatement argues that any statute that grants unlimited authority to partially revoke a will by physical act, approves of the natural consequences of doing so. Under this approach, the will is given effect as if the deleted words were not present regardless of the effect this has on the dispositive scheme.

3. REVOCATION BY SUBSEQUENT WILL

a. Express Revocation by Subsequent Will

Wills may be expressly revoked in whole or in part by a properly executed subsequent will. The basic requirement for revocation by subsequent will is an instrument executed with the prescribed testamentary formalities. Although no words of art are necessary to revoke, the testator must satisfy the statutory execution and capacity requirements.

If a testator executes a subsequent will without revoking a prior will, the former will continues in existence subject to interpretation. At death all of the valid wills constitute the will as a whole.

b. Revocation by Inconsistency

One of the most litigated questions is whether a subsequent will, which does not expressly revoke a prior will, entirely revokes the prior will by inconsistency, or merely supercedes some of the provisions in the prior will. Of course, if both wills are probated after the testator's death, the provisions and terms of the subsequent will prevail to the extent that they are inconsistent with the former will.

A determination whether the prior will was revoked or merely superseded is important if the subsequent will is revoked before the testator's death. The result depends on testator's intent: but often this is not adequately expressed. If the subsequent will merely superseded the prior will, revocation of the subsequent inconsistent will or its provisions reinstates the prior will or its provisions. If the prior will is held to have been revoked, however, that will or its provisions will be effective again only if reexecuted or if the doctrine of revival is applicable.

Illustration 3: T dies having properly executed valid wills with the following dispositive provisions: no express revocation of the prior will is stated.

Will #1

My wrist watch to A

$10,000 to B

Residue to C

Will #2

My automobile to D

$10,000 to E

My XYZ Corporation stock to F

Who takes what? The question is to what extent if any Will #2 revokes or supersedes Will #1. On the face of Will #2, Will #1 is revoked or superseded only to the extent of the #2's devises which would reduce the residue in Will #1.

Illustration 4: T dies having executed valid wills with the following dispositive provisions: no express revocation of the prior will is stated.

Will #1

My wrist watch to A

$10,000 to B

Residue to C

Will #2

My wrist watch to D

$5,000 to B

$10,000 to E

Residue to C

Who takes? Some courts have said that where a subsequent will is "totally inconsistent" with the prior will, it revokes it. In this situation Will #2 makes a complete disposition, but is it totally inconsistent with Will #1 or not? The answer is a matter of interpretation. Although several of the devises in Will #1 are implicitly revoked by inconsistent devises in Will #2, the will basically follows the same distribution pattern. Clearly according to Will #2 the clock will go to D and not A. But the other devises are less inconsistent. B and C are beneficiaries in both wills.

c. Revocation by Inconsistency Under the UPC

UPC Subsections 2–507(b)-(d) set specific presumptions depending on the nature of the inconsistencies between the wills. They establish reverse presumptions rebuttable by clear and convincing evidence. First, inconsistencies are revocations and replace the prior will terms if the subsequent will "makes a complete disposition" of the estate. In this situation there is no continued life to the previous will unless the will is revived under the revival doctrine. Second, inconsistencies are merely supersession and supplement to the prior will terms if the subsequent will "does not make a complete disposition" of the estate. The continuing life of the prior will depends on whether inconsistencies are effective. Both presumptions are rebuttable by clear and convincing evidence. *See* RESTATEMENT (THIRD) PROPERTY (WILLS AND OTHER DONATIVE TRANSFERS) § 4.1, cmt. d (1999).

Illustration 5: Assume the facts of Illustration 3 are applicable. Under UPC Section 2–507(d), will #2 is presumed to merely supersede Will #1 and not to revoke it. This presumption is rebuttable by clear and convincing evidence. An issue does remain, however, what does B take?: $5,000, $10,000 or $15,000. The answer depends on interpretation of the will as explained by admissible evidence of T's intent.

Illustration 6: Assume the facts of Illustration 4 are applicable. Under UPC Section 2–507(c), will #1 is revoked and is presumed to be replaced because #2 makes a complete disposition. This presumption is rebuttable by clear and convincing evidence.

4. REVOCATION BY CHANGED CIRCUMSTANCES

a. Common Law Grounds for Revocation

The common law grounds for revocation by operation of law were: A man's will was revoked if he subsequently married and had issue; A woman's will was revoked if she subsequently married. Most states have abolished these rules and have adopted a rule that the testator's will for an ex-spouse is revoked or the provisions for the ex-spouse are revoked if there has been a divorce and a property settlement.

b. Revocation by Change of Circumstance Under the UPC

UPC Section 2–802 defines the meaning of an ex-spouse. This is important for all spouse determination issues. Divorce or annulment terminates a marriage;

separation does not; remarriages existing at death of decedent reinstates a spousal relationship. The UPC defines divorce. *See infra.* Part 2.III.C.3.

UPC Section 2–804 sets out the consequences of a divorce. Although a court order or contract between the decedent and the former spouse may provide otherwise, divorce revokes:

- Dispositions and powers of appointments of property by will or other governing instrument to the former spouse and to the former spouse's relatives;
- Grants of general and nongeneral powers in a will or other governing instrument to the former spouse and the former spouse's relatives;
- Nominations to fiduciary positions in a will or other governing instrument to the former spouse and the former spouse's relatives; and,
- Severs joint survivorship interests between the decedent and the former spouse and converts them into tenancies in common.

No other change of circumstances, however, causes a revocation. Significantly, the instrument can provide otherwise.

Nonrevoked provisions are given effect as if the former spouse and relatives of the former spouse disclaimed the revoked provisions, or with regard to appointments, predeceased the decedent. Remarriage to the spouse revives provisions for spouse, etc.

Payors are protected if their action occurred prior to written notice of the divorce, annulment or remarriage. Bona fide purchasers or payees for value under a valid obligation who receive property from the former spouse or former spouse relatives and who have not received notice of the divorce are protected, others are not.

5. LOST WILLS

There is a presumption of revocation if the will is traced to the T but not found or found in a mutilated condition. Evidence is usually admissible to determine intent. Generally, a nonrevocatory destruction of a will cannot be ratified by the testator unless the testator performs a recognized revocatory act or document.

a. Lost and Destroyed Wills Statutes

Many states passed "Lost and Destroyed Wills" statutes. These statutes were intended to be remedial statutes to specifically allow probate of unintentionally lost or destroyed wills. Unfortunately they have caused problems due to their wording.

In relevant part the statute provides: "No will of any testator shall be allowed to be proved as a lost or destroyed will, unless … (1) The will is proved to have been in existence at the time of the death of the testator; or (2) The will is shown to have been fraudulently destroyed in the lifetime of the testator." ARK. CODE ANN. § 28–40–302 (1987). The principal problem with the meaning of this phrase is the meaning of the words "fraudulently destroyed" or "in existence." Some courts have interpreted these words to mean either the will had not been destroyed during the testator's lifetime or that, if destroyed during testator's lifetime, it had not been destroyed by testator or by testator's authority. Or the will continues to have "legal existence" even if it has no continuing "physical existence."

Comment: There is policy conflict between the revocation statute and the lost will statute because the latter could provide a lesser formalistic method for revocation.

b. Lost Wills Under the UPC

The UPC has no special lost will provision. It requires, however, that formal probate under Section 3–402(a) be instituted if a will is "lost, destroyed or otherwise unavailable."

6. OTHER REVOCATIONS CAUSED BY CHANGE

Revocation may occur because of the effect of other related concepts. For example, the exercise of a statutory protection for the disinherited spouse, the premarital spouse, or the pretermitted heir provisions as well as the family protections, may each have the effect of partially revoking a will, at least to the extent the protection interferes with a testator's freedom of disposition.

B. REESTABLISHING REVOKED OR APPARENTLY REVOKED WILLS

1. REVIVAL OF REVOKED WILLS

The issue whether a will that was previously revoked is revived by revoking the revoking instrument arises in at least three situations: (1) Will #2 wholly revokes Will #1 and Will #2 is revoked by physical act; (2) Will #2 partially revokes Will #1 and Will #2 is revoked by physical act; or, (3) Will #2 wholly revokes Will #1 and Will #2 is revoked by Will #3.

a. Three Theories for Revival of Wills

The three basic theories for revival are:

Common Law Rule–Revival by Operation of Law: A prior will is not revoked simply by executing a subsequent will. Consequently, if the testator revokes the subsequent will by act the prior will is still valid.

Ecclesiastical Rule–Revival Depends upon the Testator's Intent: Although revocation takes effect immediately upon execution of the revoking instrument, the earlier will is revived if the testator intended to revive it when the testator revoked the later will. Courts taking this approach generally freely admit extrinsic evidence to prove intent. When evidence is lacking, courts vary on whether the earlier will is presumed to be revived or whether it is presumed to be revoked.

Wills Act Antirevival Statute: Under the Wills Act, a prior will is revived only if that will is reexecuted or the testator executes a codicil indicating an intent to revive the former will.

b. Revival Under the UPC

UPC Section 2–509 adopts two rules: one for the case where the subsequent will wholly revokes the previous will and one for the case where the subsequent will merely partly revokes the previous will.

i. If a physically revoked subsequent will wholly revoked the previous will, revival occurs only when those who seek revival present evidence that the testator intended the previous will to be revived. UPC § 2–509(a). This puts the burden on those seeking revival of the previous will. The UPC permits extrinsic evidence, including statements by the testator, to be admissible to prove intent. If no evidence is introduced or if the evidence is inconclusive, the prior will will not be revived.

Illustration 7: If T executed Will 1 and wholly revokes it by express terms in Will 2, T's physical revocation of Will 2 is presumed not to revive Will 1 unless adequate proof of T's intent to revive is admitted into evidence. Extrinsic evidence including statements by T is admissible to determine T's intent.

ii. If a physically revoked subsequent will only partly revoked the previous will, UPC Section 2–509(b) provides that revival of the revoked provisions is presumed unless those who contend that no revival occurred introduce evidence showing the testator did not intend revival of the revoked provisions. This puts the burden on those seeking nonrevival of the revoked provisions. The UPC permits extrinsic evidence including statements by the testator to be admissible to prove intent. If no evidence is introduced or if the evidence is inconclusive, however, the prior will will be revived.

Illustration 8: If T executed Will 1 and only partially revoked it by express terms in Will 2, T's physical revocation of Will 2 will presumably revive Will 1 unless the person, who asserts that T did not intend to revive the prior will, introduces evidence of that contrary intent. Again extrinsic evidence including statements by T is admissible to determine T's intent.

The UPC's revival provision does not apply to the situation where the prior will has also been physically revoked by the testator.

iii. If the subsequent revoking will is revoked by a later will, the revoked portions of the prior will are revived only if testator's intent to revive them appears from the terms of the latest will. UPC § 2–509(c). It makes no difference whether the subsequent will wholly or partially revokes the prior will. No extrinsic evidence, including statements by T, is admissible to determine T's intent. Revival of Will 1 will occur only if the testator reexecutes Will 1 or executes a Will 3 that incorporates by reference Will 1 into Will 3.

Illustration 9: If T properly executed Will 1 but partially revoked it by properly executed Will 2, the revocation of Will 2 by properly executed Will 3 will not revive the portions of Will 1 revoked by Will 2 unless the revival of the revoked portion appears by the terms of the Will 3. Evidence of intent is limited to the words on the face of the will unless some other evidence admissibility rule applies. Assumably, statements by T regarding revival are also inadmissible.

2. DEPENDENT RELATIVE REVOCATION

As formulated in the Restatement (Third) of Property, the doctrine of dependent relative revocation is: "A partial or complete revocation of a will is presumptively ineffective if the testator made the revocation (1) in connection with an attempt to achieve a dispositive objective that fails for some reason under applicable law or (2) because of a false assumption of law, or because of a false belief about an objective fact, that is either recited in the revoking instrument or established by clear and convincing evidence." RESTATEMENT (THIRD) PROPERTY (WILLS AND OTHER DONATIVE TRANSFERS) § 4.3 (1999). This presumption is rebutted if the revocation is more consistent with testator's probable intent. The Restatement (Third) of Property suggests DRR might more aptly be called the "doctrine of ineffective revocation."

a. Common Applications of DRR

- If a testator cancels or destroys a will with the intent of making a new one *but* the new will fails of effect for any reason, *e.g.,* Rule Against Perpetuities, mortmain, execution validity, death of beneficiary, the cancellation and the making of the new will are said to be part of one scheme.

- If a testator cancels or destroys a will while laboring under a mistake of law or fact in connection therewith, it may be presumed that the testator preferred the old will to intestacy and the old will will be admitted to probate in absence of evidence overcoming the presumption provided that its contents can be ascertained. The doctrine applies to partial and/or total or complete revocation.

b. DRR Under the Restatement (Third) of Property

The Restatement (Third) of Property treats DRR as an independent doctrine, not dependent on either conditional intent or mistake analysis. It is a presumption that the revocation was ineffective due to the stated circumstances. It seeks to identify the testator's probable intention, *i.e,* does treating the revocation as ineffective come closer to testator's failed objectives than does treating the revocation as effective? *See* RESTATEMENT (THIRD) PROPERTY (WILLS AND OTHER DONATIVE TRANSFERS) § 4.3, cmt. a (1999).

C. REVIEW QUESTIONS

1. What is the principal source of permissible methods of revocation?
2. What are the three elements of revocation of a will?
3. What are some of the ways in which a testator may physically revoke a will?
4. A will cannot be partially revoked by subsequent instrument? True or false.
5. How does the UPC deal with lost will?
6. What doctrine is also referred to as the doctrine of ineffective revocation?

III

DEFINING THE SCOPE OF THE WILL

Analysis

A. POLICY OF THE STATUTE OF WILLS

1. The Statute of Wills requires that the will consist only of appropriate materials that were made a part of the execution process. Generally, a valid devise in a will must adequately describe the beneficiary and the property. If either cannot be adequately determined from the face of the will, the devise is invalid.

B. INTEGRATION OF WILLS

1. INTEGRATION OF WILLS DEFINED

Theoretically, a person might have to execute each page of a multi-page will. Although this is not required, one must satisfy the doctrine of integration. Under the doctrine of integration, when a will consists of multiple pages, only those pages that were intended by the testator to be part of the will and that were present at the time of execution are part of the will and covered by the execution process.

Normally the proponent of the multi-page will is aided in proof of integration. A presumption of integration is recognized if the pages are securely stapled together or otherwise physically attached, or exhibit a coherence of the provisions. Generally, courts will admit extrinsic evidence to determine the scope of the integration. Internal coherence and other extrinsic evidence concerning T's intent and the execution process are considered by courts

Problems of integration arise when the proponent of the will is faced with loose and unfastened pages that do not exhibit an internal coherence.

2. INTEGRATION OF HOLOGRAPHIC WILLS

The integration requirement for holographic wills varies. While some courts require that holographic wills should be written entirely as part of one transaction, a preferred approach considers all the papers which the holographic testator intended to constitute the will, regardless of the time and place of making them. Atkinson, Wills § 79. The integration requirements of existence and intent to include are considered with each page as it is written. Several cases have held that subsequent holographic alterations of a holographic will are effective even though the testator did not sign the alterations or resign the will. *See, e.g., Estate of Archer v. Moises,* 239 Cal. Rptr. 137 (Ct. App. 1987).

Illustration 1: T dies and in T's desk are found seven unattached pages that when put together appear to be a last will: all pages are in T's handwriting and at the end of one appears T's signature. The issues are whether T intended to complete and execute a will and what pages are a part of it. The first issue depends on whether T had testamentary intent. The second, concerns integration. Using extrinsic evidence, the court must determine which pages were intended to be a part of the will, and which pages were present when the will became effective.

C. REPUBLICATION BY CODICIL

1. DEFINITION OF REPUBLICATION BY CODICIL

The *Republication by Codicil Doctrine* holds that when a will is republished by codicil, it is held to speak as of the date of the republishing as though originally executed at that time. *See* RESTATEMENT (THIRD) PROPERTY (WILLS AND OTHER DONATIVE TRANSFERS) § 3.4 (1999). The doctrine has relevance anytime the date of the will is an important reference point to a rule of construction or interpretation doctrine.

2. APPLICATION OF REPUBLICATION BY CODICIL

This doctrine had its first application in cases involving after-acquired lands so that land acquired after the will and before the execution of the codicil passed under a general or residuary devise in the will. It often was applied mechanically without determining actual intent of the testator. The preferred view is that it should not be applied mechanically but should be used as a flexible instrument for effectuating the testator's intent.

3. REPUBLICATION'S UPDATING EFFECT

The updating effect of the republication doctrine can have several beneficial applications. It can assist in the inclusion of new beneficiaries; the release of new debts; the inclusion of second spouses; the inclusion of new property to avoid ademption by extinction; and, to qualify a document for incorporation by reference purposes. Its application can have adverse consequences also. For example, it might apply to preclude the application of a pretermitted heir statute; void a charitable bequest because of time of execution and death; change specific devise coverage; or, exclude the use of ademption by satisfaction. The doctrine should not be applied in cases in which its application would defeat testator's intention. *See* RESTATEMENT (THIRD) PROPERTY (WILLS AND OTHER DONATIVE TRANSFERS) § 3.4 cmt. b (1999).

D. INCORPORATION BY REFERENCE

1. DEFINITION OF INCORPORATION BY REFERENCE

The doctrine of *Incorporation by Reference* permits a document, not executed with the proper execution requirements of a will, to be made part of the will, for certain purposes only. The document itself may be anything (*e.g.*, will, codicil, deed, note, list or memorandum). It is a recognized exception to the Statute of Wills because it has its own formalities.

The requirements (in a sense its formalities) for incorporation by reference are:

(1) A will executed as required by statute.

(2) A distinct reference to a written document in the will itself. Lenient courts say the reference must be so definite and precise as to permit the document to be identified by parol evidence. Strict courts say the reference must be such as to identify the document beyond any doubt.

(3) The document must in fact be in existence at the time the will is executed.

(4) The will must show or state that the document is in existence at the time the will is executed. This requirement has not been strictly enforced, and is rejected in UPC § 2–510 and in RESTATEMENT (THIRD) PROPERTY (WILLS AND OTHER DONATIVE TRANSFERS) § 3.6 (1999).

(5) The will must show an intention to incorporate the document as part of the will. The entire document need not be incorporated: it may be incorporated in whole or part.

(6) When the document is offered it must be shown to be the document referred to in the will. It must be shown that it corresponds to the description in the will.

When the incorporated document is entirely holographic, courts show a tendency to be more liberal with the incorporation by reference doctrine even where such writings are not valid. Intuitively, holographic documents are inherently authentic, clearly expressive of the writer's intent and relatively free from fraudulent creation.

2. INCORPORATION BY REFERENCE OF HOLOGRAPHIC WILLS

If a holographic will incorporates a non-holographic writing into the will, there is a question whether this violates the necessary holographic character of the will. There is a split of authority. Some courts treat the incorporated document as a physical part of the will and therefore destroying the holographic nature of the will. These courts hold that the nonholographic document is integrated into the will. Other courts say that integration and incorporation by reference are distinct concepts with their own safeguards and that a proponent of a will need only satisfy one or the other doctrine, not both. This is the position adopted in the RESTATEMENT (THIRD) PROPERTY (WILLS AND OTHER DONATIVE TRANSFERS) § 3.6, cmt. f. (1999).

3. INCORPORATION BY REFERENCE UNDER THE UPC

The UPC substantially codifies the doctrine of incorporation by reference as described above. UPC § 2–510. The one exception is that requirement (3) is not a prerequisite. Consequently, so long as there is proof that the document was actually in existence at the time of execution [requirement (4)], the UPC does not require that there be a showing or statement in the will that the document is in existence at the time that the will is executed.

The essence of the application of the doctrine under the UPC is the determination that the testator intended to incorporate the document into the will. The UPC requires that the language of the will "manifest" this intent. The key word "manifest" when used as a verb means "to show plainly: make palpably evident or certain by showing or displaying." WEBSTER'S THIRD NEW INT'L DICTIONARY 1375. This means that although there must be some indication of an intent to incorporate by reference another document on the face of the will, it is not necessary that precise language be used such as "I intend to incorporate" as a means of showing this intent. The intent can be derived from the total meaning of the relevant clauses in the will.

Illustration 2: T *types* a document that states: "This is my last will. I devise all my property to my friend, Z." T signs and dates (7/1/95) the document but no one witnessed it. Two years later, T types a document that states: "This is a codicil to my last will of 7/1/95, I give my car to X." T signs, dates and has this document witnessed by two qualified witnesses. Because the first document is not a valid will, the question is whether the Codicil can validate it. This is not Republication by Codicil, because that doctrine is merely an updating technique between prior and subsequent validly executed documents. The doctrine necessary to save the first document is incorporation by reference. The question is whether that doctrine's requirements are met. All of the requirements are met except (5) concerning intent to incorporate. In a technical sense T did not intend to incorporate but intended to modify and update. A court might glide over this technical deficiency and allow the codicil to incorporate the "will," if the court feels that T would have preferred that result versus the alternative result that most of the estate would pass by intestacy.

E. REFERENCE TO FACTS OF INDEPENDENT SIGNIFICANCE

1. FACTS OF INDEPENDENT SIGNIFICANCE

Generally, a valid devise in a will must adequately describe the beneficiary and the property. If either cannot be adequately determined from the face of the will the devise is invalid.

There are important exceptions to this rule. The doctrine of independent significance permits certain evidence outside the will to be admitted in order to determine who receives and what property passes under the testator's will. 2 PAGE ON THE LAW OF WILLS § 19.34 (Bowe–Parker rev. ed., 1960). The Restatement (Third) of Property states the doctrine as follows: "The meaning of a dispositive or other provision in a will may be supplied or affected by an external circumstance referred to in the will, unless the external circumstance has no significance apart from its effect upon the will." RESTATEMENT (THIRD) PROPERTY (WILLS AND OTHER DONATIVE TRANSFERS) § 3.7 (1999). Significantly, this principle applies regardless of whether the testator or third persons can affect the act or event subsequent to the will's execution. ATKINSON, WILLS § 81. The degree of significance a devise is said to have, however, may depend on matters such as convenience versus whimsy and the degree of certainty from misuse.

2. EXAMPLES OF INDEPENDENT SIGNIFICANCE

Typical examples of the application of the doctrine are the common use in wills of such terms as "children," "cousins," "brothers and sisters," the "residue" and "all my property." In order to determine the meaning of each of these words or phrases, it is necessary to look at facts outside the face of the will; however, because these words have obvious significance other than to pass property at death, extrinsic evidence is admitted to show their meaning.

Illustration 3: What is the effect of the following relevant will provisions:

<table>
<tr><td>A.</td><td>I devise $5,000 to</td><td>Comment</td></tr>
<tr><td>1.</td><td>each of my children, including adopted children;</td><td>The fact that one is a child, even an adopted child, has significance other than to pass property at death.</td></tr>
<tr><td>2.</td><td>each person who may be a son-in-law or daughter-in-law of mine at my death;</td><td>The same analysis applies to in-laws since marriage has significance.</td></tr>
<tr><td>3.</td><td>the person who is my personal secretary at my death;</td><td>Subject to control by testator but without indication of manipulation, a personal secretary position has independent significance.</td></tr>
<tr><td>4.</td><td>each person listed on a paper that I shall place with this will.</td><td>Unless the paper has an independent significance, this devise would fail. The paper appears to have no purpose other than to pass property at death.</td></tr>
<tr><td>B.</td><td>I devise to X</td><td></td></tr>
<tr><td>1.</td><td>all of the furniture in my home office;</td><td>Furniture in a room has independent significance. It has a living purpose and is not arranged to pass property at death.</td></tr>
<tr><td></td><td colspan="2">Comment: But could it turn into a race to the house, e.g., all valuables are found in the office after X was in the house? Subject to evidence of misuse, most courts approve such gifts.</td></tr>
<tr><td>2</td><td>the balance of my personal checking account;</td><td>Checking accounts clearly have independent significance with a major lifetime purpose.</td></tr>
<tr><td>3.</td><td>the contents of my safe-deposit box;</td><td>Safe-deposit boxes have a lifetime purpose of providing security for assets and documents and thus have independent significance.</td></tr>
<tr><td>4.</td><td>the contents of the top drawer of my desk.</td><td>The drawer has less independent significance. It is subject to unsupervised manipulation. But with additional facts, it might have independent significance, too, e.g, the drawer is maintained in a manner and for a purpose similar to the safe-deposit box.</td></tr>
<tr><td></td><td colspan="2">Comment: The same caveat as mentioned in B.1. above is applicable here also.</td></tr>
</table>

C.	*I give the property and securities located in shoe boxes in my closet to the person whose name is written on each of them.* After death, three shoe boxes were found marked "A's devise," "B's devise," and "C's devise."	This devise lacks independent significance. Neither property nor devisee is identified in the will. The shoe boxes are apparently being used to determine who is beneficiary and to set the size of a testamentary gift. This violates the Statute of Wills. A court may say this fails. Possibly incorporation by reference may apply.
D.	*I give the residue to the person or persons, equally, named as primary beneficiary or beneficiaries of my life insurance policies or policies on my life at my death.*	This should be held to have independent significance because a life insurance policy has a purpose other than to pass testator's probatable estate at death. Some courts have had difficulty with this because the reference is to a nontestamentary document, but the concern is a confusion with the incorporation by reference doctrine. Independent significance is a separate doctrine with its own requirements and safeguards.

3. INDEPENDENT SIGNIFICANCE UNDER THE UPC

The UPC includes a provision that codifies a broad statement of the common law rule. UPC § 2–512. This provision is applicable to acts or events that occur not only before or after the execution of the will but also that occur after the testator's death. Under its test, testamentary dispositions may be controlled by these acts and events only if the latter "have significance apart from their effect upon the dispositions made by the will."

Although the UPC generally leaves to the court the determination of what comes within its test, it does expressly state that under that test the execution or revocation of another's will constitutes such an event. This separate and specific rule permits a testator to dispose of testator's property according to the terms of another's will notwithstanding that the other's will was executed before or after the testator's will.

F. REVIEW QUESTIONS

1. A valid devise in a will must adequately describe the beneficiary and the property. True or False?
2. What doctrine states that when a will consists of multiple pages only pages that were intended by the testator to be part of the will and that were present at the time of execution are part of the will and covered by the execution process?
3. What does the Republication by Codicil Doctrine hold?
4. What is a fact of independent significance?

*

IV

WILL CONTESTS AND WILL SUBSTITUTE SUITS

Analysis

b. Mental Requirement
c. Mental Deficiency
d. Insane Delusion
5. Undue Influence and Duress
a. Definition of Undue Influence
b. Elements of Undue Influence
c. Proving Undue Influence
d. Undue Influence and the Courts
e. Typical Undue Influence Situations
f. Undue Influence and Confidential Relationships
g. Undue Influence and Attorneys
h. Duress
6. Fraud
a. Fraud in the Execution
b. Fraud in the Inducement
7. Mistake
D. Inter Vivos Transfers
E. Review Questions

A. PROVING THE WILL

1. POST MORTEM PROBATE

The restricted meaning of "probate" is the judicial proof of the will. *See supra* Part 1.II.A.3. At a hearing on probate the sole question before the court is whether the propounding instrument is or is not the valid will of the decedent; the validity and meaning of its provisions are not in issue.

The two common types of probate are: *Ex parte* probate or probate in common form where no notice is given at the initiation of the proceedings; and, probate *in solemn form* where notice to all interested parties is required at initiation. By election of interested persons depending on their needs, the UPC includes both types.

2. ANTE MORTEM PROBATE

Ante mortem probate, sometime referred to as "living probate," is a statutory device that permits a person while alive to institute an adversary proceeding to declare the validity of a will including the testamentary capacity of the testator and the absence of undue influence. *See, e.g.,* ARK. CODE ANN. § 28–40–202 (1987). Generally, living probate procedures have not been used frequently where they exist. Ante mortem probate statutes have many application problems.

- What is the effect of revocation of the will probated ante mortem?
- How will subsequent wills and codicils be treated?
- If a will is denied probate under the system, what bearing does this determination have on subsequently executed wills?

B. LIMITATIONS ON THE RIGHTS OF PROBATE AND CONTEST

1. STANDING—THE REQUIREMENT OF INTEREST

A person who contests the probate of a will must be "interested" or "aggrieved." This limitation means that all such persons are entitled to contest, and no others may do so. Generally one is interested if, and only if, it is to the person's direct pecuniary advantage that the will be set aside. *See* UPC § 1–201(24).

An heir or next of kin can contest a will when the heir receives more in intestacy than from the will. If a prior will cuts off the heir or next of kin, the heir need not contest both but should at least allege that the prior will is invalid. If procedures permit, the better practice would be to make all persons connected with the prior will parties to the proceeding, then the validity of all wills could be litigated.

A legatee or devisee of a prior will can contest if the devisee receives less or nothing under the subsequent will. While such contestants need not show probate of the will under which he or she claims, the devisee must at least prove that the will exists and that it is apparently executed in due form.

Generally, an executor or administrator under a prior will is not deemed to have a sufficient pecuniary interest to contest a subsequently probated will. This rule is criticized because the rights of minor and unborn beneficiaries of future interests under a prior will could thereby be protected. This protection is particularly appropriate when there are no other *sui juris* beneficiaries under that will who desire to challenge the second will either because they benefit from the second will or otherwise do not exist. Although a guardian ad litem could be appointed to protect these potential beneficiaries, it might be more efficient to allow the executor to represent them.

A surviving spouse can contest a will only if the spouse cannot obtain as much without a contest by way of elective share. But a spouse may contest the will as guardian of any child of the deceased if the child has an interest.

While wills are ordinarily not construed upon probate, the tribunal before whom the contest takes place may render a tentative construction of the will for the purpose of determining the necessary interest of the contestants for standing purposes.

2. ANTICONTEST CLAUSES

An anticontest clause (sometimes called an *in terrorem* clause—by way of threat) is a clause in a will which provides that if a devisee under a will contests the will, the devisee forfeits that devise. A variation provides that a devise is forfeited if the devisee files a claim against the estate. The devisee is given an election: either take under the will as provided or contest and defeat will. If devisee contests and loses, devisee loses the devise under the will. If the contest is successful, of course, the no-contest provision fails with the will.

There are two approaches courts take regarding the validity of these clauses: (1) enforce the condition whether or not there is probable cause for the contest, or (2) enforce the condition only if there was no probable cause for the contest. There are some courts that require the testator to indicate to whom the property is to go if the devisee contests the will.

"What is a Contest?": A threshold question is "What is a contest?" Courts have had to deal with a wide range of issues. For example, aiding the contestants, or even claiming title to land or chattels which the testator gave by testator's will, or a suit to set aside the will because it violated the Rule Against Perpetuities, have been held to activate the clause. On the other hand, for example, a suit to construe a will, or an objection to the jurisdiction or venue of the probate court, or suit to obtain one's share under the will from the executor have not activated the clause.

UPC Anticontest Clauses: The UPC Section 2–517 adopts the "probable cause" rule. It is broadly phrased to permit comprehensive forfeiture provisions: it goes beyond mere anticontest of will clauses and includes forfeiture for claims against the estate.

C. GROUNDS OF CONTEST

1. GENERAL MATTERS CONCERNING WILL CONTESTS

In a will contest, the proponent is a person favoring the will; the contestant is one trying to contest it. The general grounds for contesting a will include:

- improper execution,
- forgery,
- failure of capacity,
- nontestamentary intent,
- revocation,
- undue influence,
- fraud, and
- illegality.

The burden of proof or risk of nonpersuasion varies depending on the ground. The following table shows the prevailing approach.

Ground	Burden on
Execution (including testamentary intent)	Proponent
Testamentary capacity	Split of authority
Fraud	Contestant
Revocation	Contestant
Undue influence	Contestant

When undue influence is the ground, contestant may be aided by certain presumptions when a confidential relation is involved. Even in this situation, however, the shift of burden to proponents may merely be a burden of going forward with the evidence and not a shift in the risk of nonpersuasion. *See* Part 1.III.B.1.

2. CONTESTS CONCERNING EXECUTION AND REVOCATION OF WILLS

a. Execution

For a will to be valid, it must be executed according to the proper formalities of the applicable statute of wills. *See supra* Part 3.I.B. What makes the execution process so vulnerable to contest is that each act or condition required by the relevant wills statute must be satisfied. One must dissect the statutory requirements of the applicable wills statute. Each "action" word may have importance.

b. Revocation

Revocation of the will is also a valid ground for contest. The contestant must prove that the testator revoked his or her will. The precise terms of the applicable revocation statute must be meticulously obeyed. *See supra* Part 3.II.

c. Forgery

If any of the necessary signatures or writings were forged by another person, the will is not valid. The validity of signatures arises in numerous probate proceedings, but few of the instruments are actually found to be forged. Proponents are required to prove proper execution including identifying signatures. Forgery contentions usually concern expert testimony over the validity of signatures.

3. TESTAMENTARY INTENT

To be a valid will, the testator must have executed the document with testamentary intent. This usually is not a problem because most wills state that they are wills or otherwise clearly indicate they are wills. On the other hand, an instrument does not have to state it is a will: any instrument may be a will if there is testamentary intent. Testamentary intent must exist when testator signed the instrument, or when the last act of execution was performed.

a. Proving Testamentary Intent

If testamentary intent is an issue, the first place to look for it is on the face of the instrument. If that does not adequately indicate the necessary intent, proof of intent may depend on the admissibility of relevant evidence. Some courts have limited the admissibility of evidence. These courts limited the evidence to the instrument in question—no evidence *aliunde* (from outside) unless there is an ambiguity. Finding an ambiguity is often the problem. Other courts freely admit extrinsic evidence concerning testamentary intent.

b. Sham Will

Extrinsic evidence has been held admissible to prove that a testator did not intend that an instrument be executed as a will but was a sham and thus lacked testamentary intent. *See Fleming v. Morrison,* 72 N.E. 499 (Mass. 1904). In this case testator made a will passing T's property to A. Testator tells his attorney, who prepared the will, that it was a fake made only to induce A to have sex with T. The court held the will lacked testamentary intent despite its appearance and form. The court allowed extrinsic evidence to rebut that apparent testamentary intent.

c. Conditional Will

Sometimes a testator may state in the wills that the will was executed in anticipation of a particular event. For example, T's will states: "Because I am going on a long and dangerous trip, I am executing this will and I devise my property as follows.... " What is the effect of this will if testator returns safely from the trip and never executes another will? If the will clearly states that its validity is conditional on whether testator die during the trip, then the court would enforce the condition and not probate the will. Many courts, however, interpret language of this nature to be an inducement to write the will and not a condition for its validity. If it is merely an inducement, it remains valid even if the testator survives the mentioned event. These courts often emphasize that there is a presumption against intestacy. Surrounding circumstances, *e.g.*, where the will was found, may also aid the court with this interpretation.

4. TESTAMENTARY CAPACITY

a. Age Qualification

Generally it is a chronologically determined age and usually requires 18 years.

b. Mental Requirement

There are several reasons why the law denies probate to a will that was executed by a mentally deficient person. It is socially undesirable (against public policy) to give freedom of testation to one who is so deficient or unbalanced mentally that he or she does not appreciate the significance of the disposition. It is better to distribute property according to intestate laws or to a prior valid will than according to the caprice of an unsound mind. For the protection of the family, the system's legitimacy and reputation, society in general, and the incompetent, the law must demand true intent, not deranged intent.

c. Mental Deficiency

Mental deficiency concerns the basic mental ability to execute a will. It is said to go to total capacity. The appropriate time for considering this ability is at the time of execution. The statement of its test is well established:

Testator is of sound mind for testamentary purposes only when:

Testator has the ability to know (can understand and carry in testator's mind in a general way):

(1) The nature and extent of testator's property;

(2) The persons who are the natural objects of his or her bounty; and,

(3) The disposition which testator is making of testator's property.

Testator must also be capable of:

(4) Appreciating these elements in relation to each other; and,

(5) Forming an orderly desire as to the disposition of testator's property.

Atkinson, Wills § 51.

A person who fails the above test of ability is mentally deficient and cannot execute a valid will. The test is subjective and pragmatic. Various objective standards are considered too demanding, *e.g.,* a standard of average intelligence or of prudent person's intelligence would be too high. The test must consider eccentricities and peculiarities. The real problems in these cases are typically those of fact and proof and in some states of the province of the trier of fact.

Compare the capacity one must have to make a contract, which is said to require mutual assent, with the capacity to execute a will, which is an unilateral act. The former is often said to require more than the latter. Compare, however, an agreement to have a haircut with writing a will that gives away $3,000,000. Testamentary capacity is also compared to capacity to make an inter vivos gift. Because of the immediacy of the consequences, the capacity to make a gift might be higher than to make a will.

Common attributes of mental deficiency include paranoia (delusions of persecution and extreme jealousy), paresis (delusions of great wealth, strength, etc.), flightiness, irresponsibility, forgetfulness, short attention span, irritability, and slovenliness. Most people exhibit at one time or another, one or more of these attributes. Setting a definite line when these attributes constitute mental deficiency, and when they do not, is not easy. The decision will be a subjective one based on a combination of attributes and conduct. Typically, expert witnesses will testify in the dispute and frequently they will disagree.

Abnormal Distributions in Wills: One of the pervasive issues in mental deficiency cases is the relevance of an abnormal distribution plan in the will. Generally, abnormal means the testator did not follow the normal order of distribution for an estate using the intestacy statutes as a guide.

The hornbook answer is that an "abnormal" will does not equal mental deficiency, *e.g.,* disinheriting one's heirs does not, without more proof, constitute mental deficiency. A person can have capacity to write a will even though the person is mean or ignorant or both. "The right of a testator to dispose of his estate depends neither on the justice of his prejudices nor the soundness of his reasoning." *Clapp v. Fullerton*, 34 N.Y. 190 (1866). The ultimate question is that of the rational character of the testator's mind rather than the objective reasonableness of the will itself. On the other hand, the will of a person of unsound mind is not valid even though the provisions are exactly the same as they would be if the testator had possessed capacity.

Comment: Despite the hornbook answer, in practice abnormality of the distribution scheme is going to have an effect on whether a testator is found to be mentally deficient. As mentioned, one part of the test for mental capacity is knowledge of the natural object of one's bounty; consequently, an unusual distribution may raise questions whether the testator held that knowledge. In states which decide capacity by juries, the tendency of juries to favor normal distribution and to suspect abnormal distribution have caused tensions between jury determinations of incapacity and appellate courts applications of the legal standard. Consequently, appellate courts are more willing to throw out a jury decision on mental incapacities than they do in other cases. The fear seems to be that juries have a tendency to overemphasize the importance of who gets the property.

d. Insane Delusion

An insane delusion is a false belief which is the product of a diseased mind unto which one adheres against evidence and reason and which affects the disposition. It is said that one should compare an irrational belief which is adhered to without reason with a rational belief to which one unreasonably adheres. The former is an insane delusion, the latter valid behavior. It is also said that a false belief, however unfounded, does not constitute an insane delusion if based on any evidence. The mistake must be one to which no rational person, in testator's place, would entertain. Instinctive prejudices are not insane delusions. The question is whether, considering all the facts and circumstances, it is fairly shown that the will proceeded from and on account of a deranged mind. ATKINSON, WILLS § 52, at p. 245.

Illustration 1: T believes that all drugs, legal or illegal, are harmful to people. T's daughter, D, takes prescription drugs. T disinherits D and devises entire estate to S, T's son. T's belief is not an insane delusion because it is only a rational belief to which T unreasonably adheres. *See Kirkpatrick v. Union Nat'l Bank,* 601 S.W.2d 607 (Ark. Ct. App. 1980), *rev'd unpublished opinion* (Sup. Ct. 1981).

There is a significant difference between "mental deficiency" and "insane delusion" with respect to the disposition made in the will. If the testator is mentally deficient, testator's will is invalid notwithstanding that the disposition of the property is rational: it goes to total capacity. An insane delusion, however, invalidates a will only if the insane delusion affects the disposition made by the deceased: it relates solely to one issue. Mental capacity may be there but the mind is warped or deranged. This is a nonscientific and nonpsychiatric standard that recognizes partial incapacity or monomania.

If the insane delusion affects the will, normally the whole will is denied probate. An English case has held that only the part affected will be denied probate and the remainder may stand: there is American dicta to the same effect.

Determining whether the insane delusion affects the will has been crucial in some cases. If the effect of the insane delusion is unmistakably indicated on the face of the will, this requirement is met.

Illustration 2: T believes that people are living in the trees outside his house. If T's will devises $10,000 to hire a person to evict them, the clause of the will is invalid because it is the effect of an insane delusion.

If the insane delusion is one that directly affects a relationship or asset of the testator, proof of the effect on the will may be more difficult, particularly when the will is not irrational. When the insane delusion goes directly to the core of the relationship, some courts have shown a lack of concern about evidence of direct effect.

Illustration 3: T suffers from an insane delusion that his only child is not biologically his child. T's will devises the entire estate to a charity in which T had great interest. Courts might not require much evidence of effect because if one holds to such a belief, the person presumably could not form a rational or orderly desire as to the disposition of his property. A similar analysis may be found when testator holds to a groundless or unjust belief with regard to a spouse's fidelity. *See In re Honigman's Will*, 168 N.E.2d 676 (N.Y. 1960). Even under these circumstance, however, some courts might require that the delusion's effect on the will be proved: that the will was a product of deranged mind.

5. UNDUE INFLUENCE AND DURESS

a. Definition of Undue Influence

Undue influence is not influence but an exercise of control over the testator that causes the will to recite the desires of the influencer rather than the desires of the testator. The undue influencer is said to destroy "the free agency of the testator, at the time when the instrument is made, and which, in effect, substitutes the will of another for that of the testator." *Toombs v. Matthesen*, 241 P.2d 937, 940 (Okla. 1952). The distinction is made between a testator acting as a free agency versus one acting as a captive of another.

Undue influence is not based on an objective test based on the average testator. It is a subjective evaluation determining whether *this testator* was overcome, not whether an average testator would be overcome.

Undue influence does not spring merely from kindness, persuasion, pleas, friendship, advice or courting favors even if the intent is to obtain testamentary benefits. On the other hand, physical coercion is sufficient but not necessary.

If a will was the result of undue influence and the influence is removed, testator's voluntary acquiescence in the will does not revalidate it. The will would have to be reexecuted or otherwise validated.

b. Elements of Undue Influence

Four elements are often mentioned as necessary to establish undue influence:

i. A testator subject to such influence because of age, personality, physical, or mental health and ability;

ii. An opportunity to exercise the influence through access, communication, and contacts;

iii. A disposition to exercise the influence or a willingness to do something wrong or unfair; and,

iv. A will appearing to be the effect of the influence because it contains an "unnatural" distribution pattern or unusual inclusion or exclusion.

ATKINSON, WILLS § 55, at p. 256.

c. Proving Undue Influence

Undue influence is generally proved by inference with circumstantial evidence. The risk of nonpersuasion is by the great weight of authority on the contestant. Generally, proof by a preponderance of the evidence is all that is needed, although some courts say "clear and convincing" evidence. *See Estate of Kamesar,* 259 N.W.2d 733 (Wis. 1977). The effect on the will of a finding of undue influence is it invalidates the portion of the will procured thereby but the unaffected portions of the will *may* be allowed to stand as written.

d. Undue Influence and the Courts

The many inconsistent appellate decisions, including affirmed and overturned jury verdicts, indicate that the courts have difficulty balancing conflicting considerations. Courts know that disappointed heirs will contest a will on any available ground, including undue influence even though evidence of the ground is meager. On the other hand, courts know there are circumstances where the evidence indicates a person was so influential with the testator that there is a high degree of probability the will was the result of undue influence. Consequently, courts have avoided mechanical tests and relied primarily on fact analysis. The ultimate goal for the contestant in an undue influence case is to produce enough evidence of influence that the finder of fact's decision of undue influence will be sustained on appeal.

e. Typical Undue Influence Situations

- The elderly person cared for by a nonrelative where that person's will gives all or a substantial portion of the estate to the caretaker and disinherits or greatly reduces the shares of the heirs;
- The elderly person cared for by a young new spouse where that person's will gives all or a substantial portion of the estate to the new spouse and disinherits or greatly reduces the shares of the person's descendants or other heirs;
- The elderly person who is cared for by a child or grandchild where that person's will gives all or a substantial portion of the estate to the child caretaker and disinherits or greatly reduces the shares of the other heirs;
- In a will executed shortly before death, the person who devises all or substantially all of his or her estate to a lover or live in who is not married to the person.

Although the vast majority of cases hold that the existence of illicit relations between a testator and his or her beneficiary does not, of itself, raise a presumption of undue influence, other cases have held it to be a factor depending on the condition of the testator and the terms of the will.

f. Undue Influence and Confidential Relationships

Courts vary greatly on the effect of a confidential relationship between testator and a devisee. The typical confidential relationships include attorney-client, clergy-parishioner, physician-patient, trustee-beneficiary, guardian/conservator-ward, close business associates, and principal-agent. Courts have not always stayed within these relational categories if the facts indicated a close trusting relationship between two persons. On the other hand, the husband-wife relationship has not been found to be a confidential relationship.

<u>The Effect of a Confidential Relationship:</u> Most courts do not presume undue influence merely because a person, who is in a confidential relationship to the testator, is a devisee of that person's will. An automatic presumption from the relationship would raise the undue influence issue in too many cases. Consequently, some suspicious circumstances need be shown to raise the presumption. By comparison, there is a presumption of undue influence for inter vivos gifts made to one in a confidential relation with the donor.

Other courts find that a presumption of undue influence may arise and the burden may shift to the proponent, if there is evidence that there was activity by the person procuring the will unduly in his or her favor particularly if the beneficiary is a legal stranger. Also, a presumption may arise if the alleged undue influencer and confidant drafts testator's will. This is particularly applicable to attorneys who draft wills for clients and who are beneficiaries in the will. Preparation of the will is not essential if the undue influencer participated in procuring and executing the will.

g. Undue Influence and Attorneys

An attorney may draft a will for persons who want to make the attorney a beneficiary only under certain circumstances. An attorney cannot ethically draft a will for a legal stranger in which the attorney is a devisee. *See supra* Part 1.IV. Because the imputation rule attaches, an attorney's other firm members may not draft the will either. If an attorney is an heir of the client, the attorney may draft the will for the client and be a devisee if the attorney does not receive a disproportionate share in relation to the legal relationship.

The presumption may also arise where the beneficiary was in a confidential relationship with testator such as attorney-client, and there was a meretricious relationship between the two. It appears that the longer the relationship lasted, the less likely undue influence should be found. A sustained relationship provides a donative foundation because in time the partner would thereby become a "natural object" of the testator's bounty.

h. Duress

Duress concerns the imposition of improper pressure on the testator which overcomes testator's will and takes away testator's free agency. The pressure may be manifested by physical coercion or some other improper threat. Duress is not a common ground for will contests.

6. FRAUD

Fraud as a ground of contest concerns the situation when it can be shown that false representations were designed to and did deceive the testator into making a will different in its terms from that which he or she would have made had he or she not been misled. The ground is similar to a tort action for deceit. Fraud must relate either to fraud in the execution of a will or to fraud in its inducement. There must be intent to deceive the testator and thus an innocent misrepresentation of the fact does not constitute fraud. The "risk of non persuasion" in a fraud contest is on the contestants.

a. Fraud in the Execution

Fraud in the execution concerns a fraud perpetrated in the execution or misrepresentations as to the character or contents of the instrument. Fraud must be made directly upon the testator: Fraud on the witnesses is not enough. Misrepresentation of contents not induced by the beneficiary is not ground for judicial relief, unless under the circumstances redress would be given for mistake alone.

Courts apply varying remedies depending on the nature of the fraud. If it is fraudulent execution of the will, the will will be denied probate. If it is fraudulent nonexecution, the will is not probated and the harmed parties must seek a remedy such as a constructive trust. If the concern is fraudulent revocation, the court may grant probate. On the other hand, fraudulent nonrevocation does not prevent probate and the harmed persons must seek a remedy such as a constructive trust. It seems that the probate process will undo what was done because of fraud but will not do what was not done. The constructive trust remedy replaces or supplements inadequate probate remedy.

b. Fraud in the Inducement

i. For fraud in the inducement (falsification of facts dehors the instrument) to be a contestable ground the representation must be made directly or indirectly to the testator before the execution. It must be made either by a person benefitting under the will or at least by someone on that person's behalf. The statements must be false although under some circumstances suppression of the facts may be sufficient. The representation must be known to be false. The fraud must be to a *material* point and thus have caused the deception. The testator should have been deceived by the representation.

ii. The judicially preferred test applied to the question of whether the fraud caused the disposition to be made is that the gift is invalid if the testator would not have made the provision had he or she known the true facts. This test requires some speculation on the part of the court or jury as to what the testator would have done had he or she known the true facts at the time of the making of the will. Consequently, the matter is for the jury or trier of fact to determine under close review of the appellate courts.

7. MISTAKE

The effect of a mistake made on a will has many aspects to will validity. Testator may have been mistaken as to the nature of the instrument executed, called a "mistake in the execution." Or, a testator may have been mistaken as to facts outside the instrument itself, called a "mistake in the inducement." Mistake in the execution would be a ground for contest whereas mistake in the inducement ordinarily would not be.

Mistake in Execution of a Will: If the testator mistakenly executes the wrong document, it should be denied probate because testamentary intent is entirely lacking. Mistakes of this nature are capable of satisfactory proof because the error generally appears upon the face of the document signed, *e.g.*, mutual wills misexecuted. This issue is litigated at probate or contest of the will. Some, but not all, courts seem to be more liberal in admitting evidence at probate. This may be justified because evidence has to be admitted to prove the validity of the will. Some have called it a "foot in the door" approach.

Illustration 4: H and W, a married couple, agree to execute mutual wills both of which transfer all the assets of the first spouse to die to the surviving spouse, then to selected relatives. In the execution process, H signs W's will and W signs H's will. The error is not discovered until H dies. The issues are whether H's Will can be probated since he executed the wrong will and thus may be said to lack testamentary intent; or, if probated can it be reformed to comply with the original wishes. Whereas the court in *In re Estate of Pavlinko*, 148 A.2d 528, (Pa. 1959) refused to allow probate of such a will, the court in *In re Snide*, 418 N.E.2d 656 (N.Y. 1981) allowed probate and reformation of the will. These cases are ripe for judicial reformation because will execution formalities have been satisfied, the intent of the testators is clear and there is no indication of fraud or undue influence.

D. INTER VIVOS TRANSFERS

Inter vivos transfers such as a trusts can be reformed or rescinded upon the same grounds as transfers free of trust, *i.e.*, fraud, duress, undue influence and sometimes unilateral mistake. Unilateral mistake is ordinarily a sufficient ground for rescission or reformation although some courts have been more restrictive depending upon the situation. The question in each case is whether the transfer was made under such circumstances that it would be inequitable not to permit the settlor to set it aside. Clear and convincing evidence is the standard for the burden of proof and is put on the party seeking reformation or rescission. Cases fail where testimony is conflicting.

E. REVIEW QUESTIONS

1. What are the two common types of probate?
2. When can an heir or next of kin or surviving spouse contest a will?
3. List some of the general grounds for contesting a will.
4. What is the appropriate time for considering the basic mental ability of the testator to execute a will?
5. What is the differences between mental deficiency and mental derangement?
6. What constitutes undue influence?

*

V

CONSTRUCTIONAL PROBLEMS OF DISPOSITIONS

Analysis

A. GENERAL COMMENT

1. The application or nonapplication of the following rules of construction can be controlled by the testator by express provisions in the will. *See* UPC § 2–601.

B. CLASSIFICATION OF TESTAMENTARY GIFTS

1. TYPES OF DEVISES

It is important to determine whether a testamentary gift is of one class or type or of another because many of the distributive rules depend upon such characterization. In fact the particular distributive problem involved may influence a court in defining what type of gift is involved. Even tax law is involved. The term "devise" is used for devises, legacies, and bequests. The four types on testamentary gifts are as follows:

- Specific devises are gifts of some particular thing or parcel of land. Many times the description of the property in the specific gifts are accompanied with the word "my" or "the," *e.g.*, "my automobile."
- General devises are ones which are payable out of the general estate, *e.g.,* $1,000 to A; 100 shares of ABC stock to B. The latter gift is an order to the personal representative to purchase the asset devised out of general estate assets if that asset is not in the estate at death.
- Demonstrative devises are devises, typically of an amount of money, payable primarily from a particular source, fund or container and if that source fails or is inadequate, then from the general assets of the estate. Courts sometimes classify a devise as demonstrative in order to avoid ademption by extinction, even when the language is not specifically clear. It is usually a fiction invented by the courts for this purpose when the strict language of the will suggests either a general or a specific legacy.
- Residuary gifts are gifts of whatever remains of the estate after the payment of all obligations and after all other bequests and devises have been satisfied.

2. CHARACTERIZING DEVISES

When characterizing gifts, one must consider all possibilities and be flexible. Issues concern the importance of and existence of evidence of intent of the testator versus doctrinal avoidance.

Examples of Classification of Devises	
Devise	**Devise Type**
"I give all of my china to A"	Specific bequest
"I give $15,000 to A"	General devise (A charge on the general estate)
"I give A $10,000 out of my account at X Bank"	Demonstrative legacy or specific (or general)
"I give the residue of my estate to A"	Residuary (A gift of what is remaining in the estate after all creditors and other devises are satisfied)
"I give A $2,000 worth of my X corporation stock"	Specific or demonstrative bequest (or general)
"I give A all my personal property"	Specific bequest (or residuary—it has even been held to be general)
"I give the rest of my land to A"	Specific bequest (or residuary)
"I give A 100 shares of X Corporation stock"	Specific or general bequest.
Consider—T owned 0, 100, or 200 shares when will was executed.	If T owned no stock, the devise appears to be a general devise; if T owned 100 or 200, a court might prefer a specific characterization.
"I give A the money X owes me at my death"	Specific legacy but this could be general if interpreted to mean the amount due comes out of general estate, *e.g.*, debtor can't pay.
Consider potentially relevant facts: X owed T $1,000 when will was executed; but at death X owed T $0, $500, or $10,000.	The distribution issue may be significant, *e.g.*, ademption by extinction or abatement.

3. CLASS GIFTS

A class gift is a gift to a group of persons such as "children," "grandchildren," "brothers," "sisters," "nephews," "nieces," "cousins," "issue," "descendants," and "family." *See* Part 8.III. Class gifts inherently possess lapse avoidance capabilities. They are useful and flexible estate planning devices.

C. LAPSE AND ANTILAPSE

1. GENERAL RULES

A devisee must survive the decedent to take under a will. When the question of survival materially affects the distribution of the testator's estate, the timing of death becomes an extremely disrupting and litigable issue.

2. SURVIVORSHIP AND SIMULTANEOUS DEATH

a. Common Law Survival Requirement

To take at common law, a devisee must survive the decedent "for an instant of time." Mere survival by any measurable time was enough. When a question arises whether a person survived for inheritance purposes, the answer depends on the matter of evidence and the standard of proof. The same problems with evidence and proof can arise in regard to survivorship of devisees as with heirs. *See supra* Part 2.II.B. The one significant difference is that testators can control the terms of survival. Wills sometimes include a clause requiring devisees to survive by a specified period of time after the death of the testator, *e.g.*, thirty days.

b. Statutory Survival Periods

Drawing upon this estate planning technique, Section 2–702 of the UPC adopts a default survivorship rule for all types of gratuitous transfers, including wills and all other governing instruments. This rule of construction requires all takers to survive by 120 hours of decedent's death or the transfer activating event. This provision covers a wide range of property interests including wills, joint ownership and contractual rights.

Although similar to the comparable rule for intestacy, [*See supra* Part 2.II.B.], it has a significant difference. Whereas the rule for intestacy is irrebuttable, the Section 2–702 requirement is alterable by the terms of the document. The UPC is very specific, however, in regards to what is necessary to rebut the statutory rule of construction. UPC § 2–702(d).

The UPC itemizes four general situations where the statutory rule of construction will not apply:

- If the governing instrument contains language explicitly dealing with simultaneous death or with deaths in a common disaster and that language is operable under the facts of the case.
- If the governing instrument expressly indicates that the beneficiary is not required to survive to a particular time or event, by any specific length of time or that expressly requires the individual to survive an event or time by a specific period. The specific period in the above exception includes a reference to the death of another individual.
- If the rule's application would cause the transfer to fail to qualify as a valid transfer under the Uniform Statutory Rule Against Perpetuities. *See* UPC § 2–901; Part 8.IV.C.
- If the rule's application would result in an unintended failure or unintended duplication of a disposition.

Notwithstanding the waiver of the 120 hour survivorship requirement, survival of an event or time must be established by clear and convincing evidence.

Third parties dealing with, and bona fide purchasers from, transferees who subsequently fail to survive the necessary period of time are protected under the UPC. This includes protection for payors and payees for consideration.

3. LAPSED AND VOID DEVISES

In older usage, lapse occurs when a legatee or devisee dies between the execution of a will and the death of the testator. A devise is said to be void when the devisee died before the execution of the will. Today, both situations come under the term "lapse." When a devise lapses, the devise either: (1) passes to a specifically named alternative devisee (a gift-over); (2) if no gift-over devise, to the residuary devise; or, (3) if no gift-over or residuary devise, by intestacy.

Drafters of instruments that are subject to lapse usually attempt to control the disposition of a lapsed devise by one or more of the following techniques: (1) Gift to more than one person by joint tenancy; (2) Gifts over to another beneficiary; and (3) Gift to a class, especially a multiple-generation class such as "issue" or "descendants."

4. LAPSE AND TESTATOR'S INTENT

Lapse cases raise jurisprudential issues as to how courts should deal with rules of construction in relation to their consideration of what the testator would want or at least what an average testator would want. The opinions go all over the place. Some courts mechanically apply the applicable rule of construction. Others appear to consider matters of testator's intent.

Courts might improve decisions and results if they sought answers to several questions before applying the rule of construction in lapse cases. For example, relevant questions would include:

- What would a reasonable person think T would want?
- Who are the beneficiaries?
- What happens if lapse occurs?
- Does lapse make sense?
- Are some heirs disinherited whereas other similar heirs take?

Antilapse Statutes: Antilapse statutes exist in all states. In effect, antilapse statutes do not reverse the rule of lapse, but create a substitutional gift. The statutes do not save the gift for the original devisee so as to permit the property to become an asset of that devisee's estate. The statutes substitute the devisee's issue for the devisee, with the issue taking in their own right. The statutes usually limit the antilapse protection to certain relatives such as children, descendants, relatives (undefined or defined); or relatives by affinity, *i.e.*, stepchildren. In addition the statutes do not apply if the testator adequately indicates a contrary intent.

Class Gifts and Antilapse Statutes: When the antilapse statute is silent in regard to its application to class gifts, litigation has developed over the application of antilapse statutes to class gifts. There are strong arguments for all the various approaches.

Against application:

- The statutes apply only to lapsed devises, they do not apply to class gifts because class gifts do not lapse;
- The statutes do not apply because the purpose of class gifts shows intent not to apply statute.

For application:

- Class gift rules are only rules of construction to avoid intestacy which should be viewed in light of the statutory rule of construction which also avoids intestacy;
- The Statutes apply to any applicable devise that fails because devisee predeceases;
- In regard to void gifts, the statutes should apply because otherwise an unequal distribution may occur merely because of a fortuitous event, *i.e.*, death of ancestor.

5. ANTILAPSE UNDER THE UPC

The UPC contains a comprehensive set of provisions dealing with the problems of lapse. UPC §§ 2–603, 2–604. Section 2–603 applies to any devisee who is a grandparent or lineal descendant of a grandparent of the testator or the donor of a power of appointment. This includes parents, uncles and aunts, first cousins and their children, brothers and sisters, nephews and nieces, children and all other descendants of the testator. In addition the provision covers devises to a person who is a stepchild of the testator or the donor of a power of appointment. It applies if the devisee dies before the will, after the will or, if a devisee is treated as predeceased or disclaimed. It applies both to void and lapsed class gifts but not to class gifts that are inherently representational, *e.g.*, "heirs," "issue."

If lapse still occurs, the devised property becomes part of the residue. UPC § 2–604(a). If the residue is to more than one person, but one dies and the devise fails, the lapsed devise is divided among the other residuary beneficiaries in proportion to their interests in the residue. UPC 2–604(b).

Illustrations of Applications of UPC Antilapse Provisions

Question: Using the UPC provisions for lapse and antilapse, who takes what property under the following problems:

Assume that when a person is said to survive, it means that person satisfies all requirements of survivorship, including the 120 hour rule, and is not treated as having predeceased. *See* UPC §§ 2–702, 2–801(d), 2–803, 2–804.

Problem 1:

1. T's properly executed Will provides:

   "The coin collection to A,

   My rings to B

   $10,000 to C and D or to the survivor,

   $10,000 to E's surviving children, and

   the residue to F and G."

2. A is a neighbor and friend; B is second cousin; C and D are T's siblings; E is a first cousin; and F and G are friends of T.

3. A, B, C, E and F predecease T, each leaving surviving descendants. D and G survived T. E had three children, H, I, and J. H predeceased T leaving M and N as descendants. M died 100 hours after T.

Answer and Analysis:

Because A and B predeceased T, their devises lapse. Their descendants do not take a substitute gift because neither is a protected relative (grandparent or descendant of a grandparent). [*See supra* Chart 2–2–1 at Part 2.I.A.4.] A is not a relative and B is too distant a relative. The lapsed devises become part of the residue.

D takes the entire devise of $10,000. C's devise lapses because C predeceased T. C's descendants are not substituted for C although C is a protected relative because the words "or the survivor" create an alternative gift of C's ½ to D. The alternative devise takes precedence over both the substitute gift and the residuary devise. If both C and D predeceased T and both left surviving descendants, C's descendants would share half and D's descendants would share half.

The devise to E's children is covered by the presumption. The presumption of a substitute devise applies to class devises such as to children and here the children are members of the protected relational umbrella. Consequently, H's descendants, M and N, are eligible to receive the substitute devise in place of their ancestor H. The words "surviving children" are considered to be mere words of survivorship and do not on their own rebut the substituted devise. M died 100 hours after T and under Section 2–702 failed to survive T and thus the substitute devise to M lapses. The end result is that N, I and J will share equally the devise. The substitute gift takes precedence over the residuary devise.

F's devise lapses because F predeceased T. F's descendants will not take a substitute devise under Section 2–603 because F is not a protected relative. Even though G is not a protected relative, G takes the entire residuary devise (including F's lapsed share) because Section 2–604 applies and it does not require a particular relationship to the testator. That section creates a presumption that applies from the circumstance and in order to avoid intestacy.

Problem 2:

1. T's properly executed Will provides:

   "$10,000 to A, but if A does not survive me, to A's children

   $10,000 to B and C, equally, and

   the residue, including all lapsed or failed nonresiduary devises, to D."

2. A and B are T's siblings; C is T's stepchild from a prior marriage; and D is T's spouse. E, T's adopted child, survived T.

3. A, B, C, and D predecease T, each leaving surviving descendants. A's three children, F, G, and H, predecease T but left one, three, and four grandchildren, respectively, who survived T.

4. D's two children survived T but are from a prior marriage and are only T's stepchildren.

Answer and Analysis:

A's devise lapses because A predeceased T. The alternative devise to A's children also lapses because none survived T. Although A is a protected relative and A's grandchildren would be entitled to a substitute gift, the substitute gift is rebutted by specific inclusion of lapsed devises into the residuary devise. The entire lapsed devise becomes part of the residue. On the other hand, if the devise had said "to A's descendants" A's grandchildren would take ⅛ each by representation or as alternative devisees. *See* UPC § 2–705. A devise to A's descendants does not becomes part of the residuary even though the residuary devise specifically includes lapsed devises because devisees take directly as alternative devisees and not as substitute devisees.

B's and C's devises lapse because they both predeceased T. The lapsed devises become part of the residue. Although B is a protected relative and C is specifically protected as a stepchild and thus substitute devises would ordinarily be presumed in favor of their descendants, the devise lapses into the residuary because of the specific language included in the residuary clause captures lapsed devises.

D's devise lapses because D predeceased T. D's children do not take a substitute devise because they are not protected relatives. The protection for a stepchild does not apply here because it only applies when a stepchild is the named devisee not a substitute devisee under the statutory presumption. The residue will pass by intestacy. Consequently, T's unprovided for adopted child, E, will take the entire residuary estate in intestacy as sole surviving child. *See* UPC § 2–103. It is doubtful that the negative will provision of Section 2–101(b) would apply since the disinheritance was silent. Even if applicable, it would pass the residue to T's collateral relation, by representation and not to T's stepchildren.

6. SURVIVORSHIP RULES FOR WILL SUBSTITUTES

Survivorship problems can arise in inter vivos gratuitous transfers. The law in nonUPC states is usually undeveloped.

The UPC contains several important provisions dealing with issues raised by questions of survivorship, lapse and related problems for will substitutes as well as for wills. Because of the estate planning importance of will substitutes, the UPC extends these constructional rules beyond testamentary instruments and includes constructional rules concerning any "governing instrument." UPC § 2–701. A governing instrument includes deeds, wills, and trusts, life insurance and other related policies, POD accounts, TOD security registrations, pension, retirement and other related plans; any other "dispositive, appointive, or nominative instrument." UPC § 1–201(19). The UPC establishes a set of rules of construction that apply in default but are subject to alteration either by proof of clear and convincing evidence contrary to the default rule or by explicit language superseding the default rule in the governing instrument. UPC § 2–701.

D. ADEMPTION

1. ADEMPTION BY EXTINCTION

The common law rule of "ademption by extinction" holds that when the subject of a specific devise, *i.e.,* the property given, is not a part of the testator's estate at death, the gift fails by ademption.

a. Intent of Testator

Most but not all courts also hold that the intent of the testator is not important in whether a gift is adeemed. Courts generally apply the "identity theory": is or is not the item devised in the estate. Ademption is avoided only if avoidance is expressed on the face of the will. Some recent decisions, however, have adopted the "intent theory" and considered extrinsic evidence of testator's intent. The Restatement (Third) of Property supports the "intent theory." *See* RESTATEMENT (THIRD) OF PROPERTY (WILLS AND OTHER DONATIVE TRANSFERS) § 5.2 (1999).

Even under the identity theory, intent can sometimes come in through the back door with the use of the exceptions. The escape devices used by the courts to avoid ademption include: (1) classifying a questionable bequest as general or demonstrative rather than specific when confronted with the question of ademption; (2) applying the testamentary expression of the gift to the situation as it exists at the time of the testator's death and thus passing the property then owned by testator, *e.g.*, "the automobile I now own" (These constructional preferences have limited scope and do not apply if the description is so detailed and specific as to foreclose such construction); (3) tracing the object of the gift to another asset in the estate, *e.g.*, simultaneous death of T and destruction of gift, insurance on devise is payable to estate; and, (4) ignoring ademption caused by a guardian and converting specific gifts into general devises.

b. Change of Form

The courts have also held that changes in form, if not substantial, do not cause an ademption. Relevant factors include the degree of physical change and whether affirmative (voluntary) or automatic (involuntary) action was taken or necessary to make the change. Usually, the intent of the testator is neither mentioned nor apparently considered on the face of the decisions.

Changes of Form or Substance		
T's will provides: "I give my piano to A."		
After date of will, T:		**Analysis**
	Paints it	Mere change in form.
	Sells old, buys new	Piano exists at death, no ademption unless T intended a particular piano.
	Sells it, buys a spinet piano	There still is a piano in the estate, only its type changed. Probably merely a change in form if ademption is found at all.
	Sells it to buy an organ or a harp	Clearly the piano no longer exists in the estate and it has changed form. Liberal courts might allow A to trace the piano funds to new purchase. It is a musical instrument and a court might define this as a mere change in form.
Or, after date of will:		**Analysis**
	Piano is destroyed in a fire (insurance)	Courts have allowed devisee to take insurance proceeds for destroyed piano if they had not been paid during T's lifetime. If insurance proceeds are commingled into other assets, tracing would be unlikely.
	Conservator sells piano to pay T's bills	Courts have allowed a devisee to take the value of the devisee if the devise is sold be a conservator because T had no part in the transaction.

Corporate Security Metamorphoses: The effect of corporate structural reorganizations on specific devises of corporate securities has been litigated frequently and the results have varied. Courts have held that a devise is adeemed when the stock devised was converted to bonds and when stocks or bonds were converted to notes. On the other hand, devises of stocks that split or that were only reclassified have been held not to be adeemed.

Illustration 1: T devises 100 shares of X Corporation Stock to A. Between the date of the will and the date of T's death the stock splits five shares for each share owned. No action is required on the part of the T: X Corp. automatically issues the additional share to each shareholder. When T dies T owns 500 shares of X Corp. stock.

> What, if anything, does A take? If the devise is a general devise, A will take 100 shares of the stock. If the devise is characterized as a specific stock, the first issue is whether the devise is adeemed. If it is adeemed, A takes nothing. The issue of ademption is whether the 100 shares devised, now represented by 500 shares, is merely a change in form. In this situation, courts have allowed devisees to take the full 500 shares. *In re Mandelle's*

Estate, 233 N.W. 230 (Mich. 1930); *Shriners Hosp. for Crippled Children v. Coltrane,* 465 So.2d 1073 (Miss. 1985).

If the change in security had been from stock to debentures and the T had to affirmatively requested the change, a court may find the devise adeemed. *First National Bank v. Perkins Institute*, 176 N.E. 532 (Mass. 1931). A change from stock ownership to debenture ownership is more substantial than a change in the number of the shares of stock, particularly if the testator had to perform affirmative acts.

A line of authority that has recently emerged disregards the classification of a devise of a specific number of shares of stock or other securities. Whether the devise is specific or general is deemed to be irrelevant. Any devise of a specific number of shares is treated as a value devise that carries with it any additional securities acquired by the testator after executing the will, to the extent that the post-execution acquisitions resulted from the testator's ownership of the devised securities. *See Watson v. Santalucia,* 427 S.E.2d 466 (W. Va. 1993); *Bostwick v. Hurstel,* 304 N.E.2d 186 (Mass. 1973); *Egavian v. Egavian*, 232 A.2d 789 (R.I. 1967); RESTATEMENT (THIRD) OF PROPERTY (WILLS AND OTHER DONATIVE TRANSFERS) § 5.3 (1999). *See also* UPC § 2–605. For more on this question, *see infra* Part 3.V.F. on Accessions.

c. Ademption by Extinction and the UPC

The UPC significantly alters and clarifies the common law rule concerning ademption by extinction of specific devises. UPC § 2–606.

Under the UPC the specific devisee has a right to specifically devised property or any part of it that exists in testator's estate at death. UPC § 2–606(a). Concomitantly, the specific devisee has a right to assets that represent, in part or in whole, the remaining interest which the testator retains at death in the specifically devised property.

Five situations are delineated as constituting a testator's remaining interest at death:

- The unpaid balance of the purchase price, plus any accompanying security agreement, owed to the testator;
- The unpaid amount of a condemnation award owed to the testator;
- The unpaid fire or casualty insurance proceeds or recovery for injury to the specifically devised property;
- The property received by foreclosure or obtained in lieu of foreclosure on a specifically devised obligation; and,
- The real or personal property acquired by testator as a replacement for the specifically devised property.

UPC § 2–606(a)(1)–(5). These rules are not subject to contradiction by extrinsic evidence of testator's unexpressed intent.

If the specifically devised property is not in the testator's estate at death, the devisee is entitled to a general pecuniary devise equal to the value of the specifically devised property (less the value of any actual portion of the devise remaining in the estate at testator's death and of the five representative remaining interests described above), but only to the extent that it is established by clear and convincing evidence that ademption would be inconsistent with the testator's intent. UPC § 2–606(a)(6) (as amended in 1997).

Extrinsic Evidence: The UPC adopts a broad extrinsic evidence rule to permit proof of testator's intent concerning ademption. The presumption for ademption in (a) (6), as revised, may be rebutted either when the facts and circumstances indicate testator did not intend ademption, or if ademption is inconsistent with the testator's manifested plan of distribution. The latter proviso permits extrinsic evidence to be admitted to determine testator's intent and to permit the court to consider the entire estate plan in order to determine what the testator desired.

Conservator Transactions: Transactions made for an incapacitated testator by a lifetime conservator or agent under a durable power of attorney are covered by a specific provision. UPC § 2–606(b)–(e). The three specific situations covered by the provision include when a conservator or agent: (1) sold the specifically devised property; (2) received a condemnation award for the specifically devised property; and (3) received insurance proceeds for loss of the property due to fire or casualty. In all three situations, the specific devisee is entitled to a general pecuniary devise equal to the net sale price, condemnation award, or the value of the insurance proceeds. This right exists even when the conservator has already received the amounts and has integrated them into the testator's other assets. These rules are not subject to contradiction by extrinsic evidence of testator's unexpressed intent. If the testator survives a judicial determination that testator's disability ceased for one year or more, however, the protection provided to the specific devisee by this provision no longer applies.

Protecting the specific devisee from conservator and agent transactions is consistent with the concept that ademption or nonademption should be related to testator's intent. Acts of a third person, including a testator's conservator or agent under a durable power, do not reveal testator's desires and should not materially and unfairly affect a specific devisee's interest.

Illustrations of Ademption by Extinction

Question: Using both Common Law principles and UPC provisions concerning ademption by extinction, who takes what property under the following problems?

Problem 1

T's properly executed Will provides:

> "The wristwatch I own at my death to A, but if I do not own one, $1,000 to A;
>
> my automobile to B;
>
> my 100 shares of XYZ, Inc., common stock to C;
>
> the residue to D."
>
> T lost the watch and did not replace it.
> T's automobile was destroyed in a major accident; the insurance company has agreed to pay $2,000 but had not paid at T's death.
> T sold the XYZ, Inc., stock and used the proceeds to buy WVU, Inc., stock.
>
> T's residue is valued at $100,000.
>
> All devisees survived T.

Answer and Analysis:

The specifically devised wrist watch is adeemed and T's expressed intent devises A the alternate $1,000. This result is true under Common Law and under the UPC.

Even under the Common Law, B is entitled to the unpaid insurance proceeds on the wrecked automobile. In addition to the proceeds, if the unpaid insurance proceeds do not equal the value of the devise, B might be entitled under the UPC to a pecuniary devise equal to the difference between the value of the devise less the unpaid insurance proceeds from the estate if B can establish by clear and convincing evidence that ademption would be inconsistent with T's intent.

Under the Common Law C's devise would be adeemed unless the court accepted a tracing argument that the WVU stock is merely T's replacement for the XYZ stock. Under the UPC, C is entitled to the WVU stock as T's replacement for the XYZ stock. In addition, if the WVU stock does not equal the value of the devise, C might be entitled to a pecuniary devise equal to the difference between the value of the devise less the value of the WVU stock from the estate, if C can establish by clear and convincing evidence that ademption would be inconsistent with T's intent.

D is entitled to the residue which is the remaining estate after the deductions for expenses of administration and the payment of all the above devises. Unless the facts and circumstances indicate or it is found that the will or T manifests an intent not to apply ademption, the specific devises will adeem to the extent they are not satisfied by the property remaining in the estate and the adeemed portion will pass to D as part of the residue.

Problem 2

All facts are the same as problem 1, except that all the actions and events were performed by T's conservator or attorney in fact under a valid durable power of attorney.

Answers and Analysis:

Under the UPC the analysis for Problem 1 is the same with two exceptions. First A might take the greater of the value of the wristwatch or the $1,000. The other specific devisees will take whatever remains of their devise plus a general pecuniary devise of the difference of the original value of the devise less the value of the remaining portion of the devise. When a conservator or attorney in fact carries out the adeeming action, there is no residual relevance of T's intent. Therefore, the general pecuniary devises would be absolute and not require proof with extrinsic evidence. Under the Common Law, courts vary as to the effect of a conservator causing the ademption. Some have treated the issue similarly, some have converted the adeemed devises into general devises.

---

2. ADEMPTION BY SATISFACTION

The ademption by satisfaction doctrine is the testamentary counterpart of the advancement doctrine under intestate succession. *See supra* Part 2.II.A. Under the common law, the doctrine provides that a general or residuary devise is adeemed in whole or in part when a testator makes an inter vivos gift to the devisee after the execution of the will. ATKINSON, WILLS § 133. As with advancements, the purpose of the doctrine is to prevent a devisee from receiving a double share.

a. Satisfaction under the Common Law

Although the application of ademption by satisfaction in any situation depends on proof of the testator's subjective intent, that intent is difficult to judicially establish. When intent is not clearly manifested, courts use presumptions to settle the issue.

Presumptions: When the testator stands in loco parentis (in place of the parent) to the legatee, testator's gift is presumed to be intended as satisfaction. The common law doctrine does not apply to devises of land (but most of them are specific which are adeemed if transferred inter vivos).

When the thing given is not of the same nature as the thing bequeathed, a presumption arises that the doctrine was not intended to apply. Some courts have limited the rule to inter vivos gifts that are in the nature of a "portion" of the devise: some identifiable proportionate share of the devise. Depending on testator intent, partial satisfaction may constitute full satisfaction.

b. Satisfaction and the UPC

The UPC codifies the ademption by satisfaction doctrine and formalizes its proof requirements. UPC § 2–609. Paralleling its provision concerning advancements, the UPC provides that a gift is satisfaction of a devise only if one of several formalities is satisfied. A gift is a formal satisfaction if either (1) the will provides for the deduction, or (2) the testator "declared in a contemporaneous writing," or (3) the devisee "acknowledged in writing" that the gift is in satisfaction of the devise. UPC § 2–609(a). Under the UPC, the doctrine applies to devises of land and to devises of personalty.

Rather than declaring the gift is in satisfaction, the required writing may merely indicate that the gift must be deducted from the value of the devise. No words of art such as "satisfaction" need be used by the testator. The gist of the declaration must indicate the testator intended that the gift constitutes what lawyers call a gift in satisfaction of a devise. It is also not specifically required that the written expression of intent to make a formal satisfaction be communicated to the devisee at the time of the gift. Informal contemporaneous written notes in testator's personal records should be sufficient. The writing must be available or provable after the testator's death when distribution decisions are made. It cannot be a blanket written but nontestamentary statement that attempts to categorize future gifts as satisfaction. *Estate of McFayden v. Sample*, 454 N.W.2d 676 (Neb. 1990).

According to the comment to the section there is no requirement that the gift must be made directly to the devisee or that it even be an outright gift. UPC § 2–609, Comment. If the formality of satisfaction is satisfied and the necessary intent is declared, gifts to others and of less than full ownership can be satisfaction. In addition the UPC does not require that the relevant actions take place in a certain sequence. Formal satisfaction might be accomplished before the will is executed although most cases will concern the reverse sequence.

Valuation of formal satisfaction is determined as of the time of the devisee's possession or enjoyment or as of the testator's death, whichever occurs first. UPC § 2–609(c).

Devisee's Descendants: The UPC specifically provides that when a devisee of a formal satisfaction fails to survive the donor, the formal satisfaction affects the share that the devisee's descendants take from testator's estate if the descendants take as substitute devisees under the UPC's antilapse provisions, unless the testator's contemporaneous writing expressly provides that the gift is not to affect the descendants' devise. UPC § 2–609(c). This is the opposite rule from the UPC's advancement provision. The distinction is justifiable on the basis that satisfaction concerns the testator's intent whereas advancement concerns intestacy and therefore legislative intent. The gift in satisfaction does not affect the devisee's descendants if they take as alternative devisees unless the testator's contemporaneous writing expressly provides that the gift affects the descendants' devise.

Illustration 2: T's will, in relevant part, states: "I devise $10,000 to A" Before T's death, T made an inter vivos gift to A of $5,000. In a writing T stated that this gift was in full satisfaction of the devise in T's Will. A, who is T's child, dies before T and leaves a descendant, G who survives T. Does G take the $10,000 from the will?

Under the UPC's antilapse provision, G would be a substitute devisee and would take the $10,000 but under the UPC satisfaction provision, the satisfied gift to G's ancestor prevents G from taking the devise. In this situation the satisfaction provision trumps the antilapse provision.

Illustration 3: T's will, in relevant part, states: "I devise $10,000 to A but if A does not survive me, to A's children" Before T's death, T made an inter vivos gift to A of $5,000. In a writing T stated that this gift was in full satisfaction of the devise in T's Will. A, who is T's child, dies before T and leaves a descendant, G who survives T. Does G take the $10,000 from the will?

G is an alternate devisee and takes the devise in his or her own right; consequently, G does not take under the UPC's antilapse provision. Because G takes as a specific devisee and not as substitute devisee, G takes the $10,000 despite the satisfied gift to G's ancestor, A. In this situation the satisfaction provision does not trump the direct devise to G unless the satisfaction writing expressly provides that the gift affects that descendant's devise.

c. Will Substitutes

Although the law is not as well developed, similar issues concerning inter vivos gifts to persons who are beneficiaries of will substitutes, such as trusts, can arise.

E. ACCESSIONS

1. ACCESSION DEFINITION

Accessions issues concern the definition of the property owned or devised. It is generally agreed that the owner of an asset is entitled to all wealth that it produces, and to all wealth that is added or united to it, either naturally or artificially, even when the changes actually change the asset's form or composition. For example, the owner of a piece of real estate owns the piece with improvements added after acquisition. Or, stock purchased at $1.00 per share is the purchaser's property even if it increases in value 100 fold. Rental income and dividends from these assets are also considered to be the owner's property.

2. ACCESSION TIMING

Accession issues raised at time of distribution from a decedent's estate may concern changes in the property that arise both before and after the death of the testator. Before death accessions include the rules that specific devisee takes property at its distribution market value, the devisee takes land with improvements, and the devisee takes stock splits of specific devise of stock.

For many accession issues, there is a close relationship between accession rules and ademption by extinction rules.

Illustration 4: T's will states: "I give 500 shares of my XYZ corporation stock to A." Before death, XYZ corporation is merged with MNO corporation to form MOZ corporation. Each XYZ share is converted to 5 MOZ shares. T owns 2,000 MOZ shares at death. What does A take? There are several possible answers. (1) A takes nothing because of ademption by extinction. The XYZ stock is no longer in the estate. (2) A takes 500 shares of MOZ stock. This conforms to the number of share originally devised. (3) A takes all 2,000 shares of MOZ stock with the rest being adeemed. Answer (3) applies the normal accession concept and comes closest to giving A the value of the original devise.

3. ACCESSIONS UNDER THE UPC

Litigation is common concerning the scope and validity of devises of securities that, between the time of the will's execution and the testator's death, have undergone changes of form such as stock splits, reformulations or other accessions. In Section 2–605 the UPC provides answers to the common issues raised by such devises. The UPC's provision applies to devises of securities which are broadly defined to include not only all types of notes, stocks, bonds and loans but also mineral interest agreements and leases as well as "any interest or instrument commonly known as a security" and the right to purchase any of the above. UPC § 1–201(43).

The threshold requirements include: (1) testator's will devised securities; (2) at the time the will was executed, testator owned securities that met the description of the devised securities; (3) the additional securities owned by testator at death were acquired after the will was executed; and, (4) the additional securities owned by testator at death were acquired as a result of testator's ownership of the devised securities. UPC § 2–605(a). It makes no difference whether the devise is characterized as specific or general. UPC § 2–605, Comment.

Cash distributions prior to death are not part of the devise, however. UPC § 2–605(b). Thus, cash dividends declared prior to death, but not paid until after death, are not part of the specific devise. UPC § 2–605, Comment. In addition, the provision does not apply to nonsecurity devises that may be subject to accessions. The Comment states that the section is not intended to be exclusive as to accessions affecting securities and assumably it would not preclude similar accession interpretations in regard to other nonsecurity devises that raise similar problems.

If these conditions are satisfied, the devisee, in addition to being entitled to as many of the shares of the devised security as are part of the estate at the testator's death, is entitled to additional or other securities in the following three situations:

(1) when the additional securities of the same entity were issued by reason of action initiated by the entity but not including securities acquired by the exercise of purchase options; (2) when securities of other entities are the result of a merger, consolidation, reorganization or other similar action; or, (3) when securities of the same entity are acquired as the result of reinvestment. UPC § 2–605(a)(1)–(3).

4. ACCESSIONS AFTER DEATH

Accessions issues that arise after the death of the testator concern the productivity of assets devised and how that productivity must be distributed. Classification of testamentary gifts may be necessary to determine who benefits from the post death increase and interest. Thus, on distribution devisees of specific devises receive all post death accessions, income, etc, attributable to the asset. Cash devises or legacies earn interest after one year after death. Under UPC Section 3–904 "[g]eneral pecuniary devises bear interest at the legal rate beginning one year after the first appointment of a personal representative until payment, unless a contrary intent is indicated by the will."

F. ABATEMENT

1. ABATEMENT DEFINITION

Abatement problems arise in some estates that lack sufficient funds to satisfy all devises in a will. It may be caused by creditors' claims, an election by the spouse or pretermitted children, expenses of administration, taxes or a general insufficiency of funds. Under the common law, in the absence of a specific order indicated in the testator's will, the order of abatement for personal property was as follows: (1) intestate property; (2) residuary legacies; (3) general legacies; and (4) specific and demonstrative legacies. ATKINSON, WILLS § 136. Within each of the classes of testamentary gifts, the assets would contribute and abate ratably. Although subject to specific statutory or judicial exceptions today, real property was not subject to debts.

2. UPC ABATEMENT RULE

Except that there is no preference between real and personal property, UPC Section 3–902(a) follows the Common Law approach. The UPC also permits the testator to expressly control the order and manner by which devises shall abate. UPC § 3–902(b). In addition, several exceptions to the general rule require emphasis. First, if the abatement problem is caused by a surviving spouse taking under the elective share provisions, the UPC provides that all beneficiaries under the will are to suffer the reduction pro rata and not according to the UPC's general order of abatement. UPC §§ 3–902(a), 2–210. Second, if the personal representative determines that an express or implied purpose of the testamentary plan would be defeated by following the general order of abatement, the abatement must be made in a manner necessary to carry out the testator's intent. UPC § 3–902(b). Third, the UPC contains a special provision dealing with the apportionment of estate taxes which does not follow the general order of abatement. UPC § 3–916, *see also* UPC § 2–302(a)(2)(iv)(pretermitted children).

Illustration 5: T's will devises $30,000 to X Charity and the residue to T's children. Because of significant cost of care in T's last few years, the estate only has $40,000 for distribution. Under the Common Law order, the residue would receive $10,000 from the estate and the charity, which is a general devisee, would receive the full $30,000 devise. Under these facts, a personal representative under the UPC could determine that it was the testator's implied purpose to favor the residuary beneficiaries to the detriment of the other general and specific devisees. The personal representative should seek court approval for whatever abatement plan is recommended.

3. DEBT ABATEMENT

Another abatement problem that applies to estates that are bankrupt is the order of paying debts. All jurisdictions have provisions that determine the proper order for paying debts, claims, and expenses when funds are insufficient to pay all. They may vary, particularly in regard to what priority is given for claims of the state.

<u>UPC Abatement Provision:</u> Section 3–805 of UPC provides that if the applicable assets of the estate are insufficient to pay all claims in full, the personal representative shall make payment in the following order:

(1) costs and expenses of administration;

(2) reasonable funeral expenses;

(3) debts and taxes with preference under federal law;

(4) reasonable and necessary medical and hospital expenses of the last illness of the decedent, including compensation of persons attending him;

(5) debts and taxes with preference under other laws of this state; and,

(6) all other claims.

No preference is given in the payment of any claim over any other claim of the same class, and a claim due and payable is not entitled to a preference over claims not due.

G. MISCELLANEOUS MATTERS

1. EXONERATION

The common law presumed that loans or liens on property given by will should be discharged. The rationale was that the personal estate benefitted from the loan. The presumption was rebuttable.

The modern trend is to abolish the presumption or to reverse it. UPC Section 2–607 calls its relevant section "Nonexoneration" and provides that specific devises pass "subject to any mortgage interest existing at the date of death, without right of exoneration, regardless of a general directive in the will to pay debts." This reverse rule may be too broad and too difficult to rebut.

Illustration 6: T's will devises T's residence to X and T's personal property to Y. After the will was executed, T borrows money to buy a new automobile. Because of tax advantages, T uses the equity on the residence. To get the loan, T mortgages the residence. T dies. What will X and Y take?

> X would take the residence subject to the mortgage even though the mortgage was not used for the purposes of acquiring or improving the property. Y will take the personal property including the automobile without being subject to the debt. This result is probably not what T would have wanted. The UPC requires an expression that exoneration was intended.

Estate planners must be aware and anticipate exoneration. Joint tenancy and tenancies by the entireties have caused problems under an exoneration rule where the estate must pay off the mortgage on the property but the property passes by survivorship to a nonestate beneficiary.

2. RIGHT OF RETAINER

Right of retainer refers to the right of a personal representative of a decedent's estate to reduce a devise by an amount equal to the debt owed to the estate by the devisee. The rule has broad application and a majority of courts have permitted the retainer even if the debt is barred by the Statute of Limitations or if the devisee has declared bankruptcy.

UPC Section 3–903 provides that the amount of a non-contingent indebtedness of a successor to the estate if due, or its present value if not due, must be offset against the successor's interest. The successor, however, has the benefit of any defense which would be available to him in a direct proceeding for recovery of the debt.

H. BENEFICIARY STATUS

Dispositive instruments, such as wills and trusts, commonly use class gifts as a means of describing certain beneficiaries. For example, a will might provide: "I give my residuary estate to my" "children," or "grandchildren," or "brothers and sisters." When a testator in a will uses terms such as "children" or "brothers," it is necessary to determine who is to be included within the named classes of persons. For full-blooded marital persons, it is merely a matter of proof of relationship and survivorship. Relations who are half-bloods, adopted, nonmarital, afterborn persons, or related by affinity, however, are included only if the testator intended that they be included. Unfortunately, a specific indication of intent in the instrument is often lacking. In addition the law in many jurisdictions is not clear on these matters. The resultant litigation has not only been costly and bitter but has also resulted in uncertainties and inconsistencies.

The UPC includes a provision concerning the status of adopted, nonmarital, half blooded individuals and individuals related by affinity. UPC § 2 705. This rule of construction provides that class gift language in dispositive instruments is to be construed in a manner similar to the meaning given to similar terms under the status definitions for intestacy. Thus, relations of the half blood are are included in class gifts to collateral reactions but relations by affinity are excluded from class gifts that refer to relationship by blood whether or not the term commonly differentiates between blood and affinity relationship. § 2 705(a). For example, class gifts to "brothers" or "aunts" will include half blooded brothers or aunts but exclude brothers or aunts who are related merely by marriage.

The rule of construction is more complex for adopted and nonmarital class members. If the class gift is used in an instrument executed by the adopting or natural parent, an adopted or nonmarital child of that person takes unless an intent to exclude is discovered. If the class gift is used in an instrument by someone other than the adopting or natural parent, (1) a nonmarital class member will not take unless the child is expressly included or unless the child lived while a minor with the natural parent or that parent's parent, brother, sister, spouse or surviving spouse [2 705(b)], and (2) an adopted class member will not take unless the adopted person lived with the adopting parent either before or after the adoption as a regular member of the adopting parent's household. UPC 2 705(c). These provisions attempt to accord what some contend conforms to the desires of most people faced with these situations. UPC 2 705, cmt.

I. REVIEW QUESTIONS

1. What are the four types of testamentary gifts?
2. What type of devise gives an amount of money that is payable primarily from a particular source, but if that source is inadequate, is a charge against the general assets of the estate?
3. What occurs when a legatee or devisee dies between the execution of a will and the death of the testator?
4. What Common Law rule holds that a specific devise fails if the devise is not a part of the testator's estate at the time of testator's death?
5. What is a right of retainer?

PART FOUR

LIFETIME TRANSFERS

*

I

WILL SUBSTITUTES

Analysis

E. Nondocumented Gratuitous Transfers
- *1. Formal Requirements of Gifts*
  - *a. Inter Vivos Gifts of Personal Property*
  - *b. Gifts Causa Mortis*

F. Gifts to Minors
- *1. Consequences of a Minor's Incapacity*
- *2. Uniform Transfer to Minors Act*

G. Review Questions

A. TESTAMENTARINESS AND WILL SUBSTITUTES

1. WILL SUBSTITUTE DEFINITION

A will substitute is a property transfer device that passes title at death without being subject (1) to the formalities of the Statute of Wills, or (2) to the probate administration processes. An ideal will substitute is one that allows title to pass to others at death although control remains with the transferor. Common examples of valid will substitutes include gifts, joint ownership, contracts, life insurance, deeds, and inter vivos trusts.

2. TESTAMENTARINESS

A basic problem is to determine what powers reserved by the grantor in a will substitute causes the transfer to be declared testamentary and thus, subject to the requirements of the Statute of Wills.

3. PRESENT TRANSFER OF AN INTEREST

When evaluating a transfer, a common factor referred to by the courts is whether the evidence shows the donor made a present transfer of an interest. This is called the "present transfer" test. Relevant to this determination is the degree to which the donor retained interests or controls. The creation of a future or executory interest is to be contrasted with the future creation of an interest. It is held that if an instrument is intended to become presently binding and nothing is left for the grantor to do to complete the transaction, then it need not be regarded as of a testamentary character. It is sufficient to convey any estate or interest whatever, though it be future or contingent.

4. DOCUMENT FORMALITY

Some commentators argue it is inaccurate to say "a document is testamentary if it passes economic benefits at death." They contend that strict adherence to this analysis would theoretically cause a large number of commonly accepted will substitutes to be ineffective, *e.g.*, life insurance, bank accounts, retirement contracts. They propose that the proper question is "does the will substitute under consideration satisfy the policies of the Statute of Wills."

The two most significant factors that courts take into consideration are (1) the extent of the powers, and (2) the nature of the instrument, if any, which directs the disposition of the property to be made on the donor's death. Imparting importance to the form of the instrument is logical considering that one of the purposes of the formalities of the Statute of Wills is to prevent fraudulent claims. If the inter vivos disposition is evidenced by a formal trust instrument, the danger of fraud, mistake, or undue influence is not increased by the fact that the settlor may have reserved extensive powers.

B. JOINT OWNERSHIP

1. JOINT TENANCY WITH RIGHT OF SURVIVORSHIP

Joint tenancy with right of survivorship is a widely recognized form of ownership. Frequently, the requirements for forming such a relationship are precise, *e.g.*, the necessity of stating that the ownership is a "joint tenancy." A wide range of interests can be held in joint ownership, *e.g.,* real property, tangible personal property and chose in actions. For estate planning purposes, it is necessary to determine how much joint property a client possesses. Joint tenancies can have both income and estate tax consequences.

Transfer of Title: When a joint tenant dies, that tenant's title passes to the surviving joint tenant outside the probate process and without court administration. Although title does not pass until death, this transfer is valid and is not testamentary. Commonly, title is transferred merely by filing an affidavit and a copy of the decedent's death certificate.

Scope of the Survivorship Interest: With some assets held in joint tenancy, it is sometimes difficult to determine the scope of the survivorship interest. For example, it is common for persons to jointly lease safe deposit boxes. This gives the joint tenants the authority to gain access to the box before and after death of one of the tenants. An issue arises, however, whether the joint rights include not only access to the box but also ownership of the contents of the box. Some courts held it did. The error of this holding is that it is not clear that a joint lessor intends ownership to be determined merely by putting an asset in the box. Furthermore the rental agreement is usually prepared by the safe deposit box company on its printed form and designed for its protection. Often, therefore, it does not represent the true understanding of the lessee. It is thus reasonable to deny that a joint tenancy can be created by this method or at least permit proof that such was or was not intended.

2. TENANCY IN COMMON

Another form of joint ownership is tenancy in common. This ownership is merely a form of co-ownership in a piece of property. On the death of a cotenant, the cotenant's interest passes through the cotenant's probate estate.

C. CONTRACTUAL SURVIVORSHIP

1. PAY ON DEATH PROVISIONS

a. General Description of Pay on Death Provisions

It is common for persons to insert in various contractual arrangements provisions concerning the consequences of the death of the parties or the primary party to the contract. For example, partners in their partnership agreement might agree that on the death of a partner the deceased partner's partnership interest passes automatically to the surviving partner or to a another designated person. *See Estate of Hillowitz v. Hillowitz*, 238 N.E.2d 723 (N.Y. 1968). Another arrangement, found particularly in family dealings, concerns a parent who loans money to a child. The parent and child execute a promissory note that, in relevant part, provides the note ceases upon the death of the promisor or promisee, or that on the death of the promisor the debt is to be paid to another person. Courts have characterized the transfer that occurs on death as contractual in nature. The POD beneficiary is said to be a third party beneficiary under contract principles. POD provisions in life insurance and retirement agreements have also been approved, sometimes because they are recognized by statute. *See* N.Y. EPTL § 13–3.2.

POD provisions used in purely gratuitous arrangements have not fared as well. POD provisions under these circumstances have been held by some courts to be invalid because they are characterized as testamentary. *See, e.g., Wilhoit v. Peoples Life Ins. Co.*, 218 F.2d 887 (7th Cir. 1955); Atkinson, Wills § 44. Under these decisions, the POD provisions fail unless the instrument in question was executed with the same formalities as a will including testamentary intent.

Comment: The POD provision constitutes a very convenient way to pass an interest in property outside the probate process. Because they are ordinarily described in a written instrument, they carry with them many of the same protections as the Statute of Wills provides. The law needs to validate these instruments.

Federal Savings Bond: For federal savings bonds two arrangements for their payment on the death of an owner are set out in the Treasury regulations: (1) The name of the purchaser and a co-owner, in which case the bonds are payable to either and at the death of either, the survivor is considered the absolute owner; and, (2) The name of the purchaser and a beneficiary so that if the purchaser dies survived by the beneficiary the latter is considered the absolute owner. The prevailing view is that the regulations are *not* merely for the protection of the government in making the payment, but that the co-owner or beneficiary is absolutely entitled to the bond and its proceeds—either as a third party beneficiary or because the regulations have the effect of federal law, which prevails over the state law.

b. Pay on Death Provisions Under the UPC

In a broadly phrased provision, the UPC accords nontestamentary status to three types of provisions sometimes found in inter vivos transactions. UPC § 6–101. The UPC recognizes three different provisions as nontestamentary and permit an instrument:

(1) to pay money or other benefits due to, controlled, or owned by an obligee to a designated person on the death of the obligee;

(2) to waive a debt on the event of the death of the obligee; and

(3) to permit the obligee to designate the beneficiary of contractual or property rights which are the subject of an instrument.

UPC § 6–101(a)(1)–(3). The first and third provisions above may be included within either the instrument of creation of the transaction or a separate writing, including a will, executed at the same time or subsequently.

This section establishes the validity of many common provisions found in insurance policies, pension plans, annuity contracts, trust agreements and other family arrangements. It will also validate the use of these provisions in a wide range of commercial transactions including bonds, mortgages, promissory notes, and conveyances. With their guaranteed validity and because the effect of the provision is to avoid the estate administration process, use of these provisions in all forms of written instruments may become extremely popular. Although the assets passing by the terms of the provisions are valid and avoid the burden of administration, they do not infringe upon the rights of a creditor established under other laws of the UPC state. UPC § 6–101(b).

The UPC provision does not intend to bootstrap the validity of the underlying document, financial arrangement, or instrument. *See* UPC § 6–101, Comment. It is not designed to convert an ineffective lifetime transfer into a transfer on death. For example, the section did not eliminate the necessity of the delivery of deed to effectuate a lifetime gift of an asset. *See First Nat'l Bank v. Bloom*, 264 N.W.2d 208 (N.D. 1978).

2. MULTIPLE PARTY ACCOUNTS

a. General Description of Accounts

It is common for individuals to hold accounts at financial institutions in the names of more than one person. These arrangements are called multiple-party accounts and typically have taken one of the following forms:

- Joint accounts, *e.g.,* an account payable to "A or B";
- Trust accounts, *e.g.*, an account held as "A in trust for B"; and,
- Accounts payable on death or POD accounts, *e.g.*, an account held as "A payable on death to B."

A wide range of ownership designations are used on these accounts: Joint tenancy with survivorship, tenancy in common, in trust for another, and agency arrangements.

b. Litigation Proclivity of Multiple Party Accounts

Unfortunately, multiple party accounts generate an inordinate amount of litigation concerning various legal problems. *See* Austin W. Scott & William F.

FRATCHER, THE LAW OF TRUSTS §§ 58–58 (4th ed. 1987). The pervasive issue in this litigation is whether each account form is effective to pass the interest to the non-contributing party at the death of the donor or to the donor's estate. Issues in this litigation involve testamentariness, donor's intent, and the meanings of the account forms.

All three types of multiple-party accounts generate litigation over other issues as well. These issues relate to problems arising before the donor's death or after donor's death or at both times.

- Pre-death problems include the rights in the account between the donor and the donee and the rights of the donor's and the donee's creditors in the account.
- Post-death problems include, in addition to the validity question, the rights of the decedent's creditors and the rights of the donor's surviving spouse or other persons protected from disinheritance.
- Excluding the many tax issues raised by these accounts, the other pervasive issues include the manner and time of revocation, the sufficiency of evidence to rebut survivorship, and the relationship of the fiduciary institution which holds the account to the persons named on the account and their successors.

c. Joint Accounts

The ordinary joint bank deposit arrangement differs from an ordinary joint tenancy in that either joint tenant can withdraw all the funds from the account without the other's permission or knowledge. This withdrawal power rebuts the existence of a true joint tenancy with right of survivorship. Despite this, the survivor has been permitted to take.

Various theories have been used by the courts. The bank can be regarded as promising to pay the deposit to the survivor of the donor and the donee with such right of withdrawal in either, both, or neither as may be stipulated in the agreement. A trust theory is sometimes used also. In both situations, the transfer avoids probate in the decedent's estate.

Many states have statutes that simply authorizes the bank to pay such deposits to the survivor. These are for the bank's protection and are not determinative of contests between the donor's personal representative and the surviving spouse or other person. Such provisions have influenced some courts to find for the donee and personal representatives do not usually contest the above transactions.

d. Trust Accounts

The trust account refers to an account, usually a savings type account, that is held in the name of one or more parties as trustee for one or more beneficiaries. Sometimes called a "Totten Trust" they concern a relationship that is established by the form of the account and the deposit agreement with the financial institution and that is not the subject of the trust other than the sums on deposit in the account. *See In re Totten*, 71 N.E.748 (N.Y. 1904). Thus, a trust account does not refer to a regular trust account under a testamentary trust or a trust agreement which has significance apart from the account, or a fiduciary account arising from a fiduciary relation such as attorney-client.

Despite the unlimited control over the account by the depositor, and that the sole purpose of the arrangement is to pay the remainder of the account to the "beneficiary," these accounts have been readily upheld under the characterization of being a revocable trust. In effect, these are pay-on death accounts.

e. Pay-on Death Accounts

A pay-on death, commonly called a POD account, refers to an account that is payable on request to one person, usually the depositor, during his or her lifetime and on that person's death, to one or more POD payees to whom the account is payable. There is a split of authority as to validity of these accounts. Some courts have rejected them as testamentary transfers, others have approved them.

f. Multiple Party Accounts Under the UPC

The UPC addresses the question of the validity of multiple-party, POD, and trust accounts as well as their pre-and post-death problems, including the protection of financial institutions. UPC Art. VI, Part 2; *see generally* LAWRENCE H. AVERILL, UNIFORM PROBATE CODE IN A NUTSHELL §§ 34.01–07 (4th ed. 1996). The UPC's technique (1) eliminates references to the "joint" account and substitutes the more generic term "multiple-party account" and (2) consolidates treatment of the POD account and the trust account so that the same rules apply to both. UPC Prefatory Note, Art. 6. Its provisions are divisible into three categories:

(1) General and clarifying definitions of terms;

(2) Ownership issues as between the parties of the multiple-party accounts and other persons including creditors and successors; and,

(3) Issues concerning the liability of the financial institutions.

The latter two categories are intentionally separated so that differing intentions of the parties may affect arrangements in the second category without endangering the element of definiteness needed for the third category to induce financial institutions to offer such accounts to their customers. *See* UPC § 6–206. One of the UPC's primary goals is to provide a menu of options that could be handed to new depositors to enable them to intelligently select the kind of account they want. *See* UPC § 6–204. With intent firmly set by the selection, the hope is the process will avoid the amount of litigation that developed under nonUPC law.

Definitions of Accounts: An "account" is defined as any type of contractual arrangement for the deposit of funds between a depositor and a financial institution including the ordinary checking account, savings account, certificate of deposit and the share account. A "multiple-party account" includes any account having more than one owner with a present interest in the account. UPC § 6–201, Comment. This broad definition does not encompass, however, any account in which the relationship is established by separate instrument or arrangement. UPC § 6–202.

Types of Accounts: The definitions cover the primary types of accounts including joint, POD, trust, and agency accounts. Because of their similar substantive attributes, the rules of POD and trust accounts are combined. An agency account is an account on which an agent is authorized to make account transactions but holds no beneficial right to sums in the account. UPC §§ 6–201(2); 6–205(a); 6–211(d). Any account may be for a single party or multiple parties. Joint and POD accounts may have a POD designation, an agency designation, or both. UPC § 6–203. Joint accounts can be with or without survivorship: POD and trust accounts must include a right of survivorship.

Ownership During Lifetime of Multiple–Party Accounts: An account is presumed to belong to the parties, during their lifetimes, in proportion to the net contribution of each. UPC § 6–211(b). This presumption is rebuttable by clear and convincing evidence of a different intent such as an intent to make a gift to the non-contributing party. UPC § 6–211, Comment.

A beneficiary in an account with a POD designation, however, has no right to the sums on deposit during the lifetime of any party. UPC § 6–211(c). Similarly, an agent in an account with an agency designation has no beneficial right to sums on deposit. UPC § 6–211(d).

When ownership belongs to more than one party, the division of this ownership during the lifetime of the parties is in proportion to the net contribution of each. UPC § 6–206(b). "Net contribution" of any party at any given time is an amount equal to the sum of all deposits made by or for that party and a pro rata share of any interest or dividends remaining in the account, less any withdrawals from the account made by or for the party that have not been paid to or applied to the use of any other party. UPC § 6–211(a). For spouses, the "net contribution" for each is presumed be an equal amount, subject to contrary proof. UPC § 6–211(b).

Rights at Death for Multiple–Party Accounts: Unless a nonsurvivorship arrangement is specified by the terms of the account, a presumption of a right of survivorship exists for interests in the account. UPC § 2–612. Thus, on the death of a party to a multiple-party account, ownership to the sums on deposit belong to the surviving party or parties. Special ownership allocation presumptions are made when two or more parties survive. These presumptions of, and calculation for, survivorship continue until only one party survives.

Any interest of a decedent, who is a named party in a single-party or multiple-party account that has no effective POD designation or right of survivorship, passes through the decedent's estate. UPC § 6–212(c) . A tenancy in common designation on an account establishes that the account is without right of survivorship.

Rights of survivorship are determined by the form of the account as it exists at the death of a party. Alteration to this form may be made only by a party who gives written notice of the alteration and this notice must be received by the financial institution during the party's lifetime. UPC § 6–213(a). Significantly, the right of survivorship cannot be changed by the will of a party or of any other person. UPC § 6–213(b).

Nontestamentariness of Accounts: Except as the surviving spouse is protected by a spouse's elective share [UPC §§ 2–201 to 2–214], and creditors and others are protected in insolvent estates [UPC § 6–215], transfers resulting from these rules are nontestamentary. UPC § 6–214. This provision means that for purposes of passing an interest to survivors at death, the accounts need not satisfy the execution requirements for wills and are not subject to administration procedures required for assets passing through the decedent's estate. UPC § 6–214, Comment.

3. LIFE INSURANCE, ANNUITIES, AND RELATED ARRANGEMENTS

Within limits of affordability, life insurance presents perhaps the most satisfactory method of limiting the estate which is subject to probate and administration. The amount and beneficiaries may be kept secret. The insured can cash in or borrow against the policy and can change the beneficiaries at will. Despite this control, beneficiaries take at death without court proceedings. Unless fraud is shown, the proceeds payable to a named beneficiary are free of creditors.

Clearly and consistently life insurance of all kinds is held not to be testamentary. The beneficiary obtains his or her interest upon the theory of a contract or a trust for his or her benefit. The *Kansas City Life Ins. Co. v. Rainey*, 182 S.W.2d 624 (Mo. 1944), case is typical of the decisions in this area, *i.e.*, a contract for the benefit of a third persons (donee third party beneficiary) effective before death of the promisee. Other retirement contractual arrangements have been treated similarly. Their beneficiary clauses have been upheld. There still may be Federal and State estate tax consequences.

With only a few exceptions, life insurance and related beneficiary designations are not alterable by will and must be changed according to the terms of the contract.

D. CONDITIONAL DEEDS

1. DEFINITION OF CONDITIONAL DEEDS

Grantors of deeds to real estate sometimes want to personally reserve control of the property transferred. Even when there has been irrevocable delivery, courts have had to determine whether these reservations of control in the deed make the deed testamentary. These reservations usually take the following forms:

- The transfer was upon the condition that the grantee survive the grantor;
- The conveyance was to take effect only upon the grantor's death;
- The instrument was revocable upon the part of the grantor.

2. TESTAMENTARINESS OF CONDITIONAL DEEDS

When all three reservations appear in the same instrument, the deed has usually been held testamentary. *See* ATKINSON, WILLS § 43. There is a decided split of authority as to the effect of each one of these provisions taken singly. Some recognize that a present contingent interest is created sufficient to sustain the instrument as a deed while others declare that there is no present passing of any interest and that the transfer instrument is testamentary. Sometimes delivery of the deed to the donee helps persuade courts that a transfer took place.

Generally, courts say that the key to the issue is whether the deed presently passes an interest on its execution. *See* Part 4.I.A.3. The creation of a future or executory interest is to be contrasted with the future creation of an interest. If an instrument is intended to become presently binding and nothing is left for the grantor to do in order to complete the transaction, then it should not be regarded as of a testamentary character. It is sufficient to convey any estate or interest whatever, though it be future or contingent.

Others contend that the real issue is whether the formality used for executing deeds is sufficient to prevent fraudulent claims and thus satisfy the purposes of the will statutes. If the deed execution procedure is secure, the danger of fraud, mistake, or undue influence is not increased by the fact that the settlor may have reserved extensive powers. Courts have not been satisfied that the deed form is sufficient.

Illustration: D executes an ordinary deed form naming A as grantee. D has two uninterested persons witness the signature. D retains possession of the deed until D's death. If A contends the gift was complete in a quiet title action, a court might say that because the deed was not delivered, a necessary requirement for an inter vivos gift, the gift fails. Consequently, it will be treated as a transaction of "testamentary" character and one that could not pass property during the donor's lifetime. If D attempts to probate the deed because it was signed and witnessed, it may fail because it lacks testamentary intent: that the donor had intended an inter vivos transfer although he had not successfully accomplished the gift. If D can convince the court that an ambiguity exists because the "deed" was executed with two witnesses, D might be able to satisfy the Statute of Wills requirements. *See Noble v. Tipton,* 76 N.E. 151 (Ill. 1905); *Tennant v. John Tennant Memorial Home,* 140 P. 242 (Cal. 1914).

In other words, one can have a testamentary transfer which does not satisfy the requirements of testamentary intent. In litigation such as was involved in the

Noble cases, the original theory may have to be the best one because proof of an incomplete inter vivos transfer can negate the subsequent attempt to prove testamentary intent.

E. NONDOCUMENTED GRATUITOUS TRANSFERS

1. FORMAL REQUIREMENTS OF GIFTS

a. Inter Vivos Gifts of Personal Property

An owner (donor) of personal property may make a gift of that property to another person (the donee) by delivering it to the donee, or to a third person for the donee, with the manifested intention that the donee be the owner of the personal property. The donee's acceptance of the gift is required to complete the gift. RESTATEMENT (SECOND) PROPERTY, DONATIVE TRANSFERS § 31.1 (1992).

The delivery requirement is the formality that explains the act of the donor. It emphasizes to the donor the significance of the act of giving. It confirms what is being done and provides evidence of the rights of the donee in the property. Mechem, *The Requirement of Delivery in Gifts of Chattels*, 21 ILL. L. REV. 341 (1926).

Delivery may be merely the actual physical delivery of the item of personal property to the intended donee. Delivery may be satisfied in other ways as well. Generally, if the donor has completed all that normally could be done under the circumstances to put the intended donee in control of the personal property, delivery to that person has been accomplished.

In addition, delivery to the donee may be constructive or symbolic. Constructive delivery takes place when the donor delivers to the donee something that gives the donee access to the place where the subject matter of the gift is located, *e.g.,* the key to that item of property. Symbolic delivery concerns the indelible inscription of the donee's name on the subject matter of the gift, *e.g.,* the inscription of donee's name on a ring donor intends to give to donee. Delivery of intangible personal property is satisfied if the evidence of the claim is delivered.

B. GIFTS CAUSA MORTIS

A gift causa mortis concerns the situation where an owner of personal property properly makes a gift to another person in apprehension of imminent death. In this situation, a presumption arises that the donor intends a revocable gift. *See* ATKINSON, WILLS § 45. If the donor fails to revoke within a reasonable time after the donor is no longer in apprehension of imminent death the right of revocation is terminated.

A gift causa mortis is not subject to the probate process but is subject to creditors if the donor's estate is insufficient. In addition, a surviving spouse can attack the gift if taking the surviving spouse's elective share. They are not revocable by will, however. At times they may be useful for federal gift and estate tax purposes in order to obtain the $10,000 per person per year exclusion.

F. GIFTS TO MINORS

1. CONSEQUENCES OF A MINOR'S INCAPACITY

Minors lack legal capacity to manage property; consequently, property ownership by minors requires that a system of property management be established. *See* Part 9.I.D. This property management system is usually called guardianship of the property or a conservatorship. The conservator is the manager of the minor's property. Because conservatorship requires court involvement, many estate planners believe that one of the goals of a proper estate plan for clients who have minor or otherwise incompetent children is to avoid guardianship. They recommend use of trusts and other property management systems.

2. UNIFORM TRANSFER TO MINORS ACT

Every state has enacted either the Uniform Transfer to Minors Act (1983) or its version issued in 1956 and revised in 1966. These Acts provide a convenient and efficient system for managing the property gifted to minors. To take advantage of the system, all the transfer document must state is that the gift is made to a custodian in the name of the minor according to the terms of the Act. For example, D may give an asset "to C, as custodian, for M [the name of the minor] under the [State name] Uniform Transfers to Minors Act." This gift is then covered by the terms of the Act which fully defines the custodian's duties and powers and the rights of the minor.

The custodian is provided under the Act with sufficient powers to fulfill the responsibilities of the position without court direction including the power to manage and invest the custodial property and to exercise broad discretion in using the custodial property for the minor's benefit. Under the Act when the minor attains the age of 21 or dies, the conservatorship ends and the property is transferred to the beneficiary, or to his or her estate, if dead. Generally, the Act offers a reasonable solution for small to modest gifts to minors. For substantial sums and assets, the trust device offers a preferred method.

G. REVIEW QUESTIONS

1. An ideal will substitute is one that allows title to pass to others at death although control remains with the transferor. True or False?

2. What is the type of joint ownership where the ownership is merely a form of co-ownership in a piece of property?

3. List three types of multiple-party accounts.

4. An "account" is defined as any type of contractual arrangement for the deposit of funds between a depositor and a financial institution including the ordinary checking account, savings account, certificate of deposit and the share account. True or False?

5. What three acts are required to complete a gift?

6. What is the term for a gift made by an owner of personal property who properly makes a gift to another person in apprehension of imminent death?

7. What is the Uniform Transfer to Minors Act designed to do?

II

PLANNING FOR RETIREMENT AND INCAPACITY

Analysis

        a. *Types of Health Care Directives*
        b. *Scope and Exercise of Living Will*
        c. *Health Care Instructions*
        d. *Notice of the Living Will*
        e. *Formalities for Execution and Revocation of Living Wills*
    3. *Health Care Durable Power of Attorney or Health Care Proxy*
        a. *Content of the Power or Proxy*
        b. *Agent's Authority*
        c. *Agent's Appointment*
        d. *Proxy Form*
D. *Physician Assisted Suicide*
    1. *The Assisted Suicide Issue*
    2. *Lower Federal Court Decisions*
    3. *Supreme Court Decisions*
    4. *Assisted Suicide Legislation*
E. *Public Programs for Incapacity and Retirement*
    1. *The Programs*
    2. *Social Security*
    3. *Medicare*
        a. *Medicare Parts*
        b. *Medicare Coverage*
    4. *Supplemental Security Income (SSI)*
    5. *Medicaid*
        a. *Medicaid Coverage*
F. *Long Term Care Planning*
    1. *The Long Term Care Planning Setting*
        a. *Estate Depletion*
        b. *Estate Planning Goal*
    2. *Qualifying for Medicaid*
        a. *Asset Requirement*
        b. *Income Requirements*
        c. *Smart Spend–Down*
        d. *Transfer Restrictions*
        e. *Ineligibility Period*
        f. *Qualifying Trusts*
        g. *Estate Recovery Program*
    3. *Federal Crime for Advising Certain Asset Transfers*
    4. *Third Party Special Needs Trusts*
G. *Organ Donation*
    1. *Summary of the Law*
    2. *Organ Donation Benefit*
    3. *Need for Organs*
    4. *Estate Planning for Organ Donations*
H. *Review Questions*

A. GENERAL CONCEPTS AND TECHNIQUES

1. SCOPE OF THE PROBLEM

All persons will suffer from incapacity at least once in their lives and some will suffer twice. All minors are presumed to be incapacitated in regard to their personal and financial decision making. Some adults, either because of physical or mental decline, will need assistance in either personal or financial decision making or both. Planning ahead for these potential incapacities is an important responsibility for the estate planner.

2. ANTICIPATING THE INCAPACITY

Common anticipatory devices employed to deal with this problem include the revocable inter vivos trust, the durable power of attorney, and the advanced healthcare directives, *e.g.*, a living will.

The uses and substance of the revocable inter vivos trust is discussed at *infra,* Part 6.IV.

Welfare and other public funding devices that deal with incapacity and retirement are discussed at *infra* Part 4.II.E–F.

B. DURABLE POWERS OF ATTORNEY

1. AUTHORIZING STATUTES

Durable power statutes exist in all states and equivalent jurisdictions in this country. *See* Francis J. Collin, Albert L. Moses, & John J. Lombard, Jr., Drafting the Durable Power of Attorney: A Systems Approach. They have become a significant alternative for conservatorships. They permit persons to anticipate the problem of partial or full incapacity without the need for court involvement. For many estate planners, the durable power is as an essential document for their clients as is the will.

2. THE UPC MODEL

The UPC incorporates the Uniform Durable Power of Attorney Act, as amended, into §§ 5–501 to 5–505. *See* Unif. Durable Power of Attorney Act, 8A U.L.A.—Estate, Probate and Related Laws 309–33 (1993).

a. Common Law Rules Altered

Two principles are adopted that make powers of attorney more durable than under the common law. First, the civil law rule with regard to the effect of the principal's death, disability or incompetence applies to all written powers of attorney. UPC § 5–504. It provides that actions by the attorney in fact in good faith and according to the written power of attorney are valid even though such actions take place after the principal's death, disability or incompetence so long as the attorney in fact did not have actual knowledge of the happening of such an event. Any such valid action taken binds the principal and the principal's heirs, devisees and personal representative. For the protection of third parties dealing with the attorney in fact and in the absence of fraud, an affidavit executed by the attorney in fact stating that the attorney in fact did not have knowledge at the time of his or her action of a revocation or termination caused by death, disability or incompetence is conclusive proof of nonrevocation or nontermination of the power to act at that time. UPC § 5–505. If the action taken requires the execution and delivery of a recordable instrument, the affidavit is also recordable when authenticated. Significantly, this provision does not alter or effect any inconsistent provision in the power of attorney dealing with revocation or termination.

b. True Durable Power

The UPC permits the creation of a true durable power of attorney in the instrument creating the power merely by the inclusion of specific provisions. UPC §§ 5–501 to 5–503. Under the relevant sections, a written power of attorney may specifically provide that the disability of the principal does not affect the power of the appointed attorney in fact to act. UPC § 5–502.

3. SUGGESTED PHRASEOLOGY

The UPC Section 5–501 suggests the following phrases for creating durable powers.

For a power of attorney that is immediately effective:

> "This power of attorney shall not be affected by disability or incapacity of the principal or lapse of time."

For a power which will become effective in the future due to disability, called a "springing power":

> "This power of attorney shall become effective upon the disability or incapacity of the principal."

Neither phrase constitutes words of art and the substance of their purpose and effect may be stated with other similar words.

4. EXERCISES OF THE POWER

Under a true durable power, all actions taken according to the power by the attorney in fact during a period of disability or incompetence of the principal have the same binding and beneficial effect as if the principal was not disabled. UPC § 5–502. In addition, the same effect applies to actions taken under circumstances where it is uncertain whether the principal is dead or alive. These durable powers remain effective until a time explicitly expressed in the instrument, if any is expressed, or until terminated by the death of the principal, whichever first occurs.

5. OTHER RESPONSIBILITIES

If a conservator is appointed for the principal, the attorney in fact must account to the conservator as well as the principal. UPC § 5–503(a). The conservator now has the same power over the attorney in fact as the principal would have had if incapacity or disappearance had not occurred, including the power to revoke, suspend or terminate any part or all of the power. This power over the attorney in fact does not apply to a guardian of the person for the principal.

6. ATTORNEY IN FACT AS CONSERVATOR

In the durable power document the principal may nominate the person whom the principal desires to serve as conservator if protective proceedings are commenced. UPC § 5–503(b). Usually, a principal names the attorney in fact as the nominee in order to prevent any conflict that might arise between two persons serving in different fiduciary roles. The principal may also nominate in the durable power the person to serve as guardian of the person. The court must appoint the nominee unless good cause or disqualification is shown.

C. HEALTH CARE DECISIONS

1. THE HEALTH CARE DILEMMA

"[T]he timing of death–once a matter of fate–is now a matter of human choice." Office of Technology Assessment Task Force, Life Sustaining Technologies and the Elderly 41 (1988). As ex Governor Lamm of Colorado remarked "We can now keep a corpse alive" Richard D. Lamm, "The Ten Commandments of an Aging Society," speech delivered to the Eddy Foundation, Troy, New York, November 6, 1987.

If suicide is not the goal, no one wants "the plug" pulled too soon. All the data on living or dying is not yet available. Reports of unexplained recovery from coma or terminal diseases and the miracle cure abound.

On the other hand there are reasons for pulling the plug including pain and suffering (although this generally need not be a problem today), concern over one's quality of life, and even concern that it is too costly to stay alive.

a. Constitutional Protection of Liberty to Body Integrity

Justice Cardozo, while on the Court of Appeals of New York, described the liberty to body integrity:

> Every human being of adult years and sound mind has a right to determine what shall be done with his own body; and a surgeon who performs an operation without his patient's consent commits an assault, for which he is liable in damages.

Schloendorff v. Society of New York Hospital, 105 N.E. 92, 93 (N.Y. 1914).

Consequently with only limited exceptions, a conscious person has complete domain over the person and no one can administer care that is not wanted.

Furthermore, if one is unable to make one's own health care decisions, decisions concerning health care will be made notwithstanding the presence or absence of personal or health care instructions.

b. The Need for an Advanced Health Care Directive

The essence of having an Advanced Health Care Directive is for the person who wants to have some input into health care decisions once the ability to make one's own decision is gone.

In *Cruzan v. Director, Missouri Department of Health,* 497 U.S. 261 (1990), the United States Supreme Court held that when a person is no longer capable of making health care decision, the state is allowed to establish a procedure and to set a burden of proof for determining the desires of the person. Thus, the existence or nonexistence of a health care directive is significant.

c. Uniform Acts Concerning Advanced Health Care Directives

There have been three uniform acts dealing with advance health care directives, *i.e.,* Uniform Health Care Decisions Act (1993), §§ 1–19, 9(Pt. 1) U.L.A. 311 (West Supp. 1999); Uniform Rights of the Terminally Ill Act (1989), §§ 1–19, 9B U.L.A. 163 (West Supp. 1999); Uniform Rights of the Terminally Ill Act (1985), §§ 1–13, 9B U.L.A. 183 (West Supp. 1999). They show a progression of thinking and attitude about the subject. The newer the version, the greater the discretion accorded the declarant, the greater the protection so that the expressed intent will be carried out, and the lesser the execution formalities.

2. ADVANCED HEALTH CARE DIRECTIVES

Although advanced health care directives are recognized in all states, the law suffers from a significant lack of uniformity. Bretton J. Horttor, *A Survey of Living Will And Advanced Health Care Directives*, 74 N.D. L. Rev. 233 (1998). In addition, many of the statutes address only narrow health care direction issues and are too formalistic and procedurally complex.

Despite the variations and deficiencies of the laws, persons, who want to have some say in the use of life support systems, should execute whatever advance directive for medical care that is permitted by the law of the state in which the person most likely may require its use, *i.e.,* state or domicile or primary residence.

a. Types of Health Care Directives

There are two basic types of health care directives recognized: the living will and the health care durable power of attorney or health care proxy.

Living Will: A living will is a document that expresses an individual's desires for health care, including the withholding or withdrawal of life-sustaining treatment, under certain prescribed circumstances when the individual is no longer personally able to make those decisions.

Health Care Durable Power of Attorney or Health Care Proxy: The health care durable power of attorney or health care proxy is a device, used instead of or in conjunction with a living will, that appoints a person as agent who is empowered to make health care decisions, including the withholding or withdrawal of life-sustaining treatment, for the principal under certain prescribed circumstances when the individual is no longer personally able to make those decisions.

b. Scope and Exercise of Living Will

The typical living will statute permits any competent adult to complete a written declaration (in some states an oral statement in front of witnesses) directing the withholding or withdrawal of life sustaining procedures under certain circumstances. For example, UNIFORM HEALTH CARE DECISIONS ACT OF 1993 allows the individual to choose not to prolong his or her life if the individual:

(1) has "an incurable and irreversible condition" that will result in declarant's death within a relatively short time; or

(2) becomes unconscious and, to a reasonable degree of medical certainty, will not regain consciousness, or

(3) faces likely risks and burdens of treatment that would outweigh the expected benefits.

Unif. Health Care Decisions Act 1993 § 4, 9(Pt. 1) U.L.A. 318–27 (West Supp. 1999).

c. Health Care Instructions

The Act allows the declarant to choose what procedures may be required, withheld or withdrawn. This includes instructions regarding the use or nonuse of:

- life support systems like artificial respirators or ventilators that maintain continued operation of the heart and lungs after the cessation of brain function;
- artificial nutrition and hydration systems or procedures; and
- the treatment for alleviation of pain or discomfort and whether it should be provided at all times even if it hastens death;

The declarant may include additional instructions if the declarant does not agree with the choices listed on the form or wishes to elaborate on the instructions given in the form.

A few persons want to and may specify that everything should be done to prolong life regardless of the cognitive or physiological condition.

d. Notice of the Living Will

Not only should lawyers advise their elder clients to execute living wills but they should also emphasize that the client must inform other relevant family members and health care providers of the existence of their living wills.

A 1990 federal law requires all hospitals to inquire on admission of a patient about the existence of a living will. The living will should be made a part of the medical record. Some states even have a formal registry for individuals to register their living wills, to which health care providers have access.

e. Formalities for Execution and Revocation of Living Wills

Living wills usually have to be in writing and signed by the declarant. Many statutes mandate that witnesses sign the declaration. The 1993 Uniform Act makes the use of witnesses discretionary.

Revocation by the declarant must also follow the prescribed formality which is often that it must be in writing and signed by the declarant.

3. HEALTH CARE DURABLE POWER OF ATTORNEY OR HEALTH CARE PROXY

A health care durable power or proxy concerns the appointment of an agent or surrogate who has authority to make decisions concerning medical treatment and health care when the attending physician has determined that those decisions can no longer be made by the individual.

a. Content of the Power or Proxy

Whereas a living will provides specific instructions as to the health care decisions to be made, a health care power may merely leave those decisions to the agent to make. It is prudent and helpful, however, for the principal to communicate a sense of the principal's particular desires, if any, concerning medical care. For example, it can be significant to know whether the principal wants or does not want to receive artificial nutrition and hydration by nasogastric, abdominal, or other tube feeding.

When specific instructions are not provided the agent is to do what is in the individual's best interests, taking into account the principal's personal values. *See* Unif. Health Care Decisions Act 1993 § 4, 9(Pt. 1) U.L.A. 318–27 (West Supp. 1999).

b. Agent's Authority

Under most laws, the agent's authority becomes effective on the primary physician's diagnosis that the individual is no longer able to make his or her own health care decisions. Under the 1993 Uniform Act, the declarant can opt to check a box which makes the agent's authority effective immediately, regardless of the declarant's capacity to make his or her own health care decisions. *See* Unif. Health Care Decisions Act 1993 § 4, 9(Pt. 1) U.L.A. 318–27 (West Supp. 1999).

c. Agent's Appointment

Most statutes allow only one agent to be named at a time, but one or two alternate agents should be designated in case the agent of first choice is not available or cannot act.

d. Proxy Form

Although not mandatory, if a form is provided by the applicable statute, it is generally recommended that it be used so that medical care providers will easily recognize it as a health care power. The appointed agent(s) addresses and telephone numbers should also be included.

D. PHYSICIAN ASSISTED SUICIDE

1. THE ASSISTED SUICIDE ISSUE

The basic legal issue is whether state laws making assisted suicide a felony violate the terminally ill patient's constitutional rights. The argument is that where the patient is in the final stage of terminal illness, the state has no business prohibiting a physician from prescribing medication to be self administered for the purpose of hastening death particularly where those who are on life support systems are permitted to hasten their deaths by withdrawing live maintaining support systems.

2. LOWER FEDERAL COURT DECISIONS

In *Compassion in Dying v. Washington*, 49 F.3d 586, 591 (9th Cir. 1995), the Ninth Circuit held that the Washington statute, which makes it a felony to aid another to commit suicide, violates liberty interest of terminally ill patients under the Fourteenth Amendment due process clause. The Second Circuit in *Quill v. Vacco*, 80 F.3d 716 (2d Cir. 1996), *rev'd,* 521 U.S. 793 (1997), held that a similar state statute violates the equal protection clause of the Fourteenth Amendment.

3. SUPREME COURT DECISIONS

Washington v. Glucksberg: In *Washington v. Glucksberg,* 521 U.S. 702, 117 S.Ct. 2258 (1997), Washington's prohibition against "caus[ing]" or "aid[ing]" a suicide was held not to violate the Due Process Clause. Referring to the Nation's history, legal traditions, and practices, the Court stated that respondents' asserted "right" to assistance in committing suicide is not a fundamental liberty interest protected by the Due Process Clause. Washington's assisted suicide ban rationally relates to legitimate government interests. The Court list several interests include prohibiting intentional killing and preserving human life; protecting the medical profession's integrity and ethics and maintaining physicians' role as their patients' healers; protecting the poor, the elderly, disabled persons, the terminally ill, and persons in other vulnerable groups from indifference, prejudice, and psychological and financial pressure to end their lives; and avoiding a possible slide towards voluntary and perhaps even involuntary euthanasia.

Vacco v. Quill: In *Vacco v. Quill*, 521 U.S. 793 (1997), the Court reversed the Second Circuit and held that the New York laws did not violate the equal protection clause of the Fourteenth Amendment. The Court found that neither the assisted suicide ban nor the law permitting patients to refuse medical treatment treats anyone differently from anyone else or draws any distinctions between persons. Everyone, regardless of physical condition, is entitled, if competent, to refuse unwanted lifesaving medical treatment; no one is permitted to assist a suicide. The distinction between letting a patient die and making that patient die is important, logical, rational, and well established: It comports with fundamental legal principles of causation.

4. ASSISTED SUICIDE LEGISLATION

In 1994, Oregon voters enacted through a ballot initiative a "Death With Dignity Act," which legalized physician assisted suicide for competent, terminally ill adults. Other states, *e.g.,* California, Iowa, and Rhode Island, have rejected such proposals either by popular vote or statute. The Federal Assisted Suicide Funding Restriction Act of 1997, prohibits the use of federal funds in support of physician assisted suicide. *See* 42 U.S.C. § 14401 et seq.

As Chief Justice Rehnquist said "the States are currently engaged in serious, thoughtful examinations of physician assisted suicide and other similar issues." *Glucksberg*, 117 S.Ct. at 2267. It will take some time to see whether the legal environment concerning assisted suicide will change in the 21st Century.

E. PUBLIC PROGRAMS FOR INCAPACITY AND RETIREMENT

1. THE PROGRAMS

Social Security, Medicare, Supplemental Security Income[1] and Medicaid[2] are the primary sources of governmental benefits for retired and disabled persons. SSI and Medicaid are financial need based programs.

1. 42 U.S.C.A. § 1382 et seq.; 20 C.F.R. § 416.101 et seq.

2. 42 U.S.C.A. § 1396 et seq.; 42 C.F.R. § 430 et seq.

SSI And Social Security: SSI and Social Security are different programs. When people talk about disability benefits, there is often confusion about Social Security and SSI. The confusion arises because the Social Security Administration administers both programs.

2. SOCIAL SECURITY

Social Security is a retirement program that workers, employers and the self-employed pay for with their Social Security taxes. You qualify for these benefits based on your work history and the amount of your benefit is based on your earnings.

Social Security also protects a worker who becomes severely disabled. Under Social Security, workers are considered disabled if they have a severe physical or mental condition that prevents them from working. The condition must be expected to last for at least 12 months or to result in death. Once benefits begin, they continue for as long as the worker is disabled and cannot work. The disabled worker and his or her eligible family members receive monthly checks.

3. MEDICARE

As part of the Social Security Amendments of 1965, the Medicare legislation established a health insurance program for aged persons to complement the retirement, survivors and disability insurance benefits. Although it originally covered only most persons age 65 and over, it has been expanded to include a few other selected persons.

a. Medicare Parts

Medicare consists of three parts: Hospital Insurance (HI), known as "Part A," Supplementary Medical insurance (SMI), known as "Part B, and the Medicare+Choice program, "Part C," which was established by the Balanced Budget Act of 1997 and began to provide services on January 1, 1998.

The Part A program financing is primarily through a mandatory payroll deduction ("FICA tax"). Almost all employees and self-employed workers in the U.S. work in employment covered by the Part A program and pay taxes to support the cost of benefits for aged and disabled beneficiaries.[3]

The Part B program is financed through: (1) premium payments ($43.80 per month in 1998) which are usually deducted from the monthly Social Security benefit checks of those who are enrolled in Part B program, and (2) through contributions from general revenue of the U.S. Treasury. Part B benefits may also be "bought" for persons by a third party directly paying the monthly

3. The FICA tax is 1.45 percent of earnings (paid by each employee and by the employer for each), as well as 2.90 percent for self-employed persons. Since 1994, this tax is paid on all covered wages and self-employment income without limit.

premium on behalf of the enrollee. Beneficiary premiums are currently set at a level that covers 25 percent of the average expenditures for aged beneficiaries.

The Part C program is financed from the Part A and Part B trust funds in proportion to the relative weights of benefits of those Parts to the total benefits paid by the Medicare program.

b. Medicare Coverage

Part A is provided automatically to persons age 65 and over who are entitled to Social Security or Railroad Retirement Board benefits. Similarly, individuals who have received such benefits based on their disability, for a period of at least 24 months, are also entitled to these benefits.

Part B primarily covers the cost for physician services (in both hospital and non-hospital settings). It also covers certain other non-physician services, including: ambulance services, clinical laboratory tests, diagnostic tests, durable medical equipment, flu vaccinations, most supplies, prescription drugs which cannot be self-administered, certain self-administered anticancer drugs, some other therapy services, certain other health services, and blood which was not supplied by Part A.

Part C provides that medicare beneficiaries who have both Part A and Part B can choose to get their benefits through a variety of risk-based plans. To participate in this Part C, the beneficiaries must be entitled to Part A and be enrolled in Part B. Organizations that are seeking to contract as Medicare+Choice plans must meet specific organizational, financial, and other requirements. The primary entities that will offer Part C plans include Qualified Health Maintenance Organizations, Provider–Sponsored Organizations, Preferred Provider Organizations, and other certified public or private coordinated care plans and entities.

Non-covered Services: Medicare does not include long term nursing care or custodial care, and certain other health care needs, *e.g.,* dentures and dental care, eyeglasses, hearing aids, most prescription drugs, etc. Some of these noncovered services may be offered in Part C plans.

4. SUPPLEMENTAL SECURITY INCOME (SSI)

SSI is a program financed through general tax revenues and not through Social Security trust funds. SSI disability benefits are paid to people who have a disability and who do not own much or have a lot of income. To qualify for SSI the applicant must have limited countable monthly income of countable assets, *e.g.,* \$2,000. Thus, the receipt of a personal injury award, an inheritance, or some other increase in resources can jeopardize eligibility for SSI.

SSI Eligibility: Under SSI eligibility rules, assets held in trust are not countable if the applicant has no power to revoke the trust and use the trust funds for applicant's own support and maintenance or cannot direct the use of the trust principal for applicant's support and maintenance under the terms of the trust, whether the trust is created with the applicant's own funds or someone else's funds for the benefit of the applicant. Actual income payments from the trust to the beneficiary will be counted under the SSI income limit test. Distribution of in-kind income that does not result in the beneficiary's direct receipt of a basic needs, *e.g.,* food, clothing or shelter, is not counted.

5. MEDICAID

Medicaid, which is Title XIX of the Social Security Act, is a Federal–State matching entitlement program that pays for medical assistance for certain vulnerable and needy individuals and families with low incomes and resources. Medicaid is the largest source of funding for medical and health-related services for America's poorest people. Medicaid currently pays for approximately forty percent of the costs of the nation's long term nursing home care.

a. Medicaid Coverage

Within broad national guidelines established by Federal statutes, regulations and policies, each State: (1) establishes its own eligibility standards; (2) determines the type, amount, duration, and scope of services; (3) sets the rate of payment for services; and (4) administers its own program.

Medicaid policies for eligibility, services, and payment are complex, and vary considerably even between similar sized or adjacent States. Thus, a person who is eligible for Medicaid in one State might not be eligible in another State; and the services provided by one State may differ considerably in amount, duration, or scope from services provided in a similar or neighboring State. In addition, Medicaid eligibility or services, or both, within a State can change during the year.

In general terms, an applicant seeking the Medicaid entitlement must (1) be eligible according to the categorically needy test; (2) have income below the state's income test; and (3) have assets valued below the state's asset test.

For qualification purposes, there are either "SSI states" or "section 209(b) states." SSI states base their Medicaid eligibility criteria on the criteria for federal SSI. Section 209(b) states may use a more restrictive criteria for Medicaid entitlement than the federal SSI standards, but may not be more restrictive than the criteria used to determine Medicaid eligibility as they existed in 1972. *See* Roger A. McEowen, *Estate Planning for Farm and Ranch Families Facing Long–Term Health Care*, 73 NEB. L. REV. 104, 107–08 (1994); 42 U.S.C. § 1396a(f) (1988). Only thirteen states use section 209(b) criteria.

F. LONG TERM CARE PLANNING

1. THE LONG TERM CARE PLANNING SETTING

Financing the costs of long term care is of crucial importance to elderly individuals. Depending on location, nursing home costs can range from thirty-thousand to more than ninety-thousand dollars annually. Cost of this magnitude can quickly exhaust an elderly person's lifetime savings. Other than long term care insurance, the alternative to personally financing nursing home care is the federal Medicaid program.

a. Estate Depletion

Because public assistance through medicaid is only available to help poverty level individuals finance long term care, middle class individuals in need of long term care must dispose of their assets exceeding poverty limits either to pay for their care or, in the alternative, to qualify for public assistance. Thus, unlike the affluent (who can provide for their own Health care needs) and low income individuals (who qualify for public assistance), middle class individuals must forfeit any wealth accumulated through a lifetime of hard work and savings to pay for long term care. This forfeiture is a harsh result for an individual who has saved for a lifetime to provide for the future and who has paid taxes to support government programs like Medicaid. ARMOND D. BUDISH, AVOIDING THE MEDICAID TRAP: HOW TO BEAT THE CATASTROPHIC COSTS OF NURSING–HOME CARE 14 (3d ed. 1995).

Approximately one-half of Medicaid recipients become eligible for benefits only after becoming impoverished in an attempt to finance nursing home care. *See* ARMOND D. BUDISH, AVOIDING THE MEDICAID TRAP: HOW TO BEAT THE CATASTROPHIC COSTS OF NURSING–HOME CARE 13–14 (3d ed. 1995). Longer life expectancies increase both the number of persons affected and the chances of impoverishment.

b. Estate Planning Goal

Efforts both to preserve the client's access to public benefits, and to preserve assets and control, are important goals in elder law estate planning.

2. QUALIFYING FOR MEDICAID

For Medicaid eligibility purposes, the goal is to reduce the value of nonexempt assets in the applicant's Medicaid estate below the specified limits. Asset protection planning may involve the transfer of assets, creation of certain trusts, conversion of excess resources to exempt assets, and outright gifts.

a. Asset Requirement

Unless exempt, all assets that could be liquidated to provide for the individual's basic needs, such as food, shelter and clothing are considered. Exempt assets for eligibility purposes under both SSI and Medicaid include the family home, household goods and personal effects with a total equity of $2,000 or less, and burial spaces and up to $1,500 for a burial fund.

b. Income Requirements

In many states if the applicant receives too much income, Medicaid is denied. For example, the 1997 "income cap" in most states was $1,452. When an applicant has $1,453 in income, a Medicaid application would be denied.

c. Smart Spend–Down

An individual may become Medicaid eligible by spending excess resources. A "smart spend-down" concerns a effort to purchase or make exempt expenditures including, *e.g.*, medical equipment, adapted or new vehicle, TV set, prepay health insurance or utility charges, repairs on the home, etc.

d. Transfer Restrictions

The Omnibus Budget Reconciliation Act of 1993, Pub. L. No. 103–66, 107 Stat. 312 (OBRA '93) greatly limited the ability for an individual to qualify merely by transferring assets to a trust and retaining an interest in income or principal. Inter vivos transfers to trusts by the applicant from that person's assets (or spouse), the applicant's spouse, a applicant's legal representative or a court acting on behalf of the applicant are counted for Medicaid eligibility purposes if payment could be made to or for the applicant under any circumstance (including the exercise of trustee's discretion).

e. Ineligibility Period

In addition, under OBRA '93 any gift of assets by the applicant to individuals within 36 months of Medicaid application (or within 60 months for transfers to trusts), triggers a period of Medicaid ineligibility, even if the applicant retains no interest in the donated property.

f. Qualifying Trusts

OBRA '93 recognized two types of trusts created with the applicant's own assets that will not be counted for Medicaid eligibility purposes.

<u>Under Age 65 Disability Trust:</u> A trust created by a parent, grandparent, legal guardian or a court to hold the disabled individual's assets or the assets of others for the benefit of a disabled individual under the age of 65 are exempt if the trust provides that, at the beneficiary's death, the state will receive amounts remaining in the trust up to Medicaid benefits provided by such state. Additional amounts may be added to the trust until the beneficiary reaches age 65. The assets in the trust continue to be an excluded resource in determining Medicaid eligibility even after the beneficiary reaches age 65 but additional assets added after age 65 will be counted.

<u>Pooled Account Trust:</u> A Pooled Account Trust is a trust established and managed by a non-profit association and designed to hold the assets of disabled individuals in separate accounts, although the trust may pool the accounts for investment and management purposes. The separate account must be established by the beneficiary's parent, grandparent, legal guardian or a court. If any amount remains in the account at the beneficiary's death that is not retained by the trust, such amount must be paid to the state up to the benefits provided by Medicaid.

g. Estate Recovery Program

OBRA '93 requires that states establish an estate recovery program to recover the cost of Medicaid benefits from the probate estates of deceased recipients who:

(1) were in-patients in a nursing facility, intermediate care facility for the mentally retarded, or other medical institution; or

(2) have received nursing home care or other long term care services, including home and community based services and community supported living arrangements, if the recipient was 55 years or older when the recipient received such benefits.

States may expand the recoverable estate to include nonprobate property in which the individual had any legal title or interest at the time of death (to the extent of such interest), including assets conveyed through joint tenancy, tenancy in common, survivorship, life estate, living trust or other arrangements.

Recovery of benefits from the applicant's estate may be obtained only after the death of the applicant's surviving spouse, if any, and only where there is no surviving child who is under age 21, blind or disabled.

3. FEDERAL CRIME FOR ADVISING CERTAIN ASSET TRANSFERS

Section 217 of the Health Insurance Portability and Accountabiliy Act of 1996, made it a federal crime to "knowingly and willfully dispose of assets (including by any transfer in trust) in order for an individual to become eligible" for Medicaid. In the Balanced Budget Act of 1997 Congress changed the focus from the transferor to his or her attorney. The new section makes it a crime for one who "for a fee knowingly and willfully counsels or assists an individual to dispose of assets ... in order for the individual to become eligible for medical assistance ... if disposing of the assets results in the imposition of a period of ineligibility for such assistance." *See* 42 U.S.C. § 1320a–7B(a). Violation of the section is a misdemeanor and conviction may result in a fine of not more than $10,000 or imprisonment for not more than one year, or both.

Effect of the Law: The scope and application of the section is not sufficiently known for planning purposes. Whatever the section's eventual interpretation is or whether it is eventually repealed, Congress has probably successfully discouraged many prospective Medicaid applicants from transferring their assets before qualifying for public medical benefits.

4. THIRD PARTY SPECIAL NEEDS TRUSTS (SNT)

If an inter vivos or testamentary trust is created by a third party for the benefit of a disabled individual and funded solely with the assets of such third party, the assets may not be counted in determining the beneficiary's eligibility for Medicaid, depending upon the distribution restrictions contained in the trust. Testamentary trusts are not subject to the Medicaid trust rules of OBRA '93 but are governed by SSI rules.

A SNT provides that the purpose of the trust is to improve upon the beneficiary's quality of life by providing for those supplemental needs, such as more sophisticated medical, rehabilitative, recreational or educational aid, not provided by other sources of assistance, including governmental assistance. The trustee's distribution discretion is limited to considering all other funds available to meet the beneficiary's needs, including governmental assistance. The trustee is prohibited from making distributions for basic support provided under governmental assistance programs. Therefore, a SNT should not be counted under the asset test for Medicaid, but actual income distributions from the trust will be counted under the income test.

The mandatory estate recovery rules should not apply to a SNT established by a parent and funded with the parent's assets for the benefit of a disabled child where the disabled child is merely the income beneficiary of the trust (even if the trustee can invade the principal for the disabled child's benefit) and other persons, such as the disabled child's siblings, are designated as principal beneficiaries because the disabled child's interest is not probate property of such child.

G. ORGAN DONATION

1. SUMMARY OF THE LAW

In the United States, the presumption is that when a person dies that person's organs may not be taken without the person's prior consent or the consent of the relevant survivors. State law controls the requirements for making an effective organ and tissue donation. All states have enacted the Uniform Anatomical Gift Act or its 1987 revision. Under these acts, an intention to make a gift may be indicated by signing a donor card. Some states require that the card also be witnessed. Organ donations can also be made by will or by a designation on a driver's license. The donor may specify which organs and tissue are to be donated and whether the donation is made for purposes of transplant, therapy, research or education.

2. ORGAN DONATION BENEFIT

"Organ and tissue donation is truly the gift of life. One person can donate up to eight organs (the heart, liver, pancreas, kidneys, lungs and small intestine), as well as tissue (skin, bone, bone marrow, corneas and heart valves). A single donor will on average benefit three or more recipients." David M. English, *Gift of Life: The Lawyer's Role in Organ And Tissue Donation*, 8 Prob. & Prop. 10, 11 (April 1994).

3. NEED FOR ORGANS

The dramatic increase in organ transplants has created an escalating shortage of available human organs. Waiting lists for organs are unconscionably long.

4. ESTATE PLANNING FOR ORGAN DONATIONS

As part of the process of ascertaining the client's wishes, the client should be asked concerning the client's desires about organ donating. Cultural, religious, and ethnic differences that might influence specific decisions by clients, as well as knowledge of the client biases, might guide the lawyer in this process. If the client desires to make donations, the appropriate procedures and documents should be prepared. As with living wills, it is essential that appropriate relations and others responsible for health care decisions for the client be informed of the desires.

H. REVIEW QUESTIONS

1. In the anticipation of incapacity, name some of the devices used to deal with the problem.
2. In a durable power document, who nominates the conservator in the event that protective proceedings are commenced?
3. Define the term "living will."
4. Name the primary sources of governmental benefits for retired and disabled persons.
5. In the United States, the presumption is that when a person dies that person's organs may be taken without the person's prior consent or the consent of the relevant survivors. True or False?

PART FIVE

POWERS OF APPOINTMENT

*

I

INTRODUCTION TO POWERS

Analysis

A. DEFINITION OF POWER OF APPOINTMENT

1. DEFINITION

A power of appointment is generally defined as the authority, held by a nonowner, to designate recipients of beneficial interests in or powers of appointment over the appointive property. See RESTATEMENT (SECOND) PROPERTY (DONATIVE TRANSFERS) § 11.1 (1986). The appointive property is the property or property interest subject to a power of appointment. The property interest subject to appointment need not be an absolute-ownership interest. In fact, powers of appointment frequently authorize appointment of only a remainder interest in the property, as in the following example.

Illustration 1: G transferred property in trust, income to A for life, remainder in corpus to those of A's descendants as A shall by will appoint; in default of appointment, to X–Charity. A subsequently dies, leaving a will that appoints the remainder interest to her adult child, B.

A major purpose served by powers of appointment is to put some flexibility into the donor's original disposition to allow it to be molded to meet changing conditions.

2. PARTIES TO A POWER OF APPOINTMENT

- Donor: The donor (creator) is the person who created the power of appointment: G in *Illustration 1.*
- Donee: The donee (powerholder) is the person upon whom the power of appointment was conferred: A in *Illustration 1.*
- Objects: The objects or permissible appointees are the persons to whom the power can be exercised: A's descendants in *Illustration 1.* The donor determines who the objects are by expressly designating them in the instrument creating the power.
- Appointee: The appointee is the person the donee appoints: B in *Illustration 1.* The appointment makes the appointee the owner of the appointed property interest.
- Takers in Default: The taker in default is the person who takes the appointive property to the extent the power is not effectively exercised: X–Charity in *Illustration 1.* The taker in default has a property interest that is subject to the power of appointment. Upon A's death, X–Charity's property interest was divested in favor of the appointee, B.

3. NECESSARY AND NON-NECESSARY PARTIES

Powers of appointment must have a donor, a donee, and someone in whose favor an appointment can be made. The other parties are common but not necessary for a valid power of appointment. Because the donee might not exercise a power of appointment, appointees might never be designated. Also, the donor need not expressly designate takers in default.

4. THE DOCTRINE OF "RELATION BACK"

Technically, the donee of a power of appointment is not recognized as the owner of the appointive property. The distinction between beneficial ownership and a power is that the beneficial owner of an interest in property ordinarily has the power to transfer to others beneficial rights in the owned interest whereas a power is the authority to designate beneficial interests in property other than as an incident of the beneficial ownership of the property. When the power is exercised, it is the completion of the terms of a transfer that started with the creator of the power. Thus the exercise of a power of appointment passes the appointed interest directly from the donor to the appointee. This is called the doctrine of "relation back": the donee's appointment is deemed to relate back to and become part of the donor's original instrument.

Illustration 2: *S* transferred property in trust, income to A for life, remainder to such of A's descendants as A shall appoint. A makes an inter-vivos appointment to his child, C. Under the doctrine of relation back, A's appointment is viewed as changing *S*'s original disposition to read: "income to A for life, remainder to C."

5. PERSONAL NATURE OF POWERS OF APPOINTMENT

Powers of appointment are personal to the donee. Unless the power is a trust power and the donee is the trustee, the donee is not a fiduciary and is under no duty to exercise a power of appointment. If the donee dies without having exercised the power, the power expires. Upon the donee's death, an unexercised power is not and cannot be passed to the donee's successors in interest.

B. CREATION OF A POWER OF APPOINTMENT

1. INTENT TO CREATE A POWER OF APPOINTMENT

A power of appointment is created when the transferor manifests an intent to create one in an otherwise effective transfer. No particular words or phrases are necessary so long as the language establishes that the transferor intended what the law calls a power of appointment.

Illustration 3: By will, S transfers property to T in trust. T is to pay the net income to D for life–

Consider the following examples:

"Remainder as D shall appoint by deed or by will." A clear expression of the creation of a power of appointment that is presently exercisable or exercisable by will.

"D shall have the right to dispose of the remainder among her children as she pleases." Although express words indicating a power of appointment are not used, the legal meaning of the quoted language gives D a non-general power to appoint to her children which may be presently exercisable.

"D shall have the right to devise the remainder among her children as she pleases." Although express words indicating a power of appointment are not used, the legal meaning of the quoted language gives D a non-general power to appoint to her children that is exercisable only by her will and is not a power presently exercisable.

2. FORMALITIES FOR CREATING POWERS OF APPOINTMENT

The requisite formalities for creating a power of appointment are the formalities required by law for the type of transfer made by the donor. If the power is created in a will, the will must satisfy testamentary formalities. If the power is created in an inter vivos transfer, the instrument must satisfy the formalities prescribed for the transfer, including the Statute of Frauds.

3. DETERMINING THE DONEE'S INTENT

Whether a donee of a power of appointment intends to exercise the power depends upon a manifestation of intent by the donee in a deed or will. The intent is provable by any relevant admissible evidence.

Properly drafted instruments of appointment should make specific reference to the creating instrument and unequivocally indicate whether the power is exercised.

4. EXERCISE FORMALITIES

In order for a donee to exercise a power effectively it must be established (1) That the donee intended to exercise it; and (2) That the expression of the intention complies with the requirements of exercise imposed by the donor and by rules of law.

C. DIFFERENT KINDS OF POWERS OF APPOINTMENT

1. GENERAL VERSUS SPECIAL (NONGENERAL) POWERS

There are several types of powers. RESTATEMENT (SECOND) PROPERTY (DONATIVE TRANSFERS) § 11.4 (1986). First, a general power is defined as a power that permits the donee to appoint the property to the donee, personally, to the donee's creditors, to the donee's estate, or to creditors of the donee's estate. Second, a special power, or what the Restatement (Second) Property calls a nongeneral power, is defined by the Restatement as any power that is not a general power. Usually the donee of a nongeneral power is permitted to appoint only to a particular group of persons, such as one's children or descendants. Because of federal gift and estate tax benefits, nongeneral powers may include as objects, everyone except the donee, the donee's creditors, the donee's estate, and the creditors of the donee's estate.

In almost all states, the scope of the donee's authority is presumptively unlimited. Thus, the donee's authority regarding appointees and the time and manner of appointment is limited only to the extent the donor effectively manifests an intent to impose limits. Restatement (Second) Property (Donative Transfers) § 12.2 (1986). Depending upon donor's exercise instructions, powers are categorized as to when they may be exercised. Restatement (Second) Property (Donative Transfers) § 11.5 (1986).

2. PRESENTLY EXERCISABLE AND TESTAMENTARY POWERS

All powers must be in existence before they are exercisable. Restatement (Second) Property (Donative Transfers) § 11.5, Cmt. a (1986). A power of appointment created in a living person's will does not come into existence until that person dies and the will becomes effective.

A power of appointment is presently exercisable if the donee may immediately exercise it at the time in question by deed or by will. When it is stated that the donee may exercise it by deed, a "deed" is merely any formally sufficient and legally operative act or instrument under applicable law that is effective during the donee's lifetime to accomplish an inter-vivos transfer.

A power of appointment is not presently exercisable if it may only (1) be exercised by a will, called a testamentary power, or (2) at the time in question cannot be exercised until some event or passage of time occurs. Although from a practical position a power that is exercisable by deed alone could be called presently exercisable, it is characterized as not presently exercisable and is accordingly called a "power exercisable by deed alone."

3. EXCLUSIVE AND NON–EXCLUSIVE SPECIAL POWERS

Whether a power of appointment is exclusive or non-exclusive depends upon the intent of the donor. A special power in which the donee is required to appoint some part to each of the members of the class is described as a "non-exclusive" power. A special power in which the donee may appoint to some members of the class and exclude others is called an "exclusive" power. Because objects of the power are unlimited in a general power, they are necessarily characterized as exclusive powers. Restatement (Second) Property (Donative Transfers) § 21.1, cmt. b (1986).

If there is ambiguity in what the donor intended, some courts have adopted a constructional preference for the "non-exclusive" power while others have adopted a constructional preference for the "exclusive" power. The latter is the prevailing and preferred modern construction.

If the donee of a non-exclusive power appoints in a manner inconsistent with the principles of the non-exclusive power, the appointment is invalid in toto, and the property passes to the takers in default, or if there are no takers in default provided for, the appointed property passes in equal parts to the class of permissible appointees. *See* RESTATEMENT (SECOND) PROPERTY (DONATIVE TRANSFERS) § 21.1 (1986).

4. COLLATERAL POWERS AND POWERS IN GROSS

The donee has a purely collateral power if the donee holds no interest in the property except the power. The donee has a power in gross if the donee holds both an interest in the property and a power that if exercised would dispose of the interest that the donee does not hold. RESTATEMENT (SECOND) PROPERTY (DONATIVE TRANSFERS) § 11.4, Cmt. c (1986).

Illustration 4. G transferred land "to A for life, remainder to such person or persons as A shall appoint; in default of appointment, remainder to B."

A's power is a presently exercisable general power. It is a power in gross. It is presently exercisable because the donor, G, did not expressly restrict the exercise of the power to a will. With few exceptions, courts would hold this power as general because the donor did not forbid A from exercising the power in A's own favor.

Illustration 5. G transferred land "to A for life, remainder to such of A's descendants as A shall by will appoint; in default of appointment, remainder to B."

A's power is a nongeneral testamentary power. It is a power in gross. It is testamentary because of the donor's insertion of the phrase "by will." Thus any purported intervivos exercise of this power by A would be invalid. A's power is nongeneral because A is authorized to appoint only among her own descendants, a group that does not include A.

Illustration 6. G transferred land "to A for life, remainder to such person or persons except A, A's estate, A's creditors, or the creditors of A's estate, as A shall by will appoint; in default of appointment, remainder to B."

In accordance with the Restatement (SECOND) of Property's categories, A's power is in the same category as A's power in Illustration 3, *supra*—a nongeneral testamentary power.

D. REVIEW QUESTIONS

1. What is the authority, held by a nonowner, to designate recipients of beneficial interests in or powers of appointment over the appointive property?
2. How is a power of appointment created?
3. Powers of appointment must name a donor, a donee, someone in whose favor an appointment can be made and takers in default. True or False?
4. A power of appointment is presently exercisable if the donee may immediately exercise it at the time in question by deed or by will. True or False?
5. Distinguish between collateral powers and powers in gross.

II

EXERCISE OF A POWER OF APPOINTMENT

Analysis

A. EXERCISE OF A POWER OF APPOINTMENT

1. EXERCISE REQUIREMENTS IMPOSED BY THE DONOR

A donor may impose restrictions on how and when the donee may exercise the power. A donee may only be able to exercise a power by inter vivos deed, or by the donee's will. Other restrictions may be imposed also. The donor may require that the donee make a specific reference to the power in order to exercise it. The donor may also require that the donee's exercise be made in an instrument executed after the date of the power's creation. If the donee fails to comply with any formal requirement imposed by the donor, the donee may not have effectively exercised it even though the donee's intention to exercise the power is clearly manifested.

Illustration 1: S by will transfers property to T in trust. T is directed to pay the income to D for life. On D's death "T shall pay the trust property to or hold the same for the benefit of such person or persons or the estate of D in such amounts and proportions and for such estates and interests and outright or upon such terms, trusts, conditions, and limitations as D shall appoint by a will referring specifically to the power herein given to D." S's will makes provision for the disposition of the trust property on D's death in default of her exercise of her general power to appoint by will. The residuary clause in D's will provides: "All the rest and residue of my property, wheresoever the same is situated, including any property over which I may have any power of appointment, I hereby bequeath, devise and appoint as follows." Although D's blanket exercise of all powers the donee holds manifests an intention to exercise all of them, some courts hold that D's general language in the residuary clause and its reference to "any power of appointment" does not satisfy the requirement imposed by S that specific reference to the power must be made in any exercise of it. D has not effectively exercised her power to appoint, and the appointive property passes to the takers in default of appointment. *See First Nat'l Bank v. Walker*, 607 S.W.2d 469 (Tenn 1980). *Contra, Motes/Henes Trust v. Motes*, 761 S.W.2d 938 (Ark 1988).

2. BLANKET APPOINTMENTS

When a donee by deed or will manifests an intention to dispose of all of the donee's property, this does not manifest of itself an intention to exercise any power possessed by the donee. When the donee by deed or will manifests an intention to exercise all powers the donee holds, this manifestation of intent indicates that donee intends to exercise both general and non-general powers that are exercisable by the deed or the will. The donee's manifested intention, however, may not be effective to exercise a power because of the formal limits imposed by the donor on the exercise of the power. *See Illustration 1, supra.*

3. APPOINTIVE ASSETS IDENTIFIED IN DISPOSITIVE INSTRUMENT OF DONEE

When a donee, by deed or will, purports to dispose of the property that is covered by a power, it is inferred that the donee manifests an intent to exercise the power.

Although it may be necessary to resolve construction issues about whether the property is adequately described, technical accuracy of identification is not required.

Illustration 2: T, owner of Meadowacre in fee simple, devises Meadowacre "to D for life, remainder to such one or more of D's children as D shall appoint by D's will, and in default of appointment to D's children who survive her and their heirs as tenants in common." D dies leaving a will that provides: "I devise Meadowacre to my daughter M." D has manifested an intent to exercise the non-general power to appoint Meadowacre by devise in the will.

4. OTHER CIRCUMSTANCES INDICATING DONEE'S INTENDED EXERCISE OF POWER

Circumstances existing at the time of the execution of the donee's deed or will may also indicate that the donee intends to exercise the power. All surrounding circumstances concerning the formulation of the deed or will are relevant. For example, the donee's knowledge about the power and its exercise as well as the relationship of the donee's personal estate *vis à vis* the property covered by the power may be considered. The question is what can be inferred by the surrounding circumstances regarding the donee's intent to exercise a power when the donee has not clearly or specifically exercised it. Sympathies for the appointee will be a factor.

Illustration 3: T's will transferred $500,000 to T in trust. T is directed "to pay the income to D for life and on D's death to pay the trust property to such persons as D may appoint and in default of appointment to pay the same to T's other children who survive D." D executes a will containing $5,000 in pecuniary bequests to a local charity, $15,000 in pecuniary bequests to distant relatives and a residuary disposition in favor of her three children. At the time D executed her will, she owned assets worth $40,000; D's children were 24, 20, and 18; the children had no property of their own and their father was dead; D's relationship with her children is most affectionate. The inference is justified that the children were the primary objects of D's bounty and that in giving $20,000 to charity and distant relatives D had at her disposal much more than $40,000. D may be found to have exercised the general power.

5. TESTAMENTARY EXERCISE OF AFTER-ACQUIRED POWER

When the donee's will manifests the intent to exercise powers, this manifestation includes powers acquired after the execution of the donee's will unless the exercise of the after-acquired powers is specifically excluded. Two factors justify this rule: (1) a will becomes legally operative on the date the testator dies; and, (2) since wills are held to dispose of after-acquired owned property, they should also dispose of after-acquired powers. When the donee dies before the donor, however, the power never comes into existence and thus the donee's will does not exercise it.

Illustration 4: D executes a will exercising all powers of appointment. T writes a will granting D a power of appointment. T dies. D dies. The power is exercised.

Illustration 5: D executes a will exercising all powers of appointment. T writes a will granting D a power of appointment. D dies. T dies. The power is not exercised.

6. EXERCISE OF POWER OF APPOINTMENT UNDER THE UPC

There are several situations that must be distinguished. The following three factors guide the application of the rules of construction adopted in the UPC: (1) whether the governing instrument that created the power of appointment expressly requires that a power is exercised by the will only if the donee makes a reference to the power or its source in the will; (2) whether the power of appointment is a general or a nongeneral power; and, (3) whether the testator-donee's will expresses an intention to exercise the power of appointment.

a. No Specific Reference Requirement

If the document creating a power of appointment does not explicitly require "reference" or "specific reference," a will that contains a "general residuary clause" or that makes a "general disposition of all the testator's property" exercises the power only if either of two conditions is met. UPC § 2–608.

First, a will containing a general residuary clause or a comparable clause exercises a general testamentary power if the document creating the power fails to contain an effective gift in default of exercise. This rule permits the donee's will to control the disposition of the property subject to the power rather than allowing the takers of the donor's estate to take. A contrary rule can create unintended and unanticipated results, including the need to reopen a donor's closed estate and to cause estate tax consequences to an otherwise settled estate.

Second, any general and nongeneral testamentary power is exercised if the testator-donee's will manifests an intention to include the property that is subject to the power as part of the residuary or general disposition clause.

These rules prevent unintended exercises of powers from occurring merely because a residue clause is included in a donee's will but provide a broad exception if admissible evidence indicates that the testator desired to exercise the power. The distinction between interpretations can be illustrated by comparing its application to two typical drafting examples: (1) if the residuary clause in testators's will merely devises "all the rest, residue and remainder" of testator's estate, presumably the power is not exercised; but (2) if the residuary clause in testators's will devises "all the rest, residue and remainder of my estate, including any property over which I hold a power of appointment," presumably the power is exercised. UPC § 2–608, cmt. The latter is called a "blending" or "blanket exercise" clause. The inclusion of such a clause in a will raises a presumption under the UPC that testator intended to exercise a power if that power does not require a particular reference to it to be exercised. When the residuary clause omits the reference to powers of appointment, the presumption is that the testator does not intend to exercise a power. Either presumption is subject to rebuttal with extrinsic evidence under the principle of Section 2–601. UPC § 2–608, cmt.

b. Specific Reference to Power of Appointment Requirement

If the document creating a power of appointment explicitly states that the power may only be exercised "by a reference, or by an express or specific reference" to the power in the exercising document, the language is presumed to indicate that the donor only wanted to prevent an inadvertent exercise of the power. UPC § 2–704. This presumption relates to the exercise of all explicit powers whether they are general or nongeneral and to all exercising documents whether they are wills or other will substitutes.

Beyond the mere presumption, the questions of the donor's intent as to the requirements for exercise, and the donee's intent as to the exercise, is left to extrinsic evidence. *See* UPC § 2–701. Relevant extrinsic evidence may swing the determination either way: in one direction it may show that the donee intended to exercise although the donee did not make an otherwise sufficient reference to the power; or, in the other direction, it may show that the donor desired a specific reference to the power and any reference that fails to satisfy this requirement fails to exercise the power. The provision has the apparent purpose of both preventing inadvertent exercise but leaving open the question of proof of intent by inferentially relying on extrinsic evidence to supply that intent.

B. EXCESSIVE APPOINTMENT–FRAUD ON POWER OF APPOINTMENT

1. APPOINTMENT TO NON-OBJECT OF NON-GENERAL POWER

The donor defines the donee's range of choice of beneficiaries in the description of the objects of the power. Because the donee of a power of appointment is acting to complete a transfer made by the donor, an appointment of a beneficial interest by the donee to a non-object is ineffective. Attempts to benefit non-objects through the appointment have been traditionally described as a "fraud on the power" or "fraudulent appointment." An appointment of a beneficial interest to a non-object fails.

In determining whether an appointment is to a non-object, the definition of the limited class is significant. The broader the class of objects, the less likely an appointment will be ineffective. A distinction is recognized between a positively defined limited class and a very wide range of objects. Compare a non-general power that merely prohibits appointment to the donee, donee's creditors, the donee's estate, and the creditors of the donee's estate with one that limits appointment to a narrow class of objects such as "children," "grandchildren," "issue," "brothers and sisters," "nephews and nieces," or "heirs." The former gives the donee an almost unlimited choice of objects whereas the latter significantly limits the choice.

When relational class terms are used, questions arise regarding the inclusion of adopted children, children born out of wedlock, stepchildren, and persons related by affinity. Proper drafting would define these terms, but when they have not been defined, rules of construction operative in the controlling jurisdiction are used to give meaning to these terms in determining the objects of the power.

2. GENERAL POWER EXCLUSION

Because under a general power the donee is free to appoint by deed to the donee personally or by will to the donee's estate, there are no non-objects. Thus the excessive appointment doctrine is inapplicable even if the instrument creating such a general power expressly excludes certain persons as objects of the power. Because the power could be exercised in favor of the donee or the donee's estate, it can be made to the excluded persons.

C. INTERESTS CREATABLE BY EXERCISE OF POWER OF APPOINTMENT

1. PERMISSIBLE APPOINTMENT UNDER GENERAL POWER

When the donee holds a general power of appointment, "there is no restriction on the quantum or character of the estate to be appointed, the donee may appoint a fee or any lesser or qualified legal estate," *Massey v. Guaranty Trust Co.*, 5 N.W.2d 279 (Neb. 1942). The court further stated that:

> The donor having indicated complete indifference as to the ultimate beneficiary of the power, it would be illogical, unreasonable and contrary to common knowledge of human nature to attribute to him concern about the nature of the estate they were to receive and especially in the absence of any language indicating any such concern.

Id. at 286.

When the general power allows outright appointments to the donee or to the donee's estate, the donee is permitted to create any power in another directly that could be created indirectly in another by appointing to the donee or the donee's estate and then creating the power in connection with a disposition of owned property. RESTATEMENT (SECOND) PROPERTY § 19.1–.2 (1984).

2. PERMISSIBLE APPOINTMENT UNDER NON-GENERAL POWER

Unless the donor has manifested a contrary intent, a donee of a non-general power is permitted to make any appointment benefitting objects of the power that the donee could make of owned property in favor of those objects. The inference is that, unless the donor indicates otherwise, the donor of a non-general power intends the donee to have the same breadth of discretion in appointment to objects that he or she has in disposing of his or her own property to objects of the power. RESTATEMENT (SECOND) PROPERTY § 19.3 (1984).

In addition, unless the donor has manifested a contrary intent, a donee of a non-general power may exercise that power by: (1) Creating a general power in an object of the non-general power, or (2) Creating a non-general power in any person to appoint to an object of the original non-general power. RESTATEMENT (SECOND) PROPERTY § 19.4 (1984). If the donee can appoint outright to an object, the creation of a general power in the object to appoint by deed is, in substance, the equivalent of a permissible outright appointment. If the general power created in the object is to appoint by will, even though the object does not have, in substance, the equivalent of ownership, the object is close to having the equivalent of ownership, especially when the object is given a life interest in the appointive assets.

A donee of the non-general power may create a power in another to appoint only to objects authorized in the original power. In the absence of a contrary manifestation of intent by the donor, it is to be inferred that the donor does not intend to do more than to keep appointments within the objects of the original power. As long as this is the case, the donee or another the donee selects may make the final selection of the objects. The donor might consider the appointment personal to the donee and then the donee should not be allowed to exercise the power by creating a power. RESTATEMENT (SECOND) PROPERTY § 19.4, cmt. a (1984).

D. CONTRACT TO APPOINT POWER OF APPOINTMENT

1. CONTRACT TO APPOINT

A contract to appoint to a particular object of the power, if the contract is valid, is a release that eliminates as objects of the power all objects but the one to whom the donee is obligated to appoint under the contract.

2. POWER PRESENTLY EXERCISABLE

When a donee holds a presently exercisable power of appointment, a contract to make an appointment in the future is enforceable by the promisee, if neither the contract nor the promised appointment confers a benefit upon one not an object of the power. In this situation an appointment in the future that the donee could make immediately does not threaten the accomplishment of purposes indirectly that could not be accomplished directly. RESTATEMENT (SECOND) PROPERTY § 16.1 (1984).

A contract to appoint relating to a power presently exercisable is not valid if the contract or the promised appointment confers a benefit on a non-object. When the donee holds a presently exercisable non-general power of appointment, the objects of the power may be so inclusive that only the donee of the power and the donee's creditors are non-objects. On the other hand, when the objects of the power are a defined limited class that does not include the donee, the non-objects are very numerous. *Id.*

3. POWER NOT PRESENTLY EXERCISABLE

When a donee holds a power of appointment that is not presently exercisable, the donee cannot contract to make an appointment in the future that is enforceable by the promisee. RESTATEMENT (SECOND) PROPERTY § 16.2 (1984)

E. TIME OF EXERCISE OF POWER OF APPOINTMENT

1. ATTEMPTED APPOINTMENT BEFORE CREATION OF POWER

A power of appointment cannot be effectively exercised by an otherwise legally effective instrument of appointment that attempts to exercise the power before the power is created or before a condition precedent to the power's exercise has been satisfied. RESTATEMENT (SECOND) PROPERTY § 18.4 (1984). An attempted exercise of a nonexistent power or a nonexercisable power cannot produce an appointment. This rule does not prevent the exercise of a testamentary power by a will executed prior to the creation of the a power so long as the will becomes effective after the power's creation. *See supra* Part 5.II.A.5.

F. APPOINTMENT TO DECEASED PERSONS

1. DEATH OF OBJECTS PRIOR TO EFFECTIVE EXERCISE

When a donee makes an appointment to a person who is dead, it is ineffective except as provided by an applicable antilapse statute. If the appointment is to the dead person's estate, the appointment is effective if the dead person's estate is a proper object of the power. RESTATEMENT (SECOND) PROPERTY § 18.5 (1984).

The donee may appoint to an alternative taker if the originally named appointee dies before some specified time but only if the alternative appointee is an object of the power and is not dead at the time of appointment.

2. ANTILAPSE STATUTES AND POWERS OF APPOINTMENTS

Although antilapse statutes exist in nearly all states, many of these statutes are silent about their application to powers of appointment and their exercise. The

Restatement and other authorities contend that they should apply if not expressly inapplicable. RESTATEMENT (SECOND) PROPERTY § 18.6 (1984).

3. UPC ANTILAPSE PROVISION

The UPC specifically applies its substitute gift protection to the exercise of powers of appointment. UPC § 2–603. Under this section the exercise of a testamentary power of appointment is a devise and an appointee of an exercised testamentary power of appointment is a devisee. UPC § 2–603(a)(3), (4). Exercised testamentary powers are protected by the substitute gift presumption if the appointee comes within the protected class of a grandparent or a lineal descendant of a grandparent or a stepchild of the donor of a power of appointment exercised by the testator's will or of the testator who is donee of the power. UPC § 2–603(b).

Illustration 6: If D devised or deeded property "to T for life, remainder to G's children as T shall appoint," and T exercised the power in favor of A but A predeceased T leaving surviving descendants, A's surviving descendants would take a substitute devise if A is a member of the protected relatives of either D or T.

It makes no difference whether the power of appointment is a general or special power so long as the appointee is in the protected class. The exercise may be to an individual or a class. If the substitute gift presumption applies, it does not matter that the substitute taker is not a member of the class of permissible appointees so long as the appointee is a permissible appointee and meets the relational threshold requirement.

G. REVIEW QUESTIONS

1. A donor may impose restrictions on how and when the donee may exercise the power. True or False?

2. A donee of the non-general power may not create a power in another to appoint only to objects authorized in the original power. True or False?

3. When a donee holds a power of appointment that is not presently exercisable, the donee cannot contract to make an appointment in the future that is enforceable by the promisee. True or False?

III

NONEXERCISE OF POWERS OF APPOINTMENT

Analysis

A. RELEASE AND DISCLAIMER OF POWERS OF APPOINTMENT

1. GENERAL CONCEPTS

When a power is released or disclaimed by the donee of the power, the uncertainty concerning who the ultimate takers is removed.

2. RELEASE OF POWERS OF APPOINTMENT

A donee of a general or a non-general power of appointment created by the donee can be released, in whole or in part, by the donee of the power. When a general or non-general power of appointment is created by another, however, the donee can release it, in whole or in part, only to the extent that the donor did not effectively manifest an intent that it not be releasable RESTATEMENT (SECOND) PROPERTY § 14.1 (1984). If the release is effective the property passes at the time and to the persons who would have taken if the power were never exercised.

Several state statutes recognize that a prohibition on release manifested by the donor of the power will be given effect. *See, e.g.,* TEXAS REV. CIV. STAT. ANN. art. 7425c (1960).

Authorities uniformly uphold the release of general powers to appoint by will. *In re Haskell's Trust,* 300 N.Y.S.2d 711 (Sup. Ct. 1969) (under New York case law, a donee may release a general power to appoint by will).

3. DISCLAIMER OF POWER BY DONEE

A person named donee of a power of appointment can disclaim all or some part of the power. A power of appointment is similar to any other property interest and thus, is disclaimable. The procedures established by disclaimer statutes must be followed.

4. LAPSE OF POWER

The donor of a power of appointment may provide that the power is to be exercised within a specified time or it will cease to exist. The failure of the donee to exercise the power within the specified period of time causes the power to lapse. Such lapse is the equivalent of a release of the power by the donee.

5. METHODS OF RELEASE

A releasable power may be released by:

a. Completing any method authorized by the donor of the power;

b. Delivering a writing declaring the extent to which the power is released to a person who could be adversely affected by an exercise of the power;

c. Joining with some or all of the takers in default of an exercise of the power in making an otherwise effective transfer of an interest in the property that is subject to the power;

d. Contracting with a person who could be adversely affected by an exercise of the power not to exercise the power;

e. Communicating an intent to release the power in any other appropriate manner.

Restatement (Second) Property § 14.5 (1984).

B. DISCLAIMER BY OBJECT OR APPOINTEE

1. DISCLAIMER BY OBJECT OF POWER

A person who otherwise would be an object of the power may disclaim within a reasonable time after the creation of the power. Restatement (Second) Property § 14.6 (1984).

2. DISCLAIMER BY AN APPOINTEE

An object of the power who becomes an appointee when the power is exercised can disclaim the interest appointed in the object's favor. Restatement (Second) Property § 14.6 (1984). Because the status of an appointee does not arise until an exercise of the power, a disclaimer of the interest appointed can be made within a reasonable time after the exercise of the power. The fact that a person accepted the status of being an object of the power does not prevent a disclaimer of the status of an appointee.

C. REVIEW QUESTIONS

1. The donor of a power of appointment may provide that the power is to be exercised within a specified period of time or it will cease to exist. What is this called?

2. Unless subject to a valid restraint on alienation, the interest in property that an object of a power might receive under an exercise of the power is transferable. True or False?

3. Who can disclaim an interest in a power of appointment?

*

IV

DONEE'S CREDITORS AND SPOUSAL ELECTIONS

Analysis

A. GENERAL APPLICATION

1. THIRD PERSON RIGHTS AGAINST THE DONEE

The issue considered here is under what circumstances can creditors and spouses of donees of powers of appointment reach appointive assets to satisfy their claims.

2. SIGNIFICANT LIMITING DISTINCTIONS

Access to the appointive assets may depend on whether the power of appointment held by the donee is a general or special power, and whether it has been exercised.

B. CREDITORS OF THE DONEE

1. NON-GENERAL POWER

Creditors of the donee of a non-general power cannot subject the appointive assets to the payment of the claims of or to the expenses of administration of the donee's estate. The same rule applies even if the donee exercises the power. The donee of a non-general power is not considered to be the owner of the appointive assets. The donee serves as a kind of fiduciary to the power and is not permitted to derive personal benefit from its exercise.

Illustration 1: D as life beneficiary of a trust is granted a power of appointment "to appoint by a deed or will to such person or persons, other than D, D's estate, D's creditors, and creditors of D's estate, in such amounts and proportions and for such estates and interests and outright or upon such terms, trusts, conditions, and limitations as D shall specify and on D's death, to the extent the trust property is not otherwise disposed of by an exercise of D's power to appoint, the trust property shall pass to settlor's issue then living, such issue to take per stirpes, and if no issue of D is then living, to the X charity." D dies. D's creditors cannot reach the appointive assets during D's lifetime or on D's death whether or not D exercises his power to appoint. The same rule applies even if the donee is in bankruptcy.

Fraudulent Conveyance: If an owner of property makes a transfer of assets into a trust that is in fraud of the owner's creditors and personally reserves a non-general power, the owner's creditors can reach the appointive assets under the rules relating to fraudulent conveyances even though the owner only reserved a non-general power.

2. GENERAL POWER NOT CREATED BY DONEE

a. Unexercised General Powers

In the absence of a controlling statute, courts have commonly held that appointive assets covered by an unexercised general power of appointment, created by some person other than the donee, cannot be subjected to payment of claims of creditors of the donee. RESTATEMENT (SECOND) PROPERTY § 13.2 (1984). The rationale is that until the donee exercises the power, the donee has not accepted sufficient control over the appointive assets to give the donee the equivalent of ownership.

A power may be exercised in part and unexercised in part. In such case, the rule is applicable to the part that is unexercised. A partial exercise of the power occurs if the exercise relates to some percentage of the appointive assets. The power is also only partially exercised if some of the interests created by the exercise violate the Rule Against Perpetuities and some do not.

Several state statutes provide that property over which a debtor holds a general power of appointment may be subject to the claims of creditors to the extent that other property available for the payment of the claims is insufficient, whether or not the power has been exercised. *See, e.g.,* CALIF. PROB. CODE § 682 (West 1992)

b. Exercised General Powers

An exercised power is one that has been effectively exercised in favor of appointees other than takers in default. A power is "unexercised" if a purported exercise is ineffective due to the failure of the donee to comply with the required formalities of an exercise of the power or to the death of the appointee. If the purported appointee is the same person that would take the appointive assets if the power is not exercised, the power is an unexercised power.

- Exercised General Testamentary Powers: The appointive assets covered by an exercised general power to appoint by will are subject to the payment of claims against the donee's estate.
- Exercised General Inter Vivos Powers: The appointive assets covered by an exercised general power to appoint by deed are subject to the payment of the claims of donee's creditors to the same extent as any transfer by donee of personally owned assets would be subject to those claims as fraudulent conveyances.
- Rationale: The donee's exercise of a general power, whether testamentary or inter vivos, exhibits a dominion over the appointive assets that is in its practical aspects identical to the dominion exercised by the donee over owned assets disposed of by the donee's will.
- Expressions of Contrary Intent: These rules apply regardless of whether the donor or the donee manifested a contrary intent.

3. GENERAL POWER CREATED BY DONEE

Appointive assets covered by a general power of appointment created by the donee can be subjected to the claims of creditors of the donee or claims against the donee's estate. The general power created by the donee may be one presently exercisable or one not presently exercisable. The rule applies if the donee paid the purchase price for the transfer, or otherwise contributed the value represented by the transfer. The rule only applies to the portion of the transfer that is subject to the general power of appointment.

Illustration 2: D transfers Meadowacre "to D for life, then to such person or persons, including D's estate, as D may appoint by deed or by will, and in default of appointment to D's child C and her heirs." A creditor of D can subject D's life estate and the remainder in fee simple to the payment of the creditor's claim. On D's death, the claims against D's estate can be satisfied out of Meadowacre to the same extent as if D owned Meadowacre at D's death. The same result occurs even if D's power to appoint is exercisable by deed only or by will only.

The rationale for the rule is that it would be contrary to sound public policy to allow a person to put one's property beyond the reach of one's creditors merely by transferring the assets to a trust and retaining a general power of appointment over the transferred property.

This rule applies (1) even if a spendthrift provision is included, (2) whether the claim of the creditor seeking relief arose prior to the transfer, (3) whether there is a gift in default of appointment; and (4) whether the transfer constituted a fraudulent conveyance.

Illustration 3: D purchases Meadowacre from A and pursuant to D's request, A transfers Meadowacre "to D for life, then as D may appoint by will to anyone, including D's estate, and in default of appointment to C and her heirs." The rule of this section applies to the power in D although the transaction was set up to make it appear that a third person, A, created the general power in D.

4. CONSEQUENCES OF DONEE'S BANKRUPTCY

Section 541(b)(1) of the Bankruptcy Code of 1978 (11 U.S.C. § 541(b)(1)) provides that "Property of the estate does not ... include any power that the debtor may exercise solely for the benefit of an entity other than the debtor." Thus the Bankruptcy Act clearly excludes from the bankruptcy estate all non-general powers of the bankrupt. In addition, a general power to appoint by will is excluded from the bankruptcy estate under the quoted language because it is exercisable "solely for the benefit of an entity other than the debtor."

The bankruptcy estate includes general powers of the bankrupt that are presently exercisable because they are inherently exercisable for the benefit of the bankrupt. This authority exists notwithstanding express statements in the drafting instrument that "no interest of any beneficiary, whether in principal or income shall be assignable or subject to the claims of creditors." This gives the bankruptcy trustee the ability to exercise the power for the benefit of the creditors of the bankrupt.

C. SPOUSAL RIGHTS IN APPOINTIVE ASSETS

1. SPOUSES RIGHTS ABSENT A STATUTE

The generally accepted rule is that the spouse of a donee of the power is not entitled to treat the appointive assets as owned by the donee if those assets are subject to a power not created by the donee. Similarly, appointive assets are not included as part of the donee's estate for purposes of the surviving spouse's right of election when the donor and donee were different persons. Restatement (Second) Property § 13.7 (1984).

2. STATUTORY SPOUSAL RIGHTS OF SURVIVING SPOUSE

Some spousal protection statutes are clear that if the deceased spouse was both the donor and donee of the power, the deceased spouse's estate, for purposes of a spouse' elective share, includes property over which the deceased spouse had a general power of appointment. *See* UPC § 2–205(2)(ii).

Other statutes dealing with the right of election of the surviving spouse do not specify what is included in the deceased spouse's estate for the purpose of the spouse's right of election. Common law right of dower does not attach to appointive assets.

Illustration 4: T by will transfers Meadowacre "to my son D for life, then as D may appoint by will to anyone, including D's estate, and in default of appointment to D's issue by representation, and if no issue of D survives D, then in default of appointment, to the X charity." D's surviving spouse, W elects to take her elective share. Meadowacre is not included in the assets of D's estate for the purpose of determining W's statutory share because the general power was not created by D but by T.

D. REVIEW QUESTIONS

1. The donee of a non-general power is considered to be the owner of the appointive assets. True or False?
2. A power may be exercised in part and unexercised in part. True or False?
3. When can a surviving spouse exercise rights in an interest in which the decedent spouse holds a power of appointment?

*

PART SIX

TRUSTS

*

I

TRUSTS: DEFINITIONS AND CHARACTERISTICS

Analysis

- 3. *Justification for a Definite Beneficiary Rule*
- 4. *Relational Terminology*
- 5. *Problem Categories*

E. *Trust Purposes*

- 1. *Trusts Contrary to Public Policy*
- 2. *Common Public Policy Prohibitions:*
- 3. *No Standard Definition of Public Policy*
- 4. *Effect of Illegal Condition*

F. *Comparisons with Other Transactions*

- 1. *Constructive Trusts*
- 2. *Resulting Trusts*

G. *Review Questions*

A. TRUST CHARACTERISTICS

1. DEFINITION

The THIRD RESTATEMENT OF TRUSTS defines the express trust as follows:

> [An express] trust ... is a fiduciary relationship with respect to property, arising as a result of a manifestation of an intention to create that relationship and subjecting the person who holds title to the property to duties to deal with it for the benefit of charity or for one or more persons, at least one of whom is not the sole trustee.

RESTATEMENT (THIRD) OF TRUSTS § 2. Definition of Trust (T.D. No. 1, 1996).

2. SPECIAL CHARACTERISTICS

An express trusts possesses the following characteristics:

- It arises from a manifestation of intention to create the relationship. It is the manifestation of intention which controls and not the actual intention where that differs from the manifestation of intention.
- It is a legal relationship between the parties concerning the trustee's duties owed to the beneficiary and to the rest of the world. Legal duties that arise are imposed by law.
- It is a relationship with respect to property, not one involving merely personal duties. There is always property held by the trustee for the benefit of the cestui que trust.
- It is a legal relationship between the parties concerning the rights, privileges, powers and immunities that the beneficiary holds against the trustee and against the rest of the world.
- It is a relationship of a fiduciary character. It concerns the duty on the trustee to act for the benefit of the beneficiary concerning matters within the scope of the relationship.
- It involves equitable duties enforced in a court of equity. The interests of the beneficiary, being an equitable interest, means that its principles, standards and rules are developed by a court of equity, *e.g.*, creation, enforcement, extinguishment and third party relations.

3. FRAGMENTATION OF TRUST INTERESTS

Trusts always separate "legal ownership" from "equitable ownership." If legal and equitable ownership are not effectively separated, no trust exists. In addition, trusts usually have their equitable trust interests divided between present and future beneficiaries. The typical private express trust creates a life interest in the corpus in favor of one or more beneficiaries, followed by equitable future interests in favor of one or more beneficiaries (or classes of beneficiaries). The existence of a trust does not depend upon fragmentation in this second sense.

4. TRUST DISTINCTIONS

Ordinarily, it is clear that a trust is intended because it is evident from the general nature of the relationship created or is apparent from the written or spoken terms of the transfer. Occasionally, the nature of a transaction is unclear and the question arises whether it creates an express trust or some other device. This problem arises only with transactions that concern property that might be identified as trust property.

Sometimes it is beneficial for a party to the transaction to contend a trust exists, sometimes another legal device. Characterization of the arrangement may be determinative of rights and duties between the parties to the transaction or of liabilities or priorities regarding third parties.

Courts have not consistently characterized ambiguous transactions. Some decisions appear to analyze the facts of the relevant transaction and objectively compare these facts to trust law requirements. Other decisions appear to find the outcome desired and fashion the facts to fit the type of transaction that will come to that result. Usually, but not always, a trust characterization is desired by the "beneficiary" because trusts principles generally protect beneficiaries better than other devices.

Illustration 1: S hands T $1,000 of cash with the understanding T will pay the cash to B at particular intervals. On the way to the bank to deposit the money, T is robbed. Is the transaction a debt or a trust? There is a person who could be called the settlor, the trustee and the beneficiary. In addition, there is an identifiable res. If this transaction creates a trust, T will not be liable for the stolen money unless T was negligent. If the subject matter of a trust is lost or destroyed without fault of the trustee, the trustee is not liable to the beneficiaries. If the transaction is a loan, however, the debt is not discharged by the theft and the liability to B, the lender's third part beneficiary, continues.

Illustration 2: Assuming the same transaction between S and T but that T is unable to pay because of bankruptcy rather than theft. If the transaction is characterized as a trust, B would be a preferred creditor if B can trace and identify the trust property. On the other hand, if this were merely a debt, B would be an ordinary creditor with no priority and would have to share with all other creditors.

Nontrust Security Arrangements: Generally, security arrangements are not "trusts" even when trust concepts are used and some rules applicable to trust relationships are applied. This includes security interests such as mortgages, pledges and legal or equitable liens. Where a person deposits money with another as security for the faithful performance of obligations owed to the other, however, a trust may be found for the depositor if it is understood that the money deposited is to be segregated for the depositor and returned when the depositor has performed the obligations. If the deposit is to be commingled with the holder's own assets, the relationship is one of debt. The nature of the duties between the depositor and the holder may depend upon the classification of the relationship. *See* RESTATEMENT (THIRD) OF TRUSTS § 5 (T.D. No. 1, 1996).

5. ESTATE PLANNING USES OF TRUSTS

Testamentary Trusts

- Property management–Trusts are frequently used with regard to minor beneficiaries and surviving spouses who are elderly or inexperienced in business matters.
- Providing for successive estates–Trusts are more flexible and secure devices than are legal life estates for dividing the life interest for one set of beneficiaries and reserving the remainder for another set.
- Greater protection of future interests.
- Greater flexibility regarding unanticipated situations–Discretion can be granted to the trustee to deal with unanticipated events.
- Tax Purposes–Where substantial amounts are involved, trusts can cut down estate taxes on death of primary beneficiaries. Trusts may also cut down income tax consequences by permitting income distributions among lower income beneficiaries.

Inter Vivos Trusts

- Avoidance of probate–Trusts can lower costs of administration, provide for greater continuity, and provide greater privacy for successors than will the administration of a decedent's estate.
- Avoid agency pitfalls–Terms of the trust can anticipate incapacity or death and the trust may continue to operate: Trusts can anticipate and handle problems caused by future incompetency.
- Tax Purposes–Inter vivos trusts may suffer gift taxes but not estate tax if irrevocable and settlor does not retain control.

B. THE TRUSTEE

1. DEFINITION OF THE TRUSTEE

The trustee is the one who holds legal title to the property and who administers the trust property. A trustee is a fiduciary. "[A] fiduciary relation is one in which the law demands of one party an unusually high standard of ethical and moral conduct with reference to another." GEORGE G. BOGERT & GEORGE T. BOGERT, THE LAW OF TRUSTS AND TRUSTEES § 1 (Rev. 2d ed. 1984).

2. APPOINTMENT OF A TRUSTEE

Ordinarily, the trustee or successor trustees are named in the trust. If not, a court may appoint the trustee. A wide range of persons or entities are eligible to serve as trustee including: individuals, corporate fiduciaries, and governments. Depending on state law, special capacity problems may arise if any of the following are named as trustee: infants, incompetents, aliens, nonresidents/foreign corporations, and unincorporated associations. Once appointed and accepted, a trustee can only terminate the relationship by court order or by following the resignation and replacement procedures set out in the instrument or by law.

3. NECESSITY OF A TRUSTEE

Although a trust must have a trustee, the cardinal rule is that "A trust will not fail for want of a trustee." Once a trust is established, the failure or absence of a trustee will not affect the continuation of the trust since a successor will ordinarily be appointed to carry out the settlor's intention. Failure or absence may occur because no trustee was appointed, or because the named trustee fails to qualify, lacks legal capacity, or dies, resigns or is removed.

Two exceptions to this rule have been mentioned. First, the rare circumstance when the trusteeship (its duties) is considered personal to the person appointed. This would have to be clearly shown on the face of the trust. Second, in regard to an inter vivos trust, there may be a validity problem when a trustee is not appointed and there is a question whether there has been a transfer. This is a technical problem and of very limited scope. It does not apply to a testamentary trust created in a valid will.

Illustration 3: A executes and records a deed to real estate that names T as trustee of an irrevocable trust for W. The deed is never delivered. Several years later, A seeks to rescind the deed. T, who never had been informed of the trust, disclaimed trusteeship upon notification of the transfer. A contends that because there was no delivery of the deed, there was no trust established and thus A holds fee simple title to the property. *Held:* Trust is valid and enforceable. The court held that a trust was created. Although there was no actual delivery, all the necessary steps were taken to transfer legal title to the trustee. The recordation of the deed constituted symbolic delivery. Although T's disclaimer of title caused a resulting trust back to A, A held as a constructive trustee until the court could appoint a new trustee. Failure to transfer legal title to T did not prevent a trust from arising because the deed effected a present transfer of the equitable title to W. Transferring equitable title to the beneficiary does not require delivery or even notice to the beneficiary. *See Adams v. Adams*, 88 U.S. (21 Wall.) 185 (1874).

4. SUCCESSOR AND SUBSTITUTE TRUSTEES

The selection of a successor trustee depends upon the intention of the settlor. A successor named in a trust will ordinarily be selected as trustee, if competent. If a court makes the selection, it will consider the desires of beneficiaries, settlor's intent, and furtherance of sound administration

C. THE TRUST PROPERTY

1. IDENTIFIABLE RES

A trust must have a specific identifiable res. Thus the trust res must be transferable and be ascertainable. A common question to ask is, "Does the trust res have value?" The basic issue is whether the property of the trust is described with such definiteness and certainty that the trustee and the court can be sure that the intended trust is carried out. Sometimes courts apply the requirements mechanically and determine whether the relationship fits the trust mold. Other courts take the requirements and mold them to the result desired.

Most types of interests can be held in trust including fee simple, term of years, life estate, contingent remainders (some states prohibit this), vested remainders, other future interests, and contractual rights.

Some interests can be held in a trust but not transferred to a trust, *e.g.*, tort claims and contingent remainders.

Other invalid examples:

> "Such property as I may own at my death" for an inter vivos trust
>
> "Most of my property"
>
> "What I will inherit from Aunt Bertha when she dies." (Aunt Bertha is alive.)

2. TRUST OF FUTURE PROFITS

Since a trust must have property in order to be valid, the trust naturally includes future profits generated by the trustee's investment and reinvestment of that property. For example, a trust of certain shares of stock or of certain capital including all future profits realized from trading that stock or capital would be effective at the date of creation. In addition, a person may immediately transfer in trust for another an enforceable contract including future earnings from the contract.

Compare *Brainard v. Commissioner*, 91 F.2d 880 (7th Cir. 1937): In December 1927, Brainard announced to his wife and mother that he declared a trust for his wife and children of his profits in stock trading during the next year. A self-declaration of trust entails a transfer of an equitable interest in the trust property and no formalities are necessary for such a transfer other than a manifestation of an intent to make the transfer. The issue in the case concerned at what time was the trust created. Three dates were considered: (1) time of declaration; (2) time of receipt of profits; (3) time of crediting of profits to beneficiaries. The court held it was the latter.

> *Answer:* It was not the first date because the "declaration" was merely a gratuitous promise in the future. No trust was then created because there was no specific trust property, only an "expectancy" at that date.
>
> It was not the second date or dates because there was no remanifestation of trust intent as each profit transaction occurred. Consequently, Brainard's profits did not automatically come under the prior declaration upon being realized. To bring them under the prior declaration, Brainard himself had to remanifest trust intent.
>
> Note that under ordinary principles of property law, a purported transfer of property to be acquired in the future becomes enforceable, *i.e.*, takes place automatically, when the property is later acquired, but only if:
>
> (1) the transfer was by warranty deed, under the doctrine of estoppel by deed [*See* Roger A. Cunningham, William B. Stoebuck & Dale A. Whitman, Property § 11.5 (West Group 2d Ed. 1993)]; or
>
> (2) the purported transfer was for adequate consideration.
>
> Neither of these applied in *Brainard*.

It was the third date when Brainard remanifested trust intent, *i.e.*, transferred the equitable interest in the property to the beneficiaries.

Illustration 4: If *S* orally declares herself trustee of all stocks she currently owns with any profits from stock trading to go to *A*, is a valid trust created?

> *Answer Illustration 4:* Yes. There is a specific res from which future profits may be derived.

Illustration 5: If *S* orally declares a trust of all royalties from patents *S* may receive from *S*'s future inventions, is a valid trust created?

> *Answer Illustration* 5: No. This is merely a gratuitous promise and no trust exists until royalties are received and transferred into the trust.

3. JUSTIFICATION FOR THE RES REQUIREMENT

The res requirement is not a matter of mere formalism because it serves both evidentiary and cautionary purposes. The existence of an identifiable res improves the reliability of proof and probative safeguards for the settlor, trustee and beneficiary against unworthy disputes over rights, responsibilities and title. In addition, the act of transferring an identifiable res provides a cautionary function by emphasizing the importance of the act, thus providing a clearer expression of finality of intent. It also serves to limit and focus the trustee's substantial fiduciary duties.

D. THE BENEFICIARIES

1. CESTUI QUE TRUST

The cestui que trust, or today what is more commonly called the beneficiary, is the one for whom the trust property is held. Most trusts have both an income and a remainder beneficiary. The beneficiary has in personam and in rem rights; personal rights against the trustee; and equitable ownership of the trust res. *See Chemical Bank New York Trust Co. v. Steamship Westhampton*, 358 F.2d 574, 584 (4th Cir. 1965).

2. DEFINITE BENEFICIARY REQUIREMENT

There must be a definite beneficiary identifiable at the time of creation or within the Rule Against Perpetuities who can receive the beneficial interest from and judicially enforce the trust against the trustee. RESTATEMENT (SECOND) OF TRUSTS § 112 (1959). Either the beneficiary must be (1) specifically named, (2) ascertainable from facts existing at the trust's creation, or (3) ascertainable from facts which must exist at some time within the Rule Against Perpetuities or other statutory period.

Note: in regard to charitable trusts the beneficiary rule is opposite. A charitable trust may fail because the class of persons who are to benefit is so narrow that the community has no interest in the performance of the trust. *See infra* Part 6.VI.E.

A valid trust does not require that the extent of the beneficiary's interest be definite or definitely ascertainable at the trust's creation. RESTATEMENT (SECOND) OF TRUSTS § 129 (1959). The beneficiary's interest may be a vested or contingent future interest or depend solely upon the discretion of the trustee or some third person. The beneficial interest must be definitely ascertainable within the period of the Rule Against Perpetuities, however.

3. JUSTIFICATION FOR A DEFINITE BENEFICIARY RULE

There would be no one able to enforce the administration of the trust because only those who stand in the position of a beneficiary under a private trust have the right to come into court and challenge the way it is administered.

Standing Issue: Just because one benefits from a trust does not give that person authority to enforce it, *e.g.,* creditor. Any member of an ascertainable class can enforce the trust. The proper question might be : "Is there at least one clear beneficiary?"

4. RELATIONAL TERMINOLOGY

When terminology such as children, grandchildren, descendants, or siblings is used to describe the trust beneficiary, the beneficiaries must be identifiable on the basis of facts of independent significance for trusts created in wills. Merely because a description has independent significance does not necessarily mean that the extrinsic evidence will adequately prove to whom or to what it applies. Generally, the trier of fact may be aided by evidence of the surrounding facts and circumstances. Definiteness depends on provable intent of the settlor.

5. PROBLEM CATEGORIES

Problem categories include "relatives," "family," "neighbors," "friends," and the like. "Relatives," for example, is ambiguous. Does it include "all" relatives or family or is it limited to relatives as defined by intestacy statutes? If the former, the group is too indefinite: if the latter, it is definite. *See Clark v. Campbell*, 133 A. 166 (N.H. 1926). "Family" requires similar distinctions. "Neighbors" and "friends" are too indefinite unless the settlor provides an adequate definition for court delineation.

Unborn and Unascertained Beneficiaries: There has been some controversy whether a trust can be validly created if all beneficiaries are unborn, unascertained, or both. The Restatement (Third) of Trusts takes the position that it can. *See* Restatement (Third) of Trusts § 44, Reporters' Note (Council D. No. 2, 1998).

Illustration 6: S transfers assets "to T, in trust, for T and his children for the life of T, remainder to T's children." At time of transfer T was childless. A valid trust is established. If T dies childless, S or S's estate will take the defeasibly vested reversion.

Illustration 7: S declares herself trustee of certain assets to accumulate income for 5 years, then to pay income to herself for life, remainder to her issue, and if none, to her spouse, and if none, to her heirs. A valid trust is established. If S dies childless, S's heirs will take the defeasibly vested reversion.

On facts similar to *Illustration 7*, the court in *Morsman v. Commissioner*, 90 F.2d 18 (8th Cir. 1937) held that a trust was not established. The case has been characterized as a tax decision designed to prevent tax avoidance. *See* Restatement (Third) of Trusts § 44, Reporters' Note (Council Dft. No. 2, 1998).

E. TRUST PURPOSES

1. TRUSTS CONTRARY TO PUBLIC POLICY

Generally, trusts can be created for any purpose that is not deemed contrary to public policy. The typical purposes found to make a trust illegal include, when the performance of the trust or its provisions involve—

- the commission of a criminal or tortious act by the trustee, or
- an activity that is against "public policy."

2. COMMON PUBLIC POLICY PROHIBITIONS

Public policy prohibitions include trust purposes that:

- Restrict marriage (But some courts allow remarriage prohibitions and requirements that one marry a person in a particular faith);
- Encourage divorce;
- Encourage the neglect of parental responsibilities;
- Change of religious beliefs.

3. NO STANDARD DEFINITION OF PUBLIC POLICY

There is no standard definition for "public policy" because the definition depends upon the conceptions (ideas) of public policy which are prevalent in the community at the time the issue is in question. These conceptions change almost as rapidly as society in general changes. It has been stated that the exercise of public policy by a court goes to the maximum of the exercise of its inherent powers.

4. EFFECT OF ILLEGAL CONDITION

When conditions are found to be illegal, court remedies vary. Some refuse to enforce the condition, others remove the condition. In some cases, the court held that the trust fails and thus the condition fails too.

The RESTATEMENT (SECOND) OF PROPERTY: DONATIVE TRANSFERS § 6.1, cmt. c, (1983) provides that before a trust purpose is invalid two conditions must be met. (1) There must be an otherwise effective present disposition of an interest in property whether that interest be present or a future interest. (2) The acquisition or retention of the interest must be dependent upon future conduct of the devisee which the disposition is intended to influence. Consequently, an invalid condition in a testamentary trust will not invalidate the trust if the condition must be met at the testator's death and there is no attempt to affect future conduct after death. The will is not a present transfer until the testator's death.

In most cases, the courts will follow the settlor's intent. If the settlor anticipates that the originally suggested trust may be held to be invalid and provides for an alternate gift, generally the law contains no punitive refusal to give effect to that which the testator probably would have wished had testator known the condition would fail. See RESTATEMENT (SECOND) OF TRUST § 65, cmt. f (1959).

Where the settlor properly manifested an intention as to the disposition to be made of the property in case the condition should be held illegal, his or her manifestation of intention determines whether the beneficiary is entitled to the interest even though the event does not happen, or is not entitled to the interest even though the event happens.

Illustration 8: Settlor creates an irrevocable trust which requires the beneficiary to divorce a spouse in order to receive benefits under the trust. If encouraging divorce is against public policy, a court might strike or refuse to enforce the condition. The trust might even be held invalid and fail thus causing the trust property to pass according to the residuary clause of the will or in intestacy if the trust is the residuary. If the settlor included a clause which provided that if the condition is found to be invalid the property goes to other persons, courts will follow the testator's intent.

Illustration 9: If the testator executes a will that includes a testamentary trust which requires the beneficiary to be divorced at the testator's death, the condition is enforceable because its threat does not require conduct against public policy after the effective date of the will.

Subjective Purpose: A particular condition may be valid or invalid depending on the subjective purpose of the settlor in inserting it in the trust terms even though the effect of the condition would be the same regardless of the settlor's motivation.

Illustration 10: In Illustration 8, if the settlor's intent is to protect the beneficiary from financial difficulties if divorce occurred rather than to encourage divorce, the condition may be valid and enforced.

F. COMPARISONS WITH OTHER TRANSACTIONS

1. CONSTRUCTIVE TRUSTS

A constructive trust is a judicial remedy. Courts impose a constructive trust in a wide range of litigation situations including: fraud, mistake, breach of implied or express promise, justified reliance, unjust enrichment, wrongful acquisition. The decree establishing a constructive trust ordinarily requires the defendant to deliver possession of and convey title to the property and to pay the plaintiff profits received or rental value during the period of wrongful holding and otherwise to adjust the equities of the parties after taking an accounting.

It is called a trust because there must be property, and someone who could be called a settlor, a trustee and a cestui que trust. It is also always up to the plaintiff to identify the property. A constructive trust does not require trust intent: the court implies the intent to prevent an "unjust enrichment."

2. RESULTING TRUSTS

From the nature of the circumstance, a court might presume, if no particular indication to the contrary is found, that the "settlor" did not intend to confer a beneficial interest upon the trustee. The character of the transaction raises an inference that the transferor did not intend for the transferee or "trustee" to receive the beneficial interest. Consequently, the "trustee" is held to hold the property or appropriate portions thereof subject to a duty to reconvey to the settlor, settlor's estate or successors in interest. With respect to the question of *trust intent*, the resulting trust is an intent enforcing device–a presumption or inference is found from the nature of the transaction. No actual intent but an implied probable intent is found. The risk of non persuasion is upon the alleged beneficiary.

The most typical types of resulting trusts include: (1) One which arises because an express trust fails or makes an incomplete disposition of the trust property; and (2) One in which the presumption is found in the situation where A buys land but has title put in B's name. The latter is commonly called a purchase money resulting trust.

In the purchase money resulting trust courts have used two contrasting presumptions or inferences. When there is a gratuitous transfer to one who is the natural object of such a transfer, *e.g.*, wife or other close relation but maybe not a husband or a parent, the presumption is not that it is a trust but a gift. On the other hand, when it is a transfer to a legal stranger rather than a close relation, the presumption is one of trust.

But even when there is a close relationship between the transferor and the transferee and also an express oral agreement that the land is held in trust for the transferor, and this oral agreement cannot be used to establish a trust because of the Statute of Frauds, the oral agreement can be used as evidence to rebut the presumption of a gift thereby leaving the alternative of a resulting trust.

When the presumption of gift is rebutted, the presumption that the one paying the money intends to create for himself a beneficial interest in the land is controlling.

G. REVIEW QUESTIONS

1. Trusts always separate "legal ownership" from "equitable ownership." True or False?

2. List some uses for testamentary trusts.

3. List some uses of inter vivos trusts.

4. What person holds legal title to the property and administers the trust property?

5. A settlor is a fiduciary. True or False?

6. A trust must have a specific identifiable res. True or False?

7. What is the person called for whom trust property is held?

*

II

TRUST FORMALITIES: CREATION AND TERMINATION

Analysis

A. INTENT TO CREATE A TRUST

1. TRUST INTENT

"A trust is created only if the settlor properly manifests an intention to create a trust relationship." RESTATEMENT (THIRD) OF TRUSTS § 13 (T.D. No. 1, 1996). The intention must exist at the time of transfer or creation. The manifestation of intent to create an inter vivos trust ordinarily must exist at the time of trust creation. The intention to create a testamentary trust must be ascertainable from the will or other provable source under the law of wills.

2. INFORMALITY OF INTENT

Words "in trust" are not necessary. No particular words or phrases need be used but there must be an outward expression of the settlor's intention: "a manifestation." It is not enough that the settlor secretly intends to create a trust.

It is immaterial whether the settlor knows the legal name of the relationship that the settlor intends to create, or knows the precise characteristics of a trust relationship. A trust is created if in substance the settlor intends to create the relationship that lawyers know as a trust.

Illustration 1: S declares that she holds certain bonds she owns "for B." Unless evidence to the contrary is introduced, S holds the bonds in trust for B. Other details of the trust relationship will be determined as necessary through interpretation.

Illustration 2: S tells others he is going to transfers bonds in trust for B. S never completes the transfer. No trust is created. Intent to transfer in trust in the future does not create a present trust.

3. PRECATORY WORDS

Precatory words that merely express a wish or hope but not a command do not satisfy the trust intent requirement. The transferor must manifest an intention to impose enforceable duties on the transferee. RESTATEMENT (THIRD) OF TRUSTS § 13 cmt. d (T.D. No. 1, 1996).

When precatory words are used, a question of interpretation arises whether the transferor intended to impose the necessary obligation or merely tried to explain the motivation for the transfer. The ordinary inference is that no trust intent was expressed and the transferor relies on the transferee's discretion to carry out the wishes. Despite this inference, it is a question of interpretation of the language used in light of all of the circumstances. Overcoming the inference depends on the admissibility of available extrinsic evidence. Courts indicate a reluctance to reach a result which produces an "unnatural" distribution of a testator's wealth under the circumstances.

Illustration 3: A's will devises residue to her daughter D and adds a "request that she use whatever of it she thinks necessary for the care of my brother, B." In the absence of other evidence of A's intention, D is entitled to the property beneficially and does not take it in trust.

Illustration 4: Same facts. The surrounding circumstances indicate that B is elderly, in poor health, and unable to provide for his own needs. B had been supported by A for several years. Despite the inference that precatory words do not create a trust, this inference may be overcome by admissible evidence of surrounding circumstances. Whether D takes outright or as trustee for B will depend on the admissibility of relevant evidence and the degree of proof available.

Relevant Surrounding Circumstances: Evidence that might be relevant include–

- Who is the fiduciary of the estate? Is devisee named as executor of testator's will?

  A "request" to one who is already nominated for some fiduciary role might indicate an expression of something other than mere precatory intent.

- What disposition is made of the residuary estate, and what other provision is made for the devisee and testator's other natural objects, if any?

  If devisee takes the residuary or other property, it might be inferred that the transferor expressed something more than mere precatory intent.

- What is the situation of the precatory legatee? How needy is this person and had testator been supporting him or her during testator's lifetime?

  A precatory devise for one whom the transferor knows needs support or has been supporting may indicate an expression of something more than mere precatory intent.

4. ACTIVE AND PASSIVE TRUSTS

Although the Statute of Uses applies to the trust concept, it does not apply to the active trust. RESTATEMENT (THIRD) OF TRUSTS § 6 cmt. c (T.D. No. 1, 1996). If a trustee merely holds title as custodian for the beneficiary, or holds title as custodian and makes nondiscretionary distribution of the trust property to the beneficiary or beneficiaries, the trust is passive. Trusts may be passive when created or may become passive later. If the trust is passive, the Statute of Uses executes it.

If by the terms of the trust the trustee has affirmative duties, the trust is active. Affirmative duties include actions such as collecting rents and profits, exercising responsibility for trust investments, and generally managing the trust property.

B. FORMALITIES FOR TRUSTS

1. FORMALITIES IN GENERAL

A trust may be created if the least possible formalities applicable to the situation are satisfied. *Matter of Brown*, 169 N.E. 612 (N.Y. 1930). There are tensions, however, between the trust requirements versus the imperfect gift problem. An imperfect gift will not be converted into a trust because the transfer lacks trust intent.

a. Settlor's Capacity

The settlor need only have the capacity to make the basic arrangement used to create the trust. If the trust is created by will, settlor must have testamentary capacity; if by gift, settlor must have the same capacity as one needs to make a gift; and if by contract, then contractual capacity suffices.

b. Possible Remedies

When formalities are a problem, a court may provide three possible remedies. (1) Enforce the trust. This permits proof of intent and prevents unjust enrichment. (2) Let the "trustee" take personally. Although this result may permit unjust enrichment to the "trustee," it abides by the formality and prevents the risks of "fraudulent" litigation. (3) Reinstate the status quo. This puts the parties back in their previous position and prevents unjust enrichment of the transferee but may cause unjust enrichment for transferor's successors. All formality controversies raise the specter of the veracity of the claimants and the actual intent of the "settlor" who is usually not available or is an interested person. There are innocent transferors as well as innocent transferees.

2. INTER VIVOS TRUSTS

The three general ways of creating a trust are (1) By transfer, (2) By declaration of trust, or (3) By contract.

a. Distinct Circumstances

There are three distinct factual situations that need to be considered:

$A \rightarrow T \rightarrow C$

$A \rightarrow \ \ T$
$\ \nwarrow \leftarrow \swarrow$

$A \rightarrow A \rightarrow C$

Depending on the formality in question, some courts distinguish between trusts for the transferor and trusts for third persons.

b. Formalities in Creation

No Writing Requirement: If neither the Statute of Frauds nor the Parol Evidence Rule is applicable, there is no writing requirement and an oral trust may be proved. RESTATEMENT (THIRD) OF TRUSTS § 20 (T.D. No. 1, 1996). When the issue has arisen, courts usually state, without explanation, that the burden of proof standard is by clear and convincing evidence.

Parol Evidence Rule: If there is no Statute of Frauds, but the parol evidence rule applies, the provability of an oral trust depends on the terms of the writing. In the absence of fraud, duress, undue influence, mistake, or other ground for reformation or rescission, extrinsic evidence is not admissible to contradict or vary the terms of an instrument which states the complete expression of the settlor's intention. RESTATEMENT (THIRD) OF TRUSTS § 21(1)1(a) (T.D. No. 1, 1996). If the terms of the instrument show that no trust is intended, extrinsic evidence may not be used to show that the transferee was intended to hold the property in trust. Concomitantly, if the instrument's terms show that a trust is intended, extrinsic evidence may not be used to show that the transferee was intended to hold the property upon a different trust or to take it beneficially. RESTATEMENT (THIRD) OF TRUSTS § 21(1)(b) (T.D. No. 1, 1996).

If no Statute of Frauds is applicable and if the instrument's expression of the settlor's intention or meaning is incomplete, ambiguous or otherwise uncertain, extrinsic evidence of the circumstances and other indications of the transferor's intent are admissible to complete the terms of the writing or to clarify or ascertain its meaning. RESTATEMENT (THIRD) OF TRUSTS § 21(2), and Reporter's Notes (T.D. No. 1, 1996). Under this circumstance an oral trust may be proved.

In addition, the Parol Evidence Rule does not bar evidence of an agreement to hold in trust even when a writing makes a transfer which is absolute on its face and includes no mention of a trust. RESTATEMENT (THIRD) OF TRUSTS § 21, Reporter's Notes (T.D. No. 1, 1996). Courts take the view that even an absolute conveyance does not unequivocally manifest an intention that the grantee should take the property for his or her own benefit, because it does not purport to show whether the grantee is to take it for personal benefit or for the benefit of someone else. The trust, therefore, is supplemental with regard to a matter on which the instrument is silent. The standard of proof has been held to require clear and convincing evidence.

Some courts distinguish between oral trusts for the transferor and trusts for third persons, the former are said not to be provable because of the parol evidence rule. *Guy v. Guy,* 104 N.C. App. 753, 411 S.E.2d 403 (1991). This is a confusion caused by the same rule when the Statute of Frauds is involved. The considerations are not the same, however.

Statute of Frauds: With a few exceptions and some variations, states have Statutes of Frauds that basically requires all trusts of real property to be in writing and signed by the settlor. RESTATEMENT (THIRD) OF TRUSTS § 22 cmt. a (T.D. No. 1, 1996). The writing must be signed by the settlor, manifest trust intent, identify the trust property, the beneficiaries, and the purposes of the trust. RESTATEMENT (THIRD) OF TRUSTS § 22 cmt. f (T.D. No. 1, 1996). Generally, trust agreements that do not comply with the Statute are not void but merely unenforceable. *See* Restatement (Second) Contracts § 110 (1981).

Illustration 5: If a person transfers property to another upon an oral express trust that is unenforceable because of the requirements of the Statute of Frauds and the transferee refuses to perform the trust, does the transferee hold the property free of trust or can the transferee be compelled to hold the property upon a constructive trust either for the transferor or for the intended beneficiaries and purposes? The answer may depend on whether restitution or specific restitution is the remedy sought by the parties.

Restitution: The Statute of Frauds is generally not a barrier to proving an oral trust if restitution to the transferor is the remedy sought. This remedy is based on the principle of preventing unjust enrichment. The "trustee" who orally promised to hold the property in trust would be unjustly enriched if permitted to keep the property for personal benefit. This is referred to as "going backwards" and is said to neither offend the letter nor the spirit of the Statute of Frauds.

Specific Enforcement: The direct or specific enforcement of the oral promise for the intended beneficiaries and of the trust purposes is more problematical. The Statute of Frauds is meant to prevent this remedy. Consequently, as a general rule, the oral trust cannot be proved to hold the transferee upon a constructive trust for the intended beneficiaries and purposes. Restatement (Third) of Trusts § 24(2) (T.D. No. 1, 1996). Exceptions are generally recognized, however.

Part Performance: Part performance may take the trust out of the Statute and permit the oral trust to be directly proved and enforced. *Id.* at § 24(1)(b). For example, part performance has been found where the beneficiary took possession of the property and changed position in reliance on the trust's existence. The part performance must provide sufficient corroboration of the parol evidence of the trust. A memorandum properly evidencing the trust is sufficient to satisfy the requirements of the Statute of Frauds, if it is signed by the settlor prior to the transfer of the interest.

Fraud or Duress: If the transfer was procured by fraud or duress, the transferee will be compelled to hold the property on constructive trust for the transferor or for the intended beneficiaries and purposes. Fraud requires proof that the transferee made a conscious misrepresentation and did not intend to perform the trust at the time of the agreement. Restatement (Third) of Trusts § 24 cmt. d (T.D. No. 1, 1996). Thus, it must be a misrepresentation as to the fact of the state of mind of the transferee. A mere breach of contract will not suffice.

Undue Influence: If the transferee at the time of the transfer and oral trust exercised undue influence over the transferor, the transferee will be held to hold the property on constructive trust for the intended beneficiaries and purposes. See Restatement (First) of Contracts § 497 (1997 App.); Restatement (First) of Restitution § 70 (1937).

Confidential Relationship: If the transferee at the time of the transfer and the oral trust stood in a confidential or fiduciary relationship with respect to the transferor, the transferee will be held to hold the property on constructive trust for the intended beneficiaries and purposes. The usual fiduciary relationships include attorney and client, guardian and ward, trustee and beneficiary, agent and principal, partners in a partnership and persons engaging in a joint enterprise. The term "confidential relationship" is broader and concerns any relationship when one person gains the confidence of another and purports to act or advise with the latter's interest in mind. RESTATEMENT (FIRST) OF RESTITUTION § 166 cmt. d (1937). Such a relationship may exist, for example, between physician and patient or priest and penitent. A close family relationship or friendship might constitute a confidential relationship under certain circumstances. The doctrine seems to be an optional excuse for courts to find a constructive trust. *See Person* v Pagnotta, 541 P.2d 483 (Or. 1975).

Contemplation of Death: The contemplation of death exception to the Statute of Frauds is based on the idea that a transferor who is in fear of fairly imminent death can be taken advantage of by a transferee who orally promises to hold the transferred property in trust.

Illustration 6: A, in contemplation of death, transfers Blackacre to B who orally agrees that on A's death B will convey Blackacre to C. If after A's death, B refuses to convey Blackacre to C, B can be held to hold Blackacre in a constructive trust for C.

Two Separate Agreements: Normally, the applicability of the Statute of Frauds is determined at the time of the transfer and a subsequent change of the nature of the property is immaterial. By the weight of authority, however, it is held that where an oral trust of land was declared and the trustee agreed to sell the land and to hold the proceeds in trust, the two understandings of the trustee are severable. The transferee's oral promise to hold the land in trust is unenforceable because of the failure to comply with the Statute of Frauds; but the transferee's oral promise in regard to the proceeds is not within the Statute of Frauds and is enforceable.

Limitations on Taking Advantage of the Statute of Frauds Defense: The trustee who still has title to the property can voluntarily carry out the trust. The trustee, by signing a memorandum evidencing the trust, can perform the trust as orally intended. Only the trustee and the trustee's successors in interest can take advantage of any failure to comply with the Statute of Frauds. Successors include a purchaser or other transferee, the personal representative of transferee-decedent's estate, the transferee's heirs, devisees, and bankruptcy trustee. Other persons cannot raise the Statute of Frauds if the trustee agrees to perform the trust because an oral trust of land is voidable, not void, under the Statute of Frauds and thus is merely unenforceable against the trustee. Other persons include creditors, attached or otherwise, of the trustee, third persons sued by the trustee and even the transferor. *Cf. Person v. Pagnotta,* 541 P.2d 483 (Or. 1975).

3. TRUSTS CREATED BY WILL

a. General Formality Requirements for Testamentary Trusts

Testamentary trusts generally must satisfy all the requirements of an express inter vivos trust and be included in a valid will. Thus the general formality requirement is that of the Statute of Wills. Ordinarily, identification of the trust property, the beneficiaries, and the purposes of the trust must be ascertainable from the face of the will or from other recognized wills' doctrines such as incorporation by reference. RESTATEMENT (THIRD) OF TRUSTS § 18(2) (T.D. No. 1, 1996).

b. Secret and Semi–Secret Trusts

Secret Trust: A "secret trust" is a devise of property to a person absolutely, without reference to any intended trust, where the devisee prior to the testator's death agreed with the testator to hold the property upon a certain trust. RESTATEMENT (THIRD) OF TRUSTS § 18 cmt. a (T.D. No. 1, 1996). The "secret trust" doctrine holds that when a testator devises property in reliance upon an agreement or understanding with a devisee either before or after the will was executed, that the devisee will hold the devised property in trust, the devisee holds the property upon a constructive trust for the person for whom the devisee agreed to hold it. The constructive trust is enforced purely on the basis of the promise with no additional requirements as usually required under the Statute of Frauds, *e.g.,* fraud, confidential relationship. In addition, relief is given for the intended beneficiary whereas under the Statute of Frauds, restitutional relief is often granted for grantor. The same result has applied where the heir orally agrees with an intestate to hold in trust for another. RESTATEMENT (THIRD) OF TRUSTS § 18(2) (T.D. No. 1, 1996).

Semi-Secret Trust: A partially-secret or semi-secret trust is a bequest or devise which clearly provides that the devisee is not to get the beneficial interest but does not adequately indicate the true beneficiary under the appropriate Statute of Wills. RESTATEMENT (THIRD) OF TRUSTS § 18 cmt. a (T.D. No. 1, 1996). Some courts have declared these trusts ineffective because of the Statute of Wills and have mandated a resulting trust for the decedent's estate. *See Olliffe v. Wells*, 130 Mass. 221 (1881). Under this approach, an unconditional resulting trust is enforced regardless of what the devisee agrees to do. There is comparable opposing authority that holds the trust property should be held upon a constructive trust for the agreed purposes and persons. *See* RESTATEMENT (THIRD) OF TRUSTS § 18 cmt. c. (T.D. No. 1, 1996).

Analysis of the Rules: The court's distinction in *Olliffe v. Wells* ignores the argument that non-enforcement of the testator's intent in partially secret trusts results in unjust enrichment, not of the trustee, but of the testator's heirs, whom she in fact never intended to benefit. The avoidance of unjust enrichment rationale suggests that partially secret trusts should be treated the same as secret trusts. In England both secret and semi-secret trusts are enforced for the beneficiaries using the constructive trust device.

The secret and partially secret trust doctrines are anomalous in several respects:

- Constructive trust relief is granted solely on the basis of evidence that a promise was made. The American doctrine regarding oral inter vivos trusts of land is that a constructive trust is not available on the basis of a broken promise alone; fraud or a confidential relationship is required. Why is the same not true of secret testamentary trusts? Is the policy behind the Statute of Frauds stronger than that of the Statute of Wills? That is hard to believe. This anomaly does not exist in English law, where constructive trust is granted in both inter vivos and testamentary trust cases on the same basis.

- In cases of secret testamentary trusts, relief is granted in favor of the intended third-party beneficiaries, on the basis of the unjust enrichment principle. But as to oral inter vivos trusts of land, if constructive trust relief is granted, some courts have held that it runs in favor of the grantor, not the intended third party beneficiary. The difference might be explained on the basis of the fact that in testamentary trust cases, there is no longer an opportunity for the testator to give it to the intended beneficiaries, as there is if the trust is inter vivos. But there still remains the argument that unjust enrichment is avoided only if, *in both* situations, relief is given to the persons who, clear and convincing evidence indicates, were the intended beneficiaries. Only if relief always runs in favor of the intended beneficiaries can the unjust enrichment principle be consistently applied.

- No meaningful distinction can be drawn between secret and partially secret trusts. In both situations, the trust should be carried out if the trustee is willing and in cases where the trustee balks, constructive trust relief should be in favor of the intended beneficiary.

Estate Planning Aspects: Despite general recognition of secret trusts, their litigation risks are too great to use them as a planning device. The trustee may refuse to carry out the trust and thereby require a law suit to enforce it. The trustee might predecease the testator-settlor or die before completion of the trust, causing the gift to lapse. If a law suit happens, the secret becomes public.

c. Pour-over Trusts

A pour-over devise is a provision in a will that directs the distribution of property into a trust. A person who has created an inter vivos trust frequently desires that his or her will "pour-over" additional property into the trust. The desire is to pass the property according to the terms of the trust without reciting the whole trust.

Common Pour-over Situations:

T → Inter Vivos Trust

↓ ↗ Pour-over devise

Will

Testator executes both a will and an inter vivos trust. On death the will makes a devise that "pours over" assets of the estate to the trust as a devisee.

Death #1 Death #2

HT WT

↓ ↓

Will Will

↓ ↙ Pour-over devise

Trust

Husband and Wife execute reciprocal wills that provide for a trust to be established in the will of the first spouse to die and a "pour-over" devise to the trust in the will of the second spouse to die.

Common Law Validation Problems: Before the common enactment of authorizing legislation, pour-over devises were contested on the basis that they did not comply with the Statute of Wills because the will did not identify the beneficiaries. Where the trust was irrevocable and not subject to amendment, two doctrines were applicable to save the devise: (1) Incorporation by reference: if all of its tests are fulfilled; and (2) independent significance: since the original trust is a fact having significance apart from its effect on the property devised or bequeathed in the will. When the trust was amendable or revocable but neither event occurred, these same grounds could be used to sustain the will provisions. The testamentariness issue typically arose when the trust was amended or changed after the execution of the will. Early authority held the trust to be an invalid testamentary disposition, because the property under the will was being disposed of by an instrument not duly executed as a will or codicil. *E.g., Atwood v. Rhode Island Trust Co.*, 275 F. 513 (1st Cir. 1921).

Under the doctrine of incorporation by reference, the devise might be upheld according to the terms of the trust that existed at the time the will was executed. *But see President and Directors of Manhattan Co. v. Janowitz,* 21 N.Y.S.2d 232 (App. Div. 1940). The preferred holding was to find that the amended trust had independent significance and thus the devise was valid and passed to the trust as it existed at death. If the trust (not the trust instrument) held substantial assets, it clearly had an active independent life of its own separate from passing property at death and thus had independent significance. *E.g., Canal Nat'l Bank v. Chapman,* 171 A.2d 919 (Me. 1961).

Use of the doctrine of independent significance raised questions, however, whether a pour-over devise to an amended unfunded life insurance trust would be valid. Since such a trust has only a nominal subject matter and does not really have an independent existence at the time of death, some authorities argued that only incorporation by reference could be used to save such a pour-over provision into the trust. *See* Restatement (Third) of Property Trusts § 19 cmt. h (T.D. No. 1, 1996).

Pour–Over Statutes: The threshold validity problems have been eliminated by authorizing pour-over statutes which exist in one form or other in all or nearly all states. *See* Restatement (Third) of Property (Wills and Other Donative Transfers) § 3.8, Statutory Note (1999). The UPC's provisions have been converted into Section 1 of the Uniform Testamentary Additions to Trusts Act (1990). *See* UPC § 2–511 cmt. Under the Act, the devise is valid when the trust is amendable or revocable or even if the trust is actually amended after the execution of the will or the testator's death. The devise is valid notwithstanding the existence, size or character of the corpus of the trust during the testator's lifetime. The trust can be established during the testator's lifetime either by the testator, or by the testator and some other person, or by some other person; or the trust can be established at the testator's death if the trust is identified in the testator's will and the trust's terms are (a) recited in a non-testamentary written instrument that was executed at any time before, with or after the testator executed the will, or (b) recited in the will of another individual who has predeceased the testator. If the trust is created during the testator's lifetime, it may be a funded or unfunded life insurance trust even if the trustor has reserved all rights of ownership in the insurance contracts.

Inter–Vivos or Testamentary Trust: Assuming the pour-over devise is valid, a question sometimes arises whether the trustee should be treated merely as a devisee and the trust would continue as an inter vivos trust or whether a new testamentary trust was established. If a separate testamentary trust is established, it might be subjected to supervision by the probate court or to double accounting. The Uniform Act gives the testator the option whether to treat the trust as a testamentary trust under the testator's will or to allow it to be governed by the terms of the trust and by its terms and provisions including amendments made to the trust before or after the testator's death. The presumption is that unless the testator's will indicates otherwise, the property devised will be administered under the terms and conditions of the trust and not as a new testamentary trust. *Accord*, Restatement (Third) of Property (Wills and Other Donative Transfers) § 3.8 cmt. e (1999).

Revocation: Clearly, if both the trust and the will are revoked, the pour-over trust is revoked too. A problem might arise where the trust is revoked but the will is not: what happens to the pour-over devise into the trust? It would seem that the pour-over devise should fail, because the testator presumably only wanted to add the property to a trust in existence at testator's death. The incorporation by reference doctrine and the issue of how one revokes a will may raise arguments that the trust should be created as a testamentary trust. The Uniform Act declares the trust is revoked in this situation.

C. REVOCATION AND TERMINATION OF TRUSTS

1. GENERAL RULE OF IRREVOCABILITY

In the absence of grounds for reformation or rescission, a trust created or declared by a written instrument cannot be revoked by the settlor unless a power of revocation is expressly reserved or may be implied from language contained in the instrument. California, Oklahoma, and Texas reverse this rule by statute. In these states, a trust is revocable unless it is expressly made irrevocable. *See infra*, Part 6.V.A.

2. TERMINATION BY THE TERMS OF THE TRUST

A trust terminates if the terms of the trust provide it is to terminate at the end of a certain period of time or upon the happening of a certain event. RESTATEMENT (SECOND) OF TRUSTS § 334 (1957). For example, if a trust is created to continue for a definite period of years or for the duration of a life or lives, the trust will be terminated upon the expiration of the designated period. *See infra* Part 6.V.B.

3. TRUST PURPOSE IMPOSSIBILITY OR ILLEGALITY

If the trust's purposes become impossible or illegal to accomplish, the trust will be terminated. RESTATEMENT (SECOND) OF TRUSTS § 335 (1957). *See* Part 6.I.E.

4. MERGER: BENEFICIARY AS TRUSTEE

The merger doctrine of trust law provides that one can not be sole trustee and sole beneficiary. If one becomes sole trustee and sole beneficiary, then the title merges and the beneficiary holds fee simple title. The Claflin doctrine may postpone termination, however. *See infra*, Part 6.V.C.1.

If there is more than one trustee, beneficiary, or settlor of a trust, there is no merger because the courts generally treat them as three different persons. Some courts have held differently. For example, in New York if S transfers to A in trust for A for life, remainder to B, no trust is created. The equitable and legal life estates merge and the legal life and remainder estates are subject to termination. *See Reed v. Browne*, 66 N.E.2d 47 (N.Y. 1946).

5. SETTLOR TERMINATION

A trust can be terminated by the settlor if the settlor is the sole beneficiary of a trust and is not under an incapacity, even though the purposes of the trust have not been accomplished and even though the settlor has not retained a power to revoke. RESTATEMENT (SECOND) OF TRUSTS § 339 (1957).

6. BENEFICIARY TERMINATION

Except when the continuance of the trust is necessary to carry out a material purpose of the trust, the beneficiaries can compel the termination of the trust if all beneficiaries consent and none is under an incapacity. RESTATEMENT (SECOND) OF TRUSTS § 337 (1957). *See infra*, Part 6.V.C.

7. TRUSTEE TERMINATION

A trustee can terminate a trust when this power is expressly or impliedly conferred upon trustee by the terms of the trust (*e.g.*, when the purpose is no longer present). For example, invasion of principal by the trustee of a discretionary trust would cause termination because all of the property is distributed. Powers of invasion are reviewable on exercise. *See infra*, Part 6.V.B.2.

D. REVIEW QUESTIONS

1. In order to create a trust, what intent must the settlor manifest?
2. Name the three general ways to create a trust.
3. An imperfect gift can be converted into a declaration of trust. True or False?
4. The Statute of Uses applies to the trust concept, but does not apply to the active trust. True or False?
5. What is the difference between a semi-secret trust and a secret trust?
6. If both the trust and the will are revoked, the pour over trust is revoked as well. True or False?

III

REVOCABLE TRUSTS

Analysis

A. DEFINITION AND APPLICATION OF REVOCABLE TRUSTS

1. DEFINITION

A revocable trust is an inter vivos trust in which the settlor either expressly, impliedly or by law, holds and reserves the right to revoke.

2. BASIC FORMALITIES

Revocable trusts require the same formalities as other inter vivos trusts. *See supra,* Part 6.II.B.2.

3. APPLICATIONS

Revocable trusts have become mainstays in estate planning. Generally, they serve as a will substitute with respect to all or part of the settlor's estate. In addition, they have their primary significance in the determination of interests and shares that persons receive at the settlor's death.

Revocable trusts are used because they:

- Avoid the costs and delays typically associated with the processes of administering decedents' estates in this country;
- Provide property management for settlor's contingent or actual incompetence;
- Offer greater privacy for the estate plan;
- Avoid continual probate court supervision applicable to testamentary trusts; and,
- Save or postpone taxes both at the federal and state level.

See RESTATEMENT (THIRD) OF TRUSTS § 25 cmt. a (T.D. No. 1, 1996).

B. SETTLOR CONTROL OVER REVOCABLE TRUSTS

1. METHOD OF REVOCATION

When the settlor reserves a power to revoke the trust only in a particular manner or under particular circumstances, the settlor can revoke the trust only if the manner or circumstances are met. RESTATEMENT (SECOND) OF TRUSTS § 330 cmt. j. When the settlor reserves a power to revoke the trust but does not specify the mode of revocation, the settlor may revoke the trust in any manner that sufficiently manifests the intention of the settlor to revoke the trust. For example, any definitive manifestation that the settlor intends to revoke is sufficient. *Id.* at § 330 cmt. i.

2. CONCEPT OF TESTAMENTARINESS

The settlor of an inter vivos trust may reserve powers over the trust and its res until death. In the past, the basic problem concerned what powers reserved in the trust instrument would cause the transfer to be testamentary and thus have to be executed according to the appropriate Statute of Wills including testamentary intent. The power to revoke by itself has not caused a trust to be characterized as testamentary. When additional powers are retained, the outcomes have sometimes varied.

3. POWERS RESERVED BY SETTLOR

In addition to the power to revoke, a settlor may retain one or more or all of the following powers:

- Reservation of a life income interest.
- The combination of the two.
- Combined with additional power to alter or modify the trust terms.
- Combined with a beneficiary survivorship requirement.
- Combined with a power to control the trustee in the administration of the trust.
- Combined with settlor serving as trustee.

Generally, today courts correctly find valid inter vivos trusts "where settlors have retained complete control, and where other beneficiaries usually, if drafting is competent, have only future interests that are not only defeasible (by revocation or amendment) but also 'contingent' upon surviving the settlor and maybe other events as well.... " RESTATEMENT (THIRD) OF TRUSTS § 25 cmt. b (T.D. No. 1, 1996). Recent decisions have permitted all of the above reservations.

4. VALIDITY THEORIES

The theories expressed behind the holdings have been unsatisfactory. A common explanation is through the question whether the deed presently passes an interest on its execution. That the creation of a future interest, which is presently valid, is contrasted with the future creation of an interest, which is not valid until it is created. If the trust is intended to become presently binding and nothing is left for the settlor to do to complete the transaction, then it need not be regarded as of a testamentary character. It is sufficient to convey any estate or interest whatever, though it be future or contingent. Distinguishing between a "trust" or a "mere agency" is at best question begging.

One court tried to define the nature of the interest that passed. *See Farkas v. Williams*, 125 N.E.2d 600 (Ill. 1955). The court held that the declaration of trust immediately transferred an equitable remainder interest to the beneficiary even though the enjoyment of the interest was postponed until the death of the settlor and though the interest could be divested by the exercise of the powers reserved or by the failure of the beneficiary to survive the settlor. The court called the interest a "contingent equitable interest in remainder," but in fact it was simply a vested remainder subject to divestment. *See infra* Part 8.

In an act of sophistry the court found that the settlor did not have the right to deal with the property as settlor liked as long as settlor lived while the trust remained unrevoked but was bound by the laws imposing obligations on a trustee. Scholars have argued that the real issue is the Statute of Wills and whether the settlor satisfied the underlying purposes of the wills execution formalities. It would seem that an unexpressed factor in recognition of these trust instruments is the extreme trust or faith which the courts have in them. The fears that courts have about other supposedly inter vivos transfers are felt not to be applicable to inter vivos trusts evidenced typically by a relatively formal document.

5. VALIDITY LIMITATIONS

There are cases, however, that indicate not every trust type transfer will be upheld. *See, e.g., Osborn v. Osborn,* 226 N.E.2d 814 (Ohio C. P. 1966), *rev'd on other grounds,* 248 N.E.2d 191 (Ohio 1969). In this case, the court questioned the seriousness of a particular settlor's trust intention.

6. STATUTORY VALIDATION

Several states have statutes expressly providing that revocable trusts are not testamentary dispositions. *See* Ky. Rev. Stat. Ann. § 394.065 (Michie 1996); Wis. Stat. Ann. § 701.07 (West 1998). By necessary implication, the common pour-over legislation recognizes the validity of revocable trusts. *See* 6.II.B.3.c.

C. REVIEW QUESTIONS

1. What makes a revocable trusts distinct?
2. What are the estate planning uses of revocable trusts?
3. Name some of the powers that a settlor may retain without invalidating the trust?

IV

TRUST INTERESTS AND RELATIONSHIPS

Analysis

3. *Discretionary and Related Trusts*
    a. *Discretionary Trusts*
    b. *Support and Education Trusts*
4. *Special Limitations*
    a. *Public Policy Limitation*
    b. *Theory of Limitation*
    c. *Claimant Procedure*

C. *Review Questions*

A. ENFORCEABILITY OF BENEFICIAL INTERESTS

1. GENERAL PRINCIPLES

a. Beneficiary Rights

The beneficiary has both in personam and in rem rights: personal rights against the trustee, and equitable ownership of the trust res.

If the beneficiary is entitled to the income from the trust estate, the trustee can be compelled to make the income payments at reasonable intervals where payment dates are not fixed by the terms of the trust. And the trustee is liable for interest on accounts unreasonably withheld.

b. Impartiality Between Beneficiaries

There is an underlying policy that the trustee must be impartial between and among the beneficiaries. This obligation often requires careful consideration when payments are made to some beneficiaries and not others. In addition, it requires careful allocation of income and principal between the income and remainder beneficiaries, *e.g.*, administrative principal and income allocation problems.

c. Improper Payments

If the trustee makes an overpayment or pays the wrong person, the trustee is liable even though trustee acted in good faith. Misinterpretation of the trust instrument and mistakes of law or fact, even though reasonable, are generally no defense. The trustee should apply to the proper court for instructions when in reasonable doubt.

2. DISCRETIONARY DISTRIBUTIONS: NATURE OF THE FIDUCIARY RELATIONSHIP

a. Range of Discretion

Sometimes a life beneficiary is not given the right to income but is entitled only to such payments as are required for a certain purpose, typically support. Sometimes a trust provides that the trustee is to distribute the income, or part of the income, among a group of beneficiaries in amounts to be decided by the trustee. Sometimes a trust provides that the trustee may invade the principal for the life beneficiary or income or principal for the remainder beneficiary—called an "invasion power"

b. Reasons for Discretion

For income tax savings, the discretion allows the trustee to accumulate some or all of the income when not needed by the beneficiary or allows the trustee to distribute the income among the low income members of the class of permissible distributees. For death tax savings, the discretion avoids taxation in the life interest beneficiary's estate although there may be generation skipping tax problems. The primary nontax reason for granting discretion is to provide flexibility in order to allow adjustment to the consequences of changed circumstances that the settlor could not foresee.

c. Examples of Discretionary Powers

"The trustee shall have power in its (sole) (unlimited) (absolute) (final) (uncontrolled) discretion:"

- "to pay to or for the benefit of the above described beneficiary any or all rent, income, and profits of the trust." [Income]
- "to pay over all or a part of the trust corpus to any one or more of the above described discretionary beneficiaries, without being required to observe any precept or rule of equality." [Principal]
- "to pay to or for the benefit of the above described beneficiary any or all rent, income, and profits therefrom and any or all of the principal." [Both income and principal]
- "to pay or apply the net income to the support, maintenance and education of the above described beneficiary." [Discretion over income tested by a standard]
- "to pay or apply for the benefit of the above described beneficiary such amount or amounts of the trust corpus as may be necessary in the event of sickness, accident, misfortune or other emergency." [Discretion over principal tested by a standard]
- "to allocate receipts and expenses between principal and income." [Administrative discretion]

d. Meaning of Uncontrolled Powers

A person may vest in another the uncontrolled authority to dispose of the donor's property such as a nonfiduciary power of appointment. But, a fiduciary power in a trust is never beyond the power of the court to review. A distinction exists between the discretionary powers of a fiduciary versus nonfiduciary powers of appointment. Nonfiduciary powers of appointment are exercisable arbitrarily and without explanation so long as persons outside the class of objects are not benefitted directly or indirectly. When a trustee is given discretion, however, the preliminary question is not whether there is review but the degree of the review. All courts agree that if the power involved is a fiduciary discretion rather than a power of appointment, it cannot be placed completely beyond the control of the proper court, regardless of the words of the settlor.

e. Simple Versus Absolute Discretion

If the trustee is given simple discretion over distributions, judicial intervention is not warranted merely because the court would have differently exercised the discretion to pay out principal or income. If the settlor manifests an intention that the discretion of the trustee shall be, *e.g.*, "absolute," "uncontrolled" or "final," such words are said to dispense with the standard of reasonableness. RESTATEMENT (SECOND) TRUSTS § 187 cmt. j (1959). Courts "will interfere [only] if the trustee acts"

- "in a state of mind not contemplated by the settlor,"
- "dishonestly, or from some motive other than the accomplishment of the purposes of the trust," or
- "arbitrarily without an exercise of his judgment."

Thus, there is court review and the difference between simple and extended discretion is out of degree, not kind. *See* Edward c. Halbach, *Problems of Discretion in Discretionary Trusts*, 61 COLUM L. REV. 1425 (1961).

B. TRANSFER OF A BENEFICIARY'S INTEREST

1. TRANSFERS IN GENERAL

a. Voluntary Assignment

A beneficiary can transfer his or her trust interest. The transferee acquires only the interest which the beneficiary owned.

b. Rights of Creditors of a Beneficiary

Generally, the beneficiary's interest can be reached by creditors in satisfaction of a judgment but in some states a creditors' bill is required to reach the equitable interest of the debtor. The creditor can reach the interest of the beneficiary, but cannot reach the trust property itself except where the debtor is the sole beneficiary of a trust and can presently demand conveyance of the trust property.

2. RESTRAINTS ON ALIENATION: SPENDTHRIFT TRUSTS

a. Definition of a Spendthrift Trust

A spendthrift is one who spends improvidently or wastefully. One of the pervasive reasons for using trusts is to protect the "spendthrift" from his or her own lack of discretion or ability. Restrictions on alienation are essential to provide this protection.

A spendthrift trust is one in which, either because of a direction of the settlor or because of statute, the beneficiary is unable to transfer his or her right to future payments of income or capital (a voluntary transfer), and the beneficiary's creditors are unable to subject the beneficiary's interest to the payment of their claims (an involuntary transfer). It is sometimes called a Prodigal Trust. A majority of the states have statutes dealing with this problem in varying degrees.

In order for a spendthrift trust to be valid, there is no requirement that the beneficiary be found to be a spendthrift. In fact most beneficiaries of spendthrift trusts are not spendthrifts.

b. Scope of the Spendthrift Protection

The spendthrift provisions do not involve any restraint on alienability or creditor's rights with respect to property after it is received by the beneficiary from the trustee, but rather impose a restraint with regard to the creditor's rights to future payments under the trust.

Broadway National Bank v. Adams, 133 Mass. 170 (1882), held that spendthrift restraints on equitable life estates are valid. The court found that the only ground upon which such restraint could be held to be against public policy is that it defrauds the creditors of the beneficiary. Creditors are not defrauded because had they used proper diligence they could have ascertained the nature and extent of the beneficiary's estate. The concept of freedom of disposition prevailed. By comparison, however, when a legal life estate is created, *e.g.*, by gift, it is generally held that a direct restraint on alienation, voluntary or involuntary, is invalid.

c. Policy Considerations

The major consideration in determining the validity of restraints on involuntary transfers depends on whether property given to a person which is not otherwise exempt from the claims of creditors can be made exempt by the terms of the gift when the gift is in trust. The actual public policy involved depends on the effects produced both economically and sociologically upon both the community and the beneficiaries by permitting such restraints, and whether these effects are desirable or not. The answers to these questions depend upon the circumstances of each situation. In regard to a true spendthrift who needs the protective shield, the protection makes good policy sense. It has no justification for the person of ability who uses the protection as a devious exemption. But it is difficult as a matter of law to make one rule for one type of beneficiary and another rule for another type of beneficiary.

It can reasonably be stated that today the typical voluntary creditor is not harmed by spendthrift trusts—no one should rely on personal statements by the debtor that a trust secures a debt.

d. Statutory Spendthrift Recognition

The New York statutes automatically prohibit voluntary assignments of express trusts and protect creditors only "in excess of the sum necessary for the education and support of the beneficiary." N.Y. EST. POWERS & TRUSTS §§ 7–1.5, 7–3.4. Early court decisions interpreted "need" to mean "station in life" of the beneficiary which might permit protection for extravagance. *See, e.g. In re Brown's Estate*, 35 N.Y.S.2d 646 (Sup.Ct. 1941).

Under the California statutes, if spendthrift provisions are imposed by the settlor, they prohibit voluntary assignments of express trusts but protect creditors "in excess of the amount that is or will be necessary for the education and support of the beneficiary." CAL. PROB. CODE § 15300. Although "need" has been interpreted to mean "station in life" of the beneficiary, only reasonable amounts are protected. *See Canfield v. Security–First Nat'l Bank*, 87 P.2d 830 (Cal. 1939).

3. DISCRETIONARY AND RELATED TRUSTS

a. Discretionary Trusts

When a trust provides that the trustee shall pay to or apply for a beneficiary only so much of the income or principal, or both, as the trustee in the trustee's uncontrolled discretion shall see fit, a creditor of the beneficiary cannot compel the trustee to pay any part of the income or principal. RESTATEMENT (SECOND) OF TRUSTS § 155 (1959).

Limitation on Discretionary Payments: Although a transferee or creditor of the beneficiary cannot compel the trustee of discretionary trust to pay over any part of the trust property to him or her, a trustee should not pay over or apply any part of the trust property to the beneficiary with knowledge of the transfer of the interest or of a proceeding by a creditor of the beneficiary to reach that interest. Absent the application of a valid spendthrift provision, the trustee who makes such payments is personally liable to the transferee or creditor for the amount paid to or applied for the beneficiary. RESTATEMENT (SECOND) OF TRUSTS § 155 cmt. h (1959)

b. Support and Education Trusts

If a trust provides that the trustee must pay or apply only so much of the income and principal or either as is necessary for the education or support of the beneficiary, the beneficiary cannot transfer his or her interest and his or her creditors cannot reach it. RESTATEMENT (SECOND) OF TRUSTS § 154 (1959). A trust for support limits the beneficiary's interest by its nature and does not require a specific prohibition on alienation. The creditor cannot compel the trustee to pay anything to the creditor because the beneficiary could not compel payment or compel application in any way except according to the terms of the trust. The trustee is not liable to the creditor even though:

(1) the trustee pays to or applies for the beneficiary so much of the property as is necessary for his education or support, and

(2) the trustee has knowledge of the conveyance or has been served with process in proceedings instituted by the creditor to reach the interest of the beneficiary.

A purpose to provide for the education or support of the beneficiary may be found from circumstances showing this intention and if from the terms of the trust such an intention appears, a support trust is created.

The restriction on alienation is applicable even where the beneficiary becomes bankrupt.

4. SPECIAL LIMITATIONS

a. Public Policy Limitation

The beneficiary's interest in a spendthrift trust or a trust for support (but not a discretionary trust) may be reached by claimants if considerations of public policy so require. The SECOND RESTATEMENT OF TRUSTS provides that the beneficiary's interest can be reached by certain claimants in satisfaction of their enforceable claims. RESTATEMENT (SECOND) OF TRUSTS § 157 (1959). These claimants include (1) the beneficiary's ex-spouse for alimony, or a child for support; (2) the provider of necessary services or supplies furnished to the beneficiary; (3) the provider of services furnished to preserve or benefit the interest of the beneficiary; (4) the United States or a State for claims against the beneficiary. The Restatement does not take a position on whether other claimants, such as persons whom the beneficiary tortiously injured, are entitled to reach the beneficiary's interest.

b. Theory of Limitation

Courts have considered it against public policy to give full effect to these provisions if the particularly disadvantaged claimant is denied recovery. The concept is that the beneficiary should not be able to enjoy the interest under the trust while neglecting a responsibility to the claimant.

Illustration 1: D devises $300,000 to T upon a spendthrift trust for B. B neglects to support a spouse and several children. The spouse and children can reach B's interest for their support under the trust.

Where the beneficiary benefitted by the claimant's actions, the beneficiary is unjustly enriched if the claim is not allowed.

Illustration 2: D devises $300,000 to T upon a spendthrift trust for B. C furnishes to B necessary food, clothing and lodging. C can reach B's interest under the trust in payment of his claim.

c. Claimant Procedure

The proper court has discretion as to how much trust income may be applied for the claimant's benefit and how much the beneficiary may receive.

C. REVIEW QUESTIONS

1. The trustee must be impartial between and among the beneficiaries. True or False?

2. What is the liability of a trustee for making, in good faith, an overpayment or for paying the wrong person?

3. What are spendthrift trusts? How do they function against assignees and creditors of the beneficiary?

*

V

TRUST MODIFICATION AND TERMINATION

Analysis

A. TRUST MODIFICATION AND TERMINATION BY THE SETTLOR

1. REVOCATION AND MODIFICATION OF TRUST BY SETTLOR

Generally, if a trust represents the complete expression of the settlor's intention, the trust is not revocable or modifiable by the settlor, unless these powers were expressly or impliedly reserved. This rule is applied even though no consideration was received by the settlor for creating the trust. RESTATEMENT (SECOND) OF TRUSTS § 330 cmt. a (1959).

To the extent of the terms of the trust,[1] the settlor may exercise any power to revoke or modify reserved by the settlor. If the settlor does not specify any mode of revocation or modification, the power to revoke or modify can be exercised in any manner which sufficiently manifests the settlor's intention. When the method of revocation or modification is specified, the trust is revoked or modified only in that manner or under those specified circumstances. RESTATEMENT (SECOND) OF TRUSTS § 330 cmt. j (1959).

2. REFORMATION AND RESCISSION BY THE SETTLOR

Even if there are no specifically reserved powers, a trust can be reformed or rescinded upon the same grounds as a transfer free of trust, *i.e.*, fraud, duress, undue influence or sometimes unilateral mistake. *See* RESTATEMENT (SECOND) OF TRUSTS § 333 (1959). Unilateral mistake is ordinarily a sufficient ground for rescission or reformation although some courts have been more restrictive depending upon the situation. The question in each case is whether the trust was created under such circumstances that it would be inequitable not to permit the settlor to set it aside. The courts generally impose a clear and convincing evidence burden. Cases fail where testimony is conflicting

B. TRUST MODIFICATION AND TERMINATION BY THE TRUSTEE

1. TRUSTEE TERMINATION

A trustee may terminate a trust when a power to do so is expressly or impliedly (*e.g.*, when the purpose is no longer present) conferred upon him or her by the terms of the trust or when discretionary power of invasion of principal would cause termination because all of the property is distributed. Powers of invasion are reviewable on exercise.

2. TRUSTEE WRONGFUL TERMINATION

If the trustee wrongfully terminates the trust, consenting sui juris beneficiaries are precluded (estopped) from recovering from the trustee for breach of trust, nonconsenting and unknown beneficiaries are not estopped.

1. The phrase "terms of the trust" means the manifestation of settlor's intention as expressed at the time of the creation of the trust and as provable by competent evidence which is expressed by written or spoken words or by conduct or both. RESTATEMENT (SECOND) OF TRUSTS § 330 cmt. a (1959).

The RESTATEMENT (SECOND) OF TRUSTS also protects the trustee of a spendthrift trust. It makes the consenting beneficiaries liable to the trustee for the value of the property transferred to them. RESTATEMENT (SECOND) OF TRUSTS §§ 152 cmt i, 342 cmt. f (1959). Under the New York law, however, a trustee is not protected by beneficiaries' estoppel. But if a beneficiary can sue, the beneficiary must account for what he or she still holds from the trust although not for that which is no longer possessed. All interests must be in agreement to avoid subsequent disputes.

3. TRUSTEE MODIFICATION

A trustee can modify a trust to the extent permitted by the terms of the trust. If a power to modify is not provided by the terms of the trust, the trustee may seek modification by the appropriate court. *See infra* Part 6.V.D.1. Modification may be made without prior court approval when the trustee reasonably believes that there is an emergency and there is no opportunity to apply to the court for permission to deviate. If circumstances exist demanding modification, the trustee may be liable for failure to act or failure to apply to a court for permission to act.

C. TRUST MODIFICATION AND TERMINATION BY THE BENEFICIARIES

1. BENEFICIARY CONSENT

If all of the beneficiaries of a trust consent and none is under an incapacity (they are sui juris), they can compel the trust's termination (or modification) unless the continuance of the trust is necessary to carry out an unfulfilled material purpose of the trust. RESTATEMENT (SECOND) OF TRUSTS § 337 (1959).

Where the trust's continuance is necessary to carry out a material purpose of the trust, however, the beneficiaries cannot compel the termination of the trust even if they all consent and are sui juris. This is called the *Claflin* doctrine and it derives from the American philosophy that the owner of property can do as the owner likes with it as long as the owner makes no provision which runs counter to any rule of law or principle of public policy. *Claflin v. Claflin*, 20 N.E. 454 (Mass. 1889). It is the duty, then, of the court to carry out the owner's directions. The consequences of the doctrine is that when applicable there can be no termination of the trust even if all beneficiaries consent.

Settlor and Beneficiaries Consent: The settlor and all the beneficiaries may consent to modification or termination even if a material purpose has not been fulfilled. RESTATEMENT (SECOND) OF TRUSTS § 338 (1959).

Illustration 1: S transfers property to T in trust to pay the income to B for life and on B's death to pay the principal to C. The trust contains a spendthrift clause. If S, B, and C are all sui juris and if all they agree, S and B and C can agree to terminate the trust.

Similarly, if the settlor is or becomes the sole beneficiary of a trust and is not under an incapacity, the settlor can terminate the trust even though material purposes of the trust have not been accomplished. This power exists even if the trust is irrevocable, contains a spendthrift clause, and was intended to protect the settlor from his or her own improvidence. In cases of this nature the common problem is determining whether the settlor is the sole beneficiary or whether vested or contingent interests are held by others.

Illustration 2: S transfers property to T in trust into an irrevocable trust to pay the income to S for life and on S's death to pay the principal as S may by deed or by will appoint and in default of appointment to S's heirs or next of kin. S reserves no power of revocation. S effectively is the sole beneficiary and can compel T to terminate the trust.

2. DETERMINATION OF A MATERIAL PURPOSE

a. General Principles

If the settlor's purposes for the trust are expressed in the instrument of creation, a different purpose cannot be shown by extrinsic evidence. Restatement (Second) of Trusts § 337 cmt. e. (1959). If the purposes are not expressed in the instrument, extrinsic evidence of the surrounding circumstances to aid in the construction of the instrument is admissible in order to determine the purposes of the trust. Whether a material purpose exists is a question of interpretation of the trust instrument in light of all the circumstances. There is a presumption that there is no material purpose without language in the trust or evidence of the circumstances that the settlor desired to separate the beneficial ownership of the property from its management or to secure support for the beneficiary or to protect the beneficiary from his or her improvidence. *See In re Estate of Brown*, 528 A.2d 752 (Vt 1987); *Schmucker v. Walker*, 311 S.E.2d 108 (Va. 1984).

b. Successive Beneficiaries

The mere creation of a trust for successive beneficiaries does not of itself indicate that the trust has a material purpose that must be fulfilled. Restatement (Second) of Trusts § 337 cmt. f (1959). The inference is that the only purpose of the trust is to give the beneficial interest in the trust property to one beneficiary for a designated period and to preserve the principal for the other beneficiary. Consequently, if all of the beneficiaries are sui juris and consent to the termination of the trust, they can compel its termination.

Illustration 3: A devises property to B in trust to pay the income to C for life and on C's death to pay the principal to D. C and D can compel the termination of the trust.

c. Material Purpose Trusts

Several trust purposes have been characterized as establishing a material purpose under the *Claflin* Doctrine. Typical material purposes include:

Postponement of Enjoyment of Interest: If the trust provides that it shall not terminate until a certain time arrives or event happens, termination of the trust will not be allowed until that time happens or the event occurs.

Illustration 4: A devises securities to B in trust to pay the income to C until C reaches the age of forty years, and to pay the principal to C when he reaches that age. There is no other beneficiary who has any interest in the trust property. C is thirty years old. C cannot compel B to convey the securities to C.

If C could compel termination of the trust, the provision for postponement of the trust's termination would be a practical nullity.

Protection Against Improvidence: When a trust contains a spendthrift clause, it generally is held to contain a material purpose.

Illustration 5: A devises property to B in trust to pay the income to C for life, and on C's death to pay the principal to D. By the terms of the trust, C's interest is subject to a spendthrift clause and is thus inalienable by him. C and D cannot compel the termination of the trust.

Where one of A's purposes in creating the trust is to protect C from C's own improvidence by giving B an interest that C cannot transfer and that C's creditors cannot reach, the purpose would obviously be defeated if C and D could compel the termination of the trust. If C and D terminated the trust and they received their respective shares of the trust property, the property C receives could be transferred by C and reached by C's creditors in contravention of A's expressed intent.

Trust for Support: A support trust, which requires the trustee to make periodic payments to the beneficiary for education and support, has a material purpose that bars termination merely by beneficiary consent. RESTATEMENT (SECOND) OF TRUSTS § 337 cmt. m (1959).

Discretionary Trusts: A trust that confers discretion upon the trustee as to the method of distribution cannot be terminated by beneficiary consent. Assumably this would indicate a material purpose because the trustee is specifically given managerial powers over the distributive provisions. *See* RESTATEMENT (SECOND) OF TRUSTS § 337 cmt. n (1959).

d. Beneficiary Nonconsent

Unless the trust provides otherwise, trust beneficiaries cannot terminate a trust if one or more of the trust beneficiaries do not consent to its termination or are not sui juris. This requirement makes it difficult if not impossible for beneficiaries to terminate most modern trusts before their expressed termination date because of the typical inclusion of minor and unborn or unknown beneficiaries.

Illustration 6: A devises property to T in trust to pay the income to B for life and on B's death to pay the principal—		
a.	to C.	Neither B nor C, without the consent of the other, can compel trust termination.
b.	to C. C is an infant.	B and C cannot compel trust termination in whole or in part.
c.	to C or C's issue if C does not survive B.	B and D cannot compel trust termination in whole or in part.

e. Representing Minors, Unborns and Unascertained Beneficiaries

Because the existence of incapacitated or unknown beneficiaries prevents trust modification or termination even though those of current interest desire it, some courts and statutes permit representatives to provide the consent. If the beneficiary is a minor or other incapacitated person a guardian may be able to consent for the ward. If unborns or unknowns are involved, guardians ad litem have been appointed to represent them. *Hatch v. Riggs National Bank*, 361 F.2d 559 (D.C. Cir. 1966).

Virtual representation: When formal judicial proceedings arise involving trust termination, the doctrine of virtual representation may permit certain persons of a large group with a common interest to represent other persons with the same interest. *See* UPC § 1–403. The purpose is to allow some with similar interests to represent others. There may be a problem of independence from the other beneficiaries. Finally, is invasion or termination ever in the interests of a contingent beneficiary who might take something if no invasion but might take nothing if invasion is permitted? Of course, if termination of the trust is likely, settlement is clearly justified.

D. TRUST MODIFICATION AND TERMINATION BY THE COURT

1. EQUITABLE DEVIATION FROM TRUST ADMINISTRATIVE PROVISIONS

a. Changing Circumstances

A problem inherent with many trusts is that they are destined to exist for a significant period of time. Over time, circumstances change. Generally, the trust is a flexible enough device to adjust to change. The trustee, if properly empowered, can adjust the operation of the trust to many changed circumstances. Occasionally, changes are so drastic or the trust instrument is so inflexible that it is necessary to seek court approval to modify the trust itself to accommodate the changed circumstances. The modifications requested must concern administrative provisions in the trust such as powers to invest or to sell trust assets.

b. Proper Court Review Procedure

When a court receives such a petition to deviate, it should first look to see if the trust instrument could be interpreted to permit the requested action. If so, the trustee is found to have the power. When the court permits a deviation outside the instrument, it is conferring the power upon the trustee and is not holding that the trustee has such power.

c. Judicial Modification Criteria

Courts do not alter trusts freely. They have established a set of criteria that proponents of change must satisfy.

Unanticipated circumstance: There must be circumstances that have occurred not known to the settlor and not anticipated by settlor. If the settlor has anticipated the circumstances, the court will not ordinarily order a deviation. It is not sufficient for the court to be convinced that a change of administration would be preferable to the terms prescribed in the instrument. The English rule is opposite.

Even under the American rule, however, if the change is necessary to save the trust and its purposes from virtual destruction, the court may order a deviation.

In *Matter of Pulitzer,* 249 N.Y.S. 87 (Surr. Ct. 1931), *aff'd mem.,* 260 N.Y.S. 975 (App. Div. 1932) the court changed the trust to permit sale of an asset which the settlor had expressed should not be sold "under any circumstances." Although it would appear that the settlor anticipated the circumstances which arose, it was not entirely clear that the settlor would want the whole trust to be destroyed by keeping the asset.

Trust purposes defeated or substantially impaired: These circumstances must be such that failure to approve a modification would defeat or substantially impair the accomplishment of the purposes of the trust.

Some cases have concerned petitions to allow trustees to invest in a manner to deal with inflation. Courts have decided both ways. *Compare Stanton v. Wells Fargo Bank & Union Trust Co.*, 310 P.2d 1010 (Cal. Dist Ct. App. 1957) (Refused to grant change) *with Trusteeship with Mayo,* 105 N.W.2d 900 (Minn. 1960) (Granted change). Although these trusts performed well at times when economic times were difficult, the investment problems caused by inflation may permit a deviation from investment provisions in the extreme case.

Administrative provision modification: There must be a request to modify an administrative provision of the trust and not its distributive provisions. Usually, however, the provision sought to be changed indirectly affects the dispositive provisions, *e.g.*, investment clauses.

Court approval: Proponents of the change must get court approval.

2. DEVIATION FROM DISTRIBUTIVE PROVISIONS

a. General Rule Against Deviation

Although the court can properly authorize or direct the hastening of enjoyment of income or principal by a sole beneficiary, it cannot properly authorize this where the result would be to deprive another nonconsenting beneficiary of an interest in the trust property, even though the other beneficiary's interest is contingent.

b. Anticipating Vested Interests

The only area in which courts generally recognize a power to modify the dispositive provisions is when only the time or manner of enjoyment is modified without changing the beneficiary.

Illustration 7: Under typical construction, a trust that provides "income to A until age 30, and then principal is to be paid to A," will be interpreted to permit, in case of need, the principal to be advanced to A prior to age 30. Had the remainder been "to A if then living and otherwise to his issue," the standard rule would preclude advancement of principal to A.

c. Alternative Remedy

The alternative to court modification is to get the consent of all the beneficiaries. This may be impossible because the beneficiaries are often unknown or unborn, *e.g.*, "descendants by right of representation."

In *Petition of Wolcott*, 56 A.2d 641 (N.H 1948), the court allowed invasion of the principal although only the primary, but not all, remainder beneficiaries consented. The court emphasized the settlor's intent to benefit the life beneficiary. Other courts might deny such a petition because of contingent remainder persons and the question whether they could possibly benefit by the destruction of the trust for someone else.

d. Invasion for Support and Education

Several states have statutes that allow the court to invade principal for the life beneficiary for the beneficiaries support and education if that purpose is otherwise insufficiently provided. *See* Wis. Stat. Ann. § 701.13 (1981); N.Y. Estate, Probate & Trust § 7–1.6(b) (McKinney 1992). The settlor can expressly prohibit invasion.

E. REVIEW QUESTIONS

1. What phrase refers to the manifestation of settlor's intention as expressed at the time of the creation of the trust and as provable by competent evidence?

2. Unilateral mistake is ordinarily an insufficient ground for rescission or reformation. True or False?

3. What is a trustee's power to modify the terms of the trust called?

4. What philosophy does the *Claflin* doctrine represent?

5. What are the general criteria for a court to modify a trust?

6. What doctrine permits certain persons of a large group with a common interest to represent other persons with the same interest where formal judicial proceedings arise involving trust termination?

VI

CHARITABLE TRUSTS

Analysis

A. HISTORY OF CHARITABLE TRUSTS

1. CHARITABLE TRUSTS AT COMMON LAW

Despite early precedent holding that charitable trusts were not part of the Common Law and required authorizing statutory recognition, the Supreme Court corrected the matter and held that charitable trusts had been enforced in equity prior to the Statute of Charities of 1601 and were part of the Common Law. *Vidal v. Girard's Ex'rs,* 43 U.S. (2 How.) 127 (1844)

2. CHARITABLE TRUSTS TODAY

Charitable trusts are now recognized throughout the United States. Some states have specific statutes that define charities. *See* N.Y. Est. Powers & Trusts Law § 8–1.1 (McKinney 1992). Most states recognize them as part of their Common Law.

B. GENERAL NATURE OF CHARITABLE TRUSTS

1. GENERAL DISTINCTIONS

Although many of the rules applicable to private trusts are also applied to charitable trusts, some rules applicable to private trusts are not applicable to charitable trusts, and *vice versa.* The following table lists the major distinctions:

Chart 6–VI–1

Private Trusts	Charitable Trusts
Definitely ascertainable beneficiary required.	Indefinite beneficiary permitted: no definite or definitely ascertainable beneficiary requirement.
Any purpose permitted that is not illegal or against public policy.	Charitable purpose required.
Enforceable at the suit of one or more of the beneficiaries.	Enforceable at the suit of a public officer, usually the Attorney General.
No cy pres doctrine.	Cy pres doctrine.
Duration tested by Rule Against Perpetuities.	Perpetual duration permissible for charitable purpose.
Taxable.	Tax exempt.

2. DEFINITION OF CHARITABLE TRUST

In contrast with a private trust in which the property is devoted to the benefit of specific beneficiaries, a charitable trust is a trust in which the property is devoted to purposes the law deems appropriately beneficial to the community. Restatement (Third) of Trusts § 1 cmt. c (T.D. No. 1, 1996). In what might be considered circular, it is said that a charitable trust is a trust established for a charitable purpose.

3. SPECIAL BENEFITS OF A CHARITABLE TRUST

As inferred from the **Chart 6–VI–1**, a charitable trust has several special benefits that are not enjoyed by a private trust. Thus a charitable trust may:

- Last longer than the period of the Rule Against Perpetuities;
- Accumulate income beyond the period of the Rule Against Perpetuities;
- Have purposes changed under the *cy pres* doctrine;
- Have charitable immunity if recognized; and
- Receive special tax exemption and benefits.

4. MIXED PRIVATE AND CHARITABLE TRUSTS

Mixed private and charitable trusts are valid if the private and charitable portions or estates are separately valid as their type of trust and the private portions are limited to the Rule Against Perpetuities. *See Rice v. Morris*, 541 S.W.2d 627 (Tex. Civ. App. 1976).

C. CHARITABLE PURPOSE

1. DEFINITION OF CHARITABLE TRUST

Although a charitable trust is said to be a trust established for a charitable purpose, "charitable purpose" has no exact definition and no fixed standard. It changes from time to time and community to community.

2. APPRECIABLE SOCIAL BENEFIT

Generally a charitable trust is a trust the performance of which will, in the opinion of the court, accomplish an appreciable amount of social benefit to the public or some reasonably large class thereof. Generally, motive of the settlor is not determinative. "Morality" is not relevant either, but it is unrealistic to believe that public concepts of "morality" do not influence decisions concerning charitable purpose. The key is to evaluate the purpose to which the property is applied. *See* RESTATEMENT (SECOND) OF TRUSTS Ch. 11, Introductory Note (1959).

Additional Distinctions: It is said that charitable is not a popularity contest or limited to universal beliefs. One must also draw a line between purposes believed to be irrational and those merely believed to be unwise. The test is not what the court believes and not what the majority believe, but what rational persons *may* believe. But concepts of contemporaneous "public policy" affect decisions also.

Illustration 1: M.K. devised the residue of her estate to FNBank in trust for the establishing and maintaining of an annual Harness Horse Stake Race, named in honor of M.K.'s deceased child. Is this an attempt to memorialize a relative in perpetuity or to benefit the community? *See Barton v. Parrott*, 495 N.E.2d 973 (Ohio Common Pleas 1984). Court held it was the former and invalidated the trust.

Political Objectives: In regard to whether a charitable purpose may have a political objective, a line must be drawn, though it is not easy to draw it, between objectives which are merely political and objectives which are of general social significance.

Illustration 2: W.B, an active socialist, willed the residue of his estate to M.L. and W.S. as co-trustees, for distribution of the trust income "to persons, entities and causes advancing the principles of socialism and those causes related to socialism. This shall include, but not be limited to, subsidizing publications, establishing and conducting reading rooms, supporting radio, television and the newspaper media and candidates for public office." *See In re Estate of Breeden v. Lessner*, 256 Cal.Rptr. 813 (Ct. App. 1989). Although the cause advocated may not be encouraged by the majority of society, the issue is whether settlor had a valid underlying purpose. The determining characterization will depend on whether a court views this as merely a political purpose designed to promote a particular political group and thus noncharitable, or views it as educationally motivated and designed to "form public opinion through educational enlightenment."

3. ALL OR NOTHING RULE

Validity problems have arisen under the "all or nothing" analysis when terms of purpose such as "charitable," have been included with purpose terms such as "benevolent," "philanthropic," or "fraternal." The latter three words have been said to include more than charitable uses and thus do not qualify as charitable purposes. Thus, if all the terms of purpose used are not considered to qualify as charitable purposes, a court might hold that the whole trust fails as a charitable trust. Other courts have examined extrinsic evidence concerning the use of these words to glean the intent of the settlor. If the evidence indicates the settlor intended the ambiguous phraseology to have the legal equivalence of "charitable," the trust qualifies as a charitable trust. *See Wilson v. Flowers*, 277 A.2d 199 (N.J. 1971).

D. ILLEGAL AND PUBLIC POLICY LIMITATIONS

1. ILLEGAL PURPOSE

A trust cannot be created for an illegal purpose. If the trust's purpose is to use trust property in violation of criminal law, or it tends to induce crime, the trust is invalid. It is not always easy to characterize trust purpose, however.

Illustration 3: Consider the trust established to pay income and principal for the "care, comfort, support, medical attention, education, sustenance, maintenance or custody of such minor Negro child or children, whose father or mother, or both, have been incarcerated, imprisoned, detained or committed in any federal, state, county or local prison or penitentiary, as a result of the conviction of a crime or misdemeanor of a political nature." Is this trust invalid as against public policy? The answer depends upon whether the purpose is characterized as encouraging the commission of crime or as protecting innocent children from harm caused by incarceration of their parents. The former purpose is invalid, the latter valid. In *Estate of Robbins*, 371 P.2d 573 (Cal.1962), the court found that in this situation it was the purpose for which the property was to be used, not the motives of the testator that determines whether a trust was a valid charitable trust and that the assistance to the minor beneficiaries was a valid charitable purpose.

2. AGAINST PUBLIC POLICY

A trust purpose may not be charitable if it seeks a result contrary to public policy. RESTATEMENT (SECOND) OF TRUST, § 377 cmt. c (1959). Unfortunately, there is no standard definition for "public policy" because the definition depends upon the conceptions of public policy which are prevalent in the community at the time the issue arises. The exercise of public policy by a court in a matter of this nature goes to the maximum of the exercise of its inherent powers.

E. INDEFINITE BENEFICIARY

1. THE INDEFINITE BENEFICIARY RULE

A charitable trust may not be created for a specifically identified beneficiary. "Uncertainty of the beneficiaries is one of the characteristics of a true, technical, charitable use, because, if the beneficiaries are named with precision, the doctrine applicable to ordinary trusts is sufficient to support it." *Cowden v. Sovran Bank/Central South*, 816 S.W.2d 741 (Tenn. 1991).

That only one or a few persons actually benefit from a charitable trust does not necessarily make the trust noncharitable. The fact that a trust only benefits a small number of actual beneficiaries will not defeat a charitable trust that has an otherwise valid charitable purpose. For example, a trust to annually pay or augment a salary for a single distinguished university professorship or for the person who is currently the minister of a church would be valid because the underlying charitable purpose of benefitting education or religion is paramount.

A charitable trust may fail, however, because the class of persons who can benefit is so narrow that the community has no interest in the performance of the trust. For example, a trust to provide funds for the education of a particular person's descendants would be too specific a class of potential beneficiaries and not qualify as a charitable trust. Even so, if the purpose of the trust is to relieve poverty, promote education, advance religion or protect health, the class need not be as broad as it must be where the benefits to be conferred have no relation to any of these purposes. For example, a trust is charitable if it provides funds for the education of needy students with a preference to be given for a particular person's descendants. *See Continental Illinois Nat. Bank & Trust Co. v. Harris*, 194 N.E. 250 (Ill. 1934).

2. ACTUAL VERSUS POTENTIAL BENEFICIARIES

A trust may be valid even if all beneficiaries are known if they are part of a large enough group. Conversely, a trust may fail even if the beneficiaries are unknown if they are part of too small a group. On the other hand, a large group of beneficiaries may cause a trust to fail if the actual benefit to the public is insignificant.

3. THE TOO MANY BENEFICIARIES DICHOTOMY

When the actual benefit from the trust is de minimis or insubstantial, courts have made the distinction sometimes between being generous or benevolent but not charitable.

Illustration 4: C.B.H. devised $86,000, in trust, to divide the net income into as many equal parts as there are children in the first, second and third grades of the J.K. Elementary School and to twice a year divide and pay the income of the trust in equal amounts to each child in those grades for the purpose of "the furtherance of his or her obtainment of an education." There were approximately 450 student who qualified each year for the distribution. At an estimated 5% rate of return, the value of each share would be $4.75. Whether this is a valid charitable trust depends on the characterization given to the distributable benefit. On its face the trust is a valid charitable trust. It is for a charitable purpose (education of children), and the beneficiary is indefinite. The issue is whether the trust will accomplish an appreciable amount of social benefit to the public or some reasonable large class thereof. It may be generous but is it charitable? Although "education" was the purpose, the incidental benefits to each child greatly diminished the likelihood that the trust would accomplish any measurable educational benefit or result. *See Shenandoah Valley National Bank of Winchester v. Taylor,* 192 Va. 135, 63 S.E.2d 786 (1951). It appears the trust might have been modifiable under cy pres and converted to a more substantial public benefit, *e.g.,* accumulate the income, buy books for each child on a periodic basis. *See. infra,* Part 6.VI.H.

F. INTERRELATED FACTORS

When a "charitable trust" is analyzed to determine its charitability, there is an interrelationship between the various charitable trust criteria, *i.e.,* appreciable social benefit, legality, and indefiniteness of beneficiary. For example, the greater the perceived social benefit, the less concern the reviewer will show concerning the legality of the purpose or the size of the class of beneficiaries. *Cf.* RESTATEMENT (SECOND) OF TRUSTS § 368 (1959).

G. DISCRIMINATORY TRUSTS

1. DISCRIMINATORY CHARITABLE TRUSTS

Settlors of charitable trusts often express conditions and limitations on the use of trust funds. Normally these expressions of intent do not have special legal consequences. These desires will be enforced by courts if suit is instituted by the proper parties to require the trustee to properly carry out the terms of the trust. Occasionally, the settlor's condition or limitation concerns matters that affect conflicting public policies. The most predominant of these are charitable trusts that discriminate on the basis of race, gender, or religion.

2. LEGAL ISSUES FOR DISCRIMINATORY TRUSTS

The primary legal issue has been the application of the equal protection clause of the Fourteenth Amendment. To be applicable, the trust must concern "state action." Private action is not affected by the constitutional protection. Clearly, if a state entity is directly involved with the administration of the trust, the state action requirement is met and the trust may not discriminate. *Pennsylvania v. Brown*, 392 F.2d 120 (3d Cir. 1968).

If there is no state action, discriminatory clauses have been upheld. The fact that charitable trusts are enforced by a state official, have special state law benefits and are enforced by courts, does not constitute state action for constitutional protection. The nondiscriminatory judicial application of trust law does not itself constitute state action for purposes of the equal protection clause. *Estate of Wilson*, 452 N.E.2d 1228 (N.Y. 1983).

H. CY PRES

1. DEFINITION OF THE CY PRES DOCTRINE

It is a procedure by which if the trust purpose of a charitable trust is or becomes impossible or impracticable or illegal to carry out, or fully accomplished, and the settlor manifested a more general intention, a court may direct an application of the remaining assets in the trust to some other charitable purpose which falls within the general charitable intention of the settlor. RESTATEMENT (SECOND) OF TRUSTS § 399 (1959).

The doctrine of cy pres goes beyond the principles permitting the modification of private trusts. The cy pres doctrine, which is peculiar to charitable trusts and charitable corporations, permits the court to direct the application of the trust property to a different charitable purpose from that designated by the settlor.

2. CY PRES PROCEDURE

The first step of the process is to determine whether carrying out the originally specified purpose has become impossible, illegal, impracticable. This should require more than a mere finding that modification or broadening of the purposes would be better or more desirable.

Second, assuming impracticability, impossibility, or illegality of the continued use of the distributable interest, the court must determine whether the settlor had a general charitable intent or whether settlor's purpose in making the gift was so strictly limited to the original, stated objective that its failure to absorb all of the funds requires a finding that the excess be held upon resulting trust. If the settlor makes an express provision as to the disposition of the property in case the particular purpose fails, that provision is controlling.

Third, assuming a finding of impracticability, impossibility, or illegality and of general charitable intentions, the final step in the application of the doctrine is to determine what modifications would be made under the cy pres power. Courts recognize that in choosing among possible schemes the court is not necessarily required to adopt that scheme which is as nearly like that designated by the terms of the gift. Thus, courts seek to frame a scheme which in its opinion is the best new purpose to accomplish the general charitable purpose of the donor. This approach is particularly applicable when the designated purpose became impossible or impracticable of accomplishment after the trust was created.

Frequently the court will refer the matter to a master with directions to report back to the court with a scheme for the application of the property. The court may accept, reject or modify the scheme so proposed. The appellate court reserves wide discretion in framing a scheme for the application of the charitable fund to the new purpose.

3. CY PRES INITIATION

To obtain *cy pres*, a suit may be begun by the trustees, making the Attorney General of the state a party, as the representative of the people of the state. Alternatively, the Attorney General may institute the suit.

4. OLD TRUST INCLINATION

When the purpose of an old trust becomes impracticable, impossible, or illegal to carry out, courts seem to be more willing to find a general charitable purpose. Otherwise a resulting trust would require identification of successors to the settlor's estate. This task is frequently difficult and always expensive. On the other hand, when intent is found to have been clearly expressed, a trust might be terminated rather than *cy presed. See Evans v. Newton,* 382 U.S. 296 (1966), *aff'd, Evans v. Abney*, 396 U.S. 435 (1970) where a fifty year trust that established a segregated park was held to revert to the settlors' successors because the trust purpose had become impossible. *Cy pres* was not applicable because the impossible purpose was integral to the trust. Thus the court held that the settlor would prefer termination of the trust to termination of the purpose.

I. HONORARY TRUSTS

1. DEFINITION OF HONORARY TRUST

The honorary trust is loosely definable as a trust for a "specific non-charitable purpose" where no beneficiary is actually named and the designated purpose cannot be considered charitable. RESTATEMENT (SECOND) OF TRUST § 124, cmt c (1959). Although trusts for specific non-charitable purposes where there is no definite ascertainable beneficiary are unenforceable in the absence of statute, honorary trusts have sometimes been held valid. The legality of these devices, however, is far from secure. BOGERT, TRUSTS § 35. Recognized honorary trusts include, for example, the perpetual care of grave trusts, pet care provisions in a will, and recitation of masses. *See* RESTATEMENT (SECOND) OF TRUST § 124 (1959).

2. UPC HONORARY TRUST

The UPC both legitimatizes and limits the duration of honorary trusts. UPC § 2–907(a). Any transfer in trust that is for a lawful non-charitable purpose, either as specified in the instrument or as selected by the trustee, may be performed by the trustee regardless whether there is a beneficiary who can enforce or terminate the trust. UPC § 2–907(a). Because the UPC gives no guidance as to what a non-charitable purpose is, this provision applies to any transfer in trust that does not qualify as either private or a charitable trust. Thus, trusts for the offering of masses and for the care of personal individual grave sites would qualify.

The trustee of such an honorary trust may carry out these types of devices but only for a period of twenty-one years. The twenty-one year term is a maximum even if the instrument contemplates a longer period.

3. "BONA FIDO" LAW

Because it is well known that pet owners commonly desire that their pets be well cared for after their deaths, the UPC permits assets to be transferred in trust for the care of designated domestic or pet animals. UPC § 2–907(b). Although the provision validates trusts for pets, it limits the duration of the trust to the lives of the covered animals living when the trust is created.

Under the UPC, instruments are to be liberally construed and extrinsic evidence freely admitted to determine the transferor's intent. Income and principal of the trust must be used only for trust purposes or for covered animals unless the instrument expressly provides otherwise. UPC § 2–907(c)(1). On termination, the trust must be transferred according to its creating instrument or the relevant clauses of the transferor's will or by intestacy. UPC § 2–907(c)(2).

The settlor's intent is enforceable by the trustee or other court appointed persons. UPC § 2–907(c)(4). If no trustee is designated or no one is willing to serve, the court may name a trustee and order transfer to another trustee in order to see the intended use is carried out. UPC § 2–907(c)(7). If excessive funds are transferred into the trust, the court may adjust the funds and order the excess distributed as it would be if the trust ended. UPC § 2–907(c)(6).

J. CHARITABLE CORPORATIONS

1. CHARITABLE CORPORATIONS

Charitable corporations are non-profit corporations which were organized for charitable purposes. Generally, these corporations are structured so that they can receive tax "exempt" status under I.R.C. section 501(c)(3).

2. CHARITABLE CORPORATION'S PURPOSE

Property may be devoted to charitable purposes by transferring it to a charitable corporation. Under the terms of the gift, the property may be used for any of the purposes for which the corporation is organized or for only one of its purposes. The use of the property may be limited to income from the property and thus the duration for the use of the property would be perpetual.

3. TRUST CHARACTERISTICS

Ordinarily, principles and rules applicable to charitable trusts are also applicable to charitable corporations. The charitable corporation must use the property for the designated charitable purposes for which it was transferred. The Attorney General can enforce these purposes. In addition, the doctrine of *cy pres* is applicable to gifts to charitable corporations.

On the other hand, even though members of the managing board of a charitable corporation are called trustees, they are not technically "trustees" because they do not hold title to the property of the corporation.

K. SUPERVISION OF CHARITABLE TRUSTS

1. THE BENEFICIAL INTEREST OF A CHARITABLE TRUST

The designated beneficiaries do not hold the beneficial interest of a charitable trust. They represent the intermediaries through whom an advantage to the public is achieved. The state or the community is the actual beneficiary and thus the trust is enforced by a public officer, usually the Attorney General.

Similarly designated charitable trust beneficiaries cannot agree to terminate a charitable trust even though they may all agree. An appropriate government official might be able to seek termination. *See supra*, Part 6.VI.H.

L. REVIEW QUESTIONS

1. Charitable trusts are part of the Common law. True or False?
2. What is a charitable trust?
3. What are the special benefits of a charitable trust?
4. What is the distinction between being generous or benevolent versus being charitable.
5. What is the beneficiary rule for a charitable trust?
6. What doctrine allows the court to direct an application of the remaining assets in the trust to some other charitable purpose?
7. What are the requirements of the cy pres doctrine?
8. How do honorary trusts differ from charitable trusts?

PART SEVEN

REGULATION OF DISPOSITION

*

I

POLICY LIMITATIONS ON FREEDOM OF DISPOSITION

Analysis

A. INTERRELATED PUBLIC POLICIES

1. THREE INTERRELATED PUBLIC POLICY CONCEPTS

There are three interrelated public policy concepts that relate to the regulation of gratuitous transfers. First, intestacy, which deals with omission of an otherwise valid estate plan, reflects a policy that combines normality of intention and the supposed better intention.

Second, the family protections, which protect certain relatives from creditors of the decedent and from total disinheritance, reflect policies that combine *parens patriae* concepts or assumed intent and limited forced heirship (by type of asset or amount).

Third, forced or elective heirship, which directly limits freedom of disposition, reflects the combined policies of *parens patriae* and forced intention, usually by some specific share. Much of the world recognizes the "légitime" (lej e tem) which sets an interest in a succession of which the forced heirs may not be deprived without a legal cause.

2. LÉGITIME REJECTED

The closest concept to the civil law *légitime* in use in the states of this country is the inclusion in their statutes or codes of some form of spousal protection from unintentional and intentional disinheritance. The protection usually provides a share or percentage of the estate of which the spouse is treated as owner (Community property) or from which the surviving spouse may not be disinherited (Forced share or dower).

B. ALLOWANCES, HOMESTEADS, AND EXEMPTIONS

1. TYPES OF FAMILY PROTECTIONS

The three basic types of family protections are: allowances, homesteads and exemptions. Their purposes are threefold: to protect against testamentary omission, to protect from creditors, and to reduce financial problems caused by delay in administration.

Their effectiveness in accomplishing their purposes is limited by their design. First, the amounts that are usually specified are modest. Second, some types like the homestead and exemptions are frequently limited to specific types or values of property. Third, the scope of possible beneficiaries is limited, *e.g.*, spouse, minor children.

On the other hand, if they were significant in amount and scope, they might constitute a bar on testation (a "légitime"), coerce guardianship, or raise the cost of credit.

2. FAMILY PROTECTIONS UNDER THE UPC

The UPC includes family protection provisions for all three types. The homestead under UPC Section 2–402 protects the surviving spouse, minor children, dependent children up to the amount of $15,000. Exempt property under Section 2–403 protects the surviving spouse, children (jointly) up to $10,000. The family allowance under Sections 2–404–05 protects the surviving spouse, minor children, dependent children up to $18,000 (Adjustable on petition by court). The total family protection is a minimum of $43,000 if the estate is that large.

When a decedent's estate crosses state lines, the law of the decedent's domicile controls the scope and coverage of the family protections. UPC § 2–401. In addition, these family protections are paid before claims, intestacy, and testacy. Even multiple-party accounts may be at risk. *See UPC* § 6–215(a).

C. SURVIVING SPOUSE PROTECTION FROM DISINHERITANCE

1. JUSTIFICATION FOR SPOUSAL PROTECTION

Although studies indicate that the vast majority of married persons pass substantial portions of their estates to their surviving spouses and that spousal disinheritance is not a major problem, experience indicates that there are a sufficient number of incidents where married persons have attempted to disinherit their surviving spouses to justify regulation. Marital discord and other difficulties sometimes cause married persons to act like non-married persons. Consequently, it is worthwhile for the law to provide a safety net so that those who are unfairly disinherited will be able to protect their merited interest in the deceased spouse's estate. On the other hand, its limited utility indicates that caution should be taken to restrict protective provisions to situations deserving control and not to extend protection beyond its purpose so as to cause interference with legitimate property allocations.

2. TYPES OF PROTECTIVE DEVICES

a. Dower

Anglo–American common law initially used the dower concept to protect the wife from disinheritance. Curtesy was the similar doctrine that protected the husband. In nearly all states that retain the dower concept, dower and curtesy have been combined into one common doctrine. Common law dower was primarily a protective device to restrict disinheritance of the spouse of the decedent's real property. Typically, it was limited to a life interest in one-third of the real estate held seized by the deceased spouse during marriage. Many states expanded the concept to include personal property and have often enlarged the fractional interest in the estate from a life estate to one in fee.

b. Forced Shares

The forced share is another common protection device enacted in many states. With wide variations, a typical forced share statute provides that if a decedent spouse does not pass a minimum arbitrary percentage, usually running from one-third to one-half, of that person's probate estate, to the surviving spouse, the surviving spouse may elect to take that share under a spousal protection right. ATKINSON, WILLS § 33. The electing spouse takes the share in fee. Frequently, dower and curtsey are abolished in these states, although a few states give the surviving spouse an election to take under the will, dower, or forced share.

c. Community and Quasi Community Property

A third device, called community property, is found in ten states. This is a combined accrual and accumulation technique providing that property gained during a marriage is owned equally by each spouse. Community property goes beyond the typical spousal protection provisions that are found in common law states because it establishes a lifetime division of the property as well as a method for dividing an estate upon death of a spouse. It is actually a property division system among married persons based on a partnership theory of marriage and not merely a post-death safety-net minimum protection technique. Each spouse is treated in a sense as a tenant in common of the property earned by both spouses during the marriage. Community property operates as a protection from inter vivos disposition as well as testamentary disinheritance. All property earned and acquired during marriage is treated as owned ½ by the wife and ½ by the husband. States that have community property do not ordinarily need other spousal protection statutes although some have them to deal with noncommunity property acquired by the spouses before and during marriage.

d. Fixed Share Augmented Estate

In 1969 when the original UPC was promulgated it contained a spousal protection scheme that provided a fixed ⅓ share of an augmented estate. The augmented estate concept expanded the scope of property that is subject to the calculation of the elective share and that is subject to the obligation of satisfying the share.

e. Accrual Share Augmented Estate

The 1990 UPC, reorganized and renumbered by 1993 Technical Amendments, adopts an accrual-type elective share which employs a rational but arbitrary rising percentage scale based upon the length of the marriage. The elective share percentage ascends from a low of three percent of the augmented estate after the first year of marriage to a high of fifty percent of the augmented estate after fifteen years of marriage. *See* Chart 7–1–1.

Accrual Approach Theory: The accrual approach theorizes that marriages are similar to economic partnerships and thus the partnership interest of one spouse should increase in the other spouse's assets as the marriage endures. At the moment persons are married, little of their property has been earned as a result of the marriage in an economic partnership sense. The UPC provides that as the marriage continues each spouse earns an increasing percentage interest in the estate of the other spouse. This percentage constitutes the share that may be elected at the death of a spouse by the surviving spouse.

Scope of UPC Accrual System: This reciprocal maturing interest attaches to all of the assets of both spouses, not merely to the assets acquired during the marriage. This pervasive accrual approach differs significantly from community property states where the automatic one-half interest attaches only to assets earned during the marriage and not to "separate property" obtained prior to marriage or derived from third persons by inheritance or gratuitous transfer during marriage. Administrative efficiency is promoted because there need not be any tracing of assets to determine their source. It also roughly accords with the ways that married persons treat their assets: few spouses distinguish their separate from their marital property when making gifts or devises to others.

Monetary Minimum: The UPC also includes a supplemental or minimum safety-net monetary amount for a surviving spouse below which the elective share cannot equal regardless of the length of the marriage. Accordingly, any surviving spouse is entitled to a supplemental elective share designed to bring the surviving spouse's assets up to a minimum of $50,000.

Chart 7–1–1 Section 2–202(a) Elective Share	
If the decedent and the spouse were married to each other:	**The elective-share percentage is:**
Less than 1 year	Supplemental Amount Only.
1 year but less than 2 years	3% of the augmented estate.
2 years but less than 3 years	6% of the augmented estate.
3 years but less than 4 years	9% of the augmented estate.
4 years but less than 5 years	12% of the augmented estate.
5 years but less than 6 years	15% of the augmented estate.
6 years but less than 7 years	18% of the augmented estate.
7 years but less than 8 years	21% of the augmented estate.
8 years but less than 9 years	24% of the augmented estate.
9 years but less than 10 years	27% of the augmented estate.
10 years but less than 11 years	30% of the augmented estate.
11 years but less than 12 years	34% of the augmented estate.
12 years but less than 13 years	38% of the augmented estate.
13 years but less than 14 years	42% of the augmented estate.
14 years but less than 15 years	46% of the augmented estate.
15 years or more	50% of the augmented estate.

3. DEFINITION OF THE PROTECTABLE ESTATE

a. Probate Estate

Common law states that do not have the UPC's augmented estate concept apply their protection statutes against the decedent's estate subject to administration. As so limited, the protection may fail to adequately protect the surviving spouse because the decedent can dispose of the greater part of his or her estate through will substitutes. In addition, the surviving spouse may be over compensated by the election because the protection device does not consider the surviving spouse's personal estate derived from the decedent or others.

Unfortunately, the limited scope of the estate subject to the spousal protection encourages persons determined to disinherit their spouses to transfer their assets to third persons through the use of relatively frail inter vivos transactions or of probate estate purging transfers on their deathbed or in near deathbed situations. A law that permits easy and unburdensome avoidance establishes too vast a loophole and encourages disinheritance even in the most undesirable situation.

b. Attempts to Defeat the Spousal Protection

At Common Law a transfer of land prior to marriage could be set aside *pro tanto* upon proof that it was made fraudulently with intent to defeat dower, and there have been similar holdings in cases of transfer of personalty in fraud of the spouse's forced share. In some jurisdictions an inter vivos transfer after marriage is ineffective to deprive the surviving spouse of his or her forced share if made with intent to defraud him or her thereof. Other courts have rejected the fraud test and recently some have applied the test as to whether the transfer is real or illusory. ATKINSON, WILLS § 34. Courts have had difficulty determining what is illusory. For example, joint survivorship interests have been held valid and not illusory. Totten trusts have also been held to avoid the rule. *Allender v. Allender*, 87 A.2d 608 (Md. 1952).

The doctrine of fraud on marital rights and illusoriness represent attempts to balance the social and practical undesirability of restricting the free alienation of property against the desire to protect the legal share of a spouse. Thus, courts have permitted a married person in the absence of statutory regulation to make lifetime gifts of his or her property even though the effect is to deprive the spouse of a statutory share. If the gift is not absolute and unconditional and the donor retains dominion and control over the property until death, an increasing number of courts have granted the surviving spouse protection. This stop gap protection leaves too many escape devices available for the person who wants to defeat the relevant spousal protection. With escape devises readily available, the efficacy of the spousal protection is in question.

c. Augmented Estate Under the UPC

The UPC's augmented estate concept builds in a protection system against attempts to defeat the election. The inclusion of specified inter vivos transfers fundamentally prevents most persons from avoiding the elective share protection.

The augmented estate is a hotchpot estate in that it is not really physically assembled. It is a set of values created for purposes of calculating the amount of the elective share. Similar but separate concepts deal with the funding of the elective share amount. UPC § 2–209.

The augmented estate starts with the decedent's net probate estate. To be fully effective, however, the spousal protection statute must take into account certain inter vivos transfers of the decedent spouse. Consequently, the UPC includes in the augmented estate what it calls the decedent's non probate estate.

Concomitantly, the UPC prevents the surviving spouse from receiving more than the circumstances merit. Thus, the surviving spouse must include in the augmented estate both the assets derivable from the decedent as a result of the latter's death and all of the surviving spouse's personal assets including the surviving spouse's comparable nonprobate transfers to others. These latter inclusions discourage elections by surviving spouses in marriages of short duration or where the surviving spouse has substantial personal assets.

The sum of the value of decedent's controllable estate plus the value of the surviving spouse's controllable estate less the value of nonmarital interests and completed transfers equals the augmented estate.

Generally, the augmented estate includes all assets less liabilities owned or controlled by the decedent and by the decedent's surviving spouse plus certain gratuitous transfers made by either spouse to third persons. More specifically, it is composed of four distinct components or segments. UPC § 2–203. If the same property or interest is includable in more than one segment, it is includable in the segment that would yield the highest value; however, the value for the same interest may only be included in one segment. UPC § 2–208(c).

Segment 1 of the Augmented Estate: Segment 1 includes what normally is thought of as the decedent's net probate estate which is the gross probate estate less enforceable claims, funeral and administration expenses, and the family protections. UPC § 2–204.

Segment 2 of the Augmented Estate: Segment 2 includes all properties over which decedent immediately prior to death retained certain interests, powers or relationships. UPC § 2–205. Examples of such powers include power to revoke, presently exercisable general power of appointment, or joint tenancy with right of survivorship. Although transfers of this nature pass outside the probate estate, they may be subject to reclaim if they are required to contribute to the funding of the surviving spouse's elective share amount. UPC § 2–205. Properties that have comparable relationships to the surviving spouse are includable in the augmented estate under Segment 4. UPC § 2–207.

Segment 3 of the Augmented Estate: Segment 3 includes all of decedent's nonprobate property which the surviving spouse gratuitously received or derived from the decedent by reason of the latter's death. UPC § 2–206. This includes property received by the surviving spouse from decedent by way of survivorship, appointment, benefits of life insurance on decedent's life, benefits from retirement plans in which decedent participated and of any other property that would have been included as part of Segment 2, described above, had it passed to a third person. Social security system survivorship benefits are, however, specifically exempt. Segment 3 also does not include any Segment 1 properties received from the decedent's estate or the value of the spouse's family protections. UPC § 2–202(c).

Segment 4 of the Augmented Estate: Segment 4 includes (1) all of the surviving spouse's individual property and (2) the surviving spouse's Segment 2 property (the spouse's nonprobate transfers to others) as if that spouse predeceased decedent, to the extent these properties are not included in Segments 1 and 3. UPC § 2–207. This Segment is all inclusive and supplemental to the other segments. It includes not only assets earned during the marriage but also assets acquired prior to marriage and assets derived gratuitously from the decedent and other persons. It also includes the spouse's fractional interests in survivorship property, the ownership interests in financial accounts and security registrations and property passing to the spouse by reason of the decedent's death. Segment 4 guarantees that surviving spouses will have to account for their own estate and estate plan in opting for the elective share.

The sum of the value of these four segments equals the augmented estate and the surviving spouse's elective share equals the elective share percentage times the augmented estate. For example, if the spouses have been married 11½ years, the elective share equals 34%, and if the augmented estate equals $500,000, the elective share amount equals $170,000.

4. ELECTION PROCEDURE BY THE SURVIVING SPOUSE

Ordinarily when disinheritance is a problem, the surviving spouse is required to make an election of benefits. Either the spouse may take under the decedent's estate plan as expressed or under the elective share of the spousal protection statute. Sometimes the spouse is given a third election and that is to take a dower share. Most states presume the surviving spouse will take under the decedent's estate plan and thus, the spouse must affirmatively elect to take under the protection statutes. A few states reverse this process and presume the statutory protection is elected unless the surviving spouse affirmatively indicates otherwise.

Whatever the election is, it must be made within a specified time after the decedent's death. The time runs from three months to nine months. If no election is made, the default benefit is conferred.

Under the UPC the opportunity to take the elective share exists whether the decedent died intestate, testate with a will which disinherits the surviving spouse, or testate with a will which gives all or part of the estate to the surviving spouse. The election must be made within the later of nine months after decedent's death or six months after probate of decedent's will but in no case is the decedent's nonprobate transfers subject to the election unless the election is filed within nine months of decedent's death. UPC § 2–211(a). Extension of time may be granted by the court for cause if made within nine months of decedent's death and the extension binds all interested persons notified. UPC § 2–211(b). Court determines amount and contribution.

The decision to elect depends upon three determinations: (1) the elective share amount; (2) the determination of the augmented estate; and (3) the satisfaction of the elective share amount.

5. EFFECT OF SPOUSE'S ELECTION

When a spouse elects the spousal protection rather than the estate plan, the intended beneficiaries must suffer abatement of their devise or gift. An important concern for this abatement is the order in which the legacies, devises and bequests have to suffer the loss if any. The election by a spouse can greatly disrupt an "estate plan." The UPC employs pro rata sharing among levels of contributors. UPC § 2–209. Other states have special statutes as well.

The doctrine of acceleration: Sometimes the election of a share by a surviving spouse leaves future interests unsettled. For example, T's will devises Meadowacre to W for life, remainder to G. If W elects against the will taking a portion of the estate outright but relinquishing the life estate, the remainder interest is put into a sort of state of limbo. Under the acceleration doctrine, G's remainder interest would be accelerated and thus become immediately possessory unless the remainder is subject to some other unfilled condition precedent. Some courts have refused to apply the doctrine mechanically and have applied the equitable doctrine of sequestration to equalize any unfair burden caused by the spousal election on other persons. In this example a court might order the income from the life estate to be paid to the residuary beneficiaries for the life of W if these beneficiaries are otherwise unfairly burdened. *See Sellick v. Sellick*, 173 N.W. 609 (Mich 1919).

6. FUNDING THE ELECTIVE SHARE UNDER THE UPC

For funding purposes, the UPC divides the augmented estate into three separate hotchpots or funds. Each fund is composed of property interests that are included in the augmented estate depending on certain characterization decisions that will be explained. The ultimate goal is to fully fund the elective share amount. To accomplish this goal and to allocate the necessary contribution from each fund, the funds are arranged in an order of priority. Fund 1 interests must contribute first to satisfy the elective share amount and must be exhausted before seeking contribution from Fund 2 interests. Fund 3 interests are required to contribute if the previous two funds do not fully satisfy the elective share amount.

Fund 1: Fund 1 is composed of the amounts of the augmented estate that are received or attributable to the surviving spouse and includes the following amounts: (1) The intestate and testate portions of Segment 1 that pass to the surviving spouse from the decedent; (2) The amounts included in Segment 3; (3) Twice the elective share percentage times the amounts of Segment 4 of the augmented estate. UPC § 2–209(a). In order to properly calculate the value of the surviving spouse's portion of segment 4 assets, it is necessary to double the elective share percentage. In the economic sharing concept, the surviving spouse's personal assets are shared as well by the decedent. Therefore, if the elective share percentage is 34% and the surviving spouse's personal estate equals $1,000, 68% of this amount or $680 is attributable to the marriage: the 34% share of the surviving spouse and 34% contributed by the decedent. If after deducting the value of the surviving spouse's share, the elective share amount is satisfied, the process ends and thus the surviving spouse will take nothing further.

Fund 2: If there remains an elective share deficiency, Fund 2 must be calculated and it includes the following amounts: (1) the amounts of the nonspousal portions of Segment 1; and (2) the amount of Segment 2 of the augmented estate less the value of certain irrevocable transfers made by decedent within the two year period prior to death. UPC § 2–209(b). The third person beneficiaries of these included amounts must contribute to the funding of the elective share deficiency. All contributions from these beneficiaries are made on a pro rata basis. A pro rata share equals the value of the recipient's interest divided by total value of Fund 2. Fund 2 transfers must be fully exhausted before proceeding to Fund 3.

Fund 3: If interests in Fund 2 assets are exhausted and the elective share amount still remains unsatisfied, Fund 3 must be calculated. It includes the irrevocable transfers made by decedent within the two year period prior to death that are included in Segment 2 except for life insurance proceeds of policies irrevocably transferred by decedent during this period of time. UPC §§ 2–209(c); 2–205(3)(i) and (iii). The insurance proceeds are included in Fund 2. UPC §§ 2–209(b); 2–205(3)(ii). The recipients of Fund 3 must contribute to the remaining unsatisfied portion of elective share amount. All contributors of Fund 3 contribute on a pro rata basis. A pro rata share equals the value of recipient's interest divided by the value of Fund 3. The elective share amount should be fully funded after the three contribution steps are completed. As a practical matter, it will rarely be necessary to go into Fund 3.

Only the original recipients and their gratuitous donees are liable for contribution. UPC § 2–210(a). In addition, a recipient may either pay the value of the amount of contribution due or give up the proportional part of the nonprobate reclaimable asset received. No recipient or gratuitous donee of a recipient is required to contribute more than the pro rata portion as determined through the above funding process even though the elective share amount is not fully satisfied because some recipients are unable to contribute or are jurisdictionally unavailable. UPC § 2–211(d). For example, if a recipient of Fund 2 interests is unable or unavailable to pay the pro rata portion, the other recipients of Fund 2 amounts do not have to make up the difference. Fund 3 recipients must contribute only if Fund 2 is insufficient to satisfy assuming all recipients in Fund 2 contributed their full pro rata portion. These limitations on funding mean that some surviving spouses will not be able to collect their full elective share amount.

7. PERMISSIBLE AVOIDANCE OF THE SPOUSAL PROTECTION

The underlying philosophy of freedom of disposition and clarity of title and ownership are important policies. It is generally agreed that no spousal protection system should interfere with legitimate property transactions. For example, the UPC excludes several categories of nonmarital interests and completed lifetime transfers made by either spouse.

Because spousal protection concerns gratuitous transactions by the spouse, transfers for which either spouse received adequate and full consideration in money or money's worth are excluded from the augmented estate. UPC § 2–208(a). The augmented estate also excludes all irrevocable transfers, and exercises or releases of powers of appointment made with the written consent or joinder of the other spouse.

8. MARITAL AGREEMENTS

Premarital and marital contracts, agreements and waivers of a right of election of a surviving spouse are also specifically recognized so long as they are (a) in writing, (b) voluntary, and (c) not unconscionable. UPC § 2–213(a). The family protection allowances may similarly be waived. The surviving spouse who contests a waiver has the burden of showing that the waiver was not executed voluntarily or it was unconscionable when executed and lacked fair disclosure prior to execution. UPC § 2–213(b). Fair disclosure is explained. It must be either (a) a "fair and reasonable disclosure" of the decedent's assets and liabilities, (b) a voluntary and express waiver of any disclosure, or (c) knowledge of the decedent's assets and liabilities was possessed or reasonably available. UPC §§ 2–213(b)(2)(i)–(iii). Unconscionability is a question of law and is not a jury question. UPC § 2–213(c).

If the relevant agreement waives "all rights" or contains equivalent language, each spouse waives all rights to elective share and the family protections in the other spouse's estate and renounces all interests passing from the other spouse by intestacy or by a will executed before the agreement. UPC § 2–213(d).

9. SIMPLE ELECTIVE SHARE COMPARISONS

Hypothetical: In all of the following hypotheticals assume that decedent, D, is married at D's death to the surviving spouse, S, and that D's estate plan passes nothing to S. S takes the full value of the family protections, *i.e.,* $43,000 under UPC.

Assumption 1: D and S were married for 10 years. At death D's net estate is valued at $300,000 and S's net estate is valued at $100,000. No inter vivos transfers were made by either spouse. S petitions for the elective share in timely fashion. What result?

Comparison of UPC with NonUPC Forced Share	UPC Amount	NonUPC Amount
D's Probate Estate	$300,000	$300,000
S's Net Assets	$100,000	N.A.
Total Value of Augmented Estate	$400,000	$300,000
Elective Share Percentage	x 30%	⅓
Elective Share Amount	$120,000	$100,000
Less S's Chargeable Share (Fund 1) S's Estate (Segment 4 x (2 x 30%))	–$60,000	N.A.
Elective Share Deficiency	$60,000	$100,000

Comment: Because the marriage lasted ten years, the elective share percentage under the UPC equaled 30% of the augmented estate, yielding an elective share amount of $120,000. Sixty percent of the value of S's assets count toward satisfying the elective share amount. That leaves a deficiency of $60,000, which must be paid out of D's probate estate.

Under NonUPC forced share, only the probate estate is considered and the surviving spouse can take a full forced share from the value of that estate regardless of the economic status of the surviving spouse. In this example the elective share deficiency will come from the probate estate.

Assumption 2: D and S were married for 20 years. At death D's net estate is valued at $120,000 and S's net estate is valued at $300,000. No inter vivos transfers were made by either spouse. S petitions for the elective share in timely fashion. What result?

Comparison of UPC with NonUPC Forced Share	UPC Amount	NonUPC Amount
D's Probate Estate	$120,000	$120,000
S's Net Assets	$300,000	N.A.
Total Value of Augmented Estate	$420,000	$120,000
Elective Share Percentage	x 50%	⅓
Elective Share Amount	$210,000	$40,000
Less S's Chargeable Share (Fund 1) S's Estate (Segment 4 x (2 x 30%))	–$300,000	N.A.
Elective Share Deficiency	–$90,000	$40,000

Comment: Because the marriage lasted more than fourteen years, the elective share percentage equaled 50% of the augmented estate. In this example, D's estate will not have to pay S the value of the elective share deficiency which is a negative amount, *i.e.,*-$90,000. The UPC does not require S to pay D's estate the elective share excess amount nor forfeit the value of the family protections. It does prevent S from taking even more from D's estate.

Under NonUPC forced share, only decedent's probate estate is considered and the elective share percentage does not change. Consequently, despite the size of the surviving spouse's estate, he will get the additional sums from the decedent's estate. This might be greater protection than the protective policy requires.

10. COMPLEX ELECTIVE SHARE COMPARISON

Hypothetical: Decedent, D, is married at D's death to the surviving spouse, S. D's will passes nothing to S. At death D held a power to revoke a trust of which D was the life beneficiary and which on D's death the remainder went to Y. The trust is valued at $600,000. S is the beneficiary of D's $200,000 life insurance policy. S also had net assets valued at $300,000. D and S were married for 20 years. S petitions for the elective share in timely fashion.

Comparison of UPC with NonUPC Forced Share	UPC Amount	NonUPC Amount
D's Probate Estate (Segment 1)	$900,000	$900,000
D's Nonprobate Transfers to Others (Segment 2)	$600,000	$0
D's Nonprobate Transfers to S (Segment 3)	$200,000	$0
S's Net Assets (Segment 4)	$300,000	$0
Total Value of Augmented Estate	$2,000,000	$900,000
Elective Share Percentage	x 50%	⅓
Elective Share Amount	$1,000,000	$300,000
D's Nonprobate Transfers to S (Segment 3)	($200,000)	$0
Less S's Chargeable Share (Fund 1) S's Estate (Segment 4 x (2 x 50%))	($300,000)	N.A.
Elective Share Deficiency	$500,000	$300,000
Contributions From Segments 1 and 2		
Segment 1 pro rata portion	60%	100%
	($300,000)	($300,000)
Segment 2 pro rata portion	40%	
	($200,000)	
Balance	$0	$0

Comment: Because the marriage lasted more than fourteen years, the elective share percentage equaled 50% of the augmented estate. In this example, D's estate and the recipients of the nonprobate transfers to third persons will have to pay S a pro rata portion of the elective share deficiency. The effect of the augmented estate concept is to equalize the estates. This is a fair result of the marriage partnership concept.

Under NonUPC forced share, the surviving spouse is protected only by the size of the probate estate. Unless there is fraud or illusoriness, the $600,000 nonprobate transfers escape contribution to the elective share despite the decedent's possession of a power to revoke up to the moment of death. This result makes spousal protection avoidance too easy.

D. UNINTENTIONAL DISINHERITANCE

1. PRETERMITTED ISSUE OF DECEDENT

a. General Rule

One may disinherit one's relatives including children. *McKamey v. Watkins*, 273 N.E.2d 542 (Ind. 1971). Except for the protection of surviving spouses and a limited protection for certain children in Louisiana, forced heirship is not recognized in the states of this country. Omission from the will is generally sufficient to disinherit a relative except for pretermitted heir statutes. Omission might indicate a lack of testamentary capacity, however, *i.e.*, testator does not know the objects of one's bounty.

b. Exception—Pretermitted Heir Statutes

These statutes are designed to avoid *unintentional* disinheritance of a testator's children or other descendants. The statutes are based on a testator's natural and probable intention of including all children and descendants of deceased children. They establish rules of construction against unintentional disinheritance. Wills and the surrounding circumstances are interpreted liberally in favor of the omitted person. The original thrust of the statutes was concerned with preprocreation wills that did not consider certain relatives, usually testator's afterborn children. As indicated, intentional disinheritance is allowed.

c. Differences Among Pretermitted Heir Statutes

The pretermitted heir statutes differ as to time of application and scope of coverage:

i. Time of Birth: the statutes differ as to the time of birth of the pretermitted heir vis à vis the date of the will. Some statutes apply to those covered persons who are born both before or after the will was executed. Under these statutes, mere omission of a covered person may not be sufficient to disinherit the person. Other statutes apply only to protect those born after the will was executed. Although these allow mere omission to disinherit a covered person born before the will is executed, they may protect similarly covered persons who are born after the will was executed. Mere omission will not exclude the post-will person whereas mere omission will exclude the person born before the will was executed.

Illustration 1: T's will that devises everything to T's spouse executed after two children were born but before two other children were born. If the statute only protects children born after the will was executed, the anomalous result of a strict interpretation of the statute will be that the two children born after the will was executed will be protected but the two children born before the will will not. On the other hand, if the statute covers both pre and post born children, then mere omission will not disinherit any of these four children and they may be able to take the share provided by the statute despite the fact that the surviving spouse is clearly the preferred beneficiary.

ii. Persons Covered: Statutes also vary as to the status of the persons covered. Some statutes only cover children of the testator. A few expand coverage to grandchildren. Whether the statute protects adopted persons within the protected class is another issue with varying statutory resolutions.

iii. Admissibility of Evidence: A significant distinction between the statutes concerns the admissibility of evidence. A few statutes limit evidence of testator's intent to the face of the will. Others admit extrinsic evidence to resolve ambiguity. Whether declarations of the testator are admissible is frequently an important issue. Many courts say no. Finally, a significant number of statutes permit evidence of inter vivos transfers made to the omitted person by the testator prior to death.

iv. Effect of Pretermission: A very few states hold the entire will is revoked thus requiring the entire estate to pass by intestacy. A greater number of states permit the pretermitted person to take an intestacy forced share against the estate. Another permits the court to determine the share according to a standard of probable intention of the testator. WIS. STAT. § 853.25(5).

v. Planning Around Statutes: Because these statutes can cause unintended disruption to otherwise proper estate plans, it is important that drafting techniques be used to clearly exclude application of these statutes. The most common device is to anticipate subsequent issue and to provide for them. Specifically excluding afterborn children and grandchildren may be necessary. On the other hand a will that merely states: "to my spouse if spouse survives, if not to my children whenever born" should be sufficient.

2. OMITTED CHILDREN UNDER THE UPC

Because pretermitted heir statutes are intended and designed to prevent injustice and reduce will contests when unintentionally omitted heirs survive a testator, the statute should be designed to accomplish these goals. Unfortunately, some statutes that exist in non-UPC states have actually produced the opposite results. Accordingly, the UPC's provision contains very precise prerequisites and limitations that are designed to reduce this litigation and judicial misinterpretation. The UPC establishes conditional thresholds against which each applicable situation must be tested.

a. Threshold—Level 1 Requirements

- The protection is limited to pretermitted children and does not protect disinheritance of other descendants and relatives.
- The child must be born or adopted after the execution of the will that disinherits the child.
- Intent to disinherit must not appear on the "face of the will."
- The disinherited or omitted child must not have been provided for by transfers outside the will intended to be in lieu of testamentary provision.

UPC § 2–302(b). A liberal admissibility of extrinsic evidence rule is adopted in regard to proof of intent to use nontestamentary transfers in lieu of testamentary transfers. Extrinsic evidence may include the testator's declarations, the value of the transfer vis à vis the estate and "other evidence" that is relevant to proof of intent.

If the threshold requirements are satisfied, the omitted child must then test the section's protection against two factual circumstances.

b. Alternative Circumstances—Level 2 Requirements

If the testator had no children living when the will was executed, the omitted child takes an intestate share from the estate unless the natural or adopted child's parent is "devised all or substantially all" of the estate, survives the testator and is entitled to take under the will. The last condition concerns whether the will might have been revoked by other law. The child's parent does not have to be the spouse of the decedent: marriage between the decedent and that child's other parent is not necessary.

If the testator had one or more children living when the will was executed, the pretermitted child takes only if one or more of those existing children at the time of the will's execution received a legal or equitable interest in the estate from the will. If pre-will children take, the pretermitted child takes a representative pro rata share from the total value of the interests devised to the pre-existing children. The interest of the pre-existing children's devises abate pro rata according to their respective interests. The nature of the interest accorded, *e.g.*, legal, equitable, present, future, to the omitted child must conform to the extent possible to the character of the devises to the pre-existing children. In general, the character of the estate plan must be preserved to the maximum degree possible. In other words, the pretermitted child does not take a separate share from the estate but is a forced devisee among the gifts given to the pre-existing children. *See* Illustrations below.

3. ILLUSTRATIONS OF PRETERMITTED HEIR STATUTES

Hypothetical 1: Testator has two living children, A and B, when will was executed. Will provides nothing for A and B. Subsequent to will execution, C is born. Thereafter Testator dies.

Answer: Under the pretermitted children section of the UPC, the pretermitted child C would not be entitled to take anything from the estate because pre-existing children of the testator were not devised property under the will. This provision is included to provide equality among children who are born before and after a will is executed. Some pretermitted heir statutes in the states would give C a share although A and B would take nothing. The UPC treats equals equally.

Hypothetical 2: Testator has two children A and B when the will is executed. The will gives $9,000 to A and $9,000 to B. Subsequent to the will execution, C is born. Thereafter Testator dies.

Answer: C will be entitled to share a portion of the devises to A and B. C will not be able to take from other assets in the estate. In this example, C would be entitled to take $6,000. This is an equal portion with the other two children, A and B, from the total of the property passed to A and B in the will. A and B would each take $6,000 also and their gifts would be abated $3,000 apiece.

Hypothetical 3: Assuming the same condition as hypothetical 2 except that the will gives A $6,000 and B $12,000. Thereafter Testator dies.

Answer: C would be able to take a pro rata share of the total of the gifts to A and B. As one of the three children, C would be able to take one-third of the total gifts to A and B. This equals one-third of $18,000 or $6,000. In other words, C will take 6,000 of the total gifts to A and B. Because B received two-thirds of the total of those gifts, two-thirds of C's $6,000 will come from B's share. Concomitantly, one-third of C's $6,000 will come from A's share. This means that A's interest will be abated by $2,000 and B's interest will be abated by $4,000.

The final distribution of these gifts will be that A will take $4,000, B will take $8,000 and C will take $6,000. Although this solution does not result in perfect equality, it addresses the pretermitted heir problem, it attempts to address the presumed intent of the testator due to the pretermission, and it attempts to provide basic equality among those who do take. Although A now takes less than C, the loss was a pro rata portion of the abatement. In addition, the satisfaction of the pretermitted child's forced share has no effect on the other devises made in the will. Consequently, the total estate plan suffers minimal disruption and abatement problems are greatly diminished.

The general abatement provision of the UPC is applicable to abatement of devises caused by the application of this provision. UPC §§ 2–302(d); 3–902.

4. OMITTED OR PRETERMITTED SPOUSE

Most states do not have a special provision concerning the omitted spouse or premarital will provision. These states rely upon their spousal protection provisions.

a. UPC Omitted Spouse Provision

Believing that most testators desire to give their spouses a major portion of their estates and that failure to do so for the post testament spouse is an unintentional omission, the UPC includes a special provision. UPC § 2–301. This section does not allow an election: it is automatic. Under this provision, the surviving spouse takes an intestate share as if decedent had died intestate even if the decedent's will was executed prior to marriage. Omission is not required. The provision does not apply, however,

(1) If the will indicates or evidence indicates that the will was executed in contemplation of the marriage, or

(2) If the will expressly shows an intent to exclude the spouse from a subsequent marriage, or

(3) If the surviving spouse received transfers outside the will intended to be in lieu of a testamentary gift.

The latter intent may be inferred from the nature or amount of transfer(s), *e.g.*, life insurance proceeds, or proved by declarations of the testator or other evidence, or both.

The automatic intestate share is limited to the portion of the estate not passing to the decedent's children or descendants of those children born before marriage who are not children of the surviving spouse. In addition, the share can be satisfied from testamentary gifts to the spouse. All others devisees are subject to pro rata abatement caused by the application of this provision.

Illustration 2: T, five years ago, when unmarried and with no descendants, executed a will that devised his entire estate to his surviving parents, or if no surviving parent, to his siblings or their descendants. Last year T married W. T died a month ago without changing his will. T made no transfers to W in lieu of a testamentary gift. Under UPC Section 2–301, W will take her intestate share which will be either the first $200,000 plus ¾ of the remainder if one or more of T's parents survived [UPC § 2–101(2)], or the entire estate if no parent survives. UPC § 2–102(1)(i).

Illustration 3: Five years ago T, married with two children, executed a will that devised her entire estate to P, her spouse, if he survived her, but if he does not, to her children, C1 and C2, or their descendants. Two years ago T divorced P. Last year T married H. T died a month ago without changing her will. T made no transfers to H in lieu of a testamentary gift. Although under UPC Section 2–301 H is entitled to his intestate share, his recovery from the estate is limited to that portion of the estate not passing to devisees who are decedent's children or descendants of those children born before marriage and who are not children of the surviving spouse. Under T's will, the devise to T's former spouse, P, is revoked by the divorce and thus, the children of that marriage, C1 and C2, take the residue if they survived. Consequently, no part of T's estate passes to anyone other than C1 and C2, the children of another relationship. H takes no share under Section 2–301 and is limited to electing under the UPC's elective share provisions.

E. OTHER PUBLIC POLICY REGULATIONS AND PROHIBITIONS

1. MORTMAIN STATUTES

A very few states have sometimes imposed restrictions on charitable dispositions. Mortmain statutes are of two types: (1) monetary maximums or percentage maximums which can be left to charity, or (2) time limitations within which the gifts are invalid if made to charities. Some have both restrictions. Certain relatives must typically survive to take advantage of the Mortmain statute. Pennsylvania held that its statute which generally invalidated bequests in wills to religious and charitable organizations made within 30 days of a testator's death, was unconstitutional because it denied charitable beneficiaries equal protection of the laws. *Estate of Cavill,* 329 A.2d 503 (Pa. 1974).

2. PUBLIC POLICY LIMITATIONS

a. Wasteful Devises and Gifts

Sometimes public policy considerations are raised with certain testamentary gifts. Testators can request that very unusual actions be taken with the property they leave in their estates. For example. testators have requested that their residence be razed or that they be buried in their automobile.

b. Improper Conditions

Testators have tried to exercise "dead hand" control by requiring the beneficiary to meet certain conditions. Most of these conditions include the use of trusts and the attempt by the testator to control future activity. These matters are discussed at *supra* Part 6.I.E.

c. Testamentary Distinction

For outright devises, conditions set upon inheritance that must be satisfied at death have no *in terrorem* effect: testator is not controlling future activity. Generally, courts will enforce these types of conditions.

Illustration 4: Testator provides in will that S takes the residuary if S is divorced from W, otherwise the devise goes to Y Charity. At T's death, S is either divorced or not and thus can take or cannot take. This devise is probably valid because it does not cause S to conform in the future. If this were a devise in trust and it required S to get a divorce in the future in order to take trust benefits, the condition might be found to be against public policy if the condition were found to encourage divorce.

F. REVIEW QUESTIONS

1. What are the three basic types of family protection?
2. An common law a transfer of land prior to marriage could be set aside *pro tanto* upon proof that it was made fraudulently with intent to defeat dower. True or False?
3. What are the various types of protective systems that exist in this country for protecting the surviving spouse from disinheritance?
4. What are the four segments of the 1990 UPC augmented estate?
5. A person cannot intentionally disinherit his or her children. True or False?
6. How does the UPC protect the omitted spouse?

*

II

VOLUNTARY REGULATION OF DISPOSITION

Analysis

A. WILL CONTRACTS

1. TYPES OF WILL CONTRACTS

There are three basic types of will contracts: to will or devise; to die intestate; and not to revoke. Litigation concerning will contracts has been common. Will contracts face several substantiation barriers. First, the Statute of Frauds may require certain contracts such as contracts to will real property, to be in writing. Second, many states, including UPC states, require all will contracts to be in writing. Third, if there is no writing formality in a state, some courts require the contract to be proved by clear and convincing evidence. And fourth, because specific performance is usually the remedy sought, will contracts must be supported by fair and reasonable consideration: past consideration is not sufficient.

2. FORMALITY FOR WILL CONTRACTS

The absence of a writing does not prevent enforcement of an oral contract if there is part performance or estoppel. A common but not universal holding finds the part performance or estoppel exception satisfied where a promisor dies passing the property to the other promisor in conformity with the oral contract and the surviving promisor accepts the benefits of the agreement. Similarly, where wills are executed by both promisors in conformity with the alleged oral contract, the wills have been found to constitute part performance or a memorandum of the contract. Unfortunately, no general rules on these issues have emerged. Court decisions are so varied in analysis that they must be viewed on a case by case basis.

3. JOINT AND MUTUAL WILLS

A joint will is one in which the same paper is executed by two persons as their respective wills. Mutual wills are the separate testaments of two persons, more or less reciprocal in their provisions. Generally, without other evidence of the contract, there is no inference of a contract not to revoke if mutual wills are executed. An inference of a contract has sometimes been found from the execution of joint wills.

4. REMEDIES FOR BREACH OF WILL CONTRACTS

Generally, suits for breaches of will contracts are brought as claims against the estates and usually are for specific performance. Courts have at times, however, confused wills law and contract law. For example, in the enforcement of a contract not to revoke, courts sometimes have probated the revoked will, which is a form of specific performance as applied in a probate environment. Another mixed concept is to apply wills law and allow unilateral revocation of the contract if made before the death of either after notice to the other promisee.

5. SCOPE OF WILL CONTRACTS

Even if the contract not to revoke is provable there are numerous interpretive issues which usually are not adequately expressed in the contract whatever its form. For example, what property is covered by an agreement between spouses—decedent's property or both spouses' property? And, what are the survivor's rights and powers with contract property? Also what about survivorship property and other nonprobate transfers which will not be part of the probate process? The latter issue raises consideration of recordation requirements and bona fide purchasers. Other problems include what is the intended beneficiary's position, *e.g.*, does lapse apply. Finally, what are the rights of any subsequent spouse of the survivor. The latter issue raises a conflict between the public policy exhibited by spousal protection statutes versus the policy against interfering with the contract rights of the contract's third party beneficiaries. Courts have split on this conflict in policy

6. WILL CONTRACTS UNDER THE UPC

Section 2–514 of the UPC provides that a contract to make a will or a devise, or not to revoke a will or devise, or to die intestate, must be memorialized in writing. The will must state the material provisions of the contract, or expressly refer to a contract whose terms are provable by extrinsic evidence, or the decedent must sign a writing evidencing the contract. No presumption of a contract arises from execution of mutual or joint wills. The Comment states that the section intends no change in rules of evidence and does not preclude an action in quantum meruit.

B. SETTLEMENT AGREEMENTS

1. SETTLEMENT OF DISPUTES

The courts favor settlement of disputes. Consequently, when disputes over property arise, the persons in interest are allowed to settle the conflicting claims. For example, heirs of an intestate may agree to distribute the estate differently than the intestacy statute would. *See* UPC § 3–912. The agreement, however, binds only those made a party to it and may be invalid if it interferes with the rights of others. There may also be federal gift tax problems if the agreement is voluntary and made in a nonadvocative, nonadversarial environment.

2. SPECIAL REQUIREMENTS FOR WILL CONTEST SETTLEMENTS

Agreements can take several forms: an agreement not to contest a will or not to probate a will. If the "heir" has no right (interest) to contest, the settlement contract is void for lack of consideration. Some courts say the heir must have reasonable grounds for contest. Other courts and the preferred rule is that the heir has good faith intent to contest. Most courts say the parties in their settlement agreement may agree not to probate the will. Some courts, however, take the view that the probate court owes a duty to the testator to see that testator's will, if valid, is admitted to probate.

3. SPECIAL REQUIREMENTS FOR TRUST SETTLEMENTS

Some courts have restricted settlement agreements when trusts are involved. They might not permit a settlement if partial destruction of the trust is required to settle the controversy.

Illustration 1: T's will creates a spendthrift trust for W for life, remainder to W's adult children. T's heirs threaten to contest the will unless they receive 30% of the estate. W and the adult children agree to the settlement. A court might not let W and W's children agree to eliminate the trust as well as pay the heirs the 30% demanded. It is one thing to abate the trust to the extent necessary to settle the claim against the will, but it is quite another to destroy unnecessarily the trust with regard to that portion which could remain subject to the will. A court should approve the agreement only if it is reasonably necessary for the protection of the interests of the beneficiaries. Here the agreement could assign a portion of the beneficiaries' respective interests in the trust to the heirs. The court should then permit termination of that part of the trust which goes to the heirs, as sole beneficiary of a portion.

4. REMEDIES FOR BREACH OF SETTLEMENT AGREEMENTS

If properly executed, enforcement of the settlement agreement may take several forms when there is a breach by heir. The devisees may seek an injunction against a contest by heirs or the settlement agreement may be pleaded by the executor in bar of the contest. Under some circumstances, the devisee may be limited to a subsequent damage action against the heirs for breach of contract. Enforcement when there is a breach by the will beneficiaries has usually permitted a suit for specific performance.

5. SETTLEMENT AGREEMENTS UNDER UPC

The UPC contains both formal and informal private settlement procedures. Under the informal procedure, a written private agreement that alters the normal intestate or testate distribution pattern among all of the successors who are affected by the agreement must be followed by the personal representative subject, of course, to any fiduciary obligation. UPC § 3–912. An agreement of this nature is necessarily subject to the rights of creditors and taxing agencies. Because trustees under such an agreement are merely treated as devisees, the personal representative is not responsible for seeing to the performance of any testamentary trust. The trustee, of course, is not relieved of the duties owed to the trust beneficiaries.

The UPC also contains a formal procedure for compromising and settling controversies between persons holding the beneficial interests in a decedent's estate. UPC §§ 3–1101–02. The types of controversies that may be compromised include controversies as to:

- the admissibility of a will to formal probate;
- disputes concerning other governing instruments covering gratuitous transfers;
- construction, validity or effect of wills or other instruments; and,
- the rights or interests of any successor in the estate and to issues arising during the administration of the estate.

A compromise under this procedure is binding on all persons made parties to the procedure so long as it is approved in a formal proceeding before the Court. Unborn, unascertained, or otherwise unlocatable persons may be bound by the court order if they are virtually represented by other parties with substantially identical interests in the proceeding. *See* UPC § 1–403(2)(iii). This binding effect of an approved compromise is also applicable as against trusts or other inalienable interests.

The rights of creditors or taxing authorities who are not parties to the compromise are not impaired. The comprehensive binding effect of a formal settlement makes it a desirable settlement method where some of the successors are not competent or are unknown. The formal procedure provides the compromising parties a procedure for forcing fiduciaries concerned with the estate to execute the compromise even though the latters' approval might be against their own personal or financial interests, as employees entitled to compensation from the estate or trust. UPC § 3–1102, Comment.

C. DOCTRINE OF EQUITABLE ELECTION

1. EQUITABLE ELECTION DOCTRINE

The equitable election doctrine provides that a person cannot accept benefits accruing to him or her by a will and at the same time refuse to recognize the validity of will in other respects. BLACK'S LAW DICTIONARY. Usually two benefits are conferred by the will and a person must select one but not both. The other will go to another. The application of the doctrine is dependent on the intent of the testator. Intent may be inferred from circumstance.

Illustration 2: If A owns Blackacre, B owns Whiteacre, who takes if A's valid Will states "I give Blackacre to B and Whiteacre to C"? There is authority that B can take Blackacre only if B transfers Whiteacre to C. If competency is not a question, the will is a matter of A's intent. If A conditioned the gift of Blackacre to B on the premise that B would transfer Whiteacre to C, equity will enforce the premise if B attempts to obtain Blackacre. It would be unconscionable to let B take Blackacre unless B gives up Whiteacre because B would be unjustly enriched. B must make an equitable election.

D. REVIEW QUESTIONS

1. List the three basic types of will contracts.
2. All will contracts must be in writing. True or False?
3. What is the name for separate testaments executed by two persons and that contain more or less reciprocal provisions?
4. An inference that a contract not to revoke exists from the execution of joint and mutual wills. True or False?
5. What is the equitable election doctrine?

PART EIGHT

FUTURE INTERESTS AND PERPETUITIES

*

I

CLASSIFICATION OF ESTATES AND FUTURE INTERESTS

Analysis

- *a. The Estates in Fee Simple*
- *b. Fee Tail*
- *c. Life Estates*
- *d. Term of Years*

3. Reversionary and Nonreversionary Future Interests

- *a. Identifying Type*
- *b. Labeling Vesting Categories*
- *c. Future Possessory Estate*
- *d. Steps to Identification*
- *e. Reversionary or Nonreversionary Distinctions*

4. The Nonreversionary Future Interests–Remainders and Executory Interests

- *a. Conventional Definitions*
- *b. Differentiating Remainders from Executory Interests*
- *c. Post–Creation Changes in Classification*

D. Review Questions

A. INTRODUCTION TO ESTATES IN LAND AND FUTURE INTERESTS

1. FRAGMENTATION OF OWNERSHIP

Property law in the United States recognizes both whole and divided ownership.

a. Whole Ownership

Whole ownership is outright ownership of property and refers to ownership in fee simple absolute for land and absolute ownership for personalty. Its incidents of ownership include the right to use and exclude others from using the property and to transfer ownership of the property to others by either inter vivos transfer or testamentary devise.

b. Divided or Fragmented Ownership

Divided or Fragmented Ownership allows two or more persons to have simultaneous interests in the property as a whole. It does not mean dividing property itself into tangible segments or parcels. Fragmentation of ownership involves an abstract allocation of the incidents of ownership among the owners. The manner of allocation depends to a great extent on the form of fragmentation.

Ownership fragmentation takes three forms: (1) concurrent interests, *e.g.*, tenancy in common, joint tenancy, and tenancy by the entirety; (2) separate legal and equitable interests, *e.g.*, property held in trust; (3) sequentially ownership between present and future interests, *e.g.*, the life estate followed by the remainder estate. A future interest in property is a nonpossessory interest that might or will become possessory at some future time.

2. BASIC TERMINOLOGY

A present interest is a possessory interest or estate. It entitles the owner to possession of the property. A future interest is an interest in which the right to possession is postponed.

Illustration 1: Consider the conveyance “to A for life, remainder to B.” A has a present interest and a possessory estate in the property. B has a future interest and nonpossessory present interest. Although B’s interest has a present aspect in the sense that the interest can be transferred and attached by B’s creditors, it is not a possessory estate and thus for purposes here is called a future interest.

B. THE IMPORTANCE AND PROCESS OF CLASSIFICATION

1. CLASSIFICATION PROCESS

Classification is a process of identification, of fixing the proper label or labels to a property interest. Although only a few legal consequences turn on classification, familiarity with the terms associated with classification also aids in understanding the legal literature and communicating with others in practice.

2. HIERARCHY OF ESTATES

The hierarchy of estates is a refined, artificial structure that is a creature of historical evolution. It grew from governmental imposition of burdens on the wealthy and the wealthy's lawyers designing avoidance techniques. The result was the creation of a system of technical and almost indistinguishable distinctions. Through classification, different ways of saying the same thing were accorded different legal consequences. Form controlled over substance.

a. Quantum of Estates

Possessory estates are ordered by "quantum." In descending order of quantum, the groupings are: (1) the fee simple estates (all fee simple estates are of the same quantum), (2) the fee tail, (3) the life estate, (4) the term of years, (5) the estate from period to period, (6) the estate at will, and (7) the estate at sufferance.

b. Freehold and Nonfreehold Estates

The freehold estates are: (1) the fee simple estates, (2) the fee tail, and (3) the life estate. The nonfreehold estates are: (1) the term of years, (2) the estate from period to period, (3) the estate at will, and (4) the estate at sufferance.

c. Particular Estate

The term particular estate denotes any estate that is less than a fee simple, *e.g.,* a fee tail, a life estate, or a term of years.

3. THE IMPORTANCE OF PRESENT AND FUTURE INTERESTS

The primary importance of future interest analysis concerns trusts and the common subdivision of equitable title between income beneficiaries and corpus beneficiaries in personal property such as securities.

C. THE PROCESS OF CLASSIFICATION

1. POSSESSORY ESTATES AND FUTURE INTERESTS CLASSIFIED

Distinguishing among these estates requires an understanding of the concept of defeasance.

a. Defeasance

Defeasance means that the holder of the estate will lose that estate upon the happening of a specified event. A possessory estate that is subject to defeasance is subject to either a condition subsequent or a limitation. *See* Restatement of Property § 16 cmt. b. (1940).

b. "Condition Subsequent"

Possessory estates that are subject to a "condition subsequent" terminate by being cut short or divested upon the happening of the specified event. Language in a grant that signifies a "condition subsequent" are such words as "on condition that" or "provided that," followed by such words as "but if" or "and if." (In some grants, only the "but if" or "and if" language will appear.)

c. "Limitation"

Possessory estates that are subject to a "limitation" terminate naturally or by their own terms. Language in a grant that signifies a "limitation" are such words as "during," "until," "while," "so long as," "for so long as," or simply "for [a designated period]," followed by such words as "at," "upon," or "then." A "special" limitation subjects an estate to possible termination in addition to that normally characteristic of the estate; thus a special limitation describes an event that is not certain to happen. *See* Restatement of Property § 23 (1940).

2. POSSESSORY ESTATES

a. The Estates in Fee Simple

Although there are four fee simple estates, they can be divided into two general categories, *i.e.,* fee simple absolute and fee simple defeasible.

(1) Fee Simple Absolute. The estate in fee simple absolute is an estate in land that is not subject to termination; it is unlimited in duration. The personal property counterpart of the fee simple absolute is called absolute ownership. The fee simple absolute is not subject to any special limitations, conditions subsequent, or executory limitations. A fee simple absolute is never followed by a future interest.

Illustration 2: G conveyed land "to A and his heirs." A has a fee simple absolute; no future interest follows it. The words "and his heirs" are "words of limitation," meaning words defining the estate granted to A, not "words of purchase," meaning words granting a property interest to A's heirs.

(2) Defeasible Fee Simple: The defeasible fee simple estate terminates upon the happening of an event specified in the grant. There are three defeasible fee simple estates: (1) the fee simple determinable, (2) the fee simple subject to a condition subsequent, and (3) the fee simple subject to an executory limitation.

(a) Fee Simple Determinable: The fee simple determinable is a fee estate that is subject to a special limitation. This means that it automatically terminates or expires if the specified event happens; the terminating event is an event that is not certain to happen. The future interest following the estate in fee simple determinable is a possibility of reverter (if reversionary) or an executory interest (if nonreversionary).

Illustration 3: G conveyed land "to A and her heirs so long as A does not allow liquor to be sold on the land; upon A's allowing liquor to be sold on the land, the land reverts to me." A has a fee simple determinable. G has a possibility of reverter.

Illustration 4: G conveyed land "to A and her heirs so long as A does not allow liquor to be sold on the land; and upon A's allowing liquor to be sold on the land, the land goes to B." A has a fee simple determinable. B has an executory interest.[1]

(b) Fee Simple Subject to a Condition Subsequent. The fee simple subject to a condition subsequent is a fee estate that is subject to divestment in favor of a reversionary future interest called a right of entry (also called a power of termination). The happening of the specified event does not automatically divest the estate; rather, it empowers the grantor or his or her successor in interest to divest the estate by exercising the right of entry.

Illustration 5: G conveyed land "to A and his heirs on condition that A not allow liquor to be sold on the land, and if A allows liquor to be sold on the land, then the grantor is to have the right to re-enter and take possession." A has a fee simple subject to a condition subsequent. G has a right of entry.

(c) Fee Simple Subject to an Executory Limitation: The fee simple subject to an executory limitation is a fee estate that is subject to divestment in favor of a nonreversionary future interest called an executory interest. The happening of the specified event divests the estate.

Illustration 6: G conveyed land "to A and her heirs, but if A allows liquor to be sold on the land, the land goes to B." A has a fee simple subject to an executory limitation. B has an executory interest.

b. Fee Tail

The fee tail estate is subject to termination if and when the line of the tenant in tail's issue fails. In almost all states, the fee tail estate is abolished or altered.

Illustration 7: G conveyed land "to A and the heirs of his body." This conveyance will have different consequences in different states. The most

1. Note that the limitation regarding selling liquor applies only to A and not to A's successors in interest. Therefore, B's executory interest is valid under the Rule Against Perpetuities because it must vest or fail within A's lifetime.

likely results are that it either creates a fee simple absolute in A or that it creates a life estate in A, with a remainder in fee in A's issue.

c. Life Estates

Life estates are estates that expire naturally (by their own terms) on the death of the measuring life. Unless the life estate is measured by the life of another, the measuring life is the life tenant. Life estates are by definition defeasible estates because they are subject to a limitation. *See* RESTATEMENT OF PROPERTY § 16 cmt. b (1940). A life estate that is measured by the life of another is called a life estate *pur autre vie*.

Illustration 8: G conveyed land "to A for life." A has a life estate which ends on A's death and G has the reversion. G's reversion is indefeasibly vested.

Illustration 9: G transferred land "to A for the life of B." A predeceases B. A's will devises her entire estate to X. A has a life estate *pur autre vie*. Unlike a life estate that terminates on the life tenant's death, A can devise the remaining portion of her life estate to X. After A's death, X has a life estate *pur autre vie*—for the life of B.

The phrase "equitable life estate" is sometimes used to describe the interest of a trust beneficiary who has the right to the income from a trust for his or her lifetime.

d. Term of Years

Terms of years are estates that expire naturally (by their own terms) on the expiration of the term. Terms of years are defeasible estates because they are subject to a limitation.

Illustration 10: G transferred land "to A for 10 years." A's estate is called a "term of years."

The phrase "equitable term" is sometimes used to describe the interest of a trust beneficiary who has the right to the income from a trust for a term. Equitable terms are used most frequently in charitable lead trusts, but they are also used in trusts that give the right to the income to a family member until he or she reaches a specified age.

<u>Prematurely Defeasible Life Estates and Terms of Years</u>: Life estates and terms of years can be made prematurely defeasible, so that they might end before the expiration of the life or term, by adding a special limitation to the grant or condition subsequent.

Illustration 11: G transferred land "to A for life [for 10 years] or until A remarries." A's estate is called a "life estate subject to a special limitation" or a "determinable life estate" or [a "term of years subject to a special limitation" or a "determinable term of years."]

Illustration 12: G transferred land "to A for life, remainder to B; but if A remarries, to B immediately." A's estate is called a "life estate subject to an executory limitation" or [a "term of years subject to an executory limitation."]

Illustration 13: G transferred land "to A for life on condition that A not remarry; and if A remarries, G is to have the right to re-enter and take possession." A's estate is called a "life estate subject to a condition subsequent." or [a "term of years subject to a condition subsequent."]

3. REVERSIONARY AND NONREVERSIONARY FUTURE INTERESTS

Classifying a future interest requires identifying its type, labeling it in terms of vesting, and identifying the type of possessory estate it might or will later become.

a. Identifying Type

There are five types of future interests: (1) remainders, (2) executory interests, (3) reversions, (4) possibilities of reverter, and (5) rights of entry (also called powers of termination). Executory interests are further divided into springing and shifting executory interests.

b. Labeling Vesting Categories

There are four vesting categories: (1) indefeasibly vested, (2) vested subject to complete defeasance, (3) vested subject to open (*i.e.*, subject to partial defeasance), and (4) contingent.

c. Future Possessory Estate

When the future interest becomes possessory, the range of interests is the same as it is for interests that start out as possessory estates.

d. Steps to Identification

(1) Determine whether the future interest is reversionary or nonreversionary, (2) identify the future interest by type, and (3) classify it in terms of vesting and in terms of the type of possessory estate it might or will become.

e. Reversionary or Nonreversionary Distinctions

If a future interest is reversionary, it must be a reversion, a possibility of reverter, or a right of entry, and if a future interest is nonreversionary, it must be a remainder or an executory interest.

Reversionary Interests	*Nonreversionary Interests*
Reversion	Remainder
Possibility of reverter	Executory interest
Right of entry	

(1) Rule 1: To be reversionary, a future interest must be retained by (or created in) the transferor.

(2) Rule 2: To be nonreversionary, a future interest must be created in a transferee (someone other than the transferor).

The classification of an interest as reversionary or nonreversionary is fixed at the time of creation. A post-creation transfer of a reversionary interest to a transferee does not change the interest into a nonreversionary interest. Conversely, a post-creation transfer of a nonreversionary interest to the transferor does not change the interest into a reversionary interest. It makes no difference whether the post-creation transfer was inter vivos, testamentary, or resulted from intestate succession.

Illustration 14: G conveyed land "to A for life." Later G conveyed all his interest in the land to B. When G made the second conveyance, he no longer owned the life estate he had previously conveyed to A; G owned only a reversionary interest (a reversion in this case). Consequently, the second conveyance constitutes a conveyance of G's reversion to B. This conveyance does not change the reversion into a nonreversionary interest (a remainder). A's life estate is still followed by a reversion, but the reversion is now held by B.

4. THE NONREVERSIONARY FUTURE INTERESTS–REMAINDERS AND EXECUTORY INTERESTS

a. Conventional Definitions

If a future interest is nonreversionary, it is either a remainder or an executory interest. It cannot be a reversion, a possibility of reverter, or a right of entry.

b. Differentiating Remainders from Executory Interests

(1) Remainders are future interests created in a transferee that become possessory if at all upon the natural termination of the preceding vested estate.

The preceding vested estate must (1) have been created when the future interest was created, (2) be a possessory estate, and (3) be a "particular" estate.

(2) Executory interests are future interests created in a transferee that become possessory if at all by cutting short or divesting the preceding vested estate or interest.

The preceding vested estate or interest (1) need not have been created when the future interest was created, (2) can be a possessory estate or a future interest, and (3) can be a fee simple estate or a particular estate.

(3) Differentiation When a Possessory Estate is Followed by a Single Nonreversionary Future Interest: When a possessory estate is succeeded by a single nonreversionary future interest, the following rules apply:

(a) If the possessory estate is a fee tail, a life estate, or a term of years, the future interest is a remainder.

(b) If the possessory estate is a fee simple subject to defeasance, the future interest is an executory interest.

Illustration 15: G transferred land "to A for life, and upon A's death, the land goes to B." Or, G transferred land "to A for 10 years, and at the expiration thereof, the land goes to B." B has a remainder in both cases, not an executory interest.

Illustration 16: G transferred land "to A and her heirs on condition that A never allow liquor to be sold on the land, but if A allows liquor to be sold on the land, the land goes to B." (The disposition might omit the "on condition that" phrase, and simply say: "to A and her heirs, but if A allows liquor to be sold on the land, the land goes to B.") B has an executory interest, not a remainder.

(4) Special Case–Executory Interest Succeeds Fee Simple Determinable. In one special case, an executory interest does not "cut short" or "divest" the preceding vested estate, but takes effect on its "natural termination." Because a remainder cannot follow a fee simple estate, a fee simple must always be followed by an executory interest, even when the fee simple is subject to a special limitation.

Illustration 17: G transferred land "to A and her heirs as long as A never allows liquor to be sold on the land, and upon A's allowing liquor to be sold on the land, the land goes to B." B has an executory interest, not a remainder.

(5) Remainders and Executory Interests Differentiated When a Possessory Estate is Followed by More than One Future Interest: When a defeasible fee simple is followed by more than one nonreversionary future interest, only one of which can become possessory, all the future interests are executory interests. Because a remainder cannot follow a fee simple estate the future interests are executory interests because they cannot be anything else.

Illustration 18: G transferred land "to A and his heirs, but if A allows liquor to be sold on the land the land goes to B if B is then living, and if B is not then living the land goes to C." B and C have executory interests.

When a particular estate is followed by more than one nonreversionary future interest, only one of which can become possessory, the first future interest will always be a remainder. The other or subsequent future interests might be remainders or executory interests. In determining which they are, the following rules apply:

i. If the first future interest is a contingent (nonvested) remainder, the other future interests will also be contingent remainders.

ii. If the first future interest is a vested remainder subject to divestment, the other future interests will be executory interests.

Illustration 19: G transferred land "to A for life, remainder to B if B survives A, but if not, to C." Because B has a contingent remainder, C has a contingent remainder. For convenience, B and C's interests are called alternative contingent remainders.

Illustration 20: G transferred land "to A for life, remainder to B if B survives A, but if not, to C if C survives A, and if neither B nor C survives A, to D." Because B has a contingent remainder, C and D have contingent remainders. All three interests are alternative contingent remainders.

Illustration 21: G transferred land "to A for life, remainder to B, but if B fails to survive A, to C." Because B has a vested remainder subject to divestment, C has an executory interest.

Illustration 22: G transferred land "to A for life, remainder to B, but if B fails to survive A, to C if C survives A, and if neither B nor C survives A, to D." Because B has a vested remainder subject to divestment, C and D have executory interests.

c. Post–Creation Changes in Classification

Although reversionary future interests do not become nonreversionary by virtue of a post-creation transfer to a transferee and nonreversionary future interests do not become reversionary by virtue of a post-creation transfer to the transferor, executory interests can become remainders, contingent remainders can become vested remainders, and (if the destructibility rule is not in force in the jurisdiction or if in force does not apply for some reason) remainders can become executory interests.

Illustration 23: G transferred land "to A for life, remainder to B, but if B fails to survive A, to C." B predeceases A. At creation, B's interest is a vested remainder subject to divestment and C's interest is an executory interest. At B's death, B's vested remainder is divested and C's executory interest becomes an indefeasibly vested remainder. It is as if the disposition changes to read: "to A for life, remainder to C."

Thus although an executory interest cannot vest until it vests in possession, an executory interest can vest before becoming possessory by changing into a remainder.

Illustration 24: G transferred land "to A for life, remainder to B if B survives A, but if not, to C." B dies while A is still alive. At creation, B and C's interests are alternative contingent remainders. At B's death, her contingent remainder is defeated, G's technical reversion is divested, and C's contingent remainder becomes an indefeasibly vested remainder.

Illustration 25: G transferred land "to A for life, remainder to B if B lives to age 21." The destructibility rule has been abolished by statute in the jurisdiction. If B reaches 21 while A is still alive, B's contingent remainder becomes indefeasibly vested and G's reversion is divested. If B is younger than 21 when A dies, B's contingent remainder becomes an executory interest. G's reversion takes effect in possession upon A's death, as a fee simple subject to defeasance in favor of B if and when B later reaches 21.

D. REVIEW QUESTIONS

1. What are the three forms of ownership fragmentation?
2. Property law in the United States recognizes both whole and divided ownership. True or False?
3. What term means that the holder of the estate will lose that estate upon the happening of a specified event?
4. Name the two general categories of the four fee simple estates.
5. Name the five types of future interests.

II

CONSEQUENCES OF CLASSIFICATION

Analysis

2. *Status of the Destructibility Rule*

E. *The Rule in Shelley's Case*
   1. *Statement of the Rule in Shelley's Case*
   2. *The Present Status of the Rule in Shelley's Case*

F. *The Doctrine of Worthier Title*
   1. *Statement of the Worthier Title Doctrine*
   2. *Effect of a Worthier Title Doctrine Application*
   3. *Present Status of the Worthier Title Doctrine*
   4. *Interests Subject to the Worthier Title Doctrine*
      a. *Interests Subject to Worthier Title Doctrine*
      b. *Grantor's Heirs or Next of Kin Requirement*
   5. *Rebutting the Presumption*
      a. *Estate Planning Technique*
      b. *No Clear Expression of a Contrary Intent*

G. *Express and Implied Conditions of Survival*
   1. *Survivorship and Future Interests*
   2. *Antilapse and Future Interests*

H. *Review Questions*

A. INTRODUCTION TO CONSEQUENCES OF CLASSIFICATION

1. CURRENT CLASSIFICATION CONSEQUENCES

Although the importance of classification of future interests at common law have been widely abolished, some rules continue to turn on classification. There are basically two types of consequences.

- Those directly linked to a certain classification such as the inalienability of contingent future interests at common law. Inalienability flows directly and automatically from contingency where this rule is still followed.
- Those consequences of classification that are only possible consequences. The interest's classification makes it subject to a certain rule. Contingent future interests, for example, are subject to the common law Rule Against Perpetuities but do not necessarily violate it. Contingent remainders are subject to the common law destructibility rule but are not necessarily destroyed.

B. ALIENABILITY OF FUTURE INTERESTS

1. TWO DIVISIONS OF ALIENATION OF FUTURE INTERESTS

Alienation of future interests must be divided into transferability at death (by intestacy or will) and transferability by inter vivos transfer.

2. TRANSFERABILITY AT DEATH BY INTESTACY OR WILL

a. Descendability

All future interests are "descendible" which means they are capable of passing by intestacy. All States hold that reversions, remainders, and executory interests descend according to the same rules as those applicable to possessory estates. With one exception, all hold that possibilities of reverter and rights of entry also descend according to the same rules as those applicable to possessory estates.

b. Devisability

Reversions, remainders, and executory interests are devisable by will. Generally, possibilities of reverter and rights of entry are devisable. In some states, statutes expressly so provide. A few courts and statutes hold to the contrary. *See* SIMES & SMITH ON FUTURE INTERESTS § 1903.

c. Descendability and Devisability of Contingent or Defeasible Interests

A future interest that is either contingent or vested subject to defeasance is descendible and devisable only if the condition precedent or subsequent has not been extinguished by the beneficiary's death.

Illustration 1: G transferred land "to A for life, remainder to B, but if B fails to survive A, to C." C dies, then B, then A. C's executory interest is contingent on B's not surviving A, but not on C surviving A. Consequently, C's executory interest was not extinguished by his death before A, and it is descendible and devisable. B's vested remainder subject to divestment was, however, extinguished by her death before A, and so B's remainder is neither descendible nor devisable.

3. VOLUNTARY ALIENABILITY DURING LIFE

At common law, reversions and vested remainders, including those subject to divestment, are alienable inter vivos. Contingent remainders and executory interests are inalienable. Contingent remainders were at first likened to an expectancy; thus they were treated as a possibility of an interest arising in the future, not as an interest. Lifetime transferability of such a possibility would violate the rules against champerty and maintenance, and was not permitted. Executory interests were regarded as sufficiently analogous to contingent remainders to warrant the same treatment.

4. TRANSFERABILITY OF CONTINGENT REMAINDERS AND EXECUTORY INTERESTS

The common law recognizes two ways of transferring contingent remainders and executory interests: equity recognizes another.[1]

a. Contract to Convey

A purported transfer, if for adequate consideration, is treated in equity as a contract to convey. The contract becomes specifically enforceable if and when all conditions precedent are satisfied, so as to give the transferor an alienable interest.

b. Estoppel By Deed

At law, even without adequate consideration, the title of a purported transfer made by a deed that contained a covenant of warranty inured by estoppel to the grantee if and when the conditions precedent are later satisfied.

c. Release

At law, a release was enforceable that released an inalienable future interest to the holder of the interest which would be defeated by the satisfaction of the conditions precedent attached to the released interest.

1. These three methods of transferring inalienable future interests are also available for transferring non-existent interests such as expectancies.

Illustration 2: G transferred land "to A for life, remainder to B, but if B fails to survive A, to C." A release of C's executory interest to B would be enforceable at law.

Releases need not be contained in a warranty deed, nor made for consideration. Any instrument capable of transferring an interest in land would probably be sufficient to release a future interest unless the instrument had to be under seal.

d. Current Transferability

Either by statute or by common law decision, the vast majority of states hold that all contingent future interests are alienable. About seven states still follow the common law rule of inalienability. In these states, the above mentioned exceptions are recognized. Thus the inalienability rule followed in these few states holds that a purported transfer for inadequate consideration by quit claim deed to someone other than a person in whose favor the interest could have been released is ineffective. *See* RESTATEMENT OF PROPERTY § 157 cmt. w (1940).

By statute or decision, a small number of states hold remainders and executory interests that are contingent as to person (interests created in unborn or unascertained persons) are still inalienable, but those that are contingent as to event are alienable.

Illustration 3: G transferred land "to A for life, remainder to B if B survives A; if not, to B's heirs." B's remainder is contingent as to event, and under this rule would be alienable. The remainder in B's heirs, however, is contingent as to person and would be inalienable.

e. Understanding Alienability

A future interest that is contingent as to person is not truly alienable. Even though a guardian ad litem may represent the interests of the unborn or unascertained persons in litigation, courts seldom authorize this fiduciary to join in a transfer of a property interest on behalf of these persons.

Illustration 4: G transferred land "to A for life, remainder to A's children." If A is childless, no one is authorized to transfer the remainder interest on behalf of A's unborn children. If A has living children, they can transfer their interests. But, no one is authorized to transfer the executory interests on behalf of A's unborn children. The most that A's living children can transfer is a remainder that is subject to open (partial divestment).

Thus alienability of future interests that are contingent as to persons are alienable only in regard to unascertained persons, not in regard to unborn persons.

Illustration 5: G transferred land "to *A* for life, remainder to *B*'s heirs." *B* is alive, but if *B* died now, *B*'s sole heir would be *B*'s child, *C*.

Where contingent-as-to-person future interests are alienable, C would have a transferable interest in the subject matter of *G*'s disposition. *See* AM. L. PROP. § 4.67 n. 10 & accompanying text. But C's transferee receives an interest that is contingent on C's actually qualifying as B's heir. *See* RESTATEMENT OF PROPERTY § 162 cmt. c (1936). Thus, the remainder interest that follows A's life estate is not truly alienable even though C can transfer C's interest in the disposition.

5. INTER VIVOS ALIENABILITY OF POSSIBILITIES OF REVERTER AND RIGHTS OF ENTRY

The courts and statutes are divided on the alienability of possibilities of reverter. Rights of entry are inalienable inter vivos, however, in the absence of statute. Although several states hold that an attempt to convey a right of entry inter vivos extinguishes the right of entry, other states have repudiated and abolished this rule by statute.

6. CREDITORS' RIGHTS IN FUTURE INTERESTS

Generally, if the future interest is voluntarily alienable, it is also subject to the claims of creditors. Remainders and reversions that are indefeasibly vested or vested subject to defeasance are automatically available to creditors in the satisfaction of their claims.

In states in which contingent remainders and executory interests are voluntarily alienable, courts hold such interests to be subject to creditors's claims. *See, e.g.*, *Everson v. Everson*, 431 A.2d 889 (Pa. 1981); RESTATEMENT OF PROPERTY §§ 166, 167 (1936, 1948). A few states hold that contingent remainders and executory interests are not subject to the claims of creditors.

The "Sacrificial" Sale Problem: Because of the vast difference between the sale price of a future interest that is subject to conditions and the potential value to the debtor if the interest vests or becomes possessory, the RESTATEMENT OF PROPERTY Sections 166 and 167 take the position that although legal future interests are subject to creditors, equitable future interests are not. The RESTATEMENT (SECOND) OF TRUSTS Section 162 states:

> [I]f the interest of the beneficiary of a trust is so indefinite or contingent that it cannot be sold with fairness to both the creditors and the beneficiary, it cannot be reached by his creditors.

Rather than deny access, a court might refuse to order an immediate judgment sale of such an interest, but impose a lien on the future interest until the contingencies are satisfied, if ever.

Illustration 6: G transferred property to a trustee, in trust, to pay the corpus and accumulated income to A if he lives to age 25; if not, to B upon A's death under 25. A's creditors sought by creditors' bill to reach A's contingent remainder in the corpus and accumulated income. A court might impose a lien on A's interest in the trust, and order the trustee to satisfy the creditor's judgment, if A should reach 25, out of the trust fund before paying over the remaining corpus to A.

Creditors' Rights Against the Estate of a Deceased Debtor: Although authority is limited, when the owner of a future interest dies, creditors of the estate have the same rights as they would have if the decedent were alive.

Creditors' Rights Under the Federal Bankruptcy Law: The Bankruptcy Reform Act of 1978 treats "all legal or equitable [property] interests" owned by the debtor as part of the bankrupt's estate, "notwithstanding any provision in ... applicable nonbankruptcy law ... that restricts ... transfer of such interest by the debtor...." 11 U.S.C.A. § 541. Thus creditors of a bankrupt should be able to seek claims from all types of future interests, including those that are immune from the claims of creditors under state law.

C. SUMMARY COMPARISON OF THREE FUTURE INTEREST RULES

A table comparing the three feudally-based rules provides a preliminary review of their main points prior to individual explanation:

Destructibility Rule	Rule in Shelley's Case	Inter Vivos Worthier Title
A legal contingent remainder in land is destroyed if it has not vested by the time of the termination of the preceding freehold estate	A remainder in land that is purportedly created in the life tenant's heirs or the heirs of the life tenant's body, and that is of the same quality as that of the life estate, is held by the life tenant	When a transferor, by an inter vivos conveyance, purports to create a future interest in the transferor's own heirs, the transferor is presumed to intend to retain a reversionary interest
Rule of law	Rule of law	Rule of construction by majority view
Merger causes destructibility and if it takes place, precedes the application of the Rule	Merger usually takes place and applies after the operation of the Rule, not before	Merger is not relevant
Inter vivos and testamentary transfers	Inter vivos and testamentary transfers	Inter vivos transfers only
Only to land	Only to land	Land and personalty
Applicable only to remainders	Applicable only to remainders	Applicable to remainders and executory interests
Applicable only to legal contingent remainders	Applicable to legal and equitable remainders, but the remainder and the preceding estate must be of the same quality	Applicable to legal and equitable legal future interests; can be of different quality from prior estate
Identity of the remainder person irrelevant so long as remainder is contingent (preceding estate must be a freehold)	Remainder must purportedly be created in the heirs or heirs of the body of the ancestor who is given the preceding freehold estate	Remainder must purportedly be created in the heirs of the transferor if land, the next of kin of the transferor if personalty

Destructibility Rule	Rule in Shelley's Case	Inter Vivos Worthier Title
Abolished in well over half the states. Statutory abolition is commonly not retroactive; crucial date is when the prior freehold terminated.	Abolished in over three-fourths or more of the states. Statutory abolition is commonly not retroactive; crucial date is effective date of deed or death of testator.	Specifically abolished in only a few states. Statutory abolition is commonly not retroactive. Crucial date is effective date of deed.

D. THE DESTRUCTIBILITY OF CONTINGENT REMAINDERS

1. STATEMENT OF THE DESTRUCTIBILITY RULE

The common law destructibility rule provides: A legal contingent remainder in land is destroyed if it does not vest by the time the preceding freehold estate terminates. The destructibility rule is a rule of law, not a rule of construction, which means that it is intent-defeating rather than intent-effecting.

At early common law, no naked future interest could be created that would take effect in possession in the future, and none could be created that would divest a fee simple interest. These rules provided the technical explanation for the destructibility rule: A remainder needed a freehold estate to "support" it. When the supporting freehold estate terminated, there was no problem if the remainder was then entitled to become possessory; seisin passed to the remainder beneficiary from the life tenant. But if the remainder was not yet entitled to become possessory, *i.e.,* if, for example, a condition precedent remained unsatisfied, seisin passed to the reversioner whose interest, always regarded as vested thereupon became possessory. Lacking support, the remainder could no longer exist as a future interest, and so it was destroyed.

At its best, the rule promotes alienability of land. At its worst, the rule constitutes a hyper-technical rule that frustrates the transferor's intent.

2. STATUS OF THE DESTRUCTIBILITY RULE

In a majority of states the destructibility rule has been abolished, in whole or in part, by statute or court decision. In the remaining states, the existence of the rule is unclear. The RESTATEMENT OF PROPERTY Section 240 takes the position that the rule is not part of our common law. A few courts have on their own openly rejected the rule.

E. THE RULE IN SHELLEY'S CASE

1. STATEMENT OF THE RULE IN SHELLEY'S CASE

The Rule in Shelley's Case provides:

> A remainder interest in land in favor of the life tenant's heirs or the heirs of the life tenant's body is held by the life tenant if the remainder is of the same quality as that of the life estate.

The Rule in Shelley's Case is a rule of law, not a rule of construction. Thus, the rule is intent-defeating rather than intent-effecting. The name of the rule derives from the case of *Wolfe v. Shelley*, 76 Eng. Rep. 206 (K.B. 1581). Because of limitations on the extent to which the Rule in Shelley's case applies, classification of the future interest by type is the crucial first step. The Rule in Shelley's Case is one of the possible consequences of classification, not one of its automatic consequences.

Illustration 7: G transferred land "to A for life, remainder to A's heirs." Shelley's Rule applies to give the remainder intended for A's heirs to A. The doctrine of merger says that, once in the hands of a single individual, a life estate and a vested remainder merge to become a fee simple absolute.

Illustration 8: G transferred land "to A for life, remainder to the heirs of A's body." Shelley's Rule applies to give the remainder intended for the heirs of A's body to A. The doctrine of merger says that, once in the hands of a single individual, a life estate and a vested remainder in tail merge to become a fee tail. In states that have a fee tail statute, A's fee tail would then be changed into whatever estate or interests the statute directs.

2. THE PRESENT STATUS OF THE RULE IN SHELLEY'S CASE

The Rule apparently continues in force only in a small number of states. The vast majority of states and the District of Columbia, have abolished the Rule by statute. Section 30.1(3) of the RESTATEMENT (SECOND) OF PROPERTY states that the Rule "should be abolished by judicial decision to the extent it has not been abolished prospectively by statute." Because many of the repealing statutes are not retroactive and suffer from interpretive ambiguities, residual application continues. Of course, the Rule is potentially applicable in the few states that have not repealed it.

F. THE DOCTRINE OF WORTHIER TITLE

1. STATEMENT OF THE WORTHIER TITLE DOCTRINE

The general statement of the Doctrine of Worthier Title provides:

> When a transferor, by an inter vivos conveyance, purports to create a future interest in the transferor's heirs, the transferor is presumed to intend to retain the future interest rather than confer it on his or her heirs.

The Doctrine is a rule of construction, not a rule of law, which implies that it is intent-effecting. It will yield to a contrary intention in individual cases. As a rule of construction, it applies to both land and personalty. This is very important, because most modern future interests are created in trusts of personal property.

Illustration 9: G conveys real property "to A for life, then to my heirs." If the Worthier Title Doctrine applies and the presumption is not rebutted, the grantor owns the reversionary interest.

Although the reversionary interest usually is a reversion, the grantor's reversionary interest can be a possibility of reverter because the Worthier Title Doctrine applies to executory interests as well as remainders, and because the prior estate can be a defeasible fee simple.

Illustration 10: G conveys land "to A and his heirs so long as A never allows liquor to be sold on the land, and upon A's allowing liquor to be sold on the land, the land goes to my (G's) heirs." The executory interest purportedly granted G's heirs presumptively becomes a possibility of reverter in G.

2. EFFECT OF A WORTHIER TITLE DOCTRINE APPLICATION

Under the Worthier Title Doctrine, the grantor owns the reversionary interest during grantor's lifetime; consequently, the grantor's heirs-apparent have no interest, only an expectancy. Accordingly, the grantor (not the grantor's heirs-apparent) has an alienable interest, and the grantor's creditors (not the creditors of any of the grantor's heirs-apparent) can subject the reversionary interest to the payment of their claims. Further, if the grantor dies testate, the interest passes to the grantor's devisees (usually under the grantor's residuary clause). If grantor dies intestate, the interest passes to the grantor's heirs.

Trust Termination: The Worthier Title Doctrine enables the grantor of an inter vivos trust to revoke the trust and get the property back even when the grantor did not retain a power to revoke in the trust instrument. Under trust law, a trust can be terminated prematurely, and the trust property distributed to the beneficiaries, if the grantor and all possible beneficiaries join in a petition so requesting. *See* RESTATEMENT (SECOND) OF TRUSTS § 338.

Illustration 11: G conveyed property to a trustee, in trust, directing the trustee to pay the income to G for life, and on G's death to pay the corpus of the trust to G's heirs. The trust instrument did not empower G to revoke the trust. Some time after the trust was created, G changes her or his mind and wants the trust property returned. G's child A is at that time G's heir-apparent.

> *Answer If No Worthier Title:* If Worthier Title is not applicable, G's trust created a remainder in G's heirs, and the trust cannot be terminated. Even if A joins in G's petition, A does not own the full remainder interest. Consequently, G and A are not the only possible beneficiaries of the trust. Because G's actual heirs are as yet unascertained, and potentially include persons as yet unborn, there is no way to obtain the consent of all possible beneficiaries of the trust. *See*, 6.V.C.1 *supra*.

Answer If Worthier Title Applicable: If Worthier Title is applicable, G can terminate the trust. G is the sole beneficiary, owning both the income interest for life and the reversion that follows it. *See, supra,* 6.II.C.5.

3. PRESENT STATUS OF THE WORTHIER TITLE DOCTRINE

Although authority is sparse, the inter vivos branch of the Doctrine of Worthier Title is potentially part of the jurisprudence of most jurisdictions as a rule of construction. *See* RESTATEMENT (SECOND) OF PROPERTY § 30.2, Reporter's Note 3. In a few jurisdictions, older cases exist applying the inter vivos branch as a rule of law. *See id.*, Reporter's Note 4. Whether these decisions would be followed today is problematical.

Over twenty percent of the states abolished the Doctrine by statute or by judicial decision. The UPC also abrogates the Doctrine. UPC § 2–710.

Federal Estate Tax Consequences: Application of the Worthier Title Doctrine can cause unexpected estate tax consequences. First, if the grantor's reversion is not divested upon the grantor's death, its value is includable in grantor's gross estate under I.R.C. Section 2033. Secondly, even if the reversion is divested upon the grantor's death, the Doctrine might bring into grantor's gross estate the value of the interest of a transferee who can obtain personal possession or enjoyment of the property only by surviving the grantor; this amount could equal the value of the entire corpus. This would arise under I.R.C. Section 2037 when the value of the reversion immediately before the grantor's death exceeds 5 per cent of the value of the corpus if, in addition, certain other requirements are met. Of course, in many of the cases in which the Doctrine of Worthier Title has been applied the value of the entire corpus would be includable anyway under I.R.C. Section 2036, because the grantor retained an income interest for life. *See generally* Stanley M. Johanson, *Reversions, Remainders, and the Doctrine of Worthier Title*, 45 TEX. L. REV. 1, 16–27 (1966).

4. INTERESTS SUBJECT TO THE WORTHIER TITLE DOCTRINE

a. Interests Subject to Worthier Title Doctrine

The Doctrine of Worthier Title as a rule of construction applies to all manner of future interests, remainders and executory interests in land or personalty. The Doctrine also applies to equitable as well as legal interests. There is no requirement that the preceding interest and the future interest be of the same quality. Nor is there a requirement that the preceding interest be a freehold. Commonly, the preceding interest is a life estate, but it can be a term of years, a fee tail, or a defeasible fee simple.

b. Grantor's Heirs or Next of Kin Requirement

The Worthier Title Doctrine applies only if the future interest purportedly created is in those persons who would succeed by intestate succession to the grantor's property if the grantor died intestate, *i.e.,* the grantor's actual heirs with respect to land; the grantor's next of kin (sometimes called "distributees") with respect to personal property.

The definite line of succession concept is the exclusive criterion for determining whether the future interest gives rise to the Worthier Title presumption. If the heirs are to be determined at any time other than at the grantor's death, it is usually held that the presumption does not arise because the intended takers are not those who would take on intestacy.

A future interest in the grantor's "children" or "descendants" does not trigger the Worthier Title Doctrine, regardless of whether the grantor's children or descendants actually turn out to be his or her heirs at death.

5. REBUTTING THE PRESUMPTION

The perplexity of the presumptions is that to rebut it, it must be established that the grantor really meant what he or she clearly said: "then to my heirs."

a. Estate Planning Technique

To avoid litigation, and to rebut the presumption, attorneys, who draft trusts for clients and who create future interests in the heirs of the grantor, should expressly add to the term "heirs" a phrase such as "such persons to take as purchasers, my intention being to create a remainder interest in my heirs at law; I do not intend to retain a reversion in myself."

b. No Clear Expression of a Contrary Intent

Generally, the presumption can be rebutted with extrinsic evidence but the result in a given case can be quite unpredictable.

Certain terms of the conveyance can rebut the presumption. The presumption is usually rebutted if the grantor reserves a power of appointment over the future interest, so that the future interest created in the grantor's heirs is in the form of a gift-in-default of appointment. The retention of the power is inconsistent with a reversion. If grantor had a reversion, he or she would not have needed a power of appointment.

If the gift to the heirs is a second or third priority, courts have found that grantor intended what was said, *i.e.*, a remainder or executory interest is intended.

Beyond these points, unique factors relevant to the individual cases have rebutted the presumption, but many of the cases are difficult and probably impossible to reconcile.

G. EXPRESS AND IMPLIED CONDITIONS OF SURVIVAL

1. SURVIVORSHIP AND FUTURE INTERESTS

The survivorship of the life interest is not a problem. If one is not alive or does not survive the creation of the trust or the interest in trust, the life beneficiary does not take from the trust. Survivorship is most often a problem of the remainder beneficiaries because their interests do not mature in possession or enjoyment until the death of those who hold the life interests. The question of survivorship arises after the death of the transferor or the date of creation of the trust when the life interest or interests end. Must the remainder beneficiaries survive the time of distribution or merely the time of creation? Courts have had numerous problems with this question.

If the transferor clearly indicates that survivorship to the date of distribution is or is not required, the expressed intent will be obeyed. The problem arises when intent is not clearly expressed. What is the default rule? The general common law rule holds that survivorship to date of distribution is not presumed: that is if the remainder beneficiary died between date of creation and date of distribution, the interest passes to that beneficiary's estate for distribution according to the beneficiary's will or by intestacy if no will. This construction requires reopening of estates and the consequential complexities.

Illustration 13: At common law in a gift "to A for life, remainder to B" or "to A for life, remainder to A's children," neither B nor A's children had to survive A to take the remainder interest.

But at common law, a presumption of survivorship to the distribution date is not applied and the future interest is transmissible only with regard to remainder interests to named individuals or to single-generation classes. The common law does not give a predeceased beneficiary a transmissible future interest for remainder interests to multiple-generation classes, *e.g.* "remainder to A's issue." The common law subjects the future interest to a multiple-generation class to an implied requirement of survival to the distribution date even when the language creating the future interest does not expressly require the beneficiaries to survive to that date.

UPC Provisions: The UPC adopts a new rule of construction concerning the survivorship requirement for future interests in trust. UPC § 2–707. It reverses the presumption and provides that there is an implied requirement of survivorship to the date of distribution for future interests held in trust. UPC § 2–707(b). In addition, the survivorship requirement is extended to 120 hours after the time of distribution. UPC § 2–702.

Illustration 14: A simple trust provides "to T in trust for A for life, remainder to B." Under the UPC, B must survive A's death, the date of distribution, by 120 hours in order for B to take the remainder interest.

The new presumption is only applicable to future interests in trust and therefore does not apply to nonequitable interests such as "to A for life, remainder to B." UPC § 2–707, cmt. The common law rule would continue to apply in those cases. Despite the limitation, the new rule will apply to most future interests created today because of the dominance of the trust device as an estate planning tool. One of the arguments for the nonsurvivorship rule is the desire to permit free alienation of property as soon as possible. If persons who hold remainders do not have to survive anyone to take, the interest is more readily transferrable in comparison with a contingent remainder dependent on survivorship to an unknown date. Survivorship contingencies in regard to trust interests are not barriers to property transfer because the trustee may transfer the property of the trust during its administration.

If beneficiaries fail to survive the date of distribution and the antilapse presumption is unavailable, the UPC specifies how the lapse will be treated. If the there is a residue devise in transferor's will, the trust corpus passes to those beneficiaries. If no residue exists or the residue is in trust and its remainder beneficiaries fail to survive the date of distribution, the trust corpus passes in intestacy. The 1993 Technical Amendments added that for future interests created by the exercise of a power of appointment, the lapsed property interest passes to the donor's takers in default clause, if any, which is treated as creating a future interest in trust. UPC § 2–707(e)(1). If still no takers then, the lapsed interest passes as an ordinary future interests except the transferor means the donor of a nongeneral power and the donee of a general power. UPC § 2–707(e)(2).

2. ANTILAPSE AND FUTURE INTERESTS

The presumption that survivorship is necessary may cause interests to fail and if the nonsurviving beneficiary cannot take, might cut off the beneficiary's stock. The problem of forfeiture served in part as the reasoning behind the common law presumption against a survivorship requirement. Unfortunately, the common law remedy of passing the remainder interest through the nonsurviving beneficiary's estate did not depend upon the existence of descendants surviving the beneficiary. The UPC resolves the forfeiture problem by providing an "antilapse" presumption in favor of nonsurviving beneficiary's descendants.

UPC Provisions: The UPC provides that if a remainder beneficiary fails to survive the date of distribution, a substitute gift arises for the beneficiary's descendants, if any survive. UPC § 2–707. This is an "antilapse" rule for future interests in trust. It protects descendants of all remainder beneficiaries regardless of their relationship to the transferor. *See* UPC § 2–603. One does not have to be a grandparent or descendant of a grandparent to be entitled to the presumption of the substitute gift. It applies to remainders to specific individuals and to remainders left to classes of persons who are all in a single generation. Examples of single generation class gifts include gifts to "children," "grandchildren," "siblings," and "nephews and nieces." It does not apply to multiple-generation class gifts that inherently possess a nonlapsing affect because representation is allowed for descendants of predeceased ancestors in the class. Examples of such class gifts include gifts to "descendants," "issue," "heirs" and "next of kin." In a sense, the UPC converts all single generation class gifts in remainder to multiple generation gifts in remainder. It applies to both irrevocable inter vivos trusts and trusts that are created at death.

The antilapse protection is merely a rule of construction subject to revision by the transferor. Similar to the rule as applied to decedent's estates, a mere survivorship requirement in the instrument will not rebut the presumption. The common law rule of lapse and the UPC's modification to it are discussed previously. *See* Part 3.V.D.

H. REVIEW QUESTIONS

1. What are the three methods of transferring inalienable future interests?
2. What is the common law rule of inalienablity?
3. What rule states that a legal contingent remainder in law is destroyed if it has not vested by the time of the termination of the preceding freehold estate?
4. What is the rule in Shelley's Case?
5. What is the Worthier Title doctrine?

*

III

CLASS GIFTS

Analysis

A. DEFINITION OF A CLASS GIFT

1. WHAT IS A CLASS GIFT?

A class gift is a gift of property to a group of persons identified by a group label, such as "children," "grandchildren," "issue," "descendants," "brothers," "sisters," "nieces," "nephews," or "first cousins." Not all gifts to a group of persons are class gifts, however.

2. SUBJECT TO FLUCTUATION

The distinguishing feature of a class gift is the ability of the group to fluctuate in number. Fluctuations in number can come about through an increase in the number of takers (caused by births or adoptions), and/or through a decrease in the number of takers (caused by deaths). *See* RESTATEMENT OF PROPERTY § 279. A gift to a static group is a not a class gift; it is a series of separate gifts of a fractional share of the property to each member of the original group.

Generally speaking, then, the following rules of thumb determine whether a gift is or is not a class gift:

- A gift is likely a class gift if the group members are only identified by a group label, *e.g.*, "my children".
- A gift is likely not a class gift, although the takers are identified by a group label, if the group members are also identified by name *e.g.*, "to my children, A, B, and C" or by number *e.g.*, "to my three children" or by both name and number *e.g.*, "to my three children, A, B, and C." Because gifts like these do not allow for fluctuation in number, they are gifts of a fixed fraction to each of the designated individuals. In this case, the gift is of one-third to A, of one-third to B, and of one-third to C.

Illustration 1: G devised land "to my children in equal shares." When the will was executed, G had three children (A, B, and C). A predeceased G, but B and C survived her. Because G's will created a class gift, B and C each take an undivided one-half interest in the devised land, probably as tenants in common. If after G's death, B dies survived by C, B's one-half interest would not be divested in favor of C.

Illustration 2: G devised land "to my three children, A, B, and C in equal shares." When the will was executed, G had three children (A, B, and C). A predeceased G, but B and C survived her. Because G's will did not create a class gift, B and C each take an undivided one-third interest in the devised land, probably as tenants in common. A's lost one-third share would not be added to the shares of B and C; their shares remain constant. A's lost one-third share would goes to G's residuary devisees or, in the unlikely event that there was no residuary clause, to G's heirs by intestate succession.

Although these rules are merely presumptions that can be rebutted by a contrary intent "found from additional language or circumstances," the presumptions are seldom rebutted. *See* Restatement of Property § 280.

3. FLUCTUATION IN NUMBER LIMITED

The ability to fluctuate in number does not continue forever. Births, adoptions, or deaths can cause fluctuations only if they occur within a finite period of time. As a general proposition, once the time of possession has arrived, fluctuation comes to an end.

The ability of a given class gift to increase might expire before its ability to decrease expires, and vice versa. Indeed, some class gifts might never be able to increase, only decrease, and vice versa. The point is that the time limit on the increase feature and the one on the decrease feature must be analyzed separately in each case. Identifying these time limits is a crucial preliminary step toward determining the validity of a class gift under the common law Rule Against Perpetuities. *See, infra,* 7.IV.D.

4. DECREASE IN CLASS MEMBERSHIP

A class is subject to decrease if the gift is subject to a requirement of survival. Unless a specific provision is explicitly added to the dispositive language (such as "any class member who enrolls in law school loses his or her share"), classes do not decrease after the time to which survival is required. The prior, but not subsequent, death of a person otherwise entitled to share in the class gift property causes a decrease in the class.

The deceased class member's lost share is added to the shares of those other members of the class who do become entitled to participate. This is the part that is unique to class gifts. They inherently include a built-in or implicit gift over to the other members of the class.

Immediate Testamentary Class Gifts: If a class gift is an immediate testamentary gift in fee simple absolute, it is subject to decrease between the time of the execution of the will and of the testator's death. *See* Restatement of Property § 279 cmt. d. Once the testator has died, the ability to decrease comes to an end.

Future Interest Class Gifts: If the class gift is a future interest rather than an immediate one in fee simple absolute, courts have held that the ability to decrease does not continue beyond the testator's death. This analysis is based on the Common Law rule that a future interest is not subject to a condition of survival of the life tenant unless one is expressly imposed.

This rule may be changed by statute. UPC Section 2–707, for example, presumptively makes all future interests *in trust* subject to a condition precedent of survival and provides that the deceased person's surviving descendants take the share that the deceased person would have taken had he or she survived.

Illustration 3: G devised land "to A for life, remainder to A's children." G was survived by A and by A's three children, X, Y, and Z. Z died during A's lifetime, but X and Y survived A. The class (consisting of X, Y, and Z as of G's death) is not allowed to decrease beyond G's death. The reason is that no express condition of survival was attached to the children's remainder interest. Consequently, upon A's death, X, Y, and Z (or Z's successor in interest) each take an undivided one-third possessory estate in the devised land in fee simple absolute.

Under the UPC provision had *G*'s devise been in trust, *Z*'s one-third share would be divided among *Z*'s descendants who survived *A*, and would only go to *X* and *Y* if *Z* left no such descendants.

If, on the other hand, G's will had expressly imposed a condition of survival, *e.g.*, "to A for life, remainder to A's children who survive A," then the class would have continued to be subject to decrease beyond G's death. Z therefore would have dropped out of the class. Z's lost one-third share would have been added to the shares of X and Y. Upon A's death, X and Y would each have taken an undivided one-half possessory estate in the devised land in fee simple absolute. Had *G*'s devise been in trust, UPC Section 2–707 provides that *Z*'s one-third share would be divided among *Z*'s descendants who survived *A*, and would only go to *X* and *Y* if *Z* left no such descendants.

The ability to decrease in size comes to an end on A's death. If X died after A's death survived by Y, X's one-half interest would not have been divested in favor of Y.

5. INCREASE IN CLASS MEMBERSHIP

Class gifts also have the ability for takers to increase in number. Each time a new entrant joins a class, the shares of the existing class members are reduced.

Illustration 4: G devised land "to my children." When the will was executed, G had two children (A and B). Subsequently, G had a third child (C). G was survived by A, B, and C. No children were in gestation at G's death. Because G's will created a class gift, A, B, and C each take an undivided one-third interest in the devised land.

If, on the other hand, G's will had created individual gifts, *e.g.,* the dispositive language had been "to my two children, A and B," the result would have been different. The shares of A and B would not have been decreased to one-third each by C's birth and survival of G. The shares of A and B would have remained constant at one-half each. Not being a class gift, the devise would not have been subject to increase, and C would not have been entitled to share in the devised land.

B. CLASS CLOSING

1. SUBJECT TO OPEN

A class can increase (the class is "subject to open") as long as new entrants can join the class. The possibility of new entrants is cut off or as it is described, the class "closes" to further increase, at the earlier of two events: (1) the physiological or natural closing of the class; or (2) the artificial or premature closing of the class brought about by application of the so-called "rule of convenience".

2. PHYSIOLOGICAL CLOSING

The physiological closing of a class occurs when the possibility of births (or, if adopted members are within the class description, adoptions) becomes extinct.

A class gift created in favor of the testator's children physiologically closed when the testator died. A class gift created in favor of transferor's grandchildren would physiologically close when the transferor's last surviving child dies.

3. ARTIFICIAL OR PREMATURE CLOSING OF A CLASS

Under the "rule of convenience," a class may close artificially or prematurely. Once a class is closed by the rule of convenience, new entrants are cut off. Subsequently conceived or adopted persons cannot join the class even though they otherwise fit the class label. New entrants can join a class, therefore, only if they are conceived or adopted while the class is still open.

Although the rule of convenience is a rule of construction rather than a rule of law and yields to a contrary intent, in practice a contrary intent can seldom be shown. Thus, the results dictated by the rule of convenience typically prevail. The ensuing discussion assumes that the rule of convenience has not been rebutted.

4. THE RULE OF CONVENIENCE

A class is closed under the rule of convenience when the property must be distributed. The justification for this is that although the basic intent of the transferor is to keep the class open until it closes physiologically, the "inconveniences" that would arise from keeping the class open beyond the time of distribution would cause most transferors to prefer to close the class prematurely or artificially in order to avoid those inconveniences. Keeping a class open beyond the time of distribution would "inconvenience" the distributees by causing them to receive a defeasible possessory estate, not an absolute estate. A possessory estate that is defeasible is less marketable and, if personalty, requires some device such as the posting of security to protect the interests of unborn (or unadopted) class members.

The rule of convenience comes into play only when the class did not close physiologically by the time of distribution. If the parent is still living at the time of distribution, the rule of convenience is applied.

a. Immediate Class Gifts

When at least one member of the class is in existence, an immediate class gift closes at the date the gift becomes effective, and a class gift taking effect in possession at the termination of a life estate closes at the death of the life tenant.

Illustration 5: G devised land "to my grandchildren." When G executed her will, her only son A had a child (X). Subsequently, but before G's death, A had a second child (Y). G was survived by her son A and by her two grandchildren, X and Y. No grandchildren were in gestation at G's death.

Answer: Under the rule of convenience, the class remains open until G's death but closes when G died even though A is still alive and therefore is deemed to be capable of having more children. X and Y each take an undivided estate in one-half of the devised land in fee simple absolute. In other words, their estates are not subject to partial divestment in favor of any later born (or later adopted) child of A.

An immediate class gift by will does not close at the testator's death if at that testator's death there are no class members "in being." In this situation the class remains open until it closes physiologically.

Illustration 6: G devised land "to my grandchildren." At G's death, G's daughter A was still alive, but A had no living children and she was not pregnant.

Answer: In this case, the rule of convenience does not close the class at G's death. Rather, the class remains open until the death of A. All after-born grandchildren, if any, are entitled to participate. The only feasible alternatives to keeping the class open until A dies would be to nullify the class gift entirely or to allow A's first born child to have the whole property in fee simple absolute. It is thought that few testators would desire either of these results, and so the rule of convenience holds the class open until it closes physiologically.

b. Postponed Class Gifts

For postponed class gifts, the rule of convenience closes the class when a distribution of the property must be made. When a postponed class gift is preceded by a life estate, the general rule is that the class closes on the life tenant's death.

Illustration 7: G devised land "to A for life, remainder to B's children." G was survived by A, B, and B's child (X). B had a second child (Y) during A's lifetime. B survived A. B had a third child (Z) after A's death.

Answer: The class continues to be subject to increase beyond G's death and during A's lifetime. It closes on A's death even though B is still alive and is deemed to be capable of having more children. X and Y are clearly entitled to participate. Z will also be entitled to participate if Z was in gestation at A's death, but if Z was conceived after A's death, Z will be excluded.

If at A's death, no children had been born to B and none was then in gestation, the class would not close at A's death but would remain open until it closes physiologically, *i.e.,* at B's death.

Sequential Distribution Class Gifts: The rule of convenience for sequential distribution class gifts closes the class as soon as one class member becomes entitled to receive a share.

Illustration 8: G bequeathed $90,000 "to my grandchildren who live to age of 21." (Such a bequest would probably be in trust, and it might provide either for the accumulation of the income until distribution, or for the payment of the income to the grandchildren until that time.)

> *Answer*: If one grandchild reached 21 before G's death, the class would close when G died. If no grandchild reached 21 before G's death, the class would remain open, but only until one grandchild arrives at the age of 21. Closing the class when one grandchild reaches 21 is necessitated by the desire to give that first grandchild (X) an indefeasible interest. If, when X reaches 21, there are two other grandchildren alive but not yet 21 (Y and Z), X receives one-third of the fund indefeasibly. Later, upon attaining 21, Y receives one-half of the remaining fund. Later still, when Z attains 21, Z receives all the fund that is left. Any grandchildren born (or adopted) after X reaches 21 are excluded. If Y dies under 21, one-half of the portion Y would have received is distributed to X, and the other half is paid over to Z when Z reaches 21. Should Z later die under 21, the entire fund is given to X.

Illustration 9: G bequeathed $90,000 in trust "to pay the income to A for life, then to distribute the corpus to my nieces and nephews who live to age 21." (Again, the income after A's death but before distribution of the corpus might be either accumulated or paid out.)

> *Answer*: If one or more of the nieces or nephews reached 21 prior to A's death, the class closes at A's death, not when the first one reached 21. But if none reached 21 by the time of A's death, the class closes as soon as a niece or nephew reaches 21. Any niece or nephew born (or adopted) after the closing of the class is excluded.

C. REVIEW QUESTIONS

1. How does a class gift differ from a gift to an individual?
2. What does it mean to say a class gift is subject to fluctuation?
3. A class always closes when the donor dies. True or false?
4. What is the rule of convenience?
5. When does an immediate class gift close?
6. When does a postponed class gift close?

*

IV

RULE AGAINST PERPETUITIES AND RELATED DOCTRINES

Analysis

A. BASIC REQUIREMENTS OF THE RULE AGAINST PERPETUITIES

1. STATEMENT OF THE COMMON LAW RULE

A common formulation of the Rule provides: "No interest is good unless it must vest, if at all, not later than twenty-one years after some life in being at the creation of the interest." J. GRAY, THE RULE AGAINST PERPETUITIES, § 201, at 191 (4th ed. 1942).

Although the Common Law Rule Against Perpetuities (the Rule) is easy to state, its complexity developed from difficulties in its application. Its chief purposes are stated to be a desire to curtail the deadhand control of wealth and to facilitate the marketability of property. ROBERT J. LYNN, THE MODERN RULE AGAINST PERPETUITIES 10 (1966). Few would question its goals but many have criticized its methods. Several facets of the Rule's application engender the criticisms.

First, the Rule does not directly restrict the duration of an interest but restricts the time during which an interest can remain contingent. Comparatively speaking, a relatively short twenty-five year suspended interest could violate the Rule for failure to vest within its confines whereas a suspended interest tested against lives in being could be valid under the Rule even though it actually will last for ninety years or more.

Second, the Rule is enforced with psychic anticipation of contingencies coupled with a draconian "all or nothing" remedy if the contingencies violate the Rule. According to the common law, an interest created in a governing instrument, whether a will or other transfer device, had to be tested against the Rule at its creation. All contingencies in the interest created are tested to see whether they will become vested within the term of the Rule. There must be an initial certainty of vesting of all of the interests. If an interest is not certain of vesting within the Rule, the concept of infectious invalidity might cause the entire transfer to fail. Commentators belabor these points in emphasizing the Rule's inconsistency, nonsensical approach, draconian remedy and unjust result. *See, e.g.,* W. Barton Leach, *Perpetuities in Perspective: Ending the Rule's Reign of Terror*, 65 HARV. L. REV. 722 (1952).

2. THE PRESENT STATUS OF THE RULE AGAINST PERPETUITIES

Well over half the states have reformed the common law Rule in one way or another and, nearly fifty percent of the states have enacted the Uniform Statutory Rule Against Perpetuities (1986) (USRAP).

3. CLASSIFICATIONS AND THE RULE AGAINST PERPETUITIES

Today, the most important consequence of future interest classification concerns the Rule. Classifying the future interests in a disposition sorts out which interests, if any, are subject to the Rule.

4. TRIGGERING CONCERN OF RULE AGAINST PERPETUITIES

The sole concern of the common law Rule is whether a future interest in property is certain to vest or fail to vest (terminate) within the time allowed (the perpetuity period).

5. INTERESTS SUBJECT TO THE RULE

Only an interest that is subject to the Rule can violate it.

a. Future Interests in Property

The Rule potentially applies if a transaction creates a future interest in property. It does not make any difference whether the subject matter is land or personalty or whether the interest is legal or equitable.

Legal relationships that do not create future interests in property are not subject to the Rule. Long-term contracts are generally exempt. For example, optional modes of settlement for the payment of life insurance proceeds and annuity contracts are exempt, even though future payments may be subject to uncertainties that might not be resolved within the perpetuity period. *See Holmes v. John Hancock Mutual Life Ins. Co.*, 41 N.E.2d 909 (N.Y. 1942); *Doyle v. Massachusetts Mutual Life Ins. Co.*, 377 F.2d 19 (6th Cir. 1967).

b. Contingent versus Vested Future Interests

The Rule applies only to contingent remainders and executory interests. The Rule does not apply to reversions (because they are always vested), vested remainders (whether or not subject to defeasance), possibilities of reverter, or rights of entry.

In order for a contingent remainder or an executory interest to be valid, there cannot be any possible chain of post creation events that would permit the interest to remain nonvested beyond a life in being plus twenty-one years.

6. CLASS GIFTS AND THE ALL-OR-NOTHING RULE

Class gifts are subject to the Rule, and are treated specially. An early English decision, *Leake v. Robinson,* 35 Eng. Rep. 979 (Ch. 1817), established the rule for class gifts:

> If the interest of any potential class member might vest beyond a life in being plus twenty-one years, the entire class gift is invalid.

The rule is called the "all or nothing" rule. It provides that a class gift is either completely valid or completely invalid. The "all or nothing" rule does not allow the interest of each class member to be treated separately. This rule does not allow some class members to have valid interests if other class members have invalid interests.

7. THE "PERPETUITY PERIOD"

The common law perpetuity period is the period of time produced by the lifetime of a person in being at the creation of the interest plus twenty-one years, *i.e.,* a "life in being plus twenty-one years." It may be extended by the period of gestation of an actual pregnancy. The period of gestation is not automatically part of the perpetuity period in all cases. *See Cadell v. Palmer*, 1 Cl. & F. 372 (H.L. 1883).

The "perpetuity period" is not a set length of time. The common law Rule tests the validity of an interest as of the point of its creation. Testing the validity of an interest as of the point of its creation means that validity turns on a projection regarding the various times in the future when the interest might vest or terminate. Validity at common law does not depend on when the interest actually vests or terminates. Consequently, the common law has no need to measure off a "perpetuity period." A perpetuity period would only be necessary if validity turned on the timing of actual vesting or termination.

For valid interests the common law uses the life in being plus twenty-one years "period" in a way that does not require measuring off an actual period of time by tracing the lifespan of the so-called "measuring (validating) life."

8. THE TWENTY-ONE YEAR PART OF THE PERIOD

Although the twenty-one-year part of the perpetuity period is described by Gray as coming after the death of the measuring life, and it is often referred to as the tack-on twenty-one year period, the twenty-one year part of the period need not be preceded by a measuring life. It can stand on its own. Thus a testamentary transfer "to my grandchildren who are living twenty-one years after my death" would be valid.

Sparse authority seems to be agreed that the twenty-one-year part cannot come first, followed by a life that is in being twenty-one years after the creation of the interest. The measuring life must be in being at the creation of the interest.

Illustration 1: A testator devises property in trust "to pay the income to the testator's children for twenty-one years, then to pay the income to the testator's then living grandchildren for life, and on the death of the survivor of those grandchildren, to pay the corpus of the trust to the testator's descendants then living by representation." If the testator is survived by one or more children, the remainder interest in the corpus of the trust violates the common law Rule and is invalid.

9. THE MEANING OF "MUST VEST IF AT ALL"

The common law Rule requires that the interest, when created, must be guaranteed to vest if at all within the perpetuity period. The phrase "if at all" means that the contingencies must be guaranteed to be finally resolved within the perpetuity period. Thus the Rule prohibits interests that might remain contingent beyond the perpetuity period. Conversely, the Rule validates interests that must vest or terminate within the perpetuity period.

10. THE LIFE-IN-BEING PART OF THE PERIOD

The person who serves as the life in being is traditionally called the measuring life. The measuring life must be a person who was "in being" at the creation of the interest. This means that the measuring life must have been alive or in gestation when the interest was created. The measuring life must also be a human being. A corporation, plant, or animal cannot be used. *See* SIMES & SMITH ON FUTURE INTERESTS § 1223. Although any human being in the world who was alive or in gestation when the interest was created can be the measuring life, realistically the lives in being must be identifiable and discoverable.

11. PERSONS QUALIFIED AS THE "MEASURING" LIFE

Invalid interests fail because there is no measuring life to make them valid, not because they might remain nonvested beyond twenty-one years after the death of an identified person. The search for a "measuring life" is a search for a validating life.

a. How to Search for a Validating Life

The goal of the search is to find one person for whom there is no invalidating chain of possible post-creation events. Section 1 of the USRAP explains the process used for common law perpetuities as follows:

> The process for determining whether a validating life exists is to postulate the death of each individual connected in some way to the transaction, and ask the question: Is there with respect to this individual an invalidating chain of possible [post-creation] events? If one individual can be found for whom the answer is No, that individual can serve as the validating life. As to that individual there will be the requisite causal connection between his or her death and the questioned interest's vesting or terminating no later than twenty-one years thereafter.

Dispositions of property sometimes create more than one interest that is subject to the Rule. When this happens, you must test the validity of each interest separately. A life that validates one interest might or might not validate the other interests. Consequently, you must search for a validating life for each interest.

The converse is that if no person can be found for whom there is no invalidating chain of possible post-creation events, there is no validating life and an interest for which there is no validating life is invalid. Any invalidating chain of events that would disqualify a candidate is enough.

b. Only Insiders Need to be Considered

Insiders are persons who are connected in some way to the transaction. Although anyone in the world can be used to see if he or she has the causal connection demanded by the requirement of initial certainty, only insiders have a chance of supplying the causal connection demanded by the requirement of initial certainty.

The insiders to be tested vary from situation to situation, but would always include the transferor, if living, the beneficiaries of the disposition, including but not restricted to the taker or takers of the challenged interest, the objects and donee of a power of appointment, persons related to the foregoing by blood or adoption, especially in the ascending and descending lines, and anyone else who has any connection to the transaction.

Illustration 2: G devised land "to my son A for life, remainder to A's children who live to age 21." Of the insiders involved, A satisfies the requirement of initial certainty because no possible chain of post creation events disqualifies him. None of his children can reach twenty-one (or die under twenty-one) beyond twenty-one years after his death. Because A satisfies the test, and is a validating life, there is no need to test any of the other insiders, such as A's wife[1] or any of A's children who were alive or in gestation at G's death.

Illustration 3: G devised land "to my son A for life, remainder to A's children who live to age 21." A's wife is pregnant when A dies. Although the child born after A's death could not reach twenty-one within twenty-one years after A's death, the common law provided that, if this were to happen, the "perpetuity period" would be extended to include the period of gestation of A's child.[2] Consequently of the insiders involved, A satisfies the requirement of initial certainty because no possible chain of postcreation events disqualifies him. There is no need to test any of the other insiders, such as any of A's children who were alive or in gestation at G's death. A's wife and the mother of *A*'s new child cannot serve as the validating life because she might be born after *G*'s death.

The validating life not only need not be a devisee; the validating life need not even be mentioned in the instrument.

Illustration 4: G devised land "to my daughter B for life, remainder to my son A's children who live to age 21." The obvious insiders to test first in this case are A and B. Although B is the life tenant, she does not satisfy the requirement of initial certainty. A chain of possible postcreation events that

1. The facts of the example do not indicate whether *A* was married at *G*'s death. If he was, his current wife would not satisfy the requirement of initial certainty. An invalidating chain of possible post creation events that disqualifies her is that she might die immediately after *G*'s death and that *A* might then have a child (by another woman) who would reach twenty-one or die under twenty-one more than twenty-one years after the death of *A*'s current wife. Note also that the mother of *A*'s new child cannot serve as the validating life either because she might be born after *G*'s death.

2. The Rule did not anticipate the problem of a post death conception or implantation. Whether these afterborn persons would be counted or included depends on whether the law should favor maximum inclusion versus predictability and definiteness of determination.

disqualifies her is that A might have a child who reaches twenty-one (or dies under twenty-one) more than twenty-one years after her death. A does satisfy the requirement of initial certainty, however, even though he is not a devisee. He is the validating life and the interest is valid because the law assumes that his death terminates the possibility that he will have additional children.

c. Survivor of Group

The validating life can be a later-to-be-determined member of a group of individuals. It is common in these cases to say that the members of the group are the validating lives. This is acceptable, as long you recognize that the true meaning of the plural is singular, *i.e.*, that the validating life is the life of the member of the group who turns out to live the longest.

Illustration 5: G devised land "to my grandchildren who live to age 21." Some of G's children are living at G's death. The grandchildren's springing executory interest does not violate the common law Rule. The validating life is that one of G's children who turns out to live the longest. It is impossible for any of G's grandchildren to reach twenty-one or die under twenty-one more than twenty-one years after the death of G's last surviving child. In this situation G's children are the validating lives even though they are not devisees and are not even mentioned in the instrument.

d. Beneficiary of the Interest as the Validating Life

The beneficiary of an interest can sometimes be his or her own validating life. This point sometimes validates an interest that is contingent on the beneficiary's reaching an age exceeding twenty-one or is contingent on the beneficiary's surviving a particular point in time that exceeds or may exceed twenty-one years after the interest was created or after the death of a person in being at the date of creation.

Illustration 6: G devised land "to A's children who are living 25 years after my death." A predeceased G. At G's death, A had three living children. The executory interest created in A's children does not violate the common law Rule. A's children are their own validating lives. Each child will either survive the twenty-five year period or fail to do so within his or her own lifetime.

Illustration 7: G devised land "to A's children who live to age 25." A predeceased G. At G's death, A had three living children, all of whom were younger than twenty-five and some of whom were younger than four years of age. The executory interest created in A's children does not violate the Rule. A's children are their own validating lives. Each child will either reach age twenty-five or fail to do so within his or her own lifetime.

Illustration 8: Same facts as *Illustration 7* except that all of A's children are older than four years of age (but younger than twenty-five) at G's death. Each class member's interest would be valid because each class member's interest would be guaranteed to vest or terminate within twenty-one years after G's death.

e. Executory Interests Following Defeasible Fees

An executory interest following a defeasible fee is subject to the common law Rule and will be invalid unless there is a validating life.

Illustration 9: (1) G devised land "to A and his heirs so long as liquor is not sold on the land, and upon liquor's being sold on the land, the land goes to B." A and B survived G.

(2) G devised land "to A and his heirs on condition that no liquor be sold on the land, but if liquor is sold on the land, the land goes to B." A and B survived G.

The interest in question is B's executory interest. The interest is invalid in both cases because there is no validating life. The obvious insiders to test in both cases are A and B, but neither satisfies the requirement. B is not in possession of the land and cannot control its use. Although A is initially in possession and controls its use, he can transfer his defeasible fee to someone born after G's death. This afterborn devisee, heir, or grantee of A might allow liquor to be sold on the land more than twenty-one years after the death of either A or B. Because there is no other insider to test, the executory interest is invalid.

Illustration 10: G devised land "to A and her heirs so long as A does not allow liquor to be sold on the land, and upon A's allowing liquor to be sold on the land, the land goes to B." B's executory interest is contingent on A's personally allowing liquor to be sold on the land. Consequently, A satisfies the requirement of initial certainty and is the validating life. As of G's death, it is certain that B's executory interest will either vest or terminate during the lifetime of A. If A should die without allowing liquor to be sold on the land, A's possessory estate will ripen into a fee simple absolute and B's interest will terminate.

Illustration 11: G devised land "to A and his heirs so long as liquor is not sold on the land, and upon liquor being sold on the land, the land goes to B if B is then living." B satisfies the requirement of initial certainty and is the validating life for her own interest. If no liquor is sold on the land during B's lifetime, B's executory interest will be extinguished. If liquor is sold on the land after B's death, irrespective of who allowed the liquor to be sold, A's fee simple will terminate, but the person who received the possibility of reverter from G is the one who will then become entitled to possession, not B. Since possibilities of reverter are exempt from the Rule, the possibility of reverter is valid even though it might vest beyond a life in being plus twenty-one years.

12. TIME OF CREATION

In analyzing a perpetuity question, the time of creation of the property interest in question is crucial. The creation point fixes the time when the validating life must be "in being." The creation point also limits the facts and circumstances that can be taken into account in determining validity. Under the common-law Rule, an interest is valid only if, at the point of its creation, with the facts and circumstances then existing taken into account, the interest is certain to vest or terminate within a life in being plus twenty-one years. The facts that actually occur from that time forward, including the postcreation facts that are known at the time of the lawsuit, are disregarded—with one exception concerning interests created by the exercise of, or in default of the exercise of, certain powers of appointment.

a. Testamentary Transfers

Property interests created by will are created when the testator dies, not when the testator signs the will. Thus the validating life for testamentary transfers must be a person who was alive (or in gestation) when the testator died, and the facts and circumstances that are relevant to the validity of an interest created by will are those existing at the testator's death.

b. Inter Vivos Transfers

Property interests created by inter vivos transfer are created when the transfer becomes effective for purposes of property law generally. This would ordinarily be the date of delivery of the deed or the funding of the trust. Thus the validating life for inter vivos transfers must be a person who was alive (or in gestation) when the transfer became effective, and the facts and circumstances that are relevant to the validity of an interest created by inter vivos transfer are those existing at that time. These general rules are subject to exceptions in certain cases when an interest is subject to a power of appointment.

c. Facts and Circumstances

The facts and circumstances existing at creation can be just as important in determining the validity of an interest as the contingencies attached to that interest. By varying the facts existing on the donor's death, the remainder or executory interest created could be made valid or invalid.

Illustration 12: G devised the residue of his estate in trust, directing the trustee to pay the income "to A for life, then to A's children for the life of the survivor, and upon the death of A's last surviving child, to pay the corpus of the trust to A's grandchildren." G was survived by A's two children, X and Y. The result depends on whether A predeceased G. If A died before G, the grandchildren's remainder interest in the corpus is valid. Because A was dead at G's death, X and Y are the only children A will have. All of A's grandchildren will therefore be born or at least conceived during the lifetime of the survivor of X and Y. Thus X and Y constitute the validating lives for the grandchildren's interest. If A survived G, the grandchildren's remainder interest in the corpus is invalid.

13. POSTPONEMENT PRINCIPLE

For perpetuity purposes, the time that property interests are created in revocable inter vivos transfers, typically in trust, is postponed to the time when the power to revoke expires. A power to revoke expires at the death of the settlor, unless the power was released or fixed to expire earlier. The principle is codified in Section 2 of the USRAP.

Illustration 13: G conveyed property in trust, directing the trustee to pay the income to herself (G) for life, then to G's son A for his life, then to A's children for the life of the survivor of A's children who are living at G's death, and upon the death of such last surviving child, the corpus of the trust to be distributed among A's then-living descendants, by representation. G retained the power to revoke the trust. The interest in question is the remainder interest in the corpus created in A's then-living descendants. The postponement principle validates this interest. Under the postponement principle, the remainder interest is created at G's death, not at the creation of the trust. Treating the remainder interest as created at G's death allows A's children who are living at G's death to be the validating lives.

If the trust had been irrevocable, the creation of the remainder interest would not have been postponed, and the interest would have been invalid. A child of A might have been conceived and born between the date when the trust was created and G's death, such after-born child might have turned out to be the last surviving child of A who was alive when G died, and such child might have lived more than twenty-one years beyond the deaths of all the insiders connected to the transfer who were "in being" when the trust was created, *i.e.,* G, A, and A's then-living children. The same can also be said of all outsiders—every other person in the world who was "in being" when the trust was created.

Other Interests Subject to a Power: Although court authority is lacking, commentators and the RESTATEMENT OF PROPERTY take the position that the time of creation is postponed so long as the interest "is destructible, pursuant to the uncontrolled volition, and for the exclusive personal benefit of the person having such a power of destruction." RESTATEMENT OF PROPERTY § 373 (1944). *See* SIMES & SMITH ON FUTURE INTERESTS § 1252. Under this statement of the principle, the power need not be a power to revoke and it need not be held by the settlor or transferor. An unqualified and currently exercisable power held by any person acting alone to make himself or herself the beneficial owner of the interest in question is sufficient. Section 2(b) of the USRAP codifies this proposition.

14. CONSTRUCTIONAL PREFERENCE FOR VALIDITY

Although there are strict construction states, most courts lean toward the proposition put forth by the RESTATEMENT OF PROPERTY Section 375, which provides that where an instrument is subject to two or more plausible constructions, one of which causes a Rule violation and the other of which does not, the construction that does not result in a Rule violation should be adopted. *See, e.g., Southern Bank & Trust Co. v. Brown*, 246 S.E.2d 598 (S.C. 1978); Davis v. Rossi, 34 S.W.2d 8 (Mo. 1930).

15. THE CONSEQUENCES OF INVALIDITY

When an interest is invalid because it violates the Rule, the invalid interest is stricken from the disposition. Unless the doctrine of infectious invalidity applies, the other interests created by the disposition (assuming that none of them violates the Rule) take effect as if the invalid interest had never been created.

Striking the invalid interest does not have the same consequences in all cases. The consequences depend on whether the invalid interest was a remainder or an executory interest and on whether the invalid interest was the last one in the disposition or an intermediate one.

When the invalid interest is a remainder interest following a life estate or a term of years or is an executory interest following a fee simple determinable, its invalidity will probably (though not necessarily) cause a gap in the disposition. If the transfer was inter vivos, the gap will be filled by a reversion or a possibility of reverter. If the transfer was by will, the gap will be filled by the residuary clause or, if the invalid interest was created in the residuary clause, by intestate succession.

Illustration 14: G devised land "to A for life, then to A's children for the life of the survivor, and upon the death of A's last surviving child, to A's grandchildren." G devised her residuary estate to her husband, H. A survived G. Due to the invalidity of the remainder created in A's grandchildren, the disposition reads as if that remainder interest had never been created: "to A for life, then to A's children for the life of the survivor." Because G's devise did not validly dispose of all interests in the land, the undisposed-of interest is a remainder that passes under G's residuary clause to H. This testamentary transfer of the remainder to H is deemed to have occurred at G's death. With H's remainder added in, the disposition now reads: "to A for life, then to A's children for the life of the survivor, then to H." Thus when A's last surviving child dies, the land goes to H (or H's successors in interest).

If G's original devise had been in her residuary clause, the undisposed-of interest would have been a reversion that passed by intestacy at G's death to her heirs at law.

Illustration 15: G devised land "to A for life, then for life to A's children who live to age 25, then to B." A survived G. The remainder for life created in A's children who reach twenty-five is invalid. The effect of striking it is not to create a gap that must be filled by the residuary clause. Rather it is to accelerate B's remainder. With the invalid interest stricken, the devise reads: "to A for life, then to B."

Illustration 16: G devised land "to A and her heirs so long as no liquor is sold on the land, and upon liquor being sold on the land, the land goes to B." G devised his residuary estate to C. D is G's sole heir at law. B's executory interest is invalid. The phrase "to B" is stricken and the gap is filled by the residuary clause. Under conventional analysis, however, the residuary clause confers an executory interest on C, not a possibility of reverter. If so, C's executory interest is also invalid. The gap caused by striking C's executory interest is filled by intestate succession, which passes a valid possibility of reverter to D.

When the invalid interest is an executory interest (other than one following a fee simple determinable), the effect will not be to create a gap. Rather, the invalidity of the executory interest will cause the condition subsequent to be stricken, too.

Illustration 17: G devised land "to A for life, remainder to A's children, but if none of A's children lives to age 25, to B." G was survived by A, who had two children, X and Y, both of whom were younger than twenty-five. B's executory interest is invalid. As a result, the remainder created in A's children is not subject to the condition of divestment in case all die under twenty-five. Rather, while it still is subject to open, it is no longer subject to complete divestment. With the invalid interest stricken, the devise reads: "to A for life, remainder to A's children."

16. SEPARABILITY

When an interest is expressly subject to alternative contingencies, the courts have the option of holding that two interests are created in the same person or class. The effect of doing so is that the invalidity of one of the interests does not invalidate the other. *See* SIMES & SMITH ON FUTURE INTERESTS § 1257; AM. L. PROP. § 24.54; RESTATEMENT OF PROPERTY § 376 (1944). The principle of separability is applicable only when the transferor has expressly stated the contingencies in the alternative. Where alternative contingencies are merely implicit, no separation will be recognized.

Illustration 18: Property is devised "to B if X-event or Y-event happens." B in effect has two interests, one contingent on X-event and the other contingent on Y-event. If there is no validating life for X-event but there is one for Y-event, the consequence of separating B's interest into two interests is that only the one contingent on X-event is invalid. B still has a valid interest, *i.e.*, the one contingent on Y-event. Another way of viewing it is that the invalid contingency is stricken or excised. Thus the devise is altered to read "to B if Y-event happens."

17. INFECTIOUS INVALIDITY

Under the doctrine of infectious invalidity, the invalidity of an interest may be held to invalidate one or more otherwise valid interests. The question turns on whether the general dispositive scheme of the transferor will be better served by eliminating only the invalid interest or by eliminating other interests as well. This is a question that must be answered on a case by case basis. Several items are relevant to the question, including who takes the stricken interests in place of those designated by the transferor. Some jurisdictions have become noted for a greater willingness to apply infectious invalidity than others. *See* SIMES & SMITH ON FUTURE INTERESTS § 1262; AM. L. PROP. § 24.48 et seq.; RESTATEMENT OF PROPERTY § 402 (1944).

18. TECHNICAL VIOLATIONS

The required certainty that an interest will vest or terminate within a life in being plus twenty-one years has invalidated some interests even though they do not violate the policy of the Rule. The policy of the Rule is not violated because, realistically speaking, the likelihood that the interest will remain contingent beyond the perpetuity period is either zero or so remote as to be negligible. Such cases fall generally into three categories, which received their names from Professor Leach's article, *Perpetuities in a Nutshell*, 51 HARV. L. REV. 638 (1938): (a) the fertile octogenarian; (b) the administrative contingency; and (c) the afterborn spouse.

a. Fertile Octogenarians

In Rule Against Perpetuities parlance, the term "fertile Octogenarians" refers to persons who are infertile, young or old, male or female. Courts have almost universally held that all persons are conclusively presumed to be capable of having children throughout their entire lifetimes, regardless of their age or physical condition. Only one American common law decision has squarely rejected the rule and held in a perpetuities case that the presumption of lifetime fertility is rebuttable, not conclusive. *Lattouf's Will*, 208 A.2d 411 (N.J. Super. Ct. App. Div. 1965). The RESTATEMENT OF PROPERTY § 377 (1944) squarely supports the conclusive presumption, and there are many perpetuities cases, recent as well as not so recent, that have adhered to it. *See, e.g., Turner v. Turner*, 196 S.E.2d 498 (S.C. 1973).

Illustration 19: G devises the residue in trust, directing the trustee to pay income "to A for life, then to A's children for life of the survivor, and upon the death of A's last surviving child, to pay the corpus to A's grandchildren." If G is not survived by A, the remainder to the grandchild is valid. If G is survived by A, the remainder interest in A's grandchildren is invalid because A might have additional children who are not lives in being and who might have grandchildren who are also not lives in being and who might take beyond the period of the Rule. Under the fertile octogenarian rule, this invalidity would apply even if A is 95 years old or for any other reason is incapable of having children after G's death.

b. "Precocious Toddlers"

A small number of cases have concerned young children who have not yet reached puberty and whether they are conclusively presumed to be capable of having a child. Professor Leach called them "precocious toddlers."

Illustration 20: G devised property in trust, directing the trustee to pay the income "to A for life, corpus to A's grandchildren who are living at my death or born within five years thereafter who shall live to age twenty-one." G was survived by A, a sixty-five year old widow, and by A's two children and one grandchild. Is a child under the age of five conclusively presumed to be capable of having a child? If so, the remainder created in A's grandchildren who reach twenty-one is invalid. Although any grandchild of A's born to A's two children who were living at G's death will either live to age twenty-one or die younger no later than twenty-one years after the death of the survivor of these two children (who were "in being" at G's death, and thus, potentially were validating lives), the conclusive presumption if applicable would say that it is possible that A will conceive and bear a child who will in turn conceive a child, all within five years after G's death. Such grandchild therefore might reach twenty-one more than twenty-one years after the death of the survivor of A and A's two children and one grandchild who were living when G died.

c. The Administrative Contingency

The term "administrative contingency" refers to the performance by a fiduciary (an executor, a trustee) of some administrative function, the completion of which probably will not but might take more than twenty-one years. Typical examples are the completion of the probate of a will, the settlement of an estate, the payment of debts or taxes, the sale of estate assets, or the delivery of trust corpus on the termination of a trust.

Illustration 21: G devised land "to my grandchildren, born before or after my death, who are living upon final distribution of my estate." G was survived by children and grandchildren. The grandchildren's interest is invalid, by the majority view. Though unlikely, there is a possibility that the final distribution of G's estate will not occur within twenty-one years after G's death.

d. The Afterborn Spouse

The term "afterborn spouse" refers to the fact that an unnamed "widow," "widower," "spouse," or "surviving spouse" of a beneficiary is excluded from serving as the validating life. The beneficiary's "widow," "widower," "spouse," or "surviving spouse" might turn out to be someone who was conceived and born after the creation of the interest, no matter how improbable that possibility is. Thus, if no other validating life can be located, the questioned interest, if subject to the common law Rule, is invalid.

Illustration 22: G devised land "to my son A for life, remainder to his widow for her life, remainder to A's then-living descendants." G was survived by A, A's wife W, and their adult children, X and Y. The questioned interest is invalid, *i.e.,* the remainder created in A's descendants. RESTATEMENT OF PROPERTY § 370 cmt. k & illus. 3. Though improbable, it is possible that A's widow will not be W, but someone who was born after G's death and who will live more than twenty-one years beyond the deaths of A, W, X, Y, and any other person "in being" at G's death.

There is no violation if beneficiaries of the remainder interest following the spouse's death can be their own validating lives. The beneficiaries of the remainder interest would be their own validating lives if the remainder were created in named individuals (X and Y, perhaps) or a class that was closed at G's death (the children of G's predeceased daughter, B). Another salvation would include a remainder that was not contingent on survival.

Other courts have avoided the Afterborn Spouse problem by construing G's reference to A's "widow." "widower," "spouse," or "surviving spouse" as only referring to the person to whom A was married when the will was executed or when G died.

19. PERPETUITY SAVING CLAUSES

Estate planning lawyers protect their client's plans from invalidity by using perpetuity saving clauses. A typical perpetuity saving clause might provide:

> The trust hereby created shall terminate in any event not later than 21 years after the death of the last survivor of my descendants who are in being at the time this instrument becomes effective, and unless sooner terminated by the terms hereof, the trustee shall, at the termination of such period, make distribution to the persons then entitled to the income of this trust, and in the same shares and proportions as they are so entitled.

Formulated and used properly, perpetuity saving clauses mean that the lawyer never needs to fear that a trust or other property arrangement he or she drafts will violate the common-law Rule. In addition, the practicing lawyer need not fear that the perpetuity saving clause will have any practical effect other than to save the disposition from a common law Rule violation. Perpetuity saving clauses do not typically govern the term of the trust; they operate as a back-stop just in case the actual term of the trust exceeds the time allotted by the saving clause.

The Lives in Being Component: The persons designated in the saving clause become validating lives for all interests in the trust or other property arrangement. The saving clause confers on the last surviving member of the group the requisite causal connection demanded by the requirement of initial certainty. *See Norton v. Georgia R.R. Bank & Trust,* 322 S.E.2d 870 (Ga. 1984) (upholding the validity of a traditional perpetuity saving clause).

The Perpetuity–Period Component: The part of a perpetuity saving clause that establishes the period of time is called the perpetuity-period component.

Gift Over Component: The gift over component expressly creates a gift over that is guaranteed to vest at the termination of the period established in the perpetuity period component, but only if the interests in the trust or other arrangement have neither vested nor terminated earlier in accordance with their primary terms.

Determinable Lives in Being: The RESTATEMENT (SECOND) OF PROPERTY Section 1.3 cmt. *a* states that a perpetuity saving clause is ineffective if "the number of individuals specified as the measuring lives ... is so large that it would be an impossible administrative burden to locate them initially, let alone determine the death of the survivor.... " Section 1 cmt. pt. B of the USRAP states that designation of the group is invalid if the group is such "that it would cause it to be impracticable to determine the death of the survivor."

B. PERPETUITY REFORM

1. THE NEED TO REFORM THE RULE

Although the Rule is easy to state, significant complexity developed from difficulties in its application. As indicated, the Rule is enforced with psychic anticipation of theoretical contingencies, *e.g,* the fertile octogenarian rule, coupled with a draconian "all or nothing" remedy if the contingencies violate the Rule. Until recently and despite compelling criticisms, the Rule endured against reform. A major reason for the lack of reformation derives from disagreements over what form the reform should take. The promulgation and enactment by nearly half the states of the Uniform Statutory Rule Against Perpetuities Act (USRAP) has dramatically altered the perpetuity environment in this country and significantly eliminated its potential for harm to bona fide property transactions. The USRAP has been incorporated into the UPC as Part 9 of Article II.

2. CHECKERBOARD REFORM OF THE RULE

Prior to the USRAP, reform efforts were taken by many states but they varied in scope and procedure. Reform attempts include: (1) total repeal of the Rule, (2) creation of an immediate judicial reformation power for interests that will not vest within the Rule, (3) creation of wait and see or deferred judicial reformation power for interests that do not vest within the Rule, and (4) substitution of a specific period of time or period in gross within which all conditional interests must vest. *See generally,* Fellows, *Testing Perpetuity Reforms: A Study of Perpetuity Cases* 1984–89, 25 Real Prop. Prob. & Tr. J. 597, 602–08 (1991).

3. ABOLITION OF THE RULE

The ultimate reform is abolition of the Rule. Wisconsin abolished the common law Rule Against Perpetuities and substituted the rule against the suspension of the power of alienation which is inapplicable "if the trustee has power to sell, either expressed or implied, or if there is an unlimited power to terminate in one or more persons in being." Wis. Stat. § 700.16. *See also* S.D. Codified Laws Ann. § 43–5–8. Several other states have recently abolished the Rule in order to allow perpetual trusts that are exempt from the federal generation-skipping transfer tax.

4. THE WAIT-AND-SEE REFORM OF THE RULE

Because the common law Rule based validity upon the full array of possible post-creation events, the perpetuity reform movement proposed that the basis of validity be shifted from possible to actual post-creation events. Instead of invalidating an interest because of what might happen, waiting to see what does happen seemed then and still seems now to be more sensible. This approach is known as the wait-

and-see method of perpetuity reform. This remedy has the advantage that it allows dispositions that would have been valid under the common-law Rule to remain valid. Thus, the wait-and-see element is applied only to interests that are potentially invalid under the common-law Rule. Under wait-and-see, even these potentially invalid interests are valid if they actually vest within the permissible vesting period. They are invalid only if they remain in existence but are still nonvested at the expiration of that period.

a. Saving Clause Principle of Wait-and-See

Wait-and-see should be thought of as a perpetuity saving clause injected by law. Conversely, the perpetuity-period component of a traditional saving clause should be thought of as a privately established wait-and-see rule. The permissible vesting period under wait-and-see is, or should be, the equivalent of the perpetuity-period component of a well-conceived saving clause.

b. Criticism of Wait-and-See

An early criticism of wait-and-see was that it puts the validity of property interests in abeyance because no one can determine whether an interest is valid or not. Actually wait-and-see merely subjects the nonvested future interest to an additional contingency. To vest, the nonvested interest must not only satisfy the vesting contingencies set out in the governing instrument but must also vest within an easily determinable certain period of time. In addition, only the status of the affected future interest is deferred. During the interim, the other interests, such as the interests of current income beneficiaries, are not affected.

c. The Permissible Vesting Period

The most significant controversy over wait-and-see concerns how to determine the period of time during which contingencies can be validly satisfied, *i.e.,* the permissible vesting period. Although the permissible vesting period assumably is determined by reference to so-called measuring lives who are in being at the creation of the interest, the issue is "who are the measuring lives"? The common-law Rule contains no mechanism for identifying measuring lives under wait-and-see. Because the common law mechanism for testing the validity of an interest is at its point of its creation, actual post-creation events are disregarded. Thus, there is no "perpetuity period" during which actual post-creation events can be measured. At common law, either there is or is not a validating life: there is no common-law "perpetuity period" to wait out. A permissible vesting period is necessary only under the wait-and-see method of perpetuity reform.

d. Pre–USRAP Wait-and-See

In 1947, Pennsylvania adopted the first wait-and-see statute. 20 Pa. Cons. Stat. Ann. § 6104(b). The statute merely provided that the vesting of interest was to be "measured by actual rather than possible events" but contains no method of determining who the measuring lives were and how they were to be identified under the statute in order to apply the wait-and-see remedy.

In 1954, Massachusetts adopted a statute that measures "the validity of the interest ... on the basis of facts existing at the termination of one or more life estates or lives." By merely restricting the permissible vesting period to one or more life estates created in persons in being at the creation of the interest, it fails to reverse the invalidity in the standard administrative contingency case or to provide appropriate relief for the over age twenty-one contingency. Another statute reduces age in excess of twenty-one requirement "to twenty-one as to all persons subject to the same age contingency." The Massachusetts-style statutes are in effect in Maine and Maryland but not in Massachusetts which has enacted the USRAP.

Another version, which originated in Kentucky, adopts a permissible vesting period measured by the life of persons who have a "causal relationship" to the vesting or failure of the interest in question. The meaning of "causal relationship to the vesting or failure of the interest" is much in dispute.

> *Illustration 23*: *G* deeded real property "to *A* and his heirs, but if the property is used for nonresidential purposes, to *X* and her heirs." Although *A* is the only person whose life bears a causal relationship to whether *X*'s interest vests, it has been contended that *X* is the only permissible measuring life in this example. *X* is said to have a causal relationship to vesting because *X* is the beneficiary of the nonvested interest. A, it is argued, does not have a causal relationship to the vesting of X's interest, because he might transfer his possessory interest to unknown successors in interest. See Jesse Dukeminier, *Perpetuities: The Measuring Lives*, 85 COLUM. L. REV. 1648, 1705–06 (1985).

Finally, the RESTATEMENT (SECOND) OF PROPERTY in 1983 adopted the wait-and-see method of perpetuity reform that uses a predetermined list of lives for determining the wait-and-see measuring lives. Under Section 1.3(2), the permissible vesting period expires twenty-one years after the death of the survivor of:

- The transferor if the period of the rule begins to run in the transferor's lifetime;
- Those individuals alive when the period of the rule begins to run, if reasonable in number, who have beneficial interests vested or contingent in the property in which the nonvested interest in question exists and the parents and grandparents alive when the period of the rule begins to run of all beneficiaries of the property in which the nonvested interest exists; and,
- The donee of a nonfiduciary power of appointment alive when the period of the rule begins to run if the exercise of such power could affect the nonvested interest in question.

If a property interest is still in existence but nonvested at the expiration of the permissible vesting period, Section 1.5 provides that "the transferred property shall be disposed of in the manner which most closely effectuates the transferor's manifested plan of distribution and which is within the limits of the rule against perpetuities."

So far, the RESTATEMENT'S version of wait-and-see has not been directly adopted but was an influence in the development of the 1983 Iowa statute that designates as the measuring lives the beneficiaries and "the grandparents of all such beneficiaries and the issue of such grandparents.... " IOWA CODE § 558.68(2)(b)(2) (1992).

5. IMMEDIATE REFORMATION METHOD OF PERPETUITY REFORM

By legislation, some courts are authorized or directed to cure any violation of the common law Rule by reforming the disposition to make it valid. Reformation is permitted at any time. Immediate reformation and wait-and-see are mutually inconsistent.

a. Immediate Reformation Example

The Oklahoma statute provides that "Any interest in real or personal property that would violate the rule against perpetuities shall be reformed or construed within the limits of the rule, to give effect to the general intent of the creator of that interest whenever that general intent can be ascertained." OKLA. STAT. tit. 60, § 75 (1994). Similar statutes are in effect in Missouri and Texas. A few courts have judicially adopted the immediate reformation method. *See Edgerly v. Barker,* 31 A. 900 (N.H. 1891); *Carter v. Berry*, 140 So.2d 843 (Miss. 1962).

b. Application of Immediate Reformation

Although the reformation is supposed to be made in a way that comes as close as possible to the transferor's intent without violating the common-law Rule, the few applicable cases have merely reformed an age contingency or a period in gross exceeding twenty-one to age twenty-one. Insertion of a saving clause into the governing instrument would have been a more faithful reformation to the transferor's intention.

6. SPECIFIC–STATUTORY–REPAIR METHOD

a. Specific Reformation

Two states, Illinois and New York, have enacted precise legislative provisions directed specifically to deal with the fertile-octogenarian problem, the administrative contingency problem, the afterborn spouse problem, and age contingencies exceeding twenty-one.

b. Applications of Specific Reformation

The fertile-octogenarian problem is resolved by providing that (1) persons above 65 and below 13 are deemed incapable of having a child; (2) evidence is admissible regarding the incapacity of having a child by a living person who is under 65; and (3) the possibility of having a child or more remote descendant by adoption shall be disregarded.

The administrative-contingency problem is resolved by presuming that the probate of a will, the appointment of an executor, administrator, or trustee, the administration of an estate, the payment of debts, the sale or distribution of property, the determination of tax liabilities, or any other administrative contingency must happen, if at all, within the perpetuity period.

The afterborn-spouse problem is resolved by presuming that an interest in the "widow," "widower," or "spouse" of another person was intended to refer to a person who was living at the date that the Rule commences to run.

The age contingencies exceeding twenty-one is resolved by providing that where an interest would be invalid because it depends upon any person attaining or failing to attain an age exceeding twenty-one years, the age shall be reduced to twenty-one regarding every person to whom the age contingency applies.

C. THE UNIFORM STATUTORY RULE AGAINST PERPETUITIES (USRAP)

1. DEVELOPMENT AND STATUS OF USRAP

The National Conference of Commissioners on Uniform State Laws promulgated the USRAP in 1986, and amended it modestly and brought it into the UPC in 1990. So far, the USRAP has been enacted in Alaska, Arizona, California, Colorado, Connecticut, Florida, Georgia, Hawaii, Indiana, Kansas, Massachusetts, Michigan, Minnesota, Montana, Nebraska, Nevada, New Jersey, New Mexico, North Carolina, North Dakota, Oregon, South Carolina, Tennessee, Utah, and West Virginia.

2. BASIC OPERATION

The core of the USRAP is found in its definition of the period of time within which a non-vested interest must vest in order to be valid. Phrased in the disjunctive, a non-vested interest is valid if it is certain to vest or terminate either no later than twenty-one years after the death of a living individual or within ninety years after its creation. UPC § 2–901. The first arm of the rule is merely a codification of the common law Rule. The second arm is a form of a wait and see approach tied to a specific length of time.

The rules are specifically applicable to non-vested property interests, general powers of appointment that are not presently exercisable because of a condition precedent, and nongeneral powers of appointment which generally are testamentary powers of appointment. UPC § 2–901(a), (b), and (c).

> *Illustration 24*: G devised the residue of G's estate in trust, directing the trustee to pay the income "to A for life, then to A's children for the life of the survivor, and upon the death of A's last surviving child, to pay the corpus of the trust to A's then living descendants, by representation." G was survived by A and by A's two children, X and Y.
>
> > *Answer to Illustration*: Under the common law Rule, the remainder interest in the corpus created in *A*'s descendants would be invalid. Consequently, the remainder interest would not be initially valid under Section 1(a)(1) of the USRAP. But, unlike the common law, the remainder interest would not be initially invalid either. Section 1(a)(2) of the USRAP applies, allowing ninety years for the remainder interest to vest. If *A*'s last surviving child dies within ninety years after *G*'s death, as is very likely, the remainder interest is valid. If *A*'s last surviving child lives beyond the ninety year period, the remainder interest is invalid, but the disposition can be judicially reformed to make it valid.

3. LIVES IN BEING UNDER USRAP

Because of the broad protection provided by the provision, the USRAP specifically restricts the application of lives in being as that definition concerns post-death procreation. In determining whether an interest vests or not, the USRAP disregards the possibility that an individual may have a child born after the individual's death. This exclusion is primarily directed toward the problem raised by post-death procreation due to advances in medical science. UPC § 2–901(d), cmt. It also, however, eliminates the common law lives in being extension granted to children *en ventre sa mere*. The common law rule was intended to validate interests that might otherwise have been invalid due to the birth of a child after the death of a life in being or transferor. The new rule makes this extension unnecessary for purposes of validating interests under the perpetuity rule and therefore is eliminated.

4. DATE OF CREATION OF INTEREST

Because the perpetuity period refers to the time of creation of the non-vested interest, it is necessary to define when that interest is created. The USRAP codifies the common law on this matter with some clarification. The time of creation for most non-vested property interests or powers of appointment is determined under general principles of property law. UPC § 2–902(a) . This means that non-vested interests created in a will will have the date of the testator's death as its creation date. In regard to inter vivos transfers, an interest or power is created as of the effective date of the transfer. In addition, two special circumstances are resolved. If by the terms of the instrument a person alone and without the consent of any other person may exercise a power to become the unqualified beneficial owner of the property subject to the interest, the non-vested interest or power of appointment is created for purposes of the perpetuity period when that unqualified power terminates. For example, if a person has a power to revoke an inter vivos or testamentary trust, the perpetuity period does not begin to run and is not created until the person no longer is able to exercise the power of revocation. The period then runs from the termination of this power over the interest subject to the USRAP. UPC § 2–902(b).

When property arrangements such as trusts, which include interests subject to the USRAP, provide that additional property can be added to them during their existence, the USRAP, taking the efficient course of action, provides that its perpetuity period begins when the instrument or trust was created not from the date of subsequent transfers to it. UPC § 2–902(c). Because of the USRAP's nonforfeiture approach and generous duration, this limitation should not deny intent or cause harm to intended beneficiaries.

5. REFORMATION UNDER USRAP

The USRAP includes a judicial reformation procedure exercisable by the courts concerning transfers which are found to violate its perpetuity period. UPC § 2–903. Although this will not occur in most situations because experience informs us that most transfers will qualify under the general rule, the reformation power is reserved to correct those circumstances in which a perpetuity error has indeed been made. The USRAP adopts a deferred rather than prospective reformation power in the court. This means that there is no power to reform until the transfer is invalid under the perpetuity period. UPC § 2–903. Durationally speaking, this means the non-vested interest has not vested within either of the durational periods of the perpetuity period. The reformation suit will usually be brought by an "interested person" who would frequently be the trustee.

Deferred Reformation: A deferred reformation power was selected for several reasons. First, it will significantly reduce "temperature testing" law suits over a perpetuity question. Second, it permits the transferor's plan to fully work out. Because most transfers will vest within the allowable period, a law suit is unnecessary. Third, it rejects the prospective analysis of vesting determinations and adopts the retrospective analysis approach. At the time of reformation, the court will know more about how the donor would reform the instrument had the donor known the instrument created an invalid transfer. There is no need to predict the future. The decision needs to be made at the time it needs to be made and it is final.

Exceptions to Deferred Reformation: Two exceptions to the post-validity reformation requirement are recognized. The first exception concerns class gifts in which the vesting may still be endowed but the time for actual possession or enjoyment of a share of the estate in a class member has arrived. This exception permits those of the class entitled to immediate possession or enjoyment to seek reformation of the instrument so that their possession or enjoyment may occur immediately. UPC § 2–903(2), and cmt.

The second exception concerns the ability to institute a reformation action although the perpetuity period has not expired if it is clear it will expire before the property vests. UPC § 2–903(3). This exception would cover the unlikely case where a donor created a transfer that would not vest until a period of time has passed clearly beyond the Rule.

Illustration 25: G devised property in trust, directing the trustee to divide the income, by representation, among G's descendants living from time to time, for one hundred years. At the end of the one hundred years, the trustee is to distribute the corpus to G's then living descendants, by representation. Because the remainder interest to G's descendants living one hundred years after G's death can vest but not before 90 years, the USRAP grants a right to early reformation. The most appropriate form of reformation would be to reduce the one hundred-year period to ninety years.

Reformation Remedy: When a reformation action is permitted, the court must reform the document. It does not have the discretion to hold that the transfer is invalid. The USRAP requirement is that the court must reform the transfer in a "manner that most closely approximates the transferor's manifested plan of distribution." UPC § 2–903. This provision effectively revokes the common law doctrine of infectious invalidity. UPC § 2–903, cmt. Generally, the recommendation is that courts make as little alteration to the disposition as possible. The goal is to use a scalpel, not a butcher knife. This means that (1) the maximum number of persons who could take at the time of reformation should be permitted to take even though their interests technically were not vested within the period of the rule, and (2) other prohibitory provisions should be altered as little as possible, *e.g.*, an age requirement above twenty-one should be reduced only to the point where it will satisfy the rules. USRAP § 3, cmt.

Illustration 26: G devised the residue of his estate in trust, directing the trustee to pay the income "to A for life, then to A's children for the life of the survivor, and upon the death of A's last surviving child, to pay the corpus of the trust to A's then-living descendants, by representation." G was survived by A and by A's two children, X and Y. The USRAP allows ninety years for the remainder interest to vest. If A still has a living child or children on the ninetieth anniversary of G's death, the remainder interest becomes invalid, but, on the petition of an interested person, the disposition must be judicially reformed to make it valid.

> *Answer to Illustration*: The most appropriate form of reformation would be to vest the remainder interest in A's descendants who would take if A's last surviving child had died on the ninetieth anniversary of G's death. This would not cut short the income interest of A's living child or children. The remainder interest in A's descendants would be vested in interest as of the ninetieth

anniversary of G's death, but not vested in possession. Possession would still be postponed until the actual death of A's last surviving child.

D. CLASS GIFTS UNDER THE RULE AGAINST PERPETUITIES

1. GENERAL RULE

"All or Nothing": Class gifts pose a special problem in perpetuity law. Under the common law Rule, a class gift stands or falls as an inseparable unit. This all-or-nothing rule is commonly stated as follows:

> If the interest of any potential class member might vest beyond a life in being plus twenty-one years, the entire class gift is invalid.

The all-or-nothing rule is an offshoot of the separability doctrine. Because the transferor did not expressly separate the interests of the class members as individuals, they cannot be treated separately. Some class members cannot have valid interests if other class members have invalid interests. If any potential class member has an invalid interest, the interests of all class members are invalid (including those that are certain to vest or terminate within a life in being plus twenty-one years).

All-or-Nothing Rule under the USRAP: Although the USRAP does not abrogate the all-or-nothing rule, it validates the interests of all the actual class members in most cases. Although the interest of one or more potential class members might vest beyond a life in being plus twenty-one years, the class gift is not initially invalid; rather, the class gift is valid if the interests of all class members vest within ninety years. If the interests of some class members do not vest within ninety years, the disposition can be reformed to validate the interests of all class members who are conceived (or adopted) before the ninety-year mark.

Illustration 27: G devised land "to A for life, then to A's children who live to age 25." G was survived by A, and by A's two children, X and Y. X had reached twenty-five at G's death, but Y was under twenty-five.

> *Answer to Illustration*: Under the common law Rule, the class gift in A's children who reach twenty-five is invalid.
>
> Under the USRAP the class gift is not initially invalid. Rather, the class gift is valid if, within ninety years after G's death, all of A's children (including children born after G's death) either live to age twenty-five or die younger, as is very likely. In the very unlikely event that ninety years after G's death, A is alive, or is dead but has a child who is alive but younger than twenty-five, the disposition can be reformed to make the class gift valid. The appropriate method of reformation would be to vest the remainder interest in A's children who, ninety years after G's death, had already reached twenty-five (whether then living or not) or were then living but younger than twenty-five.

2. TWO EXEMPTIONS FROM THE ALL-OR-NOTHING RULE

Two types of class gifts are exempt from the all-or-nothing rule: (1) specific-sum class gifts and (2) gifts to subclasses. These special types of class gifts are exempt because the underlying rationale of the all-or-nothing rule does not apply to them. In both cases, the interest of each taker (or group of takers) is expressly separated by the transferor, and the share of each taker (or group of takers) is, or is certain to come within a life in being plus twenty-one years, unaffected by the total number of takers (or the total number of groups of takers).

The significance of exempting these two types of class gifts from the all-or-nothing rule is that each class member's or subclass's interest can be judged separately. Thus, under the Rule, some class members or subclasses can have valid interests even though other class members or subclasses have invalid interests. Under the USRAP, the class members or subclasses that would have valid interests under the Rule are valid and the class members or subclasses that would have invalid interests under the Rule are valid if they vest within ninety years.

Specific-Sum Class Gifts: The all-or-nothing rule does not apply to specific-sum class gifts. A specific-sum class gift is one that gives a specific sum of money to each class member. Specific-sum class gifts are to be distinguished from conventional class gifts, under which a sum of money or item of property is to be divided proportionally among however many members of the class there turn out to be.

Illustration 28: G bequeathed "$10,000 to each child of A, born before or after my death, who lives to age 25." G was survived by A and by A's two children, X and Y. X but not Y had already reached twenty-five at G's death.

> *Answer to Illustration*: If the phrase "born before or after my death" had been omitted, the rule of convenience would close the class at G's death, and the entire gift would have been valid even if the all-or-nothing rule applied. The inclusion of the "before-or-after" phrase, however, means that G intended to include afterborn children.
>
> Under the Rule, the interests of the afterborn children are invalid, but the interests of X and Y are valid because they were living at G's death. The interest of X, the child who already had reached twenty-five on G's death, is valid because it is vested. The interest of Y, the other child, is valid because Y himself is his own validating life.
>
> Under the USRAP, as under the Rule, the interests of X and Y are valid. The USRAP, however, saves the interests of any of A's children who are born (or adopted) within the ninety-year period following G's death, which would undoubtedly include all of A's children.

Gifts to Sub–Classes: For similar reasons, the all-or-nothing rule does not apply to gifts to subclasses. In order for this exemption to apply, two requirements must be met:

(1) The takers must be described as a group of subclasses; and,

(2) The share going to each subclass must be certain to be finalized within a life in being plus twenty-one years.

Illustration 29: G devised property in trust, directing the trustee to pay the income "to A for life, then in equal shares to A's children for their respective lives; on the death of each child, the proportionate share of corpus of the one so dying shall go to the children of such child." G was survived by A and by A's two children, X and Y. After G's death, another child (Z) was born to A. A has now died survived by X, Y, and Z.

Answer to Illustration: Both of the requirements of the sub-class rule are met. The takers are described as a group of sub-classes rather than as a single class: "children of the child so dying," as opposed to "grandchildren." The share going to each sub-class is certain to be finalized within a life in being plus twenty-one years: As of A's death, it is certain to be known how many children she had surviving her. In fact there were three surviving children, each sub-class's share is one-third of the corpus, neither more nor less.

Under the common law rule, as a consequence of the subclass rule, the remainder in X's children and the remainder in Y's children are valid. X is the validating life for the one, Y for the other. The remainder in Z's children, however, is invalid. Z was not a life "in being," and he could have children more than twenty-one years after the deaths of A, X, and Y.

One final point: In a case like this, where there was an afterborn child (Z), a court might apply the doctrine of infectious invalidity to invalidate the remainders in the children of X and Y. To do so would probably better carry out G's overall intent.

Under the USRAP, as under the common law Rule, the remainders in X's children and in Y's children are valid. The USRAP, however, almost certainly saves the remainder in Z's children also. If Z dies within the ninety-year period following G's death, which is very likely, the remainder in Z's children is valid.

E. POWERS OF APPOINTMENT UNDER THE RULE AGAINST PERPETUITIES

1. GENERAL APPLICATION OF THE RULE

If a power of appointment violates the Rule Against Perpetuities, the power is invalid, and the disposition takes effect as if the power had never been created. If the power itself is valid, some or all of the interests created by its exercise may violate the Rule and be invalid.

Under the USRAP, if the exercise of a power is valid under the common law it is valid. An exercise that would have been invalid at common law is not initially invalid under USRAP but instead is subject to the wait-and-see element. The ninety-year period applies, in determining the validity of appointed interests that would have been invalid at common law.

2. PRESENTLY EXERCISABLE GENERAL POWERS

Under the common-law Rule and the USRAP, a general power that is presently exercisable is treated as the equivalent of a vested property interest in the donee (rejecting relation back) and is, therefore, not subject to either rule.

a. Validity of the Exercise

In determining the validity of an exercise of a general power presently exercisable, the donee is considered to have created the appointed interests. The exercise is treated as if the donee first exercised the power in the donee's own favor and then created the appointed interests out of owned property. Consequently, the appointed interests are created, for purposes of the Rule, when the exercise becomes effective.

Illustration 30: A was the income beneficiary of a trust and the donee of a presently exercisable general power over the succeeding remainder interest. A exercised the power by deed, directing the trustee after A's death to pay the income to A's children in equal shares for the life of the survivor, and upon the death of A's last surviving child to pay the corpus of the trust to A's grandchildren. A reserved a power to revoke her appointment.

Answer to Illustration: Under the common law Rule and USRAP the remainder interest is valid. Under the postponement principle, the appointed interests are created at A's death.

Illustration 31: A was the income beneficiary of a trust and the donee of a presently exercisable general power over the succeeding remainder interest. A exercised the power by deed, directing the trustee after A's death to pay the income to A's children in equal shares for the life of the survivor, and upon the death of A's last surviving child to pay the corpus of the trust to A's grandchildren. A's appointment is irrevocable.

Answer to Illustration: Under the common law Rule the remainder interest in A's grandchildren is invalid. The appointed interests were created when the deed was delivered or otherwise became effective. Under the USRAP, however, the remainder interest in A's grandchildren is not initially invalid. Instead, it is valid if A's last surviving child dies within ninety years after A's death, which is a near certainty.

If a general power that was once not presently exercisable because of a condition precedent is valid and becomes presently exercisable, the validity of an exercise is governed by the same principles discussed above.

3. GENERAL POWERS NOT PRESENTLY EXERCISABLE BECAUSE OF A CONDITION PRECEDENT

If a general power would be presently exercisable but for the fact that its exercise is subject to a condition precedent, the power is treated by both the common law Rule and the USRAP as the equivalent of a nonvested property interest in the donee (rejecting relation back). Remember that a power of appointment expires on the donee's death and so a deferral of a power's exercisability until a future time—even a time certain—imposes a condition precedent, the condition precedent being that the donee must be alive at that future time.

a. Validity of the Power

Under the common law Rule, a general power not presently exercisable because of a condition precedent is invalid unless the condition precedent must be resolved one way or the other within a life in being plus twenty-one years. Consequently, although neither a nongeneral power nor a testamentary power can validly be conferred on an unborn person (unless some special restriction is imposed on it forbidding its exercise beyond a life in being plus twenty-one years), an unborn person can be the recipient of a valid general power that becomes presently exercisable upon the donee's birth. To be valid, of course, the donee's birth must be certain to occur, if it ever occurs, within a life in being plus twenty-one years.

Illustration 32: G devised land "to A for life, then to A's first born child for life, "then to such persons as A's first born child shall appoint after reaching the age of 25," G was survived by A, who is childless.

> *Answer to Illustration*: Under the common law Rule, the general power conferred on A's first born child is invalid. Under the USRAP, the outcome is the same, except that if the power in A's first born child was contingent on reaching age twenty-five, the power would be valid if A's first born child reaches age twenty-five within ninety years after G's death.

4. VALIDITY OF NONGENERAL POWERS AND GENERAL TESTAMENTARY POWERS

a. Common Law Rule

To be valid under the common law Rule, a nongeneral power (whether testamentary or presently exercisable) or a general testamentary power cannot be exercisable beyond a life in being plus twenty-one years.

Underpinning this rule is the theory of relation back, which is that any property interest created by the donee's exercise of a nongeneral power or of a general testamentary power is created by the donor when the donor created the power. Because no such property interest can vest until the power is exercised, the Rule requires certainty that the power cannot be exercised beyond a life in being plus twenty-one years.

b. USRAP Approach

USRAP provides that a nongeneral or a general testamentary power that would be invalid at common law is not initially invalid. Instead, the power is valid if it is actually exercised within ninety years after it was created.

Illustration 33: G devised land "to A for life, then to A's first born child for life,

(1) then to such persons as A's first born child shall by will appoint" (General Testamentary Power); or

(2) then to such of A's grandchildren as A's first born child shall appoint." (Nongeneral power).

G is survived by A, who is childless.

> *Answer to Illustration*: Under the common law Rule, each power of appointments conferred on A's first born child is invalid. The latest possible time of exercise is at the death of A's first born child, who cannot be the validating life because the child was not "in being" at the creation of the power. The lesson under the common law Rule is that a nongeneral or a general testamentary power cannot validly be conferred on an unborn person, unless a perpetuity saving clause or some other special provision limits the power's exercisability to a life in being plus twenty-one years.
>
> Under the USRAP, the power is valid if A's first born child exercises the power within ninety years after G's death. Thus, in Variation (1), A's first born child must die within ninety years after G's death in order for the child's power to valid. In Variation (2), A's first born child must also die within ninety years after G's death if the child chooses to exercise the power by will rather than by deed.

If similar separate powers are given to different donees the exercise of some of which violate the common law Rule, the preferred approach is to treat the exercises of the powers separately and to evaluate the validity of each one. If the powers cannot be treated separately, however, then all the powers are invalid. The Restatement of Property § 390 cmt. f. Under the USRAP not only is separate treatment accorded, but any invalid power will be tested by the ninety year wait-and-see rule.

5. FIDUCIARY POWERS

Discretionary powers held by fiduciaries are nongeneral powers of appointment, for perpetuity purposes. Discretionary fiduciary powers include a trustee's power to invade the corpus of the trust for the benefit of the income beneficiary or a trustee's power to accumulate the income or pay it out or to spray it among a group of beneficiaries. Under the common law Rule, such powers are invalid if they might be exercised beyond a life in being plus twenty-one years. Under the USRAP, powers that would have been invalid at common law can be exercised for ninety years.

Purely administrative fiduciary powers, however, are not subject to either the common law Rule or the USRAP.

Illustration 34: G devised property in trust, directing the trustee to pay the income to A for life, then to A's children for the life of the survivor, and on the death of A's last surviving child to pay the corpus to B. The trustee is granted the discretionary power to sell and to reinvest the trust assets and to invade the corpus on behalf of the income beneficiary or beneficiaries. G was survived by A and by A's two children, X and Y.

> *Answer to Illustration*: Under the common law Rule the trustee's power to invade the corpus is invalid. It might be exercised beyond a life in being at G's death plus twenty-one years. The trust can proceed to be carried out, but the trustee has no power to invade the corpus. The trustee's power to sell and reinvest the trust assets, however, is valid even though it, too, might be exercised beyond a life in being plus twenty-one years. The reason is that purely administrative powers, as distinguished from discretionary powers to shift beneficial enjoyment, are not subject to the Rule.
>
> Under the USRAP, the trustee's power to invade corpus can be exercised for ninety years. Regarding the trustee's power to sell and reinvest the trust assets, the USRAP follows the rule at common law and exempts purely administrative powers from the Rule.

6. VALIDITY OF THE EXERCISE OF NONGENERAL AND GENERAL TESTAMENTARY POWERS

If a nongeneral or a general testamentary power is valid, it can be validly exercised. Whether or not the exercise is valid is the next question.

a. Theory of Relation Back

The relation back theory is applicable to determining the validity of interests created by the exercise of nongeneral powers and general testamentary powers. In a majority of states and under the USRAP, any property interest created by the donee's exercise of such powers is treated, for purposes of the Rule, as created by the donor when the donor created the power. A small number of states hold that, for perpetuity purposes, the appointed interests of nongeneral and general testamentary powers are created when the donee exercised the power, not when the donor created the power. *See* DEL. CODE ANN. tit. 25, § 501.

Illustration 35: A was the life income beneficiary of a trust and the donee of a nongeneral power [or a general testamentary power] over the succeeding remainder interest. The trust was created by the will of A's mother, G, who predeceased him. A exercised the power by will, directing the income to be paid after A's death to the children of A's brother B for the life of the survivor, and upon the death of B's last surviving child, to pay the corpus of the trust to B's grandchildren. B predeceased G; B was survived by his two children, X and Y, who also survived G and A.

Answer to Illustration: A's power is treated as created by the will of A's mother, G, who predeceased him. The remainder interest in B's grandchildren was created at G's death when the power was created, not on A's death when the power was exercised. Since B was dead at G's death, the validating lives are X and Y. A's testamentary appointment is valid.

b. The Second–Look Doctrine

Although, for perpetuity purposes, the nearly unanimous view is that interests created by the exercise of nongeneral powers or of general testamentary powers are treated as created when the power was created, the facts existing when the power was exercised can be taken into account. Taking this "second look" at the facts is a well-established procedure. *See, e.g., Warren's Estate*, 182 A. 396 (Pa. 1930); *Estate of Bird*, 37 Cal. Rptr. 288 (Cal. Ct. App. 1964). Justification for the "second look" approach is based on the fact that until the appointment is made the appointed interests cannot be known and their validity cannot be litigated. Thus no useful purpose would be served by holding appointed interests to be invalid because of what might have happened after the power was created but which at the time of exercise can no longer happen. *See* RESTATEMENT OF PROPERTY § 392 cmt. a. Others find the second-look doctrine to be nothing more than viewing the facts existing when the power was exercised as relating back along with the terms of the appointment.

Illustration 36: A was the life income beneficiary of a trust and the donee of a nongeneral or a general testamentary power over the succeeding remainder interest. The trust was created by the will of A's mother, G, who predeceased him. A exercised A's power by will, directing the income to be paid after A's death to A's children for the life of the survivor, and upon the death of A's last surviving child, to pay the corpus of the trust to A's grandchildren. At G's death, A had two children, X and Y, A had no additional children after G's death, and at A's death X and Y were still living.

Answer to Illustration: If only the facts existing at G's death are taken into account, the remainder interest would be invalid under the common law Rule. Under the second-look doctrine, the facts existing at A's death can be taken into account. Taking these facts into account saves A's appointment. At A's death, it has become clear that no additional children were born to A after G's death. Thus A's last surviving child will be either X or Y, both of whom were "in being" at G's death and, therefore, constitute the validating lives. Under both the common law Rule and the USRAP, A's appointment is valid. Under the doctrine of relation back, the remainder interest in A's grandchildren is treated as having been created at G's death.

7. THE VALIDITY OF APPOINTED POWERS AND EXERCISES OF APPOINTED POWERS

The donee of a power of appointment might exercise it by creating another power of appointment. The validity of the appointed power and the validity of its exercise are governed by a combination of the principles set forth above.

F. CHARITABLE GIFTS AND COMMERCIAL TRANSACTIONS UNDER THE RULE AGAINST PERPETUITIES

1. CHARITABLE GIFTS

Whether or not a charitable future interest is subject to a remote contingency, the future interest is exempt from both the common law Rule and the USRAP if it was preceded by an interest created in another charity. The rationale for this exemption is that the law allows property to be perpetually tied up for a single charity, so it ought to accord the same treatment to shifts from one charity to another, even though the shift might take place beyond a life in being plus twenty-one years or, under the USRAP, beyond ninety years.

Illustration 37: G devised land "to the X School District so long as the land is used for school purposes, and upon the cessation of such use, to Y City." The executory interest created in Y City is exempt from both the common law Rule and the USRAP and is therefore valid.

In addition charitable future interests that are vested are not subject to the Rule.

Future interests created in charities that follow noncharitable interests are subject to both common law Rule and the USRAP. Under the common law Rule, a condition precedent that might not be satisfied within a life in being plus twenty-one years invalidates the charitable interest. Under the USRAP, a charitable interest that would have been invalid at common law is given ninety years in which to vest.

Illustration 38: G devised land "to A for life, then to A's children who live to age 25, but if none lives to 25, to X Charity." Under the common law Rule, the remainder created in X Charity is invalid. Under the USRAP, the remainder created in X Charity is valid if all of A's children die before reaching twenty-five within ninety years after G's death.

2. COMMERCIAL TRANSACTIONS

Generally, the Rule Against Perpetuities is a wholly inappropriate instrument of social policy to use as a control over commercial arrangements. Nevertheless, because some contractual arrangements do create property interests, the Rule has been applied to certain types of commercial transactions. The perpetuity argument is usually raised by one of the parties who is seeking to avoid performing on his or her part of the contract.

a. Options in Gross

An option in gross is a contract right to purchase property held by an optionee who has no possessory interest in the property, such as a leasehold interest. If the subject of an option is land or a unique chattel, the option is specifically enforceable. Specifically enforceable contracts are treated as creating equitable property interests. Since equitable property interests are subject to the common law Rule, the great majority view at common law is that options in gross are invalid if they are exercisable beyond a life in being plus twenty-one years.

Illustration 39: A, the owner of Blackacre, sells an option to B under which A obligates himself and his heirs and assigns to convey Blackacre at any time in the future to B and her heirs and assigns, for $X.00. The great majority view at common law is that the option is invalid. This means that the option is unenforceable and damages are not recoverable for its breach. Under USRAP the option is exempt.

b. Rights of First Refusal (Preemptive Rights)

Unlike options to purchase, rights of first refusal do not obligate the owner to sell. They only obligate the owner to offer the property first to the preemptioner if the owner decides to sell. The preemptioner can buy or decline. If the preemptioner declines, the owner is then free to sell to anyone else. Rights of first refusal have been held to be subject to the common law Rule, and void if they are exercisable beyond a life in being plus twenty-one years.

c. Options Appurtenant to Leasehold Interests

Options to renew a lease are not subject to the common law Rule. By the majority American view, options to purchase leased property are also exempt when held by the lessee. Thus such options, even those that are exercisable beyond a life in being plus twenty-one years, are valid. Options appurtenant to leasehold interests do not necessarily deter the lessee from improving the property, and so public policy does not require controlling their duration.

d. Leases to Commence in the Future

A lease to commence at a fixed time in the future is valid even if the time is beyond a life in being plus twenty-one years. A lease scheduled to commence in the future is invalid if it is subject to a contingency that might occur beyond the rule. There has been considerable litigation concerning the validity of so-called "on-completion" leases—leases scheduled to commence when construction of a building is completed. On-completion leases would clearly be valid if the lessor was obligated to complete construction within twenty-one years, but in the absence of an explicit obligation of this sort, some courts have held the lease to be invalid though others courts have upheld such leases on the theory that the lessee's interest was vested from the beginning.

e. USRAP and Commercial Transactions

The USRAP specifically excludes certain transactions and powers from application of its rule. UPC § 2–904. First, the provision provides that all exceptions recognized at common law or excluded by statute are excluded under the USRAP. The USRAP then defines particular situations that also are excluded. Generally, non-donative transfers are not subject to the USRAP rules. UPC § 2–904(1). Although not excepted at common law the position of the drafters of the USRAP is that this is the preferred law because a perpetuity rule that concerns gratuitous transfers is not appropriate to apply to transactions with consideration.

So that the exclusion is not interpreted beyond its intent, the USRAP excepts from the exclusion certain transactions that are in the nature of donative transfers despite their nongratuitous characterization. This would include prenuptial and postnuptial agreements, separation or divorce settlements, surviving spouses' elections, and other similar types of devices specifically enumerated.

Purely administrative or management powers that are not related to distribution are excepted from the rule. UPC § 2–904(2). In addition, the UPC excepts a power to appoint a fiduciary [UPC § 2–904(3)], and a discretionary trustee's power to distribute principal to an indefeasibly vested beneficiary. UPC § 2–904(4).

The Official Comment notes, however, that these transactions are subject to the common-law rules regarding unreasonable restraints on alienation and, in some cases, marketable title acts. Another suggested approach is to enact a separate set of statutory provisions limiting the duration of certain commercial transactions to a flat period of years, as has been done in Illinois (ILL. REV. STAT. ch. 30, § 194(a) (1993)) (Forty-year limit) and Massachusetts (MASS. GEN. LAWS ANN. ch. 184A, § 5 (1991)) (Thirty year limit).

G. REVIEW QUESTIONS

1. Define the common law Rule Against Perpetuities.
2. Define the doctrine of infectious invalidity.
3. What is the rule that states if the interest of any potential class member might vest beyond a life in being plus 21 years, the entire class gift is invalid?
4. How does the USRAP deal with reformation of transfers that violate its rules?
5. What are the two types of class gifts which are exempt from the all-or-nothing rule?
6. All commercial transactions are exempt from the Rule? True or false?

*

PART NINE

THE FIDUCIARY OBLIGATION

*

I

CONCEPT OF THE FIDUCIARY

Analysis

A. THE FIDUCIARY

1. THE FIDUCIARY RELATIONSHIP

A fiduciary is a person having a duty, created by his or her undertaking, to act primarily for another's benefit in matters connected with that undertaking. The fiduciary stands in a relation that implies and necessitates great confidence and trust on the part of the one for whom the duty is held. Concomitantly, the fiduciary owes a high degree of good faith to that person. For our purposes, the term fiduciary includes the trustee, guardian, and executor or personal representative.

B. THE PERSONAL REPRESENTATIVE

1. THE REPRESENTATIVE CONCEPT

If a decedent's estate is made subject to some form of an official administration, it is essential that a personal representative or multiple personal representatives be appointed. ATKINSON, WILLS § 103. The office of personal representative, therefore, has significant responsibilities and status in the administration of a decedent's estate. Generally and briefly, these responsibilities include collection of assets, settling of claims, and final distribution of the estate.

a. Legal Status

The attributes of a personal representative's status include recognition as the estate's legal entity, as officer of the court, as a fiduciary and as title holder of the decedent's personal property. ATKINSON, WILLS § 104. The office, itself, is considered of such extreme importance that the selection of a specific person or entity to serve as personal representative is one of the most important reasons for having a will.

b. Specific Titles

Personal representatives have generally been referred to by specific names depending upon the condition of the estate. ATKINSON, WILLS § 104. A personal representative named in the will is called an "executor." If appointed under an intestate estate, the name is "administrator." Several Latin phrases are added after the term "administrator" to describe the personal representative who is appointed under other circumstances. An administrator cum testamento annexo (c.t.a.) is a personal representative appointed when an executor fails to qualify or is not named in the will. An administrator de bonis non (d.b.n.) is the personal representative who succeeds an administrator. An administrator c.t.a. d.b.n. is the successor to the executor or an administrator c.t.a.

The primary importance of these titles concerns questions of the personal representative's qualification and authority. Laws in some states make distinctions between whether the personal representative is an executor or an administrator. For example, persons named in the will as executor may have priority of appointment, less grounds for disqualification, potential bond waiver and potential additional powers during administration.

c. UPC Terminology

Except for priority of appointment, the UPC eliminated the distinctions between a person named in a will as executor and one appointed as an administrator. All of the above titles have been eliminated because all such persons are referred to merely as the "personal representative." UPC § 1–201(36). This term is used in the UPC to refer to all persons who perform substantially the same function including executors, administrators, successor personal representatives and even special administrators.

2. PRIORITY AND DISQUALIFICATION FOR APPOINTMENT

Every state has legislation dealing with the qualification and disqualification of executors and administrators. ATKINSON, WILLS §§ 108, 109. Qualification is typically phrased in the form of a priority list and disqualification is phrased with respect to a candidate's particular prohibited status. The UPC is illustrative of both issues. UPC § 3–203.

CHART IX–I–1	
Priority Order for Appointment of a Domiciliary Personal Representative	
Priority Rank	**Description of Candidates**
1	Persons named in will (including named successors and nominated selectees under a power in the will).[1]
2	Surviving spouse who is a devisee (or the surviving spouse's selectee).
3	Other devisees (or the devisees' selectee).
4	Surviving spouse (or the surviving spouse's selectee).
5	Other heirs (or the heirs' selectee).
6	Any creditor forty-five days after death.

Several features of Chart IX–1–1 deserve additional explanation. The first three priorities concern the estate of a decedent who died testate. The next two priorities concern the decedent who died intestate. Under the last priority, creditors have priority rights only when there are no persons fitting the priority categories or persons with priorities refuse or do not apply for appointment.

Disqualification: Many non-UPC states are very specific as to when a person is disqualified or incompetent to serve either as an administrator or as an executor or both. ATKINSON, WILLS §§ 108, 110. Persons who might be disqualified or barred from appointment, for example, include minors, persons convicted of infamous crimes, or persons adjudged incompetent because of drunkenness, improvidence,

1. The typical court attitude with regard to the appointment of an executor is "Whom the testator will trust so will the law."

mental incapacity or lack of integrity. The additional status of being a non-resident commonly disqualifies a person from becoming an administrator unless a resident agent for service of process is appointed.

The UPC eliminates in its disqualification provision any distinction between administrators and executors and most of the specificity. It simply provides that persons under the age of twenty-one and those found unsuitable by a Court in a formal proceeding are disqualified. UPC § 3–203(f) . The UPC's suggested age requirement is a legislative option and the term "unsuitable" will have to be defined by the courts. Persons disqualified for either reason do not retain any priority status which they may have otherwise had. One additional temporary disqualification rule worthy of noting is that a non-resident may not be appointed as personal representative in the initial informal appointment proceeding until thirty days have elapsed from the date of the decedent's death. UPC § 3–307(a) .

The UPC gives to specific persons the authority to nominate, renounce or agree to appointment even where they would ordinarily be disqualified to serve as a personal representative.

Domiciliary Foreign Personal Representative: Under the UPC when a person dies domiciled in another state, the personal representative appointed in the decedent's domicile has priority over all other persons unless the decedent's will nominates different persons for different jurisdictions. UPC § 3–203(g). In addition, any domiciliary foreign personal representative may nominate another person who immediately assumes first priority for appointment. *See* Lawrence H. Averill, Uniform Probate Code in a Nutshell § 26.02 (4th ed. 1996) [Hereinafter Averill, U.P.C. Nutshell]

Special Administrator: A special administrator may be appointed under several circumstances. These situations include: if there is a delay in granting letters testamentary or grounds for removal of the named personal representative. *See* Averill, U.P.C. Nutshell § 21.01 (4th ed. 1996)

C. THE TRUSTEE

1. TRUSTEE QUALIFICATION

The trustee must be competent. Any competent natural person or legal entity capable of taking title to property may be a trustee. Austin W. Scott, Abridgement of Law of Trusts § 89 (1960). Capacity depends upon the extent of trustee's capacity to take or hold or administer the property for the trustee's own benefit. Eligibility includes individuals, corporate fiduciaries, and governments. In some states, special capacity problems may arise with infants, incompetents, aliens, nonresidents/foreign corporations, or unincorporated associations serving as a trustee.

The capacity of the "trustee" issue raises three questions. Whether the trustee has the capacity to:

1. Take title to property: if no capacity, the person or entity never becomes trustee of the property and a proceeding to remove him or her is unnecessary.

2. Continue to hold the title to the property: Person or entity ceases to be trustee as soon as person ceases to hold the title to the property and a proceeding to remove him or her is unnecessary.

3. Administer the trust: person or entity becomes trustee of the property but a proceeding to remove and replace the person as trustee can be maintained.

That the person nominated as trustee may be incompetent or disqualified, or may refuse to accept the trust or to continue in office, does not affect the validity of the trust, because the court in such case will appoint a successor trustee.

2. GROUNDS FOR REMOVAL

A trustee may be removed for lack of capacity to administer the trust; the commission of a serious breach of trust; refusal to give a bond, if a bond is required; refusal to account; the commission of a crime, particularly one involving dishonesty; unfitness, whether due to old age, habitual drunkenness, want of ability or other cause; permanent or long continued absence from the State; the showing of favoritism to one or more beneficiaries; unreasonable or corrupt failure to cooperate with his co-trustees. RESTATEMENT (SECOND) TRUSTS § 107, cmt. b. Unless friction interferes with the proper administration of the trust, mere friction between the trustee and the beneficiary is not a sufficient ground for removing the trustee.

Disclaiming versus Resigning: A trustee does not have to accept the trust, and therefore can disclaim the position and assume no responsibility. RESTATEMENT (SECOND) TRUSTS § 102. Once a trustee has accepted the trust, however, the trustee cannot resign except (a) with the permission of a proper court; or (b) in accordance with the terms of the trust; or (c) with the consent of all the beneficiaries, if they have capacity to give such consent. In addition, the trustee cannot disclaim in part and accept in part.

D. THE GUARDIAN

1. CONCEPT AND NECESSITY OF GUARDIANSHIP

Guardianship concepts derive from the circumstance when a person is under some type of disability which causes that person to be unable to manage his or her own personal or business affairs or both. JOHN G. WOERNER, AMERICAN LAW OF GUARDIANSHIP OF MINORS AND PERSONS OF UNSOUND MIND § 1 (1897). Through the guardianship device, such a disabled person's rights and interests can be protected. Generally, the person who suffers from such disabilities is either a minor, mental incompetent or other incompetent. The disability of a minor is presumed by legislative determination depending upon the person's age. *Id.* The other forms of disability require voluntary action by the person or some form of legal proceeding to determine the incompetency status. *See* AVERILL, U.P.C. NUTSHELL Pt. 5.

An important feature of guardianship is that it serves two distinct functions. The first and most apparent is guardianship of property. Under such a guardianship, the guardian manages (receives and expends) the ward's property or estate for the purposes of the guardianship. The second, which is particularly important in the case of minors, is the guardianship of the person. Here the guardian has custody and, therefore, physical control over the ward. The same person may be permitted to serve in both capacities.

2. GUARDIAN OF MINORS

Unless the minor is unmarried and all parental rights of custody have been terminated or suspended, no guardianship by any method may be created for a person whose incapacity is solely minority *See* UPC §§ 5–202(b), 5–204(a). Consequently, a natural or adoptive parent is automatically the guardian of the person of his or her minor natural and adopted children. Presumably, any parent would have to be removed according to removal proceedings before any other person could be appointed guardian of that parent's minor children. UPC § 5–204(a); *see* UPC § 5–212.

Some laws, including the UPC, permit the parent of an unmarried minor to appoint a guardian for the minor by will or by any other writing which is signed by the parent and attested by at least two witnesses. UPC § 5–202(a).

When court appointment of a guardian of a minor is necessary, the court is duty bound to appoint the person whose appointment would be in the best interest of the minor. UPC § 5–207. The nominee of the minor fourteen or more years of age may but need not necessarily be appointed. Temporary guardians, with full powers of general guardians, may be appointed but their terms may not run more than 6 months. UPC § 5–204(b).

3. GUARDIAN OF INCAPACITATED PERSONS

Generally, an incapacitated person is one who for any reason except minority is "lacking sufficient understanding or capacity to make or communicate responsible decisions." *See* UPC § 5–103(7). For example, this includes mental illness, mental deficiency, physical illness or disability, chronic use of drugs and chronic intoxication.

The UPC allows the spouse or parent of an incapacitated person to appoint a guardian for the person by will or by any other writing which is signed by the spouse or parent and attested by at least two witnesses. UPC § 5–301(a), and (b). A spouse's appointment takes priority over a parent's appointment if they conflict.

UPC § 5–301(b). In addition, the appointment in the will of the last parent to die has priority over the first to die unless the surviving parent has been adjudged incapacitated or the will of the last parent to die is denied probate in formal testacy proceedings. UPC § 5–301(a). Apparently any person can be appointed. *See* UPC §§ 5–301(d); 5–301, cmt.

Although any qualified person may be appointed guardian of an incapacitated person, the UPC provides a nonmandatory priority list of suggested candidates that will be followed unless a lack of qualification, good cause or the best interest of the incapacitated person dictates otherwise. UPC § 5–305(a), and (b). The suggested order for consideration is as follows:

(1) Person nominated in the most recent durable power of attorney executed by the incapacitated person;

(2) Incapacitated person's spouse;

(3) Spouse's nominee if any;

(4) An adult child of the incapacitated person;

(5) Incapacitated person's parent;

(6) Parent's nominee if any;

(7) Any relative with whom the incapacitated person resided for more than 6 months;

(8) Person nominated by incapacitated person's caretaker.

UPC § 5–305(b), and (c). The Court must select the best qualified among candidates of equal priority. UPC § 5–306(d).

4. CONSERVATOR OF THE ESTATE

It is common to separate provisions concerned with the custody and care of the ward's person from its provisions concerned with the management of the protected person's estate. This fiduciary relationship is usually called guardian of the property or conservatorship. *See* Averill, U.P.C. Nutshell § 32.01.

Usually, the conservator must be an individual or a corporation possessing trustee powers. UPC § 5–409(a). In addition, a list of specific priorities for the Court's consideration in making an appointment follows in Chart IX–1–2.

CHART IX–I–2	
Priority Order for Appointment of a Conservator	
Rank	Description of Candidates
1	Similar kind of fiduciary appointed by an appropriate court in any jurisdiction in which the protected person resides.
2	Nominee of the protected person if the latter is at least fourteen years of age and the Court determines the person has sufficient mental capacity to make an intelligent choice.
3	The spouse of the protected person.
4	Any adult child of the protected person.
5	A parent of the protected person including a deceased parent's testamentary nominee.
6	Any relative with whom the protected person resided for more than six months prior to the petition.
7	Any person nominated by the person caring for or paying benefits to the protected person.

Chart IX–1–2 requires additional explanation. The first priority would apparently include an appropriate fiduciary appointed in a foreign country. Including the nominee of the protected person, persons holding priority through the first six ranks may nominate in writing another person to serve in the nominator's stead. UPC § 5–409(b). The seventh priority would include public or governmental agencies such as the Veterans' Administration. Between persons of equal priority, the Court has discretion to select the one best qualified if more than one is willing to serve. In addition, for good cause shown, the Court has discretion to ignore these priorities and to appoint anyone, including a person with less or without any priority. UPC § 5–409(b) .

E. REVIEW QUESTIONS

1. What is the title of the person who has a duty, created by his or her undertaking, to act primarily for another's benefit in matters connected with that undertaking.
2. What are the responsibilities of a personal representative of a decedent's estate?
3. What is meant by the phrase "Whom the testator will trust so will the law"?
4. Any competent natural person or legal entity capable of taking title to property may be a trustee. True or False?
5. When is a guardianship necessary?
6. What is the primary difference between a guardian of the person and the conservator?

II

DUTIES OF FIDUCIARIES

Analysis

1. Statement of the No Delegations Rule
2. Requirement of Supervision
3. Total Delegation of Trust Duties

E. Duty to Identify and Segregate Trust Property
1. Extent of Duty to Identify and Segregate
2. Prohibition on Commingling Other Property
3. Earmarking Trust Assets
4. Consequences of Failure to Identify and Segregate

F. Duty to Take Control of Assets and to Make Accounts
1. Personal Representative Requirement to Collect and Appraise the Estate
2. Inventory
3. Appraisal Process
4. Subsequently Discovered Property

G. Duty to Account
1. Personal Representative's Accounts
a. Final Closing and Accounting
b. UPC Accountings
2. Trustee's Accounts
a. Failure to Keep Accounts
b. Court Supervised Trusts
c. Proceeding for Accounting
d. Trust Provisions Waiving Accounts
e. Trustee's Record Keeping
g. Res Judicata for Prior Accountings

H. Review Questions

A. THE GENERAL AND COMMON DUTIES OF A FIDUCIARY

1. THE GENERAL AND COMMON DUTIES OF A FIDUCIARY

An abbreviated list of duties for a fiduciary include the duties:

- Of loyalty;
- Not to delegate;
- To take control of assets and to render accounts;
- To segregate property;
- To use reasonable care and skill;
- To treat all of the beneficiaries impartially when carrying out the many duties of administration; and,
- To account.

2. TRUSTEE'S PRIMARY DUTY

The primary duty of a trustee is to administer the property of the trust for the beneficiaries.

3. PERSONAL REPRESENTATIVE'S PRIMARY DUTY

The primary duty of a personal representative is to administer the property in the estate first for the benefit of the creditors of the estate and second for the distributees. Thus, notice to creditors and completing an inventory of decedent's assets are of primary importance. Because a personal representative is primarily involved in a liquidation process, a personal representative does not ordinarily have a duty to keep the property productive. Under the UPC, for example, the general duty in the use of the authority conferred is properly to distribute and settle the estate in an expeditious and efficient manner which is consistent with the best interests of the estate. UPC § 3–703(a).

4. DRAFTING CONSIDERATIONS

Most of the duties of fiduciaries may be affected by terms of the governing instrument. For example, the standard of care can be lowered, self-dealing may be permitted, and accountings waived. Ordinarily, global exceptions and waivers to these duties should not be granted in the instrument. The exceptions and waivers should be tailored to the needs of the estate or trust.

B. STANDARD OF CARE, SKILL AND PRUDENCE

1. DEFINITION OF STANDARD OF CARE

The SECOND RESTATEMENT and the common law definition of the standard of care and skill states that a trustee must exercise the care and skill that a person of ordinary prudence would exercise in dealing with his or her own property. *See* RESTATEMENT (SECOND) OF TRUSTS § 174. Generally, courts also use this definition as a standard of care for other fiduciary relationships.

2. MEANING OF THE WORD "PRUDENCE"

In this context, prudence means "caution." In application, this means how a prudent trustee would act in administering the property of others or how he or she would act in conserving the property.

3. UPC STANDARD

The UPC provides that a personal representative, conservator, and trustee must act as a prudent person dealing with the property of another. UPC §§ 3–703(a), 5–416, 7–302.

4. DIFFERENCE BETWEEN RESTATEMENT AND UPC

The difference is more of semantics than effect. Courts in applying the RESTATEMENT standard interpreted the prudence requirements to require a trustee to act as a person handling another person's property.

5. NON–VARYING STANDARD

Unless the settlor or testator reduces the amount of skill and prudence, the standard will not be lowered. That a particular fiduciary does not possess the necessary skill or prudence is not a defense. Exculpatory clauses have been strictly construed.

6. HIGHER STANDARD ENFORCED

If a fiduciary possesses or represents that it possesses greater than ordinary skill and more than ordinary facilities, it is under a duty to exercise the skill and to utilize the facilities at its disposal. Restatement (Second) Trusts § 174, cmt. a.; U.P.C. § 7–302. *See also* RESTATEMENT (THIRD) OF TRUSTS § 227, cmt. d.

C. DUTY OF LOYALTY

1. PRINCIPLE OF LOYALTY

The principle behind the duty of loyalty is that the fiduciary must administer the estate or trust solely in the interest of the beneficiaries. The fiduciary is not permitted to place personal interests in a position where it would be for the fiduciary's own benefit to violate the duty to the beneficiaries.

The duty of loyalty is broadly applied. A trustee not only violates the duty of loyalty when the trustee purchases trust property individually but also when the trustee uses trust property for the trustee's own financial or other purposes. RESTATEMENT (THIRD) TRUSTS, PRUDENT INVESTOR RULE, § 170 (1992). A trustee, therefore, cannot properly personally borrow money or lease land held in the trust, or invest trust funds in the trustee's own business. *Id.*

2. SELF–DEALING STRICT LIABILITY

If a trustee personally purchases trust property, good faith and fair consideration are not defenses. The duty of loyalty is strictly construed against the fiduciary. Courts use what is called the "no-further-inquiry" rule. If a fiduciary engages in self-dealing, *e.g.,* sells trust property to itself personally or buys personal assets for the trust, this conduct is per se illegal. The beneficiaries can surcharge the fiduciary for any profit and any loss or return the assets if still available, regardless of the substantive fairness of the deal and regardless of the fiduciary's good faith.

The only defense to self-dealing is consent of the beneficiaries after full disclosure.

If the fiduciary places itself in a position of conflict of interest that does not include self-dealing, then fairness, reasonableness and good faith are relevant.

3. RATIONALE BEHIND THIS STRICT RULE

The strict rule against self-dealing is a prophylactic rule that attempts to eliminate a choice of loyalty. It demands that fiduciaries not allow themselves to assume a position of conflict. In this way it tries to avoid potential conflicts and requires undivided loyalty. By rigid adherence to the strict rule, all temptation is removed from one acting as a fiduciary to serve the fiduciary's own interest when in conflict with the obligations of the trust or estate.

Furthermore, to permit a defense of good faith and fairness may require the beneficiaries to offer evidence of bad faith, wrongdoing or unfairness to the estate. This may impose a difficult burden on the beneficiary particularly if the issues are presented a long time after the event and the fiduciary has had the opportunity to cover its tracks.

Besides, there are no countervailing reasons to allow a conflict. Finally, the strict rule is buttressed by the arguments of clarity and administrative efficiency.

4. ARGUMENTS AGAINST THE STRICT RULE

Some contend the strict rule gives beneficiaries a windfall when loss is caused by a decline in general market valuations. In this situation, the loss would have resulted even if the trust or estate assets had been earmarked. It is argued that it makes even the innocent non-earmarking trustee an insurer against all losses to the beneficiaries. This harshness may cause some otherwise responsible individuals and institutions to refuse to accept the fiduciary office. It is contended that a rule of reasonableness sufficiently protects beneficiaries against risks of loss.

5. COURT APPROVAL

If a situation developed where it is advantageous for a fiduciary to self-deal with the estate or trust, the appropriate action is to seek approval from the appropriate court. A court, after reviewing all of the relevant facts, could be sought to approve the transaction. Sometimes courts have approved such transactions post facto when there was insufficient time to apply to the court prior to the transaction and approval was sought immediately thereafter.

6. DRAFTING SOLUTION

It is frequently apparent to all at the time of the creation of the estate or trust, that self-dealing may be necessary or desirable for all concerned. When this is the case, provisions in the governing instrument may be advisable to permit it specifically, *e.g.*, allow a bank trustee to deposit funds in its banking department or permit the fiduciary to purchase assets from the estate or trust under prescribed circumstances.

D. DUTY NOT TO DELEGATE

1. STATEMENT OF THE NO DELEGATIONS RULE

At common law the trustee was not permitted to delegate trust responsibilities. The SECOND RESTATEMENT changed this rule to state that a trustee is under a duty not to delegate the doing of acts which the trustee can reasonably be required personally to perform. RESTATEMENT (SECOND) OF TRUSTS § 171.

The 1992 changes to the Restatement now provide that a trustee has a duty personally to perform the responsibilities of the trusteeship except as a prudent person might delegate those responsibilities to others. RESTATEMENT (PRUDENT INVESTOR RULE) TRUSTS § 171. Basically, "the trustee is under a duty to the beneficiaries to exercise fiduciary discretion and to act as a prudent person would act in similar circumstances." *Id.*

A trustee may delegate fiduciary authority when it is reasonably intended to further sound administration of the trust. The trustee has fiduciary discretion to delegate such functions and in such manner as a prudent investor would delegate under the circumstances. RESTATEMENT (PRUDENT INVESTOR RULE) OF TRUSTS § 171, cmt. f.

2. REQUIREMENT OF SUPERVISION

Even if delegation is permitted, however, the trustee cannot totally delegate the responsibility and must exercise general supervision over any agent's conduct. RESTATEMENT (PRUDENT INVESTOR RULE) OF TRUSTS § 171, cmt. k.

3. TOTAL DELEGATION OF TRUST DUTIES

Unless the trust instrument permits, a trustee may not properly commit the entire administration of the trust to an agent, co-trustee, or other person. RESTATEMENT (PRUDENT INVESTOR RULE) OF TRUSTS § 171, cmt. e.

Illustration 1: T, as trustee of a trust created in S's will, transfers the trust property to C, who agrees to perform the trust. T has breached the trustee's duty to administer the trust.

E. DUTY TO IDENTIFY AND SEGREGATE TRUST PROPERTY

1. EXTENT OF DUTY TO IDENTIFY AND SEGREGATE

Ordinarily the trustee has a duty (1) to keep the trust property separate from trustee's own property; (2) to keep the trust property separate from property held upon other trusts; and (3) to identify and earmark the trust property as property of the trust.

2. PROHIBITION ON COMMINGLING OTHER PROPERTY

The trustee must not commingle trust funds with trustee's own funds. The trustee may be permitted by the terms of the trust, however, to mingle trust property with trustee's own property

The commingling prohibition does not apply when it may be proper for the trustee to mingle funds of the different trusts by deposit thereof in a common bank account. A bank trustee when authorized can properly deposit in a single trust account in another bank the funds of several trusts, provided that it keeps an accurate record of the contributions of the separate trusts.

3. EARMARKING TRUST ASSETS

A trustee must earmark trust property as trust property. In other words, title to land acquired by the trustee as trust property should be held and recorded in the name of the trustee as trustee. Certificates of stock should be issued in the name of the trustee as trustee. If bonds held in trust are registered, they should be registered in the name of the trustee as trustee. RESTATEMENT (SECOND) OF TRUSTS § 179, cmt. d.

4. CONSEQUENCES OF FAILURE TO IDENTIFY AND SEGREGATE

A trustee will not be liable for a technical breach of trust that involves a trustee taking title to the trust property in trustee's individual name in good faith if no loss results. But, if a loss resulted from the fact that trustee took title in trustee's own name, such as trustee's personal creditors were thereby enabled to reach the property free of trust, the trustee is liable for the loss even if trustee acted in good faith. The trustee is liable for the full amount of the loss and interest thereon, if trustee took title in trustee's own name in bad faith with intent to misappropriate the property.

F. DUTY TO TAKE CONTROL OF ASSETS AND TO MAKE ACCOUNTS

1. PERSONAL REPRESENTATIVE REQUIREMENT TO COLLECT AND APPRAISE THE ESTATE

Generally, a personal representative of a decedent's estate must identify and take into his or her possession the decedent's estate as can be found. Within a set period time, frequently three months, the personal representative must prepare an inventory of the estate and must file it with the court or send it to interested persons or both. The personal representative may be subject to removal for failure to complete the inventory responsibilities. *See* UPC § 3–706, cmt.

2. INVENTORY

The inventory of the estate must list the decedent's assets with reasonable detail indicating the fair market value and the amount of any encumbrance existing as to each asset. *See, e.g.*, UPC § 3–706.

3. APPRAISAL PROCESS

In some states the personal representative must hire one or more appraisers to value the property of the estate. They may even have to be appointed by the court. Under the UPC the personal representative may personally value the assets at fair market value or may employ other qualified and disinterested appraisers as is required under the circumstances. UPC § 3–707. The UPC grants specific authority to hire different appraisers for different types of assets. If outside appraisers are employed, their names and addresses must be included and the item they appraised must be indicated on the inventory.

4. SUBSEQUENTLY DISCOVERED PROPERTY

If subsequent property is discovered or the value or description of property on the original inventory is erroneous or misleading, the personal representative must prepare a supplementary inventory and appraisement which provides the same information necessary on the original item for the subsequently discovered property or for the property revalued or redescribed. *See, e.g.*, UPC § 3–708. Supplementary inventory must be sent or filed or both as the original inventory had been.

G. DUTY TO ACCOUNT

1. PERSONAL REPRESENTATIVE'S ACCOUNTS

In states that have a formal administration procedure for the administration of estates, it is common to require the personal representative to file periodic accountings of transactions that occurred during the period.

a. Final Closing and Accounting

A full accounting of the actions and transaction occurring during the administration is usually required in a formal closing proceeding brought by the personal representative. Notice to interested persons is required. If interested persons object, a hearing will be held to resolve disputes. After all disputes are settled or if no one objects, the court then approves the accounting, closes the estate and discharges the personal representative.

b. UPC Accountings

The UPC does not contain a standard accounting requirement. Interested persons may file petitions for accountings if that remedy is desired. If a formal closing procedure is desired or required (under a supervised administration), formal proceedings terminating administration must be instituted by petition by the personal representative or any devisee under the will. A request for a final accounting is part of this formal closing process. A hearing is to be held only after notice has been given to all devisees and the personal representative. The Court is empowered to approve the accounting and order the discharge of the personal representative.

2. TRUSTEE'S ACCOUNTS

A trustee is under a duty to keep and render accounts and to furnish the beneficiary information at reasonable times. *See generally* RESTATEMENT (SECOND) TRUSTS § 172. These accounts must show in detail the nature and amount of the trust property and the administration thereof. Statutes control this in some states. *See* UPC § 7–303.

a. Failure to Keep Accounts

A trustee is liable for any loss or expense resulting from trustee's failure to keep proper accounts. The trustee has the burden of proof to show that the trustee is entitled to the claimed credits. Failure to keep proper accounts and vouchers may inhibit trustee's proof of the these credits.

b. Court Supervised Trusts

In some states when a trustee is appointed by a court such as under a testamentary trust, the trustee may be required to submit accountings at designated intervals to the proper court for its approval.

c. Proceeding for Accounting

Any person financially interested in the trust administration may bring suit to review or to force an accounting. Persons who are financially interested include both the beneficiaries presently entitled to the payment of income or principal, and the beneficiaries who will be or may be entitled to receive income or principal in the future, contingent or otherwise.

d. Trust Provisions Waiving Accounts

If the trust instrument relieves the trustee from the necessity of keeping formal accounts, a beneficiary cannot expect to receive reports concerning the trust estate. Notwithstanding that the trust instrument relieves the trustee from all obligation to account, the beneficiary may, by suit, require the trustee to account and to show that the trustee faithfully and dutifully performed the trust. The trustee will be liable to whatever remedies may be appropriate due to any revealed breach of trust.

e. Trustee's Record Keeping

Trustees must keep records that are so complete and accurate that the trustee can prove faithfulness to the trust. If the trustee does not keep records, all evidentiary presumptions and doubts are resolved against the trustee.

If a fiduciary can be rendered free from the duty of informing the beneficiaries concerning matters to which the beneficiaries are entitled to know and if the trustee can also be made immune from liability resulting from trustee's breach of trust, equity has been rendered impotent. Unless the instrument manifests an intention that the property should be held free of trust, courts are not going to allow a provision to create a virtual license to the trustee to convert the fund to trustee's own use and thereby terminate the trust.

f. Consequences for Failure to Account

If the trustee fails to account when required, the trustee may be:

- removed,
- deprived of trustee's compensation, and
- liable for costs of suit requiring him to account.

g. Res Judicata for Prior Accountings

When an accounting is approved by a court, the order of the court is final but only to matters determined by and before the court. The trustee's duty is to make the fullest measure of disclosure.

h. Informal Accounting Reports

It is common for corporate trustees to present to beneficiaries a written statement of the trust work at frequent intervals, *e.g.,* annually or bi-annually. The statements are brief condensed outlines of the work of the trustees during the stated period. The beneficiaries are asked to give express written approval of the accounts thus rendered: if no objection is received within a limited period, the trustee will consider the accounts approved. The beneficiary is bound only if the trustee made a proper disclosure in the accounting of the conduct in question in the administration of the trust.

H. REVIEW QUESTIONS

1. How does the primary duty of a trustee differ from the primary duty of a personal representative?
2. What is the standard of care of a trustee?
3. A higher standard can be imposed if a fiduciary possesses or represents that it possesses greater than ordinary skills and more than ordinary facilities. True or False?
4. What is the "no-further-inquiry" rule?
5. At common law the trustee was not permitted to delegate trust responsibilities. How does the rule in the RESTATEMENT (SECOND) OF TRUSTS differ?
6. What are the purposes of the accounting requirement for trustees?

*

III

POWERS OF FIDUCIARIES

Analysis

A. POWERS CONCEPT

1. INTERRELATIONSHIPS OF FIDUCIARY CONCEPTS

Professor Scott indicated that a fiduciary's powers, duties and liabilities are different ways of saying the same thing. AUSTIN W. SCOTT, ABRIDGEMENT OF LAW OF TRUSTS § 163A (1960) If a trustee does not have the power to act in a particular way, the trustee breaches the trust and is liable for the consequential loss if the trustee so acts. The power to act means there is no duty not to act and thus no liability. The scope of a trustee's powers depend upon the scope of the trustee's duties: liability springs only from breach of duties.

2. POWERS OF THE PERSONAL REPRESENTATIVE

Generally, non–UPC law concerned with the administration of decedents' estates frequently includes several unmeritorious characteristics. First, nearly every action taken by a personal representative requires an order by the appropriate court either when initiating the action or when obtaining approval for it, or at both times. Second, and even of a greater hindrance to efficient administration, the personal representative lacks any degree of broad powers necessary to administer the estate. Finally, the restrictiveness of the law places a burden of severe potential liability on the personal representative if one attempts to act on one's own without court order. The consequence of these characteristics is that the prudent, cautious personal representative is forced to obtain court approval for actions taken thereby substantially increasing the time and cost involved in the administration of an estate.

For example, the power of a personal representative to sell property of the estate was commonly limited by the law of many states. Unless the sale was specifically authorized by the will, if any, all sales of all types of property had to be made under court order. Modern legislation such as the UPC grants the personal representative power to sell, even for credit. *See* UPC § 3–715, (6) (23).

a. Estate Planning Relief

Significantly, provisions limiting court involvement, broadening the personal representative's powers, and exculpating the personal representative from certain liabilities typically constitute a substantial and significant portion of a well drafted will in these states.

b. UPC Approach

Many jurisdictions have greatly expanded the express and implied powers of the personal representative. The UPC is an example of this approach. Except as restricted by the terms of the will or requested of interested persons and ordered by a court, the personal representative is to administer the estate as rapidly as possible without court supervision or intervention. UPC § 3–704. In order to permit administration without continual or frequent court involvement, the UPC confers upon a personal representative significant administrative powers. First, the personal representative is given the same power over the title to decedent's property that an absolute owner would have except that it is in a trust-like relationship for the benefit of all interested in the estate including creditors and successors. UPC § 3–711. Second, in exercising proper drafting concepts, the UPC authorizes the personal representative and any successors to perform twenty-seven specified transactions. UPC § 3–715. For example, the personal representative is empowered: (1) to make extraordinary repairs or alterations on the estate's structural assets [UPC § 3–715(7)]; (2) to borrow money [UPC § 3–715(16)]; (3) to hold securities in the name of a nominee [UPC § 3–715(14)]; (4) to set reasonable compensation for the personal representative's own services [UPC § 3–715(18)]; (5) to employ agents who may perform acts of administration whether or not discretionary [UPC § 3–715(21)]; and (6) to incorporate any of decedent's businesses or ventures engaged in at the time of his death. UPC § 3–715(25) .

Exercise Standard: All of these powers must be exercised "reasonably for the benefit of interested persons." UPC § 3–715. Thus, the power is given, but it may only be exercised if the latter standard is satisfied.

3. POWERS OF TRUSTEE

A trustee may exercise all powers conferred by the specific terms of the trust and any other power necessary or appropriate to carry out the purposes of the trust which are not expressly or impliedly forbidden. The nature and extent of a trustee's duties and powers are primarily determined by the terms of the trust including any form of judicially provable intent.

It can be assumed that the settlor intends to confer upon the trustee the powers necessary to carry out the purposes of the trust. For example, if property is transferred into a trust which is to pay income to a beneficiary, the trustee can perform the acts necessary or appropriate not only to protect and preserve the property but also those acts necessary to make the property productive.

a. Trustee's Implied Powers

When a trustee has neither an express power nor statutory authority, to determine whether a trustee has a particular power, the courts generally consider:

- The language of the trust instrument;
- The purpose of the trust; and,
- The character of the trust's assets.

b. Forbidden Powers

If the terms of the trust forbid a trustee from performing an act, the trustee must not perform the act even though a trustee would normally be assumed to have the power to do so. For example, if the trust forbids the sale of an asset transferred to the trust, the trustee cannot sell it even if investment powers are otherwise granted to the trustee. If sale was necessary to save the trust, a court might order the trustee to sell the asset on the principle of equitable deviation from administrative provisions. *See supra* Part 6.V.D.1

4. UNIFORM TRUSTEES POWERS ACT (UTPA)

The UTPA impacts trust powers significantly. *See also* UPC §§ 3–711, 715. The Act applies to "trusts" that contemplate general trust administration whether they are inter vivos or testamentary, or characterized as charitable, or private trust.

Prudent Trustee Concept: The Act adopts the prudent person concept as a pervasive regulator of trustee action. UTPA § 1(3). This approach necessarily changes and liberalizes the doctrine of implied powers. Under the Act, the trustee must determine whether it has the necessary power to act: if the trustee makes this determination in good faith and within the bounds of reasonable judgment, courts should be precluded from substituting their judgment for that of the trustee. UTPA § 3(a). It is important to understand, however, that because a power is conferred does not mean the trustee should exercise it. The mere existence of power is not enough to justify its exercise. It is only if the power conferred ought to be exercised that a trustee is permitted to exercise the power.

Listed Powers: UTPA contains a long list of powers that the trustee may exercise using the standard of care required for all trustee actions. As with the UPC, the list covers every primary power a trustee would need to use to properly administer the trust. These powers include, for example, power to sell, lease and mortgage trust assets and even the power to borrow in general.

UTPA Powers That Were Prohibited at Common Law: The specific powers provided to a trustee significantly alter some of the common law rules concerning expressed or implied powers.

Regarding loyalty and other conflicts of interest, UTPA permits a trustee to

- Retain assets though the trustee has an interest in them. UTPA § 3(c)(1).
- Acquire an undivided interest in trust property. UTPA § 3(c)(4).
- Deposit trust funds in its own bank. UTPA § 3(c)(6).
- Put a lien on trust assets for reimbursement. UTPA § 3(c)(18)
- Fix its own compensation. UTPA § 3(c)(20).
- Hire persons associated with the trustee. UTPA § 3(c)(24).

Regarding the common law's limited delegation powers, UTPA permits the trustee to give proxies to someone else. UTPA § 3(c)(13). In direct contradiction to the common law, the trustee may delegate discretion to agents and act upon an agent's recommendations without independent investigation. UTPA § 3(c)(24). On the other hand, a "trustee shall not transfer his office to another or delegate the entire administration of the trust to a co-trustee or another." UTPA § 4

In regard to the common law requirement of segregation of trust property, the trustee can hold securities in the name of nominee and is only liable for the nominee's act in regard to the security. UTPA § 3(c)(16).

Although Section 3(c)(5) of the Act states it does not change the trustee's investment power, subsection (7) (sell trust asset on credit) and (8) (make extraordinary repairs or alterations to trust assets) give the trustee powers that some courts have held to fall under the investment limitations. *See* UTPA § 3(c)(5), (7), (8); *see also* UPC § 3–715(5).

5. TRUSTEE UNANIMITY

At common law multiple trustees had to act with unanimity unless otherwise provided in the instrument. *See also* UPC § 3–717. Disagreement constituted a rejection of the proposed action. Section § 6(a) of UTPA make unanimity unnecessary. If a third person requires unanimity, however, UTPA permits the trustees to achieve it without making the dissenting trustee a part of the action.

6. SETTLOR'S LIMITATION ON POWERS

It is universally agreed that a settlor may limit a trustee's powers. The UTPA recognizes this rule except that the settlor probably cannot change § 7 which requires third persons dealing with the trustee to have actual notice of a breach of trust in order to be liable. If settlor could change this power, it would destroy the purposes of the Act because it would restore the duty of inquiry even in cases where clearly not intended.

B. THE INVESTMENT FUNCTION

1. INVESTMENT STANDARD

A fiduciary must invest and manage the funds of the trust as a prudent investor would, in light of the purposes, terms, distribution requirements, and other circumstances of the trust. *See* Restatement (Third) of Trusts § 227 (1992). The trustee must possess and exercise ordinary intelligence in the investment function. *See* Restatement (Third) of Trusts § 227, cmt. d (1992). Fiduciaries, who possess a greater investment skill than an individual of ordinary ability must use that higher level of skill.

2. BASES OF JUDGING FIDUCIARY INVESTMENTS

A fiduciary's investments are judged on two bases.

- Whether the investment is of a type in which the fiduciary may properly invest. This issue is controlled by statute, judicial decision, or the terms of the specific trust. Compliance with the general fiduciary standards of care, skill and prudence is not a defense when the investment is of a type not permitted to the fiduciary.

- Whether the particular investment chosen from the permissible type is proper. The fiduciary may defend investment actions by showing compliance with the skill, care and cautions exercised by the fiduciary.

3. THE INVESTMENT FUNCTION OF AN EXECUTOR OR ADMINISTRATOR

Normally the personal representative does not have an investment function. It may be granted or implied from the will.

Interrelationship Between Powers and the Investment Function: Sometimes a question arises whether a certain action by the personal representative is an exercise of a permissible power or an act of investment. For example, even if a power of sale is conferred, would taking a mortgage as part of the purchaser's financing fall within the fiduciary's powers. A mortgage is a type of investment, and the personal representative's investment powers might have to be considered.

The UPC permits the personal representative to "deposit or invest liquid assets of the estate ... in federally insured interest-bearing accounts, readily marketable secured loan arrangements or other prudent investments which would be reasonable for use by trustees generally" if funds are not needed to meet currently payable debts and expenses or distributions.

4. THE INVESTMENT FUNCTION OF A TRUSTEE

Normally, a trustee must use reasonable care and skill to make the trust property productive in a manner that is consistent with the fiduciary duties of caution and impartiality. RESTATEMENT (THIRD) TRUSTS: PRUDENT INVESTOR RULE § 181 (1992). This means that property held in the trust should produce reasonable earnings during all appropriate investment periods. If property is unproductive, it needs to be made productive or sold unless the trust instrument requires otherwise or the circumstances indicate otherwise.

5. LIMITED INVESTMENT POLICY

A few states have statutes, called legal-list statutes, that restrict the trust investment to particular types of investments. Some of these statutes restrict investments of only a portion of the trust fund. These statutes can be avoided by the settlor granting broader investment authority in the trust.

6. PRUDENT PERSON RULE

The Massachusetts Court in a landmark decision held that in regard to trustee investments:

> "[A] trustee to invest [trust funds must] conduct himself faithfully and exercise sound discretion," and must ... "observe how men of prudence, discretion and intelligence manage their own affairs, not in regard to speculation, but in regard to the permanent disposition of their funds, considering the probable income, as well as the probable safety of the capital to be invested."

Harvard College v. Amory, 9 Pick. (26 Mass.) 446, 461 (1830).

Under the test, the Court prohibited investments into speculative ventures. In addition, as between the beneficiaries, "so far as reasonably practicable, [the trustee must] hold the balance even between the claims of the life tenant and those of the remaindermen." *See Appeal of Dickinson,* 25 N.E. 99, 100 (Mass. 1890).

SECOND RESTATEMENT OF TRUSTS Rule: Using the term "prudent-man rule," the SECOND RESTATEMENT OF TRUSTS declares that it is the trustee's duty "to make such investments and only such investments as a prudent man would make of his own property having in view the preservation of the estate and the amount and regularity of the income to be derived." RESTATEMENT (SECOND) TRUSTS § 227 (1959). Legislation has been enacted in most states codifying the rule or a close proximity to it.

When a trust document grants the trust authority to select investments "in the trustee's discretion," the trustee is limited by the "prudent trustee" rule regardless of the rule in the state.

a. Investment in Stock of Companies

The prudent investor rule allowed investments in corporate stock under certain criteria: "[W]hen the corporations have acquired by reason of the amount of their property, and the prudent management of their affairs, such a reputation that cautious and intelligent persons commonly invest their money in such stocks and bonds as permanent investments." *See Appeal of Dickinson,* 25 N.E. 99, 100 (Mass. 1890).

b. Diversification

Most states require that a trust fund be diversified. *See* RESTATEMENT (SECOND) OF TRUSTS § 228. New York is the exception. The "great weight of authority in this state is that diversification is not mandatory." *Matter of Mendleson's Will,*

261 N.Y.S.2d 525, 535 (N.Y. Surr. Ct. 1965). Within states that recognize the duty, the definition of the concept of diversification is subject to several meanings.

Restrictive Application: The concept of diversification has been linked with protecting the security of trust funds. When so characterized, a trust investment portfolio need not be diversified but invested in the most conservative investments such as federal government securities. If protection from risk of loss through default is the purpose of diversification then safety of the investment is the only consideration. *See, e.g., Commercial Trust Co. v. Barnard*, 142 A.2d 865 (N.J. 1958). Thus, it may be a breach of trust to have too large a proportion of the trust fund in a single investment if that investment fails or declines in value.

Expansive Definition: Diversification requires the trustee to invest in a wide range of investments in order to take advantage of the many attributes of the investment market place. Under the RESTATEMENT (THIRD) OF TRUST, PRUDENT INVESTOR RULE, diversification is concerned with (1) risk in the form of impaired purchasing power, (2) the duty of impartiality and (3) the objective of reducing so-called diversifiable (or uncompensated) risk. For example, under this approach a trustee might be surcharged for putting most or all of the trust's assets in long-term government bonds that carry no credit risk, if the heavy concentration of investment in these bonds subjected the trust assets "to both a market price risk and a liquidity risk." *See GIW Industries, Inc. v. Trevor, Stewart, Burton & Jacobsen, Inc.*, 10 E.B.C. 2290 (S.D.Ga.1989).

c. Non–Legal Investments

If investments become improper as to type, the trustee must get rid of them. If non-legal investments are included within the original trust, the trustee should dispose of them within a reasonable period unless specifically empowered to hold them. A trustee may be surcharged for retaining them if the trustee has not honestly exercised personal judgment based on actual consideration of existing conditions.

7. THE PRUDENT INVESTOR RULE

The RESTATEMENT (THIRD) OF TRUST, PRUDENT INVESTOR RULE (PIR) was adopted in 1992 and the UNIFORM PRUDENT INVESTORS ACT (UPIA)[1] was approved in 1994. Substantively, the UPIA and the PIR are similar. Both law sources were promulgated because the law under the prudent person rule had become stagnated with subrules. Whereas the prudent person rule had originally been adopted to provide flexibility to trustees in their investment decisions, cases under the rule had developed constructional precedents that limited that discretion. For example, an investment characterized as speculative for a trust in one case might carry that

1. As of 1999, 28 states had enacted a version of this act.

characterization through other cases where the characterization was not so appropriate. In addition, courts sometimes tested trustee liability merely on the merits of single investments rather than reviewing the merit of the entire portfolio. Prohibitions that developed under the traditional prudent man rule not only potentially imposed unjustified liability for trustees generally but also for skilled trustees in the exercise of sound judgment. For example, widely accepted theories and practices of investment management might not be properly pursued by trustees under some interpretations of the prudent person rule. The PIR and the UPIA are intended to solve these problems.

a. Purpose and Goals of the Prudent Investor Concept

The new investment rules are intended to accept modern investment experience and research, without either endorsing or excluding any particular theories of economics or investment. In addition, the rules are meant to be general and flexible enough to adapt to changes in the financial world. They try to provide both protection for the trustee and guidance for review of trustee actions by the courts. They allow the expert trustees to pursue challenging, rewarding, non-traditional strategies when appropriate to the particular trust, while providing less sophisticated trustees with reasonably clear guidance and safe harbors. This is a recognition of the importance and usefulness of modern portfolio theory.

b. First Principle of Modern Portfolio Theory

The value (price) of an asset is a function of two factors. First, the rate of total return (*i.e.*, ordinary income and capital appreciation) that the asset is anticipated to generate. Second, the risk that the actual return will fall short of the anticipated return.

The risk of shortfall of total return leads to a focus upon assets as integral parts of a whole portfolio rather than to a focus upon each asset in isolation. This analysis leads away from the labeling of any asset as inherently prudent or imprudent, per se.

Thus, the issue whether a trustee has discharged its duties focuses upon the manner in which the trustee has made investment decisions. RESTATEMENT (THIRD) OF TRUSTS § 227, cmt. b. The behavior of the trustee is judged in relation to actual circumstances, not in a vacuum. Trustee conduct is the key not portfolio performance. Thus, the risk of hindsight evaluation of assets is diminished.

Shortfall of Total Return: The risk of shortfall of return is divided into two categories: market risk and nonmarket risk.

- Market risk (sometimes known as systemic, systematic, nondiversifiable or compensated risk): This is the risk that the return in the market in which the asset is situated will fall short of the anticipated return, *e.g,* change in the monetary policy of the Board of Governors of the Federal Reserve System, or a general economic downturn. Modern portfolio theory espouses that the market compensates the investor for market risk. Compensation for this risk comes in the form of an adjustment of the return that inures to the particular asset. The market price varies directly in regard to the market's estimate of price volatility. Generally, a higher rate of return corresponds to a higher market risk of a shortfall. *See generally* RESTATEMENT (THIRD) OF TRUSTS § 227, cmt. g (1992).

An investor can regulate market risk by selecting a level of risk and (at least to some extent) reward and by selecting investments that are consistent with that level. For example, an investor might select investments that tend to rise and fall in value at a rate greater than, less than, or the same as the market as a whole, and the investor can tend to obtain rewards that vary commensurately.

The trustee should attempt to assemble a portfolio that maximizes return at any level of risk. Conversely, the trustee should attempt to assemble a portfolio that minimizes risk at any level of return.

- Nonmarket Risk (sometimes known as diversifiable, specific, unique or uncompensated risk): This is the risk that something may occur particularly with respect to the particular asset that may increase or decrease its return, *e.g,* the chief executive officer of a particular firm dies, or an earthquake or flood renders a plant inoperable. Modern portfolio theory espouses that to the extent this risk may cause a shortfall of return, it is a nonmarket risk. *See generally* RESTATEMENT (THIRD) OF TRUSTS § 227, cmt. g. (1992). Thus, the market does not compensate for the risk that an unanticipated event might reduce the fortunes of a particular company. An investor can protect against nonmarket risk by diversifying. *See generally* RESTATEMENT (THIRD) OF TRUSTS § 227, cmt. g. (1992). The duty to diversify for the purpose of eliminating nonmarket risk is a centerpiece of the Rule. The duty to diversify induces the trustee to focus upon each asset as an integral part of a portfolio and not in isolation.

Evaluating Risks: A trustee usually has a duty to incur what risk is necessary to obtain a return that preserves real values. Thus, for example, the trustee must regard inflation as a risk. Conversely, the selection of a level of reward that will cause inflation to erode the value of principal is a breach of the duty of the trustee who wants to use caution to preserve safety of capital. RESTATEMENT (THIRD) OF TRUSTS § 227, cmts. c and e (1992).

Risk Tolerance: Risk tolerance is the tolerance that a trust has to the volatility of return. This tolerance depends on an estimate of distribution obligations of the trust including both its regular distribution requirements and any irregular distributions that may in fact become necessary or appropriate. The trust obligations depend on the terms of the trust, as affected by the needs of one or more of the beneficiaries. RESTATEMENT (THIRD) OF TRUSTS § 227, cmt. e (1992).

Duty to Diversify: Generally, the Rule imposes a duty upon the trustee to eliminate the risk that is unique to each asset by imposing a duty to diversify. *See generally* RESTATEMENT (THIRD) OF TRUSTS § 227, cmt. g (1992). The duty to diversify addresses this risk problem. In addition, it reduce the importance, of nonmarket risk. No asset inherently is appropriate or inappropriate, per se. Thus, in investment selection, diversification elevates the importance of market risk and leads to the conclusion that the chief duties of the trustee are to determine and implement the mix of market risk and reward that is appropriate for the trust.

c. Second Principle of Modern Portfolio Theory

Modern portfolio theory contends that an investor is not able to outperform the market at whatever mix of risk and reward the investor is seeking. Attempts to do so are futile, counterproductive and wasteful. RESTATEMENT (THIRD) OF TRUSTS ch. 7 (Introduction, pp. 6–7; Reporter's Notes, pp. 75–76). The theory argues that capital markets are efficient, information is disseminated and reflected in prices immediately. Consequently, no asset is relatively overpriced or underpriced. The primary consequence of this theory on a trustee's investment strategy is that it prohibits the trustee from incurring costs that are not reasonable in amount. RESTATEMENT (THIRD) OF TRUSTS § 227(c)(3) (1992). A trustee who actively buys and sells investments must justify the increased transactional costs by increases in expected returns. The theory tends to sanction strategies of passive investment and to challenge active investment strategies that produce inferior returns. Investments such as index funds that tend to mimic a market as a whole are encouraged.

C. ALLOCATING RECEIPTS AND EXPENDITURES BETWEEN PRINCIPAL AND INCOME

1. THE ALLOCATION PROBLEM

All fiduciaries, including both personal representatives and trustees, often find themselves in the position of having to allocate expenses or income among beneficiaries. As there is a general duty to use reasonable care and skill and to act with impartiality between conflicting beneficiaries, the allocation decision may be difficult. *Cf.* RESTATEMENT (THIRD) TRUSTS: PRUDENT INVESTOR RULE § 181 (1992). The process is one of characterization. When the fiduciary receives property for the estate or trust, the fiduciary must determine whether that property should be characterized as income or principal. Similarly, when the fiduciary uses trust or estate assets to pay an expense, a characterization must be made to determine whether that expense is charged against the income or the corpus.

2. SOURCES OF ALLOCATION RULES

The fiduciary has three basic sources for allocation rules:

- Instructions included in the relevant transfer instrument. Instructions range in type from specific allocation rules, to the grant of discretion to the fiduciary to make the allocation.

- If no instruction or authority is included in the relevant instrument, the fiduciary must follow any relevant state statute.
- Third, if neither the instrument nor state statute specifies the proper method of allocation, the trustee must allocate in a reasonable and equitable manner, taking into account the interests of both income and principal beneficiaries.

3. UNIFORM PRINCIPAL AND INCOME ACTS

Several Uniform Acts have been promulgated and adopted by the states to deal with problems about the allocation of income and expenses among the estate or trust beneficiaries. Most states have enacted either the Uniform Principal and Income Act of 1931, its 1962 revision or its 1997 revision.

These Acts deal with four general problems affecting the rights of beneficiaries:

- The allocation of income earned during the administration of an estate that is to be distributed to trusts and to persons who receive outright bequests of specific property, pecuniary gifts, and the residue.
- The allocation of income interests between income and principal for any trust that begins when a person who creates the trust dies or transfers property to a trust during life.
- The allocation of income interests that end including who gets the income that has been received but not distributed, or that is due but not yet collected, or that has accrued but is not yet due.
- The allocation of income between principal and income for any interest that is received during administration of the estate or trust.

4. CONFLICTING INTERESTS BETWEEN BENEFICIARIES

A settlor of a trust may provide for both income and remainder beneficiaries. The income beneficiaries are granted the right to trust income: the remainder beneficiaries are granted the right to the principal when the trust terminates. With regard to the allocation of income and expenses against these beneficiaries interests, this arrangement places these two types of beneficiaries in conflict. Income beneficiaries want the trust corpus invested in property that generates high rates of return such as corporate bonds and mutual funds. Remainder beneficiaries want the trustee to invest in property that appreciates in value such as real property and growth stocks. An investment that is good for one type of beneficiary may not benefit another. Regarding expenses, each type of beneficiary wants expenses to be charged against the other beneficiaries' interest and not their own.

Illustration 1: Trustee invested in a government insured certificate of deposit that earn 7 percent interest. The income beneficiaries are pleased because the rate of return is relatively high and the investment is extremely safe. The remainder beneficiaries may be dissatisfied. Not only will the CD not grow in value because the face amount will be returned at maturity, but the actual value of the principal may decreased because of inflation. Generally, trustees must invest in investments that either benefit both types of beneficiaries or operate under a prudent investor rule where the entire investment portfolio is weighed rather than individual investments. *See* 9.III.B.

5. SPECIAL ALLOCATION RULES UNDER THE REVISED ACT

a. Income

Under Section 3 "income" is defined to include:

- Rent and other related payments;
- Interest and similar appreciation;
- Cash dividends or other distributions of value in lieu of cash dividends;
- Net business and farming profits determined under generally accepted accounting principles;
- Net receipts from interests in minerals or natural resources less the value of a specified portion allocated to principal;
- An amount from the disposition of underproductive property that equals the difference between the net proceeds and the amount, which if invested at 4% per year during the period of under-productivity, would have produced the net proceeds.

b. Principal

"Principal" is defined to include:

- Proceeds from sales of principal assets, repayments of loans and other payments in the nature of return of principal;
- Eminent domain proceeds;
- Insurance proceeds on principal assets;
- Stock dividends, stock splits, subscription rights, liquidating dividends, capital gains, depreciating or depletion distributions, and distributions pursuant to a call of shares, merger, consolidation, or reorganization.
- Receipts from the disposition of corporate securities, bonds or other obligations;
- A portion of production payments from natural resources;

- A portion of gross receipts, not exceeding 50% of net receipts (computed without allowance for depletion), received as a royalty from a working net profit or from any other interest in mineral or natural resources;
- Receipts from depletable assets, such as leaseholds, patents, copyrights, royalty rights, and rights to receive payment on a contract for deferred compensation, to the extent such receipts exceed 5% per year of the asset's inventory value;
- Profit resulting from the change in form of principal;
- Receipts from the disposition of underproductive property after allocation to income of a portion that represents delayed income.
- Any allowance for depreciation.

c. Expenses Against Income

Section 13 provides that charges against income include:

- Ordinary administration, management, or preservation of trust property expenses, including regularly recurring taxes assessed on principal, water rates, premiums on insurance covering the trust property, interest paid by the trustee, and ordinary repairs;
- A reasonable allowance under generally accepted accounting principles for depreciation upon property other than a beneficiary's residence;
- One-half of the court costs, attorney's fees, and other fees on periodic judicial accountings unless the court otherwise directs; [All such costs and fees may be charged to income if the matter primarily concerns the income interest.]
- One-half of the trustee's regular compensation, whether based on a percentage of principal or of income;
- All reasonable expenses incurred for current management of principal and application of income; and,
- Any tax assessed upon receipts defined as income under either the Revised Act or the governing instrument.

<u>Extraordinary Expense Against Income:</u> If any income charge is unusually high, it may be charged in a reasonable manner over a reasonable period of time so that income distributions can be regularly maintained.

d. Expenses Against Principal

The following are charges against principal:

- One-half of a trustee's regular compensation;

- Expenses reasonably incurred in connection with or concerning principal;
- Costs of investing and reinvesting principal;
- Payments to reduce the balance of an indebtedness;
- Expenses for the preparation of property for rental or sale;
- Expenses incurred in maintaining or defending any action for construction of a trust or to protect it or the trust property;
- Charges not charged against income;
- Extraordinary repairs or expenses incurred in making a capital improvement to principal;
- Any tax levied upon profit, gain, or other receipts allocated to principal even if classified as an income tax;
- Estate or inheritance taxes, including interest and penalties thereon; and,
- Loss sustained in a given year from the continuation of a business of which the settlor was a sole proprietor or a partner.

e. Income Earned During the Administration of an Estate under the Revised Act

- Under section 3(a)(3), net income includes all the income earned by an estate or realized from property sold to pay estate liabilities that is not payable to any beneficiary of an absolute pecuniary bequest.
- Unless the will provides otherwise, all debts, funeral expenses, estate taxes, attorney's fees, fiduciary commissions, and court costs are charged against the principal of the estate.
- Specific legatees and devisees receive the income from the property specifically devised or bequeathed to them, reduced by expenses clearly allocated to that property.
- The remaining net income is payable to all other beneficiaries except those who receive pecuniary legacies in proportion to their respective interests in the estate as of the dates of distribution and based on inventory values.

D. REVIEW QUESTIONS

1. What are the consequences to the administration of an estate, if the personal representative does not have broad express and implied powers?
2. The Uniform Trustees Powers Act (UTPA) changes and liberalizes the doctrine of implied powers. True or false.
3. Name some powers granted to trustees under UTPA not granted at common law.
4. The expressly granted powers granted to trustees under UTPA overrule a settlor's expressed contrary intent? True or false.
5. What are the three basic sources for allocation of principal and income for a fiduciary?
6. What are the four general problems affecting the rights of beneficiaries that are dealt with by the Uniform Principal and Income Acts?

*

IV

LIABILITY OF FIDUCIARIES AND OTHERS

Analysis

A. GENERAL FIDUCIARY LIABILITY

1. NATURE OF LIABILITY

Fiduciaries are not insurers of loss to the estate or trust. They are liable to beneficiaries for breaches of trust for violating a duty. They may also be liable to third persons for problems caused by contracts and torts occurring during the administration of the estate or trust.

2. PROPER PARTY

An action may be brought against a fiduciary, be it a personal representative, trustee or conservator, by a beneficiary, a creditor of the estate or trust, or a successor or co-fiduciary.

3. STATUS OF CLAIM

A judgment against a fiduciary is not a preferred claim unless the claimant is granted a lien on certain property of the fiduciary or where the claimant can trace particular trust property to particular assets or accounts owned by the fiduciary.

4. MEASURE OF DAMAGES TO BENEFICIARY

The fiduciary for breach of trust is liable for:

- Any loss or depreciation in value of the property of the estate or trust resulting from the breach.
- Any profit made by the fiduciary through the breach.
- Any profit which would have accrued to the property of the estate or trust if there had been no breach.

Offsetting a Loss by a Gain: A fiduciary can not directly offset a loss with a gain but can offset gain from sale of asset on which surcharge is made for losses.

5. JOINT AND SEVERAL LIABILITY

Multiple fiduciaries are liable jointly and severally to the beneficiaries. Fiduciaries that satisfy the claim have a right to indemnification from the other fiduciaries. The degree of indemnity will depend upon the culpability of the respective fiduciary. Innocent fiduciaries may be able to obtain complete indemnification from wrongdoing fiduciaries.

6. FIDUCIARY DEFENSES

If a fiduciary has breached the trust, good faith and reasonable exercise of care and skill are not defenses. When a fiduciary has a reasonable doubt as to the fiduciary's power and duties, it is generally recognized that the fiduciary may apply to the appropriate court for instructions at the expense of the trust. If the fiduciary acts pursuant to the court instructions that were obtained in good faith and upon full disclosure assuming the beneficiaries were parties to the proceeding, the fiduciary will then be protected.

7. BENEFICIARIES CONSENT TO THE BREACH

Beneficiaries are estopped if they consent to the fiduciary's action provided that the fiduciary has not concealed material facts and has acted in a manner consistent with its fiduciary relationship to the beneficiaries in obtaining the consent. Nonconsenting beneficiaries are not bound except under special circumstances, *e.g.*, consent of settlor of a revocable trust.

8. EXCULPATORY PROVISIONS

Clauses that attempt to relieve fiduciaries of liability for negligence are limited in effectiveness. Although they may be effective to exculpate the fiduciary from liability for nonvolitional behavior such as negligence, exculpatory clauses are not effective to relieve them of liability for:

- Breach of trust committed in bad faith, intentionally, or with reckless indifference to the interest of the beneficiary, or
- Any profit that the trustee derived from a breach of trust.

9. UPC RULE OF LIABILITY

The UPC provides that a personal representative is liable to interested persons for any damage or loss that results from a breach of a fiduciary duty in the improper exercise of a power. UPC § 3–712. This liability is characterized as the same as that of a trustee of an express trust. Consequently, prior law concerning the liability of trustees as developed by the statutes and courts is relevant.

B. A FIDUCIARY'S LIABILITY TO THIRD PARTIES

1. COMMON LAW RULE OF PERSONAL FIDUCIARY LIABILITY

The fiduciary is personally liable upon contracts, tax assessments and torts relating to the property and its management. *See* RESTATEMENT (SECOND) TRUSTS § 261 (1959). If the fiduciary pays, it will be reimbursed from the estate for its expenses if the fiduciary's administration was proper. Actions in tort or contract are brought and judgment entered in the fiduciary's individual capacity. The common law courts did not recognize the fiduciary as an individual, as being a separate entity from the fiduciary in a representative capacity.

a. Personal Liability Rationale

The rationale behind these rules was that the nature of the original liability and then the liability of the estate might cause a clash between the trustee's interests in its individual capacity versus its interests in its representative capacity. The conflict before the courts is often the need to balance the desire of assuring that injured persons are protected versus the burden on the fiduciary by liability for something not really caused by it. Holding the fiduciary personally liable is sometimes influenced by the availability of insurance for the fiduciary.

b. Avoiding Personal Liability

Generally, personal contract liability could be avoided by specific terms of the contract although this is effective only if the contract was one proper to the fiduciary's administration. RESTATEMENT (SECOND) TRUSTS § 263 (1959). In addition, contracting parties might not allow the trustee to limit liability in a contract because they desire the additional protection of another liable party or they enter the contract based on the fiduciary's personal credit and reputation. The instrument could not change the rule but only give the fiduciary the power to limit personal liability by specific terms of contracts with third persons.

c. Judgment Enforcement

The judgment creditor can reach the assets of the estate in equity through subrogation but the creditor's rights are dependent upon the fiduciary's right of indemnification.

2. UPC RULE OF LIABILITY

Under the UPC, the estate is made into a "quasi-corporation" for purposes of a personal representative's personal liability to third persons on contracts, from ownership or control of the estate's property and from torts arising out of the administration of the estate. UPC § 3–808, cmt. The personal representative becomes an agent of the entity (estate) and is liable not individually but only as an agent would be liable. UPC § 3–808.

Specific UPC Rules: A personal representative is personally liable under the following circumstances: (1) on contracts properly made in the course of the estate's administration only when expressly provided in the contract or when the representative capacity of the personal representative is not revealed in the contract. [UPC § 3–808(a)]; and, (2) for torts or for obligations arising from property ownership or control only when the personal representative is personally at fault. [UPC § 3–808(b)]. *See* UPC § 3–808 (Personal Representatives); § 5–429 (Conservators); and, § 7–306 (Trustees).

Fiduciary Liability Issue: Third persons may sue the estate for such claims in the name of the personal representative in a representative capacity regardless of the personal representative's personal liability. UPC § 3–808(c). The personal representative's personal liability to the estate may be litigated during the third person's initial action against the estate or in any other appropriate proceeding such as a proceeding for an accounting. UPC § 3–808(d).

C. THIRD PARTY LIABILITY TO TRUST OR BENEFICIARY

1. PARTIES TO THE ACTION

Normally the fiduciary brings an action against a third person who owes or has injured the estate. Two exceptions are recognized: (1) when a beneficiary has a possessory right which has been interfered with, and (2) when a trustee neglects or declines to act. In those situations the beneficiary may bring the action personally.

2. LIABILITY FOR TRUSTEE'S BREACH OF TRUST

a. Nature of the Liability

If a third person joined with a fiduciary in committing a breach of trust, that person is liable to the beneficiaries. Generally, the issues concern transactions between the third person and the trustee. If the question concerns the purchase by a third person of trust property from a trustee who commits a breach of trust in making the transfer, the third person is not liable if he or she paid value and did not have notice of the breach of trust. The third person may have to return the property or its value or the proceeds of resale if that person did not pay value or had notice of the breach. Although "value" paid need not be the fair market value it must be greater than would put a person on notice that a breach is involved or that a reasonable inquiry be made.

b. Notice of Breach of Trust

To be found to have joined, the third party must have notice of the breach of trust. There is diversity of opinion whether notice must be actual or can come from circumstances which would reasonably support knowledge of a breach. Some courts have held that a third person has notice if the third person had knowledge of facts that would cause a reasonable person to make an inquiry into the trustee's actions and it was likely that the breach of trust would have been discovered upon reasonable inquiry. Consequently, any third person who deals with a fiduciary faces the possibility of being liable for having participated in the personal representative's breach of the fiduciary responsibilities. *See* 4 AUSTIN W. SCOTT & WILLIAM F. FRATCHER, THE LAW OF TRUSTS § 279A (4th ed. 1987). Third persons have become very cautious and conservative in dealing with fiduciaries such as personal representatives.

c. Remedial Uniform Acts

A significant number of states have enacted one or more uniform laws that reduce the potential liability of third persons for the breach of trust by a fiduciary in particular commercial transactions. *See, e.g,* Uniform Commercial Code § 4–8–304 (2); Uniform Act for Simplifications of Fiduciary Security Transfers § 7; Trustees' Powers Act § 7. Under these acts, if a third person purchases for value an asset from a person known to be a trustee, the person takes good title unless he or she had actual knowledge or reason to believe that the transfer is in breach of trust. The third person is not bound to inquire whether the trustee has power to act or is properly exercising the power.

d. UPC Rule of Third Person Liability

Without changing or abandoning the basic rule, and for purposes of encouraging third persons to deal with a personal representative, the UPC reduces the potential liability of third persons in their dealings with the personal representative. If a person deals with or assists a personal representative in good faith and for value, that person is protected as if the personal representative properly exercised a power. UPC § 3–714. In addition, a third person is not required to inquire into the existence of a power or the propriety of its exercise because one knows one is dealing with a personal representative. A third person who pays or delivers assets to the personal representative is also not required to see to its proper application. Finally, unless the person had actual knowledge of a restriction on the personal representative's powers, of restrictive provisions in a will or even of court orders restricting the personal representative's power, restrictions of this nature are ineffective to cause the third person to be liable.

D. REVIEW QUESTIONS

1. Fiduciaries are insurers of loss to the estate or trust. Trust or false.
2. What are the general measures of damages to the beneficiary when the fiduciary commits a breach of trust?
3. Explain the application of estoppel to claims by a beneficiary who consented to the fiduciary's action.
4. At common law, the fiduciary is personally liable upon contracts, tax assessments and torts relating to the property and its management. True or false.
5. What is meant by the concept that under the UPC the estate is made into a "quasi-corporation"?
6. How have various remedial Uniform Acts reduced the potential liability of third persons for the breach of trust by a fiduciary in commercial transactions?

*

PART TEN

TAXATION

*

I

TAXATION OVERVIEW

Analysis

A. THE PLACE FOR TAXATION

1. ACCUMULATION OF WEALTH AND THE IMPOSITION OF TAXES

Since time immemorial, people who have accumulated wealth have battled the state, Crown, or whatever the ruling system, over duties such as taxes that the wealthy may have to pay to the government. The development of the feudal real property law was a product of this type of battle. Taxing authorities have found that the wealthy will struggle to find "loopholes" in the tax burden system. Consequently, taxes and other similar duties must be carefully drafted to avoid mere clever avoidance. The current federal gift and estate tax system is a product of careful and comprehensive draftsmanship. One clear attribute of this system is its comprehensive application to will substitutes as well as testamentary disposition. One cannot have an effective transfer tax system that does not deal with will substitutes of wide variety. Today in the federal tax system there are few "loopholes" for tax avoidance that have not been intentionally engrafted into the law.

2. TAX TRIUMVIRATE

For most estate planning purposes, the federal taxation system is composed of three basic elements: income tax, gift tax and estate tax.

Although the three types are meant to complement each other, they overlap to some extent. Thus, a transaction may be treated differently in the application of the three taxes. For example, a donor may make a gift of property that is subject to a gift tax, although its post transfer income remains taxable to the donor and its value might be included in the donor's gross estate at death for estate tax purposes. Estate planning decisions require that transactions be weighed only after three separate questions are determined:

- Is the transfer one on which a gift tax will be imposed?
- Will the transferred property be included in the donor's gross estate at the donor's death, notwithstanding the inter vivos transfer? And,
- Will the donor continue to be taxed on the post-transfer income generated by the transferred property?

3. FEDERAL TRANSFER TAX SYSTEM OVERVIEW

Under federal law, gratuitous transfers of property, including both probate and nonprobate transfers, are subject to an excise tax. This tax is usually imposed on the donor or the donor's estate. It can be derived from any of three transfer tax components: (1) the federal gift tax, (2) the federal estate tax, and (3) the federal generation skipping transfer tax.[1] As for donees, the receipt of lifetime or deathtime gifts of money or other property is not taxable to donees as income. *See* IRC § 102.

B. BLACK LETTER APPROACH

The explanation of the federal tax system in this Black Letter is only an outline of the subject matter. Its purpose is to acquaint the student with the existence of the current taxing system, to understand its importance to the law of succession, and to increase familiarity with the terminology and concepts. A full discussion of the intricacies and subtleties of the subject must be left to a separate course on federal transfer taxation.

C. REVIEW QUESTIONS

1. What are the three basic elements of the federal taxation system?
2. Under Federal law gratuitous transfers of property including both probate and nonprobate transfers are subject to an excise tax. True or false?

*

1. States have a wide variety of transfer taxes. Quite a few have inheritance taxes that tax the recipient of an after-death gratuitous transfer. Others have the estate and gift tax variety that taxes the donor. Many have a tax provision called "pick-up" or "sponge" taxes, which taxes only the portion of the tax the federal system concedes to the state of domicile. The relative importance of these state tax systems generally depend on the size of the taxable estate. They are significant enough that estate planners must consider them in designing the estate plan for an individual.

II

GIFT AND ESTATE TAXES

Analysis

A. UNIFIED TRANSFER TAX SYSTEM

1. HISTORY OF UNIFIED TAX

Prior to 1976, the federal estate and gift taxes operated independently rather than cumulatively. Each tax had its own exemption and progressive rate schedule. Gift taxes were figured on gifts made annually, less exemptions and exclusions and were accumulative up to death. On death, however, the progressive estate tax rate started over. The gift tax rate was seventy-five percent of the estate tax rate. A person with a $2 million taxable estate who transferred $1 million during the person's lifetime would incur less total taxes than the person who retained all $2 million until death. Of course, the person who transferred property inter vivos would lose any benefit and protection the transferred assets might have provided until death.

2. THE UNIFIED TAX

In 1976, Congress overhauled the federal gift and estate tax system. One of the principal changes concerned the relationship between the gift and estate taxes. Congress adopted a unified tax system that accumulates all taxable gifts over the person's lifetime and adds them to the value of the taxable estate at death. Consequently, the progressive tax system eventually extracts its maximum bite. Unification of the calculation of the estate and of the gift tax rate significantly reduces the tax advantages under old law of splitting large estates between lifetime and deathtime transfers.

Lifetime Giving Advantages: Although there is now a single cumulative tax rate and tax free exemption threshold, a few tax advantages of lifetime giving remain. Outright inter vivos gifts of $10,000 or less per donee per year are excluded from all transfer taxation. This is the most important lifetime exemption for gifts and constitutes a necessary guide for proper estate planning for the wealthy. In addition, gift taxes paid on inter vivos gifts are not included in the valuation of the taxable estate if the gift is made prior to three years before the donor's death. For estates, the tax is calculated on the value of the estate including that portion of the estate that will be used for payment of the estate taxes. For large estates, the elimination of the gift taxes from the estate can represent a significant savings. These savings must be weighed economically against loss of the investment return on the amount of any gift taxes paid. Finally, assets that are appreciating in value are excellent lifetime gift assets because the gift will lock in the date of gift value for the asset to which the transfer tax is applied whereas if the asset were retained in the estate at death, the higher date of death value would be subject to the transfer tax.

3. UNIFIED TAX RATE SCHEDULE

The following chart lists the current gift and estate tax rate schedule:

CHART 10–II–1

PROGRESSIVE RATE OF FEDERAL GIFT AND ESTATE TAXES		
TAXABLE BASE OR ESTATE	PERCENT OF TAX ON EACH DOLLAR ABOVE BASE	TAX ON TAX BASE
$1	18%	$0
$10,000	20%	$1,800
$20,000	22%	$3,800
$40,000	24%	$8,200
$60,000	26%	$13,000
$80,000	28%	$18,200
$100,000	30%	$23,800
$150,000	32%	$38,800
$250,000	34%	$70,800
$500,000	37%	$155,800
$750,000	39%	$248,300
$1,000,000	41%	$345,800
$1,250,000	43%	$448,300
$1,500,000	45%	$555,800
$2,000,000	49%	$780,800
$2,500,000	53%	$1,025,800
$3,000,000	55%	$1,290,800
$10,000,000	60%	$5,140,800
$21,040,000	55%	$11,764,800

Marginal Tax Rate: Several features of the Schedule deserve mention. The low rate tax brackets between 18 and 37 percent are irrelevant except as they are used to calculate the tax on $500,000. The marginal rate that a taxpayer will pay is 37 percent because the unified credit eliminates tax liability below its equivalent exemption value which in 2000 will be $675,000. *See infra* Chart 10–II–2. In other words, the tax on $675,000 equals $211,300, and thus that is the credit amount. The donor or estate will not pay a dime of tax until the value of taxable gifts and the estate have an accumulated value of more than $675,000. Every dollar above $675,000 will be taxed at the marginal rate of no less than 37 percent. In 2004, the marginal rate will go up to 39% because the equivalent exemption rises above $750,000. Similarly, in 2006, the marginal rate goes up to 41% as the exemption amount becomes $1 million.

1997 Tax Act: The Taxpayer Relief Act of 1997 set a calendar for increasing the equivalent deduction until the exemption equals $1,000,000 in 2006. Between 1998–2005, the unified credit and its equivalent exemption, which is exempt from the federal estate taxes, increases as follows:

CHART 10–II–2

UNIFIED TAX EXEMPTION AND CREDIT

Year	Exemption	Unified Tax Credit
Prior to 1998	$600,000	$192,800
1998	$625,000	$202,050
1999	$650,000	$211,300
2000 and 2001	$675,000	$220,550
2002 and 2003	$700,000	$229,800
2004	$850,000	$287,300
2005	$950,000	$326,300
Thereafter	$1,000,000	$345,800

Illustration 1: D died in 2000 with a taxable estate of $750,000. D made no taxable lifetime gifts. The estate tax on that taxable estate is $248,300. Applying only the unified credit, the estate would owe estate taxes of $27,750 ($248,300 minus $220,550). The $675,000 equivalent exemption calculates out as a $220,550 credit against the estate tax and reduces the tax due accordingly.

4. UNIFIED TAX MECHANICS

The process for determining the final gift and estate tax liability is outlined in the following chart:

CHART 10–II–3

COMPUTATION OF GIFT TAX

1.	Total gifts of donor during current relevant period	
2.	Less one-half of gifts attributable to spouse	
3.	Balance	
4.	Add gifts of spouse to be included	
5.	Total gifts	
6.	Less total exclusions ($10,000 per donee)	
7.	Total includable gifts	
8.	Deductions	
a.	Marital deduction	
b.	Charitable gifts	
c.	Less Total Deductions	
9.	Current taxable gifts	
10.	Add taxable gifts for preceding years and quarters	
11.	Total taxable gifts (Tentative Tax Base)	
12.	Tax on taxable gifts	
13.	Less current tax on taxable gifts for preceding years	
14.	Balance	
15.	Less Unused Unified Credit	
16.	Tax Due	

B. THE FEDERAL GIFT TAX

1. ACCUMULATIVE EFFECT OF TAXABLE GIFTS

Although taxable gifts must be reported and the tax must be paid on an annual basis, the tax rates applicable to a gift are determined by reference to the total amount of taxable lifetime gifts made by the donor, rather than by reference only to taxable gifts made in a given year.

Illustration 2: D made taxable gifts of $1 million in 1998. The tentative tax on that amount is $345,800. D must pay gift taxes of $143,750 ($345,800 minus $202,050). The $625,000 equivalent exemption calculates out as a $202,050 credit against the gift tax and reduces the tax due accordingly.

In 2000, D makes another $1 million taxable gift. The tentative tax on the accumulated gift of $2 million is $780,800. After subtracting the tentative gift tax on the previous gift or gifts, the tentative tax due equals $435,000. Although D completely used up the 1998 unified credit, that credit has increased in 2000 to $220,550. D owes gift taxes of $416,500 ($435,000 minus ($220,550 minus $202,050). D gets to deduct the additional $18,500 credit.

2. DEFINITION OF A GIFT

Although transfers for consideration are not gifts and thus are not subject to the gift tax, all transfers "for less than adequate and full consideration in money or money's worth" will be considered gifts to the extent "the value of the property exceeded the value of the consideration." IRC § 2512(b). The regulation defines adequate and full consideration in money or money's worth to require "a sale, exchange, or other transfer of property made in the ordinary course of business (a transaction which is bona fide, at arm's length, and free from donative intent.)" Reg. § 25.2512–8.

3. ANNUAL EXCLUSION

The federal gift tax law recognizes an annual exclusion that provides that qualified gifts valued up to a cumulative value of $10,000 or less made by a donor during a calendar year to each separate donee are excluded from the donor's taxable gifts.[1] IRC § 2503(b).

Gift splitting: The donor and the donor's spouse have the right to elect to treat gifts as having been made one-half by the donor and one-half by the donor's spouse. *See* IRC § 2513. This gift-splitting rule allows a married couple to transfer $20,000 per year to a donee tax free. It makes no difference whether the gift is from the property of one or both spouses.

1. In addition, certain transfers for educational expenses or medical expenses are not subject to gift taxation regardless of their amount. IRC § 2503(e). The exclusion applies only to direct payments for (1) qualifying educational expenses in the form of tuition paid to institutions defined under IRC Section 170(b)(1)(A)(ii), and (2) medical expenses listed in IRC Section 213(d)(1). Reg. § 25.2503–2(e).

4. QUALIFIED GIFTS

For purposes of the annual exclusion, the term "qualified gifts" refers to a basic requirement that the gifts must be of a present interest in property. *See* Reg. § 25.2503–3. For example, a gift of a remainder interest to a donee is a gift of a future interest and will not qualify for the annual exclusion. A gift of a present income interest, however, qualifies to the extent of the income interest's present value. Consequently, most transfers in trust do not qualify for the annual exclusion unless a beneficiary is given a nondiscretionary present interest, right to income from trust annually, or possess a necessary power over the trust property, *e.g,* beneficiary has a presently exercisable general power of appointment over trust property.

2503(c) Exception: IRC Section 2503(c) offers a structured exception to the present-interest rule for a gift to a minor. Donor can make gifts in trusts giving a trustee the discretion to distribute or accumulate the income from the property as long as the property and any accumulated income is distributed when the minor attains 21. If the minor dies before attaining 21, the trust must provide that the property and any accumulated income be paid to the minor's estate or as the minor directs under a general power of appointment.

5. VALUATIONS

When substantial gifts other than of cash are made, it is important that accurate valuation appraisals be prepared for gift tax purposes, particularly if the gifts are of assets that are not publicly traded. IRC § 2503. Even the annual exclusion raises significant valuation problems because it sets a benchmark of taxability: gifts valued above it are taxable gifts and those valued below it are not.

6. DONEE'S BASIS

Gifts of capital assets carry over the donor's basis subject to adjustment for transfer expenses and gift taxes incurred and subject to the limitation that basis cannot exceed fair market value as adjusted at the date of the gift. IRC § 1015.

7. ALLOWABLE DEDUCTIONS

In addition to the reduction of any gift by the annual exclusion, gifts are also reduced by any allowable deductions, *i.e.,* the marital deduction or the charitable deduction.

8. SPOUSAL JOINT INTERESTS

Under IRC Section 2523(d), a transfer of individually owned or purchased property by one spouse into the names of both spouses as joint tenants with right of survivorship qualifies for the gift tax marital deduction. The spouses' relative amounts of contribution to the purchase of the jointly held property are irrelevant for gift tax purposes.

9. TAXABLE GIFT

The taxable gift equals the total value of the gift less the annual exclusion and the applicable deductions. The gift tax is then calculated and any unused unified credit is deducted. The result is the tax due.

10. NONTAXABLE LIFETIME TRANSFERS

If a donor reserves a power to revoke a transfer, the transfer is not subject to gift taxation. The gift is called incomplete for gift tax purposes. Thus, the donor continues to be treated as owner of the transferred property for gift and income tax purposes. IRC § 676; Treas. Reg. § 25.2511–2(c). In addition, and notwithstanding that a donor retains no beneficial interest, a transfer may continue to be treated as an incomplete gift and the donor as owner, if the donor retained the right to choose who will enjoy the property. Treas. Reg. § 25.2511–2(b), (c).

11. POWERS OF APPOINTMENT

Releases of or exercises by a donee of a general power of appointment constitutes a gift. IRC § 2514(b). A general power of appointment is any power that the donee can exercise in favor of the donee, the donee's estate, the donee's creditors, or the creditors of the donee's estate. IRC § 2514(c). Powers to consume or to invade trust property are excluded from the definition if the power is limited by an ascertainable standard relating to the "health, education, support, or maintenance of the donee." *See* IRC § 2514(c)(1). Powers that can be exercised only in conjunction with the donor of the power or an adverse party are also excluded. *See* IRC § 2514(c)(3). *See* Part 5.I.C.

The 5 and 5 Power: An exception to the rule that a release of a general power constitutes a gift for gift tax purposes is a lapse of what is called a 5 and 5 power. The Code provides that a lapse of a general power of appointment over an amount which does not exceed the greater of $5,000 or 5 percent of the aggregate value of the property subject to the power at the time of the lapse, is not a taxable gift. *See* IRC § 2514(e).

Illustration 3: G creates a trust that gives A an income interest for life and B the remainder at A's death. Under the trust's terms, A has a lifetime power to invade the corpus up the greater of $5,000 or 5 percent of the aggregate value of the trust each year. Ordinarily if A allows the power to lapse in any year that lapse would result in a gift of the remainder interest to B, but because A's power is a 5 and 5 power, the lapse is exempt from gift taxation.

C. THE ESTATE TAX

1. LIFETIME AND DEATHTIME APPLICATION

Congress recognized from the beginning that to have an effective estate tax the law had to tax both the net probate estate and will substitutes which otherwise could be used as tax avoidance devices. Most of the estate tax statutory provisions concern the taxing of will substitutes such as life insurance, joint tenancies and joint accounts, pension death benefits, revocable trusts, and even irrevocable trusts with a retained life estate.

2. THE GROSS ESTATE DEFINITION

The decedent's gross estate includes the value of the decedent's probate estate, specified will substitutes, property over which the decedent held a general power of appointment, and certain transfers (QTIPs) for which a marital deduction was previously allowed.

3. PROBATE ESTATE

IRC Section 2033 provides that the decedent's gross estate includes "the value of all property to the extent of the interest therein of the decedent at the time of his death." This includes all of decedent's transmissible property that passes at death by will or by intestacy. Property owned by the decedent but not transferred at death such as the grave in which the decedent is interred and other valuables interred with the decedent are not included in the gross estate. Transmissible property includes property owned in fee, as tenants in common, or in a transmissible remainder interest. Income interests that expire on the death of the income beneficiary, however, are not included in the income beneficiary's probate or gross estates.

Illustration 4: S transferred property to T in trust for S's spouse for life, remainder to R. R dies before S's spouse. The includability of R's remainder interest depends on whether the remainder interest in R is dependent on R surviving the life beneficiaries. Under IRC Section 2033, if R does not have to survive, R's remainder interest is part of both R's probate estate and gross estate for federal estate tax purposes. If R had to survive the income beneficiary, R's remainder interest terminated and its value would not be included either in G's probate estate or gross estate.

4. LIFETIME GIFTS WITHIN THREE YEARS OF DEATH

The unified gift and estate tax system eliminated for most purposes the tax collector's concern about near death donative transfers. Consequently, the value of outright gifts of property that the donor owns in full are not part of the gross estate even if made minutes before death. The gift tax will extract its full share and the value of all taxable gifts will be added to the taxable estate for estate tax calculations purposes. That the donor may be able to use an additional annual $10,000 exclusion per donee per year does not alter the rule. There are two major exceptions.

a. Selected Transfers

The first exception arises where the value of the gift for estate tax purposes greatly exceeds the value of the gift for gift tax purposes. The best example of this is life insurance. *See* IRC § 2042. Whereas for gift tax purposes life insurance is valued at its replacement value or its interpolated terminal reserve value, for estate tax purposes it is valued at the full amount payable under the policy. Typically, the value for estate tax purposes would be greatly higher than for gift tax purposes. Although gifts of life insurance made three years or more prior to the date of death are not subject to the estate tax, those made within that three year period are under IRC Section 2035(a). The purpose of the three year rule for this kind of transaction is to reduce the difference in tax consequences caused by near death transfers. The same rule applies for transfers within three years of death of any interest in which the donor retained a life interest [IRC § 2936], or that takes effect at death (IRC § 2037), or is revocable. IRC § 2038.

b. Gift Tax Gross–Up Provision

IRC Section 2035(b) provides that the amount of any gift tax paid by the decedent on gifts made by the decedent (or the decedent's spouse) during the three-year period ending on the date of the decedent's death is includable in the decedent's gross estate. Thus, there will be a tax on the gift tax similar to the way the estate tax is calculated. This provision takes away one of the few tax advantages of making lifetime taxable gifts. The rule applies regardless of donor's motive or expectations of death.

5. RETAINED PROPERTY INTERESTS

When a donor does not part with complete ownership of the property, the donor is treated as owning the property at death for estate tax purposes.

a. Retention of an Income Interest

If a donor irrevocably transfers a remainder interest in property, in trust or otherwise, while retaining possession or enjoyment or the right to the income for life, the value of the transferred property at the donor's death is included in the gross estate. IRC § 2036(a)(1). The value of the remainder interest transferred is subject to the gift tax. A later transfer of the retained life estate in the property three years or more before the date of death avoids inclusion in the gross estate but subjects the value of the life estate to the gift tax. IRC § 2036(a)(1).

b. Retention of a Reversionary Interest

If a donor irrevocably transfers a life estate and retains the reversion, the value of the reversion is part of the gross estate under IRC Section 2033. If donor's retained reversionary interest terminates at the donor's death, the value of the reversion may be part of the gross estate under IRC Section 2037. These kinds of transfers are very unusual under modern estate planning practices.

Under IRC Section 2037, three requirements must be met: (1) the donor must have made a transfer of an interest in which possession or enjoyment of the property can, through ownership of the interest, be obtained only by surviving the donor; (2) the donor retained a reversionary interest in the property; and (3) the value of the reversionary interest immediately before the donor's death exceeds 5 percent of the value of the property.

c. Revocable and Other Retained Powers

If a donor transfers property and reserves a power to revoke it, the value of the property is included in the donor's gross estate under IRC Section 2038(a)(1). Usually revocable transfers are made in trust. Although a revocable trust may assist donors in asset management and avoid probate, they produce no tax savings.

The value of property over which the donor retains the power to decide who can enjoy the property or its income is included in the donor's gross estate even though the donor relinquished the right to enjoy personally the property or the income it produces. IRC §§ 2036(a)(2); 2038(a)(1). Under IRC Section 2036 the gross estate includes the entire value of the property in the decedent's gross estate. Under IRC Section 2038, the gross estate includes only that portion of the property over which the decedent had retained a power to alter, amend, revoke, or terminate.

d. Powers of Appointment

IRC Section 2041(a)(2) provides that decedent's gross estate includes the value of property over which the decedent held a general power of appointment. *See* Part 10.II.B.11 for the definition of a general power of appointment.

When a donee of a general power exercises or releases the power but retains an interest that would cause the property to be included in the donee's gross estate if the donee had owned the property, then the property over which the power is exercised or released is includable in the donee's gross estate. For example, if a donee holds a life estate and a general power of appointment in property of a trust, the lifetime exercise of the power but retention of the life interest will cause the entire value of the trust corpus be included in the donee's gross estate at the donee's death. *See* IRC §§ 2041(a)(2) and 2036(a)(1). To avoid this result, the donee must exercise the power without retaining the life estate.

Similar to the exception to the gift tax, a lapse of a general power to appoint that does not exceed the greater of $5,000 or 5 percent of the aggregate value of the trust at the time of the lapse is not included in the gross estate. The 5 and 5 power allows a donor to provide a donee limited access to the trust corpus, but not access that results in estate taxation to the donee.

Donees, who at death hold nongeneral powers of appointment over property, will not have that property included in their gross estates. Thus, donees who die owning powers to appoint property to anyone except themselves, their creditors, their estates, or the creditors of their estates will not have that property included in their gross estates.

e. Jointly Held Property

IRC Section 2040 contains special estate tax consequences for jointly held property. For estate tax purposes, only joint ownership in property that is subject to a right of survivorship is covered under this section. This includes property held in joint tenancy with right of survivorship, property held in tenancy by the entirety by spouses, joint bank accounts, and jointly held U.S. Savings Bonds.

Two rules are established by IRC Section 2040 for determining the amount includable in the decedent's gross estate: (1) a fractional-interest rule and (2) a percentage-of-consideration rule. The fractional interest rule applies in two specific situations: the percentage rule applies to the rest.

Joint Tenancy Created by Gift: If the decedent's jointly held interest was received as a gift or devise from a person who did not also become a joint tenant, decedent's estate includes a fractional share of the property equal to the decedent's fractional cotenancy interest. In effect, for estate tax purposes, the decedent's interest is treated as if it were a tenancy in common interest. For example, if T devised Meadowacre to A, B, and C as joint tenants with right of survivorship, upon A's death prior to the other two tenants, A's gross estate will include one third of the value of Meadowacre.

Spousal Joint Tenancy: For married couples who own jointly held property, IRC Section 2040(b) includes one half of the value of the property in the estate of the first spouse to die regardless of how much the decedent spouse contributed to its purchase. IRC Section 2056(a) provides that a decedent can deduct as a marital deduction the value of property included in the gross estate that passes to the surviving spouse in a qualified manner. The combination of IRC Sections 2040(b) and 2–2056(a) has the effect of excluding from taxation any portion of the jointly held property until the surviving spouse makes a lifetime gift or dies.

The percentage-of-consideration rule: The percentage-of-consideration rule of IRC Section 2040(a) applies for all jointly held property owned by unmarried tenants who acquire the property by purchase. Under this rule, the value of the portion of the jointly held property included in the decedent's gross estate is determined by multiplying the property's value by the percentage of consideration the decedent is deemed to have provided. All decedents holding joint interests under this rule are presumed to have provided all the consideration for the jointly held property. The decedent's estate has the burden of proving the amount of consideration, if any, that the surviving cotenant or cotenants provided.

f. Life Insurance

Under IRC Section 2042(2), the proceeds from life insurance on the decedent's life are included in the gross estate if at the decedent's death the decedent retained an "incident of ownership." Treas. Reg. Section 20.2042–1(c)(2) defines incidents of ownership as meaning "the right of the insured or his estate to the economic benefits of the policy." For example, a "right" that will cause includability includes the power to change the beneficiary, surrender or cancel the policy, assign the policy, revoke an assignment, pledge the policy for a loan, or obtain from the insurer a loan against the surrender value of the policy. To avoid inclusion of life insurance proceeds, decedent must (1) relinquish all rights over the policy during life, and (2) assure that the proceeds are not paid to the estate or available to pay creditors of the estate. In addition, this action must have occurred more than three years prior to decedent's death. *See* Part 10.II.C.4.a.

g. Annuities

There are four types of annuity contracts that have varying estate tax consequences.

- Nonrefund-single-life annuities that are fully exhausted at the decedent's death are not part of the decedent's probate or gross estate.
- If the annuity contract pays a refund of a portion of the cost upon the decedent's premature death, the refund is included in the gross estate under IRC Section 2033 if the refund is paid to the decedent's estate. If the refund is paid to a designated beneficiary, it is included in the gross estate under IRC Section 2039.
- If the annuity contract is a joint-and-survivor annuity that obligates the company to make payments to the annuitants and upon the death of either, to make payments to the survivor for life, IRC Section 2039 includes the value of the survivor's right to future payments in the decedent's gross estate.
- If the annuity contract is a self-and-survivor annuity by which the insurance company obligates itself to make payments to the decedent and to the designated beneficiary only after the decedent's death, IRC Section 2039 includes the value of the survivor's right to future payments in the

decedent's gross estate. If the designated beneficiary dies first, however, the annuity is not included in the decedent's gross estate because the annuity is exhausted at decedent's death.

IRC Section 2039 applies to benefits under employee retirement and pension plans and individual retirement accounts.

D. REVIEW QUESTIONS

1. What is the name of the tax system adopted by Congress in 1976 which accumulates all taxable gifts over the person's lifetime and adds them to the value of the taxable estate at death?

2. Inter vivos gifts of $20,000 or less per donee are excluded from all transfer taxation. True or False?

3. What is the unified tax exemption?

4. What is gift-splitting?

5. What must a gift be to qualify as an annual exclusion?

6. When is a general power of appointment not included in the donee's estate?

7. When are annuities taxable to the annuitant's estate?

III

DEDUCTIONS FROM THE GROSS ESTATE

Analysis

A. GENERAL SCOPE

1. THE VARIOUS DEDUCTIONS

The IRC specifically recognized several deductions which reduce the gross estate to the net estate. These deductions are the marital deduction, the charitable deduction, the deduction for funeral and administration expenses, bona fide claims against the decedent's estate, and the deduction for certain losses during administration. The estate tax payable to the federal government is not deductible.

B. EXPENSES, DEBTS, AND LOSSES

1. EXPENSES OF ADMINISTRATION

IRC Section 2053 allows decedent's allowable funeral expenses and, subject to certain limitations, the expenses of administering property that was included in the decedent's gross estate to be deducted. Some administration expenses also constitute allowable income tax deductions, and the executor must elect whether to deduct the expenses as either estate tax or income tax deductions. IRC Section 2053 also allows outstanding bona fide debts of the decedent to be deducted. If a debt is based on a promise or agreement, the deduction is limited to the extent that the liability was undertaken for an adequate and full consideration in money or money's worth.

Decedent's mortgage obligations that were incurred in a bona fide manner for adequate and full consideration in money or money's worth are either deductible or constitute a reduction in the value of the property subject to the mortgage, depending upon whether the decedent was personally liable for the payment of the underlying debt.

2. CASUALTY AND THEFT LOSSES

IRC Section 2054 permits casualty and theft losses incurred during the administration of the estate to be deducted, provided that the loss is not reflected in the valuation of the property where the alternate valuation date was elected under IRC Section 2032.

C. MARITAL DEDUCTION

1. THE UNLIMITED MARITAL DEDUCTION

Since 1981 federal estate and gift tax law allows married persons to transfer property to their spouses without gift or estate taxation so long as the property is transferred in a qualified manner. Thus, a married couple is treated as the taxable unit for transfers between themselves. For these tax purposes, interspousal transfers are ignored. An estate or gift tax is assessed only when one or the other of the spouses transfers property to someone outside the marital unit.

2. QUALIFIED DEVISE OR GIFT

IRC Section 2056(a) sets forth several requirements in order to qualify for the marital deduction:

- The decedent must be a citizen or resident of the United States. Reg. § 20.2056(a)–1(a).
- The decedent must be survived by a spouse.
- The property must "pass" from the decedent to the surviving spouse. "Passing" includes all normal transfers from the decedent to the surviving spouse such as bequests under a will, *e.g.*, by will, intestacy, or right of survivorship, as a dower or curtesy interest in the surviving spouse.
- The value of the property interest must be included in the decedent's gross estate.
- The property interest must be a type that will be included in the surviving spouse's gross estate to the extent not consumed or disposed of during that spouse's lifetime.

3. NONDEDUCTIBLE TERMINABLE INTEREST

To qualify for the marital deduction, the property interest passing to the surviving spouse cannot be a nondeductible terminable interest. A terminable interest is defined as an interest that will either fail or terminate on: (i) the mere lapse of time; (ii) on the occurrence of an event or contingency; or (iii) on the failure of an event or contingency to occur. Life estates, terms of years, and annuities are terminable interests.

Although terminable interests are generally nondeductible, there are several specific exceptions included in IRC Section 2056 and the related regulations. All exceptions require that the interests passing to the surviving spouse will result in gift or estate taxation when that spouse transfers them during life or at death. The two most popular of the exceptions are the life estate general power of appointment and the QTIP. *See* IRC §§ 2056(b)(5), (7), 2523(e), (f). Both exceptions have particular and unique requirements that must be followed. The trust mechanism is the overwhelmingly preferred method for exercising these exceptions.

4. LIFE ESTATE GENERAL POWER OF APPOINTMENT

The qualified interest rule is satisfied if the donee spouse receives an income interest for life and the power to appoint the property alone to any person and in all events. IRC §§ 2056(b)(5), 2523(e). It qualifies for the marital deduction because any unconsumed income will be subject to the estate tax [IRC § 2033] and the trust corpus will be subject to the estate tax. IRC § 2041. Even if the donee spouse makes a gift of the life estate and makes a lifetime appointment of the remainder interest, the gift of the fee will be gift taxable. IRC §§ 2511, 2514.

For the income interest to qualify, the spouse must have an absolute right to be paid the current income at least annually. In addition, the property placed in the trust must be property that produces a current income stream or, at least, that the spouse has the right to compel the trustee to convert any nonincome producing property into property that will produce a fair current return. *See* Reg. §§ 20.2056(b)–5(f)(5), 25.2523(e)-l(f)(4).

Although the power must be unrestricted, a general power only exercisable by will is sufficient. IRC §§ 2056(b)(5), 2523(e). In addition, the trustee can be given additional fiduciary powers to distribute the trust principal to the spouse so long as the trustee does not have a power to appoint any part of the property to any person other than the surviving spouse.

Furthermore, the donor spouse may supplement the spouse's right to a lifetime income interest and general testamentary power with a lifetime power to appoint to a class of beneficiaries, such as the donor's lineal descendants. The exercise of this nongeneral power during life will result in a gift tax, because its exercise operates as a release of the general testamentary power. *See* IRC § 2514(b).

5. QUALIFIED TERMINAL INTEREST PROPERTY (QTIP)

Under specified circumstances a donor can obtain a marital deduction by transferring a life estate in property to the spouse. IRC §§ 2056(b)(7), 2523(f). The qualifying condition is that the donor (for gift tax purposes) or the donor's executor (for estate tax purposes) must elect to have the life estate treated as a qualified terminable interest, and no person, not even the spouse, can have a power to appoint any part of the property to any person other than the surviving spouse during the spouse's life.

The combination of IRC §§ 2044 and 2519 makes certain that the property does not escape taxation in the donor's and the spouse's respective estates. IRC Section 2519 treats any disposition of any portion of the life estate as a transfer of the entire remainder interest and thereby assures that the remainder interest is subject to gift taxation. IRC Section 2044 includes the value of the property at the spouse's death in the spouse's gross estate, unless IRC Section 2519 applied previously. These two constructive transfer sections guarantee that property, which enjoys a marital deduction in one spouse's estate, is taxed in the other spouse's estate.

The life estate requirements permit the trustee to have a power to distribute principal to the spouse during the spouse's life. The spouse cannot have, however, a lifetime power to appoint to anyone other than the spouse.

6. ESTATE TRUST

Another but less popular device for taking the marital deduction is the estate trust. Unlike the power of appointment and QTIP marital deduction trusts, the "estate trust" does not require income to be paid to the surviving spouse. Some or all of the income may be accumulated and taxed for income purposes to the trust. Upon the death of the spouse, the trust property must then be paid to the estate of the surviving spouse. The value of the estate trust is deductible under IRC Sections 2056 and 2523 because no person other than the spouse received an interest in the property from the donor.

Accordingly, where annual payments to the surviving spouse are not desirable or necessary, or where there is a substantial amount of unproductive property, the estate trust offers an alternative to other marital deduction dispositions. The requirement that the trust assets pass through the surviving spouse's estate is a significant disadvantage in that it puts these assets through the formalities and delays of administration and subjects the property to the surviving spouse's creditors and, if the surviving spouse remarries, to the elective share of the surviving spouse's surviving spouse.

D. CHARITABLE DEDUCTION

1. GIFT AND ESTATE TAX UNLIMITED CHARITABLE DEDUCTION

The value of all outright gifts by a person to a qualifying charitable organization is deductible for estate and gift tax purposes.[1] *See* IRC §§ 2055, 2522.[2] A calculatable deduction from gift and estate taxes is available if the donor establishes a trust giving a charity either an income interest (a charitable lead trust) or a remainder interest (a charitable remainder trust). The Tax Reform Act of 1969 adopted rules requiring that the charities actually receive interests reasonably related to the amount claimed as a deduction.

2. COMBINED CHARITABLE AND MARITAL DEDUCTION

IRC Section 2056(b)(8) provides that a marital deduction is allowable for certain charitable remainder trusts as long as the trust has no noncharitable beneficiaries other than the surviving spouse. Consequently, by virtue of a combination of IRC Sections 2055 and 2056, the entire value of this type of trust is deductible by the decedent spouse's estate. The surviving spouse receives only an income interest and therefore no portion of the trust property is included in the surviving spouse's estate at death.

1. The income, gift and estate tax provisions each contain slightly different definitions of a qualifying charitable organization. IRC §§ 170(c), 2055(a), 2522(a).

2. A donor can deduct the value of property transferred to a qualifying charitable organization for income tax purposes, too. *See* IRC § 170. The income tax deduction is limited to a percentage of adjusted gross income.

E. REVIEW QUESTIONS

1. Name the deductions recognized by the IRC which reduce the gross estate to the net estate.
2. Estate tax payable to the federal government is deductible. True or False?
3. Define a terminable interest.
4. What are some examples of terminable interests?
5. The "estate trust" does not require income to be paid to the surviving spouse. True or False?

IV

FEDERAL GENERATION–SKIPPING TRANSFER TAX

Analysis

b. Predeceased Parent Exception
8. Tax Exclusive and Tax Inclusive Applications
a. Tax Exclusive Direct Skips
b. Tax Inclusive Taxable Distributions and Taxable Terminations
B. Review Questions

A. GENERATION–SKIPPING TRANSFER TAX

1. DESCRIPTION AND APPLICATION

The current version of the federal generation-skipping transfer tax (GSTT) was enacted in 1986 as an excise tax on gratuitous transfers that "skip" a generation. The tax adopts the policy that, as wealth passes from one person to another within a family, it should be subject to the federal transfer tax system at least once in each generation. Thus, the GSTT imposes a tax that is paid whenever property skips a generation or passes through a generation in a form that would allow it to escape gift or estate taxation in the skipped generation. More precisely, a generation-skipping transfer occurs when property passes to a skip person.

2. GSTT SPECIAL TERMINOLOGY

The GSTT generated a special language. The key interlocking definitions include:

a. Skip Person

A skip person is a natural person assigned to a generation two or more generations below the transferor's generation, *e.g.*, grandchildren, great-grandchildren. IRC § 2613(a). A trust can also be a skip person if all of the interests in the trust are held by skip persons and if no distributions can be made to non-skip persons. A non-skip person is a person who is not a skip person.

b. Transferor

The transferor of a testamentary bequest is the decedent: the transferor of an inter vivos gift is the donor. *See* IRC § 2652(a)(1)(B). If donor's spouse splits the gift under IRC Section 2513, both spouses are transferors. When a transfer is made to a qualified QTIP trust, either the original decedent or the surviving spouse can elect to be the transferor. All of the property qualifying for that QTIP must be covered by the election, however, if the decedent is to be the transferor.

c. Interest

A person has an interest in property held in trust if he or she has a right (other than a future right) to receive income or principal from a trust or, if he or she is a permissible recipient of income or principal from a trust. A charity has an interest if it is the remainder beneficiary of a charitable remainder trust. *See* IRC § 2652(c).

d. Generation Assignments

IRC Section 2651 assigns individuals to generations based either on their degree of relationship to the transferor or on the difference in age between the transferor and the individual. Generation assignments based on relationship extend to any lineal descendant of the transferor's grandparents, *e.g.*, transferor's descendants, siblings, aunts, uncles, cousins, nieces, nephews, and their descendants. The generation assignment of such relatives is made by simply comparing the number of generations between the individual and the transferor's grandparents with the number of generations between the grandparent and the transferor.

Spouses: Transferor's spouse is always assigned to the transferor's generation and a spouse of any lineal descendant is assigned to the generation of that descendant, no matter what the spouse's age.

Other Persons: All other people are assigned to generations based on age differences. Transferor's generation ends at an age 12½ years younger than the transferor. The next generation begins at an age 12½ years younger than the transferor and extends for 25 years. Each succeeding generation is a succeeding 25 year period.

3. GST EXEMPTION

Every transferor has a flat lifetime exemption from the GSTT called the GST exemption. *See* IRC § 2631. Originally set at $1,000,000, after December 31, 1998 the exemption is indexed for inflation. For 1999, the exemption is $1,010,000. Rev. Proc. 98–61, 1998–52 I.R.B. 18.

The transferor may allocate the GST exemption among the applicable lifetime or testamentary transfers of property as the transferor chooses including direct skips and transfers in trust. Once made, the allocation of the GST exemption is irrevocable. If the transferor makes no election, the exemption basically is allocated to direct skips first and then to trusts with respect to which a taxable distribution or taxable termination might occur. *See* IRC § 2632.

The allocation of the exemption is made by the transferor on a Federal gift return or by the transferor's executors or administrators on a Federal estate tax return filed at any time on or before the due date of such return.

4. APPLICABLE TAX RATE

The applicable rate is the maximum Federal estate tax rate at the time of the transfer (now 55%) multiplied by the inclusion ratio.

5. INCLUSION RATIO

The inclusion ratio equals the number one (1) minus a fraction, the numerator of which is the amount of the GST exemption allocated to this transfer and the denominator of which is the value of the transferred property. *See* IRC § 2642. If no GST exemption is allocated to a transfer, the inclusion ratio will be 1. When the allocated GST exemption equals or exceeds the value of generation-skipping transfer, the applicable rate equals zero and thus, the rate of tax is zero.

$$1 - \frac{\text{Allocated GST Exemption}}{\text{Value of Property Transferred}}$$

The applicable tax rate is the product of inclusion ratio and the maximum Federal estate tax rate which now is 55%. The tax is the product of the applicable rate and the value of the property transferred.

Illustration 1: T makes a direct skip of $2,020,000 to G, a grandchild. T allocates the full $1,010,000 GST exemption to this transfer. The applicable rate and tax are calculated as follows:

$$1 - \frac{\$1{,}010{,}000}{\$2{,}020{,}000} = .5 \times 55\% = 27.5\%$$

The GSTT equals 27.5% times $2,020,000 or $555,500.

6. TAXABLE EVENTS

There are three types of generation-skipping transfers: direct skips, taxable terminations, and taxable distributions. *See* IRC § 2611.

a. Direct Skips

A direct skip is a transfer to a skip person of an interest in property that is also subject to the estate or gift tax. *See* IRC § 2612(c).

b. Taxable Termination

A taxable termination occurs when an interest in trust property terminates as a result of death, lapse of time or otherwise, unless immediately after such termination, a nonskip person has an interest in the property or unless at no time after the termination may a distribution (including a distribution upon termination) be made from the trust to a skip person. *See* IRC § 2612(a).

Because the generation-skipping transfer tax is levied on the termination of any interest in trust property, a trust may have to pay the tax on more than one occasion.

Illustration 2: T's will establishes a trust to pay the income to C for life, then to G for life, with the remainder to GG. There is a taxable termination both upon C's death and G's death. The tax result is that a transfer tax is imposed three times: (1) when T dies, (2) when C dies and (3) when GC dies. Thus, in this example, a transfer tax is imposed on every generation.

c. Taxable Distributions

A taxable distribution is any distribution from a trust to a skip person other than a taxable termination or a direct skip. *See* IRC § 2612(b). Neither a direct skip transfer nor a taxable termination can be a taxable distribution. The direct skip and taxable termination rules take precedence over the taxable distribution rules. In addition, if a distribution is made from a trust that is itself a skip person, the trust distribution will not be taxed a second time by the GSTT because the creation of the trust already resulted in the imposition of the tax.

Illustration 3: S creates an irrevocable trust. Trustee is authorized to distribute income and principal among a group consisting of S's spouse, children and grandchildren: at the spouse's death the principal is to be distributed to S's then living descendants, by representation. The trustee distributes $100,000 of the corpus to S's child, C, and $100,000 to S's grandchild, G. The distribution to C is not a taxable distribution because C is not a skip person. The distribution to G is a taxable distribution: it is not a direct skip because there is no estate or gift tax incurred at the time of the distribution. G's distribution is also not a taxable termination, because there is no termination of an interest.

7. NONTAXABLE EVENTS

Not all gifts to skip persons are subject to the GSTT.

a. Gift Tax Exclusions

To the extent that a gift qualifies for the annual exclusion or the tuition-or-medical-expense exclusion, the gift is not subject to the generation-skipping transfer tax. *See* IRC §§ 2611(b)(1), 2642(c).

b. Predeceased Parent Exception

A transfer to a grandchild or a grandniece is not a generation-skipping transfer if the donee's parent was dead at the time of the transfer.[1] The exception apples to direct skips, taxable terminations, and taxable distributions. For transfers to collateral relations to qualify for the exception, the transferor must have no living descendants at the time of the transfer. *See* IRC § 2651(e).

8. TAX EXCLUSIVE AND TAX INCLUSIVE APPLICATIONS

a. Tax Exclusive Direct Skips

The GSTT on a direct skip is computed on a tax exclusive basis. Liability for payment of the tax is on the transferor or, if the direct skip came from a trust,

1. Prior to January 1, 1998, the predeceased child exception applied only to direct skip transfers to lineal descendants of the transferor. As of that date, § 511(a) of the Taxpayer Relief Act of 1997 extended the predeceased child exemption to all taxable terminations and taxable distributions and to transfers to collaterals.

on the trustee. *See* IRC § 2603(a)(2), (a)(3). The transferor's payment of the tax, however, is treated as a taxable gift for gift tax purposes. *See* IRC § 2515.

Illustration 4: S makes an outright taxable gift directly to S's grandchild, G, bypassing C, G's parent. The gift is a direct skip and is subject to the GSTT. As a taxable gift, it is subject to the gift tax. The gift tax will be calculated on the date of gift value plus the amount of GSTT paid. *See* IRC § 2515. The inclusion for gift tax purposes of the GSTT in the value of the gift from S to G approximates the tax treatment as if the transfer had been from G to C, who assumably makes a net taxable gift to G of the same amount.

b. Tax Inclusive Taxable Distributions and Taxable Terminations

For GSTT purposes, taxable distributions and taxable terminations are tax inclusive. Consequently, the GSTT is imposed on the recipient or on the trust. *See* IRC § 2603(a)(1), (2). If the trustee makes a taxable distribution and pays the tax out of the trust, the amount of the tax paid is itself a part of the taxable distribution for GSTT purposes. *See* IRC § 2621(b).

B. REVIEW QUESTIONS

1. Define a skip person.
2. What are three types of generation-skipping transfers?
3. What are tax exclusive and tax inclusive applications?

*

APPENDIX A

ANSWERS TO REVIEW QUESTIONS

End of Chapter Questions for Wills, Trusts and Future Interests Black Letter.

PART ONE: GRATUITOUS TRANSFERS IN PERSPECTIVE

II. ADMINISTRATION OF ESTATES AND TRUSTS

1. Probate. [P1.II.A.3.]

2. True. [P1.II.C.5.]

3. Opening, inventory and appraisement, creditor settlement, property management and sale, distribution, and closing. [P1.II.A.7.]

4. The distinctions between probate and nonprobate [P1.II.B.2.] include:

   a. Probate—

      i. Less efficient and slow;

ii. Interested persons have specific forum to litigate matters; and,

iii. Substantive rules are more settled and determinable.

b. Nonprobate—

i. May lack procedural protection;

ii. May offer less predictability when litigation develops; and,

iii. The cost difference usually disappears when all factors are considered.

5. Jurisdiction bases of probate [P1.II.C.4.] include:

a. Presence of the person or thing involved in the litigation within the forum's territorial boundaries; or

b. Minimum contacts with the state coupled with purposeful affiliation with the state; or

c. The party consents to jurisdiction; and,

d. Adequate notice and opportunity to be heard.

III. JUDICIAL PROCEDURE AND EVIDENCE

1. The fiduciary. [P1.III.A.1.]
2. Guardian Ad Litem. [P1.III.A.1.]
3. Burden of Proof. [P1.III.B.1.]
4. True. [P1.III.B.1.]
5. Interpretation. [P1.III.C.1.]

IV. PROFESSIONAL RESPONSIBILITY

1. Competence, diligence, communication, confidentiality and loyalty. [P1.IV.A.1.]
2. True. [P1.IV.A.3.]
3. False. [P1.IV.E.1.]
4. Competent representation requires the legal knowledge, skill, thoroughness and preparation reasonably necessary for the representation. [P1.IV.B.]
5. The attorney-client privilege. [P1.IV.C.]
6. True. [P1.IV.D.1.]

PART TWO: INTESTATE SUCCESSION AND RELATED DOCTRINES

I. ESTATE PLAN BY OPERATION OF LAW

1. True. [P2.I.A.1.]

2. False. Most protect only through grandparents and their descendants. [P2.I.A.3.]

3. True. [P2.I.A.4.]

4. True. [P2.I.B.1.]

5. Ascendant. [P2.I.B.3.]

6. True. [P2.I.C.1.]

7. Counting degrees. [P2.I.D.1.]

8. The property escheats to the state. [P2.I.E.1.]

II. TAKER QUALIFICATIONS

1. False. At common law, to take, an heir must survive the decedent "for an instant of time." [P2.II.B.1]

2. False. Affinity means relationship by marriage. [P2.II.C.1.]

3. Half blooded relations. [P2.II.C.1.]

4. Posthumous. [P2.II.C.2.]

5. Affinity means relationship by marriage, *e.g.,* spouses, step-children, brothers-in-law. [P2.II.D.]

6. The three types of adoption that affect succession [P2.II.E.1] include:

   a. Formal adoption;

   b. Virtual adoption; and,

   c. Equitable adoption.

7. The putative spouse. [P2.II.F.2.]

8. True. [P2.II.H.1.]

III. BARS TO INHERITANCE

1. An advancement. [P2.III.A.1.a.]

2. False. At common law a gift would be treated as an advancement only if the donor died totally intestate. [P2.III.A.1.b.]

3. True. [P2.III.A.3.b.]

4. True. [P2.III. B.1.]

5. It is called non spousal status. [P2.III.C.2.]

6. Under § 2–101(b), if a decedent has excluded or limited the right of an heir to succeed to that person's intestate property, the exclusion or limit is binding even if the decedent dies intestate. [P2.III.F.]

PART THREE: TESTAMENT TRANSFERS

I. EXECUTION OF WILLS

1. A codicil. [P3.I.A.1.]

2. False. A will is effective only after the death of the testator. [P3.I.A.1.]

3. Statute of Frauds, enacted in 1677. [P3.I.A.3.a.]

4. Holographic will. [P3.I.A.4.]

5. True. [P3.I.B.2.]

6. The line of sight test requires that at the time of execution the testator, if the testator had looked, must have been able to see the witness sign the will whether the testator actually sees the witness sign: the conscious presence test permits the surrounding circumstances to satisfy the visual requirement. [P3.I.B.6.b.]

II. REVOCATION OF WILL

1. The revocation statute. [P3.II.A.1.a.]

2. The three elements [P3.II.A.1.a.] are:

   a. Authorized act or instrument;

   b. Intent to revoke; and,

   c. Legal capacity of the testator.

3. A testator may physically revoke a will by either burning, tearing, canceling, obliterating, or destroying the will. [P3.II.A.2.a.]

4. False. A will can be revoked in whole or in part by a subsequent valid will. [P3.II.A.3.a.]

5. The UPC has no special lost will provision but requires that formal probate under § 3–402(a) be instituted if a will is "lost, destroyed or otherwise unavailable." [P3.II.A.5.b.]

6. Dependent Relative Revocation. [P3.II.B.2.]

III. DEFINING THE SCOPE OF THE WILL

1. True. [P3.III.A.1.]

2. Doctrine of integration. [P3.III.B.1.]

3. The Republication by Codicil Doctrine holds that when a will is republished by codicil, it is held to speak as of the date of the republishing as though originally executed at that time. [P3.III.C.1.]

4. If the fact has significance apart from its effect upon the will. [P3.III.E.1.]

IV. WILL CONTESTS AND WILL SUBSTITUTE SUITS

1. The two common types of probate [P3.IV.A.1.] are:

    a. Ex parte probate or probate in common form where no notice is given at the initiation of the proceedings; and,

    b. Probate in solemn form where notice to all interested parties is required at initiation.

2. An heir or next of kin can contest a will when the heir receives more in intestacy than from the will. [P3.IV.B.1.]

3. The general grounds [P3.IV.C.1.] for contesting a will include:

    a. Improper execution;

    b. Forgery;

    c. Failure of capacity;

    d. Nontestamentary intent;

    e. Revocation;

    f. Undue influence;

    g. Fraud; and,

    h. Legality.

4. At the time of execution. [P3.IV.C.4.c.]

5. Mental deficiency concerns the basic mental ability to execute a will: if a person who executes a will is mentally deficient at the time of the execution, the will is invalid even if it makes normal dispositions. An insane delusion is a false belief which is the product of a diseased mind unto which one adheres against evidence and reason: to invalidate a will the delusion must affect the disposition. [P3.IV.C.4.c. and d.]

6. It is an exercise of control over the testator that causes the will to recite the desires of the influencer rather than the desires of the testator. [P3.IV.C.5.a.]

V. CONSTRUCTIONAL PROBLEMS OF DISPOSITIONS

1. The four types of testamentary gifts [P3.V.B.1.] are:

a. Specific devises;

b. General devises;

c. Demonstrative devises;

d. Residuary gifts;

2. Demonstrative devises. [P3.V.B.1.]

3. The devise is said to lapse. [P3.V.D.3.]

4. Common law ademption by extinction holds that when the subject of a specific devise is not a part of the testator's estate at the time of testator's death, the gift fails. [P3.V.E.1.]

5. Right of retainer refers to the right of a personal representative of a decedent's estate to reduce a devise by an amount equal to the debt owed to the estate by the devise's devisee. [P3.V.H.2.]

PART FOUR: LIFETIME TRANSFERS

I. WILL SUBSTITUTES

1. An ideal will substitute is one that allows title to pass to others at death although control remains with the transferor. [P4.I.A.1.]

2. Tenancy in common. [P4.I.B.2.]

3. Three types of multiple-party accounts [P4.I.C.2.a.] include:

   a. Joint accounts;

   b. Trust accounts; and,

   c. Accounts payable on death or POD accounts

4. True. [P4.I.C.2.f.]

5. Three acts required to complete a gift [P4.I.E.1.a.] are:

   a. Delivery;

   b. Intent; and

   c. Acceptance.

6. The term is *Gifts Causa Mortis* [P4.I.E.1.b.]

7. It provides a convenient and efficient system for managing the property gifted to minors.

II. PLANNING FOR RETIREMENT AND INCAPACITY

1. The devices commonly used to deal with the anticipation of incapacity [P4.II.A.2.] include:

   a. Revocable inter vivos trust;

   b. Durable Power of Attorney; and

   c. Advanced Health care directives, *e.g.*, a living will.

2. The principal may nominate the conservator in the durable power document. [P4.II.B.6.]

3. The term "living will" refers to a document that expresses an individual's desire for healthcare under certain prescribed circumstances when the individual is no longer personally able to make those decisions. [P4.II.C.2.a.]

4. Social Security, Medicare, Supplemental Security Income and Medicaid are the primary sources of governmental benefits for retired and disabled persons. [P4.II.E.]

5. False. The presumption is that when a person dies that person's organs may not be taken without the person's prior consent or the consent of the relevant survivors. [P4.II.G.1.]

PART FIVE: POWERS OF APPOINTMENT

I. INTRODUCTION TO POWERS

1. The authority is called a power of appointment. [P5.I.A.1.]

2. A power of appointment is created when the transferor manifests an intent to create a relationship with property that lawyers call powers of appointment in an otherwise effective transfer. [P5.I.B.1.]

3. False. Powers of appointment need only name a donor, a donee and someone in whose favor an appointment can be made. [P5.I.C.2.]

4. True. [P5.I.D.2.]

5. The donee may hold a purely collateral power if the donee holds no interest in the property except the power. The donee may hold a power in gross if the donee holds both an interest in the property and a power that if exercised would dispose of the interest that the donee does not hold. [P5.I.D.4.]

II. EXERCISE OF A POWER OF APPOINTMENT

1. True. A donee may only be able to exercise a power by inter vivos deed, or by the donee's will. The donor may require that the donee make a specific reference to the power in order to exercise it. [P5.II.A.1.]

2. False. The donor of a non-general power intends the donee to have the same breadth of discretion in appointment to the objects of the power that the donee has in disposing of his or her own property to objects of the power. [P5.II.C.2.]

3. True. [P5.II.D.3.]

III. NONEXERCISE OF POWERS OF APPOINTMENT

1. Lapse of the power. [P5.III.A.4.]

2. Any person who otherwise would be an object of the power may disclaim within a reasonable time after the creation of the power. [P5.III.B.1.]

IV. DONEE'S CREDITORS AND SPOUSAL ELECTIONS

1. False. The donee of a non-general power is not considered to be the owner of the appointive assets. [P5.IV.B.1.]

2. True. [P5.IV.B.2.a.]

3. When power was created by donee. [P5.IV.C.]

PART SIX: TRUSTS

I. TRUSTS: DEFINITIONS AND CHARACTERISTICS

1. True. [P6.I.A.3.]

2. Uses for testamentary trusts [P6.I.A.5.] include:

   a. Property management;

   b. Providing for successive estates;

   c. Greater protection of future interests;

   d. Flexibility regarding unanticipated situations; and,

   e. Tax purposes.

3. Uses of inter vivos trusts [P6.I.A.5.] include:

   a. Avoidance of probate;

   b. Avoidance of agency pitfalls;

   c. Ability to anticipate incapacity or death; and

   d. Tax purposes.

4. The trustee. [P6.I.B.1.]

5. False. Unless the settlor is also a trustee, then the answer is True. [P6.I.]

6. True. [P6.I.C.1.]

7. The *cestui que trust* or beneficiary. [P6.I.D.1.]

II. TRUST FORMALITIES: CREATION AND TERMINATION

1. The settler must properly manifest an intention to create a trust relationship. [P6.II.A.1.]

2. A trust may be created [P6.II.B.2.] by:

    a. Transfer;

    b. Declaration of trust; or

    c. Contract.

3. False, unless trust intent was present at the time of the gift. [P6.II.B.1.]

4. True. [P6.II.A.4.]

5. A "secret trust" is a devise of property to a person absolutely, without reference to any intended trust, where the devisee prior to the testator's death agreed with the testator to hold the property upon a certain trust. A "semi-secret trust" is a bequest or devise which clearly provides that the devisee is not to get the beneficial interest but does not adequately indicate the true beneficiary under the appropriate Statutes of Wills. [P6.II.B.3.b.]

6. True. [P6.II.B.3.c.]

III. REVOCABLE TRUSTS

1. A revocable trust is a special kind of trust in which the settler reserves the right to revoke. [P6.III.A.1.]

2. Uses of revocable trusts [P6.III.A.3.] include:

    a. Avoiding the costs and delays of probate when the settlor dies;

    b. Providing property management for settlor's immediately or contingent on incompetence;

    c. Providing privacy for the estate plan; and,

    d. Saving or postponing taxes.

3. Permissible retained powers [P6.III.B.2.] include:

a. Power to revoke;

b. Reservation of a life interest;

c. The combination of the two;

d. Combined with additional power to alter or modify terms;

e. Combined with a beneficiary survivorship requirement;

f. Combined with a power to control the trustee in the administration of the trust; and,

g. Combined with settlor serving as trustee.

IV. TRUST INTERESTS AND RELATIONSHIPS

1. True. Unless the trust instrument expressly requires preference for a beneficiary over another beneficiary. [P6.IV.A.1.b.]

2. Even if the trustee acted in good faith, the trustee will be liable for any overpayment or if she pays the wrong person. [P6.IV.A.1.a.]

3. A spendthrift trust is one in which, either because of a direction of the settlor or because of statute, the beneficiary is unable to transfer his or her right to future payments of income or capital (a voluntary transfer), and the beneficiary's creditors are unable to subject the beneficiary's interest to the payment of their claims (an involuntary transfer). [P6.IV. B.2.a.]

V. TRUST MODIFICATION AND TERMINATION

1. The phrase is"terms of the trust" [P6.V.A.1.]

2. True. [P6.V.A.2.]

3. A trustee can modify to the extent permitted by the terms of the trust. [P6.V.B.3.]

4. It reflects the American philosophy that the owner of property can do as the owner likes with it as long as the owner makes no provision which runs counter to any rule of law or principle of public policy. [P6.V.C.1.]

5. The general grounds for a court to modify a trust include:

    a. Unanticipated circumstance;

    b. Trust purposes defeated or substantially impaired; and,

    c. Administrative provision modification:

6. The doctrine of Virtual Representation [P6.V.C.2.e.]

VI. CHARITABLE TRUSTS

1. True. [P6.VI.A.1.]

2. A charitable trust is a trust in which the property is devoted to a purpose the law deems appropriately beneficial to the community. [P6.VI.B.2.]

3. The special benefits of a charitable trust [P6.VI.B.3.] include:

   a. May last longer than the period of the Rule Against Perpetuities;

   b. May accumulate income beyond the period of the Rule Against Perpetuities;

   c. Purposes may be changed under the *cy pres* doctrine;

   d. If recognized, has charitable immunity; and

   e. Receives special tax exemption and benefits.

4. A charitable trust should accomplish an appreciable amount of social benefit to the public or some reasonable large class thereof. When the actual benefit from the trust is de minimis or insubstantial, courts have sometimes declared a distinction between being generous or benevolent but not charitable. [P6.VI.C.2. and E.1.]

5. The doctrine of *cy pres*. [P6.VI.H.]

6. The requirements of *cy pres* [6.VI.H.1.] are:

   a. A charitable trust that is or became impossible or impracticable or illegal to carry out, or fully accomplished;

   b. A settlor who manifested a more general intention; and,

   c. A court willing to may direct an application of the remaining assets in the trust to some other charitable purpose which falls within the general charitable intention of the settlor.

PART SEVEN: REGULATION OF DISPOSITION

I. POLICY LIMITATIONS ON FREEDOM OF DISPOSITION

1. The three basic types of family protection [P7.I.B.1.] are:

   a. Allowances;

   b. Homesteads; and,

   c. Exemptions.

2. True. [P7.I.C.3.b.]

3. The various types of protective systems in this country [P.1.C.2.] include:

   a. Dower;

   b. Forced share;

   c. Community and quasi community property;

   d. Fixed share augmented estate; and,

   e. Accrual share augmented estate.

4. The four segments of the 1990 UPC augmented estate [P7.I.3.c.] include:

   a. Segment 1 which includes what normally is thought of as the decedent's net probate estate which is the gross probate estate less enforceable claims, funeral and administration expenses, and the family protections;

   b. Segment 2 which includes all properties over which decedent immediately prior to death retained certain interests, powers or relationships;

   c. Segment 3 which includes all of decedent's nonprobate property which the surviving spouse gratuitously received or derived from the decedent by reason of the latter's death; and,

   d. Segment 4 which includes (1) all of the surviving spouse's individual property and (2) the surviving spouse's Segment 2 property (the spouse's nonprobate transfers to others) as if that spouse predeceased decedent, to the extent these properties are not included in Segments 1 and 3.

5. False. A person may disinherit one's children in this country. [P7.I.D.1.a.]

6. The UPC protects omitted spouse by granting the spouse an automatic, but qualified, intestate share as if decedent had died intestate if the decedent's will was executed prior to marriage. [P7.I.D.4.a.]

II. VOLUNTARY REGULATION OF DISPOSITION

1. The three basic types of will contracts [P7.II.A.1.] include:

   a. To will or devise;

   b. To die intestate; and,

   c. Not to revoke.

2. False. Although many states require a writing, all do not. [P7.II.A.1.]

3. Mutual wills. [P7.II.A.2.]

4. False. Some states infer a contract not to revoke from a joint will but not mutual wills. [P7.II.A.2.]

5. The equitable election doctrine provides that a person cannot accept benefits accruing to her or him by a will and at the same time refuse to recognize the validity of the will in other respects. [P7.II.C.1.]

PART EIGHT: FUTURE INTERESTS AND PERPETUITIES

I. CLASSIFICATION OF ESTATES AND FUTURE INTERESTS

1. The three forms ownership fragmentation [P8.I.A.1.b.] include:

   a. Concurrent interests;

   b. Separate legal and equitable interests; and,

   c. Sequential ownership between present and future interests.

2. True. [P8.I.A.1.]

3. This term that the holder of the estate will lose that estate upon the happening of a specified event is defeasance. [P8.I.C.1.a.]

4. The two general categories of the four fee simple estates [P8.I.C.2.] are:

   a. Fee simple absolute; and,

   b. Defeasible fee simple.

5. The five types of future interests [P8.I.C.3.a.] are:

   a. Remainders;

   b. Executory interests;

   c. Reversions;

   d. Possibilities of reverter; and,

   e. Rights of entry (also called powers of termination).

II. CONSEQUENCES OF CLASSIFICATION

1. The three methods of transferring inalienable future interests [P8.II.B.4. a-c.] are:

   a. Contract to convey (recognized in equity);

   b. Estoppel by deed (recognized by common law); and,

   c. Release (recognized by common law).

2. About seven states still follow the common law rule of inalienability that contingent remainders and executory interests are inalienable and thus a

purported transfer for inadequate consideration by quit claim deed to someone other than a person in whose favor the interest could have been released is ineffective. [P8.II.B.4.d.]

3. This Destructibility Rule states that a legal contingent remainder in law is destroyed if it has not vested by the time of the termination of the preceding freehold estate. [P8.II.D.]

4. The rule in Shelley's Case is that a remainder in land that is purportedly created in the life tenant's heirs or the heirs of the life tenant's body, and that is of the same quality as that of the life estate, is held by the life tenant. [P8.II.E.]

5. The Doctrine of Worthier Title provides that when a transferor, by an inter vivos conveyance, purports to create a future interest in the transferor's own heirs, the transferor is presumed to intend to retain a reversionary interest. [P8.II.F.]

III. CLASS GIFTS

1. A class gift is a gift of property to a group of persons identified by a group label, such as "children," or "grandchildren" rather than a gift to particular individuals. [P8.III.A.1.]

2. Class gifts can fluctuate in number through an increase in the number of takers (caused by births or adoptions), and/or through a decrease in the number of takers (caused by deaths).

3. False. Postponed class gifts may not close until the time of distribution of the gift. [P8.III.B.4.b.]

4. The Rule of Convenience provides that a class closes when the property must be distributed. [P8.III.B.4.]

5. An immediate class gifts closes when distribution is ready and at least one member of the class is in existence. [P8.III.B.4.a.]

6. A postponed class gift closes the class when distribution of the property must be made. When a postponed class gift is preceded by a life estate, the general rule is that the class closes on the life tenant's death. [P8.III.B.4.b.]

IV. RULE AGAINST PERPETUITIES AND RELATED DOCTRINES

1. The definition of the common law Rule Against Perpetuities provides that no interest is good unless it must vest, if at all, not later than twenty-one years after some life in being at the creation of the interest. [P8.IV.A.1.]

2. The definition of the doctrine of infectious invalidity states that the invalidity of an interest may be held to invalidate one or more otherwise valid interests. [P8.IV.A.17.]

3. The rule is the All-or-Nothing Rule applicable to class gifts. [P8.IV.D.1.]

4. Under the USRAP when reformation action is permitted, the court must reform the document and does not have the discretion to hold that the transfer is invalid. The court must reform the transfer in a "manner that most closely approximates the transferor's manifested plan of distribution." [P8.IV.C.5.]

5. The two types of class gifts which are exempt from the all-or-nothing rule [P8.IV.D.2.] are:

   a. Specific-sum class gifts; and,

   b. Gifts to sub-classes.

6. False. [P8.IV.F.2.]

PART NINE: THE FIDUCIARY OBLIGATION

I. CONCEPT OF THE FIDUCIARY

1. This person is generally called a fiduciary. [P9.I.A.1.]

2. The responsibilities of a personal representative of a decedent's estate [P9.I.B.1.] include:

   a. Collection of assets;

   b. Settling of claims; and,

   c. Final distribution of the estate.

3. In appointing a personal representative the court will give great deference to the person who the testator selected. [P9.I.B.]

4. True. [P9.I.C.1.]

5. A guardianship may be necessary when a person is under some type of disability which causes that person to be unable to manage his or her own personal or business affairs or both. [P9.I.D.1.]

6. The guardianship of the person has custody and physical control over the ward: the conservator manages (receives and expends) the ward's property or estate for the purposes of the guardianship. The same person may be permitted to serve in both capacities. [P9.I.D.]

II. DUTIES OF FIDUCIARIES

1. The primary duty of a trustee is to administer the property of the trust for the beneficiaries. The primary duty of a personal representative is to administer the property in the estate first for the benefit of the creditors of the estate and second for the distributees. [P9.II.A.2–3.]

2. The standard of care of a trustee is the care and skill that a person of ordinary prudence would exercise in dealing with her or his own property. [P9.II.B.1.]

3. True. This standard of care can only be lowered by the settlor or testator, but a higher standard can be enforced if a fiduciary possesses or represents that it possesses greater than ordinary skills and more than ordinary facilities. [P9.II.B.5–6.]

4. The "no-further-inquiry" rule holds that if a fiduciary engages in self-dealing, *e.g.*, sells trust property to itself personally or buys personal assets for the trust, this conduct is *per se* illegal. The beneficiaries can surcharge the fiduciary for any profit and any loss or require return of the assets if still available, regardless of the substantive fairness of the deal and regardless of the fiduciary's good faith. [P9.II.C.2.]

5. The RESTATEMENT states that a trustee is under a duty not to delegate the doing of acts which the trustee can reasonably be required personally to perform. [P9.II.D.1.]

6. The accounting requirement for the trustee is essential to protect the beneficiary's interests and the settlor's intent. [P.9.II.G.2.]

III. POWERS OF FIDUCIARIES

1. Even the prudent, cautious personal representative is forced to obtain court approval for actions taken thereby substantially increasing the time and cost involved in the administration of an estate. [P9.III.A.2.]

2. True. [P9.III.A.4.]

3. False. The UTPA recognizes that a settlor may override the Act except that the settlor probably cannot change § 7 which requires third persons dealing with the trustee to have actual notice of a breach of trust in order to be liable. [P9.A.6.]

4. The Prudent Investor Rule accepts modern investment experience and research, without either endorsing or excluding any particular theories of economics or investment. It is meant to be general and flexible enough to adapt to changes in the financial world. It tries to provide both protection for the trustee and guidance for review of trustee actions by the courts.

5. The three basic sources for allocation rules [P9.III.C.2.] include:

   a. Instructions included in the relevant transfer instrument;

   b. If none, the rules set out in relevant state statutes; and,

   c. If neither, reasonable and equitable actions that take into account the interests of both income and principal beneficiaries.

6. The four general problems affecting the rights of beneficiaries [P9.III.C.3.] include the allocation of income or principal or both:

a. Earned during and distributed by the decedent's estate;

b. For any trust that begins when a person who creates the trust dies or transfers property to a trust during life;

c. At the end of the trust; and,

d. For any interest that is received during administration of the estate or trust.

IV. LIABILITY OF FIDUCIARIES AND OTHERS

1. False. Fiduciaries are not insurers of loss to the estate or trust but are liable to beneficiaries for breaches of trust for violating a duty and to third persons for breaches of contracts and torts occurring during administration. [P9.IV.A.1.]

2. The fiduciary for breach of trust is liable [P9.IV.A.4.] for:

   a. Any loss or depreciation in value of the property of the estate or trust resulting from the breach;

   b. Any profit made by the fiduciary through the breach; and,

   c. Any profit which would have accrued to the property of the estate or trust if there had been no breach.

3. If a beneficiary consents to the fiduciary's action he or she is estopped from suit provided the fiduciary did not concealed material facts and did not act in a manner inconsistent with its fiduciary relationship to the beneficiaries in obtaining the consent. [P9.IV.A.7.]

4. True. If the fiduciary has to pay, it will be reimbursed from the estate for its expenses if the fiduciary's administration was proper. [P9.IV.B.1.]

5. For purposes of a personal representative's personal liability to third persons on contracts, from ownership or control of the estate's property and from torts arising out of the administration of the estate, the personal representative is not liable individually but only as an agent would be liable. [P9.IV.B.2.]

6. Under these acts, if a third person purchases for value an asset from a person known to be a trustee, the person takes good title unless he or she had actual knowledge or reason to believe that the transfer is in breach of trust. The third person is not bound to inquire whether the trustee has power to act or is properly exercising the power. [P9.IV.C.2.c.]

PART TEN: TAXATION

I. TAXATION OVERVIEW

1. The three basic elements of the federal taxation system [P10.I.A.2.] include:

a. Income Tax;

b. Gift Tax; and,

c. Estate Tax.

2. True. [P10.I.A.3.]

II. GIFT AND ESTATE TAXES

1. The name of the tax system adopted by Congress in 1976 is the Unified Tax System. [P10.II.A.2.]

2. False. Inter vivos gifts of $10,000 or less per donee are excluded from all transfer taxation. [P10.II.A.2.]

3. The unified tax exemption is the value of taxable transfers that will in effect be gift and estate tax free. It is calculated from the value of transfers it takes to use up the unified tax credit given to each taxpayer under the law. [P10.II.A.3.]

4. Gift-splitting concerns a gift by spouses that is treated as having been made one-half by the donor and one-half by the donor's spouse. This allows a married couple to transfer $20,000 per year to a donee tax free. [P10.II.B.3.]

5. To qualify as an annual exclusion, a gift must be one of a present interest in property. [P10.II.B.4.]

6. A general power of appointment is not included in the donee's estate if it does not exceed the greater of $5,000 or 5 percent of the aggregate value of the trust at the time of the death. [P10.C.5.d.]

7. Annuities are taxable to the annuitant's estate if the estate, a beneficiary or the contract survivor is entitled to a refund or continual payments under the annuity. [P10.C.5.g.]

III. DEDUCTIONS FROM THE GROSS ESTATE

1. The deductions recognized by the IRC to reduce the gross estate to the net estate [P10.III.A.1.] include:

a. Marital deduction;

b. Charitable deduction;

c. Deduction for funeral and administration expenses;

d. Bona fide claims against the decedent's estate; and,

e. Deduction for certain losses during administration.

2. False. Estate tax payable to the federal government is not deductible. [P10.III.A.1.]

3. A terminable interest is an interest that will either fail or terminate on: [P10.III.C.3.]

   a. The mere lapse of time;

   b. On the occurrence of an event or contingency; or,

   c. On the failure of an event or contingency to occur.

4. Some examples of terminable interests [P10.III.C.3.] include:

   a. Life estates;

   b. Term of years; and,

   c. Annuities.

5. True. The reason for this is that when the spouse dies, all of the assets in the trust including accumulated income are included in the spouse's estate for estate tax purposes. [P10.III.C.5.]

IV. FEDERAL GENERATION–SKIPPING TRANSFER TAX

1. A skip person is a natural person assigned to a generation two or more generations below the transferor's generation, *e.g.,* grandchildren, great-grandchildren. [P10.IV.A.2.a.]

2. The three types of generation-skipping transfers [P10.IV.A.6.a.-c.] are:

   a. Direct skips;

   b. Taxable terminations; and,

   c. Taxable distributions.

3. Tax exclusive application means the tax is on the transferor. Tax inclusive application means the tax is imposed on the recipient. [P10.IV.A.8.]

*

APPENDIX B

PRACTICE EXAM QUESTIONS

I. Introduction

1. Because the specific content of courses in this area offered throughout the many law schools is so diverse, it is unrealistic to provide a single full final exam that would be representative. In addition, many professors use local statutes as the relevant law applicable to the questions. Consequently, the approach will be to provide a variety of representative questions that relate to areas covered in this Black Letter. Three basic types will be included: short answer questions, problem solving fact problems, and multiple choice questions.

Note: Unless specifically provided otherwise, the Uniform Probate Code–Official 1993 Text with Comments should be used to answer all questions. If a local set of statutes is applicable for your exam, try to answer the question under that law.

II. Sample Exam Questions

A. Short Answer Questions

1. Formalism is a pervasive issue in this course. Discuss its relevance, application and appropriate standard. Give examples of the relevant formalities. (15 points)

2. The controversy between the living and the dead over control of property continues. How does current trust law deal with this issue? How should the attorney approach this issue with clients who wish to exercise control over the beneficiaries of their largess. (10 points)

3. The issue of protecting a surviving spouse from disinheritance is a policy problem that has produced many remedies. Describe briefly the system included in the Uniform Probate Code and what policies it attempts to satisfy. (15 points)

4. When discretionary trusts are used, what are the rights of the various beneficiaries. How can the interests of the settlor, trustee and beneficiaries be better protected. (10 Points)

B. Problem Solving Fact Problems

1. In a valid will, Zee devised a substantial amount of money to "my surviving grandchildren." When Zee made the will, Zee had two grandchildren, Able and Baker. After the will was executed, but before Zee died, a nonmarital grandchild, Charlie, was born. Able predeceased Zee, leaving no issue. Three days after Zee's death Baker died leaving a child, Xeno. Three months after Zee died, another grandchild, David, was born. Assuming the estate can satisfy the devise, who will take the devise to the grandchildren and in what fractional shares? Explain your answer. (15 points)

2. Wilson died in 1948. By duly probated will he devised Meadowacre, his personal residence, to his daughter Lenora for life and gave Lenora a special power to appoint Meadowacre by will among or for the benefit of descendants of her body with the right to create further life and remainder interests. Lenora was killed in an automobile accident in 1972. Her duly probated will appointed Meadowacre to her son Jules then 25 years of age, for life, remainder "to Jules' children equally." Jules' had two children: Tony born in 1971, and Pat born in 1974. Tony died unmarried in May 1994, and by duly probated will left the entire estate, real and personal, to the World's Great Charity, a corporation authorized by its charter to own real estate. Jules died six months ago, survived by Pat. Who owns Meadowacre and why?

3. Boris Bettenov died last month. The instrument that appears below was found in testator's safety deposit box along with other important documents and certificates. It was a printed form, except for the words that appear in a *bold script type face* which were handwritten. The handwriting in the will portion of the form is in Boris's hand. The notary filled out and signed the notary's certificate in her handwriting

   Between 1968 and 1997 Bettenov had been married to one Natasha Korsakov. After ten strife filled years, they were divorced in November, 1998. In January, 1999, he married Virginia Slim, who was 65 years his younger and who had been his private secretary.

   At the time of the will his oldest nephew, Stan Sampson, was killed last year. He was survived by a spouse and child. His oldest nephew at the date of death is Charles Robinson, who Boris has not seen in twenty years. Boris had a niece, Alice Bettenov Stanton and a nephew, John Sampson.

   Bettenov's estate, totaling $500,000, is composed of the following described property: $200,000 worth of corporate stock securities in his name found in his safe deposit box; $20,000 in a savings account in the Insecurity National Bank; A residence valued at $250,000; Jewelry in a jewelry box valued at $10,000 (This includes a pearl and diamond ring which is a composite of his two prior rings). $20,000 of other personal property and cash.

Wilma Whelmed consults you and asks your opinion on several matters:

a. Has the February 14, 1996 will been properly executed as a valid transfer device? Consider all possibilities. (20 Points)

b. If the will is valid, what are the validity and distribution issues raised by each of the dispositive provisions in this instruments? Assume all the beneficiaries can be identified. (15 Points)

THE LAST WILL AND TESTAMENT

I _Boris Bettenov_ a resident of _Intestate_ of _Probate_ County, State of Probate, being of sound and disposing mind and memory, do make, publish and declare this my last WILL AND TESTAMENT, hereby revoking and making null and void any and all other last Wills and Testaments heretofore by me made.

FIRST — My will is that all my just debts and funeral expenses and any Estate or Inheritance taxes shall be paid out of my Estate, as soon after my decease as shall be found convenient.

SECOND — I give devise and bequeath to

my oldest nephew the money ($15,000) out of my savings account in the Insecurity National Bank

my pearl ring to my niece, Alice Samson, and my diamond ring to my nephew, John Stanton

all the rest to my wife.

I nominate and appoint _Wilma Whelmed_ of ____________________, as execut_or_ of this my Last Will and Testament .

IN TESTIMONY WHEREOF, I have set my hand to this. My Last Will and Testament, at ____________________ this _14_ day of _February_ in the year of our Lord, One Thousand Nine Hundred _96_

____

Notary Verification

The foregoing instrument was signed by said _Boris Bettenov_ in our presence, and by __________ published and declared as and for __________ Last Will and Testament, and at __________ request, and in __________ presence, and in presence of each other, we hereunto subscribe our Names as Attesting Witnesses, at ________ This _14_ day of _February_, 19_96_

My Commission expires Jan. 16, 1999 _Ann C. McGonagill_

C. Multiple Choice Questions

A. Instructions: This portion of the sample exam consists of 35 multiple choice questions. Use only the Answer Sheet for your answers. One of these sheets is included at the end of the questions.

(a) In order to receive credit for your answers, it is essential that you follow the following instructions:

(b) Select only the one alternative answer that best completes the statement or answers the question. *Repeat*: only one answer is correct and only one alternative should be marked per question.

(c) Note: Unless specifically provided otherwise, the UNIFORM PROBATE CODE—OFFICIAL 1993 TEXT WITH COMMENTS should be used to answer all questions.

BEGINNING OF THE MULTIPLE–CHOICE QUESTIONS

Consider the following alternatives for the questions that follow:

A. The surviving spouse will receive the entire distributable estate.

B. The surviving spouse will receive $300,000 and DS's descendants will share the remaining $300,000 equally.

C. The surviving spouse will receive $350,000 and DS's descendants will share the remaining $250,000 equally.

D. The surviving spouse will receive $375,000 and DS's descendants will share the remaining $225,000 equally.

E. The surviving spouse will receive $400,000 and DS's descendants will share the remaining $200,000 equally.

Assume DS dies intestate with a net distributable estate valued at $600,000.

1. DS is survived by SS, the surviving spouse, their adult child, SS's two children from a prior marriage, and DS's parents. Under these facts, which of the above is the correct distribution?

2. DS is survived by SS, the surviving spouse, their two children, DS's two children from a prior marriage and SS's two children from a prior marriage. Under these facts, which of the above is the correct distribution?

Consider the following chart and use them to answer the questions that follow:

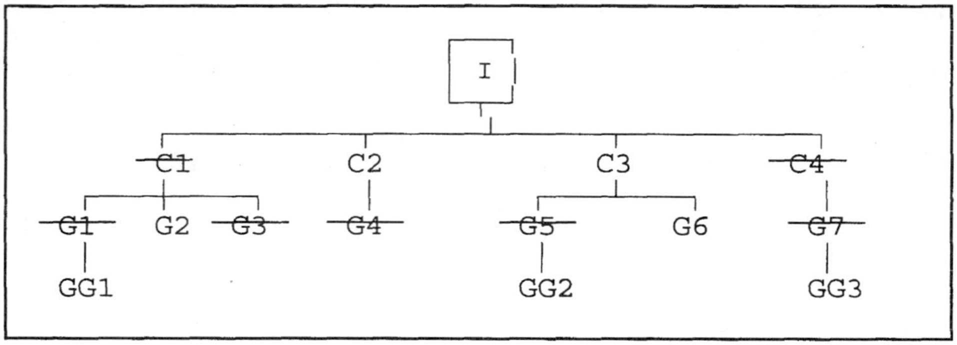

Assume (1) I died unmarried and intestate and (2) I is survived only by the following descendants: C2, C3, G2, G6, GG1, GG2 and GG3.

Alternatives	Surviving Descendants						
	C2	C3	G2	G6	GG1	GG2	GG3
A.	1/4	1/4	1/6	0	1/6	0	1/6
B.	1/5	1/5	1/5	0	1/5	0	1/5
C.	1/4	1/4	1/8	0	1/8	0	1/4
D.	1/4	0	1/6	1/8	1/6	1/8	1/6
E.	None of the Above						

Select from the above alternatives the proper pattern of distribution for intestate succession for the following methods.

3. Under per capita with per capita representation.

4. Under per capita at each generation.

5. Under per stirpes.

6. Under the UPC, if C4 feloniously murdered I, and immediately committed suicide.

Consider the following alternatives and use them to answer the questions that follow:

A. Fraud in the inducement.

B. Mistake in the inducement.

C. Undue influence.

D. Insane Delusion

E. Mental deficiency.

Determine for each of the following statements which of the above alternatives best completes or is described by the statement:

7. It is a ground for successfully contesting a will even though the will does exactly what the testator desired.

8. It is generally not a ground for contesting a will.

Consider the following alternatives and use them to answer the questions that follow:

A. Augmented Estate.

B. Community Property.

C. Dower.

D. Forced Share.

E. None of the above.

Determine for each of the following statements which of the above alternatives best completes or is described by the statement.

9. It sets a dollar amount determined on the basis of the need of the surviving spouse.

10. It adjusts both for excessive inheritance and for improper disinheritance of the surviving spouse.

Consider the following alternatives and use them to answer the questions that follow:

A. The inter vivos transfer would be made a part of Segment 1 if SS exercises the election.

B. The inter vivos transfer would be made a part of Segment 2 if SS exercises the election.

C. The inter vivos transfer would be made a part of Segment 3 if SS exercises the election.

D. The inter vivos transfer would be made a part of Segment 4 if SS exercises the election.

E. None of the above.

Determine for each of the following statements which of the above alternatives best completes or is described by the statement. Assume the UPC Elective Share provisions are applicable and that Z is survived by SS and that Z prior to death completed the following actions:

11. Changed beneficiary from X to SS on $100,000 life insurance policy owned by Z till his death.

12. Gave and delivered a diamond ring to SS ten years before Z's death.

13. Transferred three years before Z's death $500,000 of securities to T into a irrevocable trust for Z's children for life, remainder to Z's descendants.

Consider the following facts and use them to answer the questions that follow:

D's validly executed will makes the following devises:

A. $15,000 to the members of my poker group.

B. My stocks to my nephews, if they survive me.

C. $1,000 to each of my second cousins' issue.

D. Residue to my spouse, Jane Doe.

E. None of the above apply.

Using the above devises as answer alternatives select the proper devise that satisfies the following statements.

14. Which of the above devises is subject to the common law doctrine of Ademption by Extinction?

15. Which of the above devises is definitely covered by the UPC antilapse provision if a devisee dies before D and is survived by issue?

16. Which of the above constitutes a per capita class devise?

Consider the following alternatives for the questions that follow:

Alternatives	Surviving Descendants			
	W	X	Y	G
A.	0	$10,000	$20,000	$30,000
B.	0	$20,000	$20,000	$20,000
C.	0	$25,000	$35,000	0
D.	$10,000	$20,000	$30,000	0
E.	None of the above			

Assume Z died intestate and left a net distributable estate of $60,000. During Z's lifetime, she made gifts to W of $30,000, to X of $20,000, and to Y of $10,000. Each gift was accompanied by a contemporaneous written statement that it was an advancement to the donee.

17. Z is survived by two of her children (X and Y) and her only grandchild (G) a child of her predeceased child (W). When distribution is made from Z's estate which of the above alternative distributions should be made?

18. Z is survived by all three of her children (W, X and Y) and her only grandchild (G) a child of her child (W) but W properly disclaims W's interest in Z's estate. When distribution is made from Z's estate which of the above alternative distributions should be made?

Consider the following alternatives and use them to answer the questions that follow:

A. Holographic will.

B. Ordinary witnessed will.

C. Nuncupative will.

D. Self-proved will.

E. None of the above.

Determine for each of the following statements which of the above alternatives best describes the statement.

19. Testator must sign the will personally.

20. It is **not** specifically recognized.

Consider the following alternatives and use them to answer the questions that follow:

A. Accessions.

B. Ademption by extinction.

C. Ademption by satisfaction.

D. Change in form.

E. None of the above.

Assume T's will provided, inter alia, "I devise my 100 shares of XYZ stock to A." This is A's only devise in T's will.

21. Before T died, T gave these shares to A. At T's death, which alternative above will determine whether A will take from T's estate?

22. Before T died, T's XYZ stock was redeem and 1,000 shares of ZYC stock was issued in its place. If T's will is unchanged at T's death, which alternative above will determine whether A will take from T's estate?

Consider the following alternatives and use them to answer the questions that follow:

A. Claflin Doctrine.

B. Equitable Deviation Doctrine.

C. Republication by Codicil Doctrine.

D. Stranger to the Adoption Doctrine.

E. None of the above.

Determine for each of the following statements which of the above alternatives best completes or is described by the statement.

23. It permits the dispositive purposes of a charitable trust to be altered if certain conditions are met.

24. It may restrict the includability of some relations as members of class gifts in dispositive instruments.

Consider the following alternatives and use them to answer the questions that follow:

A. Dependent relative revocation.

B. Revival.

C. Revocation by inconsistency.

D. Supersession.

E. None of the above

25. Ten years ago T executed a valid will that devised his estate as follows: "To A I devise my coin collection; to B I devise $10,000; the residue I devise to C." Five years later, T executed a valid will that merely devised his coin collection to D. This year, T revoked the later will by physical act. Assuming extrinsic evidence is not available, which of the above concepts is the best rationale for allowing A now to take the coin collection?

26. Ten years ago T executed a valid will that devised his estate as follows: "To A I devise my coin collection; to B I devise $10,000; the residue I devise to C." Five years later, T executed a valid will that devised his estate as follows: "To D my coin collection; to B I devise $10,000; the residue I devise to C." This year, T revoked the later will by physical act. Assuming extrinsic evidence is not available, which of the above concepts is the best rationale for allowing A now to take the coin collection?

Consider the following alternatives for the following three questions:

A. Gift in default.

B. Fraudulent appointment.

C. Illusory appointments.

D. Second look.

E. None of the above.

For each of the following statements determine which of the above alternatives is accurately described by the statement

27. It means that the power has been exercised for a purpose beyond the scope of the instrument creating the power.

28. It is a doctrine for special powers of appointment that permits facts and circumstances existing on the date of exercise to determine the validity of the appointment under the Rule Against Perpetuities.

Consider the following alternatives and use them to answer the question that follows:

A. "Blue chip stocks."

B. Close corporation stock.

C. Bonds of federal government.

D. First mortgages.

E. None of the above.

29. Which of the above alternatives would be ordinarily prohibited under the prudent man rule for investments?

Consider the following alternatives and use them to answer the questions that follow:

A. The execution of the instrument occurred.

B. The testator died.

C. The life tenant died.

D. Distribution or actual possession occurs.

E. The first member of the class reaches or reached age twenty-one.

Determine for each of the following situations which of the above alternatives completes or answers the question asked:

30. T bequeathed 100,000 in trust to A for life, remainder to B's children. In chronological order, B had two children on the date the will was executed, and four children on A's death and six children on T's death. The class gift closes on the date on which:

31. W devised her residuary to T, in trust, income to X for life, "remainder to be divided among such of the children of my brothers and sisters as survive to age 21." X died before W. At W's death, W was survived by two brothers and two sisters and by three nieces, ages 19, 15, and 17. The class gift closes on the date on which:

32. Z devised his residuary to T, in trust, income to X for life, remainder to Y and Y's children as survive to age 21. X and Y survived Z. At Z's death Y had two children, ages 3 and 5. At X's death five years after Z's death, Y had four children, age 10, 8, 4 and 2. The class gift closes on the date on which:

33. Which of the following trusts could be terminated by the beneficiaries if they all consent:

A. S devises the residue to T in trust for W for life, remainder to S's children. S is survived by W and two adult children.

B. S devises the residue to T in trust for W for life, remainder to W's children. S is survived by W and W's two adult children.

C. S devises the residue to T in trust for W for life, remainder to S's children but if they do not survive W to S's grandchildren. S is survived only by W and two adult children.

D. S devises the residue to T in trust for W for life, remainder to S's children. S is survived by W and two adult children. W is incompetent.

E. S devises the residue to T in trust for W for life, remainder to S's children. The trust includes a spendthrift clause. S is survived by W and two adult children.

34. Ten years ago G wrotes a will leaving her entire estate to her favorite uncle, J. Five years ago, she wrotes another will, leaving her coin collection to her daughter, K, but made no other provision as to her property. Which of the following is correct?

A. If the second will contains an express revocation clause, her estate, other than the coin collection, passes by intestacy.

B. If her second will does not contain an express revocation clause, the coin collection passes to K and the rest of her estate passes to J.

C. If the second will expressly revokes the first will and she later revokes the second will, G will die intestate.

D. If the second will does not expressly revoke the first will and G later revokes the second will, the entire estate will pass to J.

E. All of the above answers are correct.

35. Under the modern common law rule, which of the following inter vivos transfers by Z would most likely be illusory if a surviving spouse claims it is an attempt to defeat the SS's spousal right?

A. Transfer of $100,000 to T into a revocable trust for Z and Z's descendants three years before Z's death.

B. Purchase of Whiteacre by Z with title being put in the name of Z and X as joint tenants with right of survivorship.

C. Transfer of Greenacre by deed to G five years before death; Z retained possession of deed till death.

D. Change of beneficiary from SS to X on $100,000 life insurance policy owned by Z till his death.

E. All of the above answers are correct.

END OF MULTIPLE CHOICE QUESTIONS

III. Answers to Sample Exam Questions

A. Outline of Answers to Short Answer Questions

1. Formalism Question

Examples of formalities include—

Statute of Will.

Statute of Frauds.

Pervasive existence.

Functions of formalities—

Protective function.

Evidentiary function.

Ritual function.

Channeling function.

Administrative function.

Constant conflict between—

Intent enforcing.

Intent denying.

Relief techniques—

Substantial compliance.

Reasonable compliance.

Strict compliance.

Dispensing power.

Going backward.

Protecting against litigation—

Higher standard of proof—

Clear and convincing evidence requirement.

2. Dead Hand Control Question

Freedom of disposition—

Power of settlor.

Power of beneficiary.

Power of trustee.

Control primarily in settlor not beneficiaries—

Spendthrift trust doctrine.

All consent, all sui juris requirement.

Claflin doctrine.

Court has some powers to change trusts—

Great deference to settlor's wishes.

Distributive provisions not changed.

Better drafting—

Detailed consideration of consequences of changes in circumstances.

Clear expressions of control issues.

3. UPC Spousal Rights Question

Accrual system—

Longer the marriage higher the percentage.

Up to 50%.

Protection against over and under protection.

Safety net minimum.

Augmented estate—

Segment 1 Probate estate.

Segment 2 Nonprobate transfers.

Segment 3 Spouse's take from estate.

Segment 4 Spouse's estate.

Satisfaction comes—

Fund 1:from spouse's take and from appropriate share doubled of spouse's assets.

Fund 2:from Segment 1 and 2 assets.

Fund 3:from irrevocable transfer within 2 years of death.

Spouse must file election—

Within the later of nine months after decedent's death or

Six months after probate of decedent's will

Decedent's nonprobate transfers not subject to the election unless the election is filed within nine months of decedent's death.

4. Discretionary Trusts Question

Discretionary trusts are used for tax management and flexibility purposes.

Courts sometimes make a distinction between a trustee's simple versus absolute discretion.

The former is tested by reasonableness but with no second guessing.

The latter is not tested by reasonableness but according to the intent of the settlor.

Courts oversees discretion regardless of its degree.

Trustee decisions are difficult to overcome, however.

If beneficiary protection is the reason for the discretion, the settlor should clearly express the intent of the power.

Standards to exercise the discretion by and examples of the exercise of discretion is recommended.

B. Outline of Answers to Problem Solving Fact Problems

1. Surviving Grandchildren Problem

Type of gift: Immediate class gift.

Include prior and post born members.

Subject to lapse.

Antilapse applicable under UPC.

Potential class members.

Able—Does not take, gift lapses, no antilapse applicable, share goes to other class members.

Baker—Does not take, gift lapses, antilapse applicable, share goes to descendant.

Charlie—May take, under UPC nonmarital class member included in class gift language if the member lived while a minor with the natural parent or that parent's parent, brother, sister, spouse or surviving spouse.

David—May take, posthumous children are included if the individual was conceived before the testator's death but born after it, if he lived 120 hours or more after their birth.

Xeno—take under UPC antilapse provision, covered relation, application not rebutted by word "surviving," mere words of survivorship.

Xeno, Charlie, David share equally.

Able, Baker do not take because they predeceased.

2. Power Of Appointment Problem

Wilson created a special power of appointment with Lenora as donee.

Lenora exercised power by adding an additional power.

Proper unless prohibited.

Lenora extended length of interest.

Rule Against Perpetuities—

Common Law—

Runs from donor's transfer for special powers.

Lives in being plus 21 years from that date with second look at exercise of power by donee.

Lenora's exercise of the power will not vest in all members of the class until Jules' death.

All or nothing rule could destroy transfer.

But Jules was a life in being when original power was created.

Thus power will totally vest in all members of class within the rule.

USRAP accepts common law rule validity.

Survivorship of Jules as a requirement.

Pat survived Jules and will take a share.

Tony died before Jules.

At common law there was no implied requirement of survivorship.

Thus Tony's estate will take Tony's share and Charity as beneficiary of the will will take that share.

Under UPC there is an implied requirement of survivorship if future interest is in trust.

No trust here thus common law applies.

If in trust, Tony must survive Jules to take.

If Tony left descendants they would take by the UPC antilapse provision.

No descendants means Pat would take all of Meadowacre.

3. Will Validity and Effectiveness Problem

a. February 14, 1996 will validity.

As ordinary witnessed will it lacks the normal two witnesses.

Even if notary can be counted as a witness, one is not enough under the standard witnessed will execution statute.

The location of the testator's signature in the exordium raises a question of execution.

Location of signature is not mandated under most statutes including the UPC.

Will might be savable under the dispensing power of the UPC—

Under UPC § 2–503, a court may dispense with one or more statutory formalities.

If testator intent the document to constitute the decedent's will is established by clear and convincing evidence.

Much evidence indicates that Boris wanted instrument to be a valid will.

Getting notary indicates importance of document.

Location of will at death indicates intent.

Will might be probatable as a holographic will.

If all printing is removed the will, the dispositive provisions as in testator's handwriting.

Under UPC, only "material provision" need be in writing.

Place of the testator's signature raises a question of testamentary intent but other evidence include type portions can be used to prove that.

Although they are problems, will should be probatable under one of the above approaches.

b. Validity and effectiveness issues. (Assuming will's validity).

The "oldest nephew" devise:

Is this a proper beneficiary description under facts of independent significance.

Did testator intend the oldest nephew at time of will or at time of death.

Description ambiguous, is extrinsic evidence admissible.

If Stan is the beneficiary, does his gift lapse because he died before testator.

Does antilapse statute will apply to protect Stan's descendants.

Is the devise a specific devise or a demonstrative devise?

Does devisee take only $10,000?

or

Does devisee take $15,000 ($10,000 from the account and $5,000 as a general charge against the estate assets)?

The devises to Alice Samson and John Stanton

Can the misdescription of these devisee be corrected?

Is extrinsic evidence admissible to correct the mistake?

Will the court rewrite the will by inserting the correct names?

The composite pearl and diamond ring:

Are the pearl and diamond devises adeemed by extinction?

Is the composite ring merely a change in form?

If adeemed, is there extrinsic evidence to rebut the presumption of ademption?

Could the devisees (assuming their identity is established) be held as tenants in common in the composite ring?

The residue to "my wife"

Who does "wife" refer to: Natasha Korsakov or Virginia Slim?

Is it the wife at the time of the will or time of death?

If Natasha is wife, is provision revoked by divorce?

Does residue pass intestate or under will to Virginia?

C. Correct Answers to Multiple Choice Questions

1. D	8. B	15. B	22. D	29. B
2. C	9. E	16. C	23. E	30. B
3. C	10. A	17. A	24. D	31. E
4. A	11. C	18. A	25. D	32. C
5. C	12. D	19. A	26. B	33. A
6. A	13. E	20. C	27. B	34. E
7. E	14. B	21. B	28. D	35. C

APPENDIX C

TEXT CORRELATION CHART

Wills, Trusts and Future Interests						
Topic in Outline	**Anderson, Gaubatz, Bloom & Solomon, Fundamentals of Trusts & Estates (2d ed. 1996)**	**Clark, Lusky, Murphy, Ascher, & McCouch, Gratuitous Transfers (4th ed. 1999)**	**Dobris & Sterk, Ritchie, Alford & Effland's, Estates and Trusts: Cases and Materials (1998)**	**Dukeminier & Johanson, Wills Trusts, and Estates (6th ed. 2000)**	**Scoles & Halbach, Decedents' Estates and Trusts (5th ed. 1993)**	**Waggoner, Alexander & Fellows, Family Property Law (2d ed. 1997)**
Part One: Gratuitous Transfers in Perspective						
I. Scope and History of Gratuitous Transfers		1-10		34-38	1-34	1-12, 23-25
II. Administration of Estates and Trusts		11-17	895-900	39-49		12-22
A. The Judicial Involvement in Property Transmission	11-17	631-637			558-582	
B. Court Versus Noncourt Transactions	17-22		43-60		573-582	
C. Jurisdictional Issues		614-624, 637-639	905-917		584-612	

Topic in Outline	ANDERSON, GAUBATZ, BLOOM & SOLOMON, FUNDAMENTALS OF TRUSTS & ESTATES (2d ed. 1996)	CLARK, LUSKY, MURPHY, ASCHER, & MCCOUCH, GRATUITOUS TRANSFERS (4th ed. 1999)	DOBRIS & STERK, RITCHIE, ALFORD &EFFLAND'S, ESTATES AND TRUSTS: CASES AND MATERIALS (1998)	DUKEMINIER & JOHANSON, WILLS TRUSTS, AND ESTATES (6th ed. 2000)	SCOLES & HALBACH, DECEDENTS' ESTATES AND TRUSTS (5th ed. 1993)	WAGGONER, ALEXANDER & FELLOWS, FAMILY PROPERTY LAW (2d ed. 1997)
III. Judicial Procedure and Evidence					166-194	615-662
A. Parties and Pleadings			903-904			
B. Burdens of Proof and Presumptions					635	
C. Introduction to Interpretation			284-290		166-171	
D. Substantive Evidence Rules: Restrictions on Admissibility	111-122	371-383	290-315	409-438	171-185	615-663
IV. Professional Responsibility					295-301	
A. General Application of Ethical Standards			27-31		295-301	
B. Competence	8-11		34-40			662-670
C. Confidentiality			32			630-631
D. Loyalty	136		31-33, 512-513	185-213, 628-29	667-669	
E. Estate Planning			34-43			253-257, 318
Part Two — Intestate Succession and Related Doctrines						
I. Estate Plan by Operation of Law					46-61	29-78
A. General Patterns of Intestate Succession	35-36	49-54	61-70	71-85	47-49	29-35
B. Shares of the Takers	38-42, 51-54	55-61	70-82	72-86	50-58	36-44
C. Representation	54-58	61-67	61-70	86-90	52-55	44-52
D. Ancestors and Collaterals		67-73	83-90	90-96	55-58	54-61
E. Escheat		72	90	74, 95-96	57	61-62
II. Taker Qualifications						79-166
A. Questions of Status	42, 361-369				61-62	
B. Survivorship and Simultaneous Death	37	59-60	125-132	77-86		34-35, 345, 449-54
C. Consanguinity	50	60-61, 72-73	91-92	96-98	2	35
D. Affinity	49-	66	98-99		2, 49	58, 159-160

	Topic in Outline	ANDERSON, GAUBATZ, BLOOM & SOLOMON, FUNDAMENTALS OF TRUSTS & ESTATES (2d ed. 1996)	CLARK, LUSKY, MURPHY, ASCHER, & MCCOUCH, GRATUITOUS TRANSFERS (4th ed. 1999)	DOBRIS & STERK, RITCHIE, ALFORD &EFFLAND'S, ESTATES AND TRUSTS: CASES AND MATERIALS (1998)	DUKEMINIER & JOHANSON, WILLS TRUSTS, AND ESTATES (6th ed. 2000)	SCOLES & HALBACH, DECEDENTS' ESTATES AND TRUSTS (5th ed. 1993)	WAGGONER, ALEXANDER & FELLOWS, FAMILY PROPERTY LAW (2d ed. 1997)
	E. Adoption	46-48	73-84	92-98, 99-106, 722-730	98-114	62-68	114-127, 148-159
	F. Definition of Spouse	42-43	58-60				80-85
	G. Cohabitors		59	417-429	77, 492-500		85-112
	H. Nonmarital Children	43-46	84-92	106-125, 730	115-128	68-74	127-147, 160-165
III.	Bars to Inheritance					74-89, 436-446	
	A. Effect of Prior Transactions on Inheritance Rights	175-179	106-108	142-144, 141-142	128-132	84-89	73-76
	B. Misconduct	193-200	92-106	16-27	141-148	74-84	462-470
	C. Termination of Marital Status	179-187	92-93				80-82
	D. Disclaimer	187-193	109-113, 864-866	132-142	148-157		65-71
	E. Alienship						
	F. Negative Wills				90		76-78
Part Three — Testament Transfers							
I.	Execution of Wills	59-63				129-154	
	A. Will Formality Overview	75-77, 92-100	252-258, 279-291	193-207	301	129-137, 152-154	167-174
	B. The Formal Requirements of Attested Wills	77-89	258-316		223-246	137-148	174-204
	C. Unattested Wills	90-91	301-316	215-224	262-176	148-142	206-212
	D. Special Wills		291	224-226	226		204-205
II.	Revocation of Wills					195-217	
	A. Revocation Requirements	122-130	344-354, 361-370	316-330	276-285	195-207	259-292
	B. Reestablishing Revoked or Apparently Revoked Wills	130-136	354-361	330-332	296-300	207-217	292-315

Topic in Outline	Anderson, Gaubatz, Bloom & Solomon, Fundamentals of Trusts & Estates (2d ed. 1996)	Clark, Lusky, Murphy, Ascher, & McCouch, Gratuitous Transfers (4th ed. 1999)	Dobris & Sterk, Ritchie, Alford & Effland's, Estates and Trusts: Cases and Materials (1998)	Dukeminier & Johanson, Wills Trusts, and Estates (6th ed. 2000)	Scoles & Halbach, Decedents' Estates and Trusts (5th ed. 1993)	Waggoner, Alexander & Fellows, Family Property Law (2d ed. 1997)
III. Defining the Scope of the Will					155-156	246-253
A. Policy of the Statute of Wills	106	252-254, 624-631	194-195	223-226	155	
B. Integration of Wills	106-107	317	226-238	301-302	155-59	246
C. Republication by Codicil		317-319	336	302-303	159-161	251
D. Incorporation by Reference	107-110	320-326	226-239	303-318	161-164	246-251
E. Reference to Facts of Independent Significance	111	319-320	240-241	318-319	164-166	251-253
IV. Will Contests and Will Substitute Suits					616-624, 634-678	
A. Proving the Will	100-101		903-904		617-620	
B. Limitations on the Rights of Probate and Contest	101-105	71-72, 233	412-416		620-630	
C. Grounds of Contest	63-75	178-251	357-412	159-222	634-678	212-246
D. Inter Vivos Transfers			45-50			425-439
V. Constructional Problems of Dispositions						
A. General Comment		371	282-290		950-951	317
B. Classification of Testamentary Gifts	200-202	383	246-252	459	951-952	319
C. Lapse and Antilapse	209-218	393-401	266-270, 272-282, 731-739	438-458	973-987	345-360, 439-449
D. Ademption	203-208	383-391	254-266	459-468, 469	952-969	319-333, 343-345, 454-457
E. Accessions	202-203				863-864	333-340

Topic in Outline	Anderson, Gaubatz, Bloom & Solomon, Fundamentals of Trusts & Estates (2d ed. 1996)	Clark, Lusky, Murphy, Ascher, & McCouch, Gratuitous Transfers (4th ed. 1999)	Dobris & Sterk, Ritchie, Alford & Effland's, Estates and Trusts: Cases and Materials (1998)	Dukeminier & Johanson, Wills Trusts, and Estates (6th ed. 2000)	Scoles & Halbach, Decedents' Estates and Trusts (5th ed. 1993)	Waggoner, Alexander & Fellows, Family Property Law (2d ed. 1997)
F. Abatement	208-209	391-392, 906-908	246-251	468	969-971	340-342
G. Miscellaneous Matters			252-253	468-69	971-972	
H. Beneficiary Status	362-367	83-84, 91	722-730	759-768	64-68, 72	148-165
Part Four — Lifetime Transfers						
I. Will Substitutes			58-60		236-279	
A. Testamentariness and Will Substitutes	145-152	402-435, 440-453			379-387	403-424
B. Joint Ownership	152-155	437-440	50-55, 843	350-351	240-242	
C. Contractual Survivorship	155-156, 166-171	435-437, 488-493	55-58	331-50	242-255	
D. Conditional Deeds		411-412			269-272	
E. Nondocumented Gratuitous Transfers		412-434				
F. Gifts to Minors		434-435		132-140	267-268	
II. Planning for Retirement and Incapacity						
A. General Concepts and Techniques	269-275		826-843			471-474
B. Durable Powers of Attorney		297-300	854-863	396-403	124-125	460-461
C. Health Care Decisions	275-286	297-300	854-863	403-405	124-125	491-507
D. Physician Assisted Suicide		300	863-874			507-510
E. Public Programs for Incapacity and Retirement	171-173, 322-323		530-543	648-51		474-481
F. Long Term Care Planning			874-876			474-481
G. Organ Donation		300-301		405-408		510-514
Part Five – Powers of Appointment						
I. Introduction to Powers						
A. Definition of Power of Appointment	377	811-813	611-612	665-666		887-888
B. Creation of a Power of Appointment	378, 381	823-824	615-621	676-677		892-894

Topic in Outline		Anderson, Gaubatz, Bloom & Solomon, Fundamentals of Trusts & Estates (2d ed. 1996)	Clark, Lusky, Murphy, Ascher, & McCouch, Gratuitous Transfers (4th ed. 1999)	Dobris & Sterk, Ritchie, Alford & Effland's, Estates and Trusts: Cases and Materials (1998)	Dukeminier & Johanson, Wills Trusts, and Estates (6th ed. 2000)	Scoles & Halbach, Decedents' Estates and Trusts (5th ed. 1993)	Waggoner, Alexander & Fellows, Family Property Law (2d ed. 1997)
	C. Different Kinds of Powers of Appointment	378	813-820	613	665-666		888-892
II.	Exercise of a Power of Appointment						
	A. Exercise of a Power of Appointment	379, 381-387	824-828	622-625	688-696		905-917
	B. Excessive Appointment – Fraud on Power of Appointment				696-702		925-926
	C. Interests Creatable by Exercise of Power of Appointment			625-628			918-919
	D. Contract to Appoint Power of Appointment		828-830	633-635			928-930
	E. Time of Exercise of Power of Appointment		813-814				
	F. Appointment to Deceased Persons						
III.	Nonexercise of Powers of Appointment				702-07		926-928
	A. Release and Disclaimer of Powers of Appointment		828-830	635-642	682-688		929-930
	B. Disclaimer by Object or Appointee						
IV.	Donee's Creditors and Spousal Elections						
	A. General Application	380-381					895
	B. Creditors of the Donee		838-841	642-645			895-898, 898-901, 903-905
	C. Spousal Rights in Appointive Assets						896-897, 901-902
Part Six — Trusts							
I.	Trusts: Definitions and Characteristics						
	A. Trust Characteristics	287-288	454-467	445-447, 543-560	553-556	302-304, 310-319	671-686
	B. The Trustee	303-305		448-450	559-561	323-325	704-707
	C. The Trust Property	294-298	493-498	456-459	581-584	325-326	687-694

	Topic in Outline	Anderson, Gaubatz, Bloom & Solomon, Fundamentals of Trusts & Estates (2d ed. 1996)	Clark, Lusky, Murphy, Ascher, & McCouch, Gratuitous Transfers (4th ed. 1999)	Dobris & Sterk, Ritchie, Alford & Effland's, Estates and Trusts: Cases and Materials (1998)	Dukeminier & Johanson, Wills Trusts, and Estates (6th ed. 2000)	Scoles & Halbach, Decedents' Estates and Trusts (5th ed. 1993)	Waggoner, Alexander & Fellows, Family Property Law (2d ed. 1997)
	D. The Beneficiaries	298-300	573-577	450-454	561-562	326-339	707-725
	E. Trust Purposes			445-446	553-556	339-349	
	F. Comparisons with Other Transactions	301-303	485-488, 568-573	446-447	562-567	304-308	
II.	Trust Formalities: Creation and Termination						
	A. Intent to Create a Trust	288-293	484, 467-85	460-465	567-581	320-323, 308-310	694-704
	B. Formalities for Trusts	162-166, 305-306	563-572	465-472	581-617	351-395	725-746, 458-460
	C. Revocation and Termination of Trusts		537-563	560-579	651-661		711-713
III.	Revocable Trusts						
	A. Definition and Application of Revocable Trusts	157		479-486	351-396		404-405
	B. Settlor Control over Revocable Trusts	157-162			394	379-395	405-415
IV.	Trust Interests and Relationships					423-471	
	A. Enforceability of Beneficial Interests	306	658-665	496-512	617-28	423-436	
	B. Transfer of a Beneficiary's Interest	306-322	498-537	513-530	631-48	436-471	747-793, 414-415
V.	Trust Modification and Termination						
	A. Trust Modification and Termination by the Settlor	324	537-542, 559-563	561-564, 573-575	651	472-477	
	B. Trust Modification and Termination by the Trustee		542-548			477	
	C. Trust Modification and Termination by the Beneficiaries	324-328	548-563	564-73	652-61	478-493	793-816
	D. Trust Modification and Termination by the Court		611	575-579, 995-1001	655-56	493-512	816-821

Topic in Outline	Anderson, Gaubatz, Bloom & Solomon, Fundamentals of Trusts & Estates (2d ed. 1996)	Clark, Lusky, Murphy, Ascher, & McCouch, Gratuitous Transfers (4th ed. 1999)	Dobris & Sterk, Ritchie, Alford & Effland's, Estates and Trusts: Cases and Materials (1998)	Dukeminier & Johanson, Wills Trusts, and Estates (6th ed. 2000)	Scoles & Halbach, Decedents' Estates and Trusts (5th ed. 1993)	Waggoner, Alexander & Fellows, Family Property Law (2d ed. 1997)
VI. Charitable Trusts						
A. History of Charitable Trusts					513-514	825-827
B. General Nature of Charitable Trusts	328		579-580	859-869	514-523	
C. Charitable Purpose	328-331	577-586	580-589	859-869		827-841
D. Illegal and Public Policy Limitations				867-869	525	841-849
E. Indefinite Beneficiary		577-586		867		
F. Interrelated Factors						
G. Discriminatory Trusts		597-607	602-610		525-537	862-883
H. Cy Pres	331-335	586-611	589-610	869-883	537-545	849-862
I. Honorary Trusts		612-613	454-456	602	523-525	725, 845
J. Charitable Corporations					548-557	826-827
K. Supervision of Charitable Trusts			589	883-901	545-548	883-884
Part Seven — Regulation of Disposition						
I. Policy Limitations on Freedom of Disposition						
A. Interrelated Public Policies		114-117, 174-177			90	515-516
B. Allowances, Homesteads, and Exemptions		117-119	175-177	476-478	90-91	575-578
C. Surviving Spouse Protection from Disinheritance	219-253	43-45, 120-159	145-175, 179-181	471-476, 478-536	91-111, 395-422	516-575
D. Unintentional Disinheritance	253-258	159-172	177-179, 181-192	530-550	112-118	578-586
E. Other Public Policy Regulations and Prohibitions	259-267	29-43, 45-48, 172-174			118-120	586-587
II. Voluntary Regulation of Disposition						
A. Will Contracts	137-143	330-344	337-352	319-329	218-235	589-613
B. Settlement Agreements					630-634	63-65, 821-824

Topic in Outline	Anderson, Gaubatz, Bloom & Solomon, Fundamentals of Trusts & Estates (2d ed. 1996)	Clark, Lusky, Murphy, Ascher, & McCouch, Gratuitous Transfers (4th ed. 1999)	Dobris & Sterk, Ritchie, Alford & Effland's, Estates and Trusts: Cases and Materials (1998)	Dukeminier & Johanson, Wills Trusts, and Estates (6th ed. 2000)	Scoles & Halbach, Decedents' Estates and Trusts (5th ed. 1993)	Waggoner, Alexander & Fellows, Family Property Law (2d ed. 1997)
C. Doctrine of Equitable Election					94-95	
Part Eight – Future Interests and Perpetuities				709-858		
I. Classification of Estates and Future Interests			669-682	710-18		
A. Introduction to Estates in Land and Future Interests	337-340	737-738				931-932
B. The Importance and Process of Classification						932-933
C. The Process of Classification	340-345	738-746				932-947
II. Consequences of Classification				718-750		
A. Introduction to Consequences of Classification			682			948-955
B. Alienability of Future Interests						955-959
C. Summary Comparison of Three Future Interest Rules						
D. The Destructibility of Contingent Remainders						970-973
E. The Rule in Shelley's Case				776-777		
F. The Doctrine of Worthier Title	372-377		739-740	775-776		1050-1063
G. Expressed and implied Condition of Survival	346-356	283-284	719-722	728-750		976-1023
III. Class Gifts				750-775		
A. Definition of a Class Gift	358-359	780-785	706-707			357-360
B. Class Closing	359-361		707-722, 740-743	777-786		1023-1050
IV. The Rule Against Perpetuities						
A. Basic Requirements of the Rule Against Perpetuities	387-395, 402-405	746-780	744-776, 801-808	787-807, 829-830		1080-1137
B. Perpetuity Reform	406-415	797-811	808-815	830-856		1137-1153
C. The Uniform Statutory Rule Against Perpetuities (USRAP)			815-825			1154-1162

Topic in Outline	Anderson, Gaubatz, Bloom & Solomon, Fundamentals of Trusts & Estates (2d ed. 1996)	Clark, Lusky, Murphy, Ascher, & McCouch, Gratuitous Transfers (4th ed. 1999)	Dobris & Sterk, Ritchie, Alford & Effland's, Estates and Trusts: Cases and Materials (1998)	Dukeminier & Johanson, Wills Trusts, and Estates (6th ed. 2000)	Scoles & Halbach, Decedents' Estates and Trusts (5th ed. 1993)	Waggoner, Alexander & Fellows, Family Property Law (2d ed. 1997)
D. Class Gifts under the Rule Against Perpetuities	396-400	785-797	776-787	807-818		1163-1171
E. Powers of Appointment Under The Rule Against Perpetuities	400-402		787-801	818-829		1172-1183
F. Charitable Gifts And Commercial Transactions Under The Rule Against Perpetuities			772-776			1183-1195
Part Nine – The Fiduciary Obligation						
I. Concept of the Fiduciary						
A. The Fiduciary		639-642				
B. The Personal Representative			77-78, 900-903	35-36	2, 679-689	1208-1213
C. The Trustee			449	661-64, 918-919		1215-1216
D. The Guardian		434-435	838-843	132-34	122-124	52-54, 1214-1215
II. Duties of Fiduciaries						
A. The General and Common Duties of a Fiduciary		645-658	905-918			1216-1221
B. Standard of Care, Skill and Prudence			953-960		704-707	
C. Duty of Loyalty	417-426	665-684	942-953	903-19, 921-22	707-729	1221-1234
D. Duty Not to Delegate	445-446	716-719	960-968	922-29	729-733	
E. Duty to Identify and Segregate Trust Property	465-474	719-	987-998	920-21	733-739	
F. Duty to Take Control of Assets				919-20	739-742	
G. Duty to Account		735-736	1011-1015	938-49	742-748	
III. Powers of Fiduciaries					781-860	
A. Powers Concept	426-430, 447-454		988-995	950-54	781-807	

Topic in Outline		Anderson, Gaubatz, Bloom & Solomon, Fundamentals of Trusts & Estates (2d ed. 1996)	Clark, Lusky, Murphy, Ascher, & McCouch, Gratuitous Transfers (4th ed. 1999)	Dobris & Sterk, Ritchie, Alford &Effland's, Estates and Trusts: Cases and Materials (1998)	Dukeminier & Johanson, Wills Trusts, and Estates (6th ed. 2000)	Scoles & Halbach, Decedents' Estates and Trusts (5th ed. 1993)	Waggoner, Alexander & Fellows, Family Property Law (2d ed. 1997)
	B. The Investment Function	430-445	684-716	968-987	954-74	807-860	1234-1264
	C. Allocating Receipts and Expenditures Between Principal and Income	454-465	722-735	1001-1011	929-38	861-949	1264-1301
IV.	Liability of Fiduciaries and Others					748-769	
	A. General Fiduciary Liability	477-484	719-722			748-762	1301-1303
	B. A Fiduciary's Liability to Third Parties	474-477			975-76	762-769	
	C. Third Party Liability to Trust or Beneficiary					769-780	
Part Ten – Taxation					977-1079	279-294	
I.	Taxation Overview		45-48, 913-914	430-432	977-81		
	A. The Place for Taxation	22-23	842-845			279-280	363-364
II.	Gift and Estate Taxes			432-441			
	A. Unified Transfer Tax System	23-25	845-848		981-85	280-281, 289-290	364-367
	B. The Federal Gift Tax	25-26	849-866		985-1004	281	367-375
	C. The Estate Tax	26-28	866-894		1005-42	281-287	375-384
III.	Deductions from the Gross Estate						
	A. General Scope		894-895			287	384
	B. Expenses, Debts, and Losses						384
	C. Marital Deduction	28-32	897-906	441-444	1042-63	288-89	384-387
	D. Charitable Deduction		895-897	579-580	1063-65	288	387-388
IV.	Federal Generation-skipping Transfer Tax						
	A. Generation-Skipping Transfer Tax	32-34	908-913	559-560	1065-78	284-286	388-392

*

APPENDIX D

TABLE OF CASES

*

APPENDIX E

INDEX OF KEY TERMS

MULTIPLE CHOICE ANSWER SHEET

No.	Multiple Choice Answers	No.	Multiple Choice Answers	No.	Multiple Choice Answers
1.	A ○ B ○ C ○ D ○ E ○	13.	A ○ B ○ C ○ D ○ E ○	25.	A ○ B ○ C ○ D ○ E ○
2.	A ○ B ○ C ○ D ○ E ○	14.	A ○ B ○ C ○ D ○ E ○	26.	A ○ B ○ C ○ D ○ E ○
3.	A ○ B ○ C ○ D ○ E ○	15.	A ○ B ○ C ○ D ○ E ○	27.	A ○ B ○ C ○ D ○ E ○
4.	A ○ B ○ C ○ D ○ E ○	16.	A ○ B ○ C ○ D ○ E ○	28.	A ○ B ○ C ○ D ○ E ○
5.	A ○ B ○ C ○ D ○ E ○	17.	A ○ B ○ C ○ D ○ E ○	29.	A ○ B ○ C ○ D ○ E ○
6.	A ○ B ○ C ○ D ○ E ○	18.	A ○ B ○ C ○ D ○ E ○	30.	A ○ B ○ C ○ D ○ E ○
7.	A ○ B ○ C ○ D ○ E ○	19.	A ○ B ○ C ○ D ○ E ○	31.	A ○ B ○ C ○ D ○ E ○
8.	A ○ B ○ C ○ D ○ E ○	20.	A ○ B ○ C ○ D ○ E ○	32.	A ○ B ○ C ○ D ○ E ○
9.	A ○ B ○ C ○ D ○ E ○	21.	A ○ B ○ C ○ D ○ E ○	33.	A ○ B ○ C ○ D ○ E ○
10.	A ○ B ○ C ○ D ○ E ○	22.	A ○ B ○ C ○ D ○ E ○	34.	A ○ B ○ C ○ D ○ E ○
11.	A ○ B ○ C ○ D ○ E ○	23.	A ○ B ○ C ○ D ○ E ○	35.	A ○ B ○ C ○ D ○ E ○
12.	A ○ B ○ C ○ D ○ E ○	24.	A ○ B ○ C ○ D ○ E ○		